W9-ABM-117

The Sociolinguistics Reader

Volume 2:
Gender and Discourse

Edited by

Jenny Cheshire
Professor of Linguistics, Queen Mary and
Westfield College, University of London
and

Peter Trudgill
Professor of English Linguistics,
University of Lausanne

A member of the Hodder Headline Group
LONDON • NEW YORK • SYDNEY • AUCKLAND

First published in Great Britain in 1998 by
Arnold, a member of the Hodder Headline Group
338 Euston Road, London NW1 3BH
175 Fifth Avenue, New York, NY10010

Distributed exlusively in the USA by
St Martin's Press, Inc.
175 Fifth Avenue, New York, NY 10010

British Library Cataloguing in Publication Data
A catalogue entry for this book is available from the British Library

Library of Congress Cataloging-in-Publication Data
A catalog entry for this book is available from the Library of Congress

ISBN 0 340 69999 X (pb)
ISBN 0 340 69182 4 (hb)

Publisher: Naomi Meredith
Production Editor: James Rabson
Production Controller: Rose James
Cover designer: Chris Halls

Composition by J&L Composition Ltd, Filey, North Yorkshire
Printed and bound in Great Britain by J W Arrowsmith, Bristol

Contents

Introduction

Sociolinguistics has changed almost out of all recognition since the 1960s, when the first readers in the subject were published. At that time the dominant branch of linguistics was generative syntax, and practising linguists could sit in their armchairs consulting their intuitions about language structure. Sociolinguistics was a peripheral, hybrid subject, a rebel discipline attracting a relatively small number of scholars who refused to consider language divorced from the social context of which it is inevitably a part. Its roots lay in the disciplines that had traditionally investigated people, society and culture, especially anthropology; and much of the emphasis in research was on the different forms and uses of language that could be observed in different cultures around the world.

Since that time a very large amount of research has been carried out on language in its social context and there have been huge advances in our understanding of how language is used, in European-type cultures as well as in those cultures more traditionally studied by anthropologists. Sociolinguistics has developed a research methodology of its own that is every bit as rigorous and scientific as that of mainstream linguistics, though it is, of course, different. It has become recognized as simply another, equally valid, way of doing linguistics, and is routinely taught as part of a wide range of degree courses, at all levels. Its coming of age has been marked by the publication of several excellent textbooks designed for teaching. There have been related developments in other branches of linguistics too, such as pragmatics, discourse analysis and corpus linguistics, all of which analyse different aspects of language in context. All these fields of linguistics – and others – now overlap with sociolinguistics in their subject-matter, both informed by it and informing it themselves.

The proliferation of interest in language and society is welcome, and has made it possible to approach the analysis of language in its social context from several different standpoints. Each approach and perspective has its own specialized journals which provide outlets for research, and the enthusiasm with which researchers investigate their subject is leading to an ever-increasing number of these specialized journals. However, while the increase in research outlets is beneficial for the development of the discipline as a whole, it makes learning about sociolinguistics more difficult for students and their teachers. The textbooks tend to discuss the same classic pieces of research, which are necessary as a first step for students, providing an overall view of the way that the subject has developed over the years. But students – and their teachers, not all of whom are specialists in sociolinguistics – also need to read more recent research reports if they are to gain an idea of the excitement of current research questions, and the interest of the controversies that inspire sociolinguists to constantly try to discover more and more about language. They need to read about more up-to-date research than they will find in their textbooks, and to read the work of leading researchers in its original form. Since the number of research journals is now so large, the task of finding relevant papers for students is daunting, even for the experts in the field. The aim of this two-volume reader is therefore to make available for students and their teachers some of the most important research papers that have appeared since 1986 in those areas of sociolinguistics where the greatest amount of research has been concentrated.

We selected 1986 as our cut-off point because, although the main purpose of the reader is to serve as a teaching resource, a secondary aim is to allow it to stand as a state-of-the-art account of the discipline of sociolinguistics in the closing years of the twentieth century. Some of the papers will stand the test of time and become classics; others may be refuted or outdated by future work. It is not possible at this stage to determine which will remain important, although in our view all the papers make valuable and timely points.

A certain amount of subjectivity is probably inevitable when choosing papers to be included in a reader, but we did not wish the volumes to represent merely our own personal favourites. In order to guard against this we carried out a survey amongst colleagues in Europe, Australasia and North America, asking them to tell us which papers they recommend most often to their students. This survey informed our eventual decision to focus on four areas within sociolinguistics where there has been a particularly large amount of influential research since 1986, to such an extent that the results have affected the development of the discipline as a whole. Although our informal survey revealed considerable variation in the papers that teachers choose to use, there were some that were mentioned again and again by the specialists in the field. These are all included in these volumes, together with some that were mentioned less often but that nevertheless seem to us to be useful in a collection of this kind. We would like to thank colleagues who replied to our questions, and especially those who sent us copies of the reading lists for their courses. While apologizing in advance to anyone whose names we have forgotten to mention, we would like to place on record our thanks to the following teachers and researchers for their suggestions and comments: Ulrich Ammon, Lars Gunnar Andersson, Allan Bell, David Britain, Jennifer Coates, Ralph Fasold, Elizabeth Gordon, David Lee, Janet Holmes, Dick Hudson, Brit Maehlum, Sharon Millar, Lesley Milroy, Dennis Preston, John Rickford, Michael Stubbs, Renee van Bezooijen, Keith Walters, Geirr Wiggen, John Wilson and Ruth Wodak.

Obviously the responsibility for the final choice rests with us. We also take responsibility for the decision only to make cuts in the papers where this seemed absolutely necessary, in accordance with our aim of providing easy access to research papers in their original form. Students will find, therefore, that some of the papers in these volumes refer to previous research with which they may not always be familiar, and that some of the papers are easier to follow than others. We make no apologies for this, since it reflects the state of the original research literature, of which these volumes provide a flavour.

Further reading

After each of the four sections in these volumes we recommend some specialized textbooks and list the main journals that are outlets for research in that area of sociolinguistics. The main general textbooks in sociolinguistics are:

Holmes, Janet (1992) *An Introduction to Sociolinguistics*, Harlow: Longman.

Hudson, R. A. (1996) *Sociolinguistics*, 2nd edn, Cambridge: Cambridge University Press.

Romaine, Suzanne (1994) *Language in Society: An Introduction to Sociolinguistics*, Oxford: Oxford University Press.

Trudgill, Peter (1995) *Sociolinguistics: An Introduction to Language and Society*, 3rd edn, Harmondsworth: Penguin.

Wardhaugh, Ronald (1992) *An Introduction to Sociolinguistics*, 2nd edn, Oxford: Blackwell.

A textbook written at a more advanced level is:

Fasold, Ralph (1984 and 1990) *The Sociolinguistics of Language: Introduction to Sociolinguistics*, 2 vols..

Section I

Gender

One of the first questions that people ask when a child is born is whether it is a girl or a boy. The question reflects the social and cultural importance of our biological sex: in all societies, being born male or female has a very significant effect on the social roles and opportunities that are available to us, and on social expectations about how we should behave. It is this social and cultural elaboration of a basic biological sex difference that is termed gender.

Gender is a major organizing principle in all societies that are known to us, so we can expect it to account for many aspects of the way that we use language. It is not surprising, therefore, that several papers in other sections of this Reader refer to gender, even where this is not their central concern. In this section, however, the authors of the papers focus specifically on gender, either to explain patterns of language variation or to examine how we accomplish our gender identities through our language. It is noteworthy that each paper closes by pointing to directions that future research might take: although there has been a great deal of research into language and gender, many of the claims that have been made are controversial and many questions remain to be answered. Some of the papers refer to the 'sex' of speakers rather than to their gender; we will use the term 'gender' in this introductory section, on the grounds that it is the social and cultural elaboration of sex that is relevant to sociolinguistic questions, and that these social and cultural processes begin at birth.

Our first paper is by **William Labov**, the leading figure in the quantitative analysis of linguistic variation and change (see the section on Variation in Volume I). One of the principal goals in this area of sociolinguistics is to discover information about the distribution of language behaviour within a community. Typically, researchers in this field group speakers into gross social categories such as socio-economic groups, age groups or female and male speakers, with the idea that these same categories can then be used over and over again to study linguistic behaviour in a range of communities. Research of this kind

1

has demonstrated the importance of gender in accounting for language behaviour (see the paper by James Milroy and Lesley Milroy in Volume I). It has also revealed two consistent patterns of gender differentiation in language behaviour, as Labov explains. To understand why these regular patterns exist in so many different communities throughout the world we obviously need to move beyond considering people in simple categories, in this case as just 'female' or 'male', and look instead at women and men as whole individuals, taking account of the complexities of the different lives that they lead and of the role of language in their lives. Penelope Eckert is one of the sociolinguists who has argued this point very cogently, and Labov wrote his paper partly in response to some of her criticisms. He agrees that the social demographic categories used in quantitative linguistics are simplistic, but points out that we can nevertheless use the evidence that has accumulated from the quantitative paradigm to increase our understanding of how language change spreads through a community. He also shows how we can use this evidence to formulate informed hypotheses about the relationship between language variation and gender, deciding which potential explanations can be ruled out from the beginning and which would be worth investigating through small-scale detailed studies that could take proper account of the complex nature of our gendered identities, including, for example, an examination of the relationship between language, gender and power.

Robert K. Herbert's paper looks at women's and men's use of compliments. Compliments are *conversational routines*, like apologies (see Janet Holmes's paper in this section), which are so important in maintaining social relationships that their form tends to remain constant. In the case of compliments this ensures that we can recognize a compliment when we receive one, and do not misinterpret the speaker's intentions. Herbert analyses a large number of compliments and compliment responses in American English, and compares his results with similar research carried out in other countries around the world. He shows that even though women and men may believe that they are speaking the same language, in fact the 'same' compliment formula often serves different social functions for women and men, used by men to give praise but by women as a way of negotiating friendship and solidarity. Interestingly, similar differences in the function of compliments exist between speakers of American English and South African English, and some revealing parallels can be drawn between the functions of compliments in the US and South Africa, and their functions for men and women. By analysing the way that people *respond* to compliments, Herbert demonstrates that women and men unconsciously cooperate in maintaining their different uses of the compliment routine. This is one indication, then, not only that women and men may have different goals in conversation but that we work together in order to allow each other to achieve our separate goals.

The idea that men and women have different conversational goals is supported by a large number of smaller-scale case studies of conversational discourse. The problem with such studies, of course, is that since they analyse the speech of only a small number of people we cannot tell whether the results hold for the speech of women and men in general, or just for the women and men who took part in the case study. Nevertheless so many case studies have now been carried out, with results all pointing in the same direction, that it seems clear that, other things being equal, women and men do have a preference for different conversational styles. Women – in most western societies at least – prefer a *collaborative speech style*, supporting other speakers and using language in a way that emphasizes their solidarity with the other person. Men, on the other hand, use a number of conversational strategies that can be described as a *competitive style*, stressing their own individuality and emphasizing the hierarchic relationships that they enter into with other people. **Amy Sheldon** and **Diane Johnson**'s paper shows that these styles can be observed even in children as young as three. They analyse conflict talk in all-male and all-female groups of friends, using the idea of 'double-voicing' for talk where speakers orient to their own agenda in the conflict but at the same time are responsive to the relationship and to the other person's point of view. Analysing the linguistic means of expressing both single-voicing and double-voicing, Sheldon and Johnson show that both girls and boys are able to use double-voicing, but that the girls do so more often in their conflicts. These findings can be related to the norms and values constraining our gender roles in wider social contexts; and Sheldon and Johnson discuss the implications of their findings for the conduct of negotiations in a range of settings, including professional organizations.

The paper by **Candace West** illustrates these points further, this time focusing on the linguistic strategies used by medical doctors to express a directive: in other words, to get someone to do something. Whereas Herbert's analysis of compliments revealed a tendency for women and men to use the same linguistic feature to fulfil a different function, West's paper shows that women and men tend to accomplish the same function using different linguistic strategies. Those strategies preferred by the male physicians in her study emphasized the hierarchic differences between their patients and themselves, whereas those preferred by the female physicians minimized status differences and stressed their connectedness to their patients. These different strategies have important implications, for West's study found that patients were more likely to comply with the directives that minimized status differences. Both Sheldon and Johnson, and West stress that it is not that speakers never use the strategies that are preferred by the other sex: both girls and boys, and men and women, can and do use the strategies that we could label as typically feminine or typically masculine. Sheldon specifically challenges our thinking of gender as a twofold category, which is inadequate for theorizing the full range of femininity (or femininities) and masculinity (or masculinities). It is difficult to think of gender other than in this dualistic manner, though, since our socialization pushes us in this direction. The fact that women and men, and girls and boys, do seem to prefer different linguistic strategies shows how we accomplish our gender identities through the interactions that we constantly engage in as part of our everyday lives.

The classic paper by **Jennifer Coates** analyses the language of women friends. Women's speech was once ignored in linguistic research, because it was considered either as uninteresting and worthless, or as no different from men's speech. Coates has been a pioneer in the analysis of the language used by women talking to women, arguing that it is important to look at same-sex conversations because whenever women talk to men language becomes part of the social process which maintains unequal power divisions between the sexes. Her research into women's friendship groups has uncovered many of the linguistic reflexes of women's collaborative speech style, and her paper demonstrates the skills that are involved in using language to create and maintain harmonious social relationships. Her paper also demonstrates how research on language and gender has advanced our understanding of the nature of spoken language generally; here she shows how linguistic forms can have many different potential functions, and how conversations are jointly created by the participants, who work together to negotiate shared meanings.

Our gender identities are undoubtedly of great importance to us, but obviously gender must interact with other social identities, so that our consciousness of ourselves as gendered beings is likely to occur in varying degrees in the interactions that make up our social lives, depending on a very wide range of contextual and other factors. Our next paper, by **Susanne Günthner**, tries to untangle some of the complex web of factors that interact with gender in different communicative situations. Her case study of interactions between speakers of Chinese and speakers of German investigates the way that cultural background and social role can interact with gender to produce different discourse styles. Women are not always cooperative and oriented to supporting their interlocutor. Günthner's paper demonstrates what we can learn from analysing matters such as how expert behaviour is activated in interactions between women and men, and how gendered behaviour may be shaped by context.

The final paper in this section, by **Susan Ehrlich** and **Ruth King**, turns to a different topic, the question of sexism in language. Experiments have shown that words like *man* in English or *l'homme* in French may be intended to have a generic sense, referring to people in general, but in fact they are interpreted as referring only to men. These words, together with a very large number of other words and expressions, encode a male perspective of the world and perpetuate social inequalities between the sexes. A strong case can therefore be made for language reform. To some extent this need has been recognized, with various social institutions in many countries issuing guidelines on the use of non-sexist language. It would be naive, however, to think that simply replacing one word by another is enough to produce a non-sexist society. Words do not come pre-endowed with meanings; instead, their meanings are socially constructed by speakers in the communities in which they live. Ehrlich and King's research demonstrates the basic sociolinguistic fact that language and society are inextricably intertwined. They document some of the uses of terms introduced as non-sexist replacements, which are not necessarily used or interpreted in a non-sexist way. By comparing language reform in two different communities they show that language reform has to be part of social reform if it is to be successful in eliminating gender inequalities.

Further reading

Jennifer Coates's *Women, Men and Language* (2nd edn, Harlow, Longman, 1993) provides a comprehensive account of research carried out into language and gender, covering all the topics represented in this section except sexism in language. She also discusses some traditional stereotypes about male and female language. Janet Holmes's book *Women, Men and Politeness* (Harlow, Longman, 1995) focuses more specifically on differences in women's and men's discourse and their use of specific linguistic features, including compliments. David Graddol and Joan Swann's *Gender Voices* (Oxford, Blackwell, 1989) includes discussion of the human voice and traditional notions of 'femininity' and 'masculinity', as well as the sexist structure of language and the implications for linguistic theory of work on language and gender. All three books discuss the implications for professional life.

Jennifer Coates's *Women Talk* (Oxford, Blackwell, 1996) analyses the language of women friends, demonstrating the linguistic reflexes of women's cooperative style and the skills involved in using language to create harmonious social relationships. Sally Johnson and Ulrike Hanna Meinhof's edited collection of papers *Language and Masculinity* (Oxford, Blackwell, 1996) looks at male ways of speaking and the role of language in the construction of masculinity in everyday life. By way of contrast, the authors in the collection edited by Victoria L. Bergvall, Janet M. Bing and Alice F. Freed, *Rethinking Language and Gender Research: Theory and Practice* (Harlow, Longman 1996) attempt to move beyond theorizing males and females as dichotomous categories.

The question of sexism in language is discussed by Deborah Cameron in her *Verbal Hygiene* (London, Routledge, 1995), along with other questions of language reform.

Journals

There is no journal devoted to language and gender, but such is the interest and importance of gender in the sociolinguistic analysis of language that research in this field is published in all the journals that publish papers on language in its social context. These include

International Journal of Applied Linguistics, Journal of Pragmatics, Journal of Sociolinguistics, Language in Society, Language Variation and Change and *Multilingua*, as well as the journals mentioned in the other sections of the Reader.

1

The intersection of sex and social class in the course of linguistic change

William Labov

Originally published in *Language Variation and Change*, 2 (1990).

Some basic findings and some basic problems

Among the clearest and most consistent results of sociolinguistic research in the speech community are the findings concerning the linguistic differentiation of men and women. These results can be summed up in two distinct principles.

(I) In stable sociolinguistic stratification, men use a higher frequency of non-standard forms than women.

(II) In the majority of linguistic changes, women use a higher frequency of the incoming forms than men.

Though these are valid and reliable findings, they do not fit into any larger framework that accounts for why men and women should be different in this way, or how sexual differentiation affects the course of language history. The two distinct patterns of behavior are difficult to reconcile with each other, and also contradict a number of well-established principles of linguistic change. The conceptual problems may be summed up under four headings.

The biological bias
Though Principles I and II are reported in terms of differences in behavior of the sexes, there is little reason to think that sex is an appropriate category to explain linguistic behavior. It follows that an intervening variable must be formulated in terms of distinct cultural roles assumed by male and female members of society (Eckert, 1989a). But there is as yet no general agreement on the identification of these roles or how to assign them to individual speakers.

The generality of gender
A well-accepted sociolinguistic principle is that the fluctuating course of linguistic change is correlated with and indirectly caused by social changes

7

that alter the structure of the speech community (Meillet, 1921). In recent years, there has been increasing evidence to reinforce the view that sudden changes in linguistic systems are associated with catastrophic social events.[1] Yet sexual relations do not show the uneven and irregular character that is typical of linguistic change. They respond more slowly than other social relations to changes in the economic, political, and demographic situations. The intimate association of sexual differentiation with linguistic change in Principle II would tend to predict long-range changes that move steadily toward completion, rather than what we often find: local movements that begin suddenly and terminate in mid-course or reverse direction.

The reversal of roles
Principles I and II show two distinct kinds of differences between men and women. In the stable situations described by Principle I, women appear to be more conservative and favor variants with overt social prestige, whereas men do the reverse.[2] But in the unstable situations described by Principle II, it is men who show a more conservative character, and women who use forms that deviate more from the standard and are in fact stigmatized when they are overtly recognized. Efforts have been made to unify these apparently conflicting behaviors under a single interpretation, such as a tendency for women to be more sensitive to symbols of social status. But so far, no such proposals have received enough support from the data available.

Intimate diversification[3]
Some of the strongest advances in our understanding of the diffusion of linguistic change depend on the principle of local density (Bloomfield, 1933). On a large scale, this principle associates dialect boundaries with weaknesses in networks of communication. It rests on the assertion that each act of communication between speakers is accompanied by a transfer of linguistic influence that makes their speech patterns more alike. This type of automatic and mechanical influence underlies the gravity model that accounts reasonably well for the spread of linguistic change from the largest to progressively smaller communities (Callary, 1975; Gerritsen & Jansen, 1980; Trudgill, 1974a). The intimate relations between men and women are associated with a very large number of acts of communication in most societies and cultures. The diversification of men's and women's speech patterns in Principles I and II is therefore difficult to reconcile with the principle of local density.

The most recent general treatment of the sexual dimension of linguistic variation is Eckert (1989a). In her review of the literature, she subjected the concepts, practices, and conclusions of sociolinguists on this matter to a searching scrutiny. Some of her arguments bear directly and indirectly on the problems just outlined and will play a role in the discussion to follow.

1.   The biological bias must be countered by substituting the social category of gender for the biological category of sex.

2. The intervening variables are not to be defined by cultural traits such as differences in the expressive character of speech, but rather in the relationships of power and dominance between men and women, based on differences in their economic and institutional roles.
3. A quantitative analysis of gender differentiation must anticipate the interaction of this dimension with socioeconomic class and other social dimensions, so that multivariate analysis must use a number of interactive categories (like "lower middle-class female") or, preferably, separate and parallel analyses of men's and women's speech.
4. Though the roots of gender differentiation of language are to be found in the possession and control of goods and authority, these patterns of behavior are not linked tightly to current patterns of economic opportunity, but are rather dependent on long-standing and more slowly changing cultural expectations of role behavior.[4]

Eckert also provided the most comprehensive report yet published on her own examination of the social matrix of sound change in a Northern Cities high school. Though many linguists have introduced an ethnographic perspective into their work, this is the first example of long-term participant observation that has produced a quantitative analysis of linguistic data. No other sociolinguistic study brings us closer to the social origins of sound change or gives us as clear a view of the sociolinguistic processes that determine and differentiate linguistic behavior. The present report takes a broader approach to resolution of the problems of sexual differentiation, drawing upon large-scale surveys of the speech community. It is therefore important to begin by relating Eckert's ethnographic view of sexual differentiation to the perspective obtained from studies of sociolinguistic stratification in the community as a whole.

Some methodological issues

There are two conflicting aims that govern our approach to the understanding of language, and they are not easily reconciled. On the one hand, our effort should be to achieve the deepest understanding by minimizing the effect of observation and maximizing our view of the social context of what is happening. This is best achieved by the full participation of the observer in the social scene, with an acute sensitivity to the norms of the local culture and the local configuration of social interaction. On the other hand, we want to achieve the largest understanding of the phenomena so that our descriptions and theories bear on the general nature of the language faculty and the general character of language change. This requires not only a representative view of the speech community, but a method of investigation that allows accurate alignment and comparison of our results with those obtained in other communities. This aim is best achieved by a controlled study of the speech production of a random sample of individuals stratified by objective measures such as occupation, education, income, residence value, age, generational status, and mobility.[5] But if the analyst is to understand how this sociolinguistic stratification comes about and how it changes in form or content, these objective data must be connected to observations of people speaking to each other in their everyday social context. Conversely, if the participant-observer is to relate interpretations of the local scene to the larger community or to language in general, a means must be found to compare such findings across social networks, dialects, and languages.

The problem of establishing these relations is severe, and no method has emerged that is completely satisfying or convincing. To see why this should be so, one must consider the opposing analytical inventories of the participant-observer and the urban survey. They share basic linguistic categories at the descriptive level and they can also converge in their theoretical approach to phonology, morphology, and syntax. Eckert drew upon the same abstract characterization of the sound change in progress that is used in our broader surveys: the Northern Cities Shift (Labov, 1991). But the two approaches to the independent variables of the social context are radically different. The urban survey takes the well-known objective categories of social life as given[6] and examines the configuration of linguistic variables across this multidimensional terrain. The goal of the procedure is to obtain new information about the distributions of linguistic behavior rather than new categories for the analysis of society. The participant-observer is guided by a much less specific social theory – one that searches for configurations of local practices, norms, rights, and obligations rooted in the local situation. It is almost inevitable that this analysis will emerge in a differnt form from those of other participant-observers, in neighboring or distant communities.[7]

The social categories used in quantitative studies are far from uniform. The approach to social class may be based on occupation, education, or a combination of these with income, residence, and membership in social institutions. But one may abstract from these differences to the more general notion of a socioeconomic hierarchy, as I do in the discussions to follow. The social categories required for a comparison of the linguistic behavior of men and women are then *highest social group, lowest social group, second highest group,* and *intermediate social group,* along with other demographic concepts that refer to population size (*urban, rural*), immigration history (*first generation, newly arrived, established*), and age. As participant-observer, Eckert located analytical categories that are specific to the local scene – *Jocks* and *Burnouts* – but achieved generality by relating them to processes that must exist to some degree in every high school. Jocks and Burnouts are taken as prototypical examples of adolescent groups who seek their goals by conforming to adult norms or by defying and escaping from them (Eckert, 1989a, 1989b). It is likely that succeeding studies of high school social life will be informed by this distinction, but it is also logical to expect that another locally rooted analysis will add new features that stem from the special features of its local situation.

The strategy that I suggest here is to distinguish between reasonably objective facts, on which we can all agree, and interpretations of those facts, on which we can only expect partial agreement. The treatment of the main independent variable under consideration here illustrates the issues involved. Eckert's reflections on the problem of biological bias (her point 1) imply that the term *gender* is to be preferred to *sex*, because the former is a social category, the latter a biological one. If this is to be a simple substitution of terms, there would not seem to be any immediate advantage. If we assign gender to our subjects by some other criterion than sex, we run the risk of losing any chance of replication by others. Thus, Eckert (1986) indicated that the use of advanced levels of the variable (aeh) by females is merely a byproduct of the fact that "brokers" – people who habitually relay information between groups – are high (aeh) speakers, and most brokers – but not all – are female. The concept of *broker* is well accepted in the literature of social anthropology. Nevertheless, we have no accepted and objective criteria for assigning the status of broker to any one individual. It would seem reasonable to retain our binary category of sex as *male* and *female*, and use a concept like *broker*, where it is applicable, to interpret and explain the objective findings about sexual differentiation.

The central focus of the present report is the interaction of two social dimensions – sex and socioeconomic class – in their joint correlation with sound change in Philadelphia. I present a number of inferences about the differentiation of men and women that go beyond the basic findings of Principles I and II, and may contribute to the resolution of the puzzling problems outlined.

First, it is necessary to review the evidence for Principles I and II of sexual differentiation, as the degree of uniformity of the evidence is an important component of the solutions that I propose.

Review of the evidence: sex as a sociolinguistic factor

Sexual differences are institutionalized in most languages as the grammatical category of *gender*. Natural gender, which corresponds directly to the sex of the referent, is usually blended, overlaid, or dominated by other arbitrary noun classifications as in French, Russian, or Swahili, but it is sometimes isolated as special pronouns and suffixes for male, female, and neuter referents. In current English, these linguistic differentia of sex are subject to overt discussion and change under the influence of the movement toward sexual equality in social life. Cross-cultural reviews of differences between linguistic forms used by men and women show a much wider range of phonological and morphological features as well as lexical differences in pronominal use (Haas, 1944). Haas' report on the situation in Koasati showed a clear connection with linguistic change; the women's form were generally regarded as archaic and were used only by older women. In Muskogee, the archaic forms used by women were preserved only in tales where a female character is talking.[8] Institutionalized differentiation of the sexes may be reflected in adjustment of forms according to the sex of the hearer as well as the speaker. These qualitative reports usually represent a sexual dimorphism that is recognized by all members of the community, is available for quotation, and is overtly taught to children by caretakers. On the other hand, the recent quantitative studies of sexual differentiation reflect patterns that are only vaguely recognized, are not taught directly, and sometimes run counter to the intuitions of linguists as well as the general public.

Principle I: For stable sociolinguistic variables, men use a higher frequency of nonstandard forms than women
This basic finding can be formulated in two complementary ways: men use more nonstandard forms, less influenced by the social stigma directed against them; or, conversely, women use more standard forms, responding to the overt prestige associated with them. Evidence for Principle I is uniform and voluminous. This section recapitulates some of the main trends summarized in Labov (1982) and presents some more recent reports that bear directly on the argument to follow.

One of the most widely studied English variables is (ing), the alternation of [n] and [ŋ] in unstressed -*ing*. Male speakers are found to use the colloquial form [in] more than females in New England (Fischer, 1958), New York City (Labov, 1966), Detroit (Wolfram, 1969), Philadelphia (Cofer, 1972), Ottawa (Woods, 1979), Norwich (Trudgill, 1974b) and 15 other cities in the British Isles (Houston, 1985), Australia (Bradley & Bradley, 1979; Shopen & Wald, 1982), and many other English-speaking regions. In a study of a single Ozark family, Mock (1979) showed that teenaged children followed the sexual differentiation of their parents in the use of (ing).

The English interdentals /θ, ð/ provide a wide range of evidence for the tendency of male speakers to use more of the nonstandard affricate and stop forms: in New York City (Labov, 1966: Ch. 8), Detroit (Shuy, Wolfram, & Riley, 1966; Wolfram, 1969), North Carolina (Anshen, 1969), and Belfast (Milroy & Milroy, 1978). Negative concord shows a strong male/female difference, with men using the stigmatized form more than women in New York City (Labov, 1966), Detroit (Shuy et al., 1966), and Anniston, Alabama (Feagin, 1979).

In a single study, Wolfram (1969) documented the operation of Principle I in Detroit for nine nonstandard variants: negative concord, (ing), stop forms of *th*, simplification of final -*t*, *d* clusters, deletion of final apical stops, vocalization of (r), absence of third singular /s/, absence of possessive /s/, and deletion of the copula. The only nonstandard variant where there were not significant differences between men and women was the use of invariant *be*.[9]

In Canadian French, the Montreal study showed Principle I operating for a number of variables (Thibault, 1983). In Ontario, Mougeon and Beniak (1987) showed that men are much more likely than women to borrow core terms, such as English *so* (59% vs. 41%), and to use such colloquial conjunctions as *ça fait que* [fak] instead of *alors* (68% vs. 32%). Mougeon, Beniak, and Valli (1988) found men more likely to use the nonstandard auxiliary [zvɔ] for *je vais* (39% vs. 26%). In all these cases, women preferred the pattern characteristic of the highest social class and of formal speech.

Perhaps the largest body of evidence on sexual differentiation is to be found in studies of Spanish in Latin America and Spain. Fontanella de Weinberg (1974) carried out a detailed study of the aspiration and deletion of (s) in Bahia Blanca in Argentina, replicating the methods of the New York City study in some detail. She found strong evidence for Principle I operating in the choice of the three variants [s], [h], and zero. Alba (1990) reported percentages and variable rule analyses of (s) in Santiago in the Dominican Republic. The most consistent finding is that men show more weakening of /s/ than women in all environments: monomorphemic, plural, and verbal /s/. In addition, men use significantly more of the traditional nonstandard forms of /l/ and /r/ than women.

In Spain, Silva-Corvalán (1986) studied the alternation of conditional and imperfect subjunctive in *si-* clauses – the same variable that was the focus of Lavandera (1975) in Buenos Aires. Men showed more than twice the frequency of the nonstandard conditional in the sociolinguistically sensitive focus of the variable: the apodosis of counterfactual sentences. Silva-Corvalán (1981) studied pleonastic clitics in Chilean Spanish and found that men had a higher tendency to use this nonstandard form. Rissel (1989) reviewed other studies in Spain that showed women using more standard forms than men.

In Glasgow, Macaulay (1977) found that male school children used the stigmatized vowels of the local dialect more than females. An even more sensitive measure of sex differentiation is found in the use of glottal stop for /t/. Preadolescent children of both sexes and all social classes show a high level of glottal stop, about 90%. Among adults, a sharp social stratification is found with middle-class women in particular showing very little glottal stop. The adolescent groups show a high reduction in this feature among middle-class girls; middle-class boys follow suit, but only in their 20s.

Perhaps the most striking differentiation of the sexes was found by Eisikovits (1981), who studied the use of a number of standard/nonstandard oppositions in a Sydney high school. The frequencies of each variable were tabulated separately according to whether the last speaker was an adult (the interviewer) or another student. For almost all variables, girls shifted toward the standard when they were responding to the interviewer, whereas boys shifted in the opposite direction.

In Taiwanese Mandarin, Lin (1988) found that the largest single variable reflecting the use of the standard retroflex consonants in careful speech was the sex of the speaker. Women moved away from the colloquial use of apical forms to a preponderant use of retroflexion in formal styles, but men showed a much more moderate style shift.

The evidence for Principle I is not limited to urban, industrialized, or Western societies. Throughout Latin America this pattern appears in isolated rural areas as well as in large cities: in the Caribbean (López, 1983) and in various countries and languages of South America (Albo, 1970).

Not all sociolinguistic variables show a sex effect. Hibiya (1988) found no significant sex differences for the several Tokyo variables that she studied. Morales (1986) found no significant difference in the velarization of /n/ in Puerto Rican Spanish. But the overwhelming majority of the variables studied do show this effect; and until recently there were no cases reported where men appeared to favor the prestige form more than women. Three such cases appeared in a contiguous area. In Amman, for all social classes, men favored the prestige form /q/ more than women (Abd-el-Jawad, 1981). This pattern was replicated in Nablus (Abd-el-Jawad, 1987). Again, in Teheran, women used the local colloquial forms of the variables (an) and (æš) more than men in all social classes (Modaressi, 1978). This appeared to represent a global reversal of the positions of men and women in two

Muslim societies, perhaps related to the fact that in general women played less of a role in public life in those societies. However, Abd-el-Jawad (1987) and Haeri (1987) challenged such an interpretation, arguing that Classical Arabic is not comparable to the standard languages of other societies. Haeri pointed out that the closest parallel to Western norms are the modern urban forms that Muslim women actually preferred: the glottal stop for /q/ in Amman and the colloquial but prestigious Teheran forms [un] and [eš]. It would follow that women in those societies do not behave differently from women in other societies.

The principle must be qualified by the observation that for women to use standard norms that differ from everyday speech, they must have access to those norms. Nichols (1976) reported that black women on the South Carolina mainland show less tendency to switch from Gullah to English than black women who live on a sea island with tourist development. In many larger studies of the speech community are found some lower class women who do not participate in the wider system of sociolinguistic norms.[10] It stands to reason that the conservative tendency of women applies only when the opportunity for it to apply is present.

Principle Ia: In change from above, women favor the incoming prestige form more than men
Many reports of linguistic change deal with alterations in the social distribution of well-known linguistic variables. These fall into the general category of *change from above*. They take place at a relatively high level of social consciousness, show a higher rate of occurrence in formal styles, are often subject to hypercorrection, and sometimes show overt stereotypes as with stable sociolinguistic variables. Because changes from above share many of the properties of stable sociolinguistic variables, it is not surprising that the role of the sexes is similar, and women lead in both the acquisition of new prestige patterns and the elimination of stigmatized forms. The importation of a new prestige pattern is essentially the adoption of a norm external to the speech community, and groups with high linguistic insecurity are most sensitive to such norms. The same groups are most susceptible to the elimination of stigmatized forms, which takes place under the vigilant stewardship of the publicly recognized dominant groups. Thus this principle is grouped under Principle I, as Ia rather than IIa.

The adoption of the (r)-pronouncing norm in New York City is led by women (Labov, 1966), and the reversal of the Parisian chain shift is equally a female-dominated change (Lennig, 1978). In Belfast, Milroy and Milroy (1985) showed that the raising of /ɛ/ from [a] toward [e] in *neck, desk*, etc., is strongly favored by women. This is actually a reversal of the traditional lowering, and the urban Belfast women follow behind the more prestigious suburbs in this process (Milroy & Milroy, 1985: 352). That it is a change from above is shown by the fact that the more advanced forms are favored in careful speech (ibid., 357).[11]

The abandonment of traditional rural dialects is normally led by women, as in the case of the Spanish village of Ucieda, documented by Holmquist (1985) for the reversal of the raising of final /a/ to /o/. Clarke (1987) demonstrates dialect shifts in Sheshatsiu, an Algonquian language of Labrador. Most of these represented the adoption of the prestigious Southwestern dialect, and women were in the lead in 5 of the 10 cases, and men in none. Thus, the sensitivity of women to prestige forms extends to societies that are not overtly stratified.

Shifts from one language to another are inevitably conscious and are always changes from above, as in the shift from Hungarian to German studied by Gal (1978, 1980). Such shifts, like the dialect redistributions, are often tightly tied to economic factors. The predominance of women therefore cannot be expected to hold when the language is associated with work situations and educational opportunities open predominantly to males, as in the case of Papua New Guinea. Here, census reports show that twice as many males as females acquire the use of English, Tok Pisin, and Hiri Motu (G. Sankoff, 1980: 123, Table 5–2).

Some possible explanations   A great deal has been written to account for the sexual differentiation of language summarized by Principle I. Most of the emphasis is on the behavior of women, who are said to be more expressive than men or use expressive symbols more than men or rely more on such symbols to assert their position. This in turn is linked to differential power relationships of men and women. Women are said to rely more on symbolic capital than men because they possess less material power. The explanations offered differ primarily in their emphasis on cultural or expressive traits as opposed to the political or economic position of women. It is interesting to note that no sociolinguistic argument views this behavior of women as a form of superiority or an advantage to them. However, this does emerge in the popular view that women speak better or more correctly than men do. In disadvantaged communities, sensitivity to exterior standards of correctness in language is associated with upward social mobility. In the inner city black community, female students show greater success than males in school and greater employability. The effects of Principle I can hardly be seen as the cause but rather a symptom of an overall readiness and opportunity to take advantage of prevailing community norms.

Those explanations that focus on the behavior of men often attribute to them a set of values that oppose the standard norms, sometimes called "covert" because they do not appear in the relatively formal context of the interview situation. Values of "masculinity" or "toughness" are often assigned forms that are stigmatized as "nonstandard" or "substandard" by writers on usage. It is easier to demonstrate the existence of the overt norms through experiments in the field, however, and the existence of such covert norms are inferred rather than demonstrated.[12]

Principle II: In change from below, women are most often the innovators
The chief focus of this discussion is not on changes from above but on changes *from below*, that is, the basic form of linguistic change that operates within the system, below the level of social awareness. These include the systematic sound changes that make up the major mechanism of linguistic

change. Changes from below offer the clearest view of the effect of sexual differentiation on the ongoing evolution of linguistic systems.

The earliest report of linguistic change in progress was that of Gauchat (1905), who showed that in the Swiss French village of Charmey women were considerably ahead of men for a number of variables: the palatalization of /l/, the aspiration of /θ/, the monophthongization of /aw/, and the diphthongization of open /o/ and /e/. Gauchat's observations were basically ethnographic and individual; his remarks on the contrast between husband and wife Laurent Rime and Brigide Rime are particularly pertinent:

ao →a   Les femmes appartenant à la première génération negligent plus facilement le son qui se perd que les hommes. J'en ai été frappé plusieurs fois surtout en confrontant les époux Laurent et Brigide Rime, lui de 59 et elle de 63 ans. Dans la phrase, *la pomme est douce*, entre outres, il prononçait da°θə, elle, daθə.

o → a°   Comme toujours, les femmes se mettent plus facilement sur la voie de la diphtongaison que les hommes. Mme. Rime, 63 ans, m'a offert trois fois autant de cas de ao que son mari, agé de 59 ans. . . . La dernière génération, c'est à dire tous les enfants, se range du coté des mères et prononce définitivement ao. On ne parle pas sans raison de toit paternel mais de la langue maternelle.

Hermann's revisit to Charmey in 1929 showed that both of these changes had gone to completion except for diphthongization before /r/, where his data clearly showed that women were in the lead. On the other hand, the aspiration of /θ/ in pronouns proved to be a stable sociolinguistic marker at the same level as at the turn of the century, opposing formal [θ] to colloquial [h], and here men showed a slight preponderance of [h].

Hermann provided enough data to allow us to construct a quantitative account, as shown in Table 1.1. This first quantitative report on sexual differentiation is particulary interesting because for those variables that proved to be true changes in progress in the real-time data, women were in the lead, whereas for those that proved to be stable cases of age-grading, there was no significant difference.

Principle II was found to be active in most of the linguistic changes in progress studied by quantitative means in the past several decades (for the English vowel notation used here and following, see Appendix 1). Women were in advance of men in the New York City raising of (aeh) and (oh) (Labov, 1966), as well as the backing of (ah) and the fronting of (aw).

Table 1.1 Sexual differentiation of three variables in Charmey in 1929

		Men ($N = 21$)(%)	Women ($N = 19$)(%)
/o/	a° before /r/	58	70
/e/	e^i before /r/	33	69
/θ/	h in -*tu*	80	86

Source: Hermann (1929).

The earliest report of the Northern Cities Shift that is the focus of Eckert's work is to be found in an unpublished analysis of Fasold (1969), which examines the fronting of (æh), (o), and (oh) by 12 men and 12 women in the Detroit survey. He found that women were leading in all three cases. Eckert (1989a) showed that girls were in advance of boys for the same three variables, though not for the more recent shifts of (e) and (ʌ).

There are fewer data available on the progression of the Southern Shift than the Northern Cities Shift, but the evidence we have indicates that women are leading. In a study of nine members of an Ozark family, Mock (in press) showed the clear advance of the younger females in the lowering and backing of the nucleus of /ey/.[13]

In the southern and western United States, some of the most active sound changes involve the laxing of vowels before /l/, yielding homonymy of *steel* and *still*, *sail* and *sell*, *fool* and *full*. Nicholas (n.d.) traced the laxing of /ey/ in the Appalachian dialect of Jackson County, North Carolina, and found that women were clearly in the lead. Di Paolo (1988) found similar results for all three vowels in her Intermountain Language Survey of Salt Lake City, Utah. Adolescents were the chief exponents of the change in pronunciation, and girls led boys: 53% to 0% for (iyl), 60% to 7% for (eyl), 47% to 20% for (uw).

The research group headed by Guy Bailey at Texas A&M has traced the relation of sex of speaker to a number of innovations in Texas speech through the Texas Poll data of 1989. The unrounding of long open *o* to [a] leading to the merger of /o/ and /oh/ was shown by 25% of the female respondents to the poll, but by only 16% of the males. For *walk*, the percentages were 23% and 16%. The merger of /iy/ and /i/ before /l/ was indicated by the laxing of the nucleus in *field*: 33% of the female respondents showed this pattern as opposed to 28% of the males. The comparable laxing of /uw/ in *school* was shown by 48% of the females compared to 40% of the males (Bailey, Bernstein, & Tillery).

The most recent sound changes to be found in the United States involve the rapid and extreme fronting of /uw/ and /ow/ on the West Coast. Luthin (1987) showed that women lead men by a considerable margin in the new fronting of (ow) in the Berkeley area. Similar observations have been made in other coastal areas, from Seattle to Los Angeles.

In England, the most detailed report we have on a new sound change in progress is from Trudgill's work in Norwich, in the backing of (el) in *belt*, *help*, and so forth (Trudgill, 1974b). There, women were clearly ahead of men (see also Labov, Yaeger, & Steiner, 1972, for instrumental displays of male and female Norwich speakers).

In Canada, Chambers and Hardwick (1985) traced the development of a new norm for (aw), a fronting that is first added to and then substituted for the traditional centralization before voiceless finals. Women are the innovators in both Toronto and Vancouver, as Fig. 1.1 shows.

Of the many studies of social variation in Latin American Spanish, only a few have found sound change in progress. Cedergren's (1973) research in Panama City found that the lenition of /č/ showed a regular increase in younger age groups and that women favored the change more than men. One of the most extensive studies of change in Spanish is the investigation

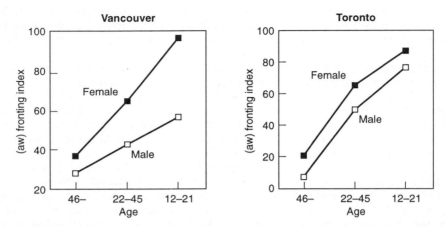

Fig. 1.1 Fronting of (aw) by age and sex in two Canadian cities (from Chambers & Hardwick, 1985)

of the devoicing of /ž/ in Buenos Aires by Wolf and Jiménez (1979). Studies of adults and high school students across social classes showed a rapid shift toward the devoiced variable in younger age groups. Fig. 1.2 shows some of the evidence that led Wolf and Jiménez to the conclusion that "females are the leaders in the spreading of the change and they are almost a whole generation farther along" (p. 16).[14] This is indeed a change from below. There is no overt reaction to the change in Buenos Aires, and there was no stylistic shift when the most formal styles were compared with interview style, casual style, and candid recording.

In Hong Kong, Bauer (1982) traced the development of syllabic /m/ for syllabic /ŋ/ in the local dialect of Cantonese. The change was initiated by women in the 30–40-year-old age range. In the next generation, most teen-aged males adopted the change categorically and passed beyond the level of most women.

These cases show sexual differentiation as a dynamic situation. Depending on the stage of the change within the purview of the investigators, we see females diverging from males, as in Vancouver, females advancing ahead of and in parallel with males, as in Toronto; or males converging with the advanced position of females, as in Buenos Aires and Hong Kong. In none of these cases do we see the creation of stable sex differentiation.

The minor tendency: men in advance   There are also a certain number of changes in progress recorded where men have been found to be in advance of women. On Martha's Vineyard, the centralization of (ay) and (aw) was led by men (Labov, 1963). As we will see, the parallel shift of (ay) before voiceless finals in Philadelphia is also dominated by men. In Norwich, Trudgill found that the unrounding of (o) was a male-dominated change. In Belfast, Milroy and Milroy (1985) found that the reverse process – the backing and rounding of /a/ – is strongly dominated by men.

The mechanism of change is therefore not linked to sex differences in any

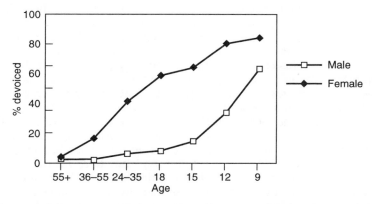

Fig. 1.2 Devoicing of /ž/ in Buenos Aires by sex and age (from Wolf & Jiménez, 1979: Table 5) (N = 12,898)

clear and simple way. Either sex can be the dominant factor. But the number of cases where men are in the lead is relatively small. Furthermore, the male-dominated changes are all relatively isolated changes, such as the centralization of /ay/ and /aw/ or the unrounding of /o/. They do not include chain shifts such as the Southern Shift or the Northern Cities Shift that rotate the sound system as a whole. All those cases of chain shifting that we have been able to examine with quantitative means are dominated by women.

Some possible explanations   It would be quite satisfying if we could arrive at a straightforward grouping of male- and female-dominated changes by their phonetic character. Some of the first sound changes studied made it seem possible that females led in the upward movement of peripheral tense vowels that increased the dispersion of the vowel system, like the raising of (aeh) and (oh), whereas males led in the opposite trend: shifts that moved toward the center corresponding to a "close-mouthed" tendency, like the centralization of (ay). But this would not account in any way for the consonantal changes that are led by women, nor for other recent female-dominated movements reported recently, such as the laxing (and centralizing) of /iy/, /ey/, and /uw/ before /l/, as both Di Paolo (1988) in Salt Lake City and Bailey's research group (in preparation) in Texas found.

If there is no simple phonetic determination of the role of the sexes, we can look to some factor that weights the choice of male or female domination toward the female. One such factor is the asymmetry of the childcare situation. In all the societies that are concerned here, children learn the rudiments of their native language from their primary caregivers, who are women. Although male models are present, and no doubt effective, early exposure to the phonetic exponents of the language categories is exposure to a female pattern.

It is well established that women have the capacity to shape the behavior of male children to a norm appropriate for males.[15] But the phonetic forms that the child is first exposed to are those used by women. Given a female-dominated change, boys and girls will hear relatively advanced forms from their female caregivers; given a male-dominated change, they will hear less advanced forms. The later influence of the peer group in accelerating or retarding these patterns can only operate on the basis of what has been first acquired. The asymmetry of the caregiving situation will therefore advance female-dominated changes and retard male-dominated changes.

It is interesting to note that Gauchat anticipated this view of the matter in his formulation of the situation in Charmey: "La dernière génération, c'est à dire tous les enfants, se range *du coté des mères.*" Gauchat might more simply have written "du coté des femmes," but here he plainly has in mind the importance of the fact that the first steps in language learning are dominated by women. Language is then literally *la langue maternelle.* The initial bias provided by this situation does not automatically produce a female-dominated situation. But as the major shifts that ultimately influence the language are drawn from a much larger set of minor local trends, it would also follow that many more female-dominated tendencies would reach the status that we call linguistic change.

The relative uniformity of Principles I and II   The overall weight of the evidence for Principle I appears to be stronger than that for Principle II. There are no significant exceptions for I but a significant group of opposing cases for II. Accordingly, the explanations advanced for I might seem to carry more weight. However, when we consider the relative uniformity of the evidence for each case, the situation will appear in a different light. Overall percentages show that women use nonstandard forms less frequently than men in every stable situation and use new prestige forms more frequently than men in every change from above. Yet the actual distribution of behavior across the community is not so uniform. More detailed analyses show that women in different sections of the community behave quite differently in regard to Principle I, and there is considerable interaction between sex and other social categories. The consequences of this fact bear strongly on the type of explanation that can be advanced and will also affect our ultimate approach to the problems previously outlined.

The interaction of sex and social class

Social class indicators
Studies of speech communities have used a variety of indicators of socio-economic class, but the robust effects of social stratification have emerged with a remarkable uniformity. Whether we use objective indicators – education, occupation, or income – some combination of these, or subjective measures of status, we will be referring to some generally recognized hierarchical organization of the speech community. It is the nature of stable sociolinguistic variables to become aligned with such class hierarchies in a monotonic fashion. For a prestige marker, the higher a speaker's socio-

economic status, the higher the frequency of use. For stigmatized markers, the reverse is true.

What is important is not the indicators of class, status, or power, but the reliability of the classification and the number of different distinctions made. Binary divisions into upper and lower class are of little value in sociolinguistic studies and conceal more information than they reveal. A useful view of the social distribution of a variable requires at least four divisions of the socioeconomic hierarchy, giving us two extreme or peripheral groups and two intermediate or central groups. We need these categories to get an accurate picture of the social stratification of language. We also need them to map the interaction of sex and social class, because the behavior of men and women in these various social groups has been found to be quite different in almost every case that has been studied.

It follows that we must analyze sexual differentiation separately for each social group – not only socioeconomic class groups, but also ethnic groups, urban and rural groups, and generations. Here, the consequences of the biological bias mentioned earlier are most evident. Of the many quantitative studies of the speech community, only a minority yields the information needed. The reasons are clear: if investigators consciously or unconsciously regard the relevant category as a biological one, they will expect the same differentials to appear everywhere. They will therefore report sex as a single category, with overall percentages for the behavior of men and women in the community that show the operation of Principle I and nothing more.

This situation could be corrected for in earlier studies that gave cross-tabulations for sex and other social factors. But the growth of multivariate analysis, with its many positive contributions, has exaggerated the problem considerably. In many of the studies cited, we find the influence of sex reported in a variable rule analysis as a single group with two factors, *male* and *female*. The degree of fit of the model is rarely reported, and the hidden interctions of sex and other social factors are irretrievably lost.[16] The next section of our analysis must therefore proceed on the basis of data from a minority of the speech communities studied – primarily the earlier studies done before multivariate analysis was introduced.

Typical interaction with stable sociolinguistic variables
The reports that show cross-tabulations by sex and social class consistently show strong interactions between these factors (Anshen, 1969; Labov, 1966; Levine & Crockett, 1966; Shuy et al., 1966; Wolfram, 1969). In general, the second highest status group shows the greatest differential of men and women, along with the highest degree of linguistic insecurity and the sharpest slope of style shifting (Labov, 1966). The tendency to avoid stigmatized forms and prefer prestige forms is greatest for the women of the lower middle class, and is often minimal for the lower class and upper middle class. Fig. 1.3 shows the characteristic pattern of stigmatized forms in the well-known pattern of negative concord for black speakers in Detroit (Wolfram, 1969). On the left is the display of percentage of negative concord. The absolute sex differences between the two intermediate groups are greater than the differences for the two extreme groups. But the important

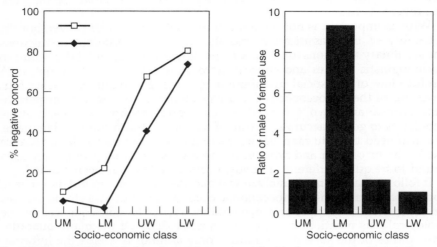

Fig. 1.3 Sexual differentiation of negative concord for black speakers in Detroit (from Wolfram, 1969: 162)

Table 1.2 Effect of sex and social group on raising of /o/ in Ucieda

	Mean closure value	Standard deviation	No. of informants
Farmers with mountain animals			
Males	227	26.88	6
Females	186	40.24	6
Farmers with dairy animals			
Males	178	38.88	14
Females	112	20.35	4
Workers			
Males	79	18.27	4
Females	79	30.16	5
Students			
Males	114	16.86	3
Females	48	22.9	3

Source: Holmquist (1988: Table 5.5).

point is the extremely low percentage for lower middle-class women. Compared to the upper middle-class norms, the male figure goes up, whereas the female use declines. The lower middle class is radically different from the others, as shown by the ratios of male to female use shown on the right.

An even more striking example of interaction is to be found in Holmquist's (1985, 1988) study of the variable (o) in rural Ucieda in northern Spain. Table 1.2 shows the effect of sex on the tendency to raise unstressed /o/ to [u]. The powerful effect of sex operates on farming families who hold close to the rural tradition (with indigenous animals), on farmers who have switched to conventional dairy stock, and even more strongly on students. But there is no difference at all among workers – men and women who do not earn a living from the land.

It is clear that no biological or universal property of women can account for distributions of this kind. Holmquist found the explanation in a rational mode of behavior: the raising of /o/ is symbolic of affiliation to a farming economy that holds far less social and economic attraction for women than for men.

Such extreme interaction of sex and social class is characteristic of well-established variables that are overtly recognized in the community and have risen to the level of publicly recognized stereotypes. They show extreme style shifting as well as class stratification. This appears clearly in Trudgill's (1974b) data on (ing) in Norwich, displayed in Fig. 1.4. Here, all social groups preserve the expected male–female relationship in both casual and careful speech, except the lower middle-class women, who cross over lower middle-class men with a dramatic shift from casual to careful speech. Figure 1.4 shows the sharp division between middle- and working-class groups that is characteristic of the Norwich data. With the shift from casual to formal speech, lower middle-class women also shift from an alignment with the working class to an alignment with the middle classes. The other groups show a very shallow slope of style

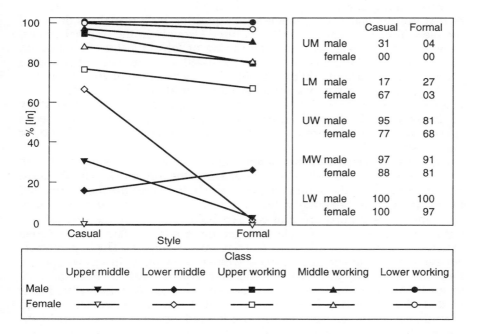

Fig. 1.4 Shifts of style in spontaneous speech by sex and class for (ing) in Norwich (adapted from Trudgill, 1974b)

shifting by comparison. In contrast to lower middle-class women, lower middle-class men show only a small, probably nonsignificant shift in the other direction.

The radical realignment of the female speakers lies at the heart of the "hypercorrect behavior of the lower middle class," which has been seen for some time as an important element in the mechanism of linguistic change (Labov, 1972: Ch. 5). All systematic style shifting is aligned toward a particular target, usually the level set by a higher status group. By "hypercorrect behavior" is meant a shift of a linguistic variable that passes beyond this target.[17] Past findings have highlighted three separate points:

1.   In sociolinguistic variation, the second highest status group shows the steepest slope of style shifting, the most self-correction and hypercorrection, the greatest difference between norms and behavior in self-report tests, highest levels in linguistic insecurity tests, and the strongest tendency to stigmatize the speech of others in subjective evaluation tests for that variable (Labov, 1972: Ch. 5).
2.   Women exceed men in all the features listed under (1).
3.   The greatest differences betwen men and women are found among members of the second highest status group.

Is this hypercorrect behavior of the second highest status group distinct from the hypercorrect behavior of women? Or is the hypercorrect behavior of the second highest group entirely a contribution of the female members of that group? Fig. 1.5 approaches that question by a reanalysis of one of the New York City variables that featured strongly in the original discussions of hypercorrect behavior: the raising of (oh) in *lost, coffee, chocolate,* and so forth. The (oh) index ranges from 10–40. A mean value of 10 would show consistent use of a high vowel [ʊː°]; a mean value of 20 corresponds to an upper mid [oː°]; a mean of 30 to a lower mid [ɔ⁴ː ə], and a mean of 40 to a low vowel [ɔ] or [ɒ]. Older conservative New York City speakers show an index around 30; most adults use values around 20 in spontaneous speech; the most advanced younger speakers reach 10 in casual and/or excited speech.[18]

Fig. 1.5 shows four stylistic contexts on the horizontal axis, ranging from casual speech to word lists. The vertical axis is the (oh) index, with the most advanced forms of the sound change at the bottom and the most corrected forms at the top. Separate values for men and women for three socio-economic class groups are plotted. The bold lines show the two groups with the greatest slope of style shifting: upper middle-class women (open squares) and lower middle-class women (open triangles). The hypercorrect behavior of the lower middle-class women is evident. In casual speech, they use the most advanced, vernacular vowels with a mean of 17.5, whereas the upper middle-class women show the most conservative forms in that style. The two lines make a parallel upward movement toward careful speech; the gap begins to close in reading style; and in word lists, lower middle-class women pass the target. The lower middle-class women also cross over the level of lower middle-class men. They begin with more advanced forms than the men, converge with them at reading style, and go

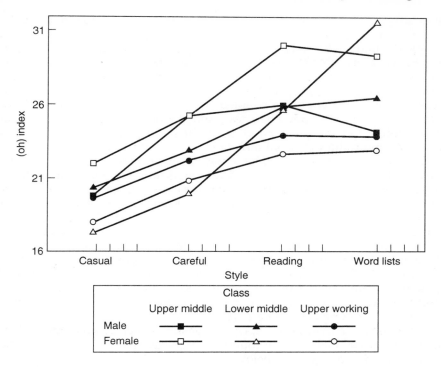

Fig. 1.5 Style shifting of (oh) by three socioeconomic groups in New York City

far beyond them in word lists. On the other hand, working-class men and women (open and solid circles) show a small parallel style shift that preserves the differences between them for all styles.

There are striking parallels between Trudgill's data in Fig. 1.4 – a stable linguistic variable – and the New York City data in Fig. 1.5 – a change in progress. The combined evidence suggests that the hypercorrect behavior of the second highest status group may be entirely a contribution of the female members of that group. On the other hand, differences between men and women are not confined to that social group but are reflected to a greater and lesser degree across the social spectrum. For a change in progress like (oh), the male–female differences are confined to a part of the social spectrum closest to the innovators; for a stable variable like (ing), these differences are found in all social groups, again to the greatest extent in the second highest status group.

Some further explanations
The extreme type of interaction seen in Figs. 1.3–5 has strong implications for our understanding of the role of women in sociolinguistic variation. As noted, the rapid shift of women away from their vernacular forms when the context of speech becomes more formal is associated with other forms of linguistic behavior, such as a comparatively high level of "linguistic

insecurity" (Labov, 1966; Owens, Thompson, & Baker, 1984; Trudgill, 1972). The index of linguistic insecurity involves the proportion of cases in which people distinguish between the way they speak and another way of speaking that is "correct."[19] This behavior may be viewed more positively as the ability to recognize an external standard of correctness[20] and to acquire new standards of appropriate symbolic behavior. Extreme attention to external standards could be coupled with the weaker economic base of women, their relative powerlessness, and the oppressive nature of social stratification. On the other hand, it might be argued that Principle I is actually a byproduct of social mobility.

The salient fact about the interaction of sex and social class is that the greatest difference between men and women is found in the group with the most extreme style shifting and the greatest recognition of external standards of correctness. This is regularly the second highest status group. In social terms, it is the lower middle class; in occupational categories, it is white-collar workers and small entrepreneurs; in educational levels, it is those who have more than high school and less than college training. Women in this group are certainly not the least powerful in the social spectrum. On the contrary, they frequently have considerably more political and economic power than working-class or lower-class women. Moreover, they frequently make more money and have more opportunity than their upper working-class male partners.

To pursue these issues further, we must ask whether a similar interaction of sex and social class can be found in linguistic change from within the system, that is, change from below.

The question of interaction in linguistic change from below
One cannot compare the interaction of sex and social class directly for stable and changing linguistic variables, because the patterns of distribution by social class are quite different. Recent research has pursued the description of these patterns vigorously, as one strategy for the explanation of change: the search for the innovators of linguistic change. The most substantial finding is that change from below is associated with a *curvilinear pattern*, where greater use of the new form is shown by the intermediate groups (upper working and lower middle) than the extreme groups (upper middle and lower working). This contrasts with the *monotonic pattern* of stable sociolinguistic variables previously examined.

The interaction of sex and social class has proved to be critical for our understanding of the curvilinear pattern and the explanation of linguistic change. The developments that have led to this situation may be outlined as follows:

1. 19th- and early 20th-century accounts of the causes of linguistic change led to the expectation that the innovators of change would be located either in the highest or the lowest social stratum, depending on the theoretical view adapted.
2. Meillet (1921) argued that the sporadic course of linguistic change can only be understood by association with sporadic changes in the composition of the speech community.

3. Sturtevant (1947) proposed that initial linguistic changes are originally associated with particular social groups, and the progress of the change depends on their adoption by neighboring groups who associate them with the social traits of the initiators. Variation between newer and older forms is associated with competition between social groups, and continues only as long as that competition endures.
4. Labov (1965) outlined a mechanism of linguistic change that may begin with a group located anywhere in the social spectrum.
5. Kroch (1978) pointed out that no change from below had been associated with an upper-class or upper middle-class group, and argued that such changes are always initiated with working-class groups, who favor more natural linguistic processes.
6. Labov (1973) – on the basis of evidence from New York City (Labov, 1966), Norwich (Trudgill, 1974b), and Panama City (Cedergren, 1973) – pointed out that, in addition, no lower-class or lower working-class group had been found to initiate change, and argued that the change from below was associated with a curvilinear pattern in the socioeconomic hierarchy.
7. The Philadelphia Project on Linguistic Change and Variation confirmed the predicted curvilinear pattern for all but one of the new and vigorous changes in that community (Labov, 1980). As the evidence to be cited shows, the innovators of change are located among the highest status members of the local community: lower middle class and upper working class.[21]

At this point, we must consider the possibility that the curvilinear pattern is a byproduct of the sexual differentiation of linguistic variables. Let us suppose that linguistic change is in general led by the working class and that a majority of these changes are more advanced among female speakers. If the advancing change is associated with female behavior, it is not unlikely that working-class men will withdraw from it and that this reaction will be greater in the lower working class. Such an interpretation would lead us to predict that a curvilinear pattern will not be found in male-dominated changes, nor among females, but only among males for female-dominated changes.[22]

If this proves to be the case, the interaction of sex and social class would be the critical organizing factor in the process of linguistic change. The balance of this article examines this question through evidence from a further analysis of the Philadelphia data.

The interaction of sex and social class in Philadelphia

The Philadelphia vowel system and its evolution
The Philadelphia speech community was selected for a detailed investigation of the social location of linguistic change because a very large section of the segmental phonology of the dialect was involved in active change.[23] As the northernmost of the southern cities, Philadelphia displayed most features of the Southern Shift (Labov, 1991): a chain shift of (ahr) → (ohr) → /uhr/ in the back,[24] and the fronting of the nuclei of (uw), (ow), and (aw), except before liquids. The upgliding diphthongs show radically different behavior according to whether the vowel is free (F) or checked (C). Free vowels are considerably in advance of checked ones. In addition,

Philadelphia shows a split of the short *a* class into a tense /æh/ and lax /æ/ in closed syllables, like most cities of the middle Atlantic and southern states, with a consequent raising and fronting of the tense form to high position.[25] This (æh) variable can be separated into three classes of tensed vowels.

(æhN): before front nasals /m/ and /n/ in *ham, man, hand,* etc.
(æhS): before voiceless front fricatives /f,θ,s/ in *laugh, bath, pass,* etc.
(æh$): before voiced stops in the three words *mad, bad, glad.*

The checked versus free distinction also affects the front upgliding vowels /iy/ and /ey/. But the traditional opening of the nuclei of these vowels is reversed for /ey/ in checked position. (eyC) shows very strong age coefficients that indicate that it is becoming higher and fronter among younger speakers.

The nucleus of /ay/ also shows a strong allophonic differentiation, but in this case, vowels before voiceless obstruents are opposed to all others. The allophone (ayO) before voiceless obstruents is strongly centralized, and usually backed, among younger speakers. The other allophones of /ay/, before voiced consonants and finally, do not participate in this movement.

The investigation of the Philadelphia sound system that produced the current evidence involved the following steps:

1. *The neighborhood study*: long-term semiparticipant studies of 10 Philadelphia neighborhoods, involving from one to four interviews with 180 speakers.[26]
2. *The telephone survey*: a random sample of 60 listed telephone users, involving relatively brief interviews of 15–20 minutes.
3. *Acoustic analysis*: analysis of the vowel systems of 116 speakers, using a linear predictive coding algorithm on the frequency domain data provided by a hardware spectrum analyzer.
4. *Normalization*: the reduction of all data to a single referential system that eliminates most of the effects of differences of vocal tract length of men and women, using the geometric mean algorithm of Nearey (1977).
5. *Regression analysis*: the normalized F1 and F2 means of the analyzed speakers were entered into a stepwise regression analysis that yielded significant correlations with 18 independent variables, including age, sex, occupation, education, income, house upkeep, mobility, ethnicity, neighborhood, foreign language use, generational status, and communication patterns.

The coefficients for the Philadelphia vowels are entered into systems of linear equations of the form:

Formant value in Hz = Constant + a * age + b * sex . . .
i.e., F2 (aw) = 2170 − 4.16 * age + 96 * sex . . .

where sex = 1 if female, 0 if male.[27] Thus, the predicted value for a group of females 35 years old would be 2170 − 4.16 * 35 + 96 = 2120 (Hz), whereas males of the same age would show, all other things being equal, a value of 2170 − 4.16 * 35 + 96 * 0 = 2024.

Age coefficients: Philadelphia sound changes in apparent time
Fig. 1.6 is a graphic portrayal of the movements of Philadelphia vowels in apparent time. The circles represent the mean values for the entire population of 116 speakers.[28] The arrows through each circle show the size of the age coefficient. The head of the arrow is at the predicted value of F1 and F2 for a group 25 years younger than the mean, and the tail of the arrow for a group 25 years older than the mean, all other things being equal. This diagram, combined with evidence from the Telephone Study and from earlier observations in real time, allows us to set up a series of five levels of sound changes: [29]

1. *completed changes*: the backing and raising of (ahr), which shows no age coefficients.
2. *almost completed changes*: the fronting and raising of (æh) along the front peripheral path; the backing and raising of (ohr) along the back peripheral path.[30]
3. *mid-range changes*: the fronting of (uw) and (ow) except before liquids.
4. *new and vigorous changes*: the fronting and raising of the nucleus of (aw);[31] the reversal of the lowering of the nucleus of checked (eyC), with fronting and raising along the front peripheral path; the centralization and backing of (ay0) before voiceless finals.
5. *incipient changes* (which are frequently below the level of significance): the lowering of (i) and (e) along the front nonperipheral path; the raising and backing of (ʌ); the raising and fronting of checked (iy).

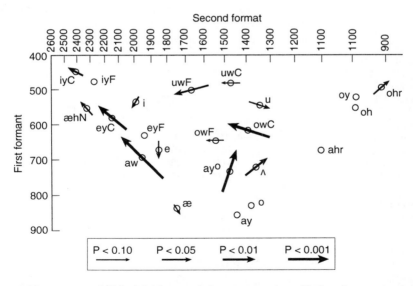

Fig. 1.6 Movements of Philadelphia vowels in apparent time. Circles show mean values for 116 speakers in the Neighborhood Study. Vectors connect values for groups 25 years older & younger than the mean. F = free vowel; C = checked vowel; 0 = before voiceless finals.

The division of these sound shifts by their relative age is an important factor in the analysis of the interaction of sex and social class with the age distributions. The new and vigorous changes show us the pattern of change from below – before any significant social reactions to them have taken place. The almost completed changes, and in particular the raising and fronting of the (æh) variables, show us the pattern of sound changes that are overtly recognized and stigmatized.[32]

The sex coefficients
The classification of sound changes by level will be useful in presenting the sexual differentiation of these processes. Table 1.3 groups the changes by their relative age as indicated by real-time data and lists the significant or near-significant regression coefficients for age and sex. In each case, the coefficient is shown for the most characteristic formant: F1 for raising and lowering, F2 for fronting. The movements along the front and back peripheral path regularly show the strongest social correlations with the fronting dimension rather than raising, and F2 coefficients are shown for these. Note that F1 effects that are numerically smaller may be proportionally larger than F2 effects because perceptually the F2 dimension is logarithmic rather than linear. The figures shown without asterisks are of questionable significance, where p is greater than .05 but less than .10. They conform to

Table 1.3 Sex and age coefficients for Philadelphia sound changes

Variable	Age	Sex	
		Female-dominated	Male-dominated
Completed			
(ahr) F2	0	43*	
Almost completed			
(æhN) F2	−1.94**	70**	
(æhS) F2	−1.64*	51	
(æh$) F2	−2.93**	124**	
(ohr) F1	.97**		17*
Mid-range			
(uwF) F2	−4.10*	60	
(uwC) F2	−2.54*	115*	
(owF) F2	−4.31**	99	
(owC) F2	−3.03**	66*	
New and vigorous			
(aw) F2	−5.08**	99**	
(eyC) F2	−3.42**	63*	
(ay0) F1	2.04**		32**
Incipient			
(i) F1	−.25		
(e) F1	−1.01*	16	
(æ) F1	−.55	35*	
(ʌ) F1	1.11**		29*

$p < .10$; *$p < .05$; **$p < .01$.

the overall pattern of Table 1.3, where the coefficient indicates that all other things being equal, females show more advanced forms of the changes for all but the raising of (ohr) and the centralization of (ay0). The centralization of (Λ) appears to be linked to the latter, as they represent parallel shifts of the same nucleus.

The completed change (ahr) shows a residual female advantage in backing. We might expect this to be replicated in the backing of (ohr) as it advances slowly in a merger with /uhr/, because this process is linked with (ahr) in a chain shift. But the only sexual differentiation of (ohr) is found in the F1 dimension.

Among the nearly completed changes, all three allophones of (æh) are listed, and all three show a female advantage, significant in two of the three cases. This, of course, represents the pattern of spontaneous speech, which is almost uncorrected in Philadelphia. Controlled styles show the same effect as in New York City, where women display the most advanced forms of a stigmatized variable in their casual speech and the least advanced forms in the corrected responses of word lists and minimal pairs.

The mid-range changes – the fronting of (uw) and (ow) – show a consistent female advantage, except for the most advanced form, which was also apparently the earliest: (uwF). This suggests that the female advantage in the fronting of these vowels will disappear as the changes reach completion with fully fronted, nonperipheral nuclei, in contrast with the case of the (æ) variables.

The strongest female advantage appears in two of the new and vigorous changes, (aw) and (eyC). But here we also find that the third of these, (ay0), shows a significant effect of male domination. This third case is parallel with the centralization of /ay/ in Martha's Vineyard, which was strongly favored by males.[33]

The overall pattern of sexual differentiation established by these figures fits the results of the earlier literature reviewed. A sizeable majority of sound changes show women in the lead. The Philadelphia data add the further information that there is some degree of correlation between the degree of activity of the sound change and the size of the female advantage. As in previous studies, there are a few cases where this tendency is reversed, and men lead women.

The curvilinear pattern in Philadelphia
Labov (1980) presented the Philadelphia evidence for the confirmation of the hypothesis of a curvilinear pattern. A significant curvilinear social class pattern appeared in two of the three new and vigorous changes – the same ones that showed a female advantage in Table 1.2. The social dimension was represented there by a combined index of socioeconomic status, made up of three equally weighted indicators: occupation, education, and residence value. Further investigation has shown that occupation has the strongest correlations with the sound changes involved, and house residence the weakest. In fact, the single indicator of occupation has a slight advantage over the combined index in consistency and strength of the correlations, and this indicator will be used throughout the presentation to follow. The occupational classification is essentially that of the U.S.

Census: Unemployed, Unskilled labor, Skilled labor, Clerical, Managerial, Professional (and owners). Women who were currently working were classified by their own occupations. Married women not working received the classification of the breadwinner of the family. Retired people were classified according to their last occupation. In the analyses to be presented, the small unemployed group is combined with unskilled labor.[34]

Fig. 1.7 presents a combined view of seven social variables across the five occupational classes. These display the results of inserting the occupational coefficients x_i in the linear equation:

$$\text{Vowel formant} = \text{Constant} + x_0 * \text{sex} + x_1 * \text{age} + x_2 * \text{unskilled}$$
$$+ x_3 * \text{clerical} + x_4 * \text{managerial} + x_5 * \text{professional},$$

where age is the numerical value for a given speaker, sex is 0 for male and 1 for female, and each of the occupational classes takes on a value of 0 or 1, depending on whether that speaker is classified in that occupational group. Thus, for a member of the managerial class, x_4 would be 1, and x_2, x_3, and x_5 would all be 0.[35] To achieve a unique solution where such dummy variables are concerned, one factor in each factor group must be a residual factor, which is always represented by 0 and is not entered into the algorithm. This will appear in the final analysis with a value of 0.00, and the significance of the other factors in the group will be measured by their degree of departure from 0.00. Thus, male is assigned 0 in the sex group, and the sex coefficient represents the effect of a speaker being female as

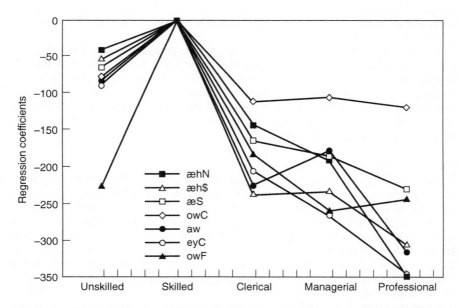

Fig. 1.7 The curvilinear pattern in the Philadelphia Neighborhood Study as reflected in occupational coefficients of multiple regression analysis, weighted for the number of tokens for each speaker. *Skilled* occupation is fixed at 0.00 as the reference group.

opposed to male. As our main purpose is to test the hypothesis of a curvilinear pattern where the *skilled* occupational group is the most advanced, it is the relationship of the surrounding occupational groups to this one that must be tested. The *skilled* group is therefore the residual group and appears with the 0.00 value in Figs 1.7–9.

Fig. 1.7 shows a curvilinear pattern for seven variables. (The numerical data on which this and the following two figures are based are given in Appendix 2.) The connected lines trace the pattern of five occupational coefficients for each variable. For all seven, there is a significant negative value for the *unskilled* class as compared with the *skilled* class.

The most advanced mean position is shown for (æhN) before nasals; behind this are (æhS) and (æh$). The rates of change also differ: (æh$) is considerably higher than the other two. It should also be noted that (æhN) is the most prominent in social awareness, most often corrected, and most often stigmatized in subjective reaction tests as an indication of the "harsh, nasal sounds" in the Philadelphia dialect. In Fig. 1.7, the three squares representing the (æh) variables are less differentiated than the others. The smallest differential between the *unskilled* and *skilled* classes is shown for the most advanced allophone, as is the greatest differential for (æh$), the variable with the highest rate of change.

A much greater differential between the *unskilled* and *skilled* class is shown for the new and vigorous changes, with a much more significant exemplification of the curvilinear pattern. The values of the *unskilled* class for the new and vigorous changes (aw) and (eyC) are grouped closely together below, along with (owC). All of these, including the very low value for (owF), are at a significance level of $p < .001$.

To the right of the *skilled* class, the values for all classes are significantly lower. For the most advanced changes, there is a very steep and regular social stratification: the higher the occupational class, the greater the negative coefficient. The middle range change (owC) does not show such a steep slope, and the only significant division of the population is between the *skilled* class and the others.

The fronting of (uw) does not show any marked social stratification. This is true of (uwC), which shows a female sex advantage, and (uwF), which does not. Though (uw) is structurally parallel to (ow) in the development of the Philadelphia dialect, it is apparently not as sensitive to social differentiation.[36]

No evidence appears of a curvilinear pattern for the (ay0) variable, which was also exceptional in its reversal of the dominant pattern of sexual differentiation.

Interaction of social class and sex

The results displayed in Fig. 1.7 provide strong support for the curvilinear pattern as the characteristic mode of development. Because the new and vigorous changes display the greatest differentiation of the *skilled* working class, it seems likely that the innovators of change are located in that group. It also appears that there is an association between female domination of a change and the curvilinear pattern. The next step in the analysis is therefore to carry out separate multivariate analyses for males and females and to see

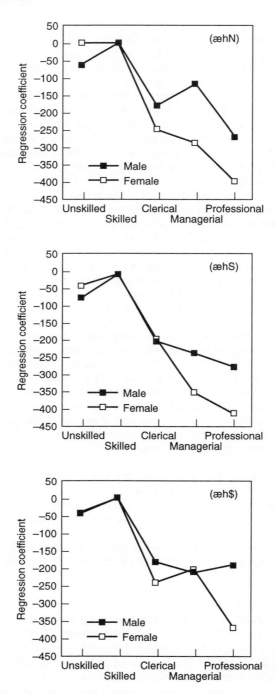

Fig. 1.8 Occupational coefficients by sex for the (æh) variables

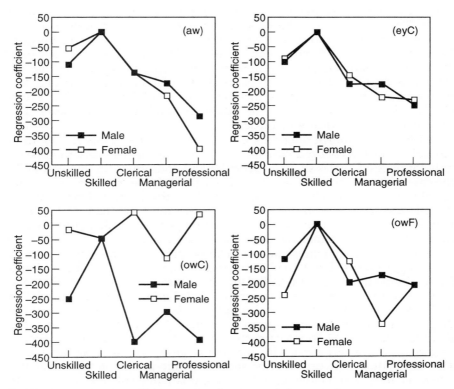

Fig. 1.9 Occupational coefficients by sex for new and vigorous changes

if the curvilinear pattern holds for both sexes. If the curvilinear pattern is a byproduct of the retreat of lower working-class males from a female-dominated change, the curvilinear relations of Fig. 1.7 will appear only in the male analysis, but not in the female.

Fig. 1.8 shows the results for the nearly completed changes, the raising and fronting of (æh) as reflected in the increase of F2 in apparent time. These showed the minimal evidence for a curvilinear pattern in Fig. 1.7, with the least effect for the most advanced changes. Fig. 1.8 shows that the ordering of these three allophones in Fig. 1.7 is also correlated with the differentiation of the sexes. The weakness of the curvilinear pattern for (æhN) seen in Fig. 1.7 is seen in Fig. 1.8 to be entirely dependent on the behavior of women, who show no differentiation at all for *unskilled* and *skilled* speakers. The difference between men and women is less for (æhS), and the sexes are identical for the (æh$), the least advanced item with the highest rate of change. On the right hand side of the three diagrams, we can see the opposite pattern: a decreasing differentiation of men and women. The most highly stigmatized item (æhN) shows the greatest differentiation of women in the *managerial* and *professional* classes, and (æh$) the least.

Fig. 1.9 displays the patterns for the new and vigorous changes, (aw) and (eyC). The case of (aw) shows a curvilinear pattern for both men and women, but with a differentiation of the sexes in the expected direction. Women show less difference between the *unskilled* and *skilled* classes than men, and a sharper slope of differentiation for the *managerial* and *professional* classes. This variable resembles the intermediate pattern of (æhS) but with a considerably greater distance between *unskilled* and *skilled* speakers. On the other hand, (eyC) shows no difference at all between the sexes. The two curves are practically identical.

The third and fourth diagrams in Fig. 1.9 show the results for the (ow) variables. For the checked variable (owC), the curvilinear pattern appears only for males; females show an irregular and nonsignificant fluctuation. In the case of (owF), both show a curvilinear pattern, the only case where the female *unskilled* group is lower than the male *unskilled* group. On the whole, there is less regularity in the fronting of (ow) and (uw) than for the front vowels, and the fluctuations for these mid-range changes do not throw any further light on the problems we are addressing here.

For a more direct representation of these differences as they appear in phonological space, Fig. 1.10 plots the mean values of (eyC) for both F1 and F2. It is evident here that the *skilled* group is clearly in advance of all others. There is a clear separation between the *skilled* group and the others. The *unskilled*, *clerical*, and *managerial* groups are associated in the center of the diagram, and the *professional* group is isolated at the lower right. Note that if we had selected F1 to measure the rate of change, the same curvilinear pattern would emerge but with the *clerical* group as the most advanced. This alternation between interior socioeconomic groups is typical of linguistic change from below. In some cases, it is white-collar workers or the lower middle class who are in the lead; whereas in others, it is the *skilled* workers or the upper working class.[37] On the whole, F2 gives us a more

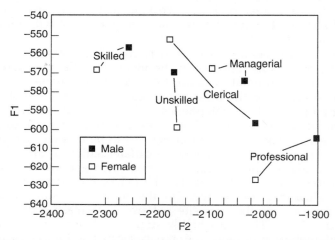

Fig. 1.10 Mean values for (eyC) F1 and F2 for five occupational groups in the Philadelphia Neighborhood Study

regular view of the tensing and raising of the front vowels in Philadelphia, with more significant coefficients for all variables.

Does sexual differentiation create the curvilinear pattern?
How can we best interpret these results? On the one hand, there is ample evidence to support the curvilinear pattern and the location of the innovators of change in an interior social group. On the other hand, there is ample evidence for the differentiation of the sexes and a closer association of the curvilinear pattern with males than with females.

The key to the situation appears to lie in the temporal stratification of the variables. The youngest change that gives us full data on change in progress is the raising and fronting of checked /ey/: the variable (eyC). There is no trace of this variable in the earlier literature. It represents the reversal of the long-standing trend to open the nuclei of front upgliding diphthongs in Philadelphia, following the pattern of the Southern Shift in the southern United States and southern England. Though we have evidence that this sound change contributes to misunderstanding within and across dialects,[38] it lies far below the level of conscious attention. No phonetician or popular writer on Philadelphia dialect detected it before our instrumental results showed the change in progress. On the other hand, the raising and fronting of (aw) is a continuation of the process of fronting that led from an earlier [ɑu] to the conservative Philadelphia [æu], and may also be associated with the raising and fronting of tense /æh/. Thus, (aw) is a further development of an old phenomenon, whereas (eyC) is a new phenomenon entirely. Subjective reaction tests show a consistent stigmatization of advanced forms of (aw). It is not surprising then that (aw) is shifted toward the pattern of the oldest changes in progress, (æhN), (æhS), and (æh$).

Fig. 1.11 shows the gradual evolution of the sexual differentiation of the Philadelphia sound changes, separating the lower class on the one hand from the middle classes on the other. The horizontal axis orders the sound changes from the newest changes on the left to the oldest on the right. The vertical axis registers the difference between the occupational coefficients found in separate multiple regression analyses of female and male speakers. The upper curve shows the differentiation of male and female speakers in the *unskilled* occupational group. No differentiation is found for the newest change, (eyC), but a distinct female advantage appears for the others. The irregularity of (æh$) is probably due to the relatively small amount of data.[39]

The lower curve in Fig. 1.11 is the female–male difference of the mean values of the coefficients for the three middle-class groups: *clerical, managerial,* and *professional*. For (eyC) there is again no significant difference between males and females, as we have seen. The rest of the sound changes show a steadily decreasing value, indicating that in the middle classes, the tendency for women to use more conservative values than men increases over time. The net result is a steady increase in sexual differentiation as sound changes become older.[40]

Fig. 1.11 should not be interpreted to mean that there is no differentiation of (eyC) for men and women. The normalized mean values for men and

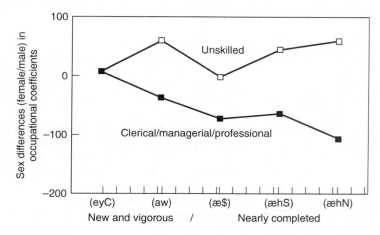

Fig. 1.11 Sex differences in occupational coefficients for five Philadelphia sound changes. Upper line = values for *unskilled* group. Lower line = mean values for *clerical, managerial,* and *professional* groups.

women for F2 of (eyC) differ by 90 Hz, and Table 1.3 indicates a significant advantage for women with a sex coefficient of 63 Hz.[41] Fig. 1.11 only shows that for (eyC), the effect of occupation does not differ by sex. As a whole, it recapitulates the view derived from Fig. 1.7 and 1.8: at the outset, sex does not interact with social class, but does so increasingly as change progresses.

The pattern of Fig. 1.11 foreshadows the gradual elimination of the curvilinear pattern in favor of a monotonic pattern, where the sociolinguistic variable becomes aligned with the socioeconomic hierarchy as well as with stable sociolinguistic variables such as negative concord or (ing). This process obviously does not operate uniformly for men and women. Fig. 1.11 shows that the first stages in this process of sexual differentiation are not the withdrawal of men from a female-dominated change, but rather a negative reaction of women to a growing social awareness of the change.

The role of women or the role of men?
In most discussions of sex differences in language, the emphasis is placed on the special behavior of women. The issue is sometimes raised as to whether one should focus on the behavior of men instead. In the case cited earlier of Australian adolescents (Eisikovits, 1981), the males seem to be the initiators of sexual differentiation. In that study, the boys reversed the normal direction of accommodation and distanced themselves even further from the speech of the interviewer in speech immediately following hers. The initial formulation of Principle I in this article describes the behavior of men, though the complementary statement about women would have served equally well. But in this section, evidence has mounted that women are as a rule the active agents of sexual differentiation. In Fig. 1.4, one group stands out from all the others: lower middle-class women, who show a very different slope of style shifting from all other groups. No male group

shows such a departure from the general pattern. The interaction of sex and social class leaves us no choice but to focus on women's behavior, and to assess its effect on linguistic change. As the innovators of most linguistic changes, women in intermediate social classes spontaneously create the differences between themselves and men. In adopting new prestige features more rapidly than men, and in reacting more sharply against the use of stigmatized forms, women are again the chief agents of differentiation. In particular, women in the second highest group respond more rapidly than men to changes in the social status of linguistic variables, and men usually follow behind with a lesser degree of investment in the social values of linguistic variation.[42]

The rise and fall of sexual differentiation
In the first section of this article, some of the general principles that emerge from Eckert's analysis of the Northern Cities Shift in the Detroit area were introduced, but her particular conclusions were not considered. Fig. 1.4 and Table 2 of Eckert (1989a) provide a remarkable parallel to Fig. 1.11 of this article. They show a similar replacement of one distributional pattern by another as one moves from the earliest stages of a sound change to the oldest. In this case, the oldest change is also the raising and tensing of short *a*, but the other stages of the Northern Cities Shift are different from the Philadelphia sound changes. The shift that Eckert documented is from social class conditioning in the early stages (in the form of a Jocks vs. Burnout difference) to sexual differentiation in the later stages. She concluded by questioning whether sexual differentiation is present in the early stages of change, because it was not significant in the backing of (e) and (ʌ) in the Detroit area. The many examples of sexual differentiation of sound change in progress that I have cited in the first half of this article may not bear crucially on the question, because in most cases they do not report the earliest stages.

Our instrumental studies allow us to attack this issue directly by adding a number of sound changes at an even earlier stage than (eyC) and (aw). Regression analyses were carried out for all Philadelphia vowels; among these it is possible to identify *incipient* changes that show small but consistent shifts across apparent time. Some of the age coefficients are significant at the .05 level, whereas others are not. But the pattern of parallel movement and the association with the more significant changes do indicate the possibility of sound change in progress. The incipient changes show only sporadic correlations with social class, ethnicity, or neighborhood – probably all the results of chance fluctuation. However, one can find some regular patterns of sexual differentiation that include incipient changes, new and vigorous changes, and changes almost completed.

The top figure in Fig. 1.12 presents such a pattern for six vowels that involve changes in F1. The horizontal axis shows three incipient changes on the left: the lowering of short (i) and (e) and the raising of (ʌ). These are followed by one new and vigorous change, the centralization of (ay0). Next is a nearly completed change, the raising of (ohr) in *more, board*, and so forth, and then a completed change: the raising of /ahr/ to lower mid position. For each vowel, empty squares show the simple difference in the

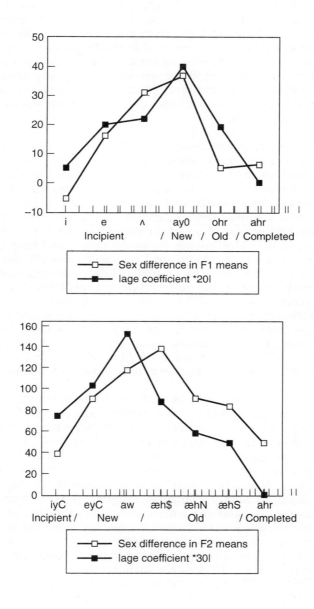

Fig. 1.12 Age coefficients and mean sex differences in Hz for six vowel changes involving F1 and seven vowel changes involving F2

F1 means in Hz for males and females (as *female–male*). A second point is plotted for each vowel, indicated by the solid squares: the absolute values of the age coefficients for the sound change as a whole for men and women combined, multiplied by 20.

The rise and fall of these two curves is very similar. The multiplier 20 was chosen mechanically for the age coefficients to allow a close comparison of the two curves, but it has an interesting interpretation. The top figure in Fig. 1.12 shows that a difference roughly equivalent to one generation is found between men and women for sound changes at all stages.

The bottom figure in Fig. 1.12 shows the corresponding data for the sound changes that crucially involve F2 movements. At the extreme left, the fronting of (iyC) is shown as an incipient change. At the extreme right, the completed change /ahr/ is supplied, this time analyzing the backing component. Again, the two curves are quite similar in contour, but they do not match as closely in value. A factor of 30 was selected to permit the best comparison. The greatest difference between the two curves is found with (æh$), which – as we have seen – is the least reliable. In general, the curves are skewed so that the age coefficients are relatively greater at the beginning, and the sex effect is relatively greater in the older changes. This suggests a parallel with Eckert's findings in Detroit, which are largely dependent on F2 differences. But it is also clear that sexual differentiation is present at the beginning in the expected direction and follows the development of the change with very similar contours. Again, the sexes differ at each stage by a value roughly equal to one generation.

Resolving problems in the sexual differentiation of language

These results may throw some light on the four problems raised in the first section.

1. *The biological bias*. Two of the findings presented here indicate that biological factors are not likely to have much value in accounting for the sexual differentiation of language: (a) the fact that Principle II does not apply in a minority of cases, and (b) the fact that Principle I interacts strongly with social factors. However biological bias, more or less unconscious, may underlie the summary treatments of sexual differentiation that conceals the crucial interactions.

   A biological bias is not avoided by dropping the category of men and women as independent variables, but rather by tracing the differential behavior of men and women through a wide variety of social factors. It is only this information that will permit the development of interpretive categories that will command general agreement.

2. *The generality of gender*. The general character of the male/female difference is manifested most clearly in the independence of sex and social class in the early stages of change. To the extent that they participate in the change, all social classes behave in roughly the same way at this stage.

   As noted at the outset, the irregular course of sound change is best correlated with fluctuations in the social class makeup of the speech community. We have also seen that the second highest status group plays a crucial role in sexual differentiation of later stages. To the extent that sexual differentiation interacts with the social class structure, the differential behavior of men and women will be correlated with local changes in space and time. As different populations move into the position of *second highest social group*, the rise and fall of sexual differentiation in that group will play a crucial role in the trajectory of the change.

3. *The reversal of roles.* Is there a single factor that would account for the opposing types of sexual differentiation in stable and changing linguistic situations? The answer that is provided here is no. Figs. 1.7–12 indicate two processes at work that are quite distinct in their history, their motivation, and their interaction with social factors. Sexual differentiation at the beginning of a linguistic change appears to be independent of other social factors. This suggests a mechanical process that is the same for all social classes. Sexual differentiation toward the end of a linguistic change interacts strongly with many social factors – not merely socioeconomic class as here and in Holmquist (1988), but local orientation (Labov, 1963) and race and ethnicity (Poplack, 1978). This points to a socially sensitive mechanism of sound change that involves the different roles that men and women play, the cultural norms that govern their behavior, and their relative power and opportunities for improving their life chances.

4. *Intimate diversification.* The problem of intimate diversification concerns the apparent inconsistency between sexual differentiation and the well-accepted principle of local density that would tend to level out any such differences at an early stage. There is a simple and mechanical process of differentiation that would resolve this inconsistency and account for the differentiation of the sexes in the early stages of sound change.

This differentiation logically begins in the acquisition of the first forms of the language by the language learner from the primary caregiver, as first implied in Gauchat's observations and developed further in the third section of this article. In all the societies studied so far, that caregiver is most often a female – a mother, grandmother, aunt, female babysitter, or daycare worker. Let us consider again the consequences of this fact. When a language learner encounters tokens of a female-dominated change in progress, it will be in the relatively advanced form used by the primary caregiver. In the case of a male-dominated feature, like the centralization of (ay0), the learner will encounter a less advanced form from the same caregiver. The simple logic of the situation will inevitably accelerate the advance of female-dominated forms and retard the advance of male-dominated forms. This process is consistent with the principle of local density, because it involves the quantitative effect of differential patterns of communication between the sexes, leading to a preponderant effect of female-dominated changes without any intersection with attitudes, emotions, or local cultural norms.

Principle I, which interacts massively with such factors, cannot be attributed to such a simple, mechanical effect. What then is the constant factor that is responsible for the gross uniformity of Principle I? It is important to note here that the differences between men and women in their reactions to linguistic change are not qualitative but quantitative. Both men and women respond to the general principle that whenever people become aware of a change in the mechanism of their language, they reject it. The right-hand sides of Figs. 1.7–9 gave us a clear view of the development of such a reaction formation in the community: class stratification becomes sharper as sound changes near completion. There is no mode of behavior shown here peculiar to women. Rather, we see that what women are doing, men are also doing, to a lesser degree. The left-hand sides of Figs. 1.7–9 appear to show that lower-class women use more of the stigmatized sound changes as time goes on. This is an unwanted consequence of the fact that we took the skilled working class as a fixed point in order to follow the curvilinear pattern. What actually seems to be happening is that the stigmatization of the sound changes affects the women of the skilled working class more strongly than the men, and the result is the leveling out of the social class coefficients for women. The sex differential that develops across the social spectrum is therefore a quantitative, not a qualitative difference between men and women.

Such quantitative differences between men and women certainly need explanation and further explorations on the basis of detailed observations of locally situated structures like that of Eckert (1989a). In this report, I have tried to reconstruct the base of objective fact that underlies Principle I in a way that will guide further interpretations. Though we are not likely to achieve any kind of unanimity in the interpretation of these social patterns, there are some directions that seem to me to be ruled out on the basis of these findings. Given the maximization of Principle I in the second highest status group, it is difficult to maintain that the cause is the relative powerlessness of women in relation to men. It seems more likely that in the United States, the forces behind this principle are associated with upward mobility and a relative increase in the power of women in this group as opposed to other sectors of society.

The explanation of Principle II is more provocative from a linguistic point of view. Principle II, as we have seen, is less regular than Principle I in the sense that there is no way to predict in any given case whether men or women lead at the beginning of a linguistic change. The suggestion I have given – that it is a result of the asymmetry of the caregiving situation – is consistent with the probabilistic character of this principle and with its independence of social factors. It is not immediately obvious how to design an empirical study that would test this idea, but it is a goal worth considering for future work.

Notes

1. The effects of such global catastrophes – wars, invasions, revolutions, migrations, and epidemics – directly affect numbers of people who are in direct communication within the speech community. Less directly, they effect changes in the socio-economic hierarchy, the dominance of ethnic groups, the relationship of the city to the countryside, and the rights and duties of generations toward each other. In turn, such social changes result in the emergence of new class dialects (Kökeritz, 1953; Wyld, 1936), the redefinition of prestige dialects (Feagin, 1979; Labov, 1966), the diversification of local dialects (Labov, Yaeger, & Steiner, 1972), the development of new racial dialects (Bailey & Maynor, 1987), the decay and disappearance of rural dialects (Alturo & Turrell, 1990; Holmquist, 1988), and the importation of rural features into an urban setting (Abd-el-Jawad, 1981; Frazer, 1983).

2. In actual fact, many of the standard forms preferred by women are not conservative but innovative, and it is men who play the conservative role in retaining a preference for older forms, like the use of *don't* with third person singular subjects or the /in/ forms of the participle. But though this view of the matter may accord with the history of the language, it is not the general view that most people have, and preference for forms with overt prestige is usually seen as a preference for the older and more established way of speaking.

3. The nature of this fourth problem was called to my attention by Gillian Sankoff.

4. These principles reflect my own interpretations of Eckert's discussion, based as much on my own findings as on her treatment, and may not have done justice to the subtlety and clarity of her thinking on these matters. The reader is referred to Eckert (1989a) for a more definitive statement.

5. For many reasons, the individual face-to-face interview is the basic means of achieving such a controlled study.

6. This is not entirely true, as it is not uncommon for analysts of variation to reverse the procedure and examine the distribution of linguistic behaviors without any reference to given linguistic categories, using the a-theoretical approach of principal components or multidimensional scaling (Horvath & Sankoff, 1987; Poplack, 1981). But the interpretation of the results is necessarily in terms of recognized social categories, and this approach is actually a complement to an analysis that focuses more directly on language with social facts as independent variables.

7. The distance between the two approaches has been reduced by a number of modifications and combinations of the two basic methods, abandoning some of the strengths of each to gain some of the advantages of the other. Thus, the Philadelphia Project on Language Change and Variation confined its random sample to a brief telephone survey and gathered the main body of information by long-term, semiparticipant investigations of selected neighborhoods. A fine-grained study of interaction was obtained by recording one speaker through an entire day (Hindle, 1980), and this was interpreted against the background of the neighborhood telephone surveys. In Eckert's study of the Detroit suburbs (1989a), the measures of sound change that form the dependent variable were gathered from recorded conversations with the investigator, rather than the free conversation of natural groups. Connections with objective measures of social status are provided in Eckert (1989b).

   Between these two polar opposites lies an approach to the study of small groups that is intermediate in several respects. Milroy and Margrain (1980) utilize general network analysis that is free of reference to the specific properties of any particular group (also Bortoni-Ricardo, 1985; Milroy & Milroy, 1985). But as the interaction of network analysis with sex has not been a major concern of this work so far, I do not consider it in this review.

8. For further references on sexual differentiation, see the reference note following Hymes' reprinting of the Haas article (1944: 228).

9. It should be pointed out that the Detroit interviews were more comparable to the interviews of the New York City Lower East Side study, carried out by whites in a relatively formal setting, than to the Harlem or Philadelphia studies in the black community, and therefore offer the maximum opportunity to observe the differential response of black men and women to a formal situation.

10. Labov (1966) presented several such cases. Silva (1988) suggested that this is the case for the reversal of the traditional backing of /a/ in São Miguel Portuguese; but the male predominance for his 12 informants was not statistically significant.

11. In contrast, the backing of /a/, a new vernacular tendency, is led by men and is favored in the least monitored styles (see later discussion).

12. The most relevant types of experiments deal with social class differences in subjective evaluation of speech rather than sex differences. Labov, Cohen, Robins and Lewis (1968) showed that evaluations of speech as an indication of fighting ability were the inverse of evaluations of job suitability, but it should be noted that this pattern of response was much clearer for middle-class subjects than for working-class subjects.

13. The same family that registered the conservative behavior of females in respect to (ing) noted earlier in Mock (1979).

14. These conclusions were based on studies across five or six years of 36 college-educated adults, 12 lower-class adults, and 240 high school students aged 9–18 years. They were verified by a separate analysis of 90 speakers from the sample of Lavandera (1975).

15. Schieffelin's examination of language socialization among the Kaluli of New Guinea (1990) is a detailed study of this process. Chapter 8 gives an ethnographically sophisticated view of "The Socialization of Gender-Appropriate Behaviors" and also reviews other anthropological work in this area. It has also been shown that women use more advanced forms for female-dominated changes when they are interacting with intimate female friends (Hindle, 1980). But this is a relatively minor adjustment compared to the difference between male and female norms.

16. This is not a weakness of the variable rule program, which was designed primarily for the analysis of internal linguistic factors where we can expect independence. Rather, it is a defect in the unreflecting use of this mode of multivariate analysis to deal with social factors. Given the assumption of independence in the operation of the variable rule program, vigorous efforts must be made to locate interaction wherever one suspects it is to be found, as in the relation between sex and social class.

17. This sense of "hypercorrect" is distinct from but related to the more traditional concept of hypercorrection, where speakers create new forms by applying the reversal of a stigmatized rule to forms that had never undergone that rule. Overshooting a quantitative target can lead to a systematic change in the language, whereas hypercorrect forms, if generalized, will alter underlying forms or introduce irregularities into paradigms.

18. The variable (oh) is not corrected by everyone; when New Yorkers do attempt to correct it, they go beyond any forms found in the New York Vernacular and produce unpredictable alternations of [a], [ɒ], and [ɔ], with mean values ranging from 30 upward.

19. In the self-report tests of Labov (1966) and Trudgill (1972), a parallel distinction appears between the way people speak and the way they report that they speak.

20. Looked at in this way, many lower-class people are handicapped in the absence of this ability, as shown by a very low index of linguistic insecurity.

21. Additional evidence for the higher status of the innovators is derived from correlations with indices of communication patterns as well as observations by the semiparticipant-observers of the neighborhood studies, but for the purposes of this article, it will be sufficient to establish their status in the hierarchical system of occupations.

22. This issue was first raised by Anthony Kroch, in response to the first presentation of this article at NWAVE-XIV in 1984.

23. The speech community being discussed here is the white community of Philadelphia and does not include the large black population (38%). With rare exceptions, black speakers do not participate in the sound changes of the white

vernacular community, and in many respects, Philadelphia is divided into two distinct speech communities with different grammars and phonologies. Within the white community, there is a very high degree of structural uniformity, with close to 100% agreement on the distribution of words in phonemic categories and the phonological rules that operate upon these categories (Labov, 1989).

24. The third element of this chain shift is shown in slashes as /uhr/ because it is not a variable, does not move further away, and the end result is a merger almost completed with the variable (ohr).

25. For a detailed account of this distribution, see Labov (1989).

26. Recordings in these series were made with a full-track Nagra IV-S or Nagra III tape recorder and Sennheiser 214 dynamic lavaliere microphones. Field methods are described in Labov (1984).

27. Each coefficient is evaluated statistically by a value of t. For the value of 4.16, $t = 4.7$, with 90 degrees of freedom, so that $p < .01$. The number of degrees of freedom represents one less than the number of speakers included in the analysis.

28. In each case, the actual number of speakers may be less than the total, because for any given vowel, a few speakers may have had less than the number of tokens required to be included in the analysis. N actually ranges from 115 for (i) to 104 for (oy).

29. The age vectors from the Telephone Study correspond well to those shown here (Labov, 1980), though the smaller amount of data and the lower quality of the phonetic signal obscure some of the smaller effects. Real time observations of De Camp (1933), Tucker (1944), and Kurath and McDavid (1961) allow us to conclude that most of these changes in apparent time correspond to changes in real time.

30. In Fig. 1.6, the (æh) variables are represented only by the /æhN/ allophone; the other two show parallel movements somewhat behind, overlapping with /eyC/.

31. This shift shows a concurrent lowering of the target of the glide from /u/ to /ɔ/.

32. The stylistic reaction to the variable (æh) in Philadelphia is by no means as vigorous as in New York City, where speakers from all social levels show correction even in spontaneous speech. In Philadelphia, correction of (æh) is confined to middle-class speakers and occurs primarily in controlled styles. But the variable is a social stereotype ("the harsh, nasal *a*") and shows very sharp stratification. (ohr) shows considerable correction in controlled styles, especially in minimal pairs, but is much less prominent than (æh). (ahr) is fixed and shows no correction at all.

33. This is parallel to the development of (aw) in Canada, studied by Chambers and Hardwick (1985). Women in Vancouver and Toronto favor the fronting of the nucleus, as well as the reversal of the traditional centralization, which is accordingly stronger among men. Chambers and Hardwick also found a new phonetic development among younger Toronto males: a phonetic backing and rounding of the nucleus to [ɔw]. Backing is also the dominant direction for Philadelphia (ay°), though the only sexual differentiation is found in the F1 dimension.

34. If the nonwhite population had been included in this survey, the unemployed and unskilled groups would be considerably larger. As our population is limited to the white residents of Philadelphia, it is skewed on the social class dimension toward the upper working class.

35. More extended analyses were conducted with other social variables such as residence value, house upkeep, foreign language knowledge, generations in the United States, ethnicity, and neighborhood. The variables listed in the text

proved to be the most robust, and in most cases, the effect of other variables was not significant. The effect of ethnicity proved to be a powerful factor in the fronting of back vowels and was included in all analyses for those variables.

36. There is also much more random fluctuation in the /uw/ values, and a higher rate of errors in measurement, due to the problems of separating the first formant from voicing energy.
37. See Cedergren (1973) for such an alternation in the development of (ch) in Panama City.
38. As, for example, a misunderstanding in which "make us slaves" was heard as "make us leave."
39. Only three words are involved with this allophone, and many speakers show only a few tokens. Thirteen of the 116 speakers have no data in spontaneous speech, and the total number of tokens is only 299, as compared to 710 for (æhN).
40. When the changes are completed, the differences between the sexes normally disappear. Thus, for the completed backing and raising of (ahr), there are no significant differences between males and females for any occupational group.
41. Fig. 1.11 does not show developments in the upper working class because the *skilled* workers were taken as the point of reference for the others in all of these analyses of sexual differences. It should therefore not be taken to mean that there is no sexual differentiation in the *skilled* working class, where women are clearly in the lead.
42. A clear illustration of this principle appears in Gal (1978). The shift from Hungarian to German was correlated with membership in nonpeasant networks for both men and women to about the same degree (78% and 74%, respectively). But the correlation with age was much less for men than women (69% and 93%, respectively).

References

Abd-el-Jawad, H. (1981) *Phonological and social variation in Arabic in Amman*, Ph.D. dissertation, University of Pennsylvania.

Abd-el-Jawad, H. (1987) 'Cross-dialectal variation in Arabic: Competing prestigious forms', *Language in Society* 16: pp. 359–368.

Alba, O. (1990) *Variación fonetica y diversidad social en el Español Dominicano de Santiago*, Santiago: Pontificia Universidad Catolica Madre Y Maestra.

Albo, X. (1970) *Social constraints on Cochabamba Quechua*, Ph.D. dissertation, Cornell University, Latin American Studies Program, Dissertation Series No. 19.

Alturo, N. and Turell, M. T. (1990) 'Linguistic change in El Pont de Suert: The study of variation of /ʒ/', *Language Variation and Change* 2: pp. 19–30.

Anshen, F. (1969) *Speech variation among Negroes in a small southern community*, Ph.D. dissertation, New York University.

Ash, S. (1984) *Variability of final consonant deletion in BEV*. Paper presented at NWAVE-XIII, Philadelphia.

Babbitt, E.H. (1896) 'The English of the lower classes in New York City and vicinity', *Dialect Notes* 1: pp. 457–464.

Bailey, G., Bernstein, C. and Tillery, J. (n.d.) *The configuration of sound changes in Texas*.

Bailey, G. and Maynor, N. (1987) 'Decreolization?' *Language in Society* 16: pp. 449–473.

Bauer, R.S. (1982a) *Cantonese sociolinguistic patterns: Correlating social characteristics of*

speakers with phonological variables in Hong Kong Cantonese, Ph.D. dissertation, University of California, Berkeley.
—— (1982b) *Lexical diffusion in Hong Kong Cantonese: "Five" leads the way.* Paper given at the 8th Annual Berkeley Linguistic Society meeting.
—— (1986) 'The microhistory of a sound change in progress in Hong Kong Cantonese', *Journal of Chinese Linguistics* 14: pp. 1–41.
Bloomfield, L. (1933) *Language*, New York: Henry Holt.
Bortoni-Ricardo, S.M. (1985) *The urbanization of rural dialect speakers: A sociolinguistic study in Brazil*, Cambridge: Cambridge University Press.
Bradley, D. and Bradley, M. (1979) 'Melbourne vowels', *University of Melbourne Working Papers in Linguistics*, No. 5.
Brouwer, D., Gerritsen, M. and de Haan, D. (1979) 'Speech differences between men and women', *Language in Society* 8: pp. 33–50.
Callary, R E. (1975) 'Phonological change and the development of an urban dialect in Illinois', *Language in Society* 4: pp. 155–170.
Cedergren, H. (1973) *The interplay of social and linguistic factors in Panama*, Ph.D. dissertation, Cornell University.
Chambers, J.K. and Hardwick, M.F. (1985) 'Dialect homogeneity and incipient variation: Changes in progress in Toronto and Vancouver', in J. Harris and R. Hawkins (eds.), *Sheffield Working Papers in Language and Linguistics 2*, Sheffield: University of Sheffield School of Modern Languages and Linguistics.
Cheshire, J. (1981) 'Variation in the use of *ain't* in an urban British English dialect', *Language in Society* 10: pp. 365–382.
Clarke, S. (1984) *Sex differences in language usage: Some further observations.* Paper presented at NWAVE XIII, Philadelphia.
Clarke, S. (1987) 'Dialect mixing and linguistic variation in a non-overtly stratified society', in Denning et al. (1987), pp. 74–85.
Cofer, T. (1972) *Linguistic variability in a Philadelphia speech community*, Ph.D. dissertation, University of Pennsylvania.
De Camp, L.S. (1933) 'Transcription of "The North Wind" as spoken by a Philadelphian', *Le Maître Phonétique*, pp. 50–51.
Denning, K.M., et al. (eds.) (1987) *Variation in language: NWAV-XV at Stanford*, Stanford: Stanford University, Department of Linguistics.
De Paolo, M. (1988) 'Pronunciation and categorization in sound change', in Ferrara et al. (1988), pp. 84–92.
Eckert, P. (1986) 'The roles of high school social structure in phonological change'. Paper presented at the Chicago Linguistic Society.
—— (1989a) *Jocks and Burnouts: Social categories and identities in the high school*, New York: Teachers College Press.
—— (1989b) The whole woman: Sex and gender differences in variation, *Language Variation and Change* 1: pp. 245–268.
—— (ed.) (1991) *New ways of analyzing sound change*, Orlando, FL: Academic.
Eisikovits, E. (1981) *Inner-Sydney English: An investigation of grammatical variation in adolescent speech*, Ph.D. dissertation, University of Sydney.
Fasold, R. (1969) *A sociolinguistic study of the pronunciation of three vowels in Detroit speech.* Manuscript.
Feagin, C. (1979) *Variation and change in Alabama English*, Washington, DC: Georgetown University Press.
Ferrara, K., Brown, B., Walters, K. and Baugh, J. (eds.) (1988) *Linguistic change and contact: NWAV XVI*, Austin: University of Texas Linguistic Forum, 30. pp. 84–92.
Fischer, J.L. (1958) 'Social influences on the choice of a linguistic variant', *Word* 14: pp. 47–56.

Frazer, T.C. (1983) 'Sound change and social structure in a rural community', *Language in Society* 12: pp. 313–328.

Gal, S. (1978) 'Peasant men can't get wives: Language change and sex roles in a bilingual community', *Language in Society* 7: pp. 1–17.

—— (1980) *Language shift: Social determinants of linguistic change in bilingual Austria*, New York: Academic.

Gauchat, L. (1905) 'L'unité phonétique dans le patois d'une commune', in *Aus Romanischen Sprachen und Literaturen: Festschrift Heinrich Morf*, Halle: Map Niemeyer, pp. 175–232.

Gerritsen, M. and Jansen, F. (1980) 'The interplay between diachronic linguistics and dialectology: Some refinements of Trudgill's formula', in P. Maher (ed.), *Proceedings of the 3rd International Congress of Historical Linguistics*, Amsterdam: John Benjamins, pp. 11–37.

Guy, G. (1984) *Social class and language change*. Paper presented at NWAVE-XIII, Philadelphia.

Guy, G., Horvath, B., Vonwiller, J., Daisley, E. and Rogers, I. (1986) 'An intonational change in progress in Australian English', *Language in Society* 15: pp. 23–52.

Haas, M.R. (1944) 'Men's and women's speech in Koasati', *Language* 20: pp. 142–149.

Haeri, N. (1987) 'Male/female differences in speech: An alternative interpretation', in Denning et al. (1987), pp. 173–182.

Hermann, E. (1929) 'Lautveränderungen in der individualsprache einer Mundart', *Nachrichten der Gesellsch. der Wissenschaften zu Göttingen. Phl.-his. Kll.* 11: pp. 195–214.

Hibiya, J. (1988) *A quantitative study of Tokyo Japanese*, University of Pennsylvania dissertation.

Hindle, D. (1980) *The social and structural conditioning of phonetic variation*, Ph.D. dissertation, University of Pennsylvania.

Holmquist, J.C. (1985) 'Social correlates of a linguistic variable: A study in a Spanish village', *Language in Society* 14: pp. 191–203.

—— (1988) *Language loyalty and linguistic variation: A study in Spanish Cantabria*, Dordrecht: Foris.

Horvath, B. and Sankoff, D. (1987) 'Delimiting the Sydney speech community', *Language in Society* 16: pp. 179–204.

Houston, A. (1985) *Continuity and change in English morphology: The variable (ING)*, Ph.D. dissertation, University of Pennsylvania.

Kökeritz, H. (1953) *Shakespeare's pronunciation*, New Haven: Yale University Press.

Kroch, A. (1978) 'Toward a theory of social dialect variation', *Language in Society* 7: pp. 17–36.

Kurath, H. and McDavid, R.I., Jr. (1961) *The pronunciation of English in the Atlantic states*, Ann Arbor: University of Michigan Press.

Labov, W. (1963) 'The social motivation of a sound change', *Word* 19: pp. 273–309.

—— (1965) 'On the mechanism of linguistic change', *Georgetown Monographs on Language and Linguistics* 18: pp. 91–114.

—— (1966) *The social stratification of English in New York City*, Washington, DC: Center for Applied Linguistics.

—— (1972) *Sociolinguistic patterns*, Philadelphia: University of Pennsylvania Press.

—— (1973) 'The social setting of linguistic change', in T.A. Sebeok (ed.), *Current Trends in Linguistics II: Diachronic, areal, and typological linguistics*, The Hague: Mouton, pp. 195–253.

—— (1980) 'The social origins of sound change', in W. Labov (ed.), *Locating language in time and space*, New York: Academic, pp. 251–266.

—— (1982) 'Building on empirical foundations', in W. Lehmann & Y. Malkiel (eds.),

Perspectives on historical linguistics, Amsterdam and Philadelphia: John Benjamins, pp. 17–92.

—— (1984) 'Field methods of the Project on Linguistic Change and Variation', in J. Baugh and J. Sherzer (eds.), *Language in Use*, Englewood Cliffs: Prentice Hall, pp. 28–53.

—— (1989) 'The exact description of the speech community: Short *a* in Philadelphia', in R. Fasold and D. Schriffrin (eds.), *Language change and variation*, Washington, DC: Georgetown University Press, pp. 1–57.

—— (1991) 'The three dialects of English', in Eckert (in press).

Labov, W., Cohen, P., Robins, C. and Lewis, J. (1968) *A study of the non-standard English of Negro and Puerto Rican speakers in New York City*, Cooperative Research Report 3288, Vols I and II. Philadelphia: U.S. Regional Survey (Linguistics Laboratory, University of Pennsylvania).

Labov, W., Yeager, M. and Steiner, R. (1972) *A quantitative study of sound change in progress*, Philadelphia: U.S. Regional Survey.

Laferriere, M. (1979) 'Ethnicity in phonological variation and change', *Language* 55: pp. 603–617.

Lavandera, B. (1975) *Linguistic structure and sociolinguistic conditioning in the use of verbal endings in si clauses*, Ph.D. dissertation, University of Pennsylvania.

Lennig, M. (1978) *Acoustic measurement of linguistic change: The modern Paris vowel system*, Ph.D. dissertation, University of Pennsylvania.

Levine, L. and Crockett, H., Jr. (1966) 'Speech variation in a Piedmont community: Post-vocalic *r*', in S. Lieberson (ed.), *Explorations in sociolinguistics. Sociological Inquiry* 36, No. 2, pp. 204–226.

Lin, Y-H. (1988) 'Consonant variation in Taiwan Mandarin', in Ferrara et al. (1988), pp. 200–208.

López, L. (1983) *A sociolinguistic analysis of /s/ variation in Honduran Spanish*, Ph.D. dissertation, University of Minnesota.

Luthin, H.W. (1987) 'The story of California (ow): The coming-of-age of English in California', in Denning et al. (1987), pp. 312–324.

Macaulay, R. (1977) *Language, social class, and education*, Edinburgh: Edinburgh University Press.

Meillet, A. (1921) *Linguistique historique et linguistique générale*, Paris: La société linguistique de Paris.

Milroy, L. and Margrain, S. (1980) 'Vernacular language loyalty and social network', *Language in Society* 9: pp. 43–70.

Milroy, J. and Milroy, L. (1978) 'Belfast: Change and variation in an urban vernacular', in P. Trudgill (ed.), *Sociolinguistic patterns in British English*, London: Edwin Arnold, pp. 19–36.

—— (1985) 'Linguistic change, social network, and speaker innovation', *Journal of Linguistics* 21: pp. 339–384.

Mock, C.C. (1979) 'The social maturation of pronunciation: A family case study', *The Rural Learner* 1: pp. 23–37. (Southwest Missouri State University, School of Education and Psychology, Springfield).

—— (1991) 'The impact of the Ozark drawl: Its role in the shift of the diphthong /ey/', in Eckert (in press).

Modaressi, Y. (1978) *A sociolinguistic investigation of modern Persian*, Ph.D. dissertation, University of Kansas.

Morales, H.L. (1986) 'Velarization of -/N/ in Puerto Rican Spanish', in D. Sankoff (1986), pp. 105–113.

Mougeon, R. and Beniak, E. (1987) 'The extralinguistic correlates of core lexical borrowing', in Denning et al. (1987), pp. 337–347.

Mougeon, R., Beniak, E. and Valli, A. (1988) 'VAIS, VAS, M'AS in Canadian French: A sociohistorical study', in Ferrara et al. (1988), pp. 250–262.

Nearey, T. (1977) *Phonetic feature system for vowels*, Ph.D. dissertation, University of Connecticut.

Nicholas, J.K. (n.d.) *Study of a sound change in progress*, University of North Carolina, Greensboro, Interdepartmental Program in Linguistics.

Owens, T.W. and Baker, P.M. (1984) 'Linguistic insecurity in Winnipeg: Validation of a Canadian Index of Insecurity', *Language in Society* 13: pp. 337–350.

Poplack, S. (1978) 'On dialect acquisition and communicative competence: The case of Puerto Rican bilinguals', *Language in Society* 7: pp. 89–104.

—— (1981) 'Mortal phonemes as plural morphemes', in D. Sankoff & H. Cedergren (eds.), *Variation omnibus*, Alberta: Lingusitic Research, pp. 59–72.

Rissel, D.A. (1989) 'Sex, attitudes, and the assibilation of /r/ among young people in San Luis Potosí, Mexico', *Language Variation and Change* 1: pp. 269–284.

Sankoff, D. (ed.) (1986) *Diachrony and diversity*, Amsterdam and Philadelphia: John Benjamins.

Sankoff, G. (1980) *The social life of language*, Philadelphia: University of Pennsylvania Press.

Schieffelin, B.B. (1990) *The give and take of everyday life: Language socialization of Kaluli children*, Cambridge: Cambridge University Press.

Shopen, T. and Wald, B. (1982) *The use of (ing) in Australian English*. Manuscript.

Shuy, R., Wolfram, W. and Riley, W.K. (1966) *A study of social dialects in Detroit*. (Final Report, Project 6-1347). Washington, DC: Office of Education.

Silva, D.J. (1988) 'The sociolinguistic variance of low vowels in Azorean Portuguese', in Ferrara et al. (1988), pp. 336–344.

Silva-Corvalán, C. (1981) 'Extending the sociolinguistic variable to syntax: The case of pleonastic clitics in Spanish', in D. Sankoff and H. Cedergren (eds.), *Variation omnibus*, Alberta: Linguistic Research, pp. 335–342.

—— (1986) 'The social profile of a syntactico-semantic variable: Three verb forms in Old Castile', in D. Sankoff (1986), pp. 279–292.

Sturtevant, E. (1947) *An introduction to linguistic science*, New Haven: Yale University Press, Ch. 8.

Thibault, P. (1983) *Equivalence et grammaticalisation*, Ph.D. dissertation, University of Montreal.

Trudgill, P. (1972) 'Sex, covert prestige, and linguistic change in the urban British English of Norwich', *Language in Society* 1: pp. 179–195.

—— (1974a) 'Linguistic change and diffusion: Description and explanation in sociolinguistic dialect geography', *Language in Society* 3: pp. 215–246.

—— (1974b) *The social differentiation of English in Norwich*, Cambridge: Cambridge University Press.

Tucker, R, W. (1944) 'Notes on the Philadelphia dialect', *American Speech* 19: pp. 39–427.

Weinberg, M.F., de. (1974) *Un aspecto sociolinguistico del Español Bonaerense: la -S en Bahia Blanca*, Bahia Blanca: Cuadernos de Linguistica.

Weinreich, U., Labov, W. and Herzog, M. (1968) 'Empirical foundations for a theory of language change', in W. Lehmann and Y. Malkiel (eds.), *Directions for historical linguistics*, Austin: University of Texas Press, pp. 97–195.

Wolf, C. and Jiménez, E. (1979) *A sound change in progress: Devoicing of Buenos Aires /z/*. Manuscript.

Wolfram, W. (1969) *A sociolinguistic description of Detroit Negro speech*, Arlington, VA; Center for Applied Linguistics.

Woods, H. (1979) *A socio-dialectology survey of the English spoken in Ottawa: A study of sociological and stylistic variation in Canadian English*, Ph.D. dissertation, University of British Columbia.

Wyld, H.C. (1936) *A history of Modern Colloquial English*, London: Basil Blackwell.

2

Sex-based differences in compliment behavior

Robert K. Herbert

Originally published in *Language in Society*, 19 (1990).

The structure of the *compliment speech event* in American English has been the subject of some careful sociolinguistic investigation.[1] This speech event has the structure of an adjacency pair operation (Schegloff & Sacks 1973: 296) or action chain event (Pomerantz 1978: 109–10). That is, the compliment event is a two-unit turn in which Utterance 1 and Utterance 2 are linked by both temporal and relevancy conditions. In an example such as

(1)   A: That's a beautiful sweater.
       B: Thanks, my sister made it for me

B is conditionally relevant and sequentially dependent on A. Note that rules of interpretation may be necessary in order to identify the relevance of B to A. Accepting that A and B are linked within a compliment event leads one to recognize that B in pairs such as

(2)   A: You look very nice today.
       B: I'm in such a hurry though

is relevant is some unspecified way to A; the use of *though* in B links it to A, that is, it is not a topic shift. One may schematize the general structure of the compliment speech event as

(3)   A: compliments B
       B: responds/acknowledges that A has spoken.

The two acts comprising the preceding event have been treated independently in the literature. For example, Wolfson and Manes have examined the structure and content of the first in a series of interesting articles on American compliments (Manes 1983; Manes & Wolfson 1980; Wolfson 1981, 1983; Wolfson & Manes 1980). They noted, for example, that compliments display a surprisingly limited range of syntactic patterns: the vast majority of compliments are produced within one of the three formulaic frames in (4a); examples appear in (4b).

(4)   a.   I like NP
           That's a ADJ NP
           NP is ADJ
      b.   Wow, I really like your hair.
           That's a neat jacket.
           Your eyes are amazingly green.

The manifest content of compliments also tends to be drawn from a limited stock of concerns, for example, personal appearance (especially clothing and hair), (new) possessions, and the results of skill or effort. Finally, Wolfson and Manes suggested that the noncreativity in form and content of compliments is a function of their role in discourse. Compliments operate within the scheme of conversational postulates such as MAKE HEARER FEEL GOOD (Goody 1978; Lakoff 1975), and their formulaic nature limits the possibility that a hearer will misinterpret the speaker's intention to offer solidarity and good will.[2] Parallel to these findings for American English, Holmes (1988a) reported broadly similar patterning for New Zealand English.

Compliment responses also have been treated independently in the literature (e.g., Herbert 1986; Pomerantz 1978). Despite their independent treatments, the acts of complimenting and responding to compliments are obviously linked in crucial ways. One of the major premises of the present article is that – at some level of analysis – both acts can serve the function of negotiating solidarity, although this claim has rarely been made explicitly for compliment responses. The actual sociology of compliment work cannot be understood without considering simultaneously the whole of the compliment event. The treatment here focuses on sex-based differences in compliments and compliment responses. The data for the present study were collected ethnographically by students at the State University of New York at Binghamton, who were instructed to collect compliments and responses within the student community, in places such as classrooms, dining halls, the student union, and so on. Fieldworkers recorded the compliment, compliment response, sex of speaker and addressee, relationship of interlocutors (if known or discernible), location, and presence of interactional bystanders.[3] A total of 1,062 compliment events comprise the data base. In the following sections, data are presented on male–female differences in American compliment behavior. The 1,062 compliments events in the corpus have the following sex-based distribution:

Male–Male	228
Male–Female	258
Female–Female	330
Female–Male	246

Just as the norms for competent complement behavior may vary from one variety of English to another, so too appropriate norms for females and males within a single speech community obviously differ. First, some differences in the actual form of compliments offered by females and males are highlighted, and the discussion then turns to observed differences in response behavior, to the integration of these two sets of differences within a single framework, and to an ethnographic investigation of the compliment event.

Sex differences in compliment behavior

Manes and Wolfson (1980: 121) offered a relative frequency analysis of American compliments, which is reproduced in Fig. 2.1. Note that the Manes and Wolfson schema relies on syntactic patterns for categorization; these syntactic formulas account for 97.2 percent of their data. Data from New Zealand English presented by Holmes (1988a) are strikingly similar. Relying on such syntactic categorization, Holmes (1988b) found that women exhibited a slight preference for the formula *I (really) like/love NP* over *PRO is (really) (a) ADJ NP* (e.g., "That's a nice coat"), as opposed to men, who used both formulas with equal frequency. The major sex-based difference in formula use was the markedly greater frequency of *What (a)*

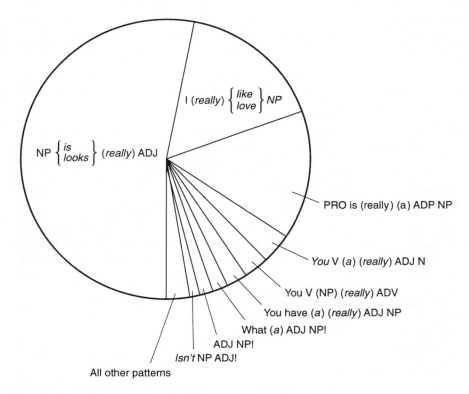

Fig. 2.1 Syntactic patterns distribution (Wolfson 1984: 238)

ADJ NP! ("What lovely earrings!") in the speech of women, whereas men use the minimal pattern ("Great shoes!") significantly more.

For present purposes, however, it may be more revealing to consider compliments according to the "personal focus" of the act, that is, whether the compliment subject is expressed with a surface 1st, 2nd, or 3rd (i.e., impersonal) person focus, for example:

(5) 1st: I like your hair that way.
      2nd: Your hair looks good short.
      3rd: Nice haircut.

In part, such a categorization overlaps with the syntactic one. *I (really) like/ love NP* examples provide the vast majority of 1st person compliments, but compliments embedded within a larger frame such as *I think . . .* (e.g., "I think that color's perfect for you") also count as 1st person focus compliments. The most common pattern *NP is (really) ADJ*, which accounts for 53.6 percent of the Manes and Wolfson data and 41.4 percent of the Holmes data (1988a), masks the distinction between 2nd and 3rd person focus in that both "That coat is really great" and "You're really gorgeous today!" exemplify this pattern. Similarly, the present schema distinguishes between "That coat is really great" and "Your coat is really great," with the latter counting as an example of 2nd person focus. There are extremely few examples of 3rd person compliments exhibiting a personal pronoun (*he/ she/it*) as subject, presumably reflecting the hearer-directed (or object/event relevant to the hearer) focus of compliments.

The literature of sex-differentiating language behavior suggests that women employ more personal focus than men in many contexts. For example, Swacker (1976) studied the behavior of female and male academics at professional meetings and found that women's questions were more often encoded in personal terms, for example, "I would like to know what evidence exists that . . . " versus the impersonal "What evidence exists . . . ?" There is a widespread general belief that women prefer personalized to impersonalized forms, paralleling the characterization of women's style as social, affiliative, other-oriented, socioemotional, supportive, and so forth (see Preisler 1986, for a review of this literature). The expectation here is that impersonal 3rd person compliments should occur more often in male than female speech. This is borne out by the data: approximately 60 percent (290 of 486) of the male-offered compliments are impersonal expressions versus 20 percent of the female compliments (114 of 576). It is more interesting to observe the interaction of speaker and hearer sex, the data of which are presented in Table 2.1.

Several interesting points emerge here. First, despite the relatively equal frequency of the three person categories, 1st person compliments predominate among female speakers regardless of sex of addressee; by contrast, 1st person compliments occur rarely in the speech of males, especially when addressed to other males. 2nd person compliments are more common from females to males, and more common from males to females than males to other males. In the latter interaction type (Male–Male), impersonal compliments predominate, and they are as rarely heard between female partici-

Table 2.1 Personal focus by sex of interactions

	1st person	2nd person	3rd person	Total
M–M	35	37	156	228
M–F	51	73	134	258
F–F	152	120	58	330
F–M	111	79	56	246
Total	349	309	404	1,062

Note: $x^2 = 203.15$, $p > .001$.

pants as 1st person compliments are between male speakers. Of the Female–Female compliments, 82.4 percent have a personal focus (1st and 2nd) as opposed to 31.6 percent of Male–Male interactions. Note that it is not only the peculiar psychosexual dynamics of Male–Male interactions that explain the infrequency of personal focus here as Male–Female interactions are also significantly more impersonal than either Female–Hearer interaction type. Compliments from females are longer than compliments from males, but this is a somewhat misleading statistic. Female verbosity is not the issue here; rather, personal focus is simply lexically costly.

Holmes (1988b: 462–63) noted that the syntactic form of women's compliments strengthens their positive force significantly and that men use a form which attenuates or hedges on complimentary force more often than women.[4] This conclusion is based, however, on the differential frequency of the *What (a) ADJ NP!* and *ADJ NP!* formulas reported earlier. Together, these two patterns account for only 15 percent of the corpus and there is otherwise no significant difference in women's and men's use of syntactic patterns in Holmes' corpus.

There is, however, a "semantic force" difference observed in "subjective" (1st person)/objective (non-1st person) focused compliments. The initial items in (6) and (7) have in some real sense less force than their objective form counterparts.

(6) a. I think you look great in blue.
     b. You look great in blue.
(7) a. I really like that shirt.
     b. (That's a) nice shirt.

In particular, (6a) and (7a) contrast with the bold assertion quality of (6b) and (7b). It is well known that utterances may have the same illocutionary point expressed with varying degrees of force. Holmes (1984: 153) noted that tag questions, for example, may have the effect of attenuating the force of a variety of speech acts, for example, "You'd better not do that again, had you?" exhibits less force of warning than the same utterance without the tag question. Similarly, directives with tags are said to be softened vis-à-vis the same directives without tags ("Put it in the box, won't you?" vs. "Put it in the box"). Links between utterance length and semantic force were noted, in different terms, by Goodwin (1980: 168), who analyzed children's directives in play. She found that boys' directives were more often expressed as imperatives, whereas girls expressed "proposals for future activity," often utilizing the 1st person plural form *Let's*. Swacker (1976) hypothesized that the use of personal focus in questions asked by women at professional conferences conspired with other features to present women as less professionally competent than male questioners. Various researchers have linked such features to a higher frequency of hedges in women's speech and to the expression of tentativeness and politeness. (See Holmes 1984, for a review of the problems inherent in the notions of "hedge" and linguistic tentativeness.)

The only other item of interest in an examination of compliment form concerns a distinction in 1st person compliments between *I like X* and *I love X* compliments. These two formulas account for greater than 90 percent of the 1st person compliments. As might be expected, the somewhat stereotypical *I love X* occurs only in women's speech, and significantly more often in Female–Female than Female–Male interactions.

(8)   *I like X   I love X*
    M–M   28   –   (M–M total 228)
    M–F   41   –   (M–F total 258)
    F–F   94   47   (F–F total 330)
    F–M   89   16   (F–M total 246)
    (n = 315; 90.3% of 1st person compliments)

No other differences in lexical choice or in lexical frequency (e.g., intensifiers) are evident at this time.

One striking fact about the data just given is the very high frequency of the *I (really) like/love NP* formula in women's speech. Manes and Wolfson (1980: 120) found that this formula accounted for 16.1 percent of their total corpus. Similarly, Holmes (1988a) noted a remarkably similar 15.9 percent frequency in her New Zealand corpus. In a later article, Holmes (1988b: 489) reported a slightly increased preference for the formula in female speech (17.8%) than in male speech (13.1%). In the present (Binghamton) corpus, the relative frequency of this formula is 29.7 percent, with a strikingly disproportionate representation in women's usage.

(9) "I like/love NP"
    Manes & Wolfson   *Holmes*   *Herbert*
       16.1%   15.9%   29.7%
              (F 17.8%)   (F 42.7%)
              (M 13.1%)   (M 14.2%)

There is no apparent reason for the markedly increased frequency of this pattern in the speech of women within the Binghamton population. Holmes (personal communication) suggested that differences in the frequency of these two formulas may interact with dialect differences. For example, *I love NP* seems to be more frequent in American than British or New Zealand English; the formula may also interact with age, with younger speakers showing a higher frequency of usage. This latter suggestion may indeed help to explain the differences in the data sets. The

Binghamton data are somewhat more homogeneous in that at least one speaker in each interchange was a university student; this appears not to have been the case in the Manes and Wolfson and Holmes corpora.

Compliment responses

There is virtual unanimity among speakers of English that the prescriptively "correct" response to a compliment is *thank you*. This judgment is collected in interviews ("What is the appropriate response to a compliment?" "What would you say if a friend said that she liked your sweater?"), in socialization advice to children ("Say 'thank you'."), and in textbook dialogues written for foreign learners of English. However, American speakers exhibit great ingenuity in avoiding simple acceptance of compliments. The enormous variation found in actual collections of compliment responses is not surprising. Etiquette books have been decrying for the past 100 years responses such as "this old rag?" and advice columns such as Dear Abby, Ask Beth, and so on often include letters from individuals whose stated problem is that they "don't know how to accept compliments." An edition of *USA Weekend*, a Sunday magazine supplement, included in its "This Weekend's Passions" column a discussion of compliments and advice from "an expert," who offered the following suggestions to persons uncomfortable with compliments:

– Be positive. Think of a reason why you deserve a compliment and say to youself "I've earned it."
– Slow down your automatic urge to reject it.
– Practice some appropriate response . . . Try "I appreciate it" or "That's very nice of you," and remember. . . . "Thank you" is always appropriate.
(*USA Weekend* 9/25/87)

Part of the difficulty speakers report in responding to compliments may derive from the dual semantico-pragmatic components of compliments, which are (a) assertions of positive valuation by the speaker, and (b) "verbal gifts" offered to the addressee insofar as the content is positive valuation of an object, appearance, achievement, and so forth, more or less directly tied to the addressee (Kerbrat-Orecchioni 1987: 15). The addressee's dilemma is to respond simultaneously to the content component of the assertion (True vs. False) and to the gift component (Acceptance vs. Rejection). Pomerantz (1978: 81–82) claimed that two general conditions (10a, b) govern the act of responding to a compliment:

(10) a. Agree with the speaker.
    b. Avoid self-praise.

These two conditions, operating simultaneously, pose an interactional dilemma for the recipient of a compliment: How can one agree with the speaker and accept the force of a compliment without seeming to praise oneself?

Based on the present Binghamton corpus, Herbert (1986, 1989) distinguished 12 types of compliment responses. The basic strategies exploited within these 12 types may be paraphrased as:

1. APPRECIATION TOKEN. A verbal or nonverbal acceptance of the compliment, acceptance not being tied to the specific semantics of the stimulus (e.g., *Thanks, Thank you,* [nod]).
2. COMMENT ACCEPTANCE – SINGLE. Addressee accepts the complimentary force and offers a relevant comment on the appreciated topic (e.g., *Yeah, it's my favorite too*).
3. PRAISE UPGRADE. Addressee accepts the compliment and asserts that the compliment force is insufficient (e.g., *Really brings out the blue in my eyes, doesn't it?*).
4. COMMENT HISTORY. Addressee offers a comment (or series of comments) on the object complimented; these comments differ from (2) in that the latter are impersonal, that is, they shift the force of the compliment from the addressee (e.g., *I bought it for the trip to Arizona*).
5. REASSIGNMENT. Addressee agrees with the compliment assertion, but the complimentary force is transferred to some third person (e.g., *My brother gave it to me*) or to the object itself (*It really knitted itself*).
6. RETURN. As with (5) except that the praise is shifted (or returned) to the first speaker (e.g., *So's yours*).
7. SCALE DOWN. Addressee disagrees with the complimentary force, pointing to some flaw in the object or claiming that the praise is overstated (e.g., *It's really quite old*).
8. QUESTION. Addressee questions the sincerity or the appropriateness of the compliment (e.g., *Do you really think so?*).
9. DISAGREEMENT. Addressee asserts that the object complimented is not worthy of praise: the first speaker's assertion is in error (e.g., *I hate it*).
10. QUALIFICATION. Weaker than (9): addressee merely qualifies the original assertion, usually with *though, but, well,* etc. (e.g., *It's alright, but Len's is nicer*).
11. NO ACKNOWLEDGMENT. Addressee gives no indication of having heard the compliment: The addressee either (a) responds with an irrelevant comment (i.e., TOPIC SHIFT) or (b) gives no response.
12. REQUEST INTERPRETATION. Addressee, consciously or not, interprets the compliments as a request rather than a simple compliment. Such responses are not compliment responses per se as the addressee does not perceive the previous speech act as a compliment (e.g., *You wanna borrow this one too?*).

The relative frequencies of these response types in American and South African English were reported in Herbert (1989). A schematization of the interrelations among the category types is presented in Fig. 2.2, and the relevant data on the actual frequencies of occurrence of the various response strategies are given in Table 2.2.

What is significant here is that only about one-third of the American responses fall into the category of ACCEPTANCE, that is, two out of three American compliments are met with something other than the prescriptively correct response. It has been argued elsewhere (Herbert 1986, 1989) that the bulk of American English compliments are not literal statements of admiration/praise/and so forth, but rather are offers of solidarity. The view that speech acts are monofunctional is obviously naive. That is, the speaker's *first intention* is not to offer positive assessment of some object or

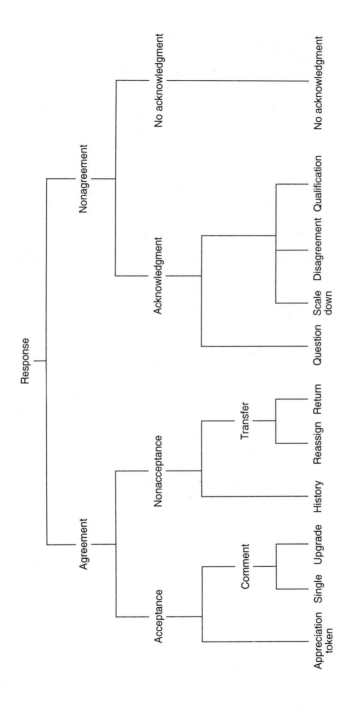

Fig. 2.2 Interrelations of compliment response types

concern relevant to the hearer. Reference here is intended to the relative prominence of some particular function. Suffice it to say that so-called literal compliments may also express/establish solidarity. Non-Americans' perception that Americans are insincere in their compliments (see later discussion) is – in a sense – correct from the perspective of their non-American cultural orientation where compliment formulas serve a much more restricted set of functions and are therefore more limited in discourse.[5] If one accepts the basic claim that compliments are (often) proffered as offers of solidarity, compliment responses other than ACCEPTANCE may be viewed as similar offers/negotiations on the part of the addressee. If the function of the compliment is, in some sense, to make the hearer feel good, the function of a response other than ACCEPTANCE may be the same. This addressee strategy may be crudely paraphrased as: "I recognize that your compliment was intended to make me feel good. I choose to avoid self-praise and thus assert that we are equal." Such an analysis predicts that ACCEPTANCES, especially APPRECIATION TOKENS such as the canonical *thank you*, should occur infrequently among close acquaintances, that is, those in the middle of the social distance scale, where (in fact) it is often indicative of suspicion on the part of the addressee.[6]

(11)   Male 1:   Nice tie.
       Male 2:   [look of dismay; checks tie] Thank you.

As noted earlier, Pomerantz (1978) attributed the form of compliment

Table 2.2 Frequency of compliment response types

	American		South African	
	No.	%	No.	%
Agreement				
Acceptance				
APPRECIATION TOKEN	312	29.4	162	32.9
COMMENT ACCEPTANCE	70	6.6	213	43.2
PRAISE UPGRADE	4	.4	1	.2
Nonacceptance				
COMMENT HISTORY	205	19.3	24	4.9
REASSIGNMENT	32	3.0	23	4.7
RETURN	77	7.3	12	2.4
Nonagreement				
SCALE DOWN	48	4.5	31	6.3
QUESTION	53	5.0	9	1.8
DISAGREEMENT	106	10.0	0	0
QUALIFICATION	70	6.6	12	2.4
NO ACKNOWLEDGMENT	54	5.1	1	.2
REQUEST INTERPRETATION	31	2.9	4	.8
Total	1,062	100.1	492	99.8

responses in American English to the two conflicting principles in (10). The analysis of compliment responses as return offers of solidarity allows one to subsume Pomerantz' two principles under a broader interpretation of the Solidarity Principle, that is, one can confirm solidarity with the previous speaker either by agreeing with that speaker's assertion or by avoiding/ negating self-directed praise, which would attribute a higher status to the complimented speaker. RETURN responses such as *So's yours, You too*, and so forth, (re)establish balance between speakers by the mutual exchange (and acceptance) of compliments. The analysis of both compliment and compliment response as gambits for signaling solidarity derives from notions of face in the sociolinguistic literature (e.g., Brown & Levinson 1978, which is discussed in greater detail in Holmes 1988b and Strecker 1988).

The view of compliment responses as a means of reestablishing balance between speakers following a compliment is related to Brown and Levinson's Balance Principle and also to the characterization of a compliment as *un cadeau verbal* by Kerbrat-Orecchioni (1987: 15) or *une action bienfaisante*. She noted further that "comme tous les cadeaux, le compliment place son bénéficiare en position de débiteur: s'il accepte le compliment, le complimenté peut se sentir 'obligé', c'est-à-dire tenu de fournir en compensation une contre-partie" (1987: 36). Similarly, Holmes (1988b: 449) noted that compliments put the addressee in the speaker's debt.

Sex-based differences in compliment responses

Perhaps more impressive than the differences in compliment form from males and females just reported are the differences in response type frequencies from the two groups. As indicated in Table 2.2, AGREEMENT responses account for about two-thirds of the American data, whereas the subcategory of ACCEPTANCE (APPRECIATION TOKEN, COMMENT ACCEPTANCE, UPGRADE) occurs in only about 35 percent of the interactions.[7] However, it is not the case that these ACCEPTANCE responses are equally distributed across interaction types. In particular, compliments offered by males are more likely to be accepted than compliments offered by females ($p < 0.001$), especially if offered to a female addressee. It is not the case that females simply accept more compliments than men: compare the roughly 40 percent acceptance rate in Male–Male interactions with the 22 percent acceptance rate in Female–Female interactions (see Table 2.3). Rather, it is the sex of the person offering the compliment that serves as a better predictor of compliment acceptance (see Table 2.4).

With regard to APPRECIATION TOKEN responses, the paradigm case of compliment acceptance, we find similarly that the best predictor of this response type is the male sex of the complimenter, with almost one-half (48.76%) of male compliments receiving this textbook response as opposed to 13 percent of compliments by females. Female complimentees offer this response almost one and one-half times as often (34.5%) as male complimentees (23%) (see Table 2.5). The generalization seems to be that male compliments are accepted, one way or another, particularly by female recipients.

Table 2.3 Response interaction data

	M–M	M–F	F–F	F–M
Agreement				
Acceptance				
APPRECIATION TOKEN	68	169	34	41
COMMENT ACCEPTANCE	23	8	37	3
PRAISE UPGRADE	1	–	2	1
Nonacceptance				
COMMENT HISTORY	41	9	85	70
REASSIGNMENT	1	8	11	12
RETURN	6	21	30	20
Nonagreement				
SCALE DOWN	–	7	23	18
DISAGREEMENT	17	13	43	34
QUALIFICATION	8	10	36	16
QUESTION	25	4	13	10
NO ACKNOWLEDGMENT	26	2	9	17
REQUEST INTERPRETATION	12	7	7	4
Total	228	258	330	246

Table 2.4 ACCEPTANCE AGREEMENT responses

	Male	Female
a. By sex of complimenter[a]	269/486 (55.3%)	118/576 (20.5%)
b. By sex of addressee[b]	137/474 (28.9%)	250/588 (42.5%)

[a]$\chi^2 = 137.917$; $p > .001$; test $u = 11.709$.
[b]$\chi^2 = 21.002$; $p > .001$; test $u = 4.579$.

Table 2.5 APPRECIATION TOKEN responses

	Male	Female
a. By sex of complimenter[a]	237/486 (48.8%)	75/576 (13.0%)
b. By sex of addressee[b]	109/474 (23.0%)	203/588 (34.5%)

[a]$\chi^2 = 162.324$; $p > .001$; test $u = 12.785$.
[b]$\chi^2 = 16.805$; $p > .001$; test $u = 4.101$.

Table 2.6 NONACCEPTANCE AGREEMENT responses

	Male	Female
By sex of complimenter[a]	86/486 (17.7%)	228/576 (39.6%)

[a]$\chi^2 = 63.936$; $p > .001$; test $u = 7.790$.

Table 2.7 AGREEMENT (ACCEPTANCE and NONACCEPTANCE) responses

	M–M	M–F	F–F	F–M
a. By sex of interactants[a]	140/228 (61.4%)	215/258 (83.3%)	199/330 (60.3%)	147/246 (59.8%)

	Male	Female
b. By sex of complimenter[b]	355/486 (73.0%)	346/576 (60.1%)
c. By sex of addressee[c]	287/474 (60.5%)	414/588 (70.4%)

[a] $\chi 2 = 45.740; p > .001.$
[b] $\chi 2 = 19.776; p > .001;$ test $u = 4.444.$
[c] $\chi^2 = 11.374; p > .001;$ test $u = 3.390.$

The larger category of AGREEMENT includes both ACCEPTANCE-type responses, already discussed, and NONACCEPTANCE agreements. In the latter case, the compliment recipient agrees with the force of the compliment proffered by the first speaker, but he or she does not explicitly accept the verbal gift. Rather, agreement with the semantic force is implicitly expressed by shifting – via a variety of mechanisms – the complimentary force from the recipient. These responses (HISTORY, RETURN, REASSIGNMENT) are clearly agreements, and the recipient's response encodes implicit agreement with the semantic content of the compliment act.

Following the increased likelihood of ACCEPTANCE as a response to male compliments, there is a high incidence of NONACCEPTANCE AGREEMENT to female compliments (see Table 2.6), especially the subtype HISTORY, in which the adressee offers a comment or series of comments on the topic of the compliment. The lesser frequency of this response type to male compliments follows as a consequence of the heightened frequency of the preferred ACCEPTANCE responses to them. Considering simultaneously the two broad subcategories of AGREEMENT (i.e., AGREEMENT and NONACCEPTANCE), in Table 2.7(a) one sees that the only interaction type in which there is a sharply greater likelihood of AGREEMENT is Male–Female interactions, which, as noted earlier, is the preferred interaction type for ACCEPTANCE responses. Male compliments are generally more likely to meet with AGREEMENT responses (see Table 2.7(b)), and female addressees are generally more likely to agree with the semantic content of a compliment act (see Table 2.7(c)).

Agreements occur in approximately two-thirds (66%) of the compliment exchanges. The remaining one-third is comprised of the large category of NONAGREEMENT (31.2%), in which the compliment recipient avoids agreeing with the semantic content of the compliment, and the smaller category of REQUEST INTERPRETATION (2.8%), to be discussed later. There is markedly less likelihood of NONAGREEMENT occurring in the Male–Female interaction type (see Table 2.8). Within the subtypes of NONAGREEMENT, there is a bifurcation such that three subtypes (SCALE DOWN, DISAGREEMENT, QUALIFICATION) attack the semantic component of the compliment, asserting that it is false or

Table 2.8 NONAGREEMENT responses

	M–M	M–F	F–F	F–M
By sex of interactants[a]	76/228 (33.3%)	36/258 (14.0%)	124/330 (37.6%)	96/246 (38.6%)

[a] $\chi^2 = 48.803; p > .001$.

Table 2.9 SCALE DOWN, DISAGREEMENT, and QUALIFICATION responses

	M–M	M–F	F–F	F–M
By sex of interactants[a]	25/228 (11.0%)	30/258 (11.6%)	102/330 (30.9%)	68/246 (27.6%)

	Male	Female
b. By sex of complimenter[b]	55/486 (11.3%)	170/576 (29.5%)
c. By sex of addressee[c]	93/474 (19.6%)	132/588 (22.4%)

[a] $\chi^2 = 53.201; p > .001$.
[b] $\chi^2 = 86.782; p > .001$; test $u = 7.222$.
[c] $\chi^2 = 1.256; p > .1$, n.s.; test $u = 1.123$, n.s.

overstated. Female compliments, especially those addressed to other females, are more likely to meet with this sort of NONAGREEMENT (see Table 2.9(a)). Sex of complimenter is a good predictor of the likelihood of these NONAGREEMENT responses (see Table 2.9(b)), but the sex of the respondent is not (see Table 2.9(c)).

The two remaining subtypes of NONAGREEMENT are QUESTION and NO ACKNOWLEDGMENT. In the former case, the recipient of a compliment questions either the appropriateness (e.g., *Why do you say that?*) of the compliment act or its sincerity (*Really?*). Holmes (1988b: 460) separated these two types of responses and reported 2.23 percent for Accuracy Questions and 0.9 percent for Sincerity Challenges. Holmes analyzed her data according to responder's sex (but not according to sex of complimenter nor to the interaction between the two), and she found no differences in responses by women and men. In the present corpus, however, QUESTION responses occur with strikingly higher incidence in Male–Male interactions (see Table 2.10). A similar pattern occurs with NO ACKNOWLEDGMENT responses, a category which accounts for 3.13 percent of Holmes' data and 5.08 percent of the Binghamton corpus. Holmes found a slightly stronger preference for these responses from men (5.3%) than women (2.4%). Analyzing the Binghamton data according to sex of participants, we see that this latter response type is most common in Male–Male interactions (see Table 2.11(a)) and that there is a significantly greater likelihood of this response type from male addressees (see Table 2.11(b)). The frequency of these two response types (QUESTION and NO ACKNOWLEDGMENT) in Male–Male interactions points

Table 2.10 QUESTION responses

	M–M	M–F	F–F	F–M
By sex of interactants[a]	25/228 (11.0%)	4/258 (1.6%)	13/330 (3.9%)	10/246 (4.1%)

[a]$\chi^2 = 22.937; p > .001$.

Table 2.11 NO ACKNOWLEDGMENT responses

	M–M	M–F	F–F	F–M
a. By sex of interactants[a]	26/228 (11.4%)	2/258 (0.8%)	9/330 (2.7%)	17/246 (6.9%)

	Male	Female
b. By sex of addressee[b]	43/474 (9.1%)	11/588 (1.9%)

[a]$\chi^2 = 31.263; p > .001$.
[b]$\chi^2 = 28.202; p > .001$; test $u = 5.368$.

to a special status for these interactions, which other analysts have noted (Holmes 1988b; Wolfson 1984). Further evidence for the special status of Male–Male interactions comes from response types such as RETURN (e.g., *So's yours, I like yours too*), which occur with least frequency here (see Table 2.12).

The category of REQUEST INTERPRETATION has been previously treated as something other than AGREEMENT or NONAGREEMENT (Herbert 1989) since, strictly speaking, the recipient of the compliment acts as if the compliment were something other than a compliment per se, treating it instead as an unrelated speech act. This response type occurs least frequently in Female–Male interactions, that is, the least likely scenario for REQUEST INTERPRETATION is a male receiving a female compliment. Such responses are most common in Male–Male interactions, where they may function as a strategy, conscious or not, to sidestep the complimentary force of the act, although the difference in frequency of occurrence is not statistically significant (see Table 2.13).

Discussion

The investigation of 1,062 compliments and compliment responses in the Binghamton corpus reveals that there are significant differences in the structuring of compliment events that depend on the sex of participants. In addition to differences in the form and the personal focus of compliments offered by men and by women, there is an important difference in the likelihood of compliment acceptance that depends most directly on the sex of the person offering the compliment. *Compliments from females will*

Table 2.12 RETURN responses

	M–M	M–F	F–F	F–M
By sex of interactants[a]	6/228 (2.6%)	21/258 (8.1%)	30/330 (9.1%)	20/246 (8.1%)

[a] $\chi^2 = 9.486; p > .025.$

Table 2.13 REQUEST INTERPRETATION responses

	M–M	M–F	F–F	F–M
By sex of interactants[a]	12/228 (5.3%)	7/258 (2.7%)	7/330 (2.1%)	4/246 (1.6%)

[a] $\chi^2 = 5.345; p > .5,$ n.s.

most likely not be accepted, whereas compliments from males will, especially by female recipients. The question then arises as to how the various differences reported earlier might be integrated into the larger literatures on sex-based differences in language use and the sociology of compliment work. The personal focus encoding seen in female compliments, as has already been mentioned, parallels personal involvement by female speakers in other situations. There do not seem to be other significant differences in the form of compliments offered by women and men, but further research may reveal such differences.

Differences in response strategies are more numerous and more interesting. The greater likelihood of male compliments being accepted is consistent with the notion that acceptances are most common among status nonequals and among those whose status in not being negotiated. The increased frequency of ACCEPTANCE responses to male compliments by female addresses may be yet another manifestation of the linguistic consequences of status differences apparent in cross-sex interactions. (See, inter alia, Cameron 1985; Preisler 1986; Smith 1985, for reviews of this literature.) In the same way that compliments usually flow from higher to lower status between status nonequals (Herbert 1989; Holmes 1988a; Wolfson 1984), ACCEPTANCE is the appropriate response in such situations. *An acceptance recognizes the compliment for the expression of good will that it is, and at the same time no return token is offered by the person of lower status.*[8] The most common case of solidarity negotiation should occur between status equals or near-equals, with the higher status person responding. Wolfson (1988: 32) noted that there are qualitative differences in the speech behavior of middle-class Americans to "intimates, status unequals, and strangers, on the one hand, and to nonintimates, status-equal friends, coworkers, and acquaintances on the other." The two extremes of social distance, minimum and maximum, evoke rather similar behaviors, whereas relationships more toward the middle of the continuum are quite different in this regard. Wolfson hypothesized that there is security in the first set of relations, where social distance can be seen as fixed. By contrast, relationships toward the center of the social distance scale are more fluid and dynamic, that is, available for negotiation. The vast majority of compliments are exchanged by speakers who are neither strangers nor intimates (Wolfson 1988: 33). Holmes (1988b) reported a quantitative study of compliment occurrences, in which almost four-fifths (78.72%) occurred between status equals.

It is not the case that frequency of the compliment act is similar in all sex-varied cell types. For example, Wolfson (1984: 241ff) noted that women receive far more compliments than men. She described compliments on appearance and possessions to males as "rare" and concluded that "women, because of their role in the social order, are seen as appropriate recipients of all manner of social judgments in the form of compliments" (243). For compliments on ability/performance among status nonequals, it was the higher status person who gave the compliment; status had little effect in the appearance/possession category. There are very few examples of compliments given to higher status males, but the relative status of women in such contexts seems not to matter, and their behavior is freely commented on by women and by men.

Holmes (1988b) reported similar findings for New Zealand English, noting that higher status females are almost twice as likely to be complimented as higher status males. In these data, however, appearance compliments occur rarely in cross-sex pairs of different status; skill compliments predominate from higher to lower status males and from men to women of different status (higher or lower) (1988b: 458–59).

Such data on the frequency of compliments as speech acts are of import in describing the sociology of compliment work. However, data on frequency of occurrence for particular speech acts are especially difficult to obtain. Both Wolfson's and Holmes' data were collected by researchers and students, the majority of whom were female. Indeed, Holmes (1988b: 450) reported that 23 of her 25 data collectors were female. Although only 12.4 percent of her data consist of compliments directed to the collectors, it is nevertheless true that male and female fieldworkers have access to different interaction types – as participants and as observers.

Impressionistic reports from those individuals who worked on the Binghamton corpus support the claims that compliments from males occur less frequently than compliments from females and that the "easiest" type of compliment to collect is Female–Female. The number of tokens in the Binghamton corpus gives no indication of this fact: [9] it simply takes longer to collect 50 male than 50 female compliments. Similar observations were made by data collectors working on South African English. It may be safe to conclude that these differences in frequency are valid, though measures of actual quantitative differences are unreliable.

Holmes (1988b) argued that there is a fundamental difference in the perception of compliments by women and men. For women, she argued, compliments are positively affective speech acts, serving "to increase or consolidate the solidarity between speaker and addressee" (1988b: 447). This view of compliments has much to commend it and virtually all researchers who have speculated about the function of compliments recognize this potential use (Herbert 1986, 1989; Kerbrat-Orecchioni 1987; Manes & Wolfson 1980; Norrick 1980; Wolfson 1988; Wolfson & Manes 1980).

In contrast to the function just mentioned, according to Holmes, is the (male) perception of a compliment as a face-threatening act: "Compliments can be regarded as face-threatening to the extent that they imply the complimenter envies the addressee in some way or would like something belonging to the addressee" (1988b: 448). Such an interpretation is well attested in a variety of cultures, for example, Samoan, where the recipient of a compliment is "obliged" to offer the complimented object to the complimenter. Holmes also noted that compliments put the addressee in the complimenter's debt, a notion akin to Kerbrat-Orecchioni's (1987) characterization of the compliment as a verbal gift. Among the evidence cited in support of this interpretation of male compliments as face-threatening acts is that offered by Holmes regarding the higher frequency of possession compliments in Male–Male interactions: 25 percent versus an average of 9.32 percent in other interaction types. Possession compliments are the most likely face-threatening act in the sense given here, but an equally plausible explanation for the high incidence of possession compliments in Male–Male interactions is simply the severe constraints on appearance compliments between males. Also, one should not make too much of the quantitative data here since the interaction types in Holmes' sample are not equally represented, for example, there are 248 Female–Female interactions and 44 Male–Male. Were such an opposition in the perception of compliments widespread among speakers of New Zealand English, one would expect that tokens of solidarity and face-threatening acts would elicit two types of responses. However, as noted earlier, Holmes found no significant differences in the compliment responses of male and female New Zealanders (1988b: 461).

The view of compliments as offers of solidarity has much to recommend it. It explains, in part, the very high frequency of this speech act in English, a fact noted by many nonnative speakers of English, particularly with reference to American English. Indeed, speakers of other varieties of English comment on the high frequency of compliments in American (e.g., New Zealand speakers [Holmes & Brown 1987] and South African speakers [Herbert & Straight 1989]). Expressions of solidarity, particularly between status equals, should be very common in speech, whereas sincere expressions of admiration, praise, and so on, are more dependent on context, that is, their occurrence in discourse is more severely constrained to the extent that a host of conditions must be met in order for a literal compliment to be appropriate; the conditions are fewer for the use of the formula to express good will.

Herbert (1989) considered differences in compliment behavior between American and South African English speakers and noted that compliment acceptance is far less common among the former than the latter. American speakers accepted only slightly more than one-third of the compliments offered (36.35%), but ACCEPTANCE was the dominant response among South African speakers (76.26%). These differences, as well as the seemingly greater frequency of the compliment act in American English, were tied to "cultural value profiles" of the two groups.

Herbert and Straight (1989) examined this opposition between high compliment expression and low acceptance (American) and lower compliment expression and high acceptance (South African) from a processual psycholinguistic perspective. They argued that American compliments are vehicles for the (re)negotiation of solidarity, a view consistent with the finding that in interactions between status nonequals compliments flow from above as do other sociolinguistic gambits of this sort, for example, the switch from formal to informal address. Note the symmetry between the claimed greater frequency of compliments in American English and the observation that Americans engage in first-name address more readily than speakers of other varieties of English. The flow from status superior to inferior is noted in etiquette books, compendia of prescriptive norms, for example, "Compliments are said by some to be inadmissible. But between equals, or from those of superior position to those of inferior station, compliments should not only be acceptable, but gratifying. It is pleasant to know that we are well thought of by those who hold higher positions, such as men of superior talent, or women of superior culture" (Young 1882: 90). Etiquette books prescribe ACCEPTANCE as the appropriate response to a compliment, a fact compatible with the interpretation offered in this article and the observation that such advice is compiled for the higher social classes, not those concerned with the daily negotiation of social solidarity among equals.

Americans are often accused of insincerity in their complimenting, that is, non-Americans seem to doubt that Americans actually believe many of the positive things they say and are falsely modest in their nonacceptance of compliments. South Africans, on the other hand, do not use compliments with the same frequency or in the same way. If a particular compliment is a genuine expression of admiration, rather than an offer of solidarity, then no amount of acceptance will threaten the social balance between speakers. Negotiating social relations is simply not the issue here. In this regard, there is a basic *functional* difference between complimenting behavior in American and South African English; compliments are used in one case to negotiate social solidarity and nonnegotiatively in the other.

It may well be that the same explanations put forward to explain differences in compliment behavior in two varieties of English may help to explain differences in male and female behavior. Compliments from males are less frequent than compliments from females, and the dominant response to the former is ACCEPTANCE. Male compliments, like South African compliments, may be unmarked with regard to the form-function relationship, that is, such compliments may be less offers of solidarity and more actual assertions of praise/admiration/and so on. They thus may conform more closely to native speakers' folk definitions of a compliment. Female compliments, on the other hand, are perhaps more often offers of solidarity/tokens of good will, and they therefore occur with greater frequency in discourse.

This distinction meshes nicely with the different response types that each set of compliments elicits. Male compliments, those which might be termed literal compliments, elicit ACCEPTANCE. Addressees recognize these speech acts for their complimentary function, and they accept that complimentary force with APPRECIATION TOKEN or COMMENT ACCEPTANCE. These responses do not function as return tokens of solidarity, and speakers are seemingly willing to abide with the "Agree with speaker" maxim of Pomerantz'

(1978) opposition and to ignore the "Avoid self-praise" maxim. On the other hand, compliments from females very often function primarily as tokens for negotiating social distance, and addressees recognize this function: they therefore do not overtly accept complimentary force. These nonacceptance responses function as return offers of solidarity, as discussed earlier. By choosing to avoid self-praise (by shifting, reducing, or disagreeing with the semantic force of the utterance), the addressee asserts solidarity with the complimenter. NONACCEPTANCE AGREEMENT shifts the complimentary force; NONAGREEMENT weakens or denies that force. Both mechanisms serve to re-establish social balance between speakers. HISTORY responses, the single most frequent response by women and men to female compliments (26.96%), are often fairly lengthy comments, and in this regard women's compliments get heavy use in conversational "work" (cf. Fishman 1980).

The greater frequency of female compliments and their exploitation in accomplishing interaction is consistent with descriptions in the literature of different conversational roles for women and men. Both men and women participate in this conversational work by *not accepting* female compliments. APPRECIATION TOKENS, which account for almost half of the responses to male compliments (48.77%) as opposed to 13.04 percent of female compliments, are the least satisfying response from a conversational point of view because they are formulas that do not easily lend themselves to follow-up comments. More than 65 percent of female responses to male compliments have this structure, a finding consistent with the notion that ACCEPTANCE should be more likely between status nonequals and with the claim that male and female compliments serve different functions in discourse.

Conclusion

The difference that is claimed to operate in male and female compliments thus parallels the difference reported for South African and American compliments. On the one hand, there is a set of formulas that serves to express admiration/praise/and so on felt by the speaker at a particular moment in time. The use of these formulas is not particularly frequent, and the dominant response to such a speech act is ACCEPTANCE. On the other hand, the same set of formulas may serve to express good will toward the addressee and act as offers of solidarity. This use, being less contextually bound, is more frequent in discourse, and the dominant response to such usage is something other than ACCEPTANCE. There is, thus, a direct relationship between the function of the speech act, the frequency of its exploitation in discourse, and the types of response that it elicits. This relationship may be sketched as:

(12) Function: offer praise   offer solidarity
     Frequency: infrequent   frequent
     Response: ACCEPTANCE   non-ACCEPTANCE
                  (South Africans; males) (Americans; females)

Such a claim requires further testing. The data presented here begin to reveal the full complexities of compliment work and the multifunctional nature of speech formulas in discourse.

Notes

1. Except when indicated to the contrary, all examples cited in the text are taken from a corpus of compliments and compliment responses collected in Binghamton, New York. The details of data collection are described briefly in the following and in detail in Herbert (1989).
2. Note that all the claims just made are language-specific, i.e., these are not universal claims about compliment events. For a discussion of cross-cultural variability in the form and content of compliments, see Manes (1983) and Wolfson (1981); on compliment responses, see Herbert (1989). Compliments in French are discussed in some detail by Kerbrat-Orecchioni (1987) and Marandin (1987); Polish compliments by Herbert (1991).
3. The South African data discussed later in the article were collected similarly at the University of the Witwatersrand Johannesburg.
4. Analysis by form only may obscure other, possibly more distinctive differences; the important paralinguistic and expressive features of speech are generally unreported and uninvestigated in the speech act literature.
5. The perception of insincerity is obviously one based on hearer's perception of the truth value of an utterance; it is not easy to divorce such an assessment from the perception of a speaker's ulterior purpose. For example, if a student, who has not spoken to an instructor during the course of a term, suddenly compliments the instructor on a lecture, an exam, etc., the latter may be justified in assuming that the student's compliment is a move to introduce a request of some sort, e.g., for a deadline extension or exemption of some sort. Non-American speakers presented with the plethora of American compliments in everyday life seek and do not find such ulterior motives generally. They sometimes conclude, then, not that Americans have broad and liberal standards of appreciation but that Americans "say anything," some of which they cannot really believe. See Apte (1974) for a similar analysis of Americans' expressions of gratitude.
6. On the basis of a suggestion by an anonymous reviewer, a check was made of the interactions in which fieldworkers had indicated such suspicion, dismay, concern, etc. Virtually all such addressees were male, and the complimenter in almost four-fifths of the exchanges were also male.
7. The categories of compliment responses proposed by Holmes (1988a) and Herbert (1986, 1989) are remarkably similar, although there is disagreement as to the relations among response types. For example, both taxonomies recognize types in which a compliment is returned to the first speaker (e.g., *I like yours too*) and in which credit for the compliment is shifted to a third party (e.g., *My mother knitted it*). Holmes counted the first within the broad category ACCEPT and the second as DEFLECT/EVADE, whereas Herbert counted both as AGREEMENT (though not as ACCEPTANCE) because both types encode implicit agreement with the force of the compliment and shift that force from the recipient. A detailed explication of the present categorization appears in Herbert (1989).
8. This distribution thus parallels the asymmetry in pronoun choice and forms of address reported widely in the sociolinguistic literature.
9. The numbers are as given in Table 2.3. Please note that the numbers cited in Herbert (1989: 9) for Female–Male and Male–Female interactions were inadvertently reversed.
   An additional caveat concerning all of the data bases on compliments is that

they may be unrepresentative of the wide national norms they purport to represent (American, New Zealand, South African) to the extent that the majority of
interactions in which the compliment was offered included at least one university
student or staff member. This skewing effect is well known throughout the social
sciences.

To add a brief comparative note at this point: Kerbrat-Orecchioni (1987: 9)
reported that among French speakers Female–Female compliments are more
common in same-sex interactions, whereas male compliments predominate in
cross-sex interactions.

References

Apte, M.L. (1974) ' "Thank you" and South Asian languages: A comparative socio-
linguistic study', *Linguistics* 136: pp. 67–89.
Brown, P. and Levinson, S. (1978) 'Universals in language usage: Politeness
phenomena', in E.N. Goody (ed.), *Questions and politeness*, Cambridge: Cambridge
University Press. pp. 56–289.
Cameron, D. (1985) *Feminism and linguistic theory*, London: Macmillan.
Fishman, P. (1980) 'Conversational insecurity', in H. Giles, W.P. Robinson and P.
Smith (eds.), *Language: Social psychological perspectives*, Elmsford, NY: Pergamon,
pp. 127–32.
Goodwin, M.H. (1980) 'Directive-response speech sequences in girls' and boys' task
activities', in S. McConnell-Ginet et al. (eds.), *Women and language in literature and
society*, New York: Praeger, pp. 157–73.
Goody, E.N. (1978) 'Toward a theory of questions', in E. Goody (ed.), *Questions and
politeness*, Cambridge: Cambridge University Press, pp. 17–43.
Herbert, R.K. (1986) 'Say "thank you" – Or something', *American Speech* 61: pp.
76–88.
—— (1989) 'The ethnography of English compliments and compliment responses: A
contrastive sketch', in W. Oleksy (ed.), *Contrastive pragmatics*, Amsterdam: John
Benjamins, pp. 3–35.
—— (in press) 'The sociology of compliment work: An ethnocontrastive study of
Polish and English compliments', *Multilingua* 10: pp. 381–402.
Herbert, R.K. and Straight, H.S. (1989) 'Compliment-rejection vs. compliment-
avoidance', *Language and Communication* 9: pp. 35–47.
Holmes, J. (1984) 'Women's language: A functional approach', *General Linguistics* 24:
pp. 149–78.
—— (1988a) 'Compliments and compliment responses in New Zealand English',
Anthropological Linguistics 28: pp. 485–508.
—— (1988b) 'Paying compliments: A sex-preferential positive politeness strategy',
Journal of Pragmatics 12: pp. 445–65.
Holmes, J. and Brown, D. (1987) 'Teachers and students learning about compli-
ments', *TESOL Quarterly* 21: pp. 523–46.
Kerbrat-Orecchioni, C. (1987) 'La description des échanges en analyse conversation-
nelle: L'exemple du compliment', *DRLAV – Revue de Linguistique* 36–37: pp. 1–53.
Lakoff, R. (1975) *Language and woman's place*, New York: Harper.
Manes, J. (1983) 'Compliments: A mirror of cultural values', in N. Wolfson and E.
Judd (eds.), *Sociolinguistics and language acquisition*, Rowley, MA: Newbury
House, pp. 96–102.
Manes, J. and Wolfson, N. (1980) 'The compliment formula', in F. Coulmas (ed.),
Conversational routine, The Hague: Mouton, pp. 115–32.

Marandin, J.M. (1987) 'Des mots et des actions: "compliment, "complimenter" et l'action de complimenter', *Lexique* 5: pp. 65–99.

Norrick, N. (1980) 'The speech act of complimenting', in E. Hovdhaugen (ed.), *The Nordic languages and modern linguistics*, Oslo: Universitetsforlaget, pp. 296–304.

Pomerantz, A. (1978) 'Compliment responses: Notes on the co-operation of multiple constraints', in J. Schenkein (ed.), *Studies in the organization of conversational interaction*, New York: Academic, pp. 79–112.

Preisler, B. (1986) *Linguistic sex roles in conversation*, Berlin: Mouton de Gruyter.

Schegloff, E. and Sacks, H. (1973) 'Opening up closings', *Semiotica* VIII(4): pp. 289–327.

Smith, P. (1985) *Language, the sexes and society*, New York: Basil Blackwell.

Strecker, I. (1988) *The social practice of symbolization*, London: Athlone.

Swacker, M. (1976) 'Women's verbal behavior at learned and professional conferences', in B.L. Dubois and I. Crouch (eds.), *The sociology of the languages of American women*, San Antonio, TX: Trinity University, pp. 155–60.

Wolfson, N. (1981) 'Compliments in cross-cultural perspective', *TESOL Quarterly* 15: pp. 117–24.

—— (1983) 'An empirically based analysis of complimenting in English', in N. Wolfson and E. Judd (eds.), *Sociolinguistics and language acquisition*, Rowley, MA: Newbury House, pp. 82–95.

—— (1984) 'Pretty is as pretty does: A speech act view of sex roles', *Applied Linguistics* 5: pp. 236–44.

—— (1988) 'The bulge: A theory of speech behavior and social distance', in J. Fine (ed.), *Second language discourse: A textbook of current research*, Norwood, NJ: Ablex, pp. 21–38.

Wolfson, N. and Manes, J. (1980) 'The compliment as a social strategy', *Papers in Linguistics* 13: pp. 391–410.

Young, J.H. (1882) *Our deportment: The manner, conduct, and dress of the most refined society*, Springfield, MA: W. C. King.

3

Preschool negotiators: linguistic differences in how girls and boys regulate the expression of dissent in same-sex groups

Amy Sheldon and Diane Johnson

Originally published in *Research on Negotiations in Organizations*, 4 (1994).

> One of the most interesting areas for investigation that emerges from a focus on cultural concepts is the possibility that women and men hold different models of language use.
>
> (Borker (1980, p. 40)

Nicole: Mom, kings are royaler than queens.
(age 6½)
Amy: Why do you think so?
Nicole: Because on Mister Rogers, when the trolley stops at the king and queen [in the Kingdom of Make Believe] the king answers the questions the most.

Sheldon (1990a)

Introduction: language, conflict, gender and feminism

The starting point for this paper is the observation that language and gender are part of every dispute and every negotiation. Language is a major force in a culture's gender ideology because through language we reflect, construct, and perpetuate gender expectations and norms. Each culture (or subculture, or community) creates an ideology of femininity and masculinity "which establishes both the imperative and the meaning of being a good or true woman [or man]" (Matthews, 1984, p. 15). As the above quote from Nicole indicates, when we learn language we are taught how to use it in ways that uphold a preferred social order. We are taught what to believe about our community and how to use language in ways that are consistent with a prevailing world view.

In this paper we examine the verbal tactics that children use to further their own interests in disputes. Our purpose is to uncover sociocultural information that is encoded in conflict talk to demonstrate how our native tongue expresses and transmits a cultural theory of gender, in this case to cultural novices. We show that young children already have complex

76

negotiating skills and use strategies that are not that different from those used by adults. Their conflicts also reveal nuanced "feminine" and "masculine" negotiating styles that reflect different social norms for acceptable behavior in female and male groups in their community. We suggest that these norms are carried into adulthood and shape adults' conflict management behavior. One important advantage in studying children is that their spontaneous conflicts and negotiations in intimate settings are observable and recordable. However, serious (nonplayful) and nonritualistic conflict and negotiation that spontaneously arises in adults' intimate settings is practically impossible to record. For this reason, the close discourse analysis of children's conflict talk and negotiation is a valuable resource that can orient us to the importance of studying the language of disputing. It can serve as a model for studying conflict and negotiation among adults.

In addition, we interpret conflict as a process that cannot avoid being influenced and shaped by implicit norms and expectations for gendered behavior that are followed, more or less, by the community being studied, whether it be a day care center or a corporate organization. Careful observation of the language of dispute management can tell us how that community is shaped and constrained by culturally mandated feminine and masculine styles of self-assertion, ways of using power and influence (e.g., ways of justifying oneself and maneuvering companions to get what one wants), ways of managing alliances and oppositions, and other complex aspects of "getting along." In other words, the social forces and values implicit in getting things done in a community can be articulated by studying the conversations in that community.

The terms *feminine* and *masculine* refer to culture bound, historically situated principles that govern social interaction – not biologically determined, essential or intrinsic personal attributes or traits – that assign different meaning and social value to females and males. As Matthews (1984, p. 8) explains, "there is no meaning of woman that is simply given for all time, an essential femininity. Every aspect of our lives is historical and changing: our bodies, our consciousness of our selves, our treatment by society, the sense of our commonality as women."

Using language creates social relations between human beings in countless everyday conversations. Vocabulary also reflects a culture's ideology. The fact that a language categorizes objects in the world according to gender indicates the importance placed by the culture on emphasizing sexual differentiation rather than similitude. Not all languages and cultures emphasize gender distinctions among humans as much as English does. For example, in traditional Yoruba culture, gender differentiation is considered a much less important principle than it is in Western cultures, whereas seniority is more important than gender (Oyeronke Oyewumi, personal communication). In highly gendered cultures, when we study the influence of gender on human lives, as a socially constructed and historically fluid concept, we are actually struggling with how to measure and interpret social difference. How, and to what extent, does a culture symbolically represent the meaning of sexual difference and how, and to what extent, do people's behaviors reflect that cultural ideology?

Western cultural ideologies represent gender relations as being about two presumably homogeneous groups of people, the ones who are expected to wear the pink diapers and booties in infancy, and the ones who are expected to wear the blue. Feminist perspectives, that is, multiple and diverse woman-centered views of social relations, can clarify and help to reformulate the working assumptions and interpretations of gender that a culture and its members bring to everyday interactions, such as disputes and negotiations. Central questions that this paper asks from a feminist perspective are: In what way does the verbal management of conflict tacitly reflect and recreate a social context for symbolizing and enacting gender in ways that are consistent with (or contrary to) cultural ideology? How does this affect negotiation in organizations? How might organizations become aware of and rethink their value systems in order to enable more produc- tive negotiation processes to take hold? The analysis of children's strategies for negotiating through conflict is relevant and helpful to the discussion of these and many other issues facing organizations today.

We start with a quote from Jeane Kirkpatrick, former Ambassador to the United Nations, because it appropriately frames our basic concern and places it in a sociocultural context. It points to a powerful way in which the normative and ideological dimension of gender is expressed in human interaction in a culture with which we are familiar:

> Now, the United Nations is an institution which specializes in talking. It's a place where people make speeches and listen to speeches. But if I make a speech, particularly a substantial speech, it has been frequently described in the media as "lecturing my colleagues," as though it were somehow particu- larly inappropriate, like an ill-tempered schoolmarm might scold her children. When I have replied to criticisms of the United States (which is an important part of my job), I have frequently been described as "confrontational." . . . In the beginning I thought that I was described as "confrontational" because we adopted a policy inside the United Nations that, when the United States was publicly attacked, we would defend ourselves. . . . I now think that being tagged as "confrontational" and being a woman in a high position are very closely related. There is a certain level of office the very occupancy of which constitutes a confrontation with conventional expectations. . . . I've come to see here a double bind: if a woman seems strong, she is called "tough", and if she doesn't seem strong, she's not found strong enough to occupy a high level job in a crunch. Terms like "tough" and "confrontational" express a certain very general surprise and disapproval at the presence of a woman in arenas in which it is necessary to be – what for males would be considered – normally assertive. (Campbell, 1988, p. 131–132)

Gender ideology and double-voice discourse

Kirkpatrick's realization of the importance of gender and its centrality in her activities of speaking, negotiating for, and representing the United States is a touchstone for this paper. The fact that a competent adult female speaker still faces socially imposed obstacles that limit her effectiveness in a community underscores the importance of understanding the social con- struction of gender and its relation to discourse. As Kirkpatrick's experi- ence indicates, the connections between language and gender are complex and not readily seen. If something as important and commonplace as negotiation is affected so centrally by gender, then surely it needs to be studied. Hopefully this can lead to practical applications.

We chose the Kirkpatrick vignette as a way to link a common experience during negotiation for some women to our analysis of girls' and boys' negotiations (see Kolb [1988a, 1988b] for a discussion of women's experiences as professional and behind-the-scene negotiators in organizations). We thus point to a possible connection between language use and gender across the life span.

The participants in this study

In this paper we demonstrate how the conflict talk of English-speaking preschool girls and boys in an urban midwestern community already reflects and perpetuates a cultural ideology which constrains girls and women from engaging in direct or confrontational conflict talk, but which permits and encourages boys and men to do so, with greater impunity. We describe some of the verbal tactics that this community of 3-, 4-, and 5-year-old advantaged middle-class children use to further their own interests in disputes. The sample was predominantly white. The conversations discussed here were videotaped while the children played unsupervised at their daycare center, in same-sex triads (see Sheldon [1990b, 1992b] for further methodological details.)

Although many aspects of children's conflicts have been studied (e.g., Shantz, 1987), descriptions of the verbal tactics children use in conflict talk are quite new. A complicating factor is that much research on children and on conflict has a male-centered bias. Thus, boys' social behavior has been well-studied, and Maccoby (1986) has pointed out that, "we have a clearer picture of what girls' groups do not do than what they do do." She calls for "a more delineated account of interaction in female groups." Male bias can also be seen in the interpretations of girls' behaviors, which have been described in the child development literature as "less forceful" (Miller, Danaher, & Forbes, 1986) or "less assertive" (Sachs, 1987), that is, something "less" than the masculine mode.

In order to address the problems due to an androcentric bias in the study of conflict, a theory of DOUBLE-VOICE DISCOURSE was proposed by Sheldon (1992a) which provides a different conceptual framework. It recognizes the complexity and effectiveness of a negotiating style of conflict talk, called double-voice discourse (the term is borrowed from Bahktin, 1971), which can be identified primarily, although not exclusively, with girls and women in the English-speaking communities studied so far. In double-voice discourse, self-assertion is accomplished with linguistic mitigation. Labov and Fanshel (1977, p. 84) define mitigation as "modifying (one's) expression to avoid creating offense." Mitigation expresses the speaker's sensitivity to the addressee. The term *double* refers to the perspective-taking stance of this style in which the speaker expresses a double orientation. The primary orientation is to the self, to one's own agenda. The other orientationn is to the conversational partner(s). The orientation to others does not mean that the speaker necessarily acts in an altruistic, accommodating, or even self-sacrificing manner. It means, rather, that the speaker is responsive to the companion's point of view and to the relationship, even while pursuing her own agenda. In this relational view of interaction, self-assertion is mitigated and contextualized. There is an expectation of mutual sensitivity and responsibility, or at least the appearance of such. As a result, the voice of the self is interconnected with and responsive to the voice of the other, but it is nevertheless forceful and very effective. The dual and interconnected voices that the theory refers to, then, are the voice of the self and the voice of the other.

There are many linguistic and pragmatic means for the expression of double-voice discourse. All of them are not present at the same time or in equal amounts in every instance, but each of them contributes to the impression of the distinctive style of double-voicing. The analysis of examples of conflict talk which follow will provide detailed descriptions of double-voicing as well as a description of how double-voicing can be jointly constructed.

Double-voice discourse is the norm in groups that are solidarity based. Such groups are constrained or governed by a social orientation which is more often, or more consistently, relationship centered. Clear cases of such groups in white, middle-class North American cultures are girls' or women's groups. In young girls' groups, the orientation is toward collaborative and reciprocal play, rather than solitary play (Black, 1989; McLoyd, 1983). Girls' and women's groups show a preference for agreement and engage in deeper levels of cooperation, consensus, and collaborative narrative (Coates, 1987; Eder, 1988; Kalčik, 1975; Tannen, 1990). Descriptions such as "competing in a cooperative mode" (Hughes, 1988), "cooperative competition" (Eckert, 1990), "enabling" (Hauser, Powers, Noam, Jacobson, Weiss, & Follansbee, 1984; Maccoby, 1990), and "affiliative" (Sheldon, 1990b) have been used to characterize girls' and women's sociolinguistic interaction, in which power is ordinarily more fluidly distributed, if not shared. Thus, mitigation and indirectness are more common in their interactions (Miller et al., 1986; Sachs, 1987). Efforts are made to protect members' face (Brown, 1980) and face-threatening acts between girls are not frequent (Connor-Linton, 1986). A cooperative talk orientation also appears in nonsolidarity-based groups during solidarity-based exchanges in which reciprocity is the speaker's focus, for example, when one speaker wants to get another to cooperate.

Solidarity-based and nonsolidarity-based groups differ in the balance they strike between reciprocity and domination and thus in double-voice and single-voice discourse. In double-voice discourse, behaviour is self-serving but it is often covertly so. Because the voice of the self is enmeshed with the voice of the other, it can be harder to hear.

Single-voice discourse, by contrast, is a talk style that is characteristic of nonsolidarity-based groups and their activities. The voice of the self is freestanding, not enmeshed with or regulated by the voice of the other, and, therefore, it may be presented more clearly and may be easier to hear. The group's orientation is toward turf-building and domination rather than affiliation and reciprocity. Resources are perceived as scarce, and efforts are made to compete for and protect both resources and turf. Power is expressed individually as power "over" other group members. Behavior is overtly self-serving because the speaker has a primary orientation to self-interest. There is less regard for the interests of others in the group or for the cost of the speaker's behavior to others. The primary goal is to win by dominating or defeating the partner. Talk is blunt and aggravated (Miller et al., 1986; Sachs, 1987), and has been called "constraining" (Hauser et al., 1984). Face-threatening acts are more common (Connor-Linton, 1986). As will be seen in the examples that follow, single-voice and double-voice discourse are similar to adult conflict negotiating styles that have been labeled, respectively, *hard*, or *hard bargaining*, and *soft*, or *mutual gains approach* (Fisher & Ury, 1981, p. 9).

Double-voice discourse is purposefully characterized as a feature of the task orientation in solidarity-based groups or solidarity-based exchanges in dominance-based groups. This is to avoid linking the concept of gender to characteristics that inhere to individuals. Double-voice discourse is not exclusively "girl talk" and single-voice discourse is not exclusively "boy talk." Instead, the use of double-voice discourse is connected to the norm for social relations in the group and to its members' task orientation, which is changeable. Therefore, boys and men can and do speak in double-voice discourse if their agenda is solidarity-based, or face-saving. In the same vein, girls and women can use single-voice discourse when their agenda involves bald self-assertion.

We will demonstrate the pragmatic effectiveness and the linguistic complexity of the double-voice discourse conflict talk style by means of a close linguistic analysis of some disputes. Examples of single-voice discourse will also be discussed. We will compare the conflict talk techniques that were found in the girls' and boys' groups. We will conclude with some remarks on how language and gender shape conflict talk and on the importance of this approach for an understanding of conflict and negotiation in organizations.

Gender and conflict

Conflict is a contest of wills. We define conflict as "an interaction which grows out of an opposition to a request for action, an assertion, or an action ... and ends with a resolution or dissipation of conflict" (Eisenberg & Garvey, 1981, p. 150). Gender ideology in American cultures gives males the license to argue in direct, demanding, and confrontative ways with unmitigated rivalry. Girls and women cannot or they will be called such things as "bossy," "confrontational," "difficult," or worse for the same behaviors that for boys and men are called "manly" or "assertive." The gender ideology of middle-class white America requires girls and women to "be nice." Sachs (1987) finds that preschool girls have already learned to "say it with a smile," pursuing their agendae and interests within the constraint that they not cause too much stress or jeopardize interpersonal harmony in their intimate groups.

Examples of single-voice discourse

First, by way of contrast, we describe some examples of a single-voice conflict style, which uses direct, unmitigated, confrontational speech acts. Notice that the interactants have the single orientation of pursuing their own self-interest without orienting to the perspective of their partner, without tempering their self-interest with mitigation. This dispute style is called single-voice discourse, because just the voice of the self, that is, just self-interest, is expressed. There is a strong resistance to being influenced and an equally strong drive to be in control.

Example 1.   Single-voice discourse in a boys' group: "You have to have a hat."
In the following conflict, three boys are riding on top of wooden trucks. Connor (4 yrs. 9 mos.) and Robert (4 yrs. 9 mos.) are wearing hard hats. Mark (4 yrs. 10 mos.) is hatless. (As is conventional in child development research, the children's ages are given in all examples. See discussion of age as a factor in these data, on page 92). Robert has told Mark to get a hat. The opposition that follows involves rounds of insistence. It also involves the exchange of threats, which is more common in boys' groups (Miller et al., 1986; Sachs, 1987).

(1) Connor: [*to Mark*] Here's your hat! [*reaches over to pick up the white hat from the floor*] Here's your hat. [*gives the hat to Mark*]
(2) Mark   No, I don't want a hat. [*said in a low key manner*]
(3) Connor: Well, you need one, 'cause – 'cause then you can't play with us.
(4) Mark: I can play if I want. [*said matter-of-factly*]
(5) Connor: Well, then, you have to have a hat.
(6) Mark: No, I don't.
(7) Connor: Uh-huh.
(8) Mark: Uh-uh.
(9) Connor: Uh-huh.
(10) Mark: Uh-uh.
(11) Connor: [*playfully*] Well, then we'll pinch you right in the nose.
(12) Mark: [*seriously*] Then we – then I'll get you back for that. I'll get – I'll get all my friends to wrestle with you.
(13) Connor: [*shouting, annoyed*] Well, then have your HAT then! [*pushes the hat on top of Mark's truck, which tilts Mark off balance; then turns away to his own truck*]
(14) Mark: No. [*pushes the hat away*]

This confrontation, over what the rules of play are, contains face-threatening acts that leave little opportunity for accommodative responses. It is constructed in ways that enhance disagreement and adversity through distancing (e.g., in 3, "cause then you can't play with us") and threatening speech acts (e.g. in 11, "Then we'll pinch you right in the nose" and in 12, "then I'll get you back for that"). Such "controlling" and "constraining" moves have been found more often in boys' groups (Hauser et al., 1984; Leaper, 1991). The use of threats here also illustrates the more heavy-handed style found in boys' conflicts (Miller et al., 1986; Sachs, 1987).

The rounds of insistence (in 7–11: "uh-huh", "uh-uh") give the disagreement a ritualistic tone.

In this example, both boys are expressing their own self-interest explicitly, directly and very clearly. Consequently, the voice of the self is expressed with a culturally familiar sense of authority. As may be expected, however, when single-voicing is carried to the extreme, it can lead to a breakdown in the social fabric. An example of how a confrontative interaction can escalate to a fragile moment during single voice exchanges is provided by the following boys' conflict.

Example 2. Boys' single-voice discourse: "That's my phone."
Charlie (4 yrs. 0 mos.) and Tony (4 yrs. 1 mo.) are together. Tony is sitting on a small foam chair/couch and pushing the buttons on a touch tone phone base that is on his lap. Charlie is nearby.

(1) Tony: I pushed two squares [*giggles*], two squares like this.
(2) Charlie: [*comes closer, puts his fist up to his ear and talks into an imaginary phone*] Hello!
(3) Tony: [*puts his fist up to his ear and talks back*] Hello.
(4) Charlie: [*picks up the receiver that is on Tony's chair*] No, that's my phone.
(5) Tony: [*grabs the telephone cord and tries to pull the receiver away from Charlie*] No, Tha-ah, it's on MY couch. It's on my couch, Charlie. It's on my couch. It's on my couch.
(6) Charlie: [*ignoring Tony, holding onto the receiver, and talking into the telephone now*] Hi. [*walks behind Tony's chair, the telephone base is still on Tony's lap*]
(7) Tony: [*gets off the couch, sets the phone base on the floor*] I'll rock the couch like this [*he turns the foam chair over on top of the telephone base and leans on it as Charlie tries to reach for it under the chair*] Don't! That's my phone!
(8) Charlie: [*pushes the chair off the telephone and moves it closer to himself*] I needa use it.
(9) Tony: [*sits back on his knees and watches Charlie playing with the phone*]

In this example the boys struggle for control over the telephone in an attempt to overpower the other child. Noticeably absent are persuasive justifications that negotiate turntaking and accommodation. In 4, Charlie grabs the receiver from Tony and in 5, Tony tries to pull the receiver away from Charlie. In 7, Tony threatens and then dumps the foam chair on top of the telephone base. In 8, Charlie pushes the chair off the phone and retrieves it for himself.

These boys use physical force, rather than verbal persuasion, to pursue their self-interest and to get control. Their direct and linguistically aggravated words increase their demands or threaten force. The only justifications given are self-serving nonreasons which are often repeated, for example, in (4) Charlie: "That's my phone!' (repeated in 7); (5) Tony: "No", . . . it's on MY couch! (repeated three times); (7) Tony: "I'll rock the couch like this. Don't! That's my phone!"; and (8) Charlie: "I needa use it." Such rigid insistence on getting one's own way (shown by Eisenberg and Garvey [1981] to be one of the least successful strategies for ending opposition), escalates the dispute, creates a stalement and an aversive atmosphere, and leads to aggressive responses and a forceful resolution that gives one boy access and leaves the other out. In short, only a limited range of problem-solving strategies are tried here, and few verbal conflict management tactics are used.

Because the interactants have the single orientation of pursuing their own self-interest without orienting to the perspective of their partner or tempering their self-interest with mitigation to maintain interpersonal harmony, this is a particularly clear example of single-voice discourse. The pattern of conflict is similar to boys' patterns found by Kyratzis (1992). Kyratzis describes such examples of conflict as reflecting an "adversarial stance" and she too finds them more frequently in boys' interaction. In a study of gender differences in the types of persuasive justifications used by same-sex pairs of 4- and 7-year-old friends she found boys using more nonreasons, ad hoc reasons, reasons that appealed to self-serving norms and challenges than girls used.

Example 3.   Single-voice discourse in a girls' group: "No, Sue's turn s'pozed to be back there."
Girls also engage in single voice discourse in same-sex groups. In the next example, Lisa (3 yrs. 11 mos.), Mary (3 yrs. 7 mos.), and Sue (3 yrs. 3 mos.) are playing with blocks that they have put in a tall pile. They are pretending that the block at the top of the pile is a camera. One person stands behind the pile and pretends to take a picture of the girl or girls on the other side. Lisa has been taking longer turns taking pictures than the others. Now she is sitting in front of the camera in position to have her picture taken; Mary is standing behind the camera; and Sue is off to the side.

   (1) Mary: No, Sue's turn s'pozed to be back there, ok Lisa?
   (2) Lisa: No, I – I – I can.
   (3) Mary: No, but Sue hasn't had a turn to be back there.
   (4) Lisa: I – I haven't had a turn to be back there.
   (5) Mary: You did.
   (6) Lisa: No I didn't.
   (7) Mary: Yes you did.
   (8) Lisa: No I didn't.
   (9) Mary: Yes you did, so –
(10) Lisa: I can – I can go there.
(11) Mary: No.

The single-voice discourse in this example, in 5–11, is composed of rounds of opposition and insistence. The girls assert themselves without mitigation. However, the conflict lacks the verbal threats or physical force that escalate and aggravate the boys' conflict in the preceding example.

Another example of girls' single-voicing from these data is similar. It too is muted in contrast to the boys'.

Example 4.   Girls' single-voice discourse: "I want the dress."
Leslie (3 yrs. 3 mos.), Tina (4 yrs. 0 mos.), and Karen (4 yrs. 0 mos.) are at the dress up corner. Tina is wearing a long, pink, filmy negligee with fuzzy

trim. Karen is dressed in a military jacket. Leslie is looking on at them. She is not in dress-up clothes.

(1) Leslie: I want the dress. [*referring to the dress Tina is wearing. Tina doesn't appear to notice that she is speaking to her*]
(2) Karen: [*in a helpful tone*] Well, there is a dress over here. [*points to a plain light-colored cotton-like dress hanging on the clothes tree*]
(3) Leslie: [*disapproving*] That's not a dress.
(4) Tina: [*in a helpful tone*] THIS is a dress. [*points to a third different dress on the rack but out of sight*]
(5) Leslie: No.
(6) Tina: THIS is a dress.
(7) Leslie: Uh-uh. [*turns her face away from Tina and doesn't face her again in this exchange*]
(8) Tina: Uh-huh.
(9) Leslie: Mm-mm.
(10) Tina: Mm-hm [*with more insistence*]
(11) Leslie: Mm-mm. [*with insistence*]
(12) Tina: Mm-mm [*with insistence*]
(13) Leslie: Mm-mm.
(14) Tina: This is! [*long pause*]
(15) Leslie: Tina, I'm playin' doctor. [*she drops her opposition*]
(16) Tina: [*rushes to the chair and sits down*] I'm the doctor and you're the kid.
(17) Leslie: Uh-huh.

This exchange contains verbal moves that are unmitigated, in particular Leslie's statements throughout are direct. In 1 she states her wishes, "I want the dress"; in 3 she contradicts Karen's statement pointing out an alternative for her, "That's not a dress"; in 5 she flatly contradicts Tina's suggestion of a third dress, "No." When Tina insists in 6, Leslie returns with insistence in 7, "Uh-uh" and rounds of insistence and contradiction by Tina and Leslie follow, until Leslie abruptly changes the topic in 15, "I'm playin' doctor." In 16 Tina claims the more favored role of doctor and allocates the lesser role of patient to Leslie.

Although it is constructed predominantly by single-voice disputing moves, this episode does have a less aversive tone than the two examples of single-voicing in the boys' group, however. The softening is accomplished first by Karen helpfully suggesting an alternative dress for Leslie in 2, and then by Tina pointing to yet another choice in 4. Although Tina gets her way and continues to wear the "fun" dress, at the same time she tries to help Leslie see that there are other dress-up choices and that she can have fun too. Tina is doing double-voice work here.

Leslie subsequently blunts her confrontation with Tina by looking away from her in 7 for the remainder of their disagreement. In 17, she agrees and does not dispute the role given to her.

Double-voice discourse

Having given you a flavor of directly insistent confrontations in girls' and boys' single-voice discourse, we will now move to an example of double-voice discourse in a girls' group.

Example 5.   Girls' double-voice discourse: simultaneous mitigation and aggravation of conflict talk: "Nurses getta do shots."
The following long and elaborate conflict takes place between Arlene (4 yrs. 9 mos.) and Elaine (4 yrs. 6 mos.); Erica (4 yrs. 2 mos.) is present briefly. They have been pretending that some dolls are sick children and they are nurses who are caring for them. A conflict develops over who will use some medical implements that are in the room. Elaine, who started enacting the role of nurse earlier than Arlene did, wants to keep control of the equipment. But Arlene wants to use something too. They each use linguistic and pragmatic techniques of double-voicing to try to get what they want. (Double-voicing moves are underlined and intense speech is indicated by capital letters.)

(1)   Arlene: Can I have that – that thing? [*referring to the blood pressure gauge in Elaine's lap*]. I'm going to take my baby's temperature.

(2)   Elaine: [*looking up from talking on the telephone*] You can use it – you can use my temperature. Just make sure you can't use anything else unless you can ask [*turns back to talking on the telephone*].

In 1, Arlene asks permission to use the blood pressure gauge. She gives a reason for her request. In 2, Elaine gives her qualified agreement. She lets Arlene use the thermometer with restrictions, telling her to ask before she uses anything else. Although the girls are competing for goods here, there is an attempt to allow for a fair distribution. Elaine shows some flexibility by offering a concession, establishing "a middle ground which moves toward the other position but still opposes it" (Vuchinich, 1990, p. 126). However, a mutual opposition subsequently unfolds.

(3)   Arlene: [*picks up thermometer from a nearby table and takes her baby's temperature*] Eighty-three! She isn't sick. Yahoo! May I? [*she asks Elaine, who is still on the telephone, if she can use the needle-less hypodermic syringe*]

(4)   Elaine: No, I'm gonna need to use the shot in a couple of minutes.

(5)   Arlene: But I – I need this though. [*picks up the hypodermic syringe*]

(6)   Elaine: [*firmly*] Okay, just use it once.

In 3, Arlene makes a polite request to use Elaine's syringe ("May I?") but in 4, Elaine denies the request with a flat "no" followed by a qualification of her refusal; she explains that she will need to use the shot soon. In 5, Arlene returns with an opposing move, adopting Elaine's reason, insisting that she also "needs" it, softening her demand with "though" while she picks up the contested syringe. In 6, Elaine reluctantly agrees to let her use it, again offering a concession that establishes a middle ground, but she firmly constrains the use to "just" one time.

(7)	Erica:	[*whispers*] Arlene, let's play doctor.
(8)	Arlene:	[*to Erica*] No. I'm gonna give her a shot on the –
(9)	Elaine:	Hey, I'm the nurse. I'm the nurse. [*she puts down the phone and comes over to Arlene and the crib in which her doll is lying*] <u>Arlene, remember, I'm the nurse, and the nurses getta do shots, remember?</u>
(10)	Arlene:	<u>But I get to do some.</u>
(11)	Elaine:	<u>Just a couple, okay?</u>

In 8, Arlene starts giving her baby a shot, but in 9 Elaine wants to be in control of the syringe. First she responds directly. She addresses Arlene by name and requests that Arlene "remember" Elaine's role. "I'm the nurse," Elaine asserts. She continues, providing a rationale: nurses have a certain authority, namely, they "getta do shots." She follows this justification with a tag question "remember?" which is intended to elicit agreement. It does elicit Arlene's token agreement and a request for another concession in 10 when Arlene says "But I get to do some." This is a mitigating response, here called a *yes but strategy*, in which agreement prefaces disagreement (discussed further in Pomerantz, 1984; Sheldon, 1992a). Arlene backs off a bit; she agrees that Elaine will use the syringe, but she still pursues her own agenda and states her intention to use it too. The yes but strategy allows for an appearance of agreement, while the partners continue to negotiate their action plans. In 11, Elaine again offers a concession, telling Arlene that she can do "just a couple." She follows this directive with a tag question that solicits agreement, "ok?"

All of Elaine's concessions with constraints allow her to hold onto her own agenda while accommodating her partner's agenda. This is a form of double-voice discourse. However, although Elaine is accommodating Arlene's wishes, the conflict is actually intensifying because Arlene is pressing to keep control of the syringe for her own use and to minister to the doll in other nurse-like ways. The opposition over who has exclusive rights to minister to the doll grows. Whereas in 3 Arlene had started out asking permission to use the needle ("May I?"), she has now moved to directly asserting what she will do, as in 12.

(12)	Arlene:	I get to do some more things too. Now don't forget – now don't touch the baby until I get back, <u>because it IS MY BABY!</u> [*said to both of the other girls*] I'll check her ears, <u>ok?</u> [*puts down the syringe and picks up the ear scope*].
(13)	Elaine:	Now I'll – and I'll give her – I'll have to give her [*the same doll*] a shot. [*picks up the syringe that Arlene has put down*]
(14)	Arlene:	<u>There can only be</u> ONE thing that you– that – NO, she – <u>she only needs</u> one SHOT.
(15)	Elaine:	<u>Well, let's pretend</u> it's <u>another day</u> that <u>we</u> have to look in her ears <u>together.</u>

At this point Elaine wants to give the doll a shot but in 12 Arlene has ordered her not to touch "her" baby. She announces she is not constrained in what she can do with the baby and that she will check the baby's ears. As Elaine has done previously, she adds a tag question – "ok?" – a marker that solicits agreement. Meanwhile, in 13, Elaine reannounces her plans to give a shot. In two indirect statements in 14, in which no agent is mentioned, and the responsibility for deciding who gives a shot is vaguely expressed, Arlene tries to cut Elaine out of the action by stating that "there can only be ONE thing . . ." and the baby "only needs one shot." Both girls are equally determined to have their own way. In 15, Elaine tries to get Arlene to consider an alternative in which they can both participate and benefit. She reframes the situation and responds in multiple mitigated ways. She opens with a delay, "well." She uses a joint directive "let's" and introduces a new, pretend, scenario: she displaces the time to "another day" and the medical problem to her "ears," in an effort to induce cooperation on a combined agenda, that is, "we" will work "together." By reframing the situation and redefining the problem, Elaine tries to take control and protect her own interests. Kyratzis notes that girls' persuasive justifications are more often framed in such a manner – in terms of benefit to the group – than boys'.

In 16, the conflict continues to heat up. In answer to Elaine's suggestion that they look in the doll's ears together, Arlene replies with a token agreement, "yeah but," and nevertheless continues to demand to examine the ears herself, ordering Elaine not to "shot her."

(16) Arlene: No, no, <u>yeah but</u> I do the ear looking. Now don't SHOT – [*lowering her voice*] DON'T SHOT HER! I'm the one who does all the shots, cause this is my baby!
(17) Elaine: [*whispers*] <u>Well</u> – I'm the nurse and nurses get to do the shots.
(18) Arlene: [*spoken very intensely*] An' me' – And men – <u>well, then men get to do the shots too even 'cause men can be nurses.</u> [*taunting, slightly sing-song*] <u>But you can't</u> shot her.

In 17, Elaine continues to mitigate by delaying, "well," and countering with a reason for why she should give a shot, "nurses get to do the shots." In 18, Arlene counters with a competing justification, that is intended to take some of the force out of Elaine's claim ". . . well, then men get to do the shots too even cause men can be nurses." In an indirect way, this statement questions whether Elaine, as a female, has an exclusive right to give shots. Arlene again orders her, somewhat indirectly, not to give a shot, "But you can't shot her."

(19) Elaine: I'll have to shot her after – <u>after</u> – after you listen – <u>after you look in the ears</u>.
(20) Erica: She [*Arlene*] already shot her even.
(21) Elaine: We have – <u>she didn't do a shot on her finger</u>.
(22) Arlene: But she did – she did – I DID TOO! Now don't shot her at all!
(23) Elaine: We hafta do it – <u>Well</u>, I'm going to keep do it after she – this baby.
(24) Arlene: [*intense but <u>lowered voice</u>*] Now DON'T YOU DARE!

In 19, Elaine continues to offer a concession, that she will give the shot "after you look in her ears." When Erica says that Arlene "already shot her," Elaine assertively persists within the pretend frame, inventively countering in 21 that "she didn't do a shot on her finger," that is, Arlene missed a spot and it needs to be done by Elaine. Thus, Elaine creatively offers alternatives in which she can share in the action too.

Although both girls are developing a complex negotiation in double-voice discourse, Arlene, however, is gaining more in this struggle than Elaine is. In line 24, Arlene persists; she intensely, directly, and threateningly orders Elaine to stop, "Now DON'T YOU DARE!" This potentially single-voice move is not delivered without mitigation, though. Arlene does not shout. Instead, she mutes her voice by lowering it. As the confrontation reaches its peak of insistence, the girls' voices get lower and lower, not louder and louder with anger. In 25, Elaine directly orders Arlene, in an even lower voice:

(25) Elaine: [*voice lowered more than Arlene's but equally intense*] Stop saying that! [*pause*] Well, then you can't come to my birthday!

(26) Arlene: [*voice still lowered*] I don't want to come to your birthday.

(27) Erica: Don't talk about birthdays.

(28) Elaine: [*makes the sound of a phone ringing and gets up from the crib to answer the phone*]

(29) Arlene: [*looking in the doll's ear*] Her ear, that ear's fine. I checked one ear and I'll check the other.

As Elaine and Arlene escalate their dispute with words, instead of raising their voices in shouts or screams, which happens in the boys' groups, their speaking voices paradoxically become more and more muted. The paradox is the lack of consonance between the girls' angry words and their quieter and quieter tone. It is a dramatic example of the mitigation of the voice of self in their double-voice discourse. It seems that the muting of the speaking voice allows them to escalate the directness of their words and the confrontational nature of their speech acts. Arlene, who has gained more in this conflict than Elaine has, uses double-voice discourse as well as Elaine. Notice also in 25, that the kind of threat that Elaine uses is one of social ostracism, ". . . you can't come to my birthday party," not one of physical attack which we saw in Example 1, ". . . we'll pinch you right in the nose," "I'll get you right back for that . . . I'll get all my friends to wrestle with you," or Example 2, "I'll rock the couch like this."

The conflict between Elaine and Arlene is enacted through a negotiational stance. It is an example of the linguistic and pragmatic complexity that is often involved in double-voice discourse and it displays a variety of verbal devices that can be used to soften conflict in order to be effective. In this example, Arlene was successful in getting what she wanted in part because Elaine was willing to accommodate after trying to negotiate numerous concessions. The balance in this negotiation was rather uneven, although it need not be (see Sheldon [1992a] for examples of more balanced double-voice negotiations). The differences in each girl's pursuit of power and their attainment of their own goals, is an important reminder that there is, of course, diversity and individual variation within same-sex groups in the extent to which children (and adults) are effective in negotiations and in getting what they want. Arlene's style here is somewhat different than Elaine's. Although both use double-voice discourse, the differences in how much they use and when they use it seem to reflect differences in their ongoing successes during the negotiation. Arlene's firm pursuit of her own self-interest is an example that should not be overlooked in discussions of how girls' and women's effectiveness in negotiations is viewed (see Sheldon [1992b] for further discussion of this issue). The example illustrates the diverse verbal resources that may be employed in double-voicing, even in childhood, and which create a more verbally complex and elaborate negotiational style than single-voice discourse.

Now let us examine an example of boys' double-voice discourse.

Example 6.   Boys' double-voice discourse example: "How 'bout if we both sit?"
Three boys have been sitting at a small table covered with eating utensils and plastic food. The following conflict between Robert (4 yrs. 9 mos.) and Connor (4 yrs. 9 mos.) arises over whose doll will sit in a high chair pulled up to their table. Both boys are very intent upon succeeding. (The features of double-voice discourse are underlined.)

(1) Robert: [*to Connor*] Go get the baby, ok? [*the next said to no one in particular*] I'll go get the baby, the baby's crying, ok?
(2) Connor: Waa![*in a high voice for the doll*] He wants to eat.
(3) Robert: I got him. [*goes over to a toy crib and picks up a doll*]
(4) Connor: No, that's not the right baby, this is. [*comes over and picks up another doll out of the same crib*]
(5) Robert: This – no, this – that's a girl. [*puts his doll in a toy high chair*]
(6) Connor: I know, but – but he can't come for dinner.
(7) Robert: No, no, she – no, he really is hungrier than her. [*tries to put his doll in the high chair too*]
(8) Connor: No. No, he's – he – he's not supposed – he's hung – she's hungrier than he is. [*pushes Robert's doll out of the high chair*]
(9) Robert: Hey, how 'bout if we both sit? [*said with an engaging tone and a big smile*]
(10) Connor: Yaa, Yaa, that's a good idea. [*he agrees in a squeaky, high pitch voice as though talking for the doll*]

The conflict begins with Connor first opposing Robert with a direct "no" in 4 but then follows with the reason that Robert's baby is not the "right" one (to put in the high chair), but rather Connor's baby is. Robert resists Connor, also with a flat "no" in 5 followed by the explanation that his doll is the right one, because Connor's is a girl. In 6, in a yes but move that is a partial agreement and a partial disagreement, Connor acknowledges that his own doll is a girl, saying "I know but," and he further explains that Robert's doll cannot come for dinner. In 7, Robert then blocks Connor's maneuver by explaining that his doll really is hungrier than Connor's doll. Connor picks up on this new theme in 8 and counters that his doll is hungrier than Robert's doll. Until this point, the boys have been quite contentious. Each boy competitively matches the other boy's objection with a new one of his own as the conflict spirals. Finally in 9, Robert dramatically reverses the tone. He grins and enthusiastically suggests a compromise with an indirect request framed as a question, "How 'bout if we both sit?" Note the inclusive words "we" and "both." In 10, Connor agrees, responding through his doll in a high pitched voice that this is "a good idea." Thus, the boys find a mutually acceptable resolution. Note also that the boys' negotiating is done within the pretend frame, which also functions to mitigate the conflict. (For further discussion, see Sheldon [1990b, 1992a].)

Comparison in amount of double-voice discourse found in girls' and boys' conflicts in the larger study

The preceding discussion has given examples of double-voice discourse and has contrasted them with an unmitigated form of conflict talk called single-voice discourse. Our intention has been to describe vivid examples of these two speech styles to give a sense of the linguistic phenomena we are observing, because they are important styles of conflict talk. The examples include a number of ways in which double-voicing is accomplished. However, in order to answer the question of how frequently the girls engage in double-voicing compared to the boys, and thus to address the issue of how characteristic one or the other styles might be for this sample, the authors coded transcripts and videotapes for conflict and double-voice discourse. We coded 6 of 24 transcripts or 25 percent of a total of 9 hours of conversation. This 25 percent contained talk produced by half of the boys and half of the girls. Interrater agreement in identifying conflict episodes was 83.3 percent, which was counted before discussion. Interrater reliability in identifying conflicts for the boys was somewhat higher (86.9%) than for the girls (80%). Interrater agreement in identifying double-voice discourse was 97 percent counted before discussion. Table 3.1 shows that of the 68 mutual conflicts that were found, 30 (44.1%) were in the girls' groups. Thirty-eight conflicts (55.9%) were in the boys' groups. Table 3.2 shows that although there were more conflicts among the boys, 44.7 percent contained double-voice discourse, compared to 60 percent of the girls' conflicts which contained double-voice discourse. Thus, we determined that the girls' conflicts more often contained some form of double-voicing. This finding is consistent with the work of Miller et al. (1986) and Sachs (1987) which found more mitigation in girls' conflict and pretend play discourses. Leaper (1991) also found more collaborative speech acts among girls (e.g., invitations to play, constructive offers, mutual affirmations), and more controlling speech acts among boys (e.g., insults, orders, refutations,

Table 3.1 Comparison of number of mutual conflicts in girls and in boys' groups as a percentage of the total number of conflicts (a mutual conflict episode is one in which each speaker opposes the other one)

	No. mutual conflicts	
Girls	30	44.1% of total number of conflicts
Boys	38	55.9% of total number of conflicts
Total	68	100%

Table 3.2 Percentage of conflicts that contained double-voice discourse (interrater reliability = 97%)

Girls	60%	(in 30 conflicts)
Boys	44.7%	(in 38 conflicts)

and nonacceptance). Kyratzis (1992) also finds more linguistic and pragmatic elaboration in girls' persuasive justifications. Our impression from having analyzed the conflicts that occurred in the full 9 hours of conversations, is that girls' double-voicing is more complex and elaborate than boys', which is reflected here by the difference in length and linguistic complexity of the girls' example in this paper compared to the boys'. We have not been able to find in these 9 hours of conversations a boys' double-voicing example that even comes close to matching the girls' for elaborateness and length. Example 6 is representative of the best boys' double-voice discourse examples in these data, whereas there are other long and shorter complex examples of girls' double-voicing similar to Example 5. Some of these are discussed in Sheldon (1990b, 1992a). Similarly, it was difficult to find "good" examples of girls' single-voice discourse in these data that did not also contain a certain amount of double-voicing sprinkled throughout, as Example 4 did here.

Finally, one might ask whether the gender differences claimed here are differences in competence and thus reflect some other developmental difference. The ability to use double-voice discourse requires skill in social perspective taking. However, there is little evidence of sex differences in perspective taking ability (Shantz, 1983). In addition, if the ability to use double-voice discourse were age-related then more, not less, double-voice should have occurred in the boys' coded discourse than in the girls', because the boys in this sample were 8 months older, on average, than the girls. Thus, it is more likely that the difference in usage is a discourse choice governed by norms in solidarity-based groups rather than a reflection of ability. Boys also are competent in double-voice discourse. But given the norms of their groups, they use it less often, with apparently less elaboration, and perhaps only when their more adversarial stance fails, as in Example 6, line 9, when Robert offers a compromise after he and Connor get nowhere trying to convince each other why their baby deserves to sit in the high chair.

Conclusion

This research provides a more delineated account of ways in which socio-linguistic norms are different in girls' and boys' groups. It suggests that children's same-sex groups are, to a certain extent, different speech communities in which different norms, expectations, and constraints on verbally and socially appropriate behavior guide interactive behavior. These norms do not mandate mutually exclusive behaviors between these groups. Rather, the differences are nuanced and fluid, and distributed between girls' and boys' groups probabilistically. The norms that produce double-voice discourse have been called solidarity-based norms (Sheldon, 1992a). They reflect a reciprocal, collaboration-based social orientation, and a focus on social perspective-taking. In such groups, maintaining harmony, sociability, and face are important. There is a preference for agreement, even token agreement. Contrary to female stereotypes mentioned earlier, the verbal conflict negotiation techniques of such groups are highly developed, elaborate, and effective. The norms that produce single-voice discourse have been called competition-oriented, dominance, adversarial, or turf-based norms. There is a higher frequency of heavy-handed persuasion tactics in such groups. Conversations that are constrained by solidarity-based or adversarial-based norms result in different verbal styles.

These differences also reflect the gender ideology of a patriarchal system which prescribes both behavioral differentiation as well as symbolic, or ideological differentiation between females and males. We should point out, first, that gender socialization is never always complete or "successful" and, therefore, we expect variation in the extent to which individual girls and boys reflect cultural expectations of gendered talk in their same-sex groups. We agree with Thorne (1993) who argues for more research devoted to describing the nature and extent of variation *within* gender categories. Second, it is not the case that boys do not know how to use double-voicing or that girls cannot use single-voicing. These data show that both styles are within the competencies of both sexes. Rather, in white, middle-class, patriarchal culture in which these children are being raised, there are social sanctions attached to boys who are nice, cooperative, or "wimpy" and to girls who are "tough," confrontational, or "sassy." These ideological injunctions can restrict girls and boys from freely using their full linguistic and pragmatic capabilities when trying to influence others. Third, studies of urban, working-class Afro-American girls and boys by Goodwin (1980), and of middle-class Afro-American women by Stanback (1985) indicate that the communicative contexts in which girls and women use single- and double-voicing can vary by race and class. Afro-American girls and women seem to be freer to express contentiousness in their cultural groups than Euro-American girls and women.

Finally, our analysis avoids theorizing gender differences as a deficit for one gender and sees them instead as variations, that is, symbolic adaptations to the different contexts, norms, and experiences that prevail in same-sex interactions. However, as we all know, these are not neutral differences; they are politically loaded. Clearly girls' (and women's) double-voicing is well-suited to the social norms that govern self-assertion in white, middle-class, solidarity-based groups. However, in mixed-sex conversations, double-voice discourse may not serve girls as well, because dominance-based norms are often operating there. Research summarized by Maccoby (1990) indicates that girls find boys aversive and hard to influence. Our focus on discourse analysis gives a new perspective on why this might be so. In mixed-sex groups, boys often dominate girls by using more heavy-handed persuasion tactics than girls, or they ignore girls altogether (Camras, 1984). In addition, single-voice discourse tactics can easily evoke similar moves from one's partner, which increases the possibility of greater polarization.

Carli (1989) also finds that men often resist being influenced by other men and are harder to influence than women. However, she notes that both men and women are influenced more by someone who agrees with them and less by someone who disagrees. She hypothesizes that men may be more inclined to agree with women than with men because they expect interactions with women to be more friendly and to produce more agreement, whereas they expect interactions with men to be more competitive and aggressive. This suggests that girls' (or women's) use of double-voicing, which is well-suited to their own social interaction, may only serve them as well in mixed-sex groups if mitigation and agreement are also highly valued *by the males* in the group. Such groups would then fit the picture of a "solidarity-based group" described earlier.

However, interaction in mixed-sex groups that are governed by masculine norms presents a painful double bind for girls and women. Single-voice discourse (i.e., unmitigated and confrontational talk) is a highly valued form of stereotypical masculine self-assertion. But such behavior is not emphasized, or is actively discouraged, for females in many American cultures. Sociolinguistic studies report that mixed-sex group interaction can require more unmitigated confrontation from females for them to influence males. Yet, ironically, when females behave in assertive ways that are *ordinary* for boys and men, they risk being labeled negatively by those males. Considering all of this, it is not surprising that professional women negotiators say that negotiation "is not about confrontation, but it's about bridge building" (Kolb, 1988b).

Clearly, gender differences in communicative style in a patriarchal culture are not neutral and are *potentially* exploitable to the advantage of the more socially dominant, entitled, and highly valued group, namely, males. Cultural restrictions on conversational style, which in same-sex groups channel females toward mitigation and concession and males to resistance to being told what to do, may facilitate girls' and women's interaction in same-sex groups. But using their preferred style can disadvantage females in mixed-sex forums, such as classrooms, playgrounds, business firms, or the United Nations, where the masculine single-voicing style (and voice) is often how power is brokered. In such circumstances, as Jeane Kirkpatrick notes, the words of boys and men are more privileged than those of girls or women, even (or perhaps especially) if the girls or women speak in the single-voice mode. On the other hand, as we have shown here, skill at double-voice discourse is a valuable asset during conflict management. The issue seems not to be one of skill then, but rather one of authorization of the female voice. In female groups women's voices are highly authorized. However, in mixed-sex groups this is not usually the case (e.g., see Hall [1982], Krupnick [n.d.], and Thorne [1989] for discussions of how mixed-sex classrooms often de-authorize and silence women's voices).

This paper is intended to challenge dualistic thinking about gender, which, because it rests on negative cultural stereotypes, is more likely to disadvantage girls. Gender dualism is also an incorrect way to theorize the full range of masculinity, or masculinities, because not all males or groups of males regularly engage in a heavy-handed conflict-style or value such. Unfortunately, it is not easy to think of gender in other than a dualistic fashion. In challenging dualistic thinking about gender, we intend to redirect attention to issues of feminine power and self-assertion which are ordinarily erased or overlooked in discussions of conflict management. We see a need for reformulating deep-seated cultural beliefs, often stereotypes, about women or girls, and men or boys. Focusing on the direct observation of spontaneous talk holds much promise for moving us toward this goal. It can yield evidence of more complex patterns of sameness and difference among and between women and men. It will no doubt uncover greater-than-imagined behavioral diversity among females and among males that will further challenge gender stereotypes and shake our dualistic thinking.

When girls and boys grow up

This paper has been a close analysis of how children talk to each other when they are in conflict. Discussing spontaneous disputes in situated interaction allows us to observe the dynamic enactment of conflict and negotiation, in context. However, it is hard to videotape spontaneous, nonplayful adult conflict. With adults we must usually be content with retellings, with accounts of disagreements rather than with the events themselves. But retellings are interpretations of events, and are often incomplete. Actual disputes and negotiations are different and independent from an account that may be constructed about them at some later time and place.

In our attempt to understand children's conflict and negotiation, we have treated language as the object to be studied. Studying conflict and negotiation in the discourse context in which the event unfolds reveals how utterances are produced as responses to another speaker's prior move and how they are framed to accommodate or distance the partner's next move. Studying the dynamic interactive process of conversations provides a richer understanding of how the conflict process and its outcomes are constructed.

We have also assumed that the verbal management of conflict reflects sociocultural knowledge. Contained in that knowledge is our understanding of cultural norms and expectations of how to use language. Gender socialization shapes the way language is used with partners of different sexes. Sociability takes different forms depending on the gender ideology of the interactants. Since gender is a primary category by which the world and our understanding of the world and ourselves are organized (at least in Western cultures), and language is our primary tool for negotiating with and understanding others, then any theory of conflict must describe the role of gender and language as *contexts* in which conflict takes shape and is managed. In short, the gender composition of the group is an important contextual variable that influences negotiation.

For these reasons, this research raises issues that are basic to analyzing adult conflict and negotiation in organizational settings. We have described two styles of conflict talk that are governed by different strategies of interaction. We hypothesize that the kind of sociocultural values that an organization actively encourages (i.e., "masculine," "feminine," or some combination of both) will be reflected and perpetuated in the kind of discourse that is tacitly encouraged during conflict and negotiation.

There are a number of questions that can be raised by this approach:

1. To what extent does an organization maintain or encourage a *predominant* style of interaction ("masculine" or "feminine") as discussed here, which results in predictable forms of conflict management and outcomes, as well as other nonconflictual patterns of social interaction? (See Martin [1990] and others cited there for excellent answers to this question.)

2. How can the important skills that females bring to conflict management, in the form of double-voice discourse, be applied to improve conflict management and negotiation in their organizations? (See Kolb, 1988a, 1988b).

3. What difficulties do women have in their day-to-day participation in organizations with predominantly "masculine" conflict management practices?

4. To what extent are women's difficulties in "masculine" organizations due to a lack of authorization of women's voice and the exclusion of "feminine" values and interactional styles?

5. To what extent do miscommunication and mismatch in an organization also develop from differences in interactional styles that are due to ethnicity, race, and class, as they interconnect with gender?

6. Finally, single-voice discourse appears to be a type of *distributive* bargaining process and double-voice discourse has features of (but may not be entirely describable as) a type of *integrative* bargaining (according to definitions in Putnam, 1990). The study of discourse in context, that is, spontaneous, unplanned, "raw" conflict and negotiation, is an important realm for further investigating the dynamic and interdependent nature and content of these bargaining processes, and for testing the validity of claims about them.

These are but a few of the research questions and directions that emerge from our approach that bear on the study of organizational conflict and negotiation.

Acknowledgements

Thanks are due to the editors of the volume in which this paper first appeared and to Cassie Drake, Sara Hayden, Becky Omdahl, Scott Poole, and Linda Puttnam for comments and suggestions raised on an earlier draft of this paper and to the conference participants for a spirited discussion of the issues contained here. This paper was originally delivered at the Fifth Research on Negotiation in Organizations Conference for the colloquium on "A Feminist Perspective on Power, Negotiation and Conflict," Fuqua School of Business, Duke University, October 18–20, 1991. Portions of this paper have appeared in Sheldon (1992a, 1992b).

References

Bahktin, M. (1971) 'Discourse typology in prose', in L. Mateja and K. Pomorska (eds.), *Readings in Russian poetics: formalist and structuralist views.* (Originally published 1929.) Cambridge, MA: MIT Press, pp. 176–196.

Black, B. (1989) 'Interactive pretense: Social and symbolic skills in preschool play groups', *Merrill-Palmer Quarterly, 35*, pp. 379–397.

Borker, R. (1980) 'Anthropology: Social and cultural perspectives', in S. McConnell-Ginet, R. Borker and N. Furman (eds.), *Women and language in literature and society,* New York: Praeger, pp. 26–44.

Brown, B. (1980) 'How and why are women more polite: Some evidence from a Mayan community', in S. McConnell-Ginet, R. Borker and N. Furman (eds.), *Women and language in literature and society,* New York: Praeger, pp. 111–149.

Campbell, K. (1988) 'Woman and speaker: A conflict in roles', in S.S. Brehm (ed.), *Seeing female: Social roles and personal lives,* Westport, CT: Greenwood Press, pp. 123–133.

Camras, L. (1984) 'Children's verbal and nonverbal communication in a conflict situation', *Ethology and Sociobiology, 5*, pp. 257–268.

Carli, L. (1989) 'Gender differences in interaction style and influence', *Journal of Personality and Social Psychology, 56*(4), pp. 565–576.

Coates, J. (1987) *Women, men and language,* New York: Longman.

Connor-Linton, J. (1986) 'Gender differences in politeness: The struggle for power among adolescents', in J. Connor-Linton, C.J. Hall and M. McGinnis (eds.), *Southern California Occasional Papers in Linguistics, 11*, pp. 64–98.

Eckert, P. (1990) 'Cooperative competition in adolescent "girl talk"', *Discourse Processes, 13*, pp. 91–122.

Eder, D. (1988) 'Building cohesion through collaborative narration', *Social Problems Quarterly, 51*, pp. 225–235.

Eisenberg, A.R. and Garvey, C. (1981) 'Children's use of verbal strategies in resolving conflicts', *Discourse Processes, 4*, pp. 149–170.

Fisher, R. and Ury, W. (1981) *Getting to yes: Negotiating agreement without giving in,* New York: Penguin.

Goodwin, M.H. (1980) 'Directive-response speech sequences in girls' and boys' task activities', in S. McConnell-Ginet, R. Borker and N. Furman (eds.), *Women and language in literature and society,* New York: Praeger, pp. 157–173.

Hall, R. (1982) 'The classroom climate: A chilly one for women?', Washington, DC: Project on the Status and Education of Women, Association of American Colleges.

Hauser, S.T., Powers, S.I., Noam, G.G., Jacobson, A.M., Weiss, B. and Follansbee, D.J. (1984) 'Familial contexts of adolescent ego development', *Child Development, 55*, pp. 195–213.

Hughes, L. (1988) 'But that's not really mean: Competing in a cooperative mode', *Sex Roles, 19*(11/12), pp. 669–687.

Kalčik, S. (1975) '". . . like Ann's gynecologist or the time I was almost raped": Personal narratives in women's rap groups', *Journal of American Folklore, 88*, pp. 3–11.

Kolb, D. (1988a) *Her place at the table: A consideration of gender issues in negotiation,* Working Paper Series 88-5, Program on Negotiation, Harvard Law School.

—— (1988b) *Her place at the table,* videotape, Program on negotiation, Harvard Law School.

Krupnick, C. (n.d.) *Women and men in the classroom: Inequality and its remedies,* Faculty Teaching Excellence Program, University of Colorado, Boulder.

Kyratzis, A. (1992) 'Gender differences in the use of persuasive justification in children's pretend play', in K. Hall, M. Bucholtz and M. Moonwomon (eds.), *Locating power,* Berkeley, CA: Berkeley Linguistic Society, vol. 2, pp. 326–337.

Labov, W. and Fanshel, D. (1977) *Therapeutic discourse.* New York: Academic Press.

98   *Amy Sheldon and Diane Johnson*

Leaper, C. (1991) 'Influence and involvement in children's discourse: Age, gender and partner effects', *Child Development*, *62*, pp. 797–811.

McLoyd, V. (1983) 'The effects of structure of play objects on the pretend play of low-income preschool children', *Child Development*, *54*, pp. 626–663.

Maccoby, E. (1986) 'Social groupings in childhood: Their relationship to prosocial and antisocial behavior in boys and girls', in D. Olweus, J. Block and M. Radke-Yarrow (eds.), *Developments of antisocial and prosocial behavior*, San Diego, CA: Academic Press, pp. 263–284.

—— (1990) 'Gender and relationships: A developmental account', *American Psychologist*, *45*, pp. 513–520.

Martin, J. (1990) 'Deconstructing organizational taboos: The suppression of gender conflict in organizations', *Organizational Science*, *I*(4), pp. 339–359.

Matthews, J.J. (1984) *Good and mad women. The historical construction of femininity in twentieth century Australia*, Boston, MA: George Allen & Unwin.

Miller, P., Danaher, D. and Forbes, D. (1986) 'Sex-related strategies for coping with interpersonal conflict in children aged five and seven', *Developmental Psychology*, *22*, pp. 543–548.

Pomerantz, A. (1984) 'Agreeing and disagreeing with assessments: Some features of preferred/dispreferred turn shapes', in J.M. Atkinson and J. Heritage (eds.), *Structures of social action: Studies in conversational analysis*, New York: Cambridge University Press, pp. 57–101.

Putnam, L. (1990) 'Reframing integrative and distributive bargaining', in B.H. Sheppard, M.H. Bazerman and R.J. Lewicki (eds.), *Research on negotiation in organizations*, Greenwich, CT: JAI Press, Vol. 2, pp. 3–30.

Sachs, J. (1987) 'Preschool boys' and girls' language use in pretend play', in S.U. Philips, S. Steele and C. Tanz (eds.), *Language, gender and sex in comparative perspective*, New York: Cambridge University Press, pp. 178–188.

Shantz, C.U. (1983) 'Social cognition', in J.H. Flavell and E.M. Markman (eds.), *Handbook of child psychology: Cognitive development*, New York: Wiley, Vol. 3, pp. 495–555.

Shantz, C. (1987) 'Conflicts between children', *Child Development*, *58*, pp. 283–305.

Sheldon, A. (1990b) '"Kings are royaler than queens". Language and socialization', *Young Children*, *45*(2), pp. 4–9.

—— (1990b) 'Pickle fights: Gendered talk in preschool disputes', *Discourse Processes*, *13*(1), pp. 5–31.

—— (1992a) 'Conflict talk: Sociolinguistic challenges to self-assertion and how young girls meet them', *Merrill-Palmer Quarterly*, *38*(1), pp. 95–117.

—— (1992b) 'Preschool girls' discourse competence: Managing conflict and negotiating power', in K. Hall, M. Bucholtz and B. Moonwomon (eds.), *Locating power*, Berkeley, CA: Berkeley Linguistic Society, vol. 2, pp. 528–539.

Stanback, M.H. (1985) 'Language and Black women's place: Evidence from the Black middle class', in P. Treichler, C. Kramarae and B. Stafford (eds.), *For alma mater: Theory and practice in feminist scholarship*, Urbana, IL.: University of Illinois Press, pp. 177–193.

Tannen, D. (1990) 'Gender differences in conversational coherence: Physical alignment and topical cohesion', in B. Dorval (ed.), *Conversational coherence and its development*, Norwood, NJ: Ablex, pp. 167–206.

Thorne, B. (1984) 'Rethinking the ways we teach', in C. Pearson, D. Shavlik and J. Touchton (ed.), *Educating the majority*, New York: Macmillan, pp. 311–325.

—— (forthcoming) *The girls and boys together*, New Brunswick, NJ: Rutgers University Press.

Vuchinich, S. (1990) 'The sequential organization of closing in verbal family conflict', in A. Grimshaw (ed.), *Conflict Talk*, New York: Cambridge University Press, pp. 118–138.

4

Not just 'doctors' orders': directive-response sequences in patients' visits to women and men physicians

Candace West

Originally published in *Discourse and Society*, 1 (1990).

Introduction

> *Doctors' Orders.* This phrase, used to describe a physician's recommendations to a patient, implies that the patient has no choice but to do whatever told (Shapiro, 1978: 170).

One of the most prevalent complaints in the literature of physician–patient communication concerns patients' failures to do as they are told (e.g., Becker and Maiman, 1975; Davis, 1966; 1968; DiMatteo and DiNicola, 1982; Francis et al., 1969; Kirscht and Rosenstock, 1977; Steele et al., 1985). Estimates suggest that 20–80 percent of patients do not follow their physicians' directives (DiMatteo and DiNocola, 1982; Sackett and Snow, 1979) and that, on average, one patient out of two does not do so (Ley, 1983). To the extent that physicians issue their directives in the interests of patients' health, one can understand why patients' failures to follow them would be deeply disturbing.

Despite this concern, the formulation of physicians' directives to patients has not been pursued as an object of investigation. As Frankel and Beckman (1989b) point out, the problem of non-adherence has traditionally been seen as a function of patients' lack of education or motivation, or as a function of physicians' failures to persuade patients of treatment benefits:

> Until very recently, little if any attention was paid to the sequences of interaction that transpire whenever a practitioner and patient meet face to face, and the possibility that non-adherence might be linked to the dynamics of speech exchange (Frankel and Beckman, 1989b: 63).

As a result, we know very little about *how* physicians formulate their directives to patients or how patients respond to them.

And yet, a growing number of studies suggest that the dynamics of speech exchange are central to our understanding of physician–patient relations. For example, Maynard (1991) reports that patients' responses to bad diagnostic news are heavily dependent on the context of discourse in which physicians deliver it. Steele et al. (1985) find that patients' adherence is directly related to the form and specificity of physicians' questions. Moreover, Frankel and Beckman (1989a) observe that more than 90 percent of patients' formal complaints about their medical care focus on ways that health professionals communicate with them. Findings such as these indicate that the forms of talk that are employed between physicians and patients may well have practical consequences for patient care (cf. West and Frankel, 1991).

In this paper, I am concerned with how physicians formulate their directives to patients and how patients respond to them. Following Goodwin (1980, 1988, 1990), I view directive–response speech sequences as a means of establishing social order between parties to talk. Hence, my analysis focuses on the various social arrangements physicians propose through their directives and the responses these elicit from patients. My study of encounters between patients and family physicians suggests that women and men physicians use very different forms to issue their directives and that these forms yield different patient responses. In discussing my findings, I consider their relationship to the issue of patient adherence more generally and to the quality of patients' relations with women and men physicians.

On giving directives

As Goodwin (1980: 157) notes, *directives* are 'speech acts that try to get another to do something'. As she also notes, alternative means of formulating directives – and responses to them – provide for a variety of social arrangements between parties to talk (Goodwin, 1990: 74). For example, the use of *aggravated* forms, such as orders and demands, implies that a speaker can legitimately impose on another by stating their requirements baldly (Labov and Fanshel, 1977: 63, 84–5). By contrast, the use of *mitigated* forms, such as pleas and suggestions, allows a speaker to avoid offending another by putting forth their wishes in downgraded ways (Labov and Fanshel, 1977: 63, 84–5).

In her ground-breaking work on the subject, Ervin-Tripp (1976) found that directive forms vary with the rank and familiarity of speakers and hearers.[1] Her study of observed directives across a broad range of settings (including homes, hospitals, adult education classrooms, offices and a Marine Corps recruiting station) showed that their distribution followed a rough stratification system – according to the explicitness of the directive and 'the relative power of speaker and addressee in conventional usage' (Ervin-Tripp, 1976: 29):

> *Need statements*, such as 'I need a match'.
> *Imperatives*, such as 'Gimme a match' and elliptical forms like 'a match'.
> *Imbedded Imperatives*, such as 'Could you gimme a match?' In these cases, agent, action, object and often beneficiary are as explicit as in direct imperatives, though they are embedded in a frame with other syntactic and semantic properties.

Permission directives, such as 'May I have a match?' Bringing about the condition stated requires an action by the hearer other than merely granting
permission.
Question directives, like 'Gotta match?' which do not specify the desired act.
Hints, such as 'The matches are all gone'.

Her findings indicate that the use of alternative directive forms varies
considerably across settings and situations and, hence, that variation is
not merely a function of politeness. Perhaps more important, they demonstrate that the interpretation of a directive *as* a directive is dependent on its
context: 'if the form is inappropriate to the context, it may not be heard as a
directive at all' (Ervin-Tripp, 1976: 59).

To be sure, 'context' often serves as a proxy for a broad range of factors in
the study of interaction, including the setting, the nature of the situation,
the task at hand (if any) and the identities of the participants involved
(Ervin-Tripp, 1976: 59; Goffman, 1964: 134; Goodwin, 1990: 88; Hymes,
1964: 10). The distribution of different directive forms across diverse settings and situations raises important questions about how these factors are
related to one another (Goodwin, 1990: 87–8). It also raises questions about
the turn-by-turn organization of conversation in which speech actions
achieve a particular meaning or delineated range of meanings in a situated
context (West and Zimmerman, 1982: 511). Goodwin's (1980, 1988, 1990)
research addresses these issues in fine detail by focusing on *how* alternative
directive forms are fitted to the specific setting, situation and conversation
in which they occur.

Her data consist of audiotapes and transcripts of conversations among
Black working-class girls and boys (ages 9–14) at play in an urban neighborhood. She recorded these conversations over an eighteen-month period
while observing the children's organization of their play groups. Goodwin's systematic analyses of these materials found that girls and boys used
distinctive directive forms to coordinate their activities in dramatically
different ways.

Among boys, tasks such as making slingshots were organized through
the use of directives that emphasized differences between parties to talk:

(Goodwin, 1980: 158)
(1) Michael: Gimme the pliers!
     Poochie: ((gives pliers to Michael))
(2) Michael: *All* right. *Gimme* some rubber bands.
     Chopper: ((giving rubber bands to Michael)) Oh.
(3) Michael: *All* right. Give me your *h*anger Tokay.
     Tokay: ((gives hanger to Michael))

Above, Michael issues his directives as explicit imperatives, his syntax
stressing the distinction between himself (me) and his addressees (Poochie
and Chopper).

Goodwin (1990) observes that the function of such directives is evident
not only from their form but from their context in particular speech
environments. For example, boys' imperatives often appeared in stretches
of talk that focused on the degraded status of their addressees:

(Goodwin, 1990: 99)
(39) Tony: Go downstairs. I don't care what you say you aren't – you ain't
                no good so go downstairs.

(Goodwin, 1990: 105)
(43) Douglas: Get outa here s: ucker
(44) Chopper: You sh: ut up your big lips.

They also appeared in utterances that used possessives (e.g. 'mine', 'yours')
to formulate differential rights of ownership or access between participants:

(Goodwin, 1990: 110)
(59) Tony: Get off my steps.

(Goodwin, 1990: 120)
(68) Malcolm: Gimme your other hangers. I'm a bend them all.

Through these means, boys arranged their activities hierarchically, their
aggravated forms establishing asymmetrical alignments between themselves and their addressees.

By contrast, girls used directives that minimized status differences
between parties to talk:

(Goodwin, 1980: 165)
((Girls are looking for bottles))
(30) Sharon: Let's go around Subs and Suds.
     Pam: Let's ask her 'Do you have any bottles.'
(31) Terry: Let's go. There may be some more on Sixty Ninth Street.
     Sharon: Come on. Let's turn back y'all so we can safe keep em.
                Come on. Let's go find some.

Here, for example, Sharon, Pam and Terry advance their plans (for making
rings from bottle rims) as proposals, using 'Let's' to formulate their suggestions as invitations to collaboration. Goodwin (1980) observes that even
these mitigated directives tended to be further modulated by the verb
forms 'can' and 'could':

(Goodwin, 1980: 166)
((Discussing how best to break bottle rims))
(41) Sharon: We *could* use a sewer.
(42) Pam: We could go around lookin for more bottles.
(43) Sharon: Uh we could um, (2.4) shell*a*c em.
((Discussing keeping the activity of finding bottles secret from boys))
(44) Terry: We can limp back so nobody know where we gettin them from.

They also were further mitigated by terms such as 'maybe':

(Goodwin, 1980: 166)
(45) Terry: Maybe we can slice them like that.
((Discussing obtaining bottles))

(46) Sharon: Hey maybe tomorrow we can come up here and see if they got
              some more.

These modulations further underscored the invitational flavor of girls'
directives, thereby proposing symmetrical relationships between speakers
and their addressees.

Of course, the issuance of a directive (in whatever form) cannot establish
a relationship between the speaker and addressee by itself, since responses
constitute the second parts of the pair. But Goodwin (1980: 160) notes that
'the format of the first pair part is characteristically implicative for the
format of the second'. Thus, when compliance was not forthcoming, aggravated directives could receive aggravated responses:

(Goodwin, 1980: 159)
(11) Huey: Gimme the *things*.
     Chopper: You sh: ut up you big lips.
(12) Juju: Terry go and get your pick.
     Terry: What pick, I'm not going in the house now.
(13) Michael: Get *out* of here Huey.
     Huey: I'm not gettin out of *no*where.

In these cases, non-compliant responses constitute both refusals of the
directives and challenges to the speakers' authority to issue them.

By contrast, non-compliant responses to mitigated directives took the
form of counters to proposals:

(Goodwin, 1990: 147)
(134)((On reaching a city creek while turtle hunting))
(1) Bea: Y'all gonna walk in it?
(2) Ruby: Walk in it, You know where
(3)   that water come from? The toilet.
(4) Bea: So, I'm a walk in it in my dirty feet.
(5)   I'm a walk in it and I don't care if it do come.=
(6)   You could ⌈ easy wash your feet.
(7) Ruby: ⌊ ((to ethnographer)) Gonna walk us across?
(8)   Yeah I'll show y'all where you can come.

In these cases, rather than refusing directives, return actions offer arguments countering the appropriateness (lines 2–3) and consequences (line 4)
of the action being proposed. Goodwin (1990: 147) observes that such
sequences do not establish hierarchical relations between parties to talk,
since 'counters to proposals are themselves counterable, and a proposal
initiated by one party may be reinstated subsequently by another'.

In sum, these findings show that both girls and boys employ directives to
organize their task activities, but they do so very differently. Whereas boys
use imperative forms to address subordinates (and requests, to those super-
ordinate to them), girls use the same mitigated forms reciprocally with one
another. Goodwin (1990: 147) concludes that *'boys' directives display distinctions between participants and stress individual rights [while] girls' directives
stress the connectedness of girls to each other and their caretaking concerns'*.

Through these means, boys and girls establish contrasting forms of social organization.

Goodwin's work affords a systematic approach to the study of directives and responses – an approach grounded in the detailed empirical examination of tape-recorded conversations. Below, I employ this approach in my examination of encounters between physicians and patients; but first I describe my methods of data collection and analysis.

Methods

Data for this analysis consist of 21 encounters between physicians and patients that were videotaped in a family practice clinic in the southern United States. The physicians in these encounters are residents in family medicine, a medical specialty that demands three years of additional training beyond medical school. Most are in their late twenties and early thirties.[2] Seventeen of the encounters involve physicians who are white men and four involve white women.

Patients in these encounters range in age from 16 to 82 years. Their backgrounds are diverse, including those of unemployed carpenter, construction worker, domestic and professional. Of the 20 patients involved (one was seen by two different physicians in the course of his visit), five are white men; six, white women; five, Black women; and four, Black men.

The encounters themselves are actual patient visits to family physicians, so they are not standardized according to length, presenting complaint, or duration of relationship between physician and patient. The clinic at which they were recorded has used videotaping for over a decade as part of the ongoing training of residents. With their signed consent, patients are taped while visiting their physicians via ceiling microphones and unobtrusive cameras placed in the corners of examining rooms. In the analysis which follows, I employ pseudonyms to ensure the confidentiality of the physician–patient relationship.

To transcribe the tapes, I used a set of conventions developed by Gail Jefferson (see Appendix). The aim of these conventions is to capture as close to a verbatim version of interaction as is possible – to record what was said and how it was said in fine detail. In all, the 21 videotaped encounters yielded 532 pages of transcript.

Elsewhere (West, 1983, 1984a, 1984b, 1984c), I have used these data for other research purposes, such as the analysis of turn-taking, question-answer sequencing and repair between physicians and patients; and, in fact, the findings reported here did not emerge from any initial plan to study 'doctors' orders'. But in the course of a related research project, I observed such striking differences in the ways that men and women physicians formulated their directives to patients that it prompted a comprehensive examination of those directives in their own right.

I began my analysis by examining the transcripts to locate all instances of physicians' directives, that is 'speech acts that try to get another to do something'. I then examined the sequential contexts of these directives to further determine: (1) the speech environments in which they occurred, and

(2) the responses – if any – they elicited from patients. Using this strategy, I encountered one problem that could not be resolved with the data at hand: it was virtually impossible to assess patients' responses to physicians' directives in the course of physical examinations. For example, when a physician told a patient to 'relax', 'loosen up' or 'tighten that muscle', I was often unable to determine what – if any – response this elicited, from examination of the videotape and transcript. And insofar as many of the directives issued during physical examinations had to do with patients' internal states, responses to them may not even have been detectable by the physicians involved. For this reason, I excluded directive-response sequences that occurred during physical examinations from the analysis which follows. With this exception, I inspected all the directive-response sequences that occurred in these data to assess how physicians formulated their directives and how patients responded to them. Because men and women physicians issued their directives in dramatically different ways, I present my findings separately for each.

Directives of men physicians

Imperatives
Among the men physicians in these encounters, directives to patients typically took the form of imperatives. For example, 49 of the 156 directives they issued (or 31 percent) were formulated as explicit commands:

(1) (Dyad 01: 749+)
     Patient: So if I fe-fee: l this coming on, an' I'm sidding up in a pl*a: ne*, 'r I'm
                 out somewhere in a *ca: r*, .h'n I c [an't lie dow-   ]
     Physician: [LIE:: DOW: N!   ]
(2) (Dyad 02: 114+)
     Patient: I'm *tryin'* tuh (.2) *sido::* n this tailbone duh try an'ged it bedder
                 an' ev'ry chance I could [I try duh   ]
     Physician: [(Oh:: don' even)] try:: :, if it *hurts*
                 when yuh *sid* on it, stay off of it.
(3) (Dyad 05: 258+)
     Physician: Go ahead an' *get* thi: s, (.) ((hands patient the x-ray order)) an'
                 then [co: me ba:] ck
     Patient: [hh-hh-hh ((audible sigh))]
     Physician: an: d um give it tuh the nurse here ut th' station.
(4) (Dyad 14: 474)
     Physician: Jus' take one of ea: ch foah times a da: y.
(5) (Dyad 16: 484+)
     Physician: Oka: y, ((while writing)) jus' rub it all over yer fa: ce in a light
                 thin fi: lm, *twice::* a da: y.

Above, for example, physicians employed imperatives to command patients with respect to future course of action: 'LIE DOWN!' (if you feel this coming on), 'stay off of it' (if it hurts when you sit on it), and 'rub it all over yer face' (twice a day). But they also used imperatives to command patients regarding immediate courses of action:

(6) (Dyad 08: 216)
    Physician: TAKE OFF YER SHOES AN' SO:: CKS.
(7) (Dyad 17: 387)
    Physician: Take yer trousers o: ff.
(8) (Dyad 18: 094+)
    Physician: .hh *Pull off a shirt* ((taps patient on the knee)) fo: r me.
(9) (Dyad 10: 252)
    Physician: °Si: t for me right there: .

In these cases, physicians' directives required return actions from patients
then and there.

One command characteristic of all these commands is the authority they
imply on the part of the speaker. As Goodwin (1980) observes, the formulation of a directive in imperative form makes implicit claims about the
speaker's right to be issuing such a directive in the first place. In excerpts
1–5, physicians' formulations propose the legitimacy of their right to command patients with respect to their physical activities ('LIE DOWN!', 'stay
off of it') and treatment ('get this' (X-ray)), 'Take one of each foah times a
day'). And in excerpts 6–9, physicians' directives assert their authority to
command patients to disrobe ('TAKE OFF YER SHOES AN' SOCKS', 'Pull
off a shirt for me') and to move ('Sit for me right there'). What they thereby
propose is an asymmetrical alignment between physician and patient, in
which the patient 'has no choice but to do whatever told' (Shapiro, 1978:
170).

Need statements
Another way in which men physicians issued directives to patients was by
stating those patients' requirements. For example, physicians frequently
told patients what they 'needed to' or 'ought to' do:

(10) (Dyad 14: 803+)
     Physician: I think yuh need duh *try*: duh ged ou: t, even if yuh- .h y'know,
                 si: t an' watch o: ther people *da: nce* 'r whatever.
(11) (Dyad 18: 208+)
     Physician: It dozen *hurt* tuh keep movin' *arou:: n*', but cha *nee: d* duh put the
                 hea: t on: it. (.6) An':: (.) yuh nee: d tuh get the *as: prun* into yuh
                 tuh sorda make it *to:* ler'ble.
(12) (Dyad 18: 261+)
     Physician: We: ll, .hh *I'll* write chew a *thy:: ung* ((meaning an excuse from
                 work)) cuz I think you oughtta . . . hh I think you oughtta knock
                 tha:: t o: ff fer awhy: ule-hhh. ((now writing))

Physicians also told patients what they 'had to' or 'had got to' do:

(13) (Dyad 02: 393)
     Physician: So yuh gotta be *ril care:* ful no: w (.) you been (.8) .h BE: IN'
                 CARE: FUL 'BOUT CUTTIN' YER TOE: NAILS?
(14) (Dyad 05: 481)
     Physician: YOU AN' [DOCKTUR] MOR: SE will hafta con: s [ult o: n] tha: t
     Patient: [Ye: ss.]   [°OKay]

(15) (Dyad 02: 708)
      Physician: An' you haf tuh sign the above: on thi: s
(16) (Dyad 07: 682)
      Physician: Lissen, I KNOW: ! Un-un, It's your problem!
                 You gotta dihci: de!

Ervin-Tripp (1976) describes 'need statements' as some of the most aggravated of directive forms, noting that they routinely occur between superiors and subordinates. However, in her data, such directives focused on the requirements of speakers themselves:

> (Ervin Tripp, 1976: 29)
> (Physician to technician):
> I'll need a routine culture and a specimen.
> (Doctor to hospital nurse):
> I'll need a 19 gauge needle, IV tubing, and a preptic swab.

In the data at hand, physicians' 'need statements' did not refer to their own requirements, but to those of the patient.

The only exceptions to this rule were directives that employed 'we' in statements of pseudo-mutual requirements:

(17) (Dyad 13: 016+)
      Physician: As I *sai:: d*, I don't think that- ((rifling through a drawer)) (.4) we
                 should use: the: (1.4) that you: should use: (1.4) an Eye Yew Dee
                 anymore. (3.6) Whi: ch'(.) mea:: : ns:: : s (.6) that wih haf tuh
                 dihcide on another method a birth control for yuh.

Above, for example, the physician first uses 'we' to refer to the-ones-who-should-be-using-an-intrauterine-device, but he quickly replaces this with 'you'. So, when he subsequently uses 'wih' to refer to the-ones-who-have-to-decide, the object of his decision-making belies the collaborative syntax he employs – here, 'we' have to decide for 'you' (not us). In this context, 'we' who-should-not-use-an-IUD-anymore is the patient, but 'we' who-need-to-decide-on-another-method-of-birth-control is the physician himself.

The next excerpt shows a similar statement of pseudo-mutual requirements:

(18) (Dyad 20: 234+)
      Physician: So yuh might wanna take some li: ddle no: tes. h Yer gunna ha:
                 f tuh .hh yer gunna take some rihsponsuhbi: lidy fer this ((taps
                 foot)) cuz we're gonna 'aftuh ((points his right index finger at
                 her)) *fig*ger ou: t whethe: r .hh we need duh do some *tes:: ts* er
                 no: t.

Here, again, the physician invokes the prospect of joint decision-making by his use of 'we' with reference to the-ones-who-are-going-to-have-to-figure-out-whether-to-do-some-tests. However, this pseudo-mutual statement appears in the same stretch of talk in which the physician tells the patient that *she's* going to take some responsibility for this, and as he formulates what 'we're' going to have to do, *he points his finger directly at the patient.*

Hence, like other statements of patients' requirements (e.g. excerpts 10–17), these directives propose the physicians' authority to assess patients' needs and determine what is best for them. What they propose simultaneously is a hierarchical relationship between physician and patient.

Want statements
Still another means of issuing directives to patients was the physician's statement of his own preferences for patient action. Typically, such statements were formatted with reference to what the physician 'wanted' or 'didn't want' the patient to do:

(19) (Dyad 05: 323+)
   Physician: Uh: m, if *you*:: in th' MEAN:: time start havin' FE:: Ver er shakin'CHI: lls (.) .h any problems like tha: t, .h then ah wa: n' uh- then I wa: n' cha duh git back with who'sever on ca:: ll
(20) (Dyad 09: 109)
   Physician: I *do*: wan' cha tuh go ahead an' *get* that Li: ght Salt.
(21) (Dyad 20: 220+)
   Physician: Whud I: wan' cha duh *do*: for me: is I wan' cha duh keep a *goo: d* record of *whe: n* yuh have that pai: n. How *o: ffun* yuh have it? (1.2) Whe: n it occu: rs? (.2) .h an' whu: t cher *do*: ing whe: n yuh *ha: ve* it.

But sometimes physicians' statements of preference were modulated by what they 'would like' patients to do:

(22) (Dyad 08: 183+)
   Physician: AH'D *AL*: SO LIKE FER YUH TUH TAKE OFF YER SHOES AN SOCKS UN- AH: ((drawing curtain to 'create' an examining/dressing room)) TROU: SERS
(23) (Dyad 09: 684+)
   Physician: Lemme *tell* yuh whud I- .h lemme tell yuh whud ah'd *like* yuh duh do: now, ah'd like you to:: : (.) *see* whut arrangemun's yuh wanna make.

And, occasionally, they were further downgraded by their formulation as physicians' own desires:

(24) (Dyad 05: 296+)
   Physician: So::. (.4) tch whud ah'd *li: ke* tuh do: (.) is
   ⎡ go ahead   ⎤ an' put cha on some asprun.
   Patient: ⎣ hh-hh-hh ((sigh)) ⎦
(25) (Dyad 05: 423+)
   Physician: A: n Uh'd like duh see yuh ba: ck on Thursday

Above, for example, the physician involved in both excerpts states what *he* would like to do (i.e., put the patient on some aspirin and see her back on Thursday). However, fulfillment of his wishes will in both cases require specific actions on the part of the patient: namely, that she *take* the aspirin and that she return to *be* seen on the appointed day. Thus, his statements function like other statements of physician preference (excerpts 19–23): that is, as directives for patient action.

As others have observed, statements that refer to the speakers' wishes are among the most aggravated of directive forms (Goodwin, 1980: 160), proposing that speakers' preferences imply an obligation on the part of their addressees (Ervin-Tripp, 1976: 29).

Quasi-question directives
Closely related to statements of preferences and needs were physicians' directives that employed 'Why don't you . . .' to preface stipulations for patient action:

(26) (Dyad 09: 266+)
   Physician: Why don' yuh ((patient rises)) take (.) .h in that case, bo: th yer
              shirt a:: n yer undershirt off.
(27) (Dyad 16: 365+)
   Physician: Why don' chew *co:: me i: n* (.2) in: (.) I guess that ·ah'm gonna
              hafta make that in two: weeks
(28) (Dyad 17: 378+)
   Physician: *Oka: y,* wull, why don't cha jump up on the table ((doctor leans
              forward to push himself out of the chair. As he does so, patient
              does too.)) (.6) An' ah'll take a loo: k ad it.

As Ervin-Tripp (1976: 29) notes, the objects of such directives are put forth as baldly as in imperatives (e.g. 'take both yer shirt an' yer undershirt off', 'come in in two weeks', and 'jump up on the table'). And despite their interrogative forms, these directives are rarely advanced with the rising intonation that characterizes questions. Indeed, physicians formulated them in ways that demanded actions – rather than answers – in return. Thus, these directives also implied an asymmetrical alignment between parties to talk, highlighting the distinction between speakers and their addressees.

Permission provisions
Yet another form of aggravated directive I observed in these data was the giving of permission for a particular course of patient action. In this case, physicians' syntax proposed a strong contrast between themselves and the patients they addressed:

(29) (Dyad 02: 249+)
   Physician: I think that's-that's alright from time-duh-time. .h I would ex::
              peck thut- prob: ably:: :: within: the next *wee: k* or so, hh you won'
              need it anymore.
(30) (Dyad 09: 126)
   Physician: *Ah'm not sa: yin' yuh never cun ha:: ve these things, it's just as a ru::*
              le, that shouldn'b e a dai: ly .hh
(31) (Dyad 13: 116+)
   Physician: Yih cun start on the three-month supply:, an' yih cun re: fill that
              three ti: mes, over the course of a ye: ar.
(32) (Dyad 17: 725+)
   Physician: (I'm) jus' gonna ((pulls the curtain open)) get *'t's all-* open for

> yuh- jus' hold o: n fer a sekkin'=.h you cun put cher trou: zers
> on:: n. (.4) In the *mean*time.

Above, for example, 'you can' and 'that's alright' specify what the patient
is permitted to do, while 'I think" and 'I'm not sayin" specify the physician's authority to be granting permission. Among these physicians, the
identity of the authority giving permission ('I', the physician) was often
omitted (as in the cases of excerpts 35 and 36), thus granting authority by
fiat.

Of course, Ervin-Tripp (1976) also discusses 'permission directives',
noting that they tend to occur between parties who differ in rank. But
there (1976: 37–8), she is dealing with directives that *request* permission
from addressees (e.g. 'Can I have my records back?', 'May I have the
salt?'); here, I am dealing with directives that *grant* it. In this sense, the
forms of directives we identify are mirror images of one another: both
propose a hierarchical relationship between speakers and their addressees, but 'permission directives' imply the speakers' subordination ('Can I
have X?') while 'permission provisions' assert their superiority ('You can
have X').

Directive by example
Another distinctive way that men physicians 'tried to get patients to do
things' was by stating what they themselves would do:

(33) (Dyad 05: 519+)
   Physician: Ah would do that. Ah'd drink *plen*'y a flu: ids, ah'd take that as:
   prun ruh*lig*: ously (.).h an' if yuh need duh stay ho: me stay
   home.

(34) (Dyad 10: 862+)
   Physician: an' ah'd take one: a tho: se *four* times a da: y, an' if *ne*: cessary, .h
   yuh cun take two: at bedti: me. (.2) .h An': (.) whut *ah*: would
   do: is tuh *sta:: y* on that fer about- .h ten da: ys 'r two wee: ks?

(35) (Dyad 18: 275+)
   Physician: Wu: ll, if tuhda:: y's Mo:: nday, hh (1.2) ah'd prob'ly lay off till
   about *Thurs*: day.

In these cases, the status of physicians' directives *as* directives is hardly
unclear. Like Ervin-Tripp's (1976: 29) need and want statements, these
assertions specify what the patient is to do as explicitly as any imperative
('drink plen'y a fluids', 'take that asprun ruhligously', 'stay on that fer
about ten days 'r two weeks', and 'lay off ((of work)) till Thursday'). But
here, the form of the directive ('I would do X') implies that the patient
should engage in a particular course of action simply because the physician
would do so. Ironically, then, this 'indirect' directive is perhaps the most
aggravated of them all: not only does it exaggerate the distinction between
speaker and addressee, but its form proposes that the speaker's inclinations
should serve as a model for others' behaviors.

Imbedded imperatives
To this point, I have focused on the most aggravated forms of directives

because these constituted the vast majority (81 percent) of the directives men physicians used. However, there were occasions on which they employed less aggravated directives, such as imbedded imperatives:

(36) (Dyad 02: 695)
    Physician: Could ju give that tuh th' bizness office on yer way ou: t?
(37) (Dyad 09: 103+)
    Physician: We: ll the *most* I cun ask yuh duh do
                 i: s ⌈ tuh cut dow: n   ⌉
    Patient: ⌊ Cut down, uh-huh ⌋
(38) (Dyad 20: 143)
    Physician: Can you: put cher fing: er on the place where yuh uj: 'ly have the
                 pa: in?

Above, the imbedding of 'can' and 'could' into otherwise explicit commands ('give that to the business office', 'cut down', and 'put cher finger on the place') downgrade the imperatives to requests – rather than demands – for patient action. The use of 'ask' in excerpt 37 and questioning intonation in excerpts 36 and 38 further modulate these directives as requests.

But as others have pointed out, such directives still explicate the agent and object of action (Ervin-Tripp, 1976: 33), and they still emphasize the distinction between the speaker who poses the request and the addressee who is asked to fulfill it (Goodwin, 1980: 160). Thus, they too propose an asymmetrical relationship between parties to talk.

False collaboratives
A final form of directive I identified in the talk of men physicians was the 'false collaborative' – a directive that is formatted as a proposal for joint action, yet actually proposes action to be undertaken by a single individual. For example, on first inspection, the excerpts just below would appear to present suggestions for collaborative activity between speakers and their addressees:

(39) (Dyad 10: 708+)
    Physician: Oka: y ((doctor walks around to the rear of the patient)) Let's
                 slip this back off, an' get chur blouse back on: n ((doctor care-
                 fully unties the patient's gown; he removes one sleeve from her
                 arm, and then removes the other))
(40) (Dyad 12: 309+)
    Physician: 'Bout uh: let's have yuh come back in about- .hh *two:* weeks.

Here, physicians employ the 'Let's do X' format that Goodwin (1980, 1990) identifies as a means of proposing joint plans of action between speakers and hearers. But in these excerpts, actions specified by the directives are *not* ones that both parties can or do engage in: in excerpt 39, it is the physician who removes the patient's gown; and in excerpt 40, it is the patient who must return in two weeks. In these contexts, 'let's' implies a form of pseudo-participation in joint action (Ervin-Tripp, 1976: 48), one that parodies, rather than enacts, a true proposal. Simultaneously, it exaggerates status differences between physician and patient by highlighting (almost satirically) the distinction between them.

In short, men physicians employed directives that functioned as comparisons, emphasizing the distinctions between their patients and themselves (Goodwin, 1990: 74). Through imperatives, imbedded imperatives and statements of their needs and wants, they made implicit claims regarding their authority to impose their demands on patients and patients' obligations to fulfill them. Moreover, physicians' 'permission provisions' and 'directives by example' afforded a stark contrast between those who have rights to issue 'doctors' orders' and those with obligations to follow them. Even physicians' use of less aggravated forms – imbedded imperatives and false collaboratives – stressed the difference between the speakers who posed the directives and the addressees who were expected to comply with them. Through these means, men physicians proposed an asymmetrical relationship between their patients and themselves – one that stressed patients' obligations in contrast to physicians' rights.

Directives of women physicians

By contrast with men, women physicians issued their directives in decidedly mitigated forms. Through such means, they minimized distinctions between themselves and their patients and proposed symmetrical physician–patient relationships.

Proposals for joint action
For example, women physicians often formulated their directives as proposals for joint action. One way of advancing these proposals was the 'Let's do X' format Goodwin (1980, 1990) describes:

(41) (Dyad 04: 370)
   Physician: .h Let's talk about ⌈ cher press: ure fer a minnit 'r two. ⌉
   Patient: ⌊ .h-.h-.h-ch-hhhhew! °Okay.   ⌋
                                       ((sounding congested))
(42) (Dyad 11: 569+)
   Physician: OKa: y! Wull *let's* make that our *pla: n,*
(43) (Dyad 04: 499+)
   Physician: *So:: :* Let's stay on- uh:: : what we're doin' right no: w. Okay?
(44) (Dyad 11: 813)
   Physician: .h Let's get a fa: sting sugar nex' time too: (.2) OKa: y?

Above, physicians use 'Let's' to include themselves and their patients as partners in the actions they propose: talking (about the patient's blood pressure), making a plan for future treatment, staying on their present plan, and getting a 'fasting sugar' on the occasion of the patient's next visit. Unlike the false collaboratives discussed earlier, these directives formulate activities that *both* parties will play a part in, be it having a conversation or planning a course of treatment. Even getting a 'fasting sugar' will in this case require the coordination of two people: the patient, who must refrain from eating prior to taking his blood test, and the physician, who must schedule the test and interpret its results.[3]

Another way of proposing joint actions was formulating them as characterizations of what 'we' can or could do:

(45) (Dyad 11: 484+)
  Physician: O: kay. hh (2.2) .h We: ll, I thi: nk- (.8) ah'll go: (.2) with tha: t (.2) along wi: th you, an'th- I think y'know, if we cun (2.) contro: l it, in fa: ct, if yuh've- been f- (.2) quite a bi:: t- uh: m (.2) off yer di: et, .h (1.0) E: n ah'm not even su: re I should u: h a' suggest yuh go u: p to (.4) .h seven hunnerd an' fi: fty. (1.6) Can yuh help me with tha: t?
(46) (Dyad 19: 682+)
  Physician: OKay, so: whadda yuh thi: nk, maybe wih'd jus' take the top of yer- yer dress o: ff?

Here, for example, 'we cun' and 'wih'd jus'h' emphasize the tentative character of what physicians and patients might undertake.

Women physicians also employed 'we' in formulations of what they and their patients 'ought to' or 'had to' do:

(47) (Dyad 11: 495+)
  Physician: Maybe whut we ought a do: is-is *sta: y* with (.2) .h the *do: se* of di(avameez) yer o: n.
(48) (Dyad 04: 393+)
  Physician: We *both* hafta take rihspon ⌊sabil⌋ ity, ⌊ri: ght?⌋

Albeit 'ought to' and 'have to' are commonly used in aggravated directives, here, their coupling with 'we' includes both the physician and the patient in the actions they propose (staying with the present dose and taking responsibility). Thus, such formulations do not construct demands, as they might if only the addressees were subjects of actions they specified (Goodwin, 1980: 167). Rather, they build proposals for joint action between speakers and addressees. Through such formulations, women physicians made implicit claims to symmetrical relationships with their patients – ones in which they '*both* had to take responsibility'.

Singular suggestions
Of course, all 'doctors' orders' cannot involve physicians as co-partners in the actions they propose. Some tasks, such as those that will be required after leaving the physician's office, can only be performed by patients. In the case of such tasks, women physicians used 'you' to formulate their directives to patients but they typically imbedded these in 'can' and 'could' modal verbs:

(49) (Dyad 04: 226+)
  Physician: One thing yuh could do o:: . . . .h is tuh ea: t, say, the *meat firs'*. Yuh know:, but if yuh have a *sal:* ud tuh eat, t' sa: ve that till *after* yuh eat the meat. (.) Cuz the sal: ud's suhpose' tuh be co: ld. .hh Somethin- like tha: t (.) °OKa: y?

(50) (Dyad 04: 243+)
    Physician: An: d u: h- (.) an' then maybe yuh can stay away from the
                 dihsserts an' stay away from the- .h foo: d in buhtwee: n meals.
                 All the snacking, °that kinda thing.
(51) (Dyad 19: 342+)
    Physician: We: ll, you could *try*: taking .h two: ev'ry four *hou:: rs* if yuh
                 needed to: . . . you could take that many an' *see:* an' that's- .h it's
                 a *ver: y strong* medicine fer arthri[: tus.]

Like the imbedded imperatives discussed earlier, these directives identify
actions to be performed in explicit terms (i.e. 'eat the meat firs'', 'stay away
from the dihsserts', and 'take that many an' see'). But here, embedded
imperatives are downgraded to the status of mere suggestions through
the inversion of subjects and verbs: not 'could you eat the meat first' but
'you could . . . eat the meat firs''; not 'can you stay away from the desserts'
but 'you can stay away from the dihsserts'; and not 'could you take that
many' but 'you could take that many'. The resulting directives advance
proposals – rather than requests – for action, thereby de-emphasizing
distinctions between speakers and addressees.

To be sure, the directives issues in excerpts 49–51 were further mitigated by the local contexts in which they occurred. Eating the meat first is
put forth as just 'one thing' among many the patient in excerpt 49 could
do; staying away from desserts is an action the patient in excerpt 50
'maybe' can take; and taking two every four hours is something the
patient in excerpt 51 'can try . . . an' see'. Such modulations were typical
of women physicians, who rarely issued their directives baldly. For example, they often used 'maybe' to underscore the suggestive nature of their
directives:

(52) (Dyad 11: 619+)
    Physician: It's good duh look, an' loo: k between yer toe: s, make sure
                 they're clea: n an' dry:, maybe yuh wanna put pow: der on um
                 . . . Depen'ing on how swe-heh-ty yer feet get! (.2) .h But
                 y'know, *check* 'um! Maybe: y'know, maybe: (.4) .h if yer *no: t*
                 feelun' (.2) the: n yuh might *see:* somp'um thet cha don't fee: l.
(53) (Dyad 04: 292+)
    Physician: *Maybe* yuh ne- yuh nee: d tuh *disc*iplun yerself a liddle bi: t? .hh
                 When yuh come ho: me from work? .h sometimes I fi: ne thet
                 when I ride my *bi: ke* home thet that's a goo: d way of unwi: n
                 ⌊ding⌋

Here, 'maybe' downgrades statements of patients' wants ('yuh wanna put
powder on um') and needs ('yuh need tuh disciplun yerself') to the status
of propositions, thereby mitigating their impact. In the process, the physicians imply a non-hierarchical alignment with their patients – one in which
patients' wants and needs are perhaps hypothesized, but left to be determined by patients themselves.

Permission directives
On occasion, women physicians even sought patients' permission to *be*

directed through the formats they employed. As Ervin-Tripp (1976: 37–8) observes, permission directives require some action by addressees beyond the granting of permission:

(54) (Dyad 11: 716+)
Physician: Could I: u: m (.) um: (.6) Ra: ther thun having yuh wai: t tuhday, since I know: yer takin' off wor: k, an' I need duh see another pa: tien', .h (.8) Could I have yer pho: ne number? an' give yuh a ca: ll then When I get that report from hi: m?

(55) (Dyad 03: 270+)
Physician: Okay:, lemme jus' say o: ne thing: at thi: s poin', an' that i: s (.6) .h no: t tuh be discouraged by whut happened.

In excerpt 54, the physician asks the patient for her telephone number, in addition to her consent to being called later on. In excerpt 55, the physician asks the patient to *listen* to her forthcoming suggestion by formulating her request ('Lemme jus' say one thing') as a 'preliminary' to the action being proposed (Schegloff, 1980). In these cases, physicians avoided comparisons between their patients' status and their own by highlighting patients' prerogatives to counter the proposals they advanced.

Inverse imperatives
As I have already noted, women physicians in these encounters made little use of aggravated directive forms. Those they did use were often noteworthy not only for their rarity but for the contexts in which they appeared:

(56) (Dyad 04: 061+)
Physician: Yih wan' me tuh- tuh- give yih some guide: lines here? (1.0) *Tell* me whut chuh *ate:* tuyday. Umka: y?

(57) (Dyad 19: 033+)
Physician: Cuz if you: duh*cide* you want it o: ff, you let me know. (.) O*kay*?

(58) (Dyad 19: 522+)
Physician: O: kay, .hh *So:* ((looking at the patient)) priddy much right *no: w*, .h you tell me if I *go: t* this, you got duh- (.2) duh pro- .h you need duh get yer me: dicine filled? . . . An' yih feel like yer pressure's okay, you are: n't having *head*ache: s, or *prob*lums *see:* ing,

Above, physicians formatted their directives as explicit commands, but they did so in contexts that implied patients should direct *them*: 'Yih wan' me to give you some guidelines here?', 'If you duhcide you want it off', and 'You tell me if I've got this'. Insofar as physicians thereby implied that patients were the ultimate authorities regarding the actions they specified, they affirmed their obligations to respect patients' rights to make the final decisions in such matters.

In sum, women physicians employed directives that minimized status differences between their patients and themselves and provided for more symmetrical arrangements of their relationships (cf. Goodwin, 1990: 74–5). Through proposals for joint action, they made implicit claims regarding the collaborative character of the activities they suggested and patients' status as co-partners in decisions to implement these. Their directives regarding patients' individual actions were modulated by 'can', 'could', and 'maybe', stressing patients' prerogatives in planning such actions. Even their aggravated directives emphasized patients' authority to direct *them*, affirming their responsibilities to patients. Thus, women physicians proposed a more egalitarian relationship between their patients and themselves – one that emphasized physicians' obligations as well as patients' rights.

Responses to directives

As noted earlier, the data at hand consist of actual patient visits, so they are not standardized by duration, presenting complaint or length of relationship between physician and patient. Some physicians and patients had sustained a three-year relationship at the time they were recorded, whereas others were meeting for the first time. Some visits were routine follow-up checks on chronic conditions; others entailed discoveries of new complaints. And although all visits were scheduled for at least 30-minute time slots, some took considerably longer than 30 minutes; others took less. For these reasons, the tasks involved in particular visits varied widely and it is difficult to classify responses to directives via a standardized coding scheme.

Moreover, as Goodwin's work (1980, 1988, 1990) demonstrates, directive-response speech sequences form adjacency pairs (Schegloff, 1972; Schegloff and Sacks, 1974), whose meaning is established through the turn-by-turn organization of talk in situated contexts. Some directives formulate future courses of action; others specify actions to be taken then and there. Some directives require verbal responses from addressees; others require no other response than performance of the action they propose. Hence, the intelligibility of responses to directives *as* responses to directives cannot be determined apart from the contexts in which they occur.

Below, I provide a detailed examination of two directive-response sequences in which it is possible to compare responses to aggravated and mitigated directive forms. Following this comparison, I present overall rates of compliance with alternative directive forms among patients in this collection.

Aggravated vs. mitigated directives
A common site for directives in these data was where physicians needed to get patients to disrobe in preparation for physical examinations. In the excerpts just below, two physicians attempt to achieve this end with patients they are meeting for the first time. Excerpt 59 involves a man physician and a man patient; excerpt 60 involves a woman physician and woman patient.

(59) (Dyad 17: 385)
Physician: You can dro: p yer trou: sers, fact, why don' cha jus' take 'um

o: ff.
(.6)

Patient: ((leans forward on the examining table, looking at the physician))

Physician: Take yer trousers o: ff.
(.6)

Patient: Eh:: :: :: -hh
(1.0)

Physician: Oh:, *o::* kay, yuh wan' the cam'ra? ((physician reaches over and draws the curtain around the table so that the patient is hidden from the camera))
(.8)

Patient: °Uh:: :: eh:: :: : -°eh-huhh! (.4) Ah don' *wa:* nna drop my trousers, at's alright-heh!
(.2)

Physician: You don' *want* to.=

Patient: =No::

(60) (Dyad 19: 682+)

Physician: Okay, so: whadda yuh thi: nk, maybe wih'd jus' take the to: p of yer-yer dress o: ff?
           [Would that be oka:: y] with [you:: ?   ]
Patient: [Uh, o:: kay,   ]   [fah: ne, go] o: d,
           ye [: s.]
Physician: [O] *kay!*

In excerpt 59, the physician issues two aggravated directives in quick succession: first, a permission provision ('You can drop yer trousers') and then, an imbedded imperative ('why don' cha jus' take 'um off'). Following a brief pause (.6), during which the patient does not undertake the action he specifies, the physician reissues his directive as an explicit command ('Take yer trousers off').

As in the case of other adjacency pairs (e.g., questions and answers or summonses and replies), directives and responses form a conditionally relevant two-part sequence (Schegloff, 1972; Schegloff and Sacks, 1974). In other words, given the occurrence of a directive, or 'first pair part', a response, or 'second pair part' is expected. And, given the occurrence of the first pair part, the absence of a second pair part is accountable – that is, it provides a warrant for repeating the first pair part or for some inference regarding the absence of the second (Schegloff, 1972: 77). In the case of excerpt 59, the patient's lack of response to the physician's initial directives provides grounds for his repetition (and, apparently, his starker formulation) of the directive in his next turn. It also provides the warrant – following the patient's further lack of response – for the physician's inference regarding the patient's reluctance to comply.

Finally, the patient issues a negative response to the physician's directive in aggravated form (he doesn't *want* to). And when the physician repeats the patient's response, thereby offering him the chance to repair it (cf. Schegloff et al., 1977), the patient instead states his refusal baldly ('no').

By contrast, the physician in excerpt 60 puts forth her directive as a proposal for joint action ('maybe wih'd jus' take the top of yer dress off?'). Before she can fully follow this up with a request for the patient's permission ('Would that be okay with you?'), the patient has already issued an affirmative response ('Okay'). Moreover, the patient provides further affirmative replies ('fahne', 'good', 'yes') as the physician's request unfolds.

The difference I want to focus on in these very rich excerpts is between the two approaches to formulating directives. In excerpt 59, the physician's aggravated forms imply that the patient has no choice but to comply with his demands; in excerpt 60, the physician's mitigated form implies that the patient can counter her proposal, should she choose to do so. In each excerpt, the physician's directive form is implicative for the formulation of the patient's response: an aggravated reply in excerpt 59, and a mitigated one, in 60.[4] And in excerpt 59, the aggravated reply is a negative response; in 60, the mitigated reply is an affirmative one.

Of course, neither response constitutes execution of the action specified by the physician's directives – namely, to disrobe. However, in the case of excerpt 60, what follows is compliance with the directive:

```
(60 cont'd) (Dyad 19: 693+)
Patient:      It- uh: m ((beginning to pull the hem of her dress up)) (2.0) It 'o:
              n' zi: p y'know, .h I gaw' no zippuh (°thad it can come o: ff) °eh-
              hunh!
              (1.0)
              ((physician walks toward the patient, who is standing by her
              chair with her dress halfway up))
Physician:    ((leaning sideways to see the patient's back)) Yih godda zi: pper
              there yih wan' me duh help with?
              (.4)
Patient:      Ain' got no sor: ta zip- ((as physician reaches over to help)) tuh
              come dow:: n?
              (.)
Physician:    Oh:: :: , the zipper's sew ⌈nu:: : p! Oh:: ! You go: dit taken   ⌉
Patient:                                 ⌊Yay:: us! .engh-hengh-hengh-hengh ⌋
Physician:    car: e of! ⌈huh: heh-heh! ⌉
Patient:                ⌊Yeah-heh-heh ⌋ heh!=
Physician:    = .h heh °Ah: kay! ((turning to walk back toward the examining
              table as the patient proceeds to undress))
```

But in the case of excerpt 59, what follow are further negotiations regarding the patient's refusal to comply. For example:

```
(59 cont'd) (Dyad 17: 406+)
Physician:    This kine a personal to: yuh?
              (.2)
Patient:      Ye:: ah! (.4) °Um-hmm.
              (1.0)
Physician:    Anything yuh'd like tuh as: k me about? 'r (uh: )=
Patient:      =°No:: :: :: (.)°engh-hh!
              (.2)
```

Physician: Cuz I ain' gonna- .h y'know, I: *ain'* gonna mess *arou:: n'* y'know.
I ⌈jes' wanna take a loo: k   ⌉ [   ] at
Patient: ⌊No:: :: ! °engh-hunh! hengh! ⌋
Physician: cher knee:: s
              (.4)
Patient: °Oh:: :: : . (.6) No:, (ah'd love tuh have yuh check 'em,) buh not
              right there, that's why I don' like tuh go duh the dock: tuh that
              much. (.4) Cuz uh:: :: (1.2) Nu: hh:: : hh (1.2) I let yih check any o:
              thuh things, but no: t down he:: ah. Drop my pa:: n's?=*no:: :: :*
              siree:: : !

Finally, following this series of unsuccessful attempts, the physician switches to a mitigated approach:

(59 cont'd) (Dyad 17: 421+)
Physician: Would juh like- (.2) .h its-*see:* , it's RI: LLY HAR: D, ay: e-
              y'know: that's yer ri: ght, it's *ri: lly hard* duh get a good look
              at cher *knee: s* .h without gettin' yer pa:: n's undone so far (1.0)
              .hh Now, if yuh'd *li:: ke* me to:, I could get a *shee:: t.* (.8) Tuh put
              over yuh, an' *then* yuh could drop yer pa: nts. (.2) An' you could
              stay covered up aroun' yer wai: st. (.6) O*ka: y*?=
Patient: =°Ye: ah, wull m ⌈ay: be, buh uh ⌉
Physician: ⌊CUZI: JUS'   ⌋ don't thi: nk I could pu: ll
              these pa:: nts up far en ⌈ough to- ⌉
Patient: ⌊°Okay.   ⌋
              (.2)
Physician: .h Cun yuh try: 'n do tha: t?
              (.2)
Patient: Yeah, I: 'll try a do: it.

And here, the patient finally issues an affirmative response: initially qualified ('wull maybe'), then mitigated ('°Okay'), and ultimately – following the physician's reiteration – in explicit terms ('I'll try a do it').

Ironically, despite the success he has just experienced with a mitigated approach, this physician closes the interchange by reverting to an aggravated directive:

(59 cont'd.) (Dyad 17: 440+)
Physician: I: 'll tell yuh wha: t. Ah: 'll close a drapes hh (1.0) ((walking over
              to the curtain pull)) Here (.6) ((sound of curtains being closed
              fully around the examining table)) hh 'N I wan' chew: (1.0)
              ((more curtain noises)) tuh drop yer trou: sers, .h jus' lay:
              them back *down: n* there on that *be: d.*

In effect, his reversion reasserts his authority to command the patient in the first instance.

The point of this detailed comparison has been to show that patients' responses to 'doctors' orders' are highly sensitive to the ways in which those orders are advanced. From this vantage point, an affirmative response is not merely the product of one individual (i.e., the patient), but the outcome of highly intricate negotiations between speakers and their addressees (cf. Frankel and Beckman, 1989b).

Patients' compliance with physicians' directives
With the data at hand, it is impossible to determine long-term patient adherence to medical advice. Videotapes and transcripts of patient visits simply do not permit access to what happens after physicians and patients part company. So, while physicians issue many instructions for future action, these data permit me to assess patients' responses to those instructions only then and there.

However, as in the case of the excerpts just presented, there is much to be learned from the detailed examination of physicians' formulations of their directives – and patients' responses to those directives – in the situated contexts in which they occur. For example, I can identify cases of compliance with physicians' directives where patients undertake actions specified by those directives in adjacent turns:

(61) (Dyad 15: 542+)
       Physician: °Ah wancha duh *gi: t* back *u: p* heah foah me pleez. hhh
                   Patient: ((walks over to and sits down on the examining
                   table))

I can also identify cases in which patients' responses to physicians' directives assert their willingness to comply in the future, either by explicit statements:

(62) (Dyad 18: 336+)
       Physician: Now, don' jus' la:: y *arou:: n'* without that *hea:: t* on it, cuz 'at
                   rilly- hh (.6) Ah cain' tell yuh how it duz:: it, but (.) it wi:: ll (1.2)
                   you'll gedda fee: lin: *bedder quicke*r. h
                   (.2)
       Patient: Ah: won't. hh

Or, by affirmation:

(63) (Dyad 11: 642+)
       Physician: *Those* 'r some a the things thut (.4) *ma:: y* be a problum layder o::
                   n, but right now: (.2) I don' see thut they *are::* . (1.2) But. °Let me
                   know: if any of 'um are:, an' we'll work tuhge: ther on thum.=
       Patient: =°Alright.

By contrast, I can identify non-compliance with physicians' directives where patients refuse or fail to undertake actions that are specified in next turns (as in excerpt 59, presented earlier). I can also identify cases of non-compliance where patients' responses display their lack of agreement with physicians' directives:

(64) (Dyad 09: 631+)
       Physician: *Why* don' yuh do thi:: s, why don' yuh *call* them, an: d u: h. (.)
                   See whut they *sa: y.* An' after tha: t, you call back here, an'- an'

talk duh Norma, an' leddum know whut they *sai: d*, an' then
ah'll get back to yuh:. (.4) .h An' we cun arrange whudever's
necessary fo: r
yu [h::, so:]
Patient: [Wull I wan] na check on it
muh: ney-wise fi: rs'.

(65) (Dyad 14: 803+)
Physician: I think yuh need duh *try:* duh ged ou: t, even if yuh- .h y'know,
si: t an' watch o: ther people *da: nce* 'r whatever
(.4)
Patient: (°M: that's-) Wull, that's-*tha: t's* the trouble with not bein' able
duh dri: ve, y'know? yer dih*pe: n*dun' on othuh people.

In excerpts 64 and 65, for example, neither patient explicitly refuses to
comply with their physician's directive. But insofar as physicians' directives constitute their assessments of what patients should do, and insofar as
agreement with assessments is strongly preferred in next turns at talk
(Pomerantz, 1984), these patients' *lack* of agreement with physicians' directives ('Wull, I wanna check on it muhney-wise firs'; and 'Wull, that's the
trouble with not bein' able duh drive') can be seen as something other than
willingness to comply with 'doctors' orders'.

Finally, I can also identify non-compliance with physicians' directives
where patients fail to respond to those directives:

(66) (Dyad 13: 116+)
Physician: Yuh cun start on the three month supply:, an' yih cun re: fill that
three ti: mes, over the course of a ye: ar.
(13.8)
((patient is silent as the physician makes notes in her medical
record))
Physician: If yih *should* have any problum with (.) pai: n an' swelling in yer
lay: gs 'r any difficuldy brea: thing, (.8) .h yuh let me know right
away. Okay?
(26.4)
((patient is still silent as the physician continues to write))

Above, the patient issues neither verbal nor nonverbal responses to the
directives her physician has issued. Given that the occurrence of a directive
warrants the occurrence of a response (Schegloff, 1972; Schegloff and Sacks,
1974), the *absence* of a response can be seen as an 'official' absence, and
hence as non-compliance with the directive.

Among patients in this collection, rates of compliance varied with the
forms of physicians' directives. For example, men physicians' imperatives
(e.g., 'LIE DOWN!') elicited compliant responses in 47 percent of the total
(49) cases in which they were used – in short, less than half the time. Their
statements of preference (e.g. 'Ah don' wan' cha duh take both') were more
successful, yielding compliance in 59 percent of the total (22) cases. However, their statements of patients' needs ('What cha need tuh do is . . .'),
permission provisions ('you can refill these three times') and directives by
example ('Ah'd take two ev'ry four hours') fared much worse, eliciting

compliance in only 38 percent of the (16) need statements; 36 percent of the (11) permission provisions; and 29 percent of the (7) directives by example. The directives of men physicians that were most successful in eliciting compliant responses were those that took less aggravated forms. False collaboratives ('Let's slip this back off') yielded compliance in 65 percent of the total (23) cases, and physician requests ('Can you put cher finger on the place?') achieved their objectives in 4 out of 5 (or 80 percent) of the cases in which they were used. As a rule, *the more aggravated the directive, the less likely it was to elicit a compliant response.*

Among women physicians, this rule also held, albeit since the vast majority of their directives took a mitigated form, there was less variation among the responses they received. For example, proposals for joint action (e.g. 'Let's make that our plan') elicited compliant responses in 67 percent of the (9) cases in which they were used. Singular suggestions for patient action ('you could try taking two ev'ry four hours') fared even better, yielding compliance in 75 percent of the total (8) cases. Perhaps most remarkable were their inverse imperatives ('You tell me if I got this'): these produced compliant responses in 8 out of 9 – or 88 percent – of the cases in which they appeared. By contrast, of the 4 cases in which women employed quasi-question directives ('Why don' chew put these away'), only one was successful in achieving its specified aim.[5]

Thus, for women physicians too, the more aggravated the directive, the less likely it was to elicit a compliant response. The difference is that women physicians *used* aggravated imperatives less often than men did. And, their overall rate of compliant responses was 67 percent – in comparison to 50 percent for men.[6]

Conclusions

'Doctors' orders' are often satirized in the admonition 'Take two aspirin and call me in the morning'. Quite apart from the banality of this directive (employed under a seemingly infinite set of circumstances), we can note that it takes the form of an imperative – an explicit command from the physician to the patient. As I have already pointed out, the formulation of a directive in this aggravated form emphasizes the distinction between the speaker and the addressee and asserts the speaker's authority to be issuing commands in the first place (Goodwin, 1980).

Among physicians in this collection, men used aggravated forms that emphasized differences between their patients and themselves, and proposed hierarchical physician–patient relationships. Women physicians employed mitigated directives, which minimized status differences between physician and patient and stressed their connectedness to one another (cf. Goodwin, 1990: 147). These alternative formulations were consequential for patients' responses: not only were aggravated forms less likely to elicit compliant responses, but women physicians elicited such responses more often than men did.

Since my data were not generated by random sampling techniques, and since there were only four women physicians in this collection, it would be inappropriate to generalize from my results to women and men physicians at large. But should these findings hold in larger systematic samples of physicians, they might prove useful in explaining why patients are more satisfied with women physicians (Linn et al., 1984) and less likely to sue them for malpractice (Holder, 1979).

To be sure, compliance with physicians' directives is not the same thing as long-term adherence to medical advice. Further research is needed to determine precisely how patients' responses to physicians' directives relate to their adherence to medical advice over time. However, in light of Carter and his colleagues' finding that patients' indicated willingness to follow medical advice is the best predictor of their actual adherence (Carter et al., 1986), my results offer a promising new direction for future work on this problem.

Finally, it would be difficult to close this paper without commenting on the significance of my findings for our understanding of the relationship between language and gender. For example, what should we make of the fact that the distribution of aggravated and mitigated directives among these white middle-class physicians is so similar to their distribution among Black working-class boys and girls (Goodwin, 1980, 1988, 1990)? The lesson to be learned here is not that the 'essential natures' of women and men determine their interactional styles – including their tendencies toward politeness (Brown, 1976); 'indirect' language (Lakoff, 1975); and 'conversational insecurity' (Fishman, 1980). After all, women physicians *can* use aggravated directives on occasions of conflict with patients (see notes 5 and 6), and girl children *do* use aggravated forms to order their younger siblings around (Goodwin, 1980, 1990). The lesson, I think, is that the mundane activities of social life – be they making slingshots or getting patients to disrobe – provide the interactional resources for 'doing gender' (West and Zimmerman, 1987), that is, exhibiting, dramatizing or celebrating our 'essential natures' as women or men in accountable ways.

Appendix

The transcript techniques and symbols are based on those devised by Gail Jefferson in the course of research undertaken with Harvey Sacks.

A: I had ⎡them⎤ B: ⎣Did ⎦ you	Brackets around portions of utterances indicate that the portions bracketed overlap one another. Segments to the left and right of these denote talk in the clear.
B: 'Swhat I said= A: =But you didn't	An equal sign is used to indicate that no time elapsed between the objects 'latched' by the marks.
?!,.'	Punctuation marks denote intonation, not grammar.
LOUDLY	Capital letters are used to mark speech that is much louder than surrounding talk.
°softly	Degree signs are used to mark speech that is much quieter than surrounding talk.
((sniff))	Double parentheses designate descriptions, rather than transcriptions.

(0.5)	Parentheses around a number mark silences in seconds and tenths of seconds.
We:: : ll	Colons indicate that the immediately prior syllable is prolonged.
But-	A hyphen marks an abrupt cut-off point in the production of the immediately prior syllable.
(word)	Single parentheses with words in them offer candidate hearings of unintelligible items.
(.)	Parentheses around a period indicate a pause of one-tenth of one second.
.hh, h .eh-heh-heh .engh-hengh	These are breathing and laughter indicators. A period followed by 'hh's' marks an inhalation. The 'hh's' alone stand for exhalation. The '.eh-heh-heh' and '.engh-hengh' are laughter syllables (inhaled when preceded by a period.)

Acknowledgement

For their helpful remarks on an earlier draft, I thank Richard Frankel, Marjorie Goodwin, Barbara Sharf, Gilly West and James West.

Notes

1. Other factors associated with variation in directive forms were 'territorial location, difficulty of task, whether or not a duty is normally expected [and] whether or not non-compliance is likely' (Ervin-Tripp, 1976: 25).
2. Two physicians in this collection are in their late thirties and are not residents. One is an alumnus of the training program who still sees patients at the clinic after completing his residency. The other is a faculty member who trains residents. In the analyses that follow, I find no differences between their directives to patients and those of the residents.
3. The patient involved in excerpt 11 is a diabetic whose blood sugar level was somewhat higher than usual on the occasion of this visit. Some people with diabetes can test their urine at home and follow their sugar levels themselves. But as this patient told her physician earlier in the encounter, 'th' sugar dudun' show up in my urine . . . Dat's why ah alweez haf tuh dipen' on the bloo: d' (Dyad 11: 501–5).
4. Here, 'okay' can be seen as a mitigated response in that it affirms but does not explicitly state the patient's willingness to comply with the physician's directive (in contrast to 'let's do that', 'we could do that' or the 'yes' that follows it).
5. Of these relatively aggravated forms, three out of four appeared in the course of a single interchange in which a man patient repeatedly interrupted his physician to dispute the wisdom of her advice (West, 1984a: 66–9). In these instances, the physician's escalation to more aggravated directive forms followed the onset of the patient's intrusions, and may have served to assert her right to be issuing directives in the first place.
6. The overall rate of compliance with women physicians' directives would have been higher, save for the patient discussed in note 5. His lack of agreement with his physician's directives and lack of responses to her directives constituted 58 percent of the 12 cases of non-compliance I observed.

References

Becker, M.H. and Maiman, L.A. (1975) 'Sociobehavioral Determinations of Compliance with Health and Medical Care Recommendations', *Medical Care* 13: pp. 10–24.

Brown, P. (1976) 'Women and Politeness: a New Perspective on Language and Society', *Reviews in Anthropology* 3: pp. 240–9.

Carter, W.B., Beach, L.R., Inui, T.S., Kirscht, J.P. and Prodzinsky, J.C. (1986) 'Developing and Testing a Decision Model for Predicting Influenza. Vaccination Compliance', *Health Services Research* 20: pp. 897–932.

Davis, M. (1966) 'Variations in Patients' Compliance with Doctors' Orders: Analysis of Congruence between Survey Responses and Results of Empirical Investigations', *Journal of Medical Education* 41: pp. 1037–48.

Davis, M. (1968) 'Variations in Patients' Compliance with Doctors' Advice: an Empirical Analysis of Patterns of Communication', *American Journal of Public Health* 58: pp. 274–88.

DiMatteo, M.R. and DiNicola, D.D. (1982) *Achieving Patient Compliance: The Psychology of the Medical Practitioner's Role*, New York: Pergamon.

Ervin-Tripp, S. (1976) 'Is Sybil There? The Structure of Some American English Directives', *Language in Society* 5: pp. 25–66.

Fishman, Pamela (1980) 'Conversational Insecurity', in *Language: Social Psychological Perspectives*, New York: Pergamon, pp. 127–32.

Francis, V., Korsch, B.M. and Morris, M.J. (1969) 'Gaps in Doctor–Patient Communication: Patients' Response to Medical Advice', *New England Journal of Medicine* 280: pp. 535–40.

Frankel, R.M. and Beckman, H.B. (1989a) 'Communication Aspects of Malpractice', Paper presented at the Midwinter Meeting of the International Communication Association, Monterey, California (February).

Frankel, R.M. and Beckman, H.B. (1989b) 'Conversation and Compliance: An Application of Microinteractional Analysis in Medicine', in B. Dervin, L. Grossberg, B. Okeefe and E. Wartella (eds) *Paradigm Dialogs in Communication*, Beverly Hills: Sage, pp. 60–74.

Goffman, E. (1964) 'The Neglected Situation', *American Anthropologist* 66: pp. 133–6.

Goodwin, M.H. (1980) 'Directive-Response Speech Sequences in Girls' and Boys' Task Activities', in S. McConnell-Ginet, R. Borker and N. Furman (eds) *Women and Language in Literature and Society*, New York: Praeger, pp. 157–73.

Goodwin, M.H. (1988) 'Cooperation and Competition across Girls' Play Activities', in A.D. Todd and S. Fisher (eds) *Gender and Discourse*, Volume 30 in the series, Advances in Discourse Processes, edited by R.O. Freedle. Norwood, NJ: Ablex, pp. 55–94.

Goodwin, M.H. (in press) *He-Said-She-Said: Talk as Social Organization among Black Children*. Bloomington, IN: Indiana University Press.

Holder, A.R. (1979) 'Women Physicians and Malpractice Suits', *Journal of the American Medical Women's Association* 34: pp. 239–40.

Hymes, D. (1964) *Language and Culture in Society*, New York: Harper and Row.

Kirscht, J. and Rosenstock, I. (1977) 'Patient Adherence to Antihypertensive Medical Regimens', *Journal of Community Health* 3: pp. 115–24.

Labov, W. and Fanshel, D. (1977) *Therapeutic Discourse: Psychotherapy as Conversation*, New York: Academic Press.

Lakoff, R. (1975) *Language and Women's Place*, New York: Harper and Row.

Ley, P. (1983) 'Patients' Understanding and Recall in Clinical Communication Failure', in D. Pendleton and D. Hasler (eds) *Doctor–Patient Communication*, London: Academic Press, pp. 89–107.

Linn, L.S., Cope, D.W. and Leake, B. (1984) 'The Effect of Gender and Training of Residents on Satisfaction Ratings by Patients', *Journal of Medical Education* 59: pp. 964–6.

Maynard, D. (1991) 'Bearing Bad News in Clinical Settings', in B. Dervin (ed.) *Progress in Communication Sciences*, Norwood, NJ: Ablex.

Pomerantz, A. (1984) 'Agreeing with Assessments: Some Features of Preferred/ Dispreferred Turn Shapes', in J.M. Atkinson and J. Heritage (eds) *Structures of Social Action: Studies in Conversation Analysis*, Cambridge: Cambridge University Press, pp. 57–101.

Sackett, D.L. and Snow, J.C. (1979) 'The Magnitude of Compliance and Non-Compliance', in R.B. Haynes (ed.) *Compliance in Health Care*, Baltimore, MD: Johns Hopkins University Press, pp. 11–22.

Schegloff, E.A. (1972) 'Discourse as an Interactional Achievement: Some Uses of 'Uh huh' and Other Things that Come between Sentences', in D. Tannen (ed.) *Analyzing Discourse: Text and Talk*, Georgetown University Round-table on Languages and Linguistics, March 1981, Washington, DC: Georgetown University Press, pp. 71–93.

Schegloff, E.A. (1980) 'Preliminaries to Preliminaries: "Can I Ask You a Question?"', *Sociological Inquiry* 50: pp. 104–52.

Schegloff, E.A., Jefferson, G. and Sacks, H. (1977) 'The Preference for Self-Correction in the Organization of Repair in Conversation', *Language* 53: pp. 361–82.

Schegloff, E.A. and Sacks, H. (1974) 'Opening Up Closings', in R. Turner (ed.) *Ethnomethodology: Selected Readings*, Baltimore, MD: Penguin, pp. 233–64 (originally published in *Semiotica* 8: pp. 289–327, 1973).

Shapiro, M. (1978) *Getting Doctored: Critical Reflections on Becoming a Physician*, Kitchener, Ontario: Between the Lines.

Steele, D.J., Jackson, T.C. and Gutmann, M.C. (1985) '"Have You Been Taking Your Pills?" The Compliance Monitoring Sequence in the Medical Interview', unpublished manuscript.

West, C. (1983) '"Ask Me No Questions" . . . an Analysis of Queries and Replies in Physician–Patient Dialogues', in S. Fisher and A.D. Todd (eds) *The Social Organization of Doctor–Patient Communication*, Georgetown: Center for Applied Linguistics, pp. 75–106.

West, C. (1984a) *Routine Complications: Troubles with Talk Between Doctors and Patients*, Bloomington, IN: Indiana University Press.

West, C. (1984b) 'When the Doctor is a "Lady": Power, Status and Gender in Physician–Patient Encounters', *Symbolic Interaction* 7: pp. 87–106.

West, C. (1984c) 'Medical Misfires: Mishearings, Misgivings and Misunderstandings in Physician–Patient Dialogues', *Discourse Processes* 7: pp. 107–34.

West, C. and Frankel, R.M. (1991) 'Miscommunication in Medicine', in N. Coupland, H. Giles, and J. Wiemann (eds) *The Handbook of Miscommunication and Problematic Talk*, Avon, UK: Multilingual Matters.

West, C. and Zimmerman, D.H. (1987) 'Conversation Analysis', in K.R. Scherer and P. Ekman (eds) *Handbook of Methods in Nonverbal Behavior Research*, Cambridge: Cambridge University Press, pp. 506–41.

5

Gossip revisited: language in all-female groups

Jennifer Coates

Originally published in J. Coates and D. Cameron, eds, *Women in their Speech Communities* (Longman, 1989).

Introduction

During the last ten years, interest in, and knowledge of, the relationship between language and sex has grown enormously. But attention has focussed on sex *differences*: sociolinguistic research has aimed to quantify differences in women's and men's usage of certain linguistic forms. The linguistic forms examined range from phonological or syntactic variables to interactive forms such as interruptions, directives and questions. Where the latter are concerned, a majority of researchers have drawn their data from mixed interaction (that is, interaction involving both male and female speakers); research has rarely focussed on women in single-sex groups. As a result, we know little about the characteristics of all-female discourse. Worse, we accept generalisations about 'the way women talk' which derive from women's behaviour in *mixed* groups, groups where the differential use of linguistic features such as interruptions, directives or questions is part of the social process which maintains gender divisions.

Deborah Jones's paper, 'Gossip: notes on women's oral culture' (1980), was a landmark. While Jones was not the first to focus on all-woman interaction (cf. Abrahams 1975; Kalcik 1975; Aries 1976; Jenkins & Kramer 1978), she was the first to locate her analysis firmly in the sociolinguistic field. Jones glosses 'female oral culture' as 'language use in women's natural groups' (using 'natural' to refer to groupings which in our *culture* are construed as 'natural'). Her paper offers a description of such language use in terms of the relations between setting, participants, topic, form and function, following Ervin-Tripp (1964). The strength of Jones's paper is that it puts women talking to women firmly centre-stage; its weakness stems from the lack of empirical data. Her common-sense description of the setting, participants and topics typical of all-woman talk provides a clear set of norms to be tested in further research. Her statement that 'Little is known about any distinctive formal features of women's language in all-female groups' is a challenge to linguists which this paper will take up.

127

Since the publication of Jones's paper, some linguists have developed the notion, originally used in inter-ethnic communication studies, that linguistic differences might be the result in part of subcultural differences rather than simply a reflection of dominant–subordinate relationships. Work adopting this model has explored miscommunication between the sexes (e.g. Maltz & Borker 1982; Tannen 1982, 1987). Such work makes the assumption, either implicitly or explicitly, that the conversational strategies which lead to miscommunication in mixed groups are acquired and developed in single-sex groups. But this assumption is unverified. The evidence presented in the few studies available (Kalcik 1975; Aries 1976; Goodwin 1980; Wodak 1981) is hardly conclusive (but does suggest that such conversational strategies may not be restricted to white middle-class women). We still know very little about the norms of spoken interaction in single-sex groups.

While they lack detail, the papers listed above all draw on a notion of **co-operativeness** to characterise all-female interaction. Early work on women's language had labelled it as 'tentative' or 'powerless'. More recently, and in reaction to this, there has been a move to value women's language more positively, using terms such as 'co-operative'. This is laudable; but in order to avoid the creation of new linguistic myths, it is important that such claims are substantiated by linguistic evidence.

In this paper, I want to analyse in detail part of a corpus of conversation between women friends. The corpus is small (135 minutes of running text), and the approach used is qualitative rather than quantitative.[1] I want firstly to see whether the evidence supports Jones's general claims, secondly to establish what formal features are typical of all-woman discourse, and thirdly to explore the notion of co-operativeness.

The data

I recorded a group of women friends over a period of nine months during 1983–4. These women were an established group who met once a fortnight at each other's houses in the evening to talk. I had belonged to this group since 1975, when it began to meet, and I recorded my friends surreptitiously each time it was my turn to have the group to my house during the period in question. All participants were informed subsequently that recordings had been made, and they agreed to this material being used for research purposes.[2] I shall discuss this data in relation to Jones's five headings, dealing briefly with setting, participants and topic, and at greater length with formal features and functions.

Setting
Jones follows Ervin-Tripp (1964) in using the term **setting** to cover both time and place. She identifies the private domain as the **place** for women's talk, and names the home, the hairdresser's, the supermarket as typical locations. Her identification of the private sphere as the setting for women's subculture seems to me to deserve more emphasis than she gives it. The division between public and private as we now understand it was estab-

lished at the beginning of the nineteenth century (see Hall (1985) for an account of the historical background). As the division became more highly demarcated, patterns of gender subdivision also changed: 'men were firmly placed in the newly defined public world of business, commerce and politics; women were placed in the private world of home and family' (Hall 1985: 12). This split was to have significant sociolinguistic consequences.

Jones describes the setting of gossip in terms of **time** as brief and fragmented: 'Time to gossip is usually snatched from work time' (1980: 194). The claim that snatched episodes are an intrinsic feature of gossip seems debatable, and depends too heavily on seeing women as mothers with small children. Old women, for example, sit on park benches or in social clubs, chatting for extended periods; adolescent girls often congregate on neutral territory (not home or school) and have considerable spare time in which to talk, especially if they are playing truant from school (see Cheshire 1982). Even mothers with small children meet in settings where the quality of the talking cannot be defined as 'snatched' – outside the school gate at the end of the day; waiting in the clinic to weigh the baby; at the mother and toddler group. According to Milroy, in traditional working-class communities such as Belfast, 'speakers valued various kinds of conversational arts very highly. *Many hours were spent simply chatting*' (my italics) (Milroy 1980: 100). Of course, some interaction between women which we would want to label as typical women's talk is brief, but it seems that length of time is not a salient feature of gossip.

The setting for the conversations I recorded was the living room of my home in Birkenhead, Merseyside. People sat on sofas or on the floor around the gas fire, drinking wine. Sessions lasted three hours or more, starting at about 9.0 in the evening. Food was served about half way through the evening; this was usually bread and cheese, but sometimes something more elaborate such as home-made soup or pizza.

Participants

'Gossip is essentially talk between women in our common role *as* women' (Jones 1980: 195). Jones argues that gossip arises from women's perception of themselves as a group with a great deal of experience in common. The members of the women's group I recorded are white, middle class, aged in their late 30s and early 40s. The group was formed (in 1975) at a time when all members had children still at school, and some had babies (who attended in carry cots). The group's *raison d'être* shifted gradually over the years: it initially provided a support network for mothers with young children; it now encourages these same women in their struggle to establish a career in their middle age. Urwin (1985) has commented on the importance for young mothers of friendships with other women. The need for contact with other women at various stages of one's life, not just as young mothers, is certainly borne out by the Birkenhead group which has now existed for 12 years.

Topic

Jones claims that the topics discussed by women are crucially related to their roles as wives, girlfriends and mothers. This claim seems to me to be over-strong, and again to overemphasise the place of motherhood in women's lives. The conversations that I recorded cover a wide range of topics, from discussions of television programmes, to mothers' funerals and child abuse. However, as I have commented in an earlier paper (Coates 1987), it seems to be typical of all-women groups that they discuss people and feelings, while men are more likely to discuss things. This finding fits Jones's general claim that 'the wider theme of gossip is always personal experience' (1980: 195).

Functions

Unlike Jones, I shall discuss the functions of gossip before I discuss its formal features, since I want to argue that the linguistic forms which characterise women's interaction can be explained in terms of the functions they serve. Jones's section on functions is weak: she merely catalogues four different types of gossip. I want to use the term **function** in relation to the **goals** of all-woman interaction. All-woman conversation, like most informal interaction between equals, has as its chief goal the maintenance of good social relationships.

Grice's conversational maxims (Grice 1975) assume that referential meaning is all-important, and that the speaker's only aim is to exchange information. The falsity of this assumption has been demonstrated by Lakoff (1973) and discussed by many other linguists subsequently (e.g. G. Brown 1977; Leech 1983; Tannen 1984). The distinction between public and private spheres, discussed earlier, leads to a distinction between public and private discourse. In public discourse, the exchange of information is an important goal. Male speakers in our culture are socialised into public discourse, while female speakers are socialised into private discourse (cf. Gilligan 1982; P. Smith 1985; G. Wells 1979). Until recently, the androcentric view that information-focussed discourse should be the object of linguistic analysis was not challenged. In private discourse, the exchange of information is not the chief goal. I hope to show in the central section of this Chapter that the formal features which are typical of women's language in all-female groups can be explained by direct reference to the functions of such interaction, that is the establishment and maintenance of social relationships, the reaffirming and strengthening of friendship.

Formal features

I shall examine in detail four aspects of the interactional pattern found in the all-female conversation I recorded. I shall look at topic development, at minimal responses, at simultaneous speech, and finally at epistemic modality. I have chosen to concentrate on these aspects of women's talk because they have been picked out by other writers as markers of co-operative style.

Topic development

It has become a truism in accounts of women's discourse that women develop topics progressively in conversation (see Maltz & Borker 1982: 213). Yet, as far as I know, this claim has not been supported by empirical evidence. The claim is multifaceted: women are said to build on each others' contributions, preferring continuity to discontinuity, and topic shift is supposed to occur gradually (rather than abruptly, as in all-male conversation). Consequently, the discussion of a single topic can last for some time (up to half an hour according to Aries 1976: 13).

In order to examine the nature of topic development in all-female conversation, I shall analyse one episode in detail from one of my recordings. This passage is about mothers' funerals and lasts just under $4\frac{1}{2}$ minutes. There are five participants. The structure of the funeral extract is as follows:

1. A introduces topic;
2. B tells anecdote on same theme;
3. C tells another anecdote on same theme; leading into:
4. general discussion;
5. D summarises;
6. A has last word.

In musical terms, (1), (2) and (3) form the exposition, (4) is the development, (5) the recapitulation, and (6) the coda. The development section is by far the longest (2 minutes 47 seconds). This pattern of topic development is typical of the material I have transcribed (see Coates 1987, where I analyse the development of a different topic).

The telling of anecdotes is a common way of introducing a new topic in conversation; sometimes one anecdote is sufficient, sometimes more than one occurs. What characterises these introductory sections, and sets them off from the central development section, is that they are **monologues**: the telling of a story gives the speaker unusual rights to speak. Example 1 below is a transcript of A's introductory anecdote. [*A key for the transcription notation used is given in the Appendix on p. 151*]

Example 1

   A: this bloke I met today who's doing (.) he he's doing some postgraduate research at at Stirling (.) anyway I asked him

(3) he he wanted to talk to me about a professional matter and I (.) I said (.) I was asking him his sort of background and

(5) he said that he'd done philosophy (.) so I was just interested with little snippets of philosophy that came my way you see+

(7) and he said one of the things that he was interested in was taboo+(.) the nature of taboo+ (.) and he said that (–) and

(9) he gave this example that um (.) if you didn't go to your mother's funeral (–) because you'd got something else to do+

(11) (.) it would be very much frowned ⌈upon um even though
                                     D: ⌊ oh god =
                                         B: = m

what you had to do could easily be more important+ and

(13) after all she's dead = (.) and wouldn't know you weren't
                          = C: m
　　　going kind of thing+

Note that A's fellow participants say nothing until the very end of her narrative. They accord her the right to establish a new topic – something she doesn't do until the end of her turn – and it is only when this point is reached that other participants volunteer supportive noises. No one attempts to make a substantive contribution until it is clear that A has finished her turn.

Once A has finished – and the group has accepted the new topic – B tells a personal anecdote which illustrates A's general theme of whether it is taboo to miss your mother's funeral. B's anecdote is reproduced below.

Example 2

(1) ⎰ B:　oh we – it's so odd you see because we had this
　　⎱ ?:　((xxx))
(2) ⎰ B:　conversation at dinner tonight =　　　= because Steve
　　⎱ A:　　　　　　　　　　　　　　　　= mm =
(3)　 B:　MacFadden's mother died at the weekend+ and she
(4)　 B:　[1] (.) well she <u>lived</u> in Brisbane+ ((they were
(5) ⎰ B:　at Brisbane+)) ⎡so he's going over there+ Australia+
　　⎱ E:　　　　　　　　⎣what (–) Australia?
(6) ⎰ B:　so he's going to the funeral+ it's obviously
　　⎱ D:　　　　　　　　　　oh my god
(7) ⎰ B:　gonna cost him a fortune+ (.) and John said
　　⎱ E:　　　　　　　　　fortune+ (whispers)
(8) ⎰ B:　(–)　　　　　　　　((he was)) just astonished+ I said
　　⎱ E:　((s' about £400))
(9)　 B:　(.) well I wouldn't go Steve+ (–) and the and the
(10)⎰ B:　[həʊ] as you say it was just taboo+ I mean as far
　　⎱ C:　　　　　　　　　　　　　　　　　mm
(11)⎧ B:　as ⎡ Steve was concerned I mean that was ⎡ just
　　⎨ C:　　⎣ mm
　　⎩ D:　　　　　　　　　　　　　　　　　⎣ you just
(12)⎧ B:　　　　　　no+ and I [s] and my response I
　　⎨ D:　can't say that+
　　⎩ ?:　　　　　　no+
(13)⎧ B:　must "oh John" (–) but sorry ((xxx)) ⎡ it's so
　　⎨ ?:　　　　　　　　　　　((xxx))
　　⎩ C:　　　　　　　　　　　　　　　　⎣ I didn't
(14)⎰ B:　odd that you should
　　⎱ C:　go over for my father . . . .

While B's right to hold the floor is never challenged, the other participants are far more active than they were during A's narrative. They support her with well placed minimal responses (lines 2, 6, 10, 11, 12), they complete her utterances either at the same time as her ('fortune', line 7) or by briefly taking over from her ('you just can't say that', lines 11–12), they ask for clarification ('what – Australia?', line 5). None of these contributions constitutes an attempt to take the floor from B – they are signals of active listenership.

B's final comment is unfinished as C starts at a point which she interprets as the end of B's turn (though co-participants were clear what B intended to say, namely, that it was a coincidence that A should bring up this subject when she herself had been discussing it that evening in relation to her neighbour). Clearly, the members of the group now feel they have established what topic is under discussion. Thus, C is granted the normal monologue rights when she begins *her* personal anecdote, but as soon as she reaches her first punch line, other speakers intervene and the discussion section begins.

Discussion sections, where speakers evaluate the topic, are multiparty in nature. Often several speakers speak at once, and speaker turns tend to be brief. Example 3 below gives C's anecdote and the opening of the general discussion.

Example 3

```
(1) ⎰ C:  I didn't go over for my father+ I asked my mother
    ⎱ B:  it's so odd that you should
(2)   C:  if she wanted me I mean (.) I I immediately said
(3)   C:  "Do you want me to come over?" (–) and she said
(4)   C:  "Well no I can't really see the point+ he's dead
(5) ⎧ C:  isn't he+ (laughs)     (.) and (.)          ⎡ and she
    ⎨ A:                    mm                        ⎢
    ⎩ B:                          well that's right+  ⎣ that's
(6) ⎧ C:  said no I mean          ((xxx))      ⎡ no point in
    ⎨ B:  what John was saying (.) that they   ⎢
    ⎩ E:                                       ⎣ you've got
(7) ⎧ C:  coming+                     so
    ⎨ E:  terribly forward-looking parents you ⎡ see+ it
    ⎩ A:                                       ⎣ yeah
(8) ⎰ C:
    ⎱ E:  depends on the attitude of (.) mean is is his
(9) ⎧ C:                                   ⎡ I don't
    ⎨ E:  father still alive?              ⎣ because
    ⎩ B:                 (pp) I don't know+
(10)⎰ C:  think I don't think they had a funeral either+
    ⎱ E:  that would have a very big bearing on it+
(11)⎧ C:
    ⎨ E:                                ⎡ yeah+
    ⎩ D:  if they were religious I mean+ yes ⎣ it would all
(12)⎧ C:  yeah I don't think they had a funeral+ (.)
    ⎨ E:         yeah+ (.) I mean ⎡ if there was if there
    ⎩ D:  depend+                ⎣ if there were life
(13) C:  they had a memorial service+
    ⎰ E:  was                    ⎡ if they if
    ⎱ D:  after death            ⎣ then they'd know
(14)⎧ C:
    ⎨ E:                     that's right ((xx))
    ⎩ D:     that you hadn't come+
```

Discussion sections are complex. At one level, individual speakers are dealing with their own feelings about the topic under discussion. In the funeral episode, C keeps returning to the theme of missing her father's funeral, expanding on the reasons for this, and hypothesising that she would go now. A says that she would be upset if her brothers and sister failed to come to her mother's funeral (and since her sister, like C's father, lives in the United States, A is implicitly challenging the assumption that the Atlantic is an insuperable barrier). E, whose parents live in Sheffield, asserts that she would definitely go to their funerals and that it is unthinkable that she wouldn't. These speakers are in effect asking for support from the group, even though their positions are to some extent mutually exclusive; they need to air their feelings in order to deal with them.

At another level, speakers are debating more general points: is it the purpose of funerals to comfort surviving relatives? or are they a public statement about one's feelings for one's dead mother? How important is distance in the decision about whether or not to attend a funeral? The general and personal are intertwined; crucially, speakers work together to sort out what they feel.

From an analytical point of view, the taken-for-granted view of conversation (originating in Sacks, Schegloff & Jefferson 1974) as interaction where one speaker speaks at a time is of little use when dealing with such material. As Example 3 illustrates, more than one speaker speaks at a time: C continues her account of not attending her father's funeral, while B ties this in with her anecdote and E adds a comment about C's parents, responding both to C ('you' in line 6 refers to C) and to B ('is his father still alive?' (lines 8 and 9). This is addressed to B – 'his' refers to B's neighbour Steve). E's comment ('that would have a very big bearing on it' at line 10) coincides with C providing further information to fit E's description of her parents as 'forward-looking'. The link between having or not having a funeral service and religious belief is picked up, slightly tongue-in-cheek, by D; E joins in with D, while C continues to refine her account.

The discussion section is long and there isn't space to give it in full nor to analyse it in detail here: specific aspects relating to minimal responses, simultaneous speech and epistemic modality will be picked up in the following three sections (4.2, 4.3 and 4.4). Example 4 gives the end of the discussion, with D's summary and A's final comment.

Example 4

```
(1)   C:   I probably I mean it would have also would have
(2)   C:   been if (.) I'd go now+ (–) Daniel was sort of
(3) ⌠ C:   (.) 18 months old+ and it would have been rather
    ⌡ A:              mm . . . . . . . . . . . . . . . . . . . . .
(4) ⌠ C:   difficult and this kind of thing =
    ⎨ A:   yes+        yes+
    ⌡ D:                              = that's right+
(5) ⌠ C:              um              I think I
    ⌡ D:   I suppose there's two things+ there's
(6)   C:   would go now because probably because I would want
```

```
(7)  ┌ C:   to go =      = cos it would be be very easy to go =
     │ E:          = mm =
     └ D:                                              = yeah =
(8)  ┌ C:          = it would have been (–) I don't know (–)
     │ A:   = yeah =
     └ D:                                        there's two
(9)  ┌ C:                        anyway ((xx perfectly all-
     └ D:   things aren't there+ there's the the other people
(10) ┌ C:   right xx))
     └ D:   like your mother or father who's left and or or
(11)   D:   siblings+ and there's also how how you feel at that
(12) ┌ D:   time about (.) the easiness of going+
     │ E:                                   mm
     │ C:                                         mm
     │ A:                                               mm
     └ B:                                                    yeah
(13) ┌ D:   I mean I would I
     └ A:                  well to go to Australia seems a
(14)   A:   bit over the top+
```

It seems that the group jointly senses that this topic has been satisfactorily dealt with: C receives lots of support in her final statement that she *would* go now since circumstances have changed. Note that D has to make two attempts to provide a summary, starting once before C has finished. C's last turn gets two *yeahs* in sequence (lines 7 and 8). D's summary, like A's initial anecdote, is notable for *lack* of interruption: only when she has completed it do the others respond, all four co-participants indicating, in a perfectly timed sequence of *mm* and *yeah*, their acceptance of what D has said. A, who initiated the topic, then has the last word.

This brief account of the development of one topic in a conversation between women friends provides an example of the way that women develop topics progressively. These women work together to produce the funeral episode, both by recognising opening and closing moves (i.e., granting one speaker the right to initiate a topic through the telling of an anecdote, or to summarise at the end), and by jointly negotiating an understanding of the problem in question (is it taboo to miss your mother's funeral?). This latter part of joint production involves both the right to speak and the duty to listen and support. The five speakers deal with their own and each other's feelings and experiences, juggling speaker and listener roles with great skill. There is no sense in which it is possible to sum up the funeral topic by saying 'A talked about taboo and funerals' or 'C talked about not going to her father's funeral'. The funeral episode is jointly produced by all speakers.

Aries' claim that topics can last up to half an hour is not apparently borne out by this example (which lasts 4 mins 29 secs), but this may depend on the definition of 'topic'. Certainly, topic shift is normally gradual rather than abrupt as the following example demonstrates (Example 5 follows on from Example 4).

Example 5

```
(1) ⎰ A:   a bit over the top =
    ⎱ E:                         = yeah what what did the oh yeah
(2) ⎧ A:                                            ⎡((xxx he
    ⎨ E:   what was your bloke saying about taboo?  ⎢
    ⎩ D:                                            ⎣ oh yeah
(3) ⎰ A:   just xxx))
    ⎱ D:   what? I've just written my chapter on taboo so I'm
(4) ⎰ A:   well          = I didn't get much more from
    ⎱ D:   terribly interested =
(5)   A:   him than that+ except um (.) he's looking at (.)
(6)   A:   er [ba] battering and his sort of thesis is and
(7)   A:   the way social services deal with these kind of
(8)   A:   problems (.) men that batter women (.) and men that
(9)   A:   (.) sexually abuse their children and um their (.)
(10)  A:   other children+ and he was just looking at (.)
(11)  A:   attitudes to that and he said that he's come across
(12)  A:   incredible taboo (.) taboos um [jə] you know this
(13)  A:   just world hypothesis (.) business
```

Note how E's question refers back to A's original anecdote (see Example 1), thus providing a very cohesive link.

In fact, this kind of gradual topic shift continues for many topics:

funerals
↓
child abuse
↓
wives' loyalty to husbands
↓
Yorkshire Ripper
↓
fear of men

These five topics are smoothly linked and overall they last for 15 minutes, 54 seconds. Perhaps Aries' figure more appropriately refers to coherent sequences of topics such as the above. At all events, my data suggest that women do build progressively on each others' contributions, that topics are developed jointly, and that shifts between topics are gradual rather than abrupt.[3]

Minimal responses

Research on the use of minimal responses is unanimous in showing that women use them more than men (Strodtbeck & Mann 1956; Hirschmann 1974; Zimmerman & West 1975; Fishman 1980). This research is, however, mainly concerned with **mixed** interaction; the finding that women use minimal responses more frequently, and with greater linguistic sensitivity, in such contexts is said to demonstrate yet again the fact that women do the 'interactional shitwork' (to use Fishman's 1977 term).

It shouldn't be automatically assumed that the use of these forms denotes powerlessness, however. The same form functions in different ways in different contexts. Certainly it is clear from my data that the use of minimal responses also characterises linguistic interaction between women who are friends and equals.

Minimal responses are used in two different ways in the women's conversations I recorded. In the interaction-focussed discussion sections, they are used to support the speaker and to indicate the listener's active attention. The opening of Example 4 (the end of the funeral discussion section) illustrates this. While C talks, first A (lines 3 and 4), then E (line 7), then D and A one after the other (lines 7 and 8) add their minimal responses. These responses are well placed: they are mostly timed to come at the end of an information unit (e.g., a tone group or clause), yet so well anticipated is this point that the speaker's flow is not interrupted. (Both Zimmerman & West and Fishman have shown how the *delayed* minimal response is used by male speakers to indicate lack of interest and/or attention.) These minimal responses signal the listeners' active participation in the conversation; that is, they are another aspect of the way text is *jointly* produced.

In the narrative or more information-focussed sections of the conversation, minimal responses seem to have another meaning. They are used far less frequently, and when they occur they signal agreement among participants that a particular stage of conversation has been reached. For example, when a speaker introduces a new topic, as in Example 1, it is only at the very end that other speakers indicate that they are attending. At this point it seems that D, B and C (lines 11 and 13, Example 1) are indicating to A that they have taken the point of her anecdote, and that they accept it as a topic.

In Example 4, D's summary is followed by minimal responses from all the other participants (line 12). Clearly the women feel the need to indicate their active agreement with D's summing-up. In both these examples, it is not just the presence of minimal responses at the end, but also their absence during the course of an anecdote or summary, which demonstrates the sensitivity of participants to the norms of interaction: speakers recognise different types of talk and use minimal responses appropriately.

So, while it is true to say that the use of minimal responses characterises women's speech in both mixed and single-sex conversation, it would be wrong to claim that you have only to say *mhm* or *yeah* every two minutes to talk like a woman. On the contrary, women's use of minimal responses demonstrates their sensitivity to interactional processes; they use them where they are appropriate. In mixed conversations, the use of minimal responses by women will only become 'weak' where women's skill as listeners is exploited by male speakers. In all-female groups, it seems that the use of these linguistic forms is further evidence of women's active participation in the joint production of text.

Simultaneous speech
The Sacks, Schegloff and Jefferson (1974) model of turn-taking in conversation views simultaneous speech by two or more co-conversationalists as an aberration. Their model assumes a norm of one speaker speaking at a time. The evidence of my data is that, on the contrary, for much of the time

(typically in discussion sections) more than one speaker speaks at a time. The same phenomenon has been observed by Edelsky (1981) and Tannen (1984), both of whom analysed mixed conversation. Edelsky's analysis of five staff meetings reveals what she describes as two types of 'floor': F1, where one speaker dominates, and F2, where several speakers speak at once to jointly produce text. Tannen's analysis of a Thanksgiving dinner involving six speakers (two women, four men) describes two kinds of talk, one more information-focussed, the other more interaction-focussed: the latter involves more than one speaker speaking at the same time.

It is certainly not the case in the conversations I have recorded that where more than one speaker speaks this normally represents an attempt to infringe the current speaker's right to a turn. I have analysed all instances of simultaneous speech which occur during the funeral episode; only a minority can be described in this way (see Table 5.1).

Type I, where more than one speaker starts at the same time, is trivial: where next speaker self-selects, such infelicities are inevitable. Types II and III are more serious: they are illustrated in Examples 6 and 7 below. In Example 6, E's interruption fails and B completes her own utterance: in Example 7, B stops talking and C claims the floor.

Example 6

```
(1)  { B:   I mean ⌈ it's not as if I'm particularly religious+
     { E:          ⌊ but if
(2)  { B:
     { E:   yeah+ but I know but if you've got a [fɑː ] if
(3)  { B:
     { E:   there's a spouse . . . .
```

Example 7

```
(1)  { B:   but sorry ((xxx)) ⌈ it's so odd that you should
     { C:                     ⌊ I didn't go over for my father+
     { sev:          ((xxx))
(2)  { B:
     { C:   I asked my mother if she wanted me . . . .
```

Table 5.1 Simultaneous speech in the funeral episode (4 mins 29 secs)

Type I.	Two speakers self-select at the same time, one stops	3
Type II.	Speaker B self-selects at TRP, A carries on, B stops	3
Type III.	Speaker B self-selects at TRP, A tails off	3
Type IV.	Speaker B completes A's utterance	5
Type V.	Speaker B asks question or comments while A is speaking	7
Type VI.	Speaker B comments, A stops speaking	2
Type VII.	Two speakers speak at the same time	7
		30

TRP = Transition Relevance Place, i.e., the end of a 'unit type' such as a phrase or clause. See Sacks, Schegloff and Jefferson 1974.

Even with these two examples, the term 'interruption' seems inappropriate. In Example 6, speaker E is guilty of what Tannen calls the 'overlap-as-enthusiasm' strategy: she is not so much trying to stop B from talking as jumping in too soon because of her enthusiasm to participate. She realises her mistake and comes in again once B has finished. (Another example of this phenomenon can be seen in Example 5 where D's enthusiasm delays the start of A's turn.) In Example 7, C assumes that B has finished, and in fact B is one of those speakers, like D (see Example 4, line 13) who typically tail off rather than finishing their turns crisply. It could be argued that B and D's personal style results from their expectation that others know what they mean (so they don't need to say it in full), and that they invite overlap by their habit of ending their turns with utterances which peter out, both syntactically and prosodically. An example of such tailing-off is given below (bold print indicates laughter):

Example 8

> E: but if there's no spouse I mean **and there's very few relatives left it doesn't really seem much of a**

In Example 8, E's contribution is not overlapped: this example therefore illustrates more starkly how such tailing-off turns are not 'unfinished', in the sense that E has made her contribution and her co-participants know what she means. (To get the full quality of this utterance, it is of course necessary to hear the tape.)

Type IV simultaneous speech is closely related to the above: if a speaker tails off, then it is open to other participants to complete the utterance. Speaker B's habit of not completing her turn often results in others (usually E) doing it for her:

Example 9

> (1)   B: I just thought "if the car breaks down on the way
> (2)   B: home I mean I'll die of fear+ (laughs) I'll never
> (3) ⎰ B: get out+ I'll just" (.)
>   ⎱ E: just sit here and die+

In this case there is no overlap, but often speakers' completion of each others' utterances results in simultaneous speech:

Example 10

> ⎰ B: I mean that ⎡ was just   = no+
> ⎱ D: ⎣ you just can't say that =

Note that B acknowledges D's contribution and in fact continues speaking: D's overlap in no way constitutes an attempt to get the floor.

Such completion-overlaps can involve more than two speakers:

Example 11

(1)   A: it'll become a [s] public statement about =
       E: = the
       D:

(2)   A: er   ((xx))   yeah +
       E: family+ ((to do with)) you
       D: yeah+   and that you're close+

Again, as in Example 10, the current speaker (A) acknowledges the others' contributions before continuing.

Type V is a very common type of simultaneous speech: it involves one of the co-participants asking the speaker a question, or commenting on what the speaker is saying, during the speaker's turn. One could describe this phenomenon as a relation of the minimal response: the questions or comments function as a sign of active listenership, and do not threaten current speaker's turn. Speakers in fact acknowledge such questions/comments while continuing to hold the floor. Examples 12 and 13 illustrate the question, where listeners seek clarification.

Example 12

(1)   B: well she lived in Brisbane+ ((they were at
       E:

(2)   B: Brisbane+)) so he's going over there+ Australia+
       E: what (–)   Australia?

(3)   B: so he's going to the funeral+
       E:

Example 13

(1)   A: and I imagine that my two far-flung sibs will
       E:

(2)   A: actually make the journey+ I'm just (.) I'm
       E: what (.) to your

(3)   A: ((almost)) yes I'm sure they will but it'll be
       E: parents? to your mother's?

(4)   A: because [1] it'll become a [s] public statement . . . .
       E:

In Example 12, B tucks 'Australia' into her exposition to satisfy E, while A, in 13, interrupts herself to say 'yes' to E before continuing her statement about her sister and brother.

Comments occur more frequently than questions and normally don't threaten a speaker's turn:

Example 14

       A: I'm absolutely sure they'll come but I mean in fact it
       E:

```
{ A:   won't make any odds but I think I (.) would be (.) hurt
{ E:                                              it'll be nicer for
{ A:   and angry if they hadn't+
{ E:   you+
```

In this example, E's comment goes unacknowledged, but speakers often do respond to listener comments:

Example 15

```
(1)  { E:   if there's a spouse then perhaps they would want
     { A:
(2)  { E:   you to go        you know but if   but if    = that's
     { A:                    yeah for their comfort+ for them =
(3)  { E:   right+ comfort for them+ but if . . .
     { A:
```

Here E acknowledges A's comment before continuing.

Occasionally comments of this kind coincide with the current speaker stopping speaking (Type VI). In the following example, C finishes making her point during E's comment about her parents, and it is E who then takes the floor. C's *so* is ambiguous: it could be a bid for a longer turn (which fails), or it could be a tailing-off noise.

Example 16

```
(1)  { C:   and she said "no" I mean ((xx))  [ no point in coming+
     { E:                                     [ you've got terribly
(2)  { C:                        so
     { E:   forward-looking parents you see+ it depends on the
(3)  { C:
     { E:   attitude . . .
```

This example is complicated by the fact that B is also talking at the same time (see example 3, lines 5–9 for the full version). However such an example is categorised, what is important is that E's contribution here is constructive: she is embellishing C's turn, putting C's mother's behaviour in context.

The final type of simultaneous speech, type VII, involves two or more speakers speaking at once; for this type it is not possible to say one speaker has the floor and the other is merely interjecting a comment. There are seven examples of this during the funeral episode (i.e., nearly a quarter of all examples of simultaneous speech). The obvious analogy is again a musical one: the speakers contribute simultaneously to the same theme, like several instruments playing contrapuntally (the notion of contrapuntal talk is also invoked in Reisman 1974). Examples 17 and 18 below illustrate this type:

Example 17

(1) { E: is his father still alive?   because that
     { B: (pp) I don't know
     { C: I don't think
(2) { E: would have a very big bearing on it+
     { C: they had a funeral either+

Example 18

(1) { A: I've [bp] for many years ((have wondered)) about my
     { E: cos that's what funerals are for
(2) { A: own (mother's funeral+
     { E: (.) they're for the relatives+

Without providing an audio-tape, it is hard to describe the quality of such passages: crucially, there is no sense of competition, or of vying for turns. Speakers do not become aggrieved when others join in. The feel of the conversation is that all the participants are familiar with each other and with the way the interaction is constructed. It is very much a joint effort, with individual speakers concerned to contribute to a jointly negotiated whole.

A final more extended example, containing four instances of simultaneous speech, will serve to give the flavour of the conversation as a whole.

Example 19

(1) C: I mean I think it really depends on the <u>atti</u>tude of
(2) { C: the survivors who are [there+ (–) if if they want
     { B: [yeah+
(3) { C: the person to [go   (–) then the person should go+
     { E: [mm+
     { A: I don't think it depends on that
(4) { C:
     { E: [oh I do+ if one of
     { A: Cathy+ I think it depends on [um
(5) { C:
     { E: mine died and (.) er I mean (–) my (.) if it were
(6) { C:
     { E: whichever one it were the other one would expect me
(7) { C:
     { E: to go (–) they'd be <u>absolutely</u> <u>staggered</u> if I
(8) { C:
     { E: didn't (–) [especially as it's only (.) (laughs) two
     { D: [mm
(9) { C: = no I mean if my mother had wanted
     { E: hours away+
     { D: Sheffield = (laughs)
(10) { C: me to come+ if she'd said "oh yes please" (.)   [or
     { A: mm   [
     { E: [you

(11) { C: "of course" or or something+   then I would've
      { A: yeah+
      { E: would've gone+
(12) { C: (.) of course I would've gone+
      { A: yeah+

At the beginning of Example 19, A's conflicting point of view overlaps with C's talking (note that C completes her utterance) and E's support for C overlaps with A, who tails off. That an interpretation of this as conflict is false is shown by A's support (given in minimal responses) for C's restatement of her point of view at the end. The contrapuntal nature of such text is exemplified by D's contribution 'Sheffield', which glosses E's 'it's only two hours away', and by E's anticipation of C's words which leads her to butt in with 'you would've gone' before C herself says it.

As someone who was a participant in this discourse, there is no doubt in my mind that the term 'interruption' is hardly ever appropriate as a description of instances of simultaneous speech which occur in gossip. In public domains, where the norm is that one speaker speaks at a time, and where the goal of participants is to grab speakership, then interruption is a strategy for gaining the floor. In private conversation between equals, on the other hand, where the chief goal of interaction is the maintenance of good social relationships, then the participation of more than one speaker is iconic of joint activity: the goal is not to take the floor *from* another speaker, but to participate in conversation *with* other speakers. The examples of simultaneous speech given here illustrate the way in which women speakers work together to produce shared meanings.

Epistemic modality
Epistemic modal forms are defined semantically as those linguistic forms which are used to indicate the speaker's confidence or lack of confidence in the truth of the proposition expressed in the utterance. If someone says *Perhaps she missed the train*, the use of the word *perhaps* indicates lack of confidence in the proposition 'she missed the train'. Lexical items such as *perhaps, I think, sort of, probably*, as well as certain prosodic and paralinguistic features, are used in English to express epistemic modality.

Such forms, however, are used by speakers not just to indicate their lack of commitment to the truth of propositions, but also to hedge assertions in order to protect both their own and addressees' face (for a full account of the role of epistemic modality in spoken discourse, see Coates 1987). It is my impression (based on an admittedly small corpus of data) that women in single-sex groups exploit these forms more than men. Table 5.2 gives the totals for the most commonly used forms in two parallel texts, each lasting about 40 minues.[4]

Utterances such as those in Examples 20 and 21 below are typical of the discussion sections of the all-women conversations recorded (epistemic modal forms in italics).

Table 5.2 Sex differences in the use of epistemic modal forms

	Women	Men
I mean	77	20
well	65	45
just	57	48
I think	36	12
sort of	35	10

Example 20
[funeral discussion]
I mean I think it *really* depends on the <u>att</u>itude of the survivors who are 'there+

Example 21
[speaker describes old friend she'd recently bumped into]
she looks very *sort of* um (–) *kind of* matronly *really*+

It is my contention (see Coates 1987: 129) that women exploit the poly-pragmatic nature of epistemic modal forms. They use them to mitigate the force of an utterance in order to respect addressees' face needs. Thus, the italicised forms in Example 21 hedge the assertion *she looks matronly* not because the speaker doubts its truth but because she does not want to offend her addressees by assuming their agreement (describing a friend in unflattering terms is controversial). Such forms also protect the speaker's face: the speaker in Example 21 can retreat from the proposition expressed there if it turns out to be unacceptable. Where sensitive topics are discussed (as in Examples 20 and 21), epistemic modal forms are used frequently. This seems to provide an explanation for women's greater use of such forms (see Table 5.2). The women's conversations I have analysed involve topics related to people and feelings (see, for example, the topic sequence given on p. 136); in the parallel all-male conversation I have analysed, the men talk about *things* – home beermaking, hi-fi systems, etc. Presumably such topics do not trigger the use of epistemic modal forms because they are not so face-threatening.

Women also use these forms to facilitate open discussion (and, as I've said, epistemic modal forms are mostly found in the discussion sections of conversation). An underlying rule of conversation between equals, where the exchange of information is not a priority, is 'Don't come into open disagreement with other participants' (see Leech 1983: 132). Examples 20 and 21 are contributions to discussion which state a point of view but allow for other points of view. More positively, epistemic modal forms can be used to invite others to speak, a function often fulfilled by the tag question.

As Perkins (1983: 111) says: 'since questions qualify the truth of a proposition by making it relative to the speaker's uncertainty, they may be regarded as expressing epistemic modality'. An analysis of the tag questions used in the conversations I have recorded shows that the vast majority are addressee-oriented rather than speaker-oriented (cf. Holmes, 1984). In one of the conversations (about 40 minutes of taped material) there are 23 tag questions, yet of these only four are used to elicit information (i.e. only four are speaker-oriented), as in Example 22:

Example 22
you don't know what colour their bluè is dó you (Note the rising intonation contour on the tag.)

Addressee-oriented tags can be used either to soften the force of a negatively affective utterance, or to facilitate interaction. Of the 19 addressee-oriented tags in the conversation, only one functions as a softener; the rest are all facilitative. Facilitative tags are given this name precisely because they are used to facilitate the participation of others; they invite them into the discourse. The following examples illustrate this (tags are italicised):

Example 23

    { E: but I mean so much research is male-dominated+ I mean
    { A:
    { E: it's just stàggering *isn't it* =
    { A: = mm+

Example 24

    { D: it was dreàdful *wàsn't it* =
    { E: = appalling Caroline
    { D:
    { E: absolutely appalling+

What is surprising about the tag questions in my data is that, while I would argue that they are facilitative, they are mostly not found in contexts like Examples 23 and 24, that is, where the tag results in another speaker taking a turn. Instead, they occur in mid-utterance, and the speaker seems to expect no verbal response (or at most a minimal response). Examples 25 and 26 illustrate this type:

Example 25
I think the most difficult thing is is that when you love someone you you half the time you forget their faults (yes) *don't you* and still maybe love them but I mean . . .

Example 26
[Discussion of Yorkshire Ripper case]

    { A: and they had they had a very accurate picture of him
    { D:
    { A: *didn't they*+ they roughly knew his age =
    { D: = at one point
    { A: = yeah =
    { D: they knew about his gap teeth too *didn't they* =

$\left\{ \begin{array}{l} \text{A:} \\ \text{D:} \end{array} \right.$ = then they got rid of that+

A further example is given in Example 4 (page 135), where D's summary at the end of the funeral discussion begins *there's twò things àren't there*. Of the 18 facilitative tags, nine occur in mid-utterance, like these; another three come at the end of a speaker's turn but elicit no overt response – for example, during the funeral discussion, E comments on the theme of missing a funeral *it's just not gòing ìsn't it*. Most of the other facilitative tags appear as comments by active listeners (Type V simultaneous speech) as in Example 27:

Example 27

$\left\{ \begin{array}{l} \text{D:} \\ \text{B:} \end{array} \right.$ cos I'm fed up of travelling to conferences ⌈ but I'm
⌊ oh it's so

$\left\{ \begin{array}{l} \text{D:} \\ \text{B:} \end{array} \right.$ giving a paper.
tỳpical ìsn't it

All these examples involve falling intonation, and all expect the answer *yes* (like *nonne* in Latin).

The women conversationalists seem to use these tags to check the taken-for-grantedness of what is being said. Paralinguistic cues, and sometimes minimal responses, signal to the speaker that what she is saying has the support of the group. Confirmation of this interpretation comes from an example where the speaker does not receive the expected response.

Example 28

A: what I can't fathom out is why children who are
A: physically battered by their parents (.) there's no,
A: there's never any suggestion that (.) they contributed
$\left\{ \begin{array}{l} \text{A:} \\ \text{E:} \end{array} \right.$ to it (.) and yet children who are sexually abused by
     yes there is
A: their parents (.) somehow that's (–) you know the [t∫ı]
$\left\{ \begin{array}{l} \text{A:} \\ \text{E:} \end{array} \right.$ the the
     well there is (–) because there's that thing of a
$\left\{ \begin{array}{l} \text{A:} \\ \text{E:} \\ \text{C:} \end{array} \right.$
     certain pitch of scrèaming ísn't there =
                                      = ah but no
$\left\{ \begin{array}{l} \text{A:} \\ \text{E:} \\ \text{C:} \end{array} \right.$
     that's logical+ ⌈ oh   = sorry =
     ⌊ genuine =   = she's um she's talking
$\left\{ \begin{array}{l} \text{A:} \\ \text{E:} \\ \text{C:} \end{array} \right.$
                              oh
     about the emotional ((sort of)) feeling+

E's *oh sorry* demonstrates her suprise and also the fact that speakers in this type of discourse are prepared to withdraw statements which turn out *not* to be accepted by others present.

I want to argue that these tags are not only addressee-oriented, in the

normal sense of 'facilitative', but that they also function, sometimes simultaneously, to mark the speaker's monitoring of the progress of the conversation. This may involve the establishment and development of new topics.
The following example is taken from the point in the conversation where
the topic shifts from child abuse to wives' loyalty to husbands.

Example 29

```
⎧ C:   and your husband has become a monster =
⎨ A:                                        = mm
⎩ B:                                        = mm (.)
⎧ C:              ‖ [end of child
⎨ A:              ‖ abuse topic]
⎨ B:    mm (.)   ‖
⎩ E:                  I mean it's like that woman who turned in (.)
  E:    was it (.) [pr ] Prime . . . one of those spy cases+ it
⎧ E:    was his wife wàsn't it who turned him in =
⎨ A:                                        = yeah+
⎩ D:                                        = oh yes+
```

E's tag question here serves to get agreement from the group to pursue a
new aspect of the topic; it functions as a *check* on the co-operative progress
of the discourse.

Co-operativeness

In some senses, co-operativeness is a taken-for-granted feature of conversation: Grice, in his well known analysis of conversational norms (Grice
1975), used the term 'co-operative' to underscore the obvious but often
overlooked fact that conversations can only occur because two or more
participants tacitly agree to co-operate in talk. The notion of co-operativeness that has become established in the literature on women's language,
however, (see, for example, Kalcik 1975; Aries 1976; Goodwin 1980; Maltz
& Borker 1982), is less general: co-operativeness in this sense refers to a
particular *type* of conversation, conversation where speakers work together
to produce shared meanings. Set against this notion of co-operativeness is
the notion of competitiveness; competitiveness is used to describe the
adversarial style of conversation where speakers vie for turns and where
participants are more likely to contradict each other than to build on each
others' contributions. (Whether competitiveness in this sense is typical of
all-male discourse is a folklinguistic myth which has still to be tested.)

At the heart of co-operativeness is a view of speakers collaborating in the
production of text: the group takes precedence over the individual. How far
does my data support the idea that women's language is co-operative in
this more specific sense? Do the formal features described in the previous
section function as collaborative devices?

At one level, we have seen that topics develop slowly and accretively
because participants build on each other's contributions and jointly arrive
at a consensus. At a more delicate level, both minimal responses and

epistemic modal forms function as enabling devices. Participants use minimal responses to signal their active listenership and support for the current speaker; they use them too to mark their recognition of the different stages of conversational development. Epistemic modal forms are used to respect the face needs of all participants, to negotiate sensitive topics, and to encourage the participation of others; the chief effect of using epistemic modal forms is that the speaker does not take a hard line. Where a group rather than an individual overview is the aim of discussion, then linguistic forms which mitigate the force of individual contributions are a valuable resource. Finally, simultaneous speech occurs in such discourse in various forms, and is rarely a sign of conversational malfunctioning. On the contrary, in much of the material I have collected, the norm of one-speaker-at-a-time clearly does not apply. Co-conversationalists ask questions or make comments which, like minimal responses, are signals of active listenership, but which more substantially help to produce joint text. Simultaneous speech also occurs when speakers complete each others' utterances: this seems to be a clear example of the primacy of text rather than speaker. Finally, simultaneous speech occurs most commonly because speakers prefer, in discussion, the affirmation of collaborative talk to the giving of the floor to one speaker. Participants in conversation can absorb more than one message at a time; simultaneous speech doesn't threaten comprehension. On the contrary, it allows for a more multilayered development of themes.

Topic development, minimal responses, epistemic modal forms and simultaneous speech are formal features of very different kinds. Yet where minimal responses and epistemic modal forms are used frequently and with sensitivity, where simultaneous speech is contrapuntal and doesn't mark conversational breakdown, and where topics develop slowly and progressively, all can be seen to function to promote co-operative talk. It seems that in conversations between women friends in an informal context, the notion of cooperativeness is not a myth.

Conclusions

In this chapter I have tried to refine Jones's description of gossip, in particular by analysing some of the formal features which characterise all-female discourse. A comprehensive account of the formal features typical of gossip remains to be carried out[5]. But it is possible on the basis of the four features analysed here to conclude that women's talk *can* be described as co-operative. This, however, brings us up against the conflicting findings of those working on women's language in the context of *mixed* interaction. Women's use of minimal responses, tag questions, and hedging devices in general (epistemic modal forms) has been interpreted as a sign of weakness, of women's subordinate position to men (see, for example, Lakoff 1975; Fishman 1977, 1980). Moreover, research on interruption and overlap in mixed and single-sex pairs has shown that men use interruptions to dominate conversation in mixed interaction, but that simultaneous speech of any kind is rare in single sex conversation (Zimmerman & West 1975; West & Zimmerman 1983).

Firstly, it is clearly not the case that any one linguistic form has one single function irrespective of contextual factors; linguists are now aware that linguistic forms are potentially multifunctional. Secondly, as I argued in the third section, the forms that characterise all-female discourse need to be understood in the framework of the goals they serve. Since it is the aim of such talk to create and maintain good social relationships, then forms which promote such ends will be preferred. I have tried to show that women's frequent use of minimal responses and epistemic modal forms, their way of developing topics progressively, and their preference for all-together-now rather than one-at-a-time discussion, all serve the function of asserting joint activity and of consolidating friendship. Women's talk at one level deals with the experiences common to women: individuals work to come to terms with that experience, and participants in conversation actively support one another in that endeavour. At another level, the *way* women negotiate talk symbolises that mutual support and co-operation: conversationalists understand that they have rights as speakers and also duties as listeners; the joint working out of a group point of view takes precedence over individual assertions.

This discussion of underlying goals should help to explain the differences between language use in same-sex and mixed interaction. It is undoubtedly the case, all other things being equal, that when women interact with other women they interact with equals, while when they interact with men they are relating to superiors. This means that analysis of mixed interaction has to be conducted in a framework which acknowledges dominance and oppression as relevant categories. Giving a minimal response to an equal in conversation, for example, is very different from giving a minimal response to a superior. Where the main goal of relaxed informal conversation between equals is the maintenance of good (equal) social relationships, one of the goals of mixed interaction is inevitably the maintenance of gender divisions, of male–female inequality.

Furthermore, it is now agreed that sociocultural presuppositions are a key factor in explaining how speakers make sense of conversation (Gumperz 1982). Since it is arguable that women and men in our culture do not share these sociocultural presuppositions, then another difference between same-sex and mixed interaction will be that the latter will exhibit communication problems similar to those found in inter-ethnic conversation.

For both these reasons, it is very important that we do not conflate the 'women's language' said to be typical of mixed interaction with the 'women's language' which characterises all-female discourse. The two need to be analysed separately. However, growing awareness of the norms of all-female discourse may help us to reassess our interpretation of the linguistic forms used by women in mixed interaction.

Jones's original paper marked the beginning of an important shift in focus in work on language and sex differences. It drew attention not just to women's language *per se*, but to the *strengths* of such discourse. This positive approach has provided an important counterbalance to the more negative tone of researchers who see women's language as weak and tentative. Much remains to be done in the study of women and language: the majority of studies so far have concentrated on white educated women in the United States and Britain. We still know very little about variation in women's language relating to age or class or ethnic group. The notion of co-operativeness needs to be tested against all these parameters. Jones's argument is that, despite differences of age or class or ethnicity, women form a speech community. In so far as human interaction is constitutive of social reality, and in so far as interaction with other women plays an important role in our dealing with our experiences as women, then the study of interaction in all-woman groups is, as Jones says, 'a key to the female subculture'.

Notes

1. I describe, and give a justification of, this approach in greater detail in Coates (1987).
2. I would like to place on record my gratitude to my friends for their tolerance and support.
3. Abrupt shifts do occur, when the emphasis switches from interaction-focussed to more information-focussed episodes. Such shifts, however, form a minority of cases.
4. The two texts used were one of my own, and one from the Survey of English Usage (University College, London). The speakers in both were white, middle-class, well educated, aged in their 30s and early 40s. Both texts were recorded in the evening in the homes of linguists who had invited their friends over for a drink. Five women are involved in the first text; three men in the other. (My thanks to Professor Greenbaum for allowing me to use SEU material.)
5. See now, however, Coates (1996). (Eds.)

References

Abrahams, R. (1975) 'Negotiating respect: patterns of presentation among black women', in C. R. Farrar (ed.), *Women in Folklore*, University of Texas Press, Austin.
Aries, E. (1976) 'Interaction patterns and themes of male, female and mixed groups', *Small Group Behaviour* 7 (1), pp. 7–18.
Brown, G. (1977) *Listening to Spoken English*, London: Longman.
Cheshire, J. (1982) *Variation in an English Dialect*, Cambridge: Cambridge University Press.
Coates, J. (1987) 'Epistemic modality and spoken discourse', *Transactions of the Philological Society*, pp. 110–131.
Coates, J. (1996) Women Talk. Oxford: Blackwell.
Edelsky, C. (1981) 'Who's got the floor?', *Language in Society* 10, pp. 383–421.
Ervin-Tripp, S. (1964) 'An analysis of the interaction of language, topic, and listener', *American Anthropologist* 66 (6; part 2), pp. 86–102.
Fishman, P.M. (1977) 'Interactional shitwork', *Heresies* 2, pp. 99–101.
—— (1980) 'Conversational insecurity', in H. Giles, W.P. Robinson and P. Smith (eds.), *Language: social psychological perspectives*, Oxford: Pergamon.
Gilligan, C. (1982) *In a Different Voice*, Cambridge, Mass: Harvard University Press.
Grice, H.P. (1975) 'Logic and conversation', in P. Cole and J.L. Morgan (eds), *Syntax and Semantics*, Vol. 3: *Speech Acts*, New York: Academic Press, pp. 41–58.
Gumperz, J. (1982a) *Discourse Strategies*, Cambridge: Cambridge University Press.

Gumperz, J. (ed.), (1982b) *Language and Social Identity*, Cambridge: Cambridge University Press.

Hall, C. (1985) 'Private persons versus public someones: class, gender and politics in England, 1780–1850', in C. Steedman, C. Urwin and V. Walkerdine (eds), *Language, Gender and Childhood*, London: Routledge & Kegan Paul, pp. 10–33.

Hirschman, L. (1974) 'Analysis of supportive and assertive behaviour in conversations', paper presented to the Linguistic Society of America, July 1974.

Holmes, J. (1984) 'Hedging your bets and sitting on the fence: some evidence for hedges as support structures', *Te Reo* 27, pp. 47–62.

Jenkins, L. and Kramer, C. (1978) 'Small group process: learning from women', *Women's Studies International Quarterly* I, pp. 67–84.

Jones, D. (1980) 'Gossip: notes on women's oral culture', in C. Kramarae (ed.), *The Voices and Words of Women and Men*, Oxford: Pergamon Press, pp. 193–8.

Kalcik, S. (1975) '". . . like Ann's gynecologist or the time I was almost raped". Personal narratives in women's rap groups', *Journal of American Folklore* 88, pp. 3–11.

Lakoff, R. (1973) 'The logic of politeness', Papers from the Ninth Regional Meeting of the Chicago Linguistics Society, pp. 292–305.

—— (1975) *Language and Woman's Place*, New York: Harper & Row.

Leech, G. (1983) *Principles of Pragmatics*, London: Longman.

Maltz, D.N. and Borker, R.A. (1982) 'A cultural approach to male–female miscommunication', in Gumperz (ed.).

Milroy, L. (1980) *Language and Social Networks*, Oxford: Basil Blackwell.

Perkins, M. (1983) *Modal Expressions in English*, London: Frances Pinter.

Sacks, H., Schegloff, E. and Jefferson, G. (1974) 'A simplest systematics for the organisation of turn-taking in conversation', *Language* 50, pp. 696–735.

Smith, P. (1985) *Language, the Sexes and Society*, Oxford: Basil Blackwell.

Strodtbeck, F. and Mann, R. (1956) 'Sex role differentiation in jury deliberations', *Sociometry* 19, pp. 3–11.

Tannen, D. (1982) 'Ethnic style in male-female conversation', in Gumperz (ed.).

—— (1984) *Conversational Style: Analysing Talk among Friends* New Jersey: Ablex, Norwood.

Thorne, B., Kramarae C. and Henley, N. (eds), (1983) *Language, Gender and Society*, Massachusetts: Newbury House, Rowley.

Urwin, C. (1985) 'Constructing motherhood: the persuasion of normal development', in C. Steedman, C. Urwin and V. Walkerdine (eds), *Language, Gender and Childhood*, London: Routledge & Kegan Paul.

Wells, G. (1979) 'Variation in child language', in V. Lee (ed.), *Language Development*, London: Croom Helm.

West, C. and Zimmerman, D. (1983) 'Small insults: a study of interruptions in cross-sex conversations between unacquainted persons', in Thorne, Kramarae and Henley (eds).

Zimmerman, D. and West, C. (1975) 'Sex roles, interruptions and silences in conversation', in Thorne and Henley (eds).

Appendix

Transcription Conventions
Extended square brackets mark overlap between utterances, e.g.:

A: he's going to the [funeral
B: [oh my god

An equals sign at the end of one speaker's utterance and at the start of the next utterance the absence of a discernable gap e.g.:

A: after all she's dead =
B: =mm

Pauses are indicated by (.) (short) or (–) (longer).
Double round parentheses indicate that there is doubt about the accuracy of the transcription:

A: she lived in Brisbane, ((they were at Brisbane))

Where material is inaudible or impossible to make out, it is represented as follows:

A: but sorry ((xxx))

Single round parentheses give clarificatory information, e.g.:

A: he's dead, isn't he (laughs).

Material in square brackets is phonetic, e.g.:

A: the [θi] the theory goes

<u>Underlining</u> indicates that words are uttered with added emphasis, e.g.:

A: then they'd <u>know</u> that you hadn't come.

A small cross indicates the end of a tone-group, e.g.:

A: I'll never get out +

The symbol (pp) precedes words where the speaker speaks very quietly, e.g.:

A: (pp) I don't know

6

The construction of gendered discourse in Chinese-German interactions

Susanne Günthner

Originally published in *Discourse and Society*, 3 (1992)

The social construction of gendered discourse

It is widely agreed that the gender of an individual is an important organizing principle in her/his everyday experience. There is, however, much debate on how gender is constructed socially.

Symbolic Interactionists consider gender is learned social behaviour, associated with a biological sex: gender 'involves the entire person in the process of becoming human. Being a man or a woman, moreover, is a social definition that is learned by individuals throughout their lives. Women and men are, therefore, social products' (Deegan, 1987: 4).

As studies in anthropology demonstrate, there are culturally specific social roles and modes of behaviour associated with a particular gender. In all cultures women and men have different social roles and certain stereotypical characteristics are associated with the 'female' and 'male' nature. There are, however – as Margaret Mead already showed – cultural-specific ways of attributing certain characteristics to a particular gender.

> If those temperamental attitudes which we have traditionally regarded as feminine – such as passivity, responsiveness, and a willingness to cherish children – can so easily be set up as the masculine pattern in one tribe, and, in another, be outlawed for the majority of women as for the majority of men, we no longer have any basis for regarding aspects of such behavior as sex linked (Mead, 1935: 279–80)

For a long period social sciences have dealt with social factors as 'objective data', which are supposedly 'given' in a society. Interpretative approaches, however, have started to ask HOW these social facts are produced by the actions of members in a society. Human interaction represents one of the central means to construct social reality, to transmit cultural structures of relevance and to create and perpetuate social identities. The means through which social identities are primarily constructed, renewed and modified are very often communicative (Luckmann, 1972).

153

The construction and confirmation of gender identity happens mainly in human interactions (Deegan, 1987: 3): the ethnomethodologist Garfinkel (1967) describes how Agnes, a person born as a male, acquired the identity of a woman. According to Garfinkel, this transformation took place in interactions: Agnes had to present herself as female in order to be treated by the others as a woman.

Interaction and communication are central means to the constitution of gendered selves. However, gender is not our only social identity. It usually interacts with others such as ethnicity, class, social role, etc. Our analysis will demonstrate that besides gender, the cultural identity (Chinese versus German) and the social role (counsellor versus student; native speaker versus learner) influences the discourse strategies of the speakers: in a lot of ways the Chinese students use communicative strageties which are associated with 'women's style' (Lakoff, 1975; Maltz and Borker, 1982; Tannen, 1990), such as interactive cooperation, non-confrontative devices, search for interactive harmony, readiness for agreement and assent and face-saving-strategies. The German speakers, on the other hand, are highly confrontative, attack their partners openly and directly, stick to their positions and employ many face-threatening acts.

Instead of postulating a stable and constant difference of styles between women and men and thereby assuming that gender is always the dominant factor in interaction, we have to look at the complex web of factors that are related in every interactive encounter. Gender is not an 'unproblematic category' (Thorne, 1986a).

As Thorne (1986b: 168) points out:

> The sex difference approach tends to abstract gender from its social context, to assume that males and females are qualitatively and permanently different . . . .. These assumptions mask the possibility that gender arrangements and patterns of similarity and difference may vary by situation, race, social class, region, or subculture.

In our society we have no kind of stable linguistic or stylistic elements that always and only indicate gender. Rather we are dealing with a variable phenomenon which is context-sensitive. The same features that in one situation may differentiate women and men may in other situations serve to differentiate lower and higher status, formality–informality, etc. As Kramarae (1981) demonstrated, gender stereotypes of speech are much stronger than actual speech differences. There are no differences in men's and women's speech that exhibit coherence across different situations, classes and subcultures. Rather, we need a concept of gendered discourse patterns that accounts for the contextual variation and the relation of linguistic, communicative strategies and social situation of the women and men interacting.

Gender-linked issues in Chinese

As we are dealing with Chinese speakers, I would like to add a few words concerning gender-linked differences in Chinese. The Chinese language does not reveal any sex-exclusive phenomena, that is, no grammatical (phonological, morphological, lexical) differences between men's and women's speech. So far, there has been no research on gender-specific ways of speaking in China. Chen and Chen (1981) refer in a short note to gender-linked ways of pronouncing certain consonants in the Beijing area. Women apparently tend to show a 'premovement, advancing the tongue forward to the front of the mouth' when they pronounce the consonants: /j/ /q/ and /x/. This pronunciation thus signals 'femininity', 'softness' and 'charm'.

Interviewing Chinese linguists about gender differences in ways of speaking, I received the following answers:

> One can perhaps say that women swear and curse less than men. Women who swear or curse are considered to be 'dirty women'. Another difference is, that women are supposed to be quiet when men speak. They are expected to sit quietly and just listen. Silence is considered to be a good female quality. It is a woman's job to listen to men. If she does not listen but speaks up, her speaking is often ignored. The men react as if she had never said a word. Generally, women are more careful of what they say and are more polite when they speak. They cannot give direct orders to men, such as 'close the door'. They will have to express this in a very polite way, otherwise they appear to be dominant. A 'dominant woman' has a very negative image in China.

> There are norms in China on how a woman should talk. For example, women should not swear or laugh loudly. We have a proverb that says: 'xiao bu luzhi, zou bu lujiao . . .', this means when you laugh, do not show your teeth, when you walk, do not show your feet . . .. Generally, a woman is supposed to be shy and very humble when she talks. She should be 'wenrou', that is, the ideal Chinese woman should be shy, timid and reserved. There is no German equivalent to wenrou.

These statements present certain impressions and expectations of women's style. One cannot say whether, generally speaking, Chinese women acutally do swear less, and are more reserved and modest. Research on naturally occurring interactions between Chinese women and men is needed in order to answer these questions.

The context of the data

Before looking at the data, let us look at some information about the ethnographic background of the situation in which I collected the material.

During the last 10 years – because of opening-up policies in China – the number of Chinese students and scholars sent to West German universities for further studies has steadily increased. Most of these scholars (at least among those who receive a scholarship from the German or Chinese government) take part in a 9-month intensive German course before leaving China. The chance of getting a scholarship to study in the West is limited and thus carries much prestige. During my own stay in China (1983–8), where I taught German at different Chinese universities, 90 percent of my students – all Chinese scientists who had received a grant to study in

Germany – were men. A Chinese engineer, who was one of the few women chosen for further studies in Germany, explained the situation as follows:

> Well, we do have equal rights for women and men in China. However, a woman only very rarely gets the chance to study abroad. Most of the scholarships for studying in the West are given to male candidates. One assumes that such an investment is more appropriate for men. 'Women can't leave their families' or 'women aren't as strong and creative', that is what one hears.

In class, I always noticed that the men mostly did the talking. The few women (usually two women per class) mainly sat in the corner and only spoke when directly addressed. Their voices were usually so soft that I could barely understand them. Female students seldom contributed to the discussions – they stayed in the background – hardly visible or audible. This kind of behaviour was explained as part of the 'restraint expected of Chinese women':

> In China one is not supposed to stick out of the group. Neither by showing that one knows more than the others – nor by showing that one knows less. A woman who attracts attention, because she speaks loudly, talks a lot or laughs loudly, is considered to have a bad character.

Traditional Confucianistic ideas of appropriate behaviour for women are still very much alive in modern China (Günthner, 1990a) – and are considered to be part of the many 'birth-marks of the feudalistic past' which have to be cut out, as the President of the All-China-Women's Association in Shanghai told me.

The data

The data of this study consists of four spontaneous interactions between Chinese students (two women and two men) and two German native speakers (both women) who work as 'counsellors' at Chinese universities (see Table 6.1). The German participants are Frau Klein and Frau Müller. The Chinese students are the two women Lu and Bu and the two Chinese men Ma and Zheng.[1] The data were collected at different universities in the People's Republic of China.

I had asked the four Chinese participants if I might tape their appoint-

Table 6.1 Interactions between Chinese students and German 'counsellors'

Chinese student	German counsellor	Length of talk (mins)
Female–female interactions:		
Ms Lu	Frau Müller	30
Ms Bu	Frau Klein	12
Male–female interactions:		
Mr Ma	Frau Klein	25
Mr Zheng	Frau Müller	18

ments with Frau Müller and Frau Klein. The Chinese participants were scientists who, at the time of the recording, were finishing a 9-months' intensive German course and getting prepared for their studies at German universities. They had each acquired a BSc. and all of them had been working as scientists at different Chinese universities. However, their official status was that of 'students' as long as they were taking the German class. The interactions took place in the offices of the two German women, who worked at different Chinese universities as 'counsellors', helping the Chinese 'students' to find a German university, helping them contact a German professor who would accept them as visiting scholars and helping them organize some of the bureaucratic steps necessary to study in Germany. Except during class, the Chinese students have little chance to practise their German or get in contact with German ways of interacting. Once in a while they consult the German counsellors in order to get more details about their possibilities of finding the appropriate university and faculty in Germany. Often they approach the counsellors with rather unrealistic views of their future stay in Germany – such as expecting to find a job at a German university or a professor who will sponsor them privately. That is why there are often conflicts during these office hours: on the one hand there are high expectations, hopes and demands of the Chinese students, on the other hand there is the German counsellor who has to tell them that she cannot help very much and who has to give these Chinese students a more realistic perspective of the problems they may face in Germany.

The consulting hours can be considered to be communicative situations within the institutional frame of the university: they offer students and counsellors a locally and timely fixed possibility to talk (in German). Further, due to the institutional context, a certain division of social roles is expected in these situations: counsellor versus student. Besides the institutional roles, these interactions reveal another asymmetry which is related to the media of communication: the counsellors are native speakers of German and thus have a much higher competence in the language used during the interaction. The students are learners of German and show certain deficiencies in their linguistic competence.

In all four interactions, the Chinese make certain requests which the Germans cannot accept or fulfil. Verbal conflict and argumentative sequences arise. A closer look at these argumentative sequences reveals striking differences in the argumentative styles of the German and Chinese speakers. Frau Müller and Frau Klein show a very offensive and confrontative discourse pattern: disagreement is produced very openly, not just attacking the other's position but also the other as a person. The Chinese way of arguing is much more indirect and face-saving. However, there are still differences in the discourse patterns between the Chinese women (Lu and Bu) and the Chinese men (Ma and Zheng).

We first look at the strategies used to organize dissent and thereby demonstrate the interactive methods applied by the participants to manage conflict and negotiate interpersonal alignments. In a second step we analyse another discourse phenomenon, which shows certain gender differences: the way of contextualizing asymmetries of knowledge, i.e. the way of orienting towards native versus non-native language abilities.

The analysis of the data

The organization of dissent
In human interaction the display of deference is an important organizational aspect. Ways of accomplishing this include the avoidance of 'dangerous' topics and the minimization of disagreement. Studies in conversation analysis argue that in everyday interactions disagreement is a dispreferred move. In her work on agreement and disagreement Pomerantz (1975) differentiates between a preferred-action-turn shape, which maximizes the salience of the preferred action, and a dispreferred-action-turn shape, which minimizes the action.

Our interactions reveal apparent differences in dealing with disagreement between the Chinese and German participants. While the Germans contextualize their dissent very directly, attack their opponents and challenge them openly, the Chinese speakers tend to use many more indirect and face-saving, 'off record' (Brown and Levinson, 1978), ways of disagreeing. They more readily show assent and offer compromises.

These findings support other research on differences in argumentative style between Western and Asian speakers (Naotsuka et al., 1981; Günthner, 1991b). In a previous study on intercultural differences in argumentation between Chinese and Germans, I demonstrated the more indirect strategies Chinese speakers use compared to the more antagonistic way of arguing among the Germans. In intercultural situations these different styles can lead to misunderstandings and frustrations: whereas for Germans a confrontative argumentation can be a sign of 'good and profound talk', where one shows that one has an opinion and is ready to defend it, Chinese etiquette demands that confrontation be avoided: it is a sign of poor education and a lack of 'limao' ('knowledge of etiquette'). Instead of facing an open confrontation, very often a 'third' person ('tiaojie ren'), is employed to act as an 'intermediary' between the opposing parties and tries to resolve the conflict. Besides these intercultural differences, that are apparent in our four interactions, the Chinese women show other ways of handling argumentation than the men do.

Argumentative sequences between German counsellors and Chinese female students
Lu intends to persuade Frau Müller that more women should be sent to Germany for further education. After a general discussion on the situation of women in China and the dual workload resting on professional women, Lu introduces the position that women should have the chance to work part-time (see pp. 158–9). In lines 6–8 M utters a very direct and personally formulated oppositional move, 'don't always say the women should. – perhaps, the men TOO', with the particle 'ne.' that reinforces what she has just said. What is opposed is not just a position but also the speaker responsible for stating such a position. The imperative form is directly addressed to Lu, telling her 'what to say'. Thus not just the trouble source in the prior talk is being called into question but also the status of the person who produced the talk (Goodwin and Goodwin, 1987: 209). Lu's giggling as a reaction to the confrontation is an often used strategy by the Chinese participants for contextualizing face-threatening situations

LU10–11

```
 1Lu:   pu'hh so. i: ich glaube wenn:: : wenn
 2      die Frau in China können zum Beispiel
 3      HALBTAGS arbeiten, dann ist BESSER
 4      hahahahhhhhaha ja/sie oder/
 5M:                    /oder/auch die MÄNNER
 6M:    /nur halbtags arbeiten. sagen Sie doch nicht immer/
 7Lu:   /hahahhhhhhhhhhhhhhhhhhhhhhhhhhhhhhihihihi/
 8M:    /die Frauen sollen. – vielleicht. die Männer genAUSO ne.
 9Lu:   /hahhhahhhhhhhhhhhhhhaahahahahahhhahh/
10Lu:   /ja'h wenn/ich glAUBE WENN en eh ich glaube
11M:    /hihihihihi/
12Lu:   wer eh wer wer ist ehm
13      (0.8)
14      wer ist ehm (1.0) ehm TÄTIG? ehm tätiger? wer
15      ist tätiger können mehr arbeiten, weil wenn
16      die/eh wenn/
17M:                /was /meinen Sie mit TÄTIGER?
18      (0.2) (das) versteh ich/nicht/
19Lu:                          /ja ich/glaube wenn
20      wenn Ma eh wenn die Frau eh GUT arbeiten
21      kann dann ka eh dann kann di Frauen arbeiten
22      und die Männer zu Haus arbei((kichern))ten hahahaha
23      wenn wenn wenn die Mann ist e TÄTIGER als die Frau', ja'
24      können die ((hi)) Frau((hi))en hhhhahahaha eh zu
25      Hause arbeiten oder die die Männer me mehr
26      konzentrieren/auf/ihr eh seine Arbeit. ja.
27M:                 /mhm/
28M:    ja'h. ja. nein, eh ich bin schon der Meinung,
29      daß – ehm (0.5) HAUSHALT HAUSHALT und KinDER –
30      eh:: : ein:: – GEMEINSAM eh von Mann und Frau
31Lu:   ja.
32M:    eh:: : ' erledigt werden sollte (0.3)
33      eh: ' weil (1.2) das ist eine Arbeit, – dié – SOVIEL
34      Arbeit ist es nicht ne?
35Lu:   ja. wenn/wenn die/
36M:           /und ich/bin auch der Meinung, dadrüber
37      braucht man gar nicht groß zu diskutieren. es –
38      MUß gemacht werden, die Wäsche MUß gewaschen
39      werden, gekocht muß werden und und und, – sonst
40      vehunGERT man /und hat nur schmutzige SACHEN zum/
41Lu:                 /hahahahhhhhhhhhhhhhhahhhhahahahh/
42M:    /anziehen/
43Lu:   /hhihihihi/
44Lu:   ja.
45M:    und das ist doch (au) Aufgabe von beiden!
46      (0.3)
47Lu:   /jajaja/
48M:    /genauso/von den MÄNNERN wie von/den/
49Lu:                                    /mhm/
50M:    FRAUEN ne=
51Lu:   =a aber diese' – diese Begriff ist noch nicht
52      au eh aufgeBAUT in China ja. / – ma/man
53M:                                 /hier ist es/
54Lu:   man ver eh man verlernt viel vond ie Frauen
55M:    mhm
56Lu:   *ja verlernt*
57M:    ehm:: : das ist i: im Westen auch nicht viel anders
58Lu:   /auch nicht viel anderes/
59M:    /Frau Lu a/lso da gibt es, DA ist der
60      Unterschied nicht so GROß/zwischen China/
61Lu:                            /jajaja jaja/
62M:    und – den – westlichen Làndern ne?
63Lu:   mhm.
```

LU 10–11

```
 1Lu:   pu'hh so. I: I believe if:: : if
 2      the woman in China can for example
 3      work PART TIME, then is BETTER
 4      hahahahhhhhaha yes she or/
 5M:                            /or/also the MEN
 6      /could only work part time don't always say/
 7Lu:   /hahahhhhhhhhhhhhhhhhhhhhhhhhhihihihi/
 8M:    /the women should. – perhaps. the men TOO (part.)/
 9Lu:   /hahhhahhhhhhhhhhhhaahahahahahhhahh/
10Lu:   /yes'h if/I THINK IF eh eh I believe
11M:    /hihihi/
12Lu:   who eh who who ever is ehm
13      (0.8)
14      who is ehm (1.0) ehm ACTIV? ehm more active? who
15      is more active can work more, because if
16      the /eh ih/
17M:        /what/do you mean by MORE ACTIVE?
18      (0.2) I don't under/stand/
19Lu:                    yes I/ believe if
20      if man eh if the woman eh works WELL
21      can then ca' eh then the women can work
22      and the men work at home hihi hahahaha
23      if if if the man is e MORE ACTIVE than the woman', yes'
24      the ((hi)) wo((hi))men can hhhahahahahaha eh
25      work at home or the the men mo' more
26      concentrate /on/ their eh his work. yes.
27M:               /mhm/
28M:    ja'h. ja. no, eh actually I have the opinion
29      that – ehm (0.5) the HOUSEHOLD HOUSEHOLD and chiLDREN –
30      eh:: : a:: – should be organized TOGETHER
31Lu:   ja.
32      eh:: : ' by the husband and wife
33      eh: ' because (1.2) this is a kind of work, – which' –
34      it isn't SO MUCH work, isn't it?
35Lu:   yes. if /if the/
36M:            and I/ also think, there
37      is nothing to discuss. it –
38      HAS to be done, the laundry HAS to be done,
39      the meals have to be cooked and and and, – otherwise
40      one STARVES and/one only has dirty CLOTHES to/
41Lu:                      /hahahahhhhhhhhhhhhhahhahahahahh/
42M:    /wear/
43Lu:   /hhihihihi/
44Lu:   ja.
45M:    and this is the job of both!
46      (0.3)
47Lu:   /jajaja/
48M:    /as well/ for the MEN as for /the/
49Lu:                                /mhm/
50      WOMEN isn't it=
51Lu:   =b but this – this concept is not yet
52      es eh estabLISHED in China ja. /one/ one
53M:                                  /here it's/
54Lu:   one de eh one demands a lot from the women
55M:    mhm
56Lu:   *yes demands*
57M:    ehm:: : this is not very different in the west
58Lu:   /not very different/
59M:    /Frau Lu we/ll there is, THERE is
60      not such a BIG difference /between China/
61Lu:                            /jajaja jaja/
62      and – the – western world is there?
63Lu:   mhm.
```

(Günthner, 1990b). Lu offers a correction of her statement 'who is more active can work more' (15). After the clarification of what 'active' means, M produces another disagreement (28): the mixture of agreement- and disagreement-signalling pre-elements (ja'h. ja. no) reflects the double direction of her utterance: on the one side she signals her understanding (ja'h. ja.), on the other side of the preface 'no' already announces the following oppositional move: 'I have the opinion that – ehm (0.5) the HOUSEHOLD HOUSEHOLD and chiLDREN eh:: : a:: – should be organized TOGETHER'. Lu's attempt to regain the floor (35) is interrupted by M's continuation of her former turn 'and I also think'. Lu does not fight for the floor but gives way to M's interruption after a short period of overlap (35). M uses the metalinguistic formula 'there is nothing to discuss' (37) as a verbal device to ward off further counter-arguments. Finally Lu offers another compromise by referring to the cultural background 'b but this' – this concept is not yet es eh estabLISHED in China ja. (51–2). Instead of accepting this statement as a possible preface to a closing up of the argumentation, M continues with an expansion of the argumentative sequence by producing another disagreement: 'ehm:: : this is not very different in the west . . .' (57ff.) and thus negates the specific Chinese situation. Lu's recipient reactions (59; 62) indicate her willingness to accept the other person's position instead of defending her own one and expanding the argumentative frame. We can recognize the negotiation of assent in this segment: Lu's first demand for part-time work for women changes – after M disagrees – into a compromise offer: the more active partner should work full-time. Finally she agrees that looking after the house is the job of both partners. And finally she decides not to defend her position concerning the special case of China.

With her consent-oriented way and her readiness to agree with the other's position and not to further the argumentation, Lu gives way to a closing down of confrontative activities. Vuchinich (1990: 121) describes the acceptance of the other's opinions as a 'submission terminal exchange': the assenter accepts a subordinate position regarding the dispute. Thus an interactive asymmetry gets established: by correcting one's statements, offering compromises and giving up her own position, Lu strengthens M's status. Interactive hierarchies and asymmetries are communicative products created and reconfirmed locally by the participants.

In the next segment of the same talk Lu and M are discussing education in China and the problem of 'the spoilt single children'. M states that children have to learn how to deal with others – they have to learn to be social. Lu continues:

LU 13

```
1Lu:    sie habeń – LEER ihr'h – /eh/sein hihi
2M:                              /ja/
3Lu:    hhhihih /ihre/KOPF is leer eh sieht leer hihi
4M:                 /ja/
5M:     ((laut)) /EH NEIN eh der KOPF ist NICHT leer/
6Lu:             /hihihihihihihihihihihihihihihihihihihihihihi/
```

7M:	Kinder sind ja nicht dumm n/e? und/
8Lu:	/eh ja/
9M:	Kinder wissen genau,

LU 13

1Lu:	*they have' – EMPTY their'h – /eh/his hihi*
2M:	*/ja/*
3Lu:	*hhhihih /their/HEAD is empty eh looks empty hihi*
4M:	*/ja/*
5M:	*((loud)) /EH NO eh the HEAD is NOT empty/*
6Lu:	*/hihihihihihihihihihihihihihihihihihihihi/*
7M:	*children are not stupid /and/*
8Lu:	*/eh ja/*
9M	*children know exactly*

M's oppositional move is built to highlight the elements of dissent. Instead of mitigating the disagreement, M organizes her utterance in an 'opposition-format'. By 'opposition-format'[2], I am referring to the organization of dissent, where a number of phenomena are used to heighten the dissent:

1. the utterance containing the disagreement repeats parts of the prior utterance and either negates it or substitutes central elements through contradictory devices:
2. the corrected item is prosodically marked by a 'contrastive stress' (Goodwin and Goodwin, 1987: 211).

In our transcript LU13, M first introduces the disagreement-signalling preface 'EH NO' (5) and increases the volume to draw special attention to the utterance, before she partially repeats the prior utterance and syntactically and prosodically focuses on the correction:

| 3LU: | their **HEAD is empty** eh looks **empty** |
| 5M: | ((loud)) EH NO eh the **HEAD is NOT empty** |

Thus M uses a variety of devices to highlight and maximize the dissent: the increase of volume already contextualizes 'otherness' – in Jacobson's sense. The direction of the change is revealed by the preface-element 'NO'. The syntactic and lexical shape of the prior utterance is reproduced with the corrected element (NOT) being prosodically marked. Instead of mitigating the disagreement by embedding it in a dispreferred-action-turn shape and leaving the speaker the opportunity of self-repair, the disagreement is produced very directly, highlighting the polarity between the utterance at hand and the prior one. Both M's and Lu's way of arguing turn out to be very different: whereas M uses direct forms to demonstrate dissent, even focussing on the opposition, Lu signals her disagreement only indirectly, often refrains from defending her positions, offers compromises and gives in to M's position.

A similar clash of styles can be found in the interaction between Bu and Frau Klein. Once an argumentative frame is established the German speaker signals her disagreement very directly, employing opposition-formats to focus on the polarity, and tries to dominate the floor by using competitive interruptions.[3]

BU3

5Bu:	aber eh man eh es gibt die Möglich
6	zu bekommen Arbeits eh'
7	genehmigung und während des Studierens
8	kann er eh man' dann arbeiten. am Abend undsoweiter
9K:	nein es gibt sicherlich KEINE solche Möglichkeit
10	einer ARBEITSGENEHMIGUNG.
11	als AUSLÄNDERIN dürfen sie NICHT arbeiten
12Bu:	*ah so ist das.*

BU3

5Bu:	*but eh one es there is the possible*
6	*to get work eh'*
7	*permission and while studying*
8	*one can eh one' then work. in the evenings and so forth*
9K:	*no there is definitely NO such possibility*
10	*of a WORK PERMIT*
11	*as a FOREIGNER you are NOT allowed to work*
12Bu:	*ah it's like that.*

In this segment the opposition turn also starts out with a preface announcing right at the beginning the up-coming disagreement (9): 'no'. The partial repeat plus the negation of the prior utterance are used to mark the opposition:

5BU:	**there is the possible** to get **work eh'-permission**
9K:	**no there is** definitely **NO** such **possibility** of a **WORK PERMIT**

Bu offers an assent 'ah it's like that' (12) and thereby signals her willingness to close the argumentative frame.

A similar opposition-format can be seen in the following segment:

BU 5

16Bu:	vielleicht eh' ja vielleicht
17	für uns Schinesen eh'
18	es ist /leichter/
19K:	/NEIN es /ist sicher NICHT leichter
20	es ist absolut NICHT LEIGHT
21	Sie werden h' sehen, die Zimmersituation
22	ist ein enormes und SEHR ERNST
23	zu nehmendes Problem in der Bundesrepublik.
24Bu:	ein eh'(. . .) zu nehmende Problem. ja.

BU 5

16Bu:	*perhaps eh' ja perhaps*
17	*for us Chinese eh'*

```
18        it is /easier/
19K:          /NO it /is definitely NOT easier
20        it is absolutely NOT EASY
21        you will h' see, the problem of finding a place to stay
22        is very enormous and has to be taken VERY SERIOUSLY
23        in the Federal Republic.
24Bu:     a eh'( . . . ) to taken problem. ja.
```

By opposition-formats speakers design their turn to fit in with not only the type of action produced by the last speaker, but also with the wording and syntactic structures she or he used (Goodwin and Goodwin, 1987: 216). The transcript segment shows the following structure:

```
18Bu:     it is easier
19K:      NO it is definitely NOT easier
20        it is absolutely NOT EASY
```

In both interactions (with Lu and Bu) the German speakers are more willing to expand the argumentative frame. However, since the Chinese women tend to offer assents and refrain from giving counter-arguments or further attacking the Germans' positions, the argumentative frame finally gets transformed in a more general discussion, where the Germans give 'advice' to the Chinese and the participant alignment changes from a confrontative to an instructive one.

Argumentative sequences between German counsellors and Chinese male students
Similarly to the preceding interactions, the Germans Frau Klein and Frau Müller use many more confrontative strategies in the interactions with Ma and Zheng, too. Instead of showing the traditionally gender-linked style elements such as 'affiliation, empathy, seeking for agreement', etc. (Sheldon, 1990: 11) and instead of masking 'their exercise of power during conflicts with the use of polite language' (Camras, 1984: 263), K and M display aggravated forms of confrontation, assert their positions, interrupt more often and build up interactive hierarchies.

However, Ma and Zheng – unlike Bu and Lu – keep on defending their positions and bringing up new arguments.

MA 3–4

```
4K:       und wenn Ihre Regierung es nicht
5         erlaubt, daß Sie länger als ein Jahr bleiben,
6         dann können Sie AUCH NICHT promovieren, Herr Ma.
7Ma:      ehm:
8         (1.0)
9         das ist n nicht sicher ( . . . . . . )
10K:      das ist GANZ sicher.
11Ma:     ganz sicher?
12K:      ja.
13Ma:     gibt es – viele' ehm solche Beispiel. Beispele
14        (0.3) die:: ' die Leute ehm (0.5) SOLL? eh
15        die Leute SOLLEN nach ein Jahr eh – zurückkommen,
```

```
•  16        aber die Tatsache' ist, sie eh – bleiben dort
   17        ehm (0.4) länger als Jahr sogar ehm – drei
   18        bis vier Jahre
   . . .
   . . .
 57Ma:       ja. eh: a ABER NACH EINE JAHR – ehm
   58        un eh ent entscheidet, eh – wie lange ehm
   59        wi:: dort bleiben können, i:: ist unsere ( . . . . . . . . tät)
   60        nicht in bei eh nicht bei Peking
 61K:        sind Sie da sicher?
 62Ma:       ja. un wenn unsere eh Universität da: MIT
   63        einverstanden ist /da/
 64K:             /dann/dürfen Sie länger
   65        bleiben.
 66Ma:       ja. (0.3) sicher.
   67        (0.6)
 68K:        glauben Sie des?
 69Ma:       ehm' ja.
 70K:        ich glaube es NICHT.
 71Ma:       eh:: m ((räuspert)) gibt es VIELE solche
   72        eh Sache.
 73K:        aber eh das gab es FRÜ:: HER, das gab es bis
```

MA 3–4

```
  4K:        and if your government doesn't
  5          give you permission to stay for more than one year
  6          then you WILL NOT be able to go for a Ph.D., Mr. Ma.
 7Ma:        ehm:
  8          (1.0)
  9          this is n not sure ( . . . . . . . . . )
 10K:        this is ABSOLUTELY sure.
 11Ma:       absolutely sure?
 12K:        ja.
 13Ma:       there are – lots of ehm such example. examples
  14         (0.3) the:: ' the people ehm (0.5) SHOULD? eh
  15         the people SHOULD come back after one year
  16         but the reality' is, they eh – stay there
  17         ehm (0.4) longer than year even ehm – three
  18         to four years
  . . .
  . . .
 57Ma:       ja. eh: a BUT AFTER ONE YEAR – ehm
  58         an eh de decide, eh – how long ehm
  59         we:: can stay there, i:: : is our ( . . . . . . . . ty)
  60         not in at eh not at Peking
 61K:        are you sure?
 62Ma:       ja. and if our eh university
  63         agrees to THAT /then/
 64K:             /then/ you may stay longer
  65         longer.
 66Ma:       ja. (0.3) sure.
  67         (0.6)
 68K:        do you believe that?
```

```
69Ma:    ehm' ja.
70K:     I do NOT believe that.
71Ma:    eh:: m ((clears his throat)) there are MANY such
72       eh thing.
73K:     but eh this happened BE:: : FORE, this happened until
```

Ma is using much more mitigated ways of disagreeing: he introduces counter-examples without formally marking the dissent. In line 7–9 Ma introduces his disagreement with hesitation particles and pauses which already contextualize[4] the following disagreement and thus give his recipient the possibility to engage in repairing. He thus produces his moves of opposition in dispreferred-action-turn shape (Pomerantz, 1975). K answers by producing an aggravated opposition-format and thus negating the prior utterance (10). The lexical tying to the prior utterance and the substitution of the negation word 'not' by 'ABSOLUTELY' even maximize the dissent:

```
9Ma:     this is n not sure( . . . )
10K:     this is ABSOLUTELY sure.
```

This kind of substitution, the 'replacement of one item in a sentence by another having a similar structural function' (Halliday and Hasan, 1976: 245), does not delay the alignment K is taking up with respect to the prior utterance, but rather it emphasizes opposition (Goodwin and Goodwin, 1987: 207).

Ma's reaction 'very sure?' shows that he does not intend to give in right away, but challenges K's utterance instead, thereby continuing the argumentative frame. In line 13ff. he provides further argument for his assertion and provides an example. In line 64–5 K produces another oppositional move, an 'opposition duet', by latching her utterance to the prior one and thus producing a syntactic and lexical continuation of the preceding utterance part:

```
62Ma:    ja. and if our eh university
63       agrees to that /then/
64K:                    /then/ you may stay longer
65       longer.
```

By producing an opposition duet, the second speaker not only attempts to take the floor, but also communicates her understanding of the prior turn and demonstrates that she has the knowledge to finish the utterance. Falk (1979: 67) talks of the 'mind-reference' that holds for duets: the co-speaker is assuming she is expressing what the other person has in mind. In the case of opposition duets, however, the continuation is used strategically in order to build up an opposition:

```
68K:     do you believe that?
69Ma:        ehm' ja.
70K:     I do NOT believe that.
```

Without offering any explanation K produces an aggravated polarity (by lexical and syntactic parallelism and prosodically focusing on the difference 'NOT') and builds up dichotomies between the 'I' and the 'you'. Ma still does not give in, but expands the argumentation by providing counter-examples (71ff.)

As the exemplary analysis demonstrated, Ma expands the argumentation, provides counter-arguments instead of offering assent. All through this interaction the argumentative frame stays activated.

In the interaction between Zheng and Frau Müller, we find very similar patterns to the ones in MA. M directly challenges Zheng's assertion by stating that it is 'not true' (15):

ZHENG 2

10Zheng:	und so weiß nicht – ehm:: und einige –
11	Universität hat (uns) verlangt, däs wir
12	sollten diese Deutschprüfung ablegen, sonst
13	werden wir nicht die eh immatrikuliert eh
14	an der Universität immatrikuliert
15M:	DA: S ist aber nicht wahr ne.

ZHENG 2

10Zheng:	*and so don't know – ehm:: and some –*
11	*university has (us) insisted, that we*
12	*should take this German exam, otherwise*
13	*we won't get eh admitted eh*
14	*to the university admitted*
15M:	*THA: T is not true, ((part.))*

However, Zheng defends himself by providing arguments for his position:

22M:	aber da Sie NUR als GASTHÖRER
23Zheng:	ja
24M:	in die Bundesrepublik gehen – ver-langen
25	die Universitäten auch diese Prüfung nicht.
26Zheng:	hm. TROTZDEM finde ich, eh finde ich,
27	daß unsere Deutsch sind nicht genug

22M:	*but since you are ONLY as a VISITING SCHOLAR*
23Zheng:	*ja*
24M:	*going to the Federal Republic – the universities*
25	*don't demand this exam.*
26Zheng:	*hm. HOWEVER I find, eh I find,*
27	*that our German is not enough*

Let's have a look at another segment of this interaction:

12Zheng:	aber eh ich glaube, wenn wir Gelegenheit,
13	werden wir einmal eh diese Prüfung eh
14	pro pro probieren. diese eh /diese Prüfung kann uns/

```
15M:                                    /wissen Sie wissen Sie/
16M:         diese Prüfung ist keine Prüfung, die man proBIERT – ne?
17          /diese/ diese Prüfung ist KEIN SPAß
18Zheng:    /j'eh/
19Zheng:    hahaha/ha/
20M:                   /ne?/ diese Prüfung ist – KNOCHENARBEIT
21Zheng:    ((kichert)) hahahh aber wir können einmal
22          versuchen eh ob eh ob, daß wir diese (kein eh)
23          diese Prüfung ablegen oder nicht. eh damit kö
24          kann ich weiß, meine Deutsche eh wie gut meine
25          Deutsche ist.
```

```
12Zheng:    but eh I believe, if we have opportunity,
13          we will eh tr' tr' try eh
14          this exam, this eh /this exam can/
15M:                          /you know you know/
16M:        this exam is not an exam that one TRIES – ((part.))
17          /this/ this this exam is NOT a joke
18Zheng:    /j'eh/
19Zheng:    hahaha/ha/
20M:               /ne?/ this exam is – TOUGH WORK
21Zheng:    ((giggles)) hahahh but we could
22          try eh if eh if, that we ( . . . eh)
23          make this exam or not. eh then
24          I can know, my German eh how good is
25          my German.
```

M demonstrates an orientation towards displaying opposition with the previous utterance:

```
12Zheng:    but eh I believe, if we have opportunity,
13          we will eh tr' tr' try eh
14          this exam. this eh /this exam can/
15M:                          /you know you know/
16M:        this exam is not an exam that one TRIES – ((part.))
17          /this/ this exam is NOT a joke
```

Although the German and Chinese speakers in my data display very different ways of arguing which might be connected partly to their different cultural background and partly to differences in status positions, we still find different ways among the Chinese women and men of dealing with the confrontative frames. Whereas Lu and Bu hardly contradict their German partners, but give up their own positions instead and offer assent, Ma and Zheng keep on fighting back. The interaction with Ma remains argumentative all the way through. In the talk with Zheng the argumentative sequences are shortly interrupted by other communicative processes or genres such as giving information, providing a narrative and making a joke.

The discourse patterns of the two German women do not confirm the general stereotypes about women's style as being more cooperative, consent-oriented, polite and aiming at conversational cooperation. The social position (counsellor and native speaker) and the cultural background could contribute to the fact that these two German women use discourse patterns that are traditionally attributed to the male and 'powerful' (O'Barr and Atkins, 1980) practices. These findings demonstrate that women's speech cannot be limited to a restricted repertoire of stereotypically classified style-components, but has to be analysed in context, in order to find out what verbal strategies women use to achieve certain communicative goals. Our observation supports the thesis of O'Barr and Atkins (1980) that the status and power position influences the discourse patterns and that women in powerful positions might also tend to use the 'powerful' language in order to reconfirm their higher status. This hypothesis would contradict the findings of West (1984), who argues that the gender of a person is more determining for their interactive behaviour than the status position. Further research on discourse patterns employed by women in high-status positions would be necessary for this discussion.

The interactive construction of social roles: experts versus learners
In our interactions German native speakers are communicating with Chinese learners of German, and consequently we find asymmetrically distributed linguistic competences. How do these specific asymmetries become interactively relevant?

It is not only within the institutional setting of language classes that participants of an interaction orient themselves to linguistic deficiencies. In everyday interactions between natives and non-natives moments of 'instruction' can appear. Situationally selected 'teachers' will provide knowledge about the medium of interaction.[5] Linguistic deficits and asymmetrically distributed knowledge in a language can thus be activated locally. Whenever such a teaching sequence is in progress, the former activity is temporarily replaced by a 'hierarchical' side sequence (Jefferson, 1972); side sequences can be seen as subsidiary sequences for some ongoing sequence. After finishing the side sequence the former activity is resumed again (Jefferson, 1972: 315). In the side sequences at hand the participant framework changes into the 'teacher' or 'master of the code' and the 'student' or 'learner of the code'.

Self-initiated instruction sequences
Instruction sequences can be initiated by the participants who lack certain knowledge (here: who have certain problems expressing themselves in German) and show their wish to acquire it. In this case the non-natives orient themselves to the asymmetrically distributed linguistic knowledge and thereby construct a temporarily hierarchical footing[6] between the experts on the one side and the learners on the other.

These initiations by the non-natives can be explicitly signalled:

LU 1

```
1Lu:    ehm: ich glaube die Frauen hat viel für die Männer tun
2       eh geTAN aber die Männer sagt-eh die eh ((kichern))
3       die Frauen sind schlecht bei der Beruf und kö eh
4       gibt es weniger hh' Perspekti?
```

```
 5M:        Perspekti?
 6Lu:       auf Inglisch?
 7M:        *Perspecktiv/      en.*/
 8Lu:                 /Perspektiv?/
 9M:        es gibt auch ein deutsches Wort (auf deutsch)
10Lu:       Perspektiv ach so. Nicht Perspectiv und hat hat gut
11          eh gut Zukunft in Wissenschaft /arBEITEN./
```

LU1

```
 1Lu:       ehm: I believe women have do a lot for men
 2          eh DONE but men say-eh the eh ((giggling))
 3          women are bad at their job and can eh
 4          there is less hh' perspecti?
 5M:        perspecti?
 6Lu:       in English?
 7M:        *Perspek/tiven.* /
 8Lu:                /Perspektiv?/
 9M:        there is also a German word (in German)
10Lu:       Perspectiv I see. there is no perspective and has has good
11          eh good future to work in/academia/
```

Lu first offers a try-marker 'perspecti?' The rising intonation contextualizes the candidate status of the term. In line 6 she then demonstrates that the candidate term is an 'English' term. M provides the German pronunciation (7). Lu's repetition of the corrected term in combination with the phrase 'I see' signal that the transfer of linguistic knowledge is now completed. By demonstrating that she has acquired the term in question, the instruction sequence can stop and the main stream of interaction can be taken up again.

The instruction phase is a dialogically produced side sequence in which both participants (the expert and the learner) take part and negotiate a transfer of knowledge.

LU 3

```
 1Lu:       und dann diese diese'ehm:
 2          eh'waiban eh'auf Deutsch?
 3          wie heißt?
 4M:        Auslandsamt
 5Lu:       ja. diese Auslands' amt'=
 6M:        =mhm.
```

LU 3

```
 1Lu:       and then this ehis'ehm:
 2          eh'waiban eh'in German?
 3          what is it called?
 4M:        office of foreign affairs
 5Lu:       ja. this office of foreign' affairs=
 6M:        =mhm.
```

In the next segment Bu appeals to the native speaker K in order to get her candidate term 'Schwägerìn?' (sister-in-law) ratified:

BU 6

14Bu:	mein Bruder, und und' meine'eh'(0.2)
15	Schwä'gerin? (0.2)
16	richtig?
17K:	ja. ja.
18Bu:	also die beiden sie wollen ja schon.

BU 6

14Bu:	*my brother, and and' my'eh' (0.2)*
15	*sister' in law? (0.2)*
16	*right?*
17K:	*ja. ja.*
18Bu:	*well both of them they wanted it.*

In the four interactions at hand the Chinese women and men handle their language problems differently: whereas the two women appeal in six cases explicitly to the native speakers for instruction, the two men never initiate any instruction sequence.

Similar results were found in an analysis of Chinese–German interactions in private settings (students meeting for tea). There, the Chinese women also oriented themselves much more to language deficiencies and appealed to the natives for help, whereas the Chinese men tried to solve their language problems (search for words, struggling with the correct syntax and pronunciation, etc.) without explicitly asking the natives for help. These differences could be interpreted in the context of gender-specific attitudes towards communicative problems in a second language. Situations that reveal communicative deficits might be more face-threatening for Chinese men. These findings support the thesis of Börsch (1982) that communicating in a foreign language is experienced differently by women and men: women tend to see such interactions much more positively, they even find the situation quite liberating, and are often more relaxed emotionally; whereas men consider the deficient communicative abilities and the fact they cannot present themselves in an 'adequate' way as 'disturbing'.

By explicitly appealing to the natives for help, the speaker reactivates her status as a learner and thereby produces unequal interactive roles: learner and student on the one side – expert and teacher on the other. Thus a learner–teacher footing is constructed.

Other-initiated instruction sequences

Not only the non-native participant but also the native speaker has the possibility to initiate an instruction sequence and thus contextualize her status as an expert. The German speakers K and M use this strategy of showing their authority as native speakers and thus 'masters of the code' only in the interactions with the Chinese men.

Conversation analysis deals with repair phenomena in everyday interaction among native speakers and shows that self-initiated self-correction is preferred (Schegloff, Jefferson and Sacks, 1977); other-initiated other-correction is dispreferred. Other-initiations yield self-correction and are produced in such a way (usually 'buffered' by various procedures, such as hesitation marks, questions, etc.) that the speaker of the trouble-source has the opportunity to self-correct.

In our data the Germans produce other-initiated instruction sequences (and thus repair) without leaving the space and opportunity for self-repair.

In the following transcript Zheng argues for extending the German course. The argumentation gets interrupted by a short side sequence, in which M corrects Zheng's prior utterance:

ZHENG 2

35	Zheng:	aber mindestens mehr an – eh wenn wir
36		mehr ein Semest eh Deutsch lernt
37		werden eh haben wir weniger Problem mit Deutsch
38		(0.8)
39		ehm besonders in Umgangssprache=
40	M:	=in DER Umgangssprache
41	Zheng:	ja.
42	M:	ja, das kann: eh wohl sein', a: ber wenn

ZHENG 2

35	Zheng:	*but at least more at – eh if we*
36		*learn more one term eh German*
37		*we will eh have less problem with German*
38		*(0.8)*
39		*ehm especially in colloquial language=*
40	M:	*=in THE colloguial language*
41	Zheng:	*ja.*
42	M:	*ja, this can: eh well bè, but if*

With the partial repetition and prosodically marked transformation (the missing definite article is highlighted by an increase of volume), 'in THE colloquial language' (40), M orients to the deficiencies of Zheng's German and thereby reactivates her status as an expert and his as a learner.

ZHENG 11

11	Zheng:	aber jetzt eh ich möchte IHNEN eh mit
12		IHNEN SPRECHEN und Ihnen fragen, ob
13		wir eine Gelegenheit haben, eh hier lang
14		langer als eh LÄNGER als eine Jahr bleiben und
15		endlich haben einmal PNDS eh: machen
16	M:	nein'hh
17	Zheng:	nein'
18	M:	NEIN.
19	Zheng:	ja das heißt ich habe keine Ch – Chance
20		eh Ihnen eh SIE überzuzeugen hihih/hhhh/
21	M:	/zu/

```
22          ((hihi)) überzeugen
23Zheng:    ((giggles)) zu überzeugen hhhihh
24M:        nein, weil das eh weil weil eh eh eh
```

ZHENG 11

```
11Zheng:    but now eh I would like to
12          TALK YOU eh with YOU and ask you, if
13          we have an opportunity, eh to stay
14          here long longer eh LONGER than one year and
15          finally have PNDS⁷ eh: make
16M:        no'hh
17Zheng:    no'
18M:        NO.
19Zheng:    ja this means I have no ch – chance
20          eh to pertosuade your eh YOU hihih/hhhh/
21M:                                          /to/
22          ((hihi)) persuade
23Zheng:    ((giggles)) to persuade hhhihh
24M:        no, because this eh because because eh eh eh
```

The incorrect verbal construction Zheng utters (20) can be considered as irrelevant to the understanding of his utterance, and could as well have remained uncorrected. However, M chooses to introduce an instruction sequence. The underlining laugh particles which are first introduced by Zheng and then taken up by M somewhat mitigate the confrontative situation. In line 23 Zheng actively accepts the instruction by repeating the offered correction, before the main stream of interaction is taken up again in line 24.

Another example of an interruption of the ongoing argumentative activity by introducing an instructive side sequence can be found in the next segment:

MA 2

```
18K:        wann war das?
19          (0.3)
20Ma:       eh:: : m
21          (0.8)
22          vor eh von ein Jahr
23K:        vor ei/nem Jahr/
24Ma:          /vor einem/ Jahr ja.
25K:        aber denken Sie, daß das für ALLE
```

MA 2

```
18K:        when was that?
19          (0.3)
20Ma:       eh:: : m
21          (0.8)
22          ago eh from one year
23K:        a/ year ago/
24Ma:          /a year/ ago ja.
25K:        but do you think, that this is possible
```

All these corrections and the transfer of correct grammar – appearing within argumentative sequences – are not necessary for the process of understanding the non-natives' utterances. Yet they do have an important interactive function: the native speaker thereby constitutes herself as an expert and focuses temporarily on the asymmetrically distributed linguistic competence. In all these cases the Germans – without any appeal for instruction from the non-native side – interrupt the ongoing argumentative activity to introduce the side sequence and thereby construct a hierarchical footing.

We can conclude that the linguistic competence forms a resource that the native speakers may activate in order to reproduce unequal status positions: the masters of the code versus the learners of the code.

In our data this resource is only used by the German women in the interactions with the Chinese men. This finding could be related to the differences in argumentative style between the Chinese women and men in our data: whereas Lu and Bu are much more consent-oriented, are willing to give up their positions and activate their learner status by appealing for help to the natives, Ma and Zheng are more confrontative, defend their opinions and thus help to expand the argumentative footing. In order to reproduce their higher-status positions in these interactions the German speakers then activate these linguistic resources and create interactive hierarchies.

Conclusion

The analysis supports the growing body of research suggesting that there are gender-related differences in interaction, but also that there are other context parameters such as social status, institutional role, cultural background, which interact with gender differences. Women are not always – in a 'context-free' sense – more cooperative, indirect and polite. Our German participants who are interacting within a certain institutional frame are 'experts' and thus 'powerful' in two ways: as counsellors and as natives. These expert roles are not just entities 'brought' into the situation, but are activated in the course of the interaction.

By studying gender-linked discourse patterns, we have to give up assumptions and stereotypes assuming that women and men are always different and behave in certain prescribed ways. Research trying to confirm folk-stereotypes of the 'cooperative, passive, personally oriented, polite, etc.' woman is responsible for the survival of traditional stereotyped dichotomies concerning gender-linked behaviour. For linguists to assume that the gender of a person is the only identity factor activated in interaction means reinforcing rigid dichotomies that treat women as a homogeneous group and ignoring the complex interaction of different social phenomena, such as setting, ethnicity, class, social role, subculture and power relations.

Instead we need more detailed analyses of the communicative strategies women and men use in specific context situations. For example, what strategies do women use to construct their higher or lower status? How do cultural identity and institutional power interact with gender? To what extent is gendered behaviour shaped and constrained by the situation and context?

Further research on the variable relationship between communicative strategies and social functions with regard to gender, ethnicity, power constellations and social roles is necessary in order to answer these questions.

Appendix: Transcription system key

/ja das/finde ich auch /du ab/	conversational overlap
(0.5)	pauses of indicated length (in seconds)
(???)	unintelligible text
(gestern)	a guess at an unclear word
=	continuous utterances
?	high rise tone
'	low rise tone
	low fall tone
;	slight rise
a:	lengthened segments
leise	low volume
sehr leise	very low volume
NEIN	extra prominence
mo((hi))mentan	laugh particles within the utterance
HAHAHA	loud laughter
hihi	giggling
((hustet))	non-lexical phenomena (e.g. coughing).

Acknowledgement

I should like to thank Jennifer Hartog for her comments on the English version of this paper.

Notes

1. The participants are all between 30 and 35 years old.
2. Kotthoff (1989).
3. In Günthner (1991a), I differentiate between cooperative and competitive forms of interruption.
4. Gumperz (1982).
5. For knowledge asymmetries in interactions see Keppler and Luckmann (1990).
6. Goffman (1986) defines 'footing' as: 'A change in footing implies a change in the alignment we take up to ourselves and the others present as expressed in the way we manage the production or reception of an utterance.'
7. The PNDS is a German language examination everyone has to take in order to study at German universities.

References

Börsch, S. (1982) *Fremdsprachenstudium–Frauenstudium?*, Tübingen: Stauffenberg Verlag.

Brown, P. and Levinson, S. (1978) 'Universals in Language Usage: Politeness Phenomena', in E.M. Goody (ed.) *Questions and Politeness*, Cambridge: Cambridge University Press, pp. 56–311.

Camras, L. (1984) 'Children's Verbal and Nonverbal Communication in a Conflict Situation', *Ethnology and Sociobiology* 5: pp. 257–68.

Chen, Z. and Chen, J. (1981) 'Sociolinguistic Research Based on Chinese Reality', *International Journal of the Sociology of Language: Sociolinguistics in the People's Republic of China* 1981: pp. 21–43.

Deegan, M.J. (1987) 'Symbolic Interaction and the Study of Women: An Introduction', in M.J. Deegan and M.R. Hill (eds) *Women and Symbolic Interaction*, Boston, MA: Allen & Unwin pp. 3–15. .

Falk, J. (1979) *The Duet as a Conversational Process*. Dissertation. Princeton University.

Garfinkel, H. (1967) *Studies in Ethnomethodology*, Englewood Cliffs, NJ: Prentice-Hall.

Goffman, E. (1986) *Frame Analysis: An Essay on the Organization of Experience*, Boston, MA: Northeastern University Press.

Goodwin, M.H. and Goodwin, C. (1987) 'Children's Arguing', in S. Philips, S. Steele and C. Tanz (eds) *Language, Gender and Sex in Comparative Perspective*, Cambridge: Cambridge University Press, pp. 200–48.

Gumperz, J.J. (1982) *Discourse Strategies*, Cambridge: Cambridge University Press.

Günthner, S. (1990a) 'Frauen an Chinas Hochschulen', in A. Gerstlacher and M. Miosga (eds), *China der Frauen*, Munich: Frauenoffensive, pp. 123–35.

—— (1990b) 'Aspekte der interkulturellen Kommunikation: Eine Analyse von Gesprächen zwischen Deutschen und chinesischen Deutschlernenden', MS. University of Konstanz.

—— (1991a) '"Eine Frau is nicht wie der Mond. Sie scheint auch ohne Sonne." Chinesinnen und Chinesen im Gespräch', in S. Günthner and H. Kotthoff (eds) *Von fremdem Stimmen: Weibliches und männliches Sprechen im Kulturvergleich*. Frankfurt: Suhrkamp, pp. 127–55.

—— (1991b) '"PI LAO ZHENG", Zur Begegnung deutscher und chinesischer Gesprächsstile', in B. Müller-Jacquier (ed.) *Formen der Wirtschaftskommunikation*, Munich: Iudicium, pp. 297–324.

Halliday, M.A.K. and Hasan, R. (1976) *Cohesion in English*, London: Longman.

Jefferson, G. (1972) 'Side Sequences', in D. Sudnow (ed.), *Studies in Social Interaction*, New York: Free Press, pp. 294–338.

Keppler, A. and Luckmann, T. (1990) '"Teaching". Conversational Transmission of Knowledge', Manuscript, University of Konstanz.

Kotthoff, H. (1989) *Pro und Kontra in der Fremdsprache*, Frankfurt: Peter Lang.

Kramarae, C. (1981) *Women and Men Speaking*, Rowley, MA: Newbury House.

Lakoff, R. (1975) *Language and Woman's Place*, New York: Harper & Row.

Luckmann, T. (1972) 'Die Konstitution der Sprache in der Welt des Alltags', in B. Badura and K. Gloy (eds), *Soziologie der Kommunikation*, Stuttgart: Metzler.

Maltz, D. and Borker, R. (1982) 'A Subcultural View on Male/Female Misunderstandings', in J.J. Gumperz (ed.), *Language and Social Identity*, Cambridge: Cambridge University Press, pp. 196–216.

Mead, M. (1935) *Sex and Temperament in Three Primitive Societies*, New York: William Morrow.

Naotsuka, R. et al. (1981) *Mutual Understanding of Different Cultures*, Osaka: Taishukan.

Naotsuka, R. and Sakamoto, N. (1983) *Mutual Knowledge of Different Cultures*, Tokyo. Taishukan.

O'Barr, W. and Atkins, B. (1980) 'Women's Language or Powerless language?', in S. McConnell-Ginet et al. (eds), *Women and Language in Literature and Society*, New York: Praeger, pp. 93–110.

Pomerantz, A. (1975) *Second Assessments. A Study of Some Features of Agreements/ Disagreements*, PhD dissertation, University of California at Irvine.

Schegloff, E., Jefferson, G. and Sacks, H. (1977) 'The Preference for Self-Correction in the Organisation of Repair in Conversation', *Language* 53: pp. 361–82.

Sheldon, A. (1990) 'Pickle Fights: Gendered Talk in Preschool Disputes', *Discourse Processes* 13 (1–4): pp. 5–31.

Tannen, D. (1990) *You Just Don't Understand: Women and Men in Conversation*, New York: Morrow.

Thorne, B. (1986a) 'Children and Gender: Constructions of Difference', in D. Rhode (ed.), *Theoretical Perspectives on Sexual Difference*, New Haven, CT: Yale University Press.

—— (1986b) 'Girls and Boys Together . . . But Mostly Apart: Gender Arrangements in Elementary Schools', in W.W. Hartup and Z. Rubin (eds), *Relationships and Development*, Hillsdale, NJ: Erlbaum, pp. 167–84.

Vuchinich, S. (1990) 'The Sequential Organization of Closing in Verbal Family Conflict', in A.D. Grimshaw (ed.) *Conflict Talk: Sociolinguistic Investigations of Arguments in Conversations*, Cambridge: Cambridge University Press, pp. 118–38.

West, C. (1984) 'Können "Damen" Ärzte sein?', in S. Trömel-Plötz (ed.), *Gewalt durch Sprache*, Frankfurt: Fischer, pp. 184–202.

7

Gender-based language reform and the (de)politicization of the lexicon

Susan Ehrlich and Ruth King

Based on 'Gender-based language reform and the social construction of meaning', *Discourse and Society*, 3(2) (1992); and 'Feminist meanings and the (de)-politicization of the lexicon', *Language in Society*, 23 (1994).

Introduction

In November 1989, Queen's University in Kingston, Ontario, Canada, sponsored its annual 'NO MEANS NO' rape awareness campaign. In reaction to the campaign, obscene and violent messages appeared in the windows of men's dormitories: 'NO MEANS HARDER', 'NO MEANS DYKE', 'NO MEANS MORE BEER', 'NO MEANS "TIE ME UP"'. In March 1991, during a nationally televised Ontario university hockey game, two University of Waterloo students held signs saying 'NO MEANS HARDER' and 'STOP MEANS PLEASE'. While these signs are extremely disturbing in terms of their normalizing and justifying of violence against women, they are also a strong illustration of the way in which meanings are socially constructed and constituted: the meaning of the word 'no' in this particular context has been appropriated by the dominant culture. As McConnell-Ginet (1989: 47) points out (in connection with women saying 'no' to men's sexual advances), 'meaning is a matter not only of individual will but of social relations embedded in political structures'. A woman will say 'no' with sincerity to a man's sexual advances but the 'no' gets filtered through a series of beliefs and attitudes that transform the woman's 'direct negative' into an 'indirect affirmative': 'She is playing hard to get, but of course she really means yes.' And, because linguistic meanings are, to a large extent, determined by the dominant culture's social values and attitudes, terms initially introduced to be non-sexist may lose such meanings in the 'mouths' of a sexist speech community and/or culture.

In arguing for the necessity of nonsexist language reform, feminist theorists have generally assumed that language is not a neutral and transparent means of representing social realities. Rather, a particular vision of social reality is assumed to get inscribed in language – a vision of reality that does not serve all of its speakers equally. Like other social institutions and practices, language is seen as serving the interests of the dominant classes (Gal, 1989, 1991); in the case of sexist language, language can be said to codify an androcentric world-view. The 'names' that a language attaches to events and activities, for example, especially those related to sex and sexuality, often encode a male perspective. Cameron (1985) discusses terms such as *penetration, fuck, screw, lay,* all of which turn heterosexual sex into something men do to women. (*Penetration* from a female perspective would be more appropriately encoded as *enclosure, surrounding,* or *engulfing.*) What becomes clear from 'names' such as these is the extent to which language serves as an ideological filter on the world – language shapes or constructs our notions of reality rather than labelling that reality in any transparent and straightforward way. In addition, as Eckert and McConnell-Ginet (1992) point out, language's ideological perspective is often naturalized, 'obscuring its status as one among many perspectives.'

While sexist language clearly reflects sexist social structures, the continuing existence of such social structures throws into question the possibility of successful language reform. Graddol and Swan (1989: 110) comment:

> Sexist language is not simply a linguistic problem. The existence of unmarked expressions 'in the language' does not mean that these will be used and interpreted in a neutral way. This may lead one to question the value of the linguistic reforms advocated in writers' and publishers' guidelines.

Cameron (1985: 90) makes a similar point:

> Therefore, in the interests of accuracy we should strive to include the female half of the human race by replacing male terms with neutral ones. But the 'reality' to which language relates is a sexist one, and in it there are no neutral terms . . .. In the mouths of sexists, language can always be sexist.

Given that language is not a neutral vehicle in the representation of reality and that it is necessarily laden with social values, the introduction of non-sexist and/or feminist terms does not guarantee such usage. In this article, we first demonstrate the way in which non-sexist and feminist linguistic innovations are redefined and depoliticized as they circulate within the larger, mainstream speech community. We then go on to argue that the relative success of attempts at gender-based language reform is dependent on the social context in which the language reform occurs. When language reform occurs within the context of a larger sociopolitical initiative whose primary goal is the eradication of sexist practices (e.g., employment equity programmes), it is more likely to succeed. By contrast, when language reform occurs within the context of a speech community that embraces sexist values and attitudes, it is less likely to succeed.

The appropriation of meaning

The appropriation of meaning by the dominant culture is by no means a phenomenon restricted to innovative forms in a language. Schulz (1975) traces the semantic derogation of terms designating women in English, showing that words, such as *hussy* and *spinster*, originally neutral or positive in interpretation took on negative connotations in a way that was unparalleled for words designating men. That is, sexist values also influence the meanings of terms that already exist in a language.

In Britain and North America today, the New Right has quite deliberately used the strategy of redefining and/or appropriating terms originally used by the Left in an attempt to delegitimize issues such as anti-sexism and anti-racism. Seidel (1988) cites examples from the *Salisbury Review in Britain*, 'a quarterly journal of conservative thought' (p. 131), in which racism is dismissed as a 'vulgar and banal catchphrase' (p. 134) and anti-racism is defined as racism in disguise:

> . . . through a combination of facile agreement, political opportunism and moral intimidation, the Left, under the specious banner of 'anti-racism', has succeeded in forcing 'institutional racism' onto the legitimate political agenda of politics and, in the process, is fostering the very racial disharmony it purports to condemn. (p. 135)

In a *Time* magazine article (Henry, 1991) on the controversial topic of 'Political Correctness' on North American campuses, it is reported with dismay that 'professors teach that while males can never be victims of racism, because racism is a form of repressive political power – and white males already hold the power in Western society'. The implication here is both that racism is *not* a form of repressive political power and that white males can suffer from racism. We see here that the term racism is being redefined by this writer as non-systemic and, in the process, its effects are trivialized, given that all individuals, in particular, even white males can now be victims of racism. This kind of redefinition is taken to an extreme in an example from Seidel where the (white) editor of the *Salisbury Review* concludes that he is 'black' because he belongs to a minority of educated people who are excluded from the power structures of the Inner London Education Authority. This type of discursive strategy where WHITE = BLACK, NO = YES, ANTIRACISM = RACISM illustrates the extent to which redefinition and even reversal of meanings operates quite independently of the intended meanings/uses of words. It should be clear from these kinds of examples why the introduction of non-sexist terms into a language will not necessarily lead to non-sexist usage.

(Mis)interpretation and (mis)use of non-sexist and feminist terms

In attempting to characterize the type of social conditions that are conducive to successful language reform, Labov's (1972) findings concerning the effect of social factors on linguistic change are relevant. Labov claims that the spread of a particular linguistic innovation is determined by the status of the social subgroup leading the change.[1]

> If the group in which the change originated was not the highest-status group in the speech community, members of the highest-status group eventually stigmatized the changed form through their control of various institutions of the communication network . . . .(p. 179)

Extrapolating from Labov's observations, we can say that the success of gender-based language reform will be determined by the extent to which high-status subgroups within a speech community adopt non-sexist values. Assuming that non-sexist language reform originates in a social subgroup that is not of the highest status within a given speech community (i.e., it originates among socially conscious women), then Labov's findings predict that, all else being equal, these linguistic innovations will be stigmatized unless the highest-status social group also displays non-sexist values. Indeed, there is much evidence to suggest that innovative, non-sexist linguistic forms do undergo a kind of deprecation. While this does not always manifest itself in overt stigmatization of the innovative forms, it does lead to the misuse and misinterpretation of non-sexist terms.[2] Examples of this misuse and misinterpretation follow.

The title *Ms* was originally popularized by feminists in the 1970s to replace *Miss* and *Mrs* and provide a parallel term to *Mr*, in that both *Ms* and *Mr* designate gender without indicating marital status. Miller and Swift (1976) see the elimination of *Mrs* and *Miss* in favor of *Ms* as a way of allowing women to be seen as people in their own right, rather than in relation to someone else. Unfortunately, while *Ms* was intended to parallel *Mr*, considerable evidence suggests that its use is often resisted, or it is not used and/or interpreted in the intended way. Fasold (1988: 190), in a survey of news organizations' style guides, reports that the *Washington Post*'s manual disallows *Ms* 'except in direct quotations, in discussing the term itself, or "for special effect"'. The Associated Press 1987 style guide (French, 1987) recommends *Ms only* if know to be the preference of the individual woman.

Examples of 'misuses' of the term *Ms* abound. Frank and Treichler (1989: 218) cite the following directive, sent to public information officers in the state of Pennsylvania: 'If you use Ms. for a female, please indicate in parentheses after the Ms. whether it's Miss or Mrs.' In a similar way, Graddol and Swann (1989: 97) explain that *Ms* is not a neutral title for women in Britain: 'in some contexts it seems to have coalesced with Miss (official forms sometimes distinguish only Mrs. and Ms)'. Atkinson (1987), in a Canadian study of attitudes towards the use of *Ms* and birthname retention among women, found that many of her respondents had a three-way distinction: they used *Mrs* for married women, *Miss* for women who had never been maried and *Ms* for divorced women. All three usages described here demonstrate the high premium placed on identifying women by their relationship (current or otherwise) to men, in spite of the intended neutrality associated with *Ms*.[3]

In a similar way, neutral terms such as *chairperson* and *spokesperson*, introduced to replace masculine generics such as *chairman* and *spokesman*, seem to have lost their neutrality in that they are often only used for women. The following example containing announcements of academics' changing jobs, cited by Dubois and Crouch (1987) (from the *Chronicle of Higher Education*, 1977), demonstrates that a woman is a *chairperson*, but a man is a *chairman*.

Margarette P. Eby, *Chairperson* of Humanities at U. of Michigan at Dearborn, to Dean of the College of Humanities and Fine Arts and Professor of Music at U. of Northern Iowa.

David W. Hamilton, Assoc. Professor of Anatomy at Harvard, to *Chairman* of Anatomy at U. of Minnesota.
Eileen T. Handeiman, *Chairperson* of Science at Sinon's Rock Early College, to Dean of Academic Affairs.
Elaine B. Harvey, Acting *Chairperson* of Graduate Pediatrics at Indiana U. to Dean of the School of Nursing at Fort Hays Kansas State U.
Philip E. Hicks, Professor of Industrial Engineering at New Mexico State U., to *Chairman* of Industrial Engineering at North Carolina A & T State U.

From this example, we can see that the attempt to replace a masculine generic with a neutral one has been somewhat unsuccessful in that neutral terms like *chairperson, spokesperson*, etc., are functioning to designate only female referents. Rather than ridding the language of a masculine generic, the introduction of neutral generic *person* forms has (in some situations, at least) led to a sex-based distinction between forms such as *chairperson* vs *chairman*.

A similar point regarding the (mis)use of neutral generics is made by Silverstein (1985). Considering the relationship between language structure and ideology, Silverstein notes that ideologically charged lexical reform 'has both a certain potential for misfire and abuse, and a certain generative force reasserting categorical homeostasis' (p. 252). He cites, as we do above, the use of neutral generics such as *chairperson* to designate female referents. Silverstein also considers cases of language reform where neutral terms such as *actor* and *waiter* are advocated as replacements for words with feminine suffixes such as *actress* and *waitress*. In Silverstein's terms, the category of gender often gets reconstituted in these cases so that a supposedly neutral term like *server* takes on the feminine suffix that the neutral term was intended to eliminate, as in serveresss. Again, while the terms involved in these oppositions may change (e.g., Mrs./Miss → Mrs./Ms, chairman/chairwoman → chairman/chairperson, waiter/waitress → server/serveress), what does persist is the linguistic encoding of social distinctions that are clearly of ideological importance to the speech community in question (e.g., the married/single distinction among women; the male/female distinction).

Concerned with interpretation rather than use, Khosroshahi (1989) investigated the effects of neutral generics vs masculine generics in terms of the mental imagery evoked. Earlier research had demonstrated that *he/man* generics do not function generically (even though they may be intended generically) to the extent that they readily evoke images of males rather than of males and females. The use of neutral generic pronouns such as *he or she, she* or *he* or singular *they* is thus advocated by supporters of language reform, given the potential negative effects of *he/man* language. Khosroshahi's subjects included both males and females with both reformed and traditional language usage (i.e., four groups of subjects). Her results are summarized below:

All groups were androcentric except the women who had reformed their language; androcentric in the sense that when they read a paragraph that was ambiguous with respect to gender, they were more likely to interpret it as referring to a male than to a female character. Even if the paragraph used *he* or *she* or *they*, feminine referents did not become more salient than masculine ones. (p. 517)

Thus, these results demonstrate that for most of the subjects in this experiment the use of masculine vs neutral generics had no significant effect on the image evoked: male referents were always more salient than female ones. Khosroshahi explains her results:

> In a literature dominated by male characters, initially sex-indefinite words must quickly develop masculine connotations. (p. 518)

Thus, like the misuse of *Ms* described above, this research shows that neutral generic terms are not readily interpreted as neutral. Again, we see that it is the prevailing values and attitudes of a culture that determine, to a large extent, how these innovative, non-sexist terms get used and interpreted, in spite of their intended neutrality. It is interesting to note here that the exceptional group in Khosroshahi's study, the reformed language women, not only interpreted neutral generics in terms of female referents but also interpreted the masculine generic mostly in terms of female referents. In other words, they displayed the opposite pattern to the three other groups: female (as opposed to male) referents were evoked regardless of the type of generic pronoun used. Again, we see that the interpretation of terms seems to be heavily influenced by the ideologies of an individual or speech community rather than by the particular pronoun used in a given context.

Feminist attempts at language reform have also involved the introduction of terms to express women's perceptions and experiences, phenomena previously unnamed. Steinem (1983: 149) sees terms such as *sexual harrassment* and *sexism* as significant in this respect: 'A few years ago, they were just called life'. Penelope (1990) cites an example of the way that one such term, *consciousness-raising* is 'perverted' when used in the film *The Billionaire Boys' Club*.

> In the made-for-television movie, *The Billionaire Boys' Club* (1989), one of the rich, white men used the phrase 'consciousness-raising' to describe his changed perception of what the club was doing when he saw the body of one of the men his friends had murdered. For all the women who participated in consciousness-raising groups in the 1960s and 1970s, the word referred very specifically (and exclusively) to the resulting process of change in how we perceived ourselves, our situation in the world, and our relationship to men. For us, consciousness-raising was a profound, mind-altering experience that impelled us to change our lives. We couldn't have imagined that that word would be so perverted as to end up describing a yuppie's shocked repulsion when he saw his first dead body.

Again we see that terms originally with very specific feminist-influenced meanings are subject to redefinition and, not accidentally, are redefined in terms of the perspective of a white male's experience. Other strategies of redefinition and depoliticization include redefining a term by eliminating or obscuring crucial aspects of the term's feminist-informed definition.[4]

The following examples illustrate how the phenomenon of sexual harrassment virtually disappears when its distinguishing characteristics are omitted from its description. In an article on sexual harassment in the *National Review*, author Morgenson (1991: 37), reports on a *Time*/CBS sexual harassment poll in which 38 per cent of the respondents said that they had been 'the object of sexual advances, propositions, or unwanted sexual discussions' from men who supervised them or could affect their position at work. However, only 4 per cent of this group actually reported the incidents at the time that they occurred. In attempting to explain the small percentage of formal complaints, Morgenson states

> Did the *Times* offer any explanation for why so few actually reported the incident? Could it be that these women did not report their "harassment" because they themselves did not regard a sexual advance as harassment?

Notice the implication here that, without a report of sexual harassment, the harassing behaviour becomes a sexual advance. (Note in this regard the quotation marks around harassment.) Reporting, then, becomes crucial to Morgenson's definition of sexual harassment. Of course, this kind of definition ignores the political dimension intrinsic to sexual harassment, specifically, that in the majority of cases women are harassed by male supervisors who have the power to affect the women's position at work. The question of whether to lodge a formal complaint is a complicated one involving economic and career considerations, among others. To imply that sexual harassment only occurs when it is reported and otherwise is merely a sexual advance is to deny the political aspect of the phenomenon and renders the majority of sexual harassment cases non-existent. This, of course, was one of the tactics used by the Republican senators in attempting to destroy Anita Hill's credibility during the Thomas/Hill hearings: How could Anita Hill say she had been sexually harassed when she didn't file a formal complaint and even followed Thomas to a new job?

A somewhat different property of sexual harassment is obscured in the following account of comments made by Brent Baker of the 'conservative Media Research Center' reported by Boot (1992: 26) in the *Columbia Journalism Review*.

> Baker argues that Phelps and Totenberg [the two reporters responsible for Anita Hill's allegations first appearing in the press] reported their leaks too hastily, recklessly jeopardizing Thomas's reputation before they had done enough reporting to justify their stories. He noted in an interview that Hill's allegation was far different from a claim that nominee X was guilty of something that definitely could be proven, such as stock fraud. Hill's allegation was an instance of her-word-against-his (as is generally the case in sexual harassment cases); there were no witnesses and real corroboration was impossible. Baker contends that, given those limitations and the inevitable damage to Thomas's reputation that disclosure would cause, Phelps and Totenberg should have held their stories until they had established, among other things, that there had been some *pattern* of misbehaviour, with other women claiming he had been guilty of sexual misconduct with them. [italics in original]

Like Morgenson, Baker disregards a crucial element of sexual harassment – that it normally occurs in private without witnesses to corroborate allegations of harassing behaviour. Because sexual harassment cannot be "proven" in the same way that stock fraud can be proven, Baker insists that sexual harassment must be subject to different criteria in the determination of guilt. This leads Baker to the conclusion that sexual harassment can only be deemed to have occurred if there is a pattern of harassing behaviour. (Notice that with other kinds of offenses such as stock fraud, a pattern of behaviour is not necessary to the determination of guilt.)

While the two examples above obscure critical aspects of the phenomenon of sexual harassment, the following examples from *Time* (Castro 1992: 37) redefine the prototypical case. It comes from a review of the book *Step Forward: Sexual Harassment in the Workplace* by Susan Webb. The book is described an 'an accessible sort of Cliffs Notes guide to the topic' and as 'refreshingly free of ideology and reproach'. The following examples of case studies from the book are given:

1) You and your boss are single and like each other a lot. You invite him to dinner, and one thing leads to another. Was someone sexually harassed? (No – though it wasn't very smart.)

2) Your boss invites you to a restaurant for dinner and – much to your surprise – spends the evening flirting with you. Just before inviting you to her house for a nightcap, she mentions that promotion you are hoping to get. (You are being sexually harassed. Whether or not you welcome her interest in you, she has implied a connection between the promotion and your response.)

Clearly, these types of examples are meant to help readers differentiate between behaviour that is sexual harassment and behaviour that is not. Of interest to us is the fact that the case that does constitute sexual harassment (#2) involves a female supervisor and presumably a male employee. (It's difficult to imagine *Time* reporting on lesbian relations.) Thus, what is presented as the prototypical case of sexual harassment is a situation where a female boss is harassing her male employee, a scenario that flies in the face of the overwhelming majority of sexual harassment cases where male supervisors or colleagues harass their female employees. This is not to say that women never harass their male employees, only that this is not the typical case of sexual harassment. Here, however, the typical case of sexual harassment comes to be reconfigured as females harassing males.

While the evidence presented above is meant to demonstrate the way in which non-sexist and feminist meanings and usages can be appropriated and depoliticized by a sexist speech community, we are not suggesting that language reform is always or ever futile. First, it should be noted that even if gender-based language reform is not immediately and/or completely successful, it does sensitize individuals to ways in which language is non-neutral and discriminatory towards women: language has become one of the many arenas in which social inequalities are elucidated. Penelope (1990: 213) maintains that 'becoming self-conscious about our linguistic choices gives us immediate access to our thought processes and that continual monitoring of what we are about to say will gradually enable us to unlearn patriarchal ways of thinking'. McConnell-Ginet (1989) takes a positive moral from the observation that non-sexist meanings and usages are very often appropriated by a sexist speech community. If meanings are socially constructed and constituted, then the existence of a speech community dedicated to the elimination of sexist practices can provide the necessary support for successful language reform. In what follows, we show that the relative success of attempts at gender-based language reform is dependent on the social context in which the language reform occurs. When language reform occurs within the context of a larger sociopolitical initiative whose primary goal is the eradication of sexist practices, it is more likely to succeed. By contrast, when language reform occurs within the context of a speech community that embraces sexist values and attitudes, it is less likely to succeed.

Successful and unsuccessful language reform

That the introduction of non-sexist and feminist terms does not guarantee non-sexist usage is clear. Along with cases of the appropriation of intended non-sexist terms such as those just discussed, there are also cases of non-sexist innovations, documented in the language and gender literature, which have not entered into (mainstream) usage; indeed, the average person has probably never heard of them. Consider in this regard the long history of attempts to reform the English pronominal system through the introduction of a third person singular indefinite pronoun. Baron (1986) cites numerous innovations dating from 1850 to the present (e.g. *thon* (1884), *hes* (1935), *hse* (1945), *tey* (1972), *hir* (1975), *E* (1977), *hiser* (1984)). These neologisms were suggested in newspaper articles and letters to the editor and in scholarly journals and books, but, as Baron (p. 241) notes, 'most coiners of new pronouns have no specific plan in mind to ensure the adoption of their creations, other than the basic attraction of the new words themselves'. Likewise, the spelling of *woman* as 'womyn' is occasionally used for political effect, but few individuals use it consistently. A similar case is *herstory*, which very clearly makes the point that mainstream *history* is essentially a history of men. Again, *herstory* is used in special contexts to highlight the contributions of women, but it is not in general usage.

A first step in achieving language reform is thus some consensus in the innovating speech community, in our case, socially conscious women, that a particular innovation is an appropriate non-sexist solution. The next step is the development of non-sexist language guidelines incorporating these solutions. In the past two decades a number of non-sexist style guides and pamphlets have appeared, some aimed at a general audience, some at specialized audiences. And, finally, the support of a non-sexist speech community is essential for the successful implementation of non-sexist language guidelines. Below we consider a number of attempts at institutional change, i.e., the implementation of language reform in agencies, companies and organizations in the form of policy statements and/or guidelines *and* the ensurance of compliance with those guidelines. We show that the extent to which language reform is couched within larger, shared sociopolitical goals is a determining factor in its degree of success.

Language reform and employment and educational equity
In Canada, non-sexist language has come to be widely regarded as an essential component in achieving employment equity in the workplace.

The term 'employment equity' was defined by Judge Rosalie Abella in 1984 as 'a strategy designed to obliterate the present and residual effects of discrimination and to open equitably the competition for employment opportunities to those arbitrarily excluded' (Government of Canada, 1984: 254). Both the 1986 Employment Equity Act and the Federal Contractors' Program, implemented the same year, identify four social groups with a history of disadvantage: women, visible minorities, native peoples and people with disabilities. The Employment Equity Act covers regulated federal employers such as crown corporations like Canada Post while the Federal Contractors' Program is binding on employers bidding for government contracts of over $200,000.00. If large federal contractors, including universities and private-sector businesses, were not already working (altruistically) to fight discrimination in the workplace, the results of lack of compliance with the FCP – loss of the possibility of bidding for government contracts – has provided added incentive. To comply, institutions must sign a certificate of commitment to implement employment equity and must establish an employment equity office to develop an employment equity policy and plan for implementation. Compliance is under regular review.

Strategies for achieving employment equity include: active recruitment and fair consideration for promotion; accessible, quality childcare; paid parental leave for both parents; pay equity (i.e., the elimination of the gap between the average wages of women and men which results from the under-valuing of women's work), equal pensions and benefits; and the introduction of supportive initiatives *such as the use of non-sexist language* (emphasis added; Ontario Women's Directorate, 1988: 2–3). The current emphasis on employment equity in the workplace has led many institutions to adopt non-sexist language policies and guidelines, if they had not already done so. For example, *Employment Equity for Women: A University Handbook*, published in 1988 by the Committee on the Status of Women of the Council of Ontario Universities, devotes a large section of its discussion of 'The University Environment' to language and visual imagery. The anti-feminist backlash on university campuses over the past few years, especially the December 1989 Montreal Massacre, has also led many institutions to attempt to deal with the negative university climate for women. Climate issues and concern over university accessibility for the four designated groups has come to be seen as part of 'educational equity'. As in the case of employment equity, non-sexist language is an issue for the task forces and committees set up over the past several years to deal with educational equity. For instance, a 1990 University of Alberta plan, intended to reduce discrimination against women on campus, calls for professors to eliminate sexist language from their educational materials. Some universities have addressed the issue of spoken as well as written language by including questions on language usage in teaching evaluations. A number of professional organizations, including the Canadian Association of University Teachers, no longer publish job advertisements using *he/man* language. In our own institution, York University, efforts to ensure that people abide by our non-sexist language policy began with the Status of Women office and only recently has the central administration taken responsibility for compliance.

In the university setting, an important area for language reform has been the naming of courses. Compliance with institutional change is not always uniform, particularly when it may be seen as conflicting with other principles and policies. For example, while sexist course titles such as '*Man* and his Environment' have virtually disappeared, some individuals and departments may still appeal to their academic freedom to name courses as they wish. Likewise, in an institution with formally adopted non-sexist guidelines, individuals may still contend that they are free to write as they choose. In our own case, York University has now a supportive climate for language reform: it was the first university in Ontario to have a Status of Women office and has had active women's studies programmes since the early 1970s. It has also been a pioneer in the development of sexual harassment policy and education.

One case of successful language reform at York took place in the early 1980s. The university's division of humanities removed, over a two-year period, all course titles with man, such as 'Modern *Man* in Search of Understanding'. Two faculty members involved remember that the general university atmosphere of the time (including support for women's studies in the humanities and social sciences, the completion of a major report of sexual harassment) was an important factor. Language reform was also facilitated by the fact that the division had already embarked on a more general curriculum reform so that, while there was some in-committee debate, change was seen in a wider context. In other sectors of the university, course titles have been the subject of heated debate and language reform has been somewhat less successful. Where change is not seen as part of a larger initiative, or where change is left to the discretion of individual instructors (as opposed to curriculum committees), reform has been less easily effected. The university's Status of Women Communications Committee, of which we are both members, worked to promote the implementation of York's non-sexist language policy. When the committee was set up in 1989, we found that the York non-sexist language policy, dating from 1985, had clearly had a positive effect. Most university documents used non-sexist alternatives to the so-called generic *he*, and *chair* rather than *chairman* was the norm. However, it was clear to us that there was still room for improvement. For instance, a number of course titles still used *man* to refer to the species as a whole. The committee wrote to each department which listed such a course title and explained the rationale for change. Responses varied widely. In some cases, we were thanked for bringing such 'anachronistic' usage to a unit's attention and the title was changed. In other cases, we received no reply but noticed the title was changed.

The one remaining area of resistance at York was within the Faculty of Science, some of whose members oppose non-sexist language reform because it challenges what they deem to be 'natural'.[5] Like much anti-feminist discourse, the opponents to language reform within our university context base their arguments on the notion that social practices (i.e., language) are grounded in nature. Biological determinism is the most prevalent example of this kind of thinking: women's biology, particularly women's reproductive biology, is used to justify women being relegated to the home. In other words, the invocation of 'nature' has been one way of rationalizing a whole range of social practices that oppress women. In a similar way, the representation of language as having a 'natural order' exemplifies the way in which 'nature' is invoked to maintain language practices that demean and diminish women.

An analysis of the university discourse surrounding non-sexist language reform in Toronto reveals at least three manifestations of the 'sexist language is natural' argument.[6] First, it is argued that the purity of the English language must be maintained:

> English is a rich language, and it seems to me that one ought to be able to overcome gender-biased problems by working within the language as such. As an editor I am as concerned with racism and sexism as I am with the purity and elegance of the English language.

In these two examples, we see that English is inherently pure and rich and elegant and that it will lose its intrinsic purity, richness and elegance if it falls victim to language reform. Like the natural environment, English is uncontaminated, but runs the risk of losing its 'natural' beauty through the infusion of atrocities:

> The guidelines [non-sexist language guidelines] . . . include some linguistic atrocities that as an editor I abhor: 's/he', her/his'.

Second, language is represented in this corpus as frozen and immutable. On the use of the 'generic' *man*, the following comments appear:

> I also personally believe that the use of 'Man' in a scientific context is correct and without any connotation of gender. The word comes directly from the dead language of Anglo Saxon in which it means person. The gender specific terms require prefixes to man, viz. weardenman, a male person, and wifman, a female person. Only the latter has come down to us in the vernacular (as woman). The word is also used in the gender free sense in other modern Germanic dialects. One of the advantages of using dead languages (such as ancient Greek and Latin) to specify scientific terms is that the meaning is more likely to remain frozen, since there is not a parallel constantly changing vernacular.

Here we see that *man* is believed to have 'no connotation of gender' just as it had no such connotation in Anglo-Saxon. In a similar example, the dictionary is invoked to justify the use of the so-called generic *man*:

> My unabridged dictionary has 25 definitions of man, 6 are gender (male) specific, 19 non-specific. I'd like to stick with the majority.

In these examples, sexist language is justified by appealing, in one case, to a dead language and, in the other case, to the dictionary. (We know that dictonaries not only reflect usages of a particular period in time but also reflect particular world-views.) Thus, language, rather than being viewed as a system that is specific to a social and historical context, is seen as unchanging just as the social roles of men and women are often represented as unchanging and inevitable, i.e., natural. Finally, we see from this corpus that language is not only unaffected by social and political forces but, like other natural entities, seems to have a life of its own. The following comments are illustrative:

> I trust, however, that in your committee's efforts to foster a greater respect for women, respect for the English language will also be demonstrated. I am appalled by some of the 'gender-neutral solutions' adopted by other institutions which reveal an almost complete disregard for the etymology of many words.
>
> What would bother me, and very deeply, would be the slightest possibility that they [the members of the University of Toronto's Ad Hoc Committee on the Status of Women] were chosen for other than their knowledge of and respect for the nuance and absurdities, richnesses and traditions of the language itself.

The suggestion here is that the language 'itself' should be respected and protected, often, it appears, at the expense of respect for half of its speakers, i.e., women.

Interestingly, this is largely from a faculty with very few women professors, few women graduate students and a reputation for vocal resistance to the university's affirmative action hiring policy. The particular division we dealt with has an unofficial policy of leaving catalogue copy, including course titles, up to the discretion of the individual who usually teaches the course. This is the opposite of the division of humanities example given above, where the climate within the faculty was more positive, course title reform was part of more general curriculum reform and decisions were taken in committee.

Language reform and mainstream media

The second example of attempted language reform we look at concerns the mainstream media. In a longitudinal study of a number of US newspapers, Fasold (1988) found that a newspaper's non-sexist language policy correlated positively with (non-)sexist language use in the newspaper. For example, he reports that 'change in language use policy over the years has succeeded in eliminating the discriminatory practice of referring to married women by their husbands' names only' (p. 202). However, while the new editions of the style books studied by Fasold and his students 'invariably decry sexism and the use of language in a discriminatory fashion' (p. 189), they are also fairly conservative. For example, while they concede that compounds with *man* may not always be appropriate, there is considerable resistance to compounds with *person*.

In March and April of 1991, the students in our language and gender course at York studied the extent to which Toronto's two major newspapers, the *Globe and Mail* and the *Star*, abided by their non-sexist language policy. Both newspapers had published new style guides in 1990 with fairly good coverage of non-sexist usage. Of course, like their US counterparts, there is a certain sensitivity to perceived public opinion in the Toronto papers: the *Toronto Star* guide proscribes *chair* on the grounds that '[it] irritates many readers'.

The 168 essays submitted on the topic all found that the newspapers' adherence to their own guidelines was sporadic: e.g. usage of the so-called generic *he* and *man* abound. For instance, while the guidelines for both newspapers tell writers not to use *he* as a generic, usages such as the following are common:

> Give your local horticulturist the dimensions of your balcony and tell *him* that you want to plant in a container that will limit growth to the size that complements, rather than overwhelms, your space. (Jeffrey Freedman, 'Tenant Gardening Trend Is to Be Beautiful and Tasty', *Toronto Star*, 17 March 1991)

> What seller would want (could afford) to lose a serious buyer who had already sold *his* existing home? (Alan Silverstein, 'Return of Conditional on Sale Offers a Good Sign', *Toronto Star*, 16 March 1991)

Similarly, the *Star* tells its writers not to use *man* as a generic and its guidelines gives a number of examples of gender-neutral usage.[7] However, a survey of one week's issues of the paper found that this guideline was not often followed. The great majority of individuals referred to that week were male and, in more than 80 percent of cases, they were referred to as *chairman, spokesman, businessman*, etc. When women were referred to, compounds with *person* or *woman* were used, never compounds with *man*. One article that week was highly reminiscent of the examples cited above from the *Chronicle of Higher Education*. In 'PM Showing CBC Contempt, Watson Charges', two sources are quoted: Canadian Broadcasting Corporation *Chairman* designate Patrick Watson and the *Chairperson* of the Council of Canadians, Maude Barlow. So we have found the opposite results from those reported by Fasold since we have widespread sexist usage in the face of non-sexist guidelines.

Some insight into the lack of enforcement of these guidelines was gained by one student on the course who interviewed a number of *Toronto Star* writers (Chelin, 1991). When asked why they used sexist language, a variety of responses were given. A gossip columnist announced that she 'wasn't performing brain surgery' but was just reporting the news and that she 'gives the audience what they want to read'. A business writer quoted from his copy of the *Star* style guide: 'it specifically says to use *chairman* or *chairwoman* but not *chairperson*', not realizing that his 1983 edition was out of date. A second business writer said he 'didn't realize there was a rule'. Attempts to justify usage included an appeal to the relative length of *man* vs *person* (this from a music writer): 'The nature of the newspaper game is to shorten; *person* has six letters and *man* has three'. There was also an argument based on the representation of women in the professions (this from another business writer): 'We are talking about men. We are talking about big companies who are all dominated by men and therefore we reflect that attitude. If we are talking about smaller companies it would be a whole different thing.' We see, then, that the (sexist) attitudes and values of individual writers have their influence. This can also be the case when a newspaper actually tries to enforce its policy. Fasold gives a revealing example from the *Washington Post*:

The reporter had just referred to a woman by last name alone in a second reference, when he added parenthetically: 'This newspaper's rules require that I call her merely that, though I would prefer Mrs.'

Clearly, then, having non-sexist language guidelines is not enough; an organization's commitment to enforcing them is crucial. As we see in the *Washington Post* case above, this enforcement may be subverted. The *Toronto Star* examples parallel the Faculty of Science course title example: language reform is less successful when it is left to the discretion of the individual to abide by the policy or not and when the speech community in question displays sexist values.[8]

Conclusion

In the first part of this article we demonstrate the extent to which linguistic meanings are determined by the social values and attitudes of the dominant culture. We argue that simply introducing non-sexist and feminist terms and phrases into a language will not necessarily lead to non-sexist usage. Just as words such as 'no' (in the context of a woman refusing a man's sexual advances), 'anti-racism' and 'racism' (among others) undergo a kind of 'semantic reversal' (Seidel's 1988 term) in the mouths and hands of a sexist, racist culture, so innovative non-sexist and feminist terms may lose their non-sexist meanings or interpretations as they are appropriated by a sexist speech community. The conclusion that we draw from this, however, is *not* that non-sexist language reform should be abandoned. Rather, we demonstrate that language reform is most successful when it takes place within the context of a non-sexist speech community, i.e., when the social values and attitudes of a speech community support non-sexist meanings rather than undermine them.

Notes

1. This is not to say that linguistic innovations will always begin with the highest status subgroup; the relative prestige associated with a particular subgroup and its linguistic innovations may be based on factors other than the socioeconomic ones typically associated with high prestige, e.g., ethnic identity, class loyalty, etc., may play a role. See Labov (1972) for discussion.
2. Henley (1987) makes a similar point regarding the possibility of successful language reform. However, Henley focuses on the way in which non-sexist forms are stigmatized and stereotyped because women, a lower prestige group, are the innovators.
3. There is also some evidence to suggest that *Ms* has been overtly stigmatized, as Labov predicts of linguistic innovations that are not introduced by the highest-status group within a speech community. Pierre Berton in a column in the *Toronto Star*, 15 June 1991, reports that a *Star* copyeditor would not allow him to use *Ms* before a woman's name because it was 'demeaning'.
4. For a fuller discussion of discursive strategies used systematically by the print media to redefine and depoliticize feminist linguistic innovations, see Ehrlich and King (1994).

5. By 1991, all but one course title within the Faculty of Science had been altered to eliminate the so-called generic 'man'. It is interesting to note that the remaining sexist course title was finally changed in 1994 through the efforts of the University's Status of Women Advisor at the time, herself, a respected biologist in the Faculty of Science.
6. Our corpus consists of letters to members of the Status of Women Communications Committee (York University) regarding course titles, letters to members of the committee regarding language reform at York more generally and articles on the subject of language reform appearing in campus newspapers.
7. The *Globe's* guidelines are less straightforward: while it advocates a number of non-sexist alternatives to *man*, it states that no satisfactory gender-neutral term exists for titles such as *chairman* or *spokesman* and that the writer should in such cases use sex-specific terms, e.g. *chairman/chairwoman*.
8. One year previously a major report by a task force on women's opportunities was commissioned by owners of the *Toronto Star*, the Southam Newspaper Group. It reported that less than 5 per cent of senior management was female and that sexist attitudes in newsrooms impeded women's chances for shattering the glass ceiling.

References

Atkinson, D. (1987) 'Names and Titles: Maiden Name Retention and the Use of Ms', *Journal of the Atlantic Provinces Linguistic Association (JAPLA)* 9: pp. 56–83.
Baron, D. (1986) *Grammar and Gender*, New Haven, CT, and London: Yale University Press.
Boot, D. (1992) 'The Clarence Thomas Hearings', *Columbia Journalism Review*, February: pp. 25–9.
Cameron, D. (1985) *Feminism and Linguistic Theory*, London: Macmillan.
Castro, J. (1992) 'Sexual Harassment: A Guide', *Time*, Jan. 20: pp. 37.
Chelin, P. (1991) 'The Inconsistencies in the Toronto Star and its 1990 Style Guide', Unpublished York University MS.
Council of Ontario Universities (1988) *Employment Equity for Women: A University Handbook*, Toronto: COU.
Dubois, B.L. and Crouch, I. (1987) 'Linguistic Disruption: He/she, S/he, He or She, He-She', in J. Penfield (ed.), *Women and Language in Transition*, Albany, NY: State University of New York.
Eckert, P. and McConnell-Ginet, S. (1992) 'Think Practically and Look Locally: Language and Gender as a Community-Based Practice', *Annual Review of Anthropology* 21: pp. 461–90.
Ehrlich, S. and King, R. (1994) 'Feminist Meanings and the (De)Politicization of the Lexicon', *Language in Society* 23: pp. 59–76.
Fasold, R. (1988) 'Language Policy and Change: Sexist Language in the Periodical News Media', in P. Lowenberg (ed.), *Language Spread and Language Policy*, Washington, DC: Georgetown University Press.
Frank, F. and Treichler, P.A. (eds.), (1989) *Language, Gender, and Professional Writing*, New York: Modern Language Association.
French, C.W. (ed.), (1987) *The Associated Press Stylebook and Libel Manual*, rev. edn. Reading, MA: Addison-Wesley.
Gal, S. (1989) 'Language and Political Economy', *Annual Review of Anthropology* 18: pp. 345–67.
Gal, S. (1991) 'Between Speech and Silence: The Problematics of Research on

Language and Gender', in M. di Leonardo (ed.), *Gender at the Crossroads of Know-ledge*, Berkeley, CA: University of California Press.

Globe and Mail (1990) *Globe and Mail Style Guide*, Toronto.

Government of Canada (1984) *Report of the Royal Commission on Equality in Employ-ment*, Ottawa: Government of Canada, Division of Supplies and Services.

Graddol, D. and Swann, J. (1989) *Gender Voices*, New York: Blackwell.

Henley, N. (1987) 'This New Species that Seeks a New Language: On Sexism in Language and Language Change', in J. Penfield (ed.), *Women and Language in Transition*, Albany, NY: State University of New York.

Henry III, W.A. (1991) 'Upside Down in the Groves of Academe', *Time* 137(13): pp. 66–9.

Khosroshahi, F. (1989) 'Penguins Don't Care, But Women Do: A Social Identity Analysis of a Whorfian Problem', *Language in Society* 18: pp. 505–25.

Labov, W. (1972) *Sociolinguistic Patterns*, Philadelphia: University of Pennsylvania Press.

McConnell-Ginet, S. (1989) 'The Sexual (Re)Production of Meaning', in F. Frank and P. Treichler (eds.), *Language, Gender and Professional Writing*, New York: Modern Language Association.

Miller, C. and Swift, K. (1976) *Words and Women: New Language New Times*, Garden City, NY: Doubleday.

Morgenson, G. (1991) 'May I have the Pleasure . . .', *National Review*, November 18: pp. 58–60.

Ontario Women's Directorate (1988) *Employment Equity in the Public Sector: A Survey Report*, Toronto: OWD.

Penelope, J. (1990) *Speaking Freely*, New York: Pergamon.

Schulz, M.R. (1975) 'The Semantic Derogation of Women', in B. Thorne and N. Henley (eds.), *Language and Sex: Difference and Dominance*, Rowley, MA: Newbury House.

Seidel, G. (1988) 'The British New Right's "Enemy Within": The Antiracists', in G. Smitherman-Donaldson and T. van Dijk (eds.), *Discourse and Discrimination*, Detroit, MI: Wayne State University Press.

Silverstein, M. (1985) 'Language and the Culture of Gender: At the Intersection of Structure, Usage and Ideology', in E. Mertz and R. Parmentier (eds.), *Semiotic Mediation*, New York: Academic Press.

Steinem, G. (1983) *Outrageous Acts and Everyday Rebellions*, New York: Holt, Rinehart & Winston.

Toronto Star (1990) *Toronto Star Style Guide*, Toronto.

Section II

Discourse

It is difficult to think of any social activities that are not accomplished through language. It is not surprising, therefore, that the analysis of discourse – stretches of speech or writing – has become an important part of many academic disciplines that aim to understand the workings of society, such as sociology, psychology, anthropology or political science. But although researchers in these different disciplines may have a common interest in analysing discourse, the questions that they aim to answer through their analyses vary, depending on their perspective. In this section we have chosen papers that address specifically sociolinguistic issues and that strengthen our understanding of the interrelationship between language and society.

The first paper, by **Janet Holmes**, tackles an assumption that has been widespread amongst linguists who analyse their intuitions about language rather than the actual language that we produce as part of our social lives. Many such linguists adopt what might seem to be a commonsense view, that the main purpose of language is to transmit objective information, or *referential meaning*. A fundamental assumption in sociolinguistics, however, is that although there may be some kinds of language use where giving and receiving information is arguably the main goal – in news broadcasts, for example – it is usually just as important to communicate *affective meaning*. Holmes presents a model of interaction which allows us to take proper account of these two aspects of meaning. She then analyses the form and function of one speech act, apologies, where the expression of affective meaning is often the only purpose of communication. Apologies are an example of a *conversational routine*. The linguistic form of a routine usually shows very little variation: its social function is so important that we need to be sure that we can recognise the routine each time that we hear it. The form of apologies is therefore relatively simple to describe, but it is more difficult to account for the function, which can be very complex. In cases such as these, sociolinguists often turn to a general model of interaction in order to explain the patterns of language use that they observe. Holmes uses the influential model of politeness developed by Penelope Brown and Stephen Levinson, which aims to account for a wide range of language behaviour in terms of the concept of face. Broadly, as Holmes explains, the idea is that there are two sides to the public face that we all present to the world. First, we have a positive face, which means that we want to be liked and approved of by other people. Certain types of language use aim to satisfy this kind of need: paying someone a compliment, for example, is usually a positive politeness strategy, showing our approval of the other person (compliments are the topic of R.K. Herbert's paper in Part I of this volume). Second, we have negative face needs, in that we do not wish to be imposed on by other people. Apologies are often negative politeness strategies, acknowledging that an imposition has occurred and attempting to put things right.

Like all theoretical models, Brown and Levinson's model of politeness makes some predictions about language use which Holmes can use her data on apologies to test. As she points out, some of her examples fit well with the politeness model, but others are better accounted for by a different model (the 'bulge' model of social relations). We see here, then, that in sociolinguistic research it is the data that have priority: our primary concern is not to construct powerful theories, as in some other branches of linguistics, but first to discover patterns of language use and then to see which theory can best explain these patterns.

The paper by **Suzanne Romaine** and **Deborah Lange** again stresses the importance of affective meaning in communication, this time in the context of language change. One recurrent and very interesting type of change is a process known as *grammaticalization*, where a word that originally had a lexical meaning takes on a grammatical meaning. The word *go*, for example, could once be glossed simply as 'to move from one place to another', but it now occurs in contemporary English as a marker of future tense, so that phrases such as *I'm going to read a book* do not necessarily imply that the speaker will change location in order to do the reading. Grammaticalization also occurs when a word that belongs to one specific grammatical category (or word class) comes to be used in additional categories also. This seems to be happening in contemporary English with the word *like*. For some time now speakers of English have used *like* as a preposition, a conjunction and an adjectival suffix, as Romaine and Lange point out; and now they are also using it as a marker of reported speech or thought. Like Holmes, Romaine and Lange interpret their results within a theoretical model, this time in terms of Traugott's principles of semantic change. These predict that linguistic forms will move from the expression of propositional (or referential) meaning towards the expression of affective meaning. Again, then, we can see the importance of these two types of meaning, this time as a first step in trying to explain some aspects of language change; we also observe the contribution that discourse analysis can make to our understanding of how language changes.

The term 'reported speech' is widely used, but we should not assume that reporting what someone has said means that we reproduce their words exactly as they were uttered. We rarely report an utterance word for word; instead, we use the strategy of reported speech to construct a mock dialogue within our own utterance, making what we say more vivid and therefore more likely to interest and involve the person to whom we are talking. Using reported speech is a profoundly social act, for it allows us to make creative use of other people's speech within our own utterances, linking what we are saying at present to what others have said on previous occasions. In this way we can connect ourselves to others, both present and absent. This *intertextuality* of discourse is the topic of the paper by **Janet Maybin**, which examines complex chaining relationships of this kind in children's conversations. Her paper makes the important point – which is mentioned in several papers in this volume – that utterances are multifunctional, simultaneously fulfilling a range of cognitive and social functions.

Much of our everyday conversation consists of recounting narratives of personal experience, reliving and retelling to others the events in which we have been involved. In this way we make sense of our past experience. Some of the linguistic characteristics of spoken narratives are universal, reflecting the fact that all speakers, in all societies, have to plan and articulate their speech as they go along, if it is to be spontaneous. This is what **James Gee** means when he writes of 'on-line planning and production', terms commonly used in psycholinguistics. Other linguistic features that occur in spoken narratives are not universal, however, but vary from one social group to another. Some characteristics, typical of oral cultures throughout the world and associated with prestigious verbal skills in those cultures, are incompatible with the discourse styles that are expected in a school context. Gee analyses the discourse styles of the narratives produced by two children from different home cultures, pointing out the implications for children learning to read and write at school. He also discusses the problems that can arise when educators do not appreciate the fact that some children have to switch from the discourse style that they have acquired at home if they are to conform to the expectations of the school. For these children, a change of speech style marks a change of their social, cultural and personal identity, and the acceptance of a different way of making sense of the world. Gee's paper should be required reading for all those who are involved in the formulation of educational language policy.

The classic paper by **Michael Clyne** continues the theme of cultural differences in discourse patterns and the problems to which they can give rise, focusing this time on written texts, and on international communication. His case study compares the writing styles of academics educated in English-dominant countries with the writing styles of academics educated in Germany. There are important differences in the organization of arguments and in the amount of digression that is considered acceptable, and in other aspects of discourse structure too. These differences, Clyne argues, reflect cultural attitudes towards learning in these countries: writers in English-speaking countries are expected to work towards making their texts intelligible for their readers, whereas the German tradition places the burden on readers to work towards understanding the knowledge and the stimulus to thought provided by academic writers. The resulting discourse strategies are so pervasive that they persist even when German speakers write in English, and even when they are aware of the differences that exist between the two traditions. These writing styles can, it seems, act as a barrier to the exchange of scholarship between Germanic and Anglophone cultures, despite their being related cultures; where cultures are more distantly related, therefore, we can expect the differences in discourse structure to be still more extreme. Discourse analysis has an important role to play, then, in a world where written communication at an international level is becoming increasingly necessary not only in the academic world but also in business, science and many other professional domains of life.

Many of the interactions that crucially affect people's lives take place in social institutions, such as the school, the workplace, doctors' surgeries, hospitals or government offices. Here too discourse analysis can play an important role in showing how language is part and parcel of the social practices that constitute our social institutions. The paper by **Michael Stubbs** deals with the courtroom where, as he points out, language has the utmost social significance, since both the verdict given by the jury and the sentencing of the judge are speech acts in the strongest sense of the word, with real power to act on individuals. Stubbs uses the techniques of *corpus linguistics*, demonstrating how computers can be used to reveal patterns of language use that are culturally significant. In this case, the methodology shows how the judge in his summing up may have unintentionally led the jury to believe that he himself thought that the defendant was guilty and, furthermore, that this was a logical way of thinking.

The final paper, by **Teun van Dijk**, represents work in the field of *critical discourse analysis*. The aim here is to use discourse analysis to understand how social dominance is achieved and maintained in key areas of social life. The analysts have the explicit goal not simply of observing, describing and explaining language but also of working towards social and political change, by seeing how inequalities of power could be removed. These, then, are far from being ivory tower academics.

It is impossible, of course, to ever be properly objective in a linguistic analysis. Van Dijk takes this point further, claiming that to even attempt to be objective when analysing language in social life is to ignore the existence of inequality and, therefore, to help to perpetuate it. For this reason, critical discourse analysts explicitly choose the perspective within which they carry out their analysis. Here Van Dijk chooses to take the perspective of supporters of multicultural education in his analysis of an extract from a debate in the British House of Commons on a specific issue relating to multiculturalism, showing how a speech that is far from being blatantly racist nevertheless indirectly supports racism in British society.

Further reading

General

Volumes III and IV of Teun Van Dijk's edited *Handbook of Discourse Analysis* (London, Academic Press, 1987) include several papers that review the main areas covered in this section (with the exception of grammaticalization). Deborah Schiffrin's *Approaches to Discourse: Language as Social Interaction* (Oxford, Blackwell, 1993) contains several chapters that examine sociolinguistic issues, though they can be hard going for beginners. A standard textbook on discourse analysis is Gillian Brown and George Yule's *Discourse Analysis* (Cambridge, Cambridge University Press, 1983).

Specific

Conversational routines:
Karin Aijmer, *Conversational Routines in English*. Harlow, Longman, 1996.
Florian Coulmas, ed., *Conversational Routine: Explorations in Standardized Communication Situations and Prepatterned Speech*. The Hague, Mouton, 1981.

Grammaticalization:
Paul Hopper and Elizabeth Closs Traugott, *Grammaticalization*. Cambridge, Cambridge University Press, 1993.

Intertextuality:
Norman Fairclough, *Discourse and Social Change*. Cambridge, Polity Press, 1992, ch. 4.

Narrative structure in oral traditions:
Dell Hymes, *'In Vain I Tried to Tell You': Essays in Native American Ethnopoetics*. Philadelphia, University of Pennsylvania Press, 1981.

A more general account of narratives is given by:
Michael J. Toolan, *Narrative: A Critical Linguistic Analysis*. London: Routledge, 1988.

Cultural differences in written discourse:
Ulla Connor, *Contrastive Rhetoric: Cross-Cultural Aspects of Second-Language Writing*. Harlow, Longman, 1996.

Corpus linguistics and discourse analysis:
Michael Stubbs, *Text and Corpus Linguistics*. Oxford, Blackwell, 1996.

Critical discourse analysis:
Norman Fairclough, *Language and Power*. Harlow, Longman, 1989.
Ruth Wodak, *Disorders of Discourse*. Harlow, Longman, 1996.

Research journals

The main journals whose specific aim is to publish sociolinguistically oriented research on discourse are *Discourse Processes, Discourse and Society* and *Text.*

8

Apologies in New Zealand English

Janet Holmes

Originally published in slightly longer form in *Language in Society*, 19 (1990).

> I'm terribly sorry. It was an accident. It really was. Don't move. I'll sort it out . . .
> No it won't happen again, I promise.

This little exchange conjures up a variety of possible scenarios. Has the speaker spilled some salt on the addressee, run into the addressee's car, caused them to drop all their papers, or forgotten to remove a cake from the oven as promised? Are the people involved complete strangers or do they live together? Is the speaker a customer, a teacher, or the bank manager? And how could one tell? There are certainly clues since appropriate remedial strategies differ in different circumstances, but totally accurate prediction is out of the question. One might, for example, think the exchange rather too elaborate and formal to have occurred between spouses, but in fact it followed the second occasion on which a woman allowed the door in her new office to close behind her just in front of her husband, who was carrying a pile of books, some of which consequently fell on the floor. The apology was provided laughingly in the wake of a vigorous but good-humored protest the first time she had forgotten the door's tendency to shut itself. Familiarity, one might think, would result in brief and casual apologies, but the circumstances are always relevant. One informant noted that after seriously offending his mother the appropriate remedial steps involved complex linguistic apology behavior, as well as an apologetic nonverbal gesture (flowers), and were spread over several days if not weeks.[1] The interaction of familiarity and the seriousness of the offense is one of the aspects of apology behavior which will be explored in this article.

The article examines some of the characteristics of apologies in informal remedial interchanges based on a New Zealand corpus. It is a wide-ranging exploration covering the functions of apologies, the range of strategies used to apologize, their semantic and syntactic structure, as well as some aspects of the sociolinguistic distribution of apologies. The discussion is developed within the broad context of Brown and Levinson's theory of politeness. Consequently, full definitions of terms such as *positive* and *negative politeness* can be found in Brown & Levinson (1978, 1987). I have explored in particular the relationship between the complexity of the apology and the weightiness of the offense which elicited it – assessed in terms of Brown and Levinson's R, P, and D, where R refers to the ranking of the imposition, P refers to the relative power of the hearer (H) over the speaker (S), and D defines the social distance between the participants (Brown & Levinson 1978: 79).[2] Brown and Levinson's model provides a means of taking account of a range of social factors which are likely to affect the way a speaker apologizes for an offense, and it is therefore possible to analyze the effect that different factors have on the apology strategies which native speakers use in different contexts.

I first discuss the function of apologies in interaction and provide a definition of what counts as an apology. Then I examine the range of strategies which served as apologies in a corpus of New Zealand remedial exchanges and the linguistic formulae used in these exchanges. Finally, the distribution of apologies is analyzed according to the type of offense they are intended to remedy and to the social relationship between the participants. Not surprisingly, apologies turn out to be a rich source of information on the ways language interacts with society.

The function of an apology

Apologies in a model of interaction
An apology is primarily and essentially a social act. It is aimed at maintaining good relations between participants. To apologize is to act politely, both in the vernacular sense and in the more technical sense of paying attention to the addressee's face needs (Brown & Levinson 1978, 1987). Apologies challenge the Gricean (1975) view of polite talk as a deviation from rational and efficient talk. Within a Gricean framework, polite ways of talking "show up as deviations, requiring rational explanation on the part of the recipient, who finds in considerations of politeness reasons for the speaker's apparent irrationality or inefficiency" (Brown & Levinson 1987: 4). It is my contention that a view of communication which regards an apology as evidence of irrationality and inefficiency on the speaker's part is scarcely illuminating. [. . .]

To provide a satisfactory analysis one needs a model which takes account of the different emphasis that participants put on referential versus social meaning in different types of interaction. It seems to me that a graphed square or two-dimensional plot provides a model which adequately represents the interdependence of these two important dimensions in any interaction: social or affective meaning on the one hand, and referential or propositional information on the other (see Fig. 8.1).[3] This model facilitates analysis of interaction as potentially permitting simultaneous expression of both content and affect.

The area within the four quadrants of the square represents interactional space. Any utterance, expression, or interaction may be located in that space according to the extent to which it expresses both referential content, on a scale from 0 to 100 percent, and affective meaning on a scale running from high solidarity at one end to maximum social distance or deference at

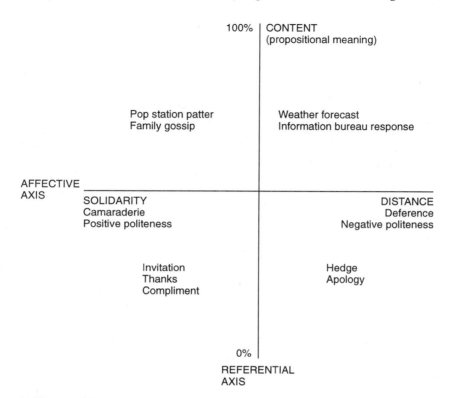

Fig. 8.1 Model for analyzing interaction

the other.[4] Such a model not only allows but requires analysis of interaction as simultaneously expressing both propositional content and affective meaning. It also recognizes that the attention paid to each will differ in degree in any particular situation. Hence, a response (such as *3 o'clock*) to an information-seeking question (such as *what time is it?*) may be placed close to the top of the vertical axis to take account of its high information content in a particular context, whereas a greeting, a compliment, or an apology may be located low on the referential axis but at the solidarity or positive politeness end of the affective dimension, reflecting the fact that such speech acts may convey little referential content but express a message high in affect or social meaning.

The form of the model has quite specific implications then. Although the referential axis represents a scale extending from minimum referential or propositional content at its base to maximum referential content at the top, the affective axis does not represent a scale of minimum to maximum affect. Rather, different points along the axis represent different kinds of affect or the degree to which the speaker takes account of the addressee's positive versus negative face needs. The affective axis thus combines Brown and Levinson's (1987) concepts of power (P) and distance (D) or

Brown and Gilman's (1960) concepts of power and solidarity. The scale makes it possible to account for utterances or expressions which express predominantly solidarity or distance/deference while also reflecting the fact that a particular utterance may have elements of each.

Defining an apology

Although it would be possible to restrict the term *apology* to expressions such as *sorry* and *I apologize*, as Owen (1983) did, it has generally been used to describe what Goffman referred to as a *remedy* (1971: 140), the one essential element in a *remedial interchange*. This term nicely highlights the central function of apologies – to provide a remedy for an offense and restore social equilibrium or harmony (cf. Edmondson 1981: 280; Leech 1983: 125). Hence, a broad definition of an apology as it is used in this article takes function as the crucial criterion:

> An apology is a speech act addressed to B's face-needs and intended to remedy an offense for which A takes responsibility, and thus to restore equilibrium between A and B (where A is the apologizer, and B is the person offended).

[. . .] The elements of the definition imply the following minimal felicity conditions:

(a)   an act has occurred;
(b)   A believes the act has offended B; and
(c)   A takes some responsibility for the act.

In these circumstances it is likely that what A says will be interpreted as an apology. But it is not possible to predict exactly what form A's utterance will take, as a wide range of forms can appropriately fit the apology slot in different circumstances. On the other hand, it is also possible that A might choose not to apologize and instead might produce one of the following utterances:

(1)   That's the way the cookie crumbles.
       Next please.
       Time for lunch.

or any number of other utterances which are unlikely to be interpreted as apologies.

Though it is not possible to specify a complete speech act set for apology, it is both possible and useful for descriptive purposes to categorize the range of strategies which were used in a corpus of apologies collected from native speakers in English, as I illustrate in the following.[5] The range includes any speech act which satisfies the definition given earlier and may therefore seem very broad. Its breadth is justified, however, by the decision to regard function as criterial. Goffman himself, in his discussion of "apologizing." initially distinguished apologies, accounts, and requests (1971: 109), restricting the term *apology* to the explicit expression of regret and repudiation of the offense. But in subsequent discussion he recognized that the underlying function of what he called a *remedy* may be achieved by any combination of these strategies: "at some level of analysis, these function in exactly the same way as does an apology" (Goffman 1971: 140).

An apology will typically address an offense performed by the apologizer, as in Example (2).

(2) [A bumps into B, who is standing still.]
A: Sorry.
B: That's OK.

It is sometimes the case, however, that an apology will be made on behalf of someone for whom the apologizer feels responsible, such as a child, a spouse, a friend, or a member of the same group as the person apologizing.

(3) [A's child spills her drink on B's carpet.]
A: Oh look I'm terribly sorry. I'll clean it up. Have you got a cloth?
B: Don't worry. I'll do it. It wasn't very much.

Thus, the definition refers to the person who takes responsibility for the offense rather than the offender.

Apologies and face
Apologies, like compliments, are primarily aimed at maintaining or supporting the addressee's, and in some cases the apologizer's, "face" (see the Introduction to Section II (p. 196), and Goffman 1967). I refer to both these speech acts, therefore, as examples of "face-supportive acts" (FSAs). Compliments focus on the addressee's positive face wants (Holmes 1986b, 1988), whereas apologies are generally aimed at face redress associated with FTAs (face-threatening acts) or offenses which have damaged the addressee's face in some respect and can therefore be regarded as negative politeness strategies (Brown & Levinson 1978: 65, 192).

It is worth noting, however, that although the speech act serving most directly as the apology functions as a negative politeness strategy, accompanying elements may address the victim's or the speaker's positive face needs (cf. Brown & Levinson 1978: 296, fn. 14).[6] The overall function of the remedial exchange is to maintain participants' face, and in order to do this elements in the exchange may address transgressions to positive or negative face wants. Since, from the speaker's point of view, an apology may itself be the FTA that damages the speaker's positive face by admitting that he or she has offended the victim, the remedial exchange may incorporate an attempt to simultaneously redress the speaker's positive face needs as well as the victim's face needs.[7]

Apologies redress negative face when the offense has ignored B's "want that his [sic] actions be unimpeded by others" (Brown & Levinson 1978: 67). Examples (2) and (3) illustrate apologies intended to remedy a threat to B's negative face. Apologies address positive face wants when the transgression offends B's need that his or her "wants be desirable to at least some others" (Brown & Levinson 1978: 67). This includes the individual's need that others recognize her or his achievements and respect them. Hence (4) redresses damage to the victim's positive face.

(4) [Introducing B to C, A has used *Mr.* instead of *Dr.* for B.]
A: Oh I am sorry – it's Dr. Hall not Mr. Forgive me.
[B smiles in an embarrassed way and addresses C.]
B: Nice to meet you.[8]

In addition to addressing the victim's face loss, apologies may simultaneously address the loss of positive face incurred by the speaker. Where a remedial exchange includes an explanation, the speaker's positive face needs are generally taken into account, as in (5).

(5) [A is phoning B to warn her of potential inconvenience.]
A: I'm sorry but I'm going to be a bit late for work. The buses aren't off strike yet and with it being a wet Friday, it'll probably be a while until my taxi arrives.
B: Uh-huh as long as you're here by six, cos I'm going then.

This remedial interchange indicates awareness of potential offense to the victim's negative face (*I'm sorry*), as well as attempting to redress the speaker's positive face loss by pointing to two reasons why the anticipated offense may be difficult to avoid.

Though FTAs are generally described and analyzed as unintentional transgressions or at least as transgressions that cannot easily be avoided, it is worth noting that apologies may in some circumstances be associated with deliberate offenses. Paddy Austin (1988) introduced the term *face attack act* (FAA) for that subcategory of FTAs which involve intentional attacks on the addressee's face, such as insults and accusations. In this context too, where apologies are used in relation to FAAs, they are concerned with face redress and function as FSAs. An apology accompanying an FAA will often be performed by someone other than the face attacker, who nevertheless takes responsibility for the offense caused, as in (6).

(6) [A's child, C has insulted her playmate, B, who is a guest at A's house.]
C: Go away you're mean and I hate you.
A: Sally! It's alright Brigid, she doesn't mean it. She's just a bit scratchy today.
B: [No visible response. Carries on playing.]

It is also possible, however, for the face attacker herself to apologize for the FAA. This involves very explicitly what Goffman described as "a splitting of the self into a blameworthy part and a part that stands back and sympathizes with the blame-giving" (Goffman 1971: 113), that is, a simultaneous recognition of the offense and an attempt to dissociate oneself from the offending action. Example (7) illustrates this.

(7) [A, reneging on an earlier agreement, tells B's family that she cannot now put them up. B can reasonably feel insulted and discounted. Apology comes some time later.]
A: Look I'm terribly sorry for what happened. I was in an impossible position. I just couldn't please everyone.
B: That's OK. I understand – though I must admit I felt pretty hurt at the time.

In concluding this discussion of the functions of apologies, it should be noted that, like many utterances, those serving as apologies can express other functions, too. They may be bivalent or plurivalent speech acts, expressing more than one illocutionary or pragmatic force (Thomas 1985). Utterances which express regret for an offense may also serve as an admission, with the addressee learning of the offense through the utterance which serves as an apology. Thus one utterance simultaneously performs the function of conveying bad news (cf. Brown & Levinson 1978: 73) and apologizing for it:

(8) [In trying to undo a bottle for B, A breaks the cap.]
A: Oh dear I'm afraid I've broken it.
B: Never mind at least it's open now!

Utterances like these illustrate the complexity of interaction, since they simultaneously express a FTA while administering face redress as a politeness strategy mitigating the effect of the FTA. The later discussion of apology strategies illustrates this point further, since it is often the case that an utterance which serves as an apology simultaneously provides an explanation or excuse for the offense, as illustrated in (9). The categorization as apology often depends on appropriate "apologetic" intonation in these cases.

(9) [A has started to eat before B, the family's guest, has served herself to all the food available.]
A: I'm just so hungry I can't wait any longer.
B: Don't worry – go ahead.

At a more general level, Norrick (1978) pointed out that, in addition to convincing the victim of the speaker's regret, apologies often serve such social functions as "to evince good manners, to assuage the addressee's wrath, or simply to get off the hook and be on one's way" (1978: 281). Clearly, then, many of the utterances with which I am concerned express more than one illocutionary force. In discussing the examples in the New Zealand corpus, however, I focus on their role as apologies.

Methodology and the corpus

[. . .] The corpus used in this analysis consists of 183 remedial interchanges, that is, apologies and apology responses, collected with the assistance of

New Zealand students who selected the task as one option in a list of possible course assignments.[9] The data collection method was the ethnographic method deriving from anthropology which has been advocated by Hymes over many years (Hymes 1962, 1964, 1972) and used very successfully by researchers such as Manes and Wolfson (1981). The students were asked to note down the next 20 apologies they heard, without selection or censorship. They noted as soon and as accurately as possible the exact words used in the apology exchange, together with relevant contextual details.

The data suffer inevitably from limitations. A number of students commented that it was much more difficult to collect examples of apologies than instances of compliments, for instance. Small short examples are not easily noticed or salient in conversation, and more elaborate apologies are comparatively infrequent. It seems likely, therefore, that the data cannot provide more than broad guidelines on the relative frequency of different types of apology. It does, however, provide a useful source of information on the range of apology strategies and the syntactic-semantic forms used to express them by New Zealand adults.

A second disadvantage of the method adopted is the reliance on a written transcription after the completion of the exchange. A small number of written apologies was included in the sample (5.5%), since they were encountered during the data collection process. They provide an interesting contrast at various points in the analysis, but the great majority of the apologies collected were spoken (94.5%). Ideally, one would wish to use taperecorded speech data, as Owen (1983) did. She provided convincing evidence that the prosodic features of what she called *primary remedial moves* are very important in a more detailed analysis of their pragmatic function in context. The analysis in this article focuses therefore on the identification of broad patterns and correlations observed within the corpus, and later I examine the question of the extent to which the data in this corpus appear to be consistent with the results of Owen's more detailed analysis. Finally, it should be noted that the apologies collected were predominantly produced by adult pakeha New Zealanders, and it is therefore the apology norms of this group that are the focus of the study.[10]

Apology strategies

A number of researchers have devised classification systems for apology strategies (Blum-Kulka & Olshtain 1984; Fraser 1981; Olshtain & Cohen 1983; Owen 1983; Trosberg 1987). Much of this research has developed from an interest in teaching second language learners, and the emphasis has frequently been comparative. As discussed in the previous section, the data on which the categorizations have been developed have often been elicited role play data.

In developing a satisfactory categorization system for the naturally occurring data in the New Zealand corpus, I have built on the work of these earlier researchers and have followed Olshtain and Cohen's (1983) framework, in particular, very closely. Four broad basic categories were used, with a number of subcategories where necessary.

(A) *An explicit expression of apology*
   – Offer apology/IFID (i.e., illocutionary force indicating device), e.g., "I apologize"
   – Express regret, e.g., "I'm afraid"; "I'm sorry"
   – Request forgiveness, e.g., "excuse me"; "forgive me"
(B) *An explanation or account, an excuse or justification*[11]
   – e.g., "I wasn't expecting it to be you"; "we're both new to this"
(C) *An acknowledgement of responsibility*
   – Accept blame, e.g., "it was my fault"
   – Express self-deficiency, e.g., "I was confused"; "I wasn't thinking"; "I didn't see you"
   – Recognize H as entitled to an apology, e.g., "you're right"; "you deserve an apology"
   – Express lack of intent, e.g., "I didn't mean to"
   – Offer repair/redress, e.g., "we'll replace it for you"; "I'll bring you another"
(D) *A promise of forebearance*
   – e.g., "I promise it won't happen again"[12]

Table 8.1 shows the total number of instances of each strategy in the data. It is important to note, however, that the strategies are not mutually exclusive; they may co-occur. Example (10) illustrates this well since it involves all four basic strategy types.

(10) [A and B are flatmates. B has asked A to put out her washing and he has forgotten.]
   B: Thanks for putting my washing out Gerry.
   A: Oops! That's right. I forgot. I'm sorry. Next time I'll remember.

It is the fact that strategies combine in this way which explains why there are more than 183 apology strategies in Table 8.1. The possible combinations are

Table 8.1 Strategies used in apologies

	Strategy	No.	%
A.	An explicit expression of apology		
	offer apology/IFID	15	5
	express regret	149	49.3
	request forgiveness	18	6
B.	An explanation or account	70	23.2
C.	An acknowledgement of responsibility		
	accept blame	8	2.6
	express self-deficiency	9	3
	recognize H as entitled to an apology	3	1
	express lack of intent	7	2.3
	offer repair/redress	18	6
D.	A promise of forbearance	5	1.7
	Total	302	100

Table 8.2 Combinations of apology strategies

Strategies	No.	%
A	79	43.2
AA	5	2.7
AAB	1	0.5
AB	47	25.7
ABA	1	0.5
ABC	5	2.7
ABCC	1	0.5
AC	17	9.3
ACC	1	0.5
ACCC	1	0.5
AD	4	2.2
Subtotal	162	88.3
B	4	2.2
BA	5	2.7
BAC	1	0.5
BACA	1	0.5
Subtotal	11	5.9
CA	2	1.1
CB	3	1.6
CC	2	1.1
CBAD	1	0.5
CCA	1	0.5
CCC	1	0.5
Subtotal	10	5.3
Total	183	99.5

A = an explicit expression of apology; B = an explanation or account; C = an acknowledgement of responsibility; D = a promise of forbearance.

discussed later and are summarized in Table 8.2. But any one strategy alone may count as an apology in the appropriate context.

Instances in category A are direct speech acts functioning as apologies, whereas, when they occur alone without an explicit apology form, those in categories B, C, and D are indirect apologies, since their surface function appears to be to make an excuse or to take responsibility for some undesirable action or to make a promise. There has been some debate over whether less direct speech acts are more polite than more direct ones. Leech (1983: 127) claimed this quite explicitly in his discussion of impositives or directives, and it is also explicit in Brown and Levinson's (1978) organization of politeness strategies from least to most direct. They too exemplified predominantly with directives, however, and it is clear that this generalization does not hold for speech acts like apologies that directly benefit rather than impose on the addressee. Politer apologies normally include an explicit apology at some point, together with another strategy. I return to this point in the discussion of the correlation of apology strategies with social factors.

The categories are also arranged in increasing order in terms of how heavily ranked they are as politeness strategies. Apologies in category A are the simplest and least heavily weighted strategies. Those in C and D are more complex and more heavily weighted apology strategies (cf. Leech 1983).

It is quite clear from Table 8.1 that an explicit expression of apology, and, in particular, the strategy of expressing regret, is the most frequent apology strategy selected. This strategy accounts for almost exactly half of all the strategies in the data. The only other strategy which is used extensively is strategy B – providing an account or excuse. Almost one quarter of the total number of strategies occurring in the corpus involved an explanation or account. No other strategy accounts for more than 6 percent of the data, so the predominance of strategies A and B is very marked.[13]

The summary provided in Table 8.1 is far from the whole story, however, since over 50 percent of the remedial interchanges in the corpus involved some combination of strategies. In fact, only strategies A and B occur alone, and although 43 percent of the remedial interchanges use strategy A on its own, strategy B occurs alone only four times. An example is given in (11).

(11) [B answers the phone and A mistakes her voice for her mother's.]
A: Hello. Margot?
B: No it's her daughter speaking.
A: Oh gosh you sound like your mother – is that the baby of the family?
B: Yes that's right.

Few researchers provide information on the ways in which strategies combine in remedial interchanges. Yet it is important to consider how strategies combine as well as which strategies native speakers use. [. . .] Just over half the apology exchanges in the corpus (54.6%) involved more than one strategy. Combining strategies results in a "weightier" apology, appropriate for more serious offenses – a point to be explored more fully later. In examining the possible combinations of strategies, there are two factors which deserve attention. First, the number of strategies which co-occur are worth comment; and second, it is interesting to note the co-occurrence patterns which characterize the data. Table 8.2 summarizes the combinations which occur using the four broad basic categories and provides information on the different patterns found in the data.

Seventeen different combinations of apology strategy occur in the data but they are far from being evenly distributed. The second most frequent pattern is one involving a combination of an explicit apology with an account or explanation (AB or BA); these account for 28.4 percent of the data. In fact, 34 percent of the remedial interchanges include a combination of A and B either alone or along with some other strategy. The only other pattern which accounts for more than 3 percent of the corpus is the combination of an explicit apology with an acknowledgment of responsibility (AC and CA: 10.4%). No other combination occurs more than five times. Moreover, only 15 (8.2%) of the remedial interchanges in this corpus involve more than two strategies in combination, and only one uses all four different strategies.

It is interesting to note that a remedial interchange may involve more than one occurrence of the *same* apology strategy. Example (5) includes two explanations or excuses, for instance, and (12) provides an example with two instances of the speaker expressing self-deficiency and one accepting the blame, all of which are C strategies (acknowledging responsibility).

(12) [A has drifted off in B's class.]
     A: I'm feeling a little muddled at the moment and I think it's my fault, maybe I wasn't listening, but what was field independence.

Strategies A and C are those which reduplicate most freely within the same interchange. There were eight exchanges that involved two or more occurrences of strategy A, illustrated in (10) as well as in (13), whereas seven involved two or more occurrences of strategy C, exemplified in (12).

(13) [A has made a mistake in marking B's assignment.]
     A: Oh I beg your pardon. I'm very sorry.

Overall, however, Table 8.2 shows that instances of exchanges where the same strategy recurs are relatively infrequent. There are only 15 instances in the corpus, that is, 8.2 percent of the total.

As mentioned earlier, about half the remedial exchanges documented involved more than one apology strategy; the remaining apology exchanges in the data (45.4%) involved just a single strategy, almost always an explicit apology. Although the precise combinations or frequencies of each strategy selected are not given, it is evident that, especially in research using role play, respondents commonly use two or more strategies (e.g., Trosberg 1987). It is possible that this is a result of the methodology. Respondents may feel under pressure to produce more than the minimum response; alternatively, the situations with which they are presented may be such that a simple apology is considered inadequate. Trosberg (1987) noted, for instance, the relatively low number of direct apologies in her data (only 7.2% of the total number of strategies used by the native speakers of English in her sample). She suggested that this may be related to "the severity of the offense" (1987: 164) and commented that the "situations chosen for role plays were of a kind that could not be easily treated as routines" (1987: 165). Given a range of naturally occurring situations, Table 8.2 demonstrates that, although native speakers do use combinations of categories most of the time, a simple explicit apology is frequently considered adequate.

Another interesting point is the relative flexibility of position that different strategies demonstrate. Table 8.3 provides a summary of the positions in the data in which each strategy occurred. It shows that strategy A (an explicit apology) and strategy C (an acknowledgement of responsibility) may occur in any position, whereas B does not occur in place 4, and D never occurs in initial position or in place 3. I am not suggesting, of course, that these patterns should be regarded as absolute co-occurrence restric-

Table 8.3 Positions in which strategies occur

Position			
1	2	3	4
A	A	A	A
B	B	B	–
C	C	C	C
–	D	–	D

A = an explicit expression of apology; B = an explanation or account; C = an acknowledgement of responsibility; D = a promise of forbearance.

tions. It seems perfectly feasible that strategy D would occur in place 3, for instance. They simply describe the patterns found in the data and provide a basis for comparing these patterns with those found in other corpora.

Finally, it is worth noting that in the small number (i.e., (10)) of written apologies in the corpus, there was *always* an explicit apology strategy at some point. Indeed, all but 5 percent of the apologies in the corpus included an explicit apology strategy (i.e., an A strategy). The only cases where there is no explicit apology are conversations between intimates, where the intonation very clearly signals the function of the utterance as an apology.[14] An example is given in (14).

(14) [B, one of A's three daughters, answers the phone.]
A: Hello.
B: Hi Mum.
A: Oh which one's that?
B: Jeannie.
A: Oh so it is – I was just waiting to hear from Em so I wasn't expecting you.
B: Huh!

In summary, then, the analysis demonstrates that an explicit apology without any elaboration or further supporting comment is the most widely occurring strategy in this corpus of naturally occurring apology exchanges. It is also evident that New Zealanders frequently combine an explicit apology with other strategies and may even reduplicate their chosen strategy on occasion.

Syntactic-semantic features of apologies

Table 8.2 demonstrates that 95 percent of the apologies in the corpus included an explicit apology strategy (i.e., an A strategy) at some point. Where an apology is explicitly expressed, it is possible to classify its form. Though Goffman commented, "[w]hether one runs over another's sentence, time, dog, or body, one is more or less reduced to saying some variant of 'I'm sorry'" (1971: 117), in fact the range of possible formulae is a little wider than that.

The most frequent variants use one of a small set of syntactic-semantic formulae and draw on a small range of lexical items. The framework used in Table 8.4 is developed from that used in Owen (1983: 63–64). Owen provided a very detailed description of the forms identified in her British corpus, hence it was possible to include in Table 8.4 a comparison of the basic patterns occurring in the New Zealand data with those in Owen's (1983) British data. I discuss and exemplify each category in turn.

Variant of 'apologize' or 'apology/ies'
Variants using the explicit performative formula are, as Owen noted, relatively rare. She found only two instances in her spoken corpus and two instances in written form, all of which she characterized as occurring in "a kind of monologue" (1983: 65), such as a lecture or a formal notice, reflecting the fact that the relationship between the participants is rather distant and formal.

In the New Zealand data too, these forms occur in more formal interactions or in writing. In speech they tended to characterize interactions where the participants did not know each other. An example is provided in (15).

Table 8.4 Syntactic-semantic patterns used for apology

Pattern	United Kingdom[a]		New Zealand	
	No.	%	No.	%
Variant of APOLOGIZE *or* APOLOGY/IES				
Verb	3	3.6	6	3.4
e.g., I { must / ought to / would like to } we apologize				
Noun	1	1.2	8	4.6
e.g., I have an apology to make . . . (accept my) apologies				
I'M AFRAID . . .	7	8.4	5	2.9
Pattern with SORRY				
(Intensifier) sorry	20	24.1	66	37.9
I'm/am (intens) sorry	21	25.3	36	20.7
(I'm) (intens) sorry to/if/for VP/(that) S	22	26.5	24	13.8
(I'm) (intens) sorry about that/it	9	10.8	12	6.9
Other patterns				
Excuse me/us	–		9	5.2
Pardon (me)/I beg your pardon	–		4	2.3
Forgive me	–		3	1.7
We regret that S	–		1	0.6
Total	83		174	

[a] Source: Owen (1983).

(15) [Waitress to customer in restaurant.]
A: Please accept our apologies sir. We'll replace it for you.

Half of the total instances of written apologies in the corpus used these explicit formal apology forms; in such cases they tended to occur not only in formal notices, but also between those who knew each other but who were not close friends.

(16) [Letter from one colleague to another.]
Dear Dave,
First apologies for taking so long to get back to you with the reading you requested . . .

(17) [Letter from writer to editor whom he knows.]
Dear Jean,
My apologies for the slightly belated arrival of this paper.

These forms are thus relatively infrequent and restricted to more formal or written interactions.

'I'm afraid' as an apology
Owen (1983: 88–92) provided an interesting account of how *I'm afraid* may serve to express an apology. She argued that when followed by a full complement sentence, the primary function of the utterance is to inform (as in (8)), though the *I'm afraid* clearly expresses regret and thus "some remedial effect may be achieved" (1983: 89). In other cases (when followed by a sentence pro-form such as *so* or *not*), she suggested the primary function is remedial, since the pro-form presupposes the addressee's knowledge of the offense. There were no examples in the original corpus, but (18) is an attested additional example.

(18) [A walks in without the parcel he was supposed to collect on his way home from school.]
B: You didn't forget it did you?
A: I'm afraid I did. I'll collect it tomorrow I promise.

Owen did not say how many instances there were in her corpus, though she cited seven examples in the discussion. In the New Zealand corpus, there were only five examples of *I'm afraid* functioning as an apology, four in speech and one in writing, that is, 2.9 percent of the syntactic patterns used to express the apology explicitly. Interestingly, this form appears to be appropriate in response to weightier offenses, though the reason for the weight, that is, P, D, or R (Brown & Levinson 1978: 79), differed in each case. This point is explored further below, in the discussion on the distribution of apologies. One instance involved a minor infraction between strangers on the telephone (i.e., where D was high), another involved participants who differed in status (i.e., high P), and another (see (19)) occurred between very close friends but involved a serious offense (i.e., high R).

(19) [A and B are close friends. A has given B a serious fright by forget-
ting to inform her of a change of arrangements.]
A: I want to make an abject apology
B: You need to.
A: I really am sorry. I'm afraid I forgot the arrangements had been
changed.

A serious offense between intimates will thus result in an overall offense
weighting that involves adopting a higher ranked remedial or negative
politeness strategy. In fact, the apologizer employs all three of the highest
ranked explicit apology strategies in combination. On a number of
grounds, then, it seems that *I'm afraid* tends to co-occur with relatively
heavily weighted offenses.

Variant of 'Sorry'
Owen (1983: 66) provided the following descriptive rule for variants in her
data involving the word *sorry*, which is clearly the most frequent form used
as an explicit apology:

I'm		(that) S
	([intensifier]) sorry	to VP
I am		if S
		about that

She commented that, "out of 24 possible combinations derivable from [the
rule], only twelve occur, and of these only several occur more than once . . .
suggesting that certain forms – roughly a third of the possibilities – predominate strongly" (Owen 1983: 67).

Table 8.4 illustrates that the New Zealand data are equally characterized
by the predominance of a few clearly identifiable patterns. Some form of
sorry accounts for more than 75 percent of the data. There is a clear
difference between speech and writing, however, reflecting the fact that
the written examples in the corpus are generally more formal and
addressed to a less familiar audience. Only one instance in the written
data uses the form *sorry*, and this one example occurs on a postcard
between two colleagues who are on very good terms.

(20) [Postcard from A to B, a colleague and friend.]
Dear Larry,
    Sorry to put you in the embarrassing position of having to ask if
you owe me money.
You do not.

Other patterns
Only four other patterns were identified in the New Zealand data as ways of
expressing an apology explicitly: *excuse me/us* (9 instances); *pardon(me)/I beg
your pardon* (4); *forgive me* (3); *we regret that S* (1). The latter two occur only
as written forms, and apart from one instance of *excuse us* observed on a
notice to customers, the first two patterns occur as speech forms. The

speech forms tend to be apologies for socially frowned on behavior, such as burping, or for actions which inconvenience addressees, such as leaning in front of them to reach something. This point is discussed further below, in the section on offense type. Example (21) illustrates an apology for an error which inconveniences B.

(21) [A is a waitress who has served B the wrong drink.]
A: I beg your pardon. I thought you said "wine and soda."
B: Never mind. I'll have it anyway.

Summing up, then, it is evident from the narrow range of syntactic-semantic patterns identified that apologies, like compliments (Holmes 1986b; Manes & Wolfson 1981: 123; Wolfson & Manes 1980: 404) are remarkably formulaic speech acts: a very small number of lexical items and syntactic patterns account for the great majority of the explicit apologies in the corpus. Since 96 percent of the apologies in the corpus involved an explicit expression of apology, the number of syntactic-semantic patterns which occurs regularly is remarkably high. This regularity is theoretically interesting in light of the debate over the relative weight to be given to Chomskyan claims of native speakers' creativity and originality, compared to suggestions that much of the language we know is stored in prefabricated chunks or "lexicalised sentence stems" (see Kuiper & Haggo 1984; Pawley 1985; Pawley & Syder 1983). Clearly, it adds to the growing body of evidence in support of the latter position.

As Table 8.4 shows, three basic categories account for 91 percent of the total New Zealand corpus of apologies. The formulae involved draw on a very narrow range of lexical items, less than 10 in total: *apology, apologize, be afraid that, excuse, forgive, sorry, regret;* and 79 percent of all the apologies collected included some form of *sorry*. Written examples always involved an explicit apology at some point and, not surprisingly, they tended to use the more formal syntactic patterns.[15] (8 out of the 10 used the very formal patterns involving some form of the words *apologize, apology,* or *regret;* only 1 example used the pattern with *sorry*, which predominated in spoken apologies.)

Overall, then, apologies appear to draw on a very narrow range of syntactic patterns and high frequency lexical items. Compared to many other speech acts, their linguistic form is relatively simple to describe. Identifying the pragmatic factors needed to account adequately for the distribution of apologies, however, is by no means so straightforward.

Distribution of apology strategies

Before examining some of the sociolinguistic features of the contexts in which different apology strategies occurred, it is worth considering what one might expect to find in the way of correlations between linguistic and nonlinguistic factors. Apologies function as remedies for offenses and are aimed at restoring social harmony between people. The crucial non-linguistic elements involved are thus the seriousness of the offense and the relationship between the participants. These factors are identified as important by a number of analysts and, most relevantly here, have been described by Brown and Levinson (1978, 1987) as factors which must be taken into account in estimating the weightiness of a face-threatening act. Using R to refer to the seriousness of the offense or the "absolute ranking of impositions in the particular culture," P to refer to the relative power of H over S, and D to define the social distance between S and H, Brown and Levinson (1978: 79) suggested that all three components contribute to an assessment of an FTA's weight. Although other factors may appear important in particular circumstances, they can often be subsumed under one of these more general factors.[16]

Brown and Levinson's model predicts that, providing the need for efficiency or urgency is not greater than the want to maintain H's face, there will be an increase in politeness in relation to the degree of face threat involved in a speech act. Assuming that an apology is quintessentially a politeness strategy (in that its predominant function relates to the maintenance of participants' face needs), variation in features of apologies presumably reflects the speaker's assessment of the appropriate balance between the support work required to maintain H's face and the inevitable face loss incurred by the apologizer. One would predict, then, that the greater the offense, the more "polite" the remedy would need to be. Indeed, Brown and Levinson commented on this quite explicitly at one point: "If a breach of face respect occurs, this constitutes a kind of debt that must be made up by positive reparation if the original level of face respect is to be maintained. Reparation should be of an appropriate kind and paid in a degree proportionate to the breach" (1987: 236).

A number of questions then arise. What linguistic means do speakers use to increase the size of an apology? Is increasing the size of an apology the same as making it more polite? Could a "big" apology be brief? Leech (1983) suggested indirectness is a means of making impositives more polite. How do speakers make apologies more polite? These are interesting questions which will require a great deal of further detailed investigation. As a first step, I have followed Brown and Levinson in using "politeness" to refer to attention to face needs, and thus I have assumed that a bigger apology which takes more account of face needs is also a more polite one. Moreover, there are clearly a number of ways in which speakers might increase the politeness of their apologies, and some at least involve easily measurable features. Speakers may select more extended rather than minimal strategies, for example, and longer rather than shorter linguistic formulae;[17] they may use intensifiers or "boosters" of the illocutionary force rather than hedges or downgraders within the formulae (Holmes 1984b); tone of voice and facial expression may contribute "feeling" or "intensity" to the expression of the apology. Moreover, particular strategies may be regarded as more polite than others in different speech communities. In this article, I offer a preliminary and relatively informal exploration of two ways in which it seems that apologizers modify the politeness of an apology in relation to the weight of the offense: they may vary the number of strategies used in any interaction, and they may vary the kinds of strategies used. A speaker may include two or more strategies in a remedial exchange and she may select higher rather than lower ranked apology strategies to increase the politeness of the apology. As a first step in this discussion, it will be useful to describe how the individual components of the model were operationalized and the correlations they revealed with the strategies speakers used.

Characteristics of the offense

The range of offenses which resulted in the apologies in the corpus was very wide, and a categorization of these into different types provides useful information for comparison with other corpora in different communities and cultures. In this section, I have also considered the crucial factor of the relative seriousness or ranking of different offenses in the contexts in which they occurred.

Type of offense
As far as I am aware, there is no formal existing classification of types of offense, though Goffman (1971) provided a very useful discussion of relevant factors, and Owen (1983) commented at various points on the effect of different types of offense on the particular form selected in her data. Building on their observations, the following categories proved workable and appeared to account for all of the instances in the New Zealand data: inconvenience, space, talk, time, possessions, and social gaffe. Table 8.5 summarizes the distribution of these in the data.

Table 8.5 Type of offense

	No.	%
Inconvenience/inadequate service	72	39.3
Space	30	16.4
Talk	30	16.4
Time	26	14.2
Possessions (including money)	20	10.9
Social gaffe	5	2.7
Total	183	100

Inconvenience. A large proportion of the apologies in the corpus (39.3%) can be described as relating to actions which have inconvenienced the addressee in some way. Where the apologizer could not provide the correct change or required information, for instance, apologies were classified in this category. It also includes examples where the apologizer had not performed adequately in a particular context or had provided inadequate service and so had inconvenienced the addressee. Examples (22) and (23) illustrate this category.

(22) [B has requested that a docket be stapled to a bankcard slip. A, the shop assistant, has been unable to find a stapler.
A: I'll just have to cellotape it on I'm sorry.
B: That's fine.

(23) [A has rung B, a friend, and waited some time for her to answer.]
A: You're puffed.
B: I've just run upstairs. I was down in the office.
A: Oh sorry. I should have rung your office.

The offenses sometimes implied a lack of respect for the addressee's positive face needs, as in example (22), whereas in other cases the offense impeded the addressee's freedom of action and so related to her negative face needs, as in example (23). The apology strategy sometimes quite explicitly addressed the relevant implication with a comment such as "I'd like to help you but . . . " or "I'm sorry to have put you out."

Table 8.6 describes the correlation of offense type with apology strategies in remedial exchanges.[18] It shows that inconvenience offenses are more likely than average to be remedied with an exchange which includes both a simple apology and an explanation (i.e., A + B), though a substantial proportion do attract just a simple explicit apology (A). The extent of the inconvenience to the victim (i.e., seriousness of the offense) and the relative power of the participants (both factors discussed further later) also appear to be relevant in accounting for the occurrence or not of an explanation.

Space. Goffman (1971) provided a detailed discussion of the range of infringements on another's personal space which may occasion apologies. Examples include walking too close to or in front of another person, bumping into them, and taking their seat or desk space. These offenses sometimes threaten the addressee's negative face by impeding

Table 8.6 Offense type by combination of apology strategies (%)

Apology strategy	Total corpus	Offense type					
		Inconvenience	Space	Talk	Time	Possessions	Social gaffe
A	43.2	33.3	83.3	36.7	30.8	30	100
B	2.2	1.4	–	10	–	–	–
A + B (+ X)	34.1	48.6	6.7	23.3	50	30	–
A + Y	17.3	15.3	6.7	20	15.4	40	–
Other	3.2	1.4	3.3	10	3.8	–	–
Total	100	100	100	100	100	100	100
N	183	72	30	30	26	20	5

A = an explicit expression of apology; B = an explanation or account; X = any strategy or strategies following A + B; A + Y = any exchange which includes strategy A except those already analyzed in this table.

her freedom of movement, though more often they are in fact very slight inconveniences and the apology addresses the "virtual offense" (Goffman 1971: 138–39). In other words, by apologizing the offender signals her wish to protect herself against being perceived negatively, for example, as lacking bodily control or initiating unwelcome advances on the victim. As Table 8.5 illustrates, there were 30 instances (16.4%) of this type of offense in the corpus.

A very high proportion of space offenses elicited just a simple apology form (83.3% compared to 43.2% in the corpus as a whole), though (24) is one of the rare examples where the seriousness of the offense warranted an explanation as well.

(24) [A bumps into B along a busy pavement and knocks a parcel out of her arms.]
A: Sorry miss. I was in a hurry.
B: You should watch where you're going.

The correlation of a space offense with a simple explicit apology strategy – almost always a form of *sorry* – is nevertheless one of the clearest patterns in the data, as Table 8.6 demonstrates.

Borkin and Reinhart (1978), who compared the use of *I'm sorry* and *excuse me*, observed that in American usage both "*excuse me* and *I'm sorry* can be used as formulaic remedies in certain situations with little difference in effect, as for instance, when two people accidentally bump into each other in the aisle of a supermarket" (Borkin & Reinhart 1978: 59). This generalization is not true for New Zealand usage, however. *Excuse me* would be distinctly odd as an apology in such a context; *sorry* would be the expected form and there are a number of instances of its use in similar contexts in the corpus.[19]

Talk. There are 30 examples (16.4%) where the offense involves some kind of intrusion on the addressee's talk or talking turn or another infringement of the rules for polite talk. The most frequent examples relate to an interruption, but others include verbal insults, the introduction of an inappropriate topic, a slip of the tongue, not hearing someone, and offenses such as talking too loud or too long. An interesting example is provided in (25).

(25) [A is apologizing to her daughter for a big argument in which she and her husband are involved.]
A: I'm sorry this happened when you were here.
B: It doesn't matter.

These offenses can often be perceived either as encroachments on the addressee's positive or negative face. An interruption, for instance, can be interpreted as implying that what the addressee is saying is not worth attention and therefore as a threat to positive face; alternatively, it can be seen as impeding the addressee's freedom to talk and thus as a threat to negative face. When an account or excuse forms part of the apology, it will often address the most obvious interpretation in the particular context as in (21), repeated here for convenience, where A adopts the strategy of self-denigration, and (26), where the explanation focuses on the negative face threat.

(21) [A is a waitress who has served B the wrong drink.]
A: I beg your pardon. I thought you said "wine and soda."

(26) [Woman to fellow student in tutorial discussion.]
A: I'm so sorry. I didn't mean to stop you.

Occasionally, a component of the remedial exchange will overtly redress the *speaker's* loss of positive face, as in the following slip of the tongue: [20]

(27) [A, a radio announcer, has mispronounced B's name.]
A: I'm sorry. That's a difficult name though you must admit.

Table 8.6 shows that talk offenses tended most often to elicit simple explicit apologies. One third involved an explanation or justification, and, predictably, these were generally the more substantial or serious offenses. An unintended interruption, or overlap, for instance, rarely elicited more than a simple "sorry" but after taking a very long turn, for instance, a speaker would tend to justify her or (more usually) his apparently inconsiderate behavior. Overall, the distribution of apology strategies used for talk offenses does not differ significantly from that in the corpus as a whole; talk offenses do not appear to elicit atypical patterns of apology strategy.

Time.   There are a number of offenses (14.2%) which involve one person wasting another person's time or in some way not taking appropriate account of the value of another's time. Where the apologizer has kept the addressee waiting, or has forgotten or arrived late for an appointment, the infringement involves an imposition on the addressee's time. Negative face is threatened by impeding the addressee's freedom of action in most cases. The addressee has remained in one place for the apologizer's benefit. Example (28) is a clear instance of this type of offense.

(28) [B is phoning her friend A.]
B: Where were you last night? I thought you said you'd meet me at 7: 45 outside Chevy's.
A: Oh no! What a nong![21] I'm really sorry. I thought you meant tonight. Oh boy I hope you're not too cheesed off with me.

Here, as in (23), self-denigration is the form the explanation takes. A intensifies the threat of her own positive face with the self-directed insult, "what a nong," thus strengthening the effect of the apology.

It is interesting to note that the most common pattern of time apologies involves a combination of an A and B strategy. Half of these apologies combined an explicit apology – usually a form of *sorry* – with an explanation or account, a much higher proportion than was typical of the whole sample (where only 34.1% involved such combinations). Moreover, less than a third of these apologies (compared to 43.2% in the total sample) involved a simple explicit apology. Apparently offenses for wasting another's time generally demand some explanation, reflecting perhaps the high value placed on time in Western culture, a point which Wolfson commented on in an American context: "The notion that [middle class Americans] consider themselves under obligation to be prompt and/or to avoid keeping another person waiting is, in fact, evidenced by the large number of apologies that refer to just this situation" (1988: 27).

Possessions. A fifth category of offense involved some damage or loss to the addressee's possessions, including money. Offenses in this category involve damage to or removal of something which belonged to the addressee, or they directly cost the addressee money. Offenses such as bumping into someone's car, spilling something on their clothes, damaging their pen, breaking their washing machine, failing to pay a bill on time, or losing a book all come into this category. These are generally offenses to positive face since they imply that the apologizer does not value the things the addressee values. Often in such cases one element in the remedial exchange directly addressed this implication.

(29) [Two friends in the library.]
    A: You know that pen you lent me, I'm afraid I've lost it. If you like I'll buy you another one.
    B: Oh don't worry. If it turns up throw it my way but if it doesn't don't worry.

There were 20 examples (10.9%) of apologies for possession offenses in the data. All included an explicit apology strategy. It is interesting to note that Y in the pattern A + Y in Table 8.6 always involved type C apology strategies in the case of possession offenses. Hence, a substantial proportion (40%) of apologies for possession offenses included an explicit acknowledgement of responsibility which took the form of an offer of repair or restitution in almost every case. This distinguishes apologies for possession offenses very clearly from apologies for space and time offenses. Moreover, possession offenses elicited twice as many apologies, including strategy C, as occurred in the sample as a whole (40% vs. 19.8%).

Social gaffe. There were a small number of apologies (5) which occurred when the apologizer broke a social etiquette rule relating to socially frowned on behavior, such as burping or speaking while eating. An example is given in (30).

(30) [A, talking to B on the phone, has just had a coughing bout.]
    A: Excuse me coughing.

These apologies can be interpreted as hearer-oriented negative politeness strategies since they acknowledge an unwelcome intrusion on the hearer.

All the examples in the data elicited a simple explicit apology which took one of the following forms: *excuse me* (3), *pardon me, I'm sorry.*

Though the number of instances is small, it is interesting to note that these examples do support Borkin and Reinhart's (1978) suggestion, made in an American context, that such breaches are likely to elicit *excuse me* rather than *sorry.* Comparing the two forms, Borkin and Reinhart suggested that the crucial difference between them is that *excuse me* "is a formula to remedy a past or immediately forthcoming breach of etiquette or other light infraction of a social rule on the part of the speaker," whereas *I'm sorry* "is an expression of dismay or regret at an unpleasantness suffered by the speaker and/or the addressee" (1978: 61). This latter formulation is so general, however, that it could be interpreted as covering all offense types.

As we saw earlier (under syntactic-semantic patterns), *excuse me* is rare in the data as a whole; there were only 9 examples. Some did occur before an offense (e.g., "excuse me but I'll have to go now"), whereas others followed the breach of a social etiquette rule (after a burp). But it is important to note two qualifications to Borkin and Reinhart's generalizations. First, whereas *excuse me* was the most common formula used in relation to etiquette breaches, there are also alternative appropriate ways of responding in New Zealand, including *pardon me* and *sorry.* Second, *excuse me* is used over a wider range of offense types than reported by Borkin and Reinhart, including anticipated intrusions on another's space or talk.

Overall, then, Table 8.6 shows that explanations (B) are most likely to accompany inconvenience offenses and time offenses, both of which are predominantly negative face-threatening acts. By contrast, an apology strategy involving an acknowledgement of responsibility (C) and more specifically an offer of redress (C5) is most likely with a possession offense, offenses that are most likely to be interpreted as threats to positive face. Space offenses and social gaffes, on the other hand, are most commonly satisfied by a simple explicit apology (A). This reflects, however, not only their nature but also their relative seriousness – a feature to which the discussion now turns.

Seriousness of offense

The relative seriousness or ranking of the offense in the relevant culture is a very important factor to be considered when examining the reasons why native speakers select particular apology strategies. Austin pointed out that what may serve as an adequate "excuse" differs in different circumstances, and that what he called our "standards of the unacceptable" (1979: 194) vary contextually: "we set very different limits in different cases. We may plead that we trod on the snail inadvertently: but not on a baby – you ought to look where you are putting your great feet" (Austin 1979: 194). The equivalent of R in Brown and Levinson's model (1978), the relative seriousness of the offense is also mentioned by researchers such as Cohen and Olshtain (1981) and Trosberg (1987) in their contrastive research as an important factor in guiding the speaker's selection of an appropriate apology strategy.

An attempt was made to calculate the seriousness of the offense independently of its overall weightiness in Brown and Levinson's terms, that is, to restrict it to an estimate of "the absolute ranking (R) of impositions in the culture" (Brown & Levinson 1978: 79), leaving P and D to be calculated independently. But the assessment of R did, of course, take into account other relevant factors of the situation (cf. Brown & Levinson 1978: 84), factors which contributed to an estimate of the relative inconvenience or embarrassment to the addressee of the offense in context. The seriousness of an offense such as losing someone's book, for instance, depends on factors such as how urgently it is needed as well as its rarity or monetary value. Spilling coffee on someone is a more heavily ranked offense if that individual is about to take part in a public performance than if he or she is at home. Insulting someone is more offensive if it is done in front of a large audience or in a formal context. Hence, ranking the imposition within the culture involves considering such features of the particular context. The effect of the relationship between the participants, which also determines the weightiness of the offense (i.e., the overall interpretation of the degree of offense caused), is discussed separately later.

A three-point scale was used to categorize the seriousness of the offense: (1) *light offense:* for example, bumped into someone; forgot to return a book to the library on time; (2) *medium offense:* for example, kept someone waiting and made them late for a film; broke someone's stapler; (3) *heavy offense:* for example, knocked someone over and hurt them; made someone miss an important engagement. In these data, the majority of offenses for which apologies occurred were light (49.7%) or medium (43.2%), with only 7.1 percent (13 instances) of offenses evaluated as heavy.

Examining the apology strategies used with offenses of different seriousness, it is clear that the great majority of light offenses elicited a simple explicit apology (58.2% compared to 43.2% in the corpus as a whole, see Table 8.7). Medium offenses, on the other hand, were much more likely than light offenses to involve an explanation as well as an explicit apology (41.8%). And medium offenses were also more likely to be accompanied by an acknowledgment of responsibility than was typical of the data as a whole (62% vs. 46%).[22] The 13 heavy offenses were much less likely than

Table 8.7 Seriousness of offense by combination of apology strategies (%)

Apology strategy	Total corpus	Seriousness of offense		
		Light	Medium	Heavy
A	43.2	58.2	29.1	23.1
B	2.2	3.3	1.3	–
A + B (+ X)	34.1	30.8	41.8	15.4
A + Y	17.3	4.4	25.3	53.8
Other	3.2	3.3	2.5	7.7
Total	100	100	100	100
N	183	91	79	13

A = an explicit expression of apology; B = an explanation or account; X = any strategy or strategies following A + B; A + Y = any exchange which includes strategy A except those already analyzed in this table.

others to be responded to with just a simple apology. They elicited a range of responses, including a majority of the more heavily ranked apology strategies (i.e., C and D). Whereas all but one included an explicit apology, accompanying it, there were acknowledgments of responsibility in four cases and two offers of restitution. This is consistent with Fraser's comment that in cases "where there was some significant injury or inconvenience, there appeared to be a change from an apology with an account to an apology with an offer of redress" (1981: 268).

There was also a tendency for the more serious offenses to elicit a more formal apology strategy, such as *I really am most terribly sorry*, and in two instances a double apology was used (i.e., AA). Overall, then, these patterns confirm what one would expect. The more serious the offense, the more likely the remedial exchange will involve an explicit apology and the more elaborated the apology is likely to be by the inclusion of an explanation, an acknowledgment of responsibility or an offer of restitution.[23]

However, these patterns cannot be considered in isolation from other relevant aspects of the situation and from the relationship between the participants, in particular. A high value for one component may offset a lower value for another. Hence, a minor infraction against a very powerful victim (e.g., keeping the Vice Chancellor, the Queen, or the President waiting for a short time) may require a response comparable to a more serious offense against a friend. Although she did not undertake any systematic correlations, Owen made a similar observation: "The same form may thus be used for insignificant offenses and more serious offenses between individuals in a closer relationship, suggesting a kind of 'trade-off' between seriousness of offense and closeness of relationship" (Owen 1983: 67). I turn now to a consideration of P and D, the most widely identified dimensions of the relationship between participants.

Relationship between the participants

Brown and Levinson's model predicts that any increase in the social distance between participants will result in a more heavily weighted FTA. Similarly, the greater the power differential between speaker and hearer, the more seriously the FTA will be assessed. It is useful, therefore, to provide a categorization of these dimensions in the data in order to interpret the correlations of choice of apology strategies with these aspects of the context in which the relevant offense occurred.

Social distance
The corpus includes apologies between participants who differ widely in terms of how well they know each other or the degree of social distance that characterizes the relationship. Three categories were used to classify the data: I – very close friends or intimates, for example, spouses, partners, family members; F – friends or colleagues; S – distant acquaintances or strangers. Though they are obviously rather broad, these categories allowed a number of useful generalizations to be made.

There were only 18 (10%) apologies in the corpus between those who could be classified as intimates, that is, people who knew each other very well indeed, whereas 74 (40%) occurred between friends and colleagues and 89 (46%) between strangers or distant acquaintances. The data on intimates should therefore be treated with circumspection and this is obviously an area where further research will be useful.

Table 8.8 shows the correlations between the degree of social distance between participants and the apology strategies they used in remedial exchanges. Using Brown and Levinson's model, one would expect (all other things being equal) that the more heavily ranked (politer) strategies would be used to the most distant addressees and the simplest strategy to those least distant. Indeed, Fraser (1981) reported this pattern for his American data, noting that "as the degree of familiarity increases between the inter-actants, the need (or at least the perceived need) to provide elaborate apologies decreases" (1981: 269). In fact, Table 8.8 shows the reverse to be the case in the New Zealand data: intimates receive fewest of the single explicit apologies (33.3%), and almost twice the norm for the more heavily ranked ones (i.e., 33.5% vs. 17.3%). The obvious explanation, given the pattern already examined for seriousness of offense (and leaving aside the possibility that Fraser's corpus is entirely different in composition), is that all other things are not equal, and that the offenses against intimates are generally among the more serious in the corpus. In fact, it makes sense that the kind of interactions one has with intimates are more likely to be risky compared to those with strangers, where lighter offenses such as bumping into them in the street predominate. This point is taken up again later.

The other pattern in Table 8.8 worth comment is the slight tendency for friends, too, to receive higher ranked apology strategies than average and, in particular, to receive an explanation (B) as one component in the reme-dial exchange more frequently than intimates or strangers do. Assuming that a more elaborate apology is generally a more polite one, one might expect that strangers would be more likely to feel entitled to an explanation for an offense than those closer to the offender. Again, much depends on the type of offense involved, as was demonstrated earlier, but the pattern in

Table 8.8 Interaction of apology with social distance (%)

Apology strategy	Total corpus	Social distance relations		
		Strangers	Friends	Intimates
A	43.2	47.2	37.8	33.3
B	2.2	2.2	1.3	5.5
A + B (+ X)	34.1	33.7	37.8	27.7
A + Y	17.3	14.7	19.1	33.5
Other	3.2	2.2	4.0	–
Total	100	100	100	100
N	181	89	74	10

A = an explicit expression of apology; B = an explanation or account; X = any strategy or strategies following A + B; A + Y = any exchange which includes strategy A except those already analyzed in this table.

Table 8.8 can be interpreted as providing interesting support for Wolfson's bulge theory of interaction (Wolfson 1988). She outlined the model as follows:

> [W]hen we examine the ways in which different speech acts are realized in actual everyday speech, and when we compare these behaviors in terms of the social relationships of the interlocuters, we find again and again that the two extremes of social distance – minimum and maximum – seem to call forth very similar behavior, while relationships which are more toward the center show marked differences. (Wolfson 1988: 32)

Wolfson pointed to the evidence that, for instance, most compliments occur between speakers who are neither total strangers nor intimates, and so do negotiated imprecise invitations. Wolfson's theory is based on the relative certainty of the relationships involved. She suggested that it is less certain relationships, that is, those between people who are neither strangers nor intimates, which need expressions of solidarity to bolster them and invitations with escape clauses to avoid rejections. The data in Table 8.8 suggest that these relationships also require explicit apologies bolstered with explanations (i.e., A + B) to protect and nurture them.

One final point which emerged from the analysis of the interaction of apology strategies and social distance relates to the order of strategies used in a remedial exchange. There was a tendency for apologies to begin with explanations, and even to consist of explanations alone, to intimates more often than to nonintimates. Intimacy evidently permits shortcuts and substitutions. Similarly, minor or light offenses between intimates require only the briefest apologetic noise. Here, Fraser's data are supportive. He noted that between intimates the utterance following a slight offense may be very brief ("Oops!") or indirectly related to the offense ("what a fool I am!"), and to interpret the utterance as an apology requires a great deal of "filling in" of the missing parts (Fraser 1981: 269). Clearly, this filling in or inferencing involves the addressee in additional conversational work; it could therefore be regarded as an imposition on the addressee and hence most reasonably demanded of intimates. On the other hand, filling in depends on shared values and mutual knowledge; thus, the assumptions revealed by a minimal apology express positive politeness or solidarity. This, too, characterizes relationships between intimates. Brief and indirect apologies for light offenses thus typify close relationships where participants may impose without worrying and where they assume shared knowledge and values.

Though the patterns of social distance are revealing, it is clear that their discussion has required reference to other factors. A very grave offense will require a very full and perhaps somewhat formal apology even between intimates. Similarly, a large power disparity will result in elaborated remedial strategies, even when the offense is not great. Before considering the complex interaction of all the factors, however, it is worth examining the final element in the equation.

Power
Determining the relative power relations in an interaction is often a difficult task. One relevant factor is the relative status of the participants, but other

factors are also important. Between children, for instance, relative size and age are important factors. In some contexts, relative experience, knowledge, or expertise will be crucial. In transactional relationships, the roles of participants, such as customer–sales assistant or teacher–student, may be more important than any considerations of relative social status (see Leach 1983: 126). The fact that the sales assistant is middle class, for instance, while her customer is working class may be irrelevant in a context where the sales assistant has the obligation to serve the customer politely.

Brown and Levinson identified the crucial criterion as "the degree to which H can impose his [sic] own plans and his own self-evaluation (face) at the expense of S's plans and self-evaluation" (1978: 82). Although this was not as easy to operationalize as one might wish, this did prove a useful guide. Based on this criterion, customers, for instance, were treated as having more P than those serving them. Again, three categories were used: U – apology was made to a person with more P; E – apology was made to a person of equal P; D – apology was made to a person with less P.

The majority of the apologies in the data (115, or 63%) occurred between equals. Among the remaining group, as one might expect, there were almost twice as many upwards as downwards. There were 43 (23.5%) apologies to a person with more power and 24 (13.1%) to a person with less power than the apologizer. Table 8.9 shows the distribution of apology strategies in the data according to the power relationship between the participants.

It is quite clear that more elaborated apology strategies are used to those with more power. Whereas on average the simple explicit apology strategy (A) characterizes 43.2% of the data, it accounts for only 25.6% of the data to those with more power. It is much more common for apologizers to go beyond the minimum strategy A to use the higher ranked strategies C and D, and especially B (explanation), in such relationships. Hence, although apology strategy A predominates between equals and downwards, this strategy is less frequently used upwards on its own than in combination – most often with an explanation. This pattern supports the prediction that

Table 8.9 Interaction of apology strategies with power (%)

Apology strategy	Total corpus	Power relations		
		Upwards	Equals	Downwards
A	43.2	25.6	47.8	50.0
B	2.2	2.3	0.9	8.3
A + B (+ X)	34.1	46.5	32.2	25.0
A + Y	17.3	18.6	16.5	16.7
Other	3.2	7.0	2.6	–
Total	100	100	100	100
N	182	43	115	24

A = an explicit expression of apology; B = an explanation or account; X = any strategy or strategies following A + B; A + Y = any exchange which includes strategy A except those already analyzed in this table.

a powerful addressee will increase the weight of an offense and consequently require higher ranked politeness strategies and is thus consistent with Brown and Levinson's theory. Apologies for offenses against those with more power clearly correlate with more elaborated strategies than apologies for offenses against power equals or inferiors.

Overall weightiness of the offense

It is now possible to consider the effect of a combination of the various nonlinguistic factors analyzed on the choice of apology strategies. The data in this corpus allowed a correlation of apology strategies with offense weight by combining the effects of the seriousness of the offense (R), the relative power of the participants (P), and their relative social distance (D). In other words, what support do the data provide for Brown and Levinson's theory of the relationship between the weight of an FTA (measured as a combination of P, D, and R) and the politeness strategies used to redress damage to face? It is clear from the preceding discussion that, in general, a serious offense elicits more elaborated apology strategies and that a powerful victim receives more elaborated strategies than an equal or less powerful one. The rogue factor assessed in terms of Brown and Levinson's model appears to be social distance. Offenses against strangers appeared less rather than more likely to elicit extensive apologies than offenses against friends and intimates. Social distance, it appears, does not increase the overall weight of an offense independently of its seriousness and the power differential between participants. What then is the effect of combining the three components?

To explore the interrelationships of the three factors, the number and range of apology strategies in particular exchanges were examined, using these as a measure of the level of politeness expressed in the exchange. First, more heavily weighted offenses were examined to see if they elicited more complex remedial behavior. Then, I examined exchanges which involved simple apology strategies and contrasted them with those which involved three or four strategies within one exchange to establish whether the latter correlated with more heavily weighted offenses than the former.

One would expect that strategy A alone, for instance, would generally not suffice for a more heavily weighted offense. It would not be rated as polite enough. And in fact the data support this prediction. There are no examples of a simple explicit apology being used with maximum P, D, and R. So, despite the prevalence of apologies using strategy A alone in the corpus as a whole (43.2%), there are no examples of strategy A in isolation in contexts where P, D, and R have maximum values.

Though the data base is not large for undertaking such extensive intercorrelations, there is also some support for the hypothesis that weightier offenses (assessed as high P, D, and R) tend to elicit more complex apologies. As Table 8.10 shows, there are just two examples in the data of apologies for offenses of maximum seriousness to more powerful and socially distant interlocuters, that is, maximum R, maximum P, and maximum D. In both cases, the remedial interchange used consists of an explicit apology combined with a promise of forebearance, the highest ranked apology strategy, and one which is relatively rare in the data as a whole. Brown and Levinson's model suggests such situations require maximally polite strategies. It seems reasonable to interpret apology strategy D as just such a strategy. These exchanges, then, go beyond the minimum required and use highly ranked politeness strategies. They provide some support for Brown and Levinson's model, though one might also have expected that such heavily weighted offenses would elicit more strategies, as well as using heavily ranked ones. The small data base may be the explanation for this.

However, further support for Brown and Levinson's model is provided by examining the strategies used in apologies between maximally distant interlocuters of different status when the less powerful person has committed an offense of medium seriousness or a lighter offense. The apology interchanges in these cases generally involve at least two strategies and sometimes three or, in the case of medium offenses four co-occurring strategies (see Table 8.10). Though strategy A does occur alone, it is clearly and decidedly outnumbered in this context by more complex remedial exchanges, reversing the pattern in the corpus as a whole, where strategy A occurs on its own considerably more frequently than the next most frequent strategy (43.2% vs. 25.7%, as shown in Table 8.2).

It appears, then, that the predictions derived from Brown and Levinson's model find some support in these data. Assuming the social factors assessed as P, D, and R contribute to the weightiness of an offense, the apology strategies which native speakers use to redress the face damage caused by a particular offense tend to reflect its relative weightiness. The

Table 8.10 P, D, and R and apology strategies

P, D, & R	Apology strategies Type	No.
1. Max D + Max P + Max R:	AD	2
2. Max D + Max P + Medium R:	A	9
	AB(C)(C)	9
	AC	2
	BA(C)(A)	2
	CB	1
	CC(A)	2
3. Max D + Max P + Minimum R:	A	2
	AB	4
	AC	1
	BA	1
	CCC	1

A = an explicit expression of apology; B = an explanation or account; C = an acknowledgement of responsibility; D = a promise of forebearance; P = power; D = social distance; R = ranking of imposition.

kind and number of apology strategies used in remedial exchanges reflect the social situation in which they are produced.

There is clear evidence too that the less weighty the offense, the more likely a single simple explicit apology will be used.[24] The highest group of apologies in the data involving the interaction of P, D, and R, were apologies between friends and equals for slight offenses (i.e., 39, or 21.3%). The predominant strategy selected in these circumstances was a simple explicit apology (i.e. 23, or 59% of this group). By contrast, the small number of remdial interchanges which involved three or four concurrent strategies tended to involve a power differential and people who did not know each other well. Overall, then, these patterns too provide some support for Brown and Levinson's theory.

There are some qualifications, however, in one particular aspect of the theory. As mentioned earlier in the discussion on social distance, an offense between friends sometimes appeared to elicit a more elaborated apology than Brown and Levinson's model would predict. Two instances of complex four-term remedial exchanges, for instance, occurred between friends for offenses which were reasonably serious but not major (i.e., forgetting to do a promised task, knocking a cup of coffee over on the rug). And though the majority of slight offenses between friends in this New Zealand corpus required little in the way of an apology, there were still a substantial proportion (41%) which elicited a more elaborated interchange. More data are needed to contrast the pattern of remedial interactions between friends and intimates in more detail, but it seems possible that Wolfson's bulge theory, referred to earlier, may serve as a more adequate model than Brown and Levinson's model in accounting for some patterns in the data. Although Brown and Levinson's claims appear to hold for low P, D, and R and for high P, D, and R, they may need to be more sensitively developed to handle exchanges between friends and especially those which involve medium offenses. In these cases, the theory would predict a medium level of politeness but in some cases good friends used very fully elaborated apology strategies, and almost half the exchanges in this group involved three or four terms or included a higher ranked strategy. Paying attention to another's face is not only a signal of concern and friendship, it is also a way of strengthening the friendship. The form of the apology appears to serve as a signal of the apologizer's concern for the other person and of the importance they attribute to the relationship.[25] As Wolfson (1988) suggested, these relationships, unlike those with strangers or those with intimates, are the ones which are least "certain." They cannot be taken for granted and require attention and face work to maintain them. Using more extended remedial exchanges in response to an offense appears to be one way in which these relationships are nurtured.

Conclusion

I have argued that apologies are essentially social or affective speech acts; they are primarily oriented to supporting the relationship between participants rather than to the expression of referential information or propositional meaning. Brown and Levinson gave away too much to those who argue that referentially oriented communication must be treated as primary and social information as secondary or derived. *Conveying social meaning may be the participants' primary or central goal, and in my view it is difficult to argue against an analysis of compliments and apologies as clear examples supporting such a view of interaction.* An adequate understanding of the contribution of an apology to interaction must take account not only of its remedial function but also its effect – in the context of the offense it is intended to remedy – on the relationship between the offender and the victim. These effects are quintessentially social.

In Brown and Levinson's terms, apologies are politeness devices expressing attention to the hearer's face needs in the context of an offense. Whereas it has been widely assumed that apologies are primarily negative politeness devices, this categorization appears to depend largely on analyses of apologies which anticipate an FTA (see, for example, Brown & Levinson 1978: 192–95; Goffman 1971: 145). I have shown here that, taking account of a wide range of offense types, apologies may also address aspects of the victim's positive face needs, such as the desire to be appreciated. Moreover, Brown and Levinson (1978: 73) pointed out that the apology itself damages the speaker's face, and I have illustrated that a remedial exchange may be oriented to attending to these face wants, too. Thus, remedial interchanges involve a complex interweaving of the face needs of S and H. Different apology strategies clearly focus on different aspects of these. It seems likely that different groups in the society emphasize different aspects of participants' face needs and that different cultures weigh the face loss engendered by an apology differently. These aspects of the way apologies function in interaction await further investigation.

I have identified a range of strategies in the New Zealand data which confirm the value for the categorization of naturalistic data of the system devised for elicitation data by Olshtain and Cohen (1983). The way strategies combine to constitute remedial exchanges of some complexity has also been described. It is clear that analyses that focus only on utterances that express explicit apologies will omit important information. And these data, too, raise further questions, such as the extent to which the combinations identified can be generalized beyond the specific population involved. How far do they represent co-occurrence rules for a particular community? Is the complexity of the data restricted by the limitations of the data collection method? To what extent are there apologies of much greater length and complexity awaiting an adequate methodology? The restrictions of an ethnographic approach on such aspects of apology behavior cannot be ignored. Even an audio- or videotaped recording will miss aspects of some interactions. One of the most complicated remedial interchanges I was involved in, for instance, continued for several days. A methodology sophisticated and sensitive enough to enable one to collect all the relevant facets of such an exchange will inevitably require a combination of techniques.

In examining the relationship between apologies and the contexts in which they occurred, the analysis explored Brown and Levinson's predictions that, assuming situational demands for efficiency and urgency do not

take precedence, the more heavily weighted the offense, the more compen-
satory attention the speaker will pay to H's face needs. It was thus predicted that apologies would increase in politeness with the size of the
offense they addressed. There is little work, however, on what constitutes
a more or less polite apology, though many researchers have made assumptions about this. Features such as apology length, the complexity of the
strategies, and the elaborateness of the linguistic formulae used have been
informally discussed by different researchers. This analysis explored the
extent to which the kind and number of strategies adopted reflected the
gravity of the offense in context. But there are many other relevant features
which need to be considered, such as prosodic and paralinguistic information; there may well be features as yet unidentified which affect our assessment of the relative politeness of an apology.

In this analysis of the relationship between apologies and the weightiness
of the offenses which occasioned them, three aspects of the context which
have been widely recognized as relevant in pragmatic and sociolinguistic
analyses were considered: the cost or ranking of the imposition on the
victim (i.e., the seriousness of the offense in the case of an apology), the
social distance between the apologizer and the victim, and the power
relations between the participants. The data suggest that the relationship
between these factors and the apology strategies used to remedy the
offense is not consistently linear as Brown and Levinson's model predicts.
For at least one group, the pattern appears to be curvilinear, a finding better
accounted for by Wolfson's bulge model. Though more research is clearly
needed to investigate this claim, it appears that apology strategies may
play a more crucial role in maintaining relationships between friends than
between intimates or strangers.

Other aspects of remedial exchanges also await further investigation. It is
clear, as Brown and Levinson (1987: 16) acknowledged, that, in relation to
at least some speech acts, factors such as whether the participants like each
other and whether there is an audience present may affect the expression
and form of the utterance. Such factors need to be systematically explored
in order to identify their importance. It is also likely that different groups in
a community will weigh the same factors differently. For example, I have
suggested elsewhere (Holmes 1988) that women and men may perceive
compliments differently; it seems equally possible that apologies function
differently for each sex. There is certainly evidence that they function
differently for different linguistic and cultural groups (e.g., Blum-Kulka
& Olshtain 1984; Coulmas 1981; Olshtain & Cohen 1983; Owen 1983; Trosberg 1987).

Previous research on apologies has provided a variety of valuable information on pragmatic patterns in English-speaking speech communities
(Owen 1983), as well as on linguistic and cross-cultural differences between
English speakers and speakers of other languages. In this article, I have
suggested some ways in which apologies may be used to identify sociolinguistic patterns and to explore in particular the relationship between
politeness and its linguistic manifestation in contexts where an offense has
occurred. Though the woman in the opening exchange may have been able
to get away with *Oops*, her choice of a more elaborated strategy probably

increased her chances of obtaining help with her books the next time she needed it.

Acknowledgements

An earlier version of this article was presented to the Lancaster Linguistics Circle in October 1988. I would like to express appreciation to Geoffrey Leech and Jenny Thomas, who read a draft and provided helpful comment. The Department of Linguistics and Modern English Language at Lancaster University provided me with comfortable facilities to complete the research. I would also like to acknowledge valuable assistance with the classification of the data from Margaret Walker and Marie Verivaki. Finally, I would like to express my gratitude to Dell Hymes for his helpful comments and his meticulous editing, both of which have improved this article.

Notes

1. Nessa Wolfson (personal communication) comments that she would not put a time limit on how far an apology (or thanking behavior) may be spread out. She also notes that the act may be repeated many times depending on what initiated it, as well as on the relationship between the interlocutors.
2. Because of the potential confusion in an analysis concerned with offenses leading to apologies between what Brown and Levinson (1978) label R, the absolute ranking of the imposition in the particular culture, and W, the overall weight of a face-threatening act or offense, I have consistently used *weight/weightiness* for the latter: i.e., the result of the calculation involving R, P, and D in any context. I have used *seriousness of the offense* or *ranking of the imposition* to refer to the culturally determined ranking of an offense independently of P and D.
3. This model is discussed in considerably greater detail in Holmes (1990), where the influence of Lakoff (1979) in particular is acknowledged. Other models which provide slightly different solutions to the same analytical problems are those of Leech (1980), Grimshaw (1980), and Halliday (1985).
4. *Solidarity* is Brown and Gilman's term (1960), whereas Lakoff (1979) used *camaraderie* and Brown and Levinson (1978, 1987) referred to *positive politeness*. Similarly, Brown and Gilman used *power*, whereas Lakoff referred to *deference*. Brown and Levinson's *negative politeness* relates to the expression of both distance and power.
5. It is perhaps worth starting explicitly that in classifying utterances as speech acts, it is the attributed underlying intention that has been the guiding criterion, rather than any surface form indicators (cf. Leech 1983).
6. Brown and Levinson included apologies in their set of negative politeness strategies, suggesting they are restricted to remedying impingements on negative face. Their examples, however, indicate that they are primarily concerned with what Goffman (1971: 114) labeled *requests* and Edmondson (1981) called *disarmers*, i.e., utterances which typically precede a potential violation of the addressee's rights. These constitute only a very small subset of what are typically regarded as apologies.
7. There are cases, of course, where the apology is largely an automatic response, "relexive and non-reflective," as one anonymous reviewer puts it. Giving weight to considerations of power and distance may seem analogous to cracking

a nut with a sledgehammer in relation to automatic and often simultaneous apologies for minor offenses. Nevertheless they are relevant. Even an apology for bumping into someone in a doorway – a situation which normally elicits an automatic and minimal apology – may vary in form if, for example, the victim's perceived status is high enough.

8. This may well be a culture-specific example, causing less offense in North America than in New Zealand or Britain.

9. The following students contributed examples to the corpus: Jane Crew, Jennifer Fouhy, Jennifer Jacob, Eletheria Lemontzi, Hedy Manders, Fiona Read, Mig Wright. Two students preferred to remain anonymous.

10. *Pakeha* is the term used for New Zealanders of European descent.

11. I have not maintained the distinction between justifications and excuses introduced by Austin (1979). Owen (1983: 93) claimed the distinction to be relevant since justifications "cannot be substituted for apologies; we do not find apologies and justifications used together because to do so would require the speaker to hold contradictory beliefs about his [sic] action." Though undoubtedly theoretically valid, the distinction seems unhelpful in analysing remedial interchanges, since in practice people do use apologies with justifications: e.g., After brushing V's hair abruptly with her hand, A says "I'm sorry but there was a wasp on your head." Though the element following the explicit apology is technically a justification rather than an excuse in Austin's terms, the exchange as a whole is remedial in intent – to avoid offense to V's face. What seems to be the crucial distinguishing feature between apologies with justifications rather than excuses is the fact that "Thanks" or "Good" might act as appropriate responses to the former but not the latter.

12. It is perhaps also worth noting that I have not included two strategies which Olshtain and Cohen (1983: 23) included in their apology speech act set:

(1) a denial of the need to apologize, e.g., "there was no need for you to get insulted"; and
(2) a denial of responsibility, such as (a) not accepting the blame, e.g., "It wasn't my fault" or (b) blaming the other participant for bringing the offense upon him/herself, e.g., "It's your own fault."
These seem to be utterances which may accompany apologies or occur as alternatives to apologies but which may not *count as* apologies, illustrating incidentally, the problem which was discussed earlier of using felicity conditions as means of identifying apologies.

13. Wolfson (personal communication; but see also Wolfson, Marmor, & Jones, 1989) suggested that the acceptability of an explanation functioning as an apology may vary cross-culturally. American respondents regarded an explanation alone as constituting an account rather than an apology – at least in some contexts (Wolfson, Marmor, & Jones, 1989). However, it is also worth noting that (as already mentioned) apologetic intonation may be crucial to the interpretation of such utterances as apologies. The small corpus of taperecorded apologies provides support for this hypothesis.

14. Though most of the data were recorded in written form only, the telephone exchanges were taperecorded, making it possible to note relevant intonational features.

15. It is interesting to note, moreover, that most of the written apologies were between people who did not know each other very well. This factor doubtless also contributed to the correlation of written apologies with more formal syntactic patterns. More formal syntactic patterns generally express more heavily

weighted negative politeness strategies, which appropriately characterize interactions between more socially distant participants. The influence of social distance on apology strategies is explored in more detail later.

16. In the introduction to the reissue of their article, Brown and Levinson (1987: 16) conceded that "there may be a residue of other factors which are not captured within the P, D, and R dimensions" and mentioned in particular the degree of "liking" between participants, the presence of an audience, and situational formality. In order to facilitate the analysis of the apology corpus, these factors have been subsumed under D for the former, and R for the latter two.

17. I am not suggesting that the correlation is always exact. An apologist may, of course, offend by overdoing an apology, but, as the term *overdoing* suggests, such usages operate against background norms. In general, I am suggesting that a longer and more elaborated apology is likely to be interpreted as a more polite one.

18. The strategies have been summarized in the form which seemed most useful for comparative purposes. Since strategy A alone is the most common, and A and B are the only two which occur in isolation, these have been separately identified. A + B (+X) allows the identification of any exchange which includes an explicit apology and an explantion, whereas A + Y identifies exchanges with an explicit apology together with the higher ranked strategies C and D. The strategies are thus ordered approximately from less to more heavily ranked apology strategies.

19. *Excuse me* is used in New Zealand to signal some unavoidable anticipated imposition on the addressee, such as the infringement on his or her space occasioned by passing in front of the addressee, or to introduce an interruption. This point is discussed further later.

20. Slips of the tongue too may address different aspects of face redress. A slip which misaddresses someone (as in example (5)) or uses an inaccurate label in the addressee's term, for instance, may offend the addressee's positive face.

21. A term of abuse or insult meaning "fool."

22. This calculation is not deducible from Table 8.7 since it involves taking account of all strategy C apologies used with medium offenses (i.e., those included in both X and Y).

23. Brown and Levinson (1978) suggested that off-record strategies are more polite than on-record strategies. However, in their more recent discussion (1987: 21) they admitted to some need to qualify this ranking. Apologies provide further support for the qualification. Only one of the most heavily ranked offenses did not include an explicit apology strategy.

24. There were no data for apologies to intimates with less power (e.g., from adults to children). To interpret this, one would need to investigate whether this was a gap in the data or whether such interchanges were characterized by the absence of apologies (see Bonikowska 1985). In other words, this may be meaningful by contrast with the norm and thus qualify as doing the FTA, behavior which would support Brown and Levinson's predictions since it could be interpreted as less polite than even the most minimal apology.

25. It is interesting to note that these patterns observed in natural interaction are consistent with the unexpected (according to Brown and Levinson's theory) elicited judgments of relative politeness obtained by Holtgraves (1984), where subjects judged a high degree of encoded politeness as indicating higher reciprocal liking, and Baxter (1984), where subjects reported they would use greater politeness for friends.

References

Austin, J.L. (1962) *How to do things with words*, Oxford: Clarendon.
—— (1979) 'A plea for excuses', in J.O. Urmson and G.J. Warnock (eds.), *Philosophical papers*, 3rd ed, Oxford: Oxford University Press, pp. 175–204.
Austin, P.J.M. (1988), *The dark side of politeness: A pragmatic analysis of noncooperative communication*, Unpublished PhD thesis, University of Canterbury, Christchurch.
Baxter, L.A. (1984) 'An investigation of compliance-gaining as politeness', *Human Communication Research* 10(3): pp. 427–56.
Bonikowska, M.P. (1985) 'Opting out: The pragmatics of what is left unsaid', *Lancaster Papers in Linguistics*, No. 32. Lancaster: University of Lancaster.
Borkin, N. and Reinhart, S.M. (1978) ' "Excuse me" and "I'm sorry" ', *TESOL Quarterly* 12(1): pp. 57–70.
Brown, P., & Levinson, S. (1978). Universals in language usage: Politeness phenomena, in E.N. Goody (ed.), *Questions and politeness*, Cambridge: Cambridge University Press, pp. 56–289.
—— (1987) *Politeness: Some universals in language usage*, Cambridge: Cambridge University Press.
Brown, R. and Gilman, A. (1960) 'The pronouns of power and solidarity', in T.A. Sebeok (ed.), *Style in language*, Cambridge, MA: MIT Press, pp. 253–76.
Cohen, A. and Olshtain, E. (1981) 'Developing a measure of sociocultural competence: The case of apology', *Language Learning*. 31(1): pp. 113–34.
Coulmas, F. (1981) 'Poison to your soul. Thanks and apologies contrastively viewed', in F. Coulmas (ed.), *Conversational routine*, The Hague: Mouton, pp. 69–91.
Edmondson, W.J. (1981) 'On saying you're sorry', in F. Coulmas (ed.), *Conversational routine*, The Hague: Mouton, pp. 273–88.
Goffman, E. (1967) *Interaction ritual*, New York: Anchor.
—— (1971) *Relations in public*, New York: Basic.
Grice, H.P. (1975) 'Logic and conversation', in P. Cole and J.L. Morgan (eds.), *Syntax and semantics*, vol. 3: *Speech acts*, New York: Academic, pp. 41–58.
Grimshaw, A.D. (1980) 'Selections and labelling of INSTRUMENTALITIES of verbal manipulation', *Discourse Processes* 3: pp. 203–29.
Halliday, M.A.K. (1985) *An introduction to functional grammar*, London: Arnold.
Holmes, J. (1984a) 'Hedging your bets and sitting on the fence: Some evidence for hedges as support structures', *Te Reo* 27: pp. 47–62.
—— (1984b) 'Modifying illocutionary force', *Journal of Pragmatics* 8: pp. 345–65.
—— (1986a) 'Functions of *you know* in women's and men's speech', *Language in Society* 15(1): pp. 1–21.
—— (1986b) 'Compliments and compliment responses in New Zealand English', *Anthropological Linguistics* 28(4): pp. 485–508.
—— (1988) 'Paying compliments: A sex-preferential positive politeness strategy', *Journal of Pragmatics* 12(3): pp. 445–65.
—— (1990) 'Politeness strategies in New Zealand women's speech', in A. Bell and J. Holmes (eds.), *New Zealand ways of speaking English*, Clevedon, Avon: Multilingual Matters.
Holtgraves, T.M. (1984) *The role of direct and indirect speech acts in social interaction*, Unpublished PhD thesis, University of Nevada, Reno.
Hymes, D. (1962) 'The ethnography of speaking', in T. Gladwin and W. Sturtevant (eds.), *Anthropology and human behaviour*, Washington, DC: Anthropological Society of Washington, pp. 15–53.
—— (1964) 'Introduction: Towards ethnograpies of communication', *American Anthropologist* 66/6, Pt 2: pp. 1–34.

—— (1972) 'An editorial introduction to *Language in Society'*, *Language in Society,* 1(1): pp. 1–14.

Kuiper, K. and Haggo, D.C. (1984) 'Livestock auctions, oral poetry, and ordinary language', *Language in Society* 13: pp. 205–34.

Lakoff, R.T. (1979) 'Stylistic strategies within a grammar of style', in J.O. Orasanu, M. Slater and L.A. Adler (eds.), *Language, sex, and gender. Annals of the New York Academy of Science* 327: pp. 53–78.

Leech, G.N. (1980) *Language and tact*, Amsterdam: John Benjamins.

—— (1983) *Principles of pragmatics*, London: Longman.

Levinson, S.C. (1983) *Pragmatics*, Cambridge: Cambridge University Press.

Norrick, N.R. (1978) 'Expressive illocutionary acts', *Journal of Pragmatics* 2: pp. 277–91.

Owen, M. (1983) *Apologies and remedial interchanges: A study of language use in social interaction*, Berlin: Mouton, Walter de Gruyter.

Pawley, A. (1985) 'On speech formulas and linguistic competence', *Lenguas Modernas* 12: pp. 84–104.

Pawley, A. and Syder, F.H. (1983) 'Two puzzles for linguistic theory: Nativelike selection and nativelike fluency', in J.C. Richards and R.W. Schmidt (eds.), *Language and communication*, London: Longman, pp. 191–226.

Thomas, J. (1985) 'Complex illocutionary acts and the analysis of discourse', *Lancaster Papers in Linguistics 11*, Lancaster: University of Lancaster.

Trosberg, A. (1987) 'Apology strategies in natives/non-natives', *Journal of Pragmatics* 11: pp. 147–67.

Wolfson, N. (1983) 'Rules of speaking', in J.C. Richards and R.W. Schmidt (eds.), *Language and communication*, London: Longman, pp. 61–87.

—— (1988) 'The bulge: A theory of speech behaviour and social distance', in J. Fine (ed.), *Second language discourse: A textbook of current research*, Norwood, NJ.: Ablex, pp. 21–38.

Wolfson, N. and Manes, J. (1980) 'The compliment as a social strategy', *Papers in Linguistics: International Journal of Human Communication* 13(3): pp. 391–410.

Wolfson, N., Marmor, T. and Jones, S. (1989) 'Problems in the comparison of speech acts across cultures, in S. Blum-Kulka, J. House-Edmondson and G. Kasper (eds.), *Cross-cultural pragmatics: Requests and apologies*, Norwood, NJ: Ablex, pp. 174–96.

9

The use of *like* as a marker of reported speech and thought: a case of grammaticalization in progress

Suzanne Romaine and Deborah Lange

Originally published in a longer version in *American Speech*, 66 (1991).

Our concern here is to document what we take to be a case of ongoing grammaticalization involving the use of *like* in American English to mark reported speech and thought. The extract in (1), which is taken from recordings of teenagers' conversations made by Lange (1985 and 1988), illustrates this innovative use of *like*.

1.   She said, "What are you doing here?"
     And I'm LIKE, "Nothing much," y'know. I explained the whole . . . weird story.
     And she's LIKE, "Um . . . Well, that's cool." [DL/SR]

Romaine observed (2) on a BBC news report in 1985; it was said by a young American woman to a reporter who was interviewing her about the Princess Di look-alike contest (being held in Washington, DC, in anticipation of a royal visit).

2.   A man came up to me and said, "You really look like Princess Di."
     And he looked at me and he's LIKE, "Are you?" [DL/SR]

It can be seen here that *like* functions much in the same way as the verb *say* does in introducing reported speech. In both these examples a form of the verb *be* followed by *like* alternates with *say*, and where *be* + *like* occurs, it appears paraphrasable by *say* with no apparent change in referential meaning. However, we will qualify this considerably in the course of our analysis, because in many, if not most, cases discourses introduced by *be* + *like* can also represent internal thought, as Butters (1982) noted. In (3), for example, it is not certain that the speaker actually SAID "no." Rather, the hearer is invited to infer that this is what the speaker was thinking or saying to himself as the girl approached.

3.   And I saw her coming, and I'm LIKE, "Noooooooooo." [DL/SR]

We draw our data from recordings and observations of teenagers and adults, and from various media sources which we have been collecting for the past few years. We have a total of almost 80 instances of *like* used in this new function as part of a quotation frame. Some of these cases are ambiguous, and we take this, too, as a sign that a reanalysis is underway.

Another indication of change in progress is a trend towards sex differentiation, which has often been cited as a major accompaniment to linguistic change (see, e.g., Trudgill 1972, 179). The majority of our examples of *like* in this new quotative function are from young women, though they use it not only to report their own dialogue but also to report the speech of men. It has often been noted that young women lead in introducing change (see, e.g., Feagin 1980). We will argue that women use *like* more because the topics they discuss are typically talked about in an involved conversational style. Clearly, a larger and more systematically collected data base is desirable, and we will suggest some directions for future research.

We will discuss here some of the current uses of *like* and the historical developments which have paved the way for change and explain the reasons why we consider it to be an instance of ongoing grammaticalization. When *like* is used in a quotative function, it allows the speaker to retain the vividness of direct speech and thought while preserving the pragmatic force of indirect speech. Thus change in the use of *like* has grammaticalized a new discourse function. To demonstrate this, however, we need to consider first some general problems posed by the representation of speech and thought and how these are resolved in discourse. This will provide a theoretical framework within which this use of *like* can be analysed.

Representation of speech and thought in discourse

Vološinov (1930, 115) noted the pivotal role that the problem of reported speech plays in our understanding of language when he wrote that "reported speech is speech within speech, utterance within utterance, and at the same time also speech about speech, utterance about utterance." Since what is reported is an utterance belonging to someone else, it has to be somehow transposed from its independent existence into the utterance of the author or speaker who reports it. This act of incorporation brings into play certain compositional, syntactic, and stylistic norms. Thus the utterance of a speaker named John, "I'll give you a call tomorrow," might be reported as follows: *John/he said, "I'll give you a call tomorrow."* In this particular case, the transpositional requirements are minimal and straightforward: the speaker is identified by name or a personal referring pronoun and a verb of saying (or what Goffman 1974 calls a LAMINATOR) is used to introduce what is assumed to be the actual speech of that person. In written language the orthographic convention of placing inverted commas around the reported speech signals that quotation is occurring, and it marks off the quotation as a syntactically independent utterance. In spoken language a variety of prosodic conventions may be employed, such as pause, change in intonation, and voice quality (see Fonagy 1986 and Kvavik 1986). This mode of reporting is usually referred to as DIRECT SPEECH or ORATIO RECTA.

The syntactic and stylistic complexities of reporting become more obvious in so-called INDIRECT SPEECH or ORATIO OBLIQUA. To take the same example, we might transform it as follows: *John/he said (that) he would give him/her a call tomorrow*. We can see that the quotation frame, *John/he said*, remains the same but that the report of what was said is subordinated to the verb of saying and becomes a dependent clause introduced by *that* (which may be absent). The second person *you* changes to the appropriate third person pronoun and the first person *I* becomes the third person. The verb is shifted from the future *will* to the conditional *would*. Stylistically, this means that what is reported can become integrated into the narrative.

Vološinov (1930, 119) observes that progress in understanding reported speech has been hindered by divorcing the reported speech from the reporting context. He suggests that the real object of inquiry ought to be the dynamic relationship between the speech being reported and the speech doing the reporting. Thus in the indirect mode the speech is that of the reporter, and its anchor point is in the speech situation of the report. Direct speech remains the speech of another, whose role is played by the reporter. In an indirect quote, speakers normally use themselves as the spatiotemporal point of reference, while in a direct quote speakers adopt the deictic orientation of those whom they quote.

It is thus generally agreed that the fundamental difference between these two modes of speech representation lies in the point of view or perspective adopted by the person who does the reporting. Leech and Short (1981, 320), for example, say that the effect produced by the use of indirect speech is one in which the reporter of the conversation intervenes as an interpreter between the person being spoken to and the words of the person being reported, instead of merely quoting verbatim the speech that occurred. This is somewhat misleading since it would be just as rare for actual speech to be quoted verbatim in conversation as it would for spontaneous speech with all its hesitations and grammatical inconsistencies to be reproduced verbatim in a novel or play. In so far as each utterance of a speaker constitutes a unique speech event realized in its own characteristic idiolect comprising idiosyncrasies of accent, grammar, prosody, and the like, even DIRECT SPEECH can be only an imperfect attempt at rendering some of the features which make any given utterance unique. Although speakers generally convey no more than an approximate version of the form and content of an utterance when reporting it directly, by convention we accept a verbatim interpretation. Often attempts are made to mimic other formal aspects, such as the intonation or voice quality of the original speech, or even the gestures of the quoted speaker. When this happens, it is usually done for (and conveys) special stylistic effect (see, e.g., Polanyi 1982, 163; Rimmer 1988). There are of course limits to what can be conveyed in speech and writing and conventions have arisen as to what and how much is reported. Moreover, the notion of what constitutes verbatim reporting varies cross-culturally.

Partly for these and other reasons, Tannen (1986) has used the term

CONSTRUCTED DIALOGUE in talking about what is generally called REPORTED SPEECH since the speech which is reported is someone's reconstruction of the speech event. It is a recollection which is often more accurate in general meaning than in precise wording. Indeed, in some cases, utterances are reported as quotations of a dialogue that either has not occurred or is never intended to occur, as in (4).

4.   She goes, "Mom wants to talk to you." It's LIKE, "Hah, hah. You're about to get in trouble." [DL/SR]

In other cases, a line of dialogue is represented as if it were the speech of a group of participants, as in (5). It is highly unlikely that a whole crowd said verbatim what is reported. By convention, however, we accept the speaker's use of *puff, puff* to mimic the crowd as an adequate representation of the sounds made by a group of breathless people. It is thus TOKEN MIMICRY rather than verbatim reporting (see Rimmer 1988 on the use of token mimicry in narrative).

5.   And then they yell, "Wait, we found it."
     And everybody goes, "Puff, puff, puff" [DL/SR]

For Leech and Short (1981), the basic stylistic opposition between direct and indirect speech is seen in terms of what speakers commit themselves to. If they use indirect speech, they commit themselves only to what was stated, while if they use direct speech, they commit themselves to what was stated and the exact form of words used to utter the statement. While we do not accept the strict requirement of a verbatim report as the main criterial feature of direct speech, the notion of "speaker commitment" is an important one in understanding the choices speakers make in reporting the discourse of others (see below).

Its relevance can be clearly seen once we consider the problem of speech reporting cross-linguistically. Consider the examples from French and English in (6). Lyons (1982, 110–12), for example, argues that the French sentences in (a) and (b) differ from one another as well as from each of the possible English translations in (c), (d), and (e). The latter not only differ truth conditionally from one another, but they also make explicit something which (a) does not say, but only implies. The difference lies in the use of the quotative conditional versus the simple present tense. The quotative conditional affects the truth conditions of (a) by expressing the speaker's restricted commitment to the truth of the proposition.

6.   a.   Le premier ministre serait malade.
     b.   Le premier ministre est malade.
     c.   The prime minister is reported to be ill.
     d.   The prime minister is believed/thought to be ill.
     e.   We (are given to) understand that the prime minister is ill.

This example illustrates the role of evidentiality, that is, the nature of the quoted source and the authenticity of the report in affecting the grammatical and lexical devices employed in reporting. Languages such as Turkish, Kwakiutl, Navajo, and Hopi have different conjugations of the verb which distinguish hearsay from what is the speaker's own knowledge (see Jakobson 1971, 135). Japanese has a sentence suffix which, when used in conjunction with a form of the copula, indicates hearsay quality, while German and Danish use modal forms of the verb for this purpose.

Frajzyngier (forthcoming) notes the widespread association between the domain of speech and the hypothetical mood. Verbs of saying are used to indicate that evidence is less than complete and that the information obtained through speech is not as reliable as information obtained through direct observation. In a number of languages the association between the domain of speech and the hypothetical is indicated by preceding the hypothetical proposition with a phrase making use of a verb of saying. Compare English LET'S SAY/SAY *you had ten dollars, what would you do*; or *If you had*, SAY, *ten dollars, what would you do?*

Languages also differ in the extent to which they maintain a grammatically distinct boundary between direct and indirect speech. The extent and nature of the cues marking reports may vary dramatically cross-linguistically, as the papers in Coulmas (1986c) show. In Swahili, for instance, Massamba (1986, 116) claims that it is always possible to distinguish grammatically between direct and indirect speech. In other languages it is considerably more problematic.

This means that most, if not all, of the features distinguishing direct from indirect speech are fairly arbitrary grammatical and pragmatic conventions rather than logical requisites. In Japanese, where the distinction between direct and indirect speech is not always marked, speakers rely more on an understanding of social factors determining the choice between registers than on grammatical rules (see Coulmas 1986b, 174–75). We will argue that discourses introduced by *like* blur the boundaries between direct and indirect representations of both speech and thought report.

Alternation between *be* + *like* and other verbs of saying

In this section we will situate our discussion of the use of *be* + *like* to introduce speech/thought by looking at such verbs of saying as *say, tell, ask, argue,* and *explain,* which speakers have at their disposal when constructing dialogue.

It is not surprising that there should be a number of verbs used to report speech, each with a slightly different function, because speakers will want to emphasize various aspects of the report. Choice of verb form therefore represents an important communicative option. This is particularly true in the written language. Page (1988, 27), for example, notes that many writers seek to "relieve the monotony of constant 'he-saids' by resorting to elegant variation," but he also draws attention to the expressiveness of variants. He goes on to point out that the opening chapter of *David Copperfield* has *returned* 8 times, *asked* and *cried* 5 times each, *exclaimed, faltered,* and *resumed* twice each, and *repeated, replied, sobbed, mused,* and *ejaculating* once each.

There are also 37 instances of *said*, and two short sentences not explicitly attributed to a speaker.

Sometimes these verbs of saying represent an attempt to inject what Page calls a spurious dramatic quality into banal writing. This can be found at an extreme in certain kinds of popular and juvenile fiction, where, according to Page, "characters rarely 'say' anything, but gasp, moan, shriek, hiss and mutter, whereas those in sentimental romances murmur, breathe, sigh and (curiously) smile their words." It is obvious that verbs of saying can be important style and genre markers.

To begin, we will highlight some general correlations between the properties of *say* and its functions. Then we will look at some examples which illustrate the motivations behind speakers' choices among *say*, *go*, and *like* and how these influence the meaning of constructed dialogue.

It is because *say* reports speech without contributing some particular pragmatic effect that it is unmarked, and therefore the most frequently used verb of saying (see Tannen 1986, 315, on the frequency of *say* in both spoken and written English and Greek). Givón (1980) characterizes *say* as involving quotation with no commitment. Its frequency is also reflected in its potential for phonological reduction. Li (1986, 35), in fact, goes so far as to suggest that, in its unstressed form, *say* is semantically "bleached" and displays the characteristics of a hearsay evidential.[1]

We noted earlier that the verb of saying can be phonologically reduced or sometimes omitted entirely, as in (7) and (8). We will call cases where dialogue appears without the support of verbs of saying BALD, UNFRAMED, or UNBRACKETED reporting.[2] In (7) the speaker, Donna, makes it clear from her intonation that her question "Can I touch you?" is the reported discourse of someone else without overtly marking it as such through the use of some verb of saying. After her friend, Vicky, expresses disbelief, Donna continues with the rest of the reported speech, "I never met anybody who's Jewish before." In Donna's final two reports the verb *say* is so phonologically reduced that it is barely audible.

> 7. Donna: In college one time I was a freshman. Somebody from a small town in Ohio came up to me and said, "Are you Jewish?"
> I said, "Yes."
> "Can I touch you?"
> Vicky: Oh, no.
> Donna: "I never met anybody who's Jewish before."
> Vicky: Are you serious?
> Donna: I'm serious.
> Vicky: Oh, wow.
> Donna: I s– "I'm just a regular person."
> She s– "Oh my God. You don't know what they told us about you in Sunday school." [DL/SR]

In (8) some teenage girls are discussing some of the differences they perceive between the way boys and girls communicate. The girls believe that the boys don't do much to hold up their end of the conversation. There are no verbs of saying.

8.   They just, "Oh, how are you?"
      "Fine."
      There you go.
      How are you?"
      "Oh I'm O.K. too."
      Then that's about it, you know? [from Eckert, 1990]

In her study of Greek and English oral and written narratives, Tannen (1986, 315) found that *say*, *go*, and *like* were the most commonly used markers which introduce constructed dialogue (see also Blyth et al. 1990 for discussion of variation among these choices). Lange (1985) suggests that while *say* and *go* show no special age-grading effects and can occur among speakers of all ages, the use of *like* tends to occur in the speech of those under 30, with the highest concentration among high-school students. It is overwhelmingly a marker of spoken rather than written discourse (but we will discuss below, 259ff., some of the few instances in print we have observed). It also appears to be used more by females than males. We have more to say about this sociolinguistic distribution below.

Tannen (1986, 323) suggests that the various ways of introducing dialogue can be placed along a continuum. At one pole is the use of no introducer at all in informal conversational narrative, as in (7) and (8), because of the greater expressive power of the human voice. At the other end is the use of explicit and graphic verbs like *say* and *tell*. The latter is typical of literary narrative, where more work has to be done by the meaning of the words than by the way they are spoken.

Given the relatively recent emergence of quotative *like*, it has not yet been studied in great detail. Butters (1982, 1989) has noted its existence in both white and black varieties of American English, while Haiman (1989, 167) remarks on its use by Midwestern teenagers but says he has no idea how general the construction is. In Tannen's study (1986), it accounts for seven instances (8%) of the markers introducing speech in American English narratives and was used by five different speakers.

We will now look at some more cases, like (1) and (2), where there is alternation between *like* and other verbs of saying. In the speaker's reported speech in (9), alternation between *go*, *said*, and *like* can be seen. In (10) there is alternation between *like* and an indirect report of another introduced with *told*. In (11) we have an instance of alternation between *like* and *say*, while (12) and (13) involve variation between *go* and *like*.

9.   When you were talking about the pillow, I thought you were talking about an old lady, you know, when you SAID it's all wrinkled up, I thought you were talking about her skin and this was on the *Today Show* and I'm LIKE, "Let me see." I'm LIKE, "Let me see," 'cause you SAID it gets old and happens all at once and I'm LIKE, "This I gotta see" and then I GO, "Where is she? What happened?" [DL/SR]

10. She TOLD me that we put that story on the front page of the newspaper. I'm LIKE, "I know." [DL/SR]

11. Vivian: So I stood on my bed.
    Marge: She pounded on the ceiling.
    Vivian: And I pounded on the ceiling.
    Marge: She was pounding.
    Vivian: And I hear Marge, and I hear Marge dash out of her room, come downstairs and open the door, and I was LIKE, "No Marge . . ."
    Marge: She said, "Marge, it's me."
    I'm LIKE, "What is . . ."
    Vivian: I was pounding on my ceiling.
    Marge: Bizzare! [from Tannen (1987, 587)]

12. He goes, "I'll give you a job anytime."
    And I'm LIKE, "Great." [DL/SR]

In (9) the only words actually spoken were "Where is she?" The speaker uses *like* to report her thoughts, *go* to introduce her own dialogue, and *say* to report the speech of her interlocutor. The reports of her friend's discourse following *said* are indirect (though syntactically indistinguishable from direct speech). In (10) and (11) the speaker uses *like* to report her own speech/thought and *say/told* for the reply of the other person(s). In (11) the speakers are Vivian and Marge, two undergraduates. We can see a similar division in (12) between the exchanges of speaker and reported discourse of another demarcated through the use of two different markers. The speaker uses *like* for her own speech and *go* for that of the person whose speech is reported. Thus, one function of the alternation between *like* and other verbs of saying is to demarcate the roles of speaker and others.

The contrast between the effect of *like* and *go* on the meaning of constructed dialogue is evident, too, in (13), where the speaker uses both. He reserves *like* for the report of his own feelings and *go* for the speech of his friend. The speaker uses *like* to convey the expressive content of his imagination rather than his precise words. He probably didn't scream, but he felt like someone who would scream "Waaa."

13. And Scott came up to the back door. He scared me half to death. He comes up and you know he looked pretty big. I was lying down on the couch, watching TV, and you know I could just see the outline of the body, and was LIKE, "Waaaaaaaaaaaa." And he comes in and go "Uh." He just walked in, scared me half to death, God – just seeing the outline of somebody's body walking in our house. [DL/SR]

In (4), which we repeat here, variation between *go* and *like* is used to distinguish a report of what was said from an interpretation of what the reported speech means rendered in dialogue form.

4. She goes, "Mom wants to talk to you." It's LIKE, "Hah, hah. You're about to get in trouble." [DL/SR]

A son is reporting to his mother a fight he had with his sister. The mother already knows of this dispute from a call her daughter made to her while it was taking place. While on the phone with her daughter, the mother told her that she wanted to speak to her son. In reporting to his mother what his sister said, the words, "Hah, hah. You're about to get in trouble," are not directly attributed to any particular speaker. It is as if the remark introduced by *it's like* is intended as a gloss of the sister's tone of voice, or what she might like to have said, when she reported, "Mom wants to talk to you." Thus, the exchange might be interpreted as: 'I am reporting that my sister told me that you want to talk to me and she led me to believe that I was about to get into trouble.' However, the use of *like* does not commit him to the actual occurrence of what is reported. Possibly the son felt he would be going too far in reporting his sister's tone as something that was said when it was not said. The son does not have the right to speak directly as and for his sister, in the presence of their mother, who is obviously in a position of authority over her children, particularly if this was not what she said or wanted the daughter to convey, but rather his own inference. Here it seems to be the pragmatic implications of *like* which make it a more appropriate choice than *say* or *go*. Thus, in (4) as well as in (1) and (2), the alternation between *like* and *say* is used for the speech of one and the same person. This indicates that there may be other important functions of the variation relating to speaker subjectivity. The marker *like* seems especially useful for reporting and/or modulating the speaker's feelings, which may or may not have been explicitly lexicalized at the time of the event, as we have seen from (4) in particular. In other words, if the same content were introduced by *say* or *go*, it would be less likely to be interpreted as a report of feelings, but as something that was really said. We have another indication of this in (14), which is the full exchange given in abbreviated form earlier in (1). After using the verb *go* to introduce Tracy's discourse, the narrator then emphasizes twice that this is actually what was *said* (i.e., "I swear she said that"). She feels she has to GO ON THE RECORD here in order to make sure her friend understands that she is to take this particular report as an accurate rendition, which is an indication that *go* lacks the explicitness of *say*. The narrator uses *go* and *like* to report her own discourse, and *say*, *go*, and *like* for introducing the speech of Tracy (cf. also 9, 10, 11, and 12).

14. We saw her huge big truck, y'know? That new scu- that new car. It's such a scandal, that car!
    [Listener: It's so tacky]
    I know.
    And so I saw it.
    And then, I didn't see Tracy. I'm like trying to cruise after the car, because I see her car. Y'know run . . . like . . . driving?
    And so I go, "Oh my God, I have to run after it and say hi to Tracy. And go, 'what's up?'" n' I look to the left. Is that scandalous?!
    Tracy's look – going [screaming], "Michelle, what's up?"
    I swear she said that. I swear she said that. And then we had the

biggest cow in front of everyone. They were all staring at us. 'cause we're like hugging.
She said, "What are you doing here?"
And I'm LIKE, "Nothing much," y'know? I explained the whole . . . weird story.
And she's LIKE, "Um . . . Well, that's cool."
And so then we had to crank over to Safeway? Because her Mom was gonna be there? Cause she was like doing groceries and stuff? [DL/SR]

Yet another example can be seen in (15), which is a conversation between two teenage girls.

15. Nancy: God, it was bad. I couldn't believe she made me go home.
      Sally: I thought it was kind of weird though, I mean one minute we were going out and the next minute Nancy's going, "Excuse me, gotta be going."
               [both laugh]
               I didn't know what was goin' on, and Mary comes up to me and she whispers, the whole place knows, "Do you know that Nancy's goin' home?"
               And I go, "What?"
               [both laugh]
               "Nancy's going' home.'"
               I go, "Why?"
               She goes, "Her Mom's makin' her."
               I go, [makes a face] "ah, ah ah."
               She comes back and goes, "Nancy's left."
               Well, I said, "Well that was a fine thing to do, she didn't even come and say goodbye."
               And she starts boiling all over me.
               I go [mimicking yelling], "All right!!"
               She was upset, Mary, I was LIKE, "God."
      Nancy: I just had to go home. I know, when I was going home, I said, I said, "Mom, could we hurry up? I want to go home and call John." I'm going, I was trying to tell her, "Look, I gotta do something or I'm going to go nuts!"
      Sally: Did she say anything?
      Nancy: Not really.
               [from Tannen, 1990]

To contrast the use of *go* with that of *like* in constructed dialogue, we can see that the verb *go* has special connections with the auditory-vocal channel. It serves as a cue for that channel and introduces sounds or onomatopoeic expressions rather than words. It is restricted to direct quotation. Thus, in the previous example, where Sally uses *go* to mimic "All right!!" and when she says, "I go, '[makes a face], ah, ah ah,'" *go* might be regarded as a channel cue. In (5), repeated below, Myra, a 30-year-old writer, uses *go* to describe the noises a crowd of passengers made while rushing to get in line after Italian airline officials lost and then found the airplane seating configuration. In such instances *go* translates loosely as "makes the sound of" (see also Butters 1980). Tannen (1986, 317) notes that *go* is associated with a very informal register; it is one marker which distinguishes conversational narratives from literary ones in English. The restriction of *go* to direct quotation is no doubt partly a reflection of the fact that sound effects cannot be reported indirectly by use of a frame which explicitly marks the subordinate relation. Thus, *everybody said/went that puff, puff, puff.*

5.   And then they yell, "Wait, we found it."
     And everybody goes, "Puff, puff, puff." [DL/SR]

This highlights at least one problem posed by the indirect mode of reporting: how to capture the emotive affective aspects of speech. Insofar as these are expressed not in the content, but in the form of the message, they are not preserved in indirect reporting. Vološinov (1930, 128), for example, observes that the direct utterance, *"Well done! What an achievement!"* cannot be rendered in indirect discourse as: **He said that well done and what an achievement.* Instead we have something like: *He said that it had been well done and was a real achievement.* It is no doubt at least partly due to these problems of incorporation that the direct speech mode is often said to be more vivid. A number of researchers (e.g., Schiffrin 1981) have said that narration is more vivid when speech is presented as first-person dialogue through direct quotation rather than as third-person report. Tannen (1986) includes the use of direct speech as one of a number of stylistic devices which create interpersonal involvement between the narrator and audience.

Nordberg (1984) has observed the use of the verb *komma* 'to come' as a marker of quotation in the conversation of Swedish adolescents, as in (16). He suggests that it may be an elliptical expression for *kom stickande med* "came up with" or *kom fram med frågan* "came out with the question". Not enough cross-linguistic work has been done on verbs of saying to enable us to offer an answer to the question of whether there is a natural tendency for verbs of motion to be used as verbs of saying (see below 267ff.). Speakers can, however, also use *like* to evoke sound effects, as we have already seen in (13) and in (17) and (18).

16.   A så KOM han då, "Va nill ni?"
      And then he came: "What do you want?" [from Nordberg (1984, 18)]
17.   These drunk guys come bustin' in – all the other patients are LIKE, "Ugh Ugh" [from Tannen (1986, 320)].
18.   that was such a bum barf. It was LIKE, "aaagh." [DL/SR]

It is the choice of *like* as an introducer, combined with the thematic content of the conversation as a whole, that makes the dialogue seem to be an expression of feeling. To see how this works, we look next at some examples of constructed dialogue where only *like* is used to mark reports of speech and thought. In some cases, like (19), it is used to mark the dialogue of both the speaker and other participants. Here its repetition adds to the point-counterpoint nature of the reported conversational exchanges.

19. Shane's *like*, "She's in Baltimore,"
     and I'm *like*, "No, she's not,"
     and Shane's *like*, "Yes, she is." [DL/SR]

In the conversation between two teenage girls, Karen and Mary, in (20), *like* is used in the retelling of an emotionally charged event. These two highschool girls are recapturing an incident, but they are also exploring their mutual fear of rejection. Mary expresses her suspicion that another girl is telling Karen secrets about her. Karen misreads Mary's expression and thinks that Mary has found fault with her in some way, perhaps in her appearance. Although Karen did not actually speak at the time of the incident, in the retelling she dramatizes her feelings by rendering them in dialogue form, thus giving them explicit verbal content. The implication appears to be that if her feelings could speak, that is what she would have said. We don't know, of course, what Karen thought precisely. By using *like*, she conveys an impression of her mood rather than an explicit report. Thus she does not commit herself to having actually said or thought this, which allows her to save face in the event that she has misinterpreted her girl-friend's actions.

20. Mary: I totally thought she was talking about me. I was a hundred
              percent positive. So I was just standing at the door – listen-
              ing to see if she was –
     Karen: I was LIKE, "Mary, what are you doing?"
              'Cause – 'cause you're LIKE you just stared at me and walked
              away.
              I'm LIKE, "Thanks. Do I look that bad today?" [DL/SR]

Our examples show that speakers have the option of changing various components of the speech event by using a variety of devices. When a quotation is explicitly marked, the verb *say* seems to be the default verb, the one the speaker chooses when there is no particular reason to choose another verb. We have also identified two important functions of *like*: (i) its use to demarcate roles in the speech event, and (ii) its use to indicate aspects of speaker subjectivity. These functions can be best understood within a perspective of the speech event which views it as a "dramatic" exchange. One such approach is found in Goffman's (1981) notion of FOOT-ING, which has to do with the alignments among interlocutors in a speech event.

Goffman argues that speaker and hearer should be considered to comprise a number of actor roles rather than seen as single entities. The hearer, for instance, can act as passive audience, active challenger, or bystander. The speaker, on the other hand, will select different styles which can be signalled by a variety of linguistic and nonlinguistic cues (such as tone of voice, eye or body movement) according to the addressee role intended or expected. The speaker can act in a number of roles, for example, as animator (recitor of someone else's discourse), author (selector of what is said), or principal (authority for what is said). It is to the personal and individual aspects of narrative that Goffman alludes when he says that any verbal performance is a presentation of self.[3]

Until recently, issues such as these have been considered mainly in the context of literary studies under the notion of "point of view."[4] They are relevant to all cases of language choice since all utterances embody the subjective component of the speaker as locutionary agent and the objective component of what is said. Stylistic choice can be seen as a question in part of the social and dramatic role of the speaker, that is, FOOTING, but also in part of the speaker's right to know and therefore talk about certain phenomena such as another person's state of mind, as in (4), where the son uses *like* rather than *say* in attributing an interpretation to his sister's tone. Goffman (1981, 150) notes that the use of quoted direct speech is one of the ways in which animators can convey words that are not their own. It also provides the speakers with a means of standing in a relation of reduced responsibility for what is said (Goffman 1974, 512). In speaking as another, we can repeat their speech without repeating their speech act (see, e.g., Haberland 1986, 220). This is one reason why, when regional dialect first appears in the novel, it is used for quotation of characters' speech rather than for the narrative itself, which represents the "voice" of the narrator, that is, standard English. Only recently has the use of non-standard English become acceptable as a mode of narration (see Traugott 1981).

Thus, at the level of discourse, alternation among *go, like,* and *say* allows the speaker to signal changes in what Goffman would call PRODUCTION FORMAT, that is, the different combinations of speaker and hearer roles. The use of one particular verb of saying as opposed to another is not uniquely tied to one particular discourse function; rather, it is the variation or shifting itself which creates meaningful stylistic oppositions.

In our data there is a tendency for *like* to be used for self-representation (58% of the cases), and *say* to be used for the speech of others (83%), while *go* is used equally for both. Insofar as only the speaker can have access to his/her own thoughts, and *like* (rather than *say* or *go*) is more likely to be used for the representation of thought, this trend is not surprising. Blyth et al. (1990, 221) also found that *be + like* was rarely used with third-person subjects. It must be remembered, however, that the choice of a verb of saying has implications which go beyond the presentation of self and extend to considerations such as what one undertakes to say/report not only TO others but OF others. When the speaker wants to stand in a relation of reduced commitment to what was actually said or thought, *like* can be used to report the discourse of others.

Thus we see that there is an asymmetrical relationship between the act of speaking and the speech act of reporting. What can be reported may not actually have been said. Not everything that was said can actually be reported. In some cases the constraints arise by dint of linguistic resources and in others, by dint of social conventions. As Vološinov (1930, 123) suggests, "the changing sociolingual conditions of verbal communication are what in fact determine the forms of reported speech."

The origin and evolution of the new use of *like*

None of the sources we noted earlier has anything to say about the historical origins of *be* + *like* in its quotative function. Blyth et al. (1990, 223)
simply speculate that it may be a pragmatically conditioned lexical change.
At least one major factor implicated in the new use of *like* to introduce
reported speech and thought is its multifunctionality. In order to shed some
light on how the new function of *like* has arisen, we will begin by making a
distinction between discourse and nondiscourse uses of *like* and proposing
a continuum which links them. Examples (21)–(25) illustrate some of the
various discourse and nondiscourse (i.e. purely grammatical or syntactic)
uses of *like* in contemporary English.

21. She looks LIKE her father. [preposition]
22. Winston tastes good LIKE a cigarette should. [conjunction]
23a. He brought along things for the picnic, food, drinks, and such-LIKE.
23b. The sculpture looked quite human-LIKE. [suffix]
24. And there were LIKE people blocking, you know? [discourse marker]
25. Maya's LIKE, "Kim come over here and be with me and Brett." [DL/
     SR] [discourse marker with quotative function]

It is evident from these and previous examples that *like* fulfills a number
of syntactic and pragmatic functions. Its grammatical uses as a preposition,
conjunction, and suffix (as in 21–23) are long-established and fairly
straightforward.[5] However, many Americans will remember the uproar
caused in the 1950s by the Winston advertisement quoted in (22) where
like is used as a conjunction. Prescriptivists complained that *like* is inappropriate here and that the correct conjunction is *as*. The usage panel of *The
American Heritage Dictionary* (1969, 757) rejected 75 percent of the examples
where *like* was used as a conjunction as inappropriate in formal written
English. Nevertheless, it is clear that, at least in colloquial English, the use
of *like* as a conjunction, by analogy with the preposition *like*, is now well-
established and may have been for centuries.[6]

Another nondiscourse use of *like* is illustrated in (23a) and (23b). Here *like*
is used as a denominal adjectivalizing suffix with the meaning 'having the
qualities of' or an approximation to the sense of the word to which it is
added. Derived adjectival and adverbial forms ending in *-like* are originally
compounds, but *like* gradually came to be felt as an independent suffix
which could be added to nouns (see Jespersen 1942, 417–18). Historically, of
course, this *like* is cognate with the modern condensed form *-ly*, used to
form adverbs from adjectives, as in *quickly*. The suffix arose through the
phonological condensation of the lexeme *liche* "body". This is a paradigm
case for grammaticalization in Meillet's (1912) sense. The process has been
complete in the sense that the suffix *-ly* is no longer an autonomous word
with full lexical meaning. It has also undergone semantic bleaching. It
functions now only as a dummy marker which signals the grammatical
meaning "adverb-forming suffix" and indicates a change of form class from
adjective to adverb.[7]

By contrast, the uses of *like* in examples (24) and (25), are not recognized as standard. For instance, under its entry for *like* as a preposition, *The American Heritage Dictionary* (1969, 757) cites as nonstandard the use of *like* as an "expletive to provide emphasis or pause," as in *The accident was like horrible*. There is no mention at all of *like* in its quotative function. This suggests that this usage was either nonexistent, too infrequent to have attracted notice, and/or so colloquial (and thus, unacceptable) that it was simply ignored.

We have called the uses of *like* in (24) and (25) discourse markers – that is, particles which are used to focus on or organize discourse structure. We have used this term because what we call the discourse uses of *like* share some similarities with those elements identified either by Schiffrin as "discourse markers" or by Östman as "pragmatic particles." Schiffrin (1987, 31–32), for example, refers to discourse markers such as *oh* or *you know* as sequentially dependent elements which bracket units of talk and which are independent of sentential structure. Similarly, Östman (1982, 149) characterizes a pragmatic particle as typically

> (a) short, and (b) prosodically subordinated to another word. It would (c) resist clear lexical specification and be propositionally empty (i.e. it would not be part of the propositional content of the sentence). Furthermore, it would (d) tend to occur in some sense cut off from, or on a higher level than, the rest of the utterance, at the same time as it tends to modify that utterance as a whole.

The uses of *like* in (22), (23b), and (24) are not instances of pragmatic particles either in Östman's or Schiffrin's sense because they are directly linked to the syntax of the clause in which they occur and have a grammatical function. However, this is less so the case for (23). In (24) *like* could be omitted without disturbing either the syntax or the propositional content of the clauses. In (25), however, it would appear to be omissible only if the whole quotation frame is deleted (see, however, examples 31, 34 and 35 below).

For Östman, true pragmatic particles have no clear syntactic function or semantic interpretation. While this may be more easily defended for some of the instances where *like* is used as a general marker, as in (24), we will argue that when *like* is used to introduce quotation, it is devoid of neither semantic meaning nor syntactic status. On the contrary, both have contributed to its functions as a discourse marker. The common semantic denominator in examples (21), (22), and (23a) is the status of *like* as a marker of comparison. It invites the hearer to infer a comparison, either actual or hypothetical, between what follows it and something preceding it. As Schiffrin points out (1987, 317), many discourse markers are used in ways which reflect their literal meanings. Conjunctions, in particular, have pragmatic effects which are closely tied to their meanings.

For Jespersen (1942, 417–18), it is the suffix *-like* as in (23a) and (23b) which is the source for the discourse use of *like* in (24). This discourse use has been noted by grammarians and condemned for some time. Jespersen, for instance, says that it is "very much used in colloquial and vulgar language to modify the whole of one's statement, a word or phrase modestly indicating that one's choice of words was not, perhaps, quite felicitous. It is generally used by inferiors addressing superiors." Among the examples he gives are those in (26)–(29), all of which are literary and none of which dates before Dickens. In these examples it is not possible to tell whether *like* modifies a word or a phrase, and it appears to be syntactically dispensable. The *OED* (1971, 285) records similar examples (all from the nineteenth century), where *like* is used "parenthetically to qualify a preceding statement." All of them contain sentence-final *like* (except one attributed to De Quincey: "Why like it's gaily nigh like to four mile like") and are labelled dialectal and vulgar.

26. You have said a faint LIKE or a fit.
27. They say she was out of her mind LIKE for six weeks.
28. She got worse all of a sudden LIKE.
29. I was a useful sort of chap LIKE.

The focusing function of *like* has also been noted by Miller (n.d.), who says that it often has the meaning of "for example", as in (30). It occurs, too, in other prepositional phrases such as *something like that* and *things like that*, which have the meaning of "for example". The phrase *for example* also has a discourse focusing function, especially when it is placed before a list of examples. In instances such as (30), it seems plausible that when *like* appears on its own, it is a condensed form of a phrase such as *everything like that, things like that, the like of that*, and so on. Examples (31) and (32) illustrate this. In (31) *like* is used along with *go* (see also 40, where *like* is used with *say*). In these examples the speaker invites the listener to imagine the remark that follows *like* as one of a number of possible things similar in form and content which could have been intended.

30. He bought several beautiful presents, LIKE a magnificent paper-weight and jewelry.
31. Matt goes something LIKE, "No way."
32. Shorty don't mean short. It just means LIKE, "Hey man what's happenin'?"

In cases like (33) through (36), it is clear from the content of what is said that *like* is used to evoke examples of what might have been said/thought or might be said/thought either on particular or repeated occasions in the past or in hypothetical instances in the future. In (36) the speaker uses the phrase *things . . . like*, to give an example of something which is predicated in the relative clause.

33. When he was first a month old and stuff I just used to want to sit there and just hold him and be around him. But now I'm *like*, "Go in the other room." [DL/SR]
34. J: Remember when we used to pretend-fight in the halls?
    M: And people would get *like*, "Oh, my God." [Dl/SR]
35. Oh because guys gotta have like, a you know, a tough image *like*, "I don't need no one's help or nothing. I can do everything by myself." Uh-huh. And girls, you know, just the opposite somewhat. [from Eckert, 1990]

36.   And the things that make her so excited are *like*, "He smiled at me today." [from Eckert, 1990]

In some of its uses (especially in Jespersen's examples), *like* seems to behave in a way similar to items which Dines (1980, 22) calls "terminal tags." These have a set marking function in that they cue the listener to interpret the preceding element as an illustrative example of some more general case (cf. 23a. He brought along things for the picnic, food, drinks, and such-LIKE).

Another similarity which the discourse uses of *like* share with elements identified by Schiffrin as discourse markers is ambiguity of scope. In (37), for instance, it is not certain how much of this, if indeed any, might be interpreted as a report of speech or thought (cf. also 38 and 50). Nor is it entirely clear what supporting role the verb *be* has when it appears as part of the quotation frame (cf. 34 and 39). Where *like* occurs with *be*, it has not become a verb of saying but retains its function as complementizer. Thus, when it is used to introduce clauses reporting speech and thought, it has become a quotative complementizer.

37.   It was LIKE, it's not wild and passionate, but it's time. [interview with Wendy Wasserstein reported in the *Washington Post*, 6 May 1985, B7]

At the moment the use of *like* as a quotative complementizer appears to be confined to American English, though there are perhaps traces of a similar development in British English. Rimmer (1988), for instance, recorded the narrative in (38), where a taxi driver uses *like* before clauses which may be intended to represent speech/thought. In the first instance it is not clear whether *like* qualifies what goes before or is used to introduce the announcement sent out from the central transmitter which gives the taxi drivers the location of passengers. The next quote, beginning with the sound effect "waah," is intended to be the speech of a group of taxi drivers who become party to embarrassing information about a colleague, and it is not introduced by an explicit verb of saying. Again, it is not possible to tell whether the next instance of *like* refers to what precedes or what follows. Part of this is repeated at the end as a coda to the story. The instances of *like* after "cab" and "who's Sylvia?" are not used for quotation, and the next quotation ("everybody was . . .") is again not introduced by a verb of saying. The occurrence of the first *like* in the quote ("woh: we've got him now like, who's Sylvia like") is ambiguous in scope and status because it may refer to what precedes or it may be seen as an introducer of the question "who's Sylvia like?" We may be seeing in these examples a major difference between British and American English with regard to the placement of certain discourse markers. Americans tend to place *like* before the part of the text they are intended to qualify or focus on, while Britons place it afterwards (cf. again Jespersen's examples in 26–29).

38. You can imagine, everybody in Birmingham, click over to channel 2,
     and it's gone across LIKE, "Can you go back to Sylvia's, she's left her
     knickers in the cab."
     So of course everybody's "waah this is it" LIKE "Now we've got him
     woh we can have him on about this." . . .
     And she'd left them [knickers, i.e. underpants] in the cab LIKE, and of
     course everybody was, "woh: we've got him now LIKE, who's Sylvia
     LIKE?" [from Rimmer (1988, 2: 91)]

Another instance of *like* recorded by Rimmer is more clearly quotative in
function, even though it is not supported by a verb in the main clause
(1988, 2: 54):

39. He says, "I know you ain't Ulysses, what's your proper name?"
     And he LIKE, "I ain't saying Ulysses I'm saying Ulilles."

In (40) we have a case where *like* appears after *say* to express the opinion
of a group of people. The fact that the noun *people* is not coreferential with
the agent of the reported event neutralizes the distinction between direct
and indirect report.

40. Yeah people say *like* they [i.e., those who run a public swimming
     pool] should keep it open but no one uses it. [from Miller, n.d.]

Schiffrin (1987, 64) also emphasizes the multifunctionality of discourse
markers; they may be used in several different discourse functions simultaneously. We have already seen some examples where *like* occurs in more
than one syntactic/discourse function within the same utterance. Thus in
(41), the speaker begins by introducing her thoughts with *like*. We can tell
that this is reported thought because of the use of the address term *Sherry*
(compare the last line where she shifts to *you*, but still uses *like*). She then
uses *like* as a discourse marker a number of times before she uses it as a
quotative complementizer in a conversation in which she explains to a
girlfriend, Sherry, how difficult it is to learn pompom routines from one
of the other girls, Betsy, and how she wishes her friend, Sherry, were the
teacher. Lange (1988) reports that the speaker used *like* at the rate of 20
times per minute in this conversation.

41. I'm LIKE, "I wish Sherry was my teacher." I mean she'll go off to one
     half of the group to show them and then say to the other half LIKE the
     half of the half. . . . All right, I'll be LIKE one, she'll go off with half
     the ones. . . . She'll LIKE be on the LIKE, . . . let's say we're all in LIKE
     two rows or something, . . . LIKE trying to learn it LIKE in a group,
     she'll go into LIKE one end of the lob and show it to them and go to
     the totally other end and be LIKE, "God, you guys, didn't you see it?"
     I mean, I couldn't see it. There were LIKE people blocking, you know?
     And she LIKE – she'll get mad at you if you ask her to do the move
     again. It's LIKE, "God, I wish you were the teacher." I wish you could
     say someting to her, LIKE "Betsy," you know, maybe you should be

LIKE, don't tell her things that other people said. But just be LIKE . . .
I'm LIKE a lost case. I'm LIKE a total lost case. [DL/SR]

More examples can be seen in (42) through (44). In (42) *like* is used for quotation, comparison, and as a verb. In (43) it is used as a general discourse marker (co-occurring with the temporal subordinator *when*) and a quotative complementizer. In (44) *like* appears as general discourse marker, quotative complementizer, and verb.

42. 'n I was LIKE, "Oh well I went up there once to see the thrift shops there, to see what they were LIKE, 'cause I LIKE used clothing sometimes too, depending on what it is. [from Jane Frank]
43. I hate it when LIKE a 60-year-old lady was LIKE "It's so cool" or a Val speak. [DL/SR]
44. . . . she started to LIKE really go for him. And she's LIKE
    And I'm LIKE, "That's so good."
    And she's LIKE, she's LIKE, "Now I'm not even sure if I LIKE him. Now when I look at him his face is kind of deformed and everything. LIKE you start seeing little flaws." [DL/SR]

Tannen (1987) has shown that speakers are more likely to use a word which has already occurred in the conversation and that repetition serves important poetic functions in discourse. Since people plan ahead even while they are speaking, it might be possible that a later use of a word in its conventional sense would inspire its earlier use as a marker of quotation and vice versa. Lange (1985) notes repetition of *go* in its conventional sense as a verb of motion and as a marker of speech. In (13) and (15) we saw instances where *come* retains its sense of verb of motion, but *go* is used to report, as in *She comes back and goes.* . . .

In (45) and (46) we have examples where *like* is used with the discourse marker *I mean*. Co-occurrences of this kind are also supportive evidence for the view that *like* is a discourse marker because messages are multiply reinforced and redundant (see Schiffrin 1987, 66). According to Schiffrin (266), *I mean* marks speakers' orientation towards their own talk. Thus, part of the meaning of *like* is derived from the context in which it occurs, namely, with events that are internally evaluative of the story's point and with external evaluation of the narrative point.

45. I mean, I was LIKE, "OK, so she thinks they're expensive, that's fine."
    [from Jane Frank]
46. And when she said that I was LIKE, I mean, "I should just go home now." [DL/SR]

The sociolinguistic distribution of *like*

In order to understand the communicative force of the various uses of *like*, we have to look more carefully at the social factors which condition its occurrence. We have already noted that the use of *like* is found most frequently in the colloquial speech of adolescents and young adults under 30. Blyth et al. (1990) also found that *be + like* was not used by those over 38. Almost all of our examples come from young people, and 83 percent were produced by women, but there are indications that its use is becoming more widespread. Thus, age-grading as well as gender marking and sty-listic distribution (i.e. spoken vs. written) require further exploration. We will offer some preliminary observations about the effects of these three factors and say why we think they are related.

Written instances of like
The finding that *like* is more often a feature of casual spoken language is consistent with its function as a discourse marker. It is not surprising that we do not find many instances of *like* used as a quotative complementizer except in transcripts of interviews and occasionally in reports of casual speech. The more general discourse *like*, however, has appeared in print for some time, as we have seen from Jespersen's examples in (26)–(29) above.

One particularly rich source of written data for this nonquotative *like* is McFadden's (1976) novel, *The Serial*, which is intended to be a polemic against "psychobabble." The characters in the book are members of a "psychologically aware set," who use expressions such as *to be where it's at, up front, get one's act together*, and so on. Among the frequent expressions used by the characters is *like*, as in (47) and (48), though none occurs in the frame *be + like* as an unequivocal marker of reported speech or thought. We have given examples of the two most frequent syntactic slots for *like*, namely, sentence initial and before or part of a verb phrase. Examples like (47) account for more than half the occurrences of *like* (i.e., 28 out of 51). However, it also occurs sentence finally and before all major constitu-ent categories – nouns, verbs, prepositions, and adjectives – as well as adverbs. The syntactic freedom of *like* in writing is supported by our spoken and written data (see, e.g., 13 and 44) and by Miller's observations about its use in conversation by Scottish adolescents (n.d.). Like the dis-course markers discussed by Schiffrin, *like* in its nonquotative function can occur in sentence locations which are often difficult to define syntactically. Underhill (1988, 242–43), however, while claiming that the scope of *like* is easy to determine, qualifies this later when he states that it "nearly always introduces a constituent." This suggests a degree of indeterminacy in both the syntactic status and scope of the elements it may modify.

47.   LIKE, this is a crisis. [McFadden 1976, 62].
48.   Tell her how I've got to LIKE take responsibility, you know? [Mcfadden 1976, 64].

We have, however, found a small number of clear instances, particularly in newspaper and magazine interviews, where *like* is used as a quotative complementizer. Two of these are in (49) and (50), which come from a newspaper interview with Lisa Bonet, who portrays a teenage daughter in the television series *The Cosby Show*. She also used *like* in her dialogue on the program. The author of the article, Trustman Senger, directs the reader's focus specifically to one of the functions of *like* in his title, "Lisa Bonet, like

Wild!" At the same time he associates *like* stereotypically with Bonet's speech style. In the interview she is quoted as having used *like* to report her own discourse as well as that of her mother.

It is interesting to see what punctuation conventions the printed language adopts in dealing with these cases. In (49) the newspaper takes Lisa Bonet's statement to be a direct quote. The use of quotation marks around the utterances of *Mom* and *What* in (50) indicates that the editor also regards these as instances of quoted speech. The third occurrence of *like*, however, is seen as the first element in a larger exchange rather than as a marker introducing the whole discourse. Thus, the punctuation suggests the interpretation that Lisa Bonet's second quote is unframed. In this case *like* would be simply a discourse marker with no implications of reporting. We feel, however, that this third instance of *like* is indeterminate in function; it may well be an ellipted frame for the following: *(I was) like: "Well, I just called to tell you. . . ."*

49. I was LIKE, "If it doesn't work, can I come back to the show?" And they said yes.
50. I was LIKE, "Mom?" She was *like* "What!"
     "Like,well, I just called to tell you that I got *The Cosby Show.* Bye."
     [from *The Washington Post*, 11 Mar. 1987, C1–C3]

Example (51) comes from a book about ape language experiments. In this extract the author, Eugene Linden, is reporting the efforts of Janis, one of the researchers, to rehabilitate chimps to the wild in the Gambia. The first two sentences are written from Linden's point of view. This orientation is evident from the use of past tense and third-person pronouns. The shift to Janis's point of view begins in the third sentence. The fact that it is her speech is indicated by the placement of quotation marks around this chunk of text as well as by the use of first-person pronouns. The discourse which is introduced by *like* is in effect a quote within a quote; it is Janis representing her thoughts in dialogue form. The "you" presumably refers to Lily, the chimp, since the other references to self are achieved through the use of *I*, but this could also be Janis addressing herself, as if telling herself that she has to perfect her ant-eating technique.

51. Her policy was not to intervene unless she thought it necessary, and so she waited until it became obvious that Lily was not going to do it unless Janis did it first. She began by practicing eating the ants without the chimps around. "Then one day it was LIKE, Today has got to be the day you do it. I was careful enough to make sure I only had a few ants on the end of the stick, and then I was careful to make sure I placed the stick in my teeth and not in my jaw so that I would be able to smash 'em immediately." [Linden 1986, 182]

In our next example, (52), the author, Lawrence Shainberg, uses *like* to report what an editor said about himself. Again, the punctuation conventions indicate that the book review editor considers what follows *like* to be a direct quote.

52.   "Or maybe I pretend I wasn't reading it for publication, only as a friend. You know, LIKE 'God, it never occured to me you wanted me to be your editor!'" [*The New York Times book Review*, 11 Sept. 1988, sec. 7: 1]

SEX DIFFERENTIATION. An exploratory survey done by Lange (1986) is suggestive of certain trends towards sex differentiation in the use of *like*. She presented teenagers with some sentences containing *like* in its various functions to see whether they thought the usages were gender marked. Although the examples containing *like* were produced by both males and females, they were often judged by teenagers of both sexes as being characteristic of female speech. There was no mention of *like* in responses to three of the four examples, but in (53) one boy singled out the use of the word *like*. He said, "Girls always use 'like.' Like boys don't talk that way. Like we don't use the word 'like' the ways girls do." Blyth et al. (1990) also found that their informants judged the quotative use of *like* to be a marker of female speech. However, their results for actual usage showed that young men used it more than women. They do not say how many instances of *like* they recorded.

53.   I can't believe you don't know what time we're leaving. It's LIKE, "Okay, we're going to New York tomorrow." Hey, I ought to put in my laundry.

It is, of course, well known that speakers often do not have very good intuitions about their own usage of certain items, and in the remark cited by Lange we can see that the boy uses *like* as a discourse marker himself. Moreover, the utterance he judged to be female on the basis of this linguistic feature is actually that of a male. It is not clear whether he is singling out the use of *like* as a marker of reported speech (rather than its use as a focuser) as a feature of female speech. It may be that speakers do not perceive that these involve different uses of *like*. The very fact that *like* is formally identical in all these uses may camouflage its use in the new function of quotative complementizer (see Spears 1982 on camouflage), and in some cases it is not possible to attribute a single function to a particular instance. This may be one reason why it has not been discussed before now. Other examples we have cited here of course show that boys (and men) do indeed use *like* to report speech (examples 3, 4, 13, 16, 18, 38, 39, 43, and 52 were all produced by males). However, it may be that what is noticed is that women tend to use more dialogue in conversation (see e.g., Johnstone 1988). They also discuss topics of a more interpersonal nature than men and in doing so use more instances of *like* to construct dialogue. Thus, *like* may be more salient as a stereotypical marker of female speech style through its use to discuss topics which women favor more than men (see Lange 1988). This requires more systematic study.

Age grading (and social class distribution)
[. . .] With regard to age grading, Nordberg (1984) considers quotation techniques to be an important style marker of adolescent speech in Sweden.

He claims that direct quotation predominates to a far greater extent in young people's speech than in adults'. Romaine (1985) found extensive use of direct quotation in children as young as ten years. What Nordberg calls "fully converted indirect speech," in other words, with consistent shifting of pronouns, tense, and adverbials of time and place, is very rare in the conversation of young people and probably not very common in adults' speech either.

He comments, too, that there is probably quite considerable social variation in adults' techniques for reporting other people's words. There have been a few studies which have shown a correlation between social status and the use of direct versus indirect speech. Macaulay's (1991) investigation of some features of narrative style in middle- and working-class speakers in Ayr, Scotland, for example, confirms Nordberg's impressionistic observation that extended indirect speech is rare in ordinary spoken discourse. Macaulay found that it occurred generally in the speech of middle-class speakers.

The use of direct speech, however, seemed to be more affected by individual factors than by social class. The lower-class speakers produced more than twice as many narratives as the middle class, but there was very little difference in the overall use of direct quotation. The greatest incidence of quotation was in the speech of a middle-class man, who also produced the highest number of narratives for his group.

The use of quoted direct speech, however, may be an important feature for the middle-class person, since it allows speakers to show knowledge of linguistic features that they do not normally use. Considering the stigma attached to some forms of working-class speech, middle-class speakers may nevertheless use stigmatized features in quotation because they can disclaim any responsibility for them (see our remarks above about the use of dialect in the novel). The same is true of taboo expressions. Macaulay (1988, 228) gives an example of one middle-class man who used working-class forms of the negative in quoted direct speech.

Rimmer (1988) found differences in the incidence of quoted speech among four occupational groups (taxi drivers, nurses, hairdressers, and chefs) in Birmingham and Liverpool. Although the groups also differed compositionally in terms of age and sex, the results suggest that those of working-class origin in occupations with less-specialized training use more direct quotation in their narratives. The hairdressers (all female) used it the most often, while taxi drivers (all male) used it the next most often. These same groups also showed the highest incidence of other features of involved style and performed narrative, as in mimicry and conversational historical present.[8] Lakoff (1973) also suggests that women tend to use more direct quotes than men. It is obvious from this brief survey that more comparative work needs to be done on narrative techniques. We will relate these findings to the historical developments we discussed above after we have considered the nature of the changes which have led to the present discourse uses of *like*.

A model of grammaticalization

We have suggested that what is happening to *like* is an instance of GRAM-MATICALIZATION. This term has generally been used in a narrow sense to refer to a unidirectional historical process whereby words acquire a new status as grammatical or morphosyntactic forms (see, e.g., Meillet 1912, Kurylo-wicz 1975, 52: and our discussion of the suffix *-ly* above). Since change is very often gradual rather than abrupt, as old forms take on new functions they must go through a stage where old and new meanings co-exist. In some cases, the new meanings may not entirely replace old ones, and this can lead to ambiguity. We noted above (254ff.) the ambiguity in scope and function of some instances of *like*. As old forms take on new functions, they may change category membership. Such category changes are some-times considered to be instances of grammaticalization. Whether *like* has changed its category membership depends on which of the syntactic uses of *like* have given rise to its discourse uses. It has in some sense become both a general discourse marker as well as a specialized complementizer. Although in its use as a quotative complement it still retains its comple-mentizer status, it is used to encode a new kind of construction which represents a compromise between the direct and indirect mode. [. . .]

Traugott (1982) sees grammaticalization as a semantic/pragmatic process rather than a syntactic one. Among her general principles for semantic shifts underlying grammaticalization are the following:

  i. from the propositional to textual to expressive components of grammar
  ii. from less personal to more personal

The first hypothesis is based on the functional-semantic theory of grammar developed in Halliday and Hasan (1976), who distinguish three functional components within the linguistic system: the ideational (or propositional), the textual, and the interpersonal.[9] Traugott (1982) uses this tripartite system as a kind of semantic space within which she traces general routes that items undergoing grammaticalization follow. "More personal" mean-ings are those which are more anchored in the context of the speech act, particularly the speaker's orientation to situation, text, and interpersonal relations. [. . .]

Presumably it is the syntactic functions of *like* as a preposition and suffix that provide the kind of grammatical context from which *like* can be extended to focus on a whole clause, sentence, or chunk of discourse. It is in this sense that the syntactic slot and grammatical function of *like* play an important role in determining the kind of grammaticalization that can take place. It seems likely that, in the case of *like* becoming a quotative complementizer, we are dealing with a case of grammaticalization which originates within the propositional and textual component and which then undergoes further specialization within the textual component. Here a marker (a preposition or conjunction which is already grammatical in function) is extended to a specific textual function of quotative comple-mentizer. In the case of the more general discourse use of *like*, however, we may be dealing with a development which illustrates movement from the textual to the interpersonal.

Using Traugott's model, we can illustrate these developments in Fig. 9.1. We will now sketch out a possible grammaticalization channel for *like*. The first stage in its route to becoming a quotative complement is its use as ə preposition, where *like* is subcategorized to take a nominal or pronominal complement. It undergoes recategorization so as to take a sentential complement.[10] This involves treating a subordinate clause as a nominal constituent so that *like* is extended to it by analogy. At this stage *like* can be used as conjunction or complementizer, as in the Winston example in (22) above. Because *like* can appear as a suffix following an item (as in 23a and 23b), as well as precede a clause or sentence, it can be reanalyzed as a discourse marker, which shows syntactic detachability and positional mobility.[11] When *like* precedes a clause or a sentence which is a quotation, it functions as part of the quotation frame. Since English does not license verbless sentences, a dummy verb *be* is required to complete syntactically the quotation frame. Here we see an element of reanalysis and "syntactic fixing" as part of the process. Heine et al. (1991) say that reanalysis may accompany grammaticalization in the sense that when an item is grammaticalized its pragmatic or syntactic position is affected in addition to that of the constituent it belongs to. Unlike *that*, which can also occur as complementizer in the frame *say that X*, *like* does not require the speaker to shift deictic perspective. The clause containing *be* + *like* is only loosely bound to the following complement which preserves the direct form (see, e.g., Givón 1980 on binding of complements).

Certainly historically, the nondiscourse uses of *like* appear to precede the discourse uses as far as we know, but that may simply reflect the nature of our evidence. Both coexist synchronically and the steps we are postulating here are almost certainly not strictly sequential since in Middle English, even where *like* was used in a clearly prepositional function, it had some positional mobility before a more rigid word order was imposed. In early use with the dative it could occur after its object.[12] A simple linear model of grammaticalization is inadequate to account for these developments. What may emerge from grammaticalization is a network of related meanings of an item (cf. Claudi and Heine 1986, 313).[13]

Once *like* occurs in its roles as a conjunction, it is only a short step to the use of *like* to introduce reported speech and thought. This happens when the speaker presents the clause created for comparison or exemplification so that it can be construed as a report of speech or thought. Thus in (54) a

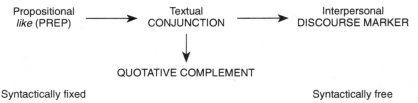

Fig. 9.1 Grammaticalization of *like*

checkout woman at the supermarket has forgotten that the customer has purchased the roll of coins she is about to put into her cash register. She imputes the question "What is she doing?" to the customer as an example of what the customer is thinking or would say if she were to comment on the checkout woman's action. The switch from *I* to *she* makes the shift in perspective clear.

54.   Why am I putting these in my drawer? These are yours. You're just standing there *like*, "What is she doing?" [DL/SR]

In this way the function of *like* is extended so that it becomes a propositional anaphor referring back to a proposition as a whole rather than to just one of its components, which is interpreted as belonging to the de dicto domain. At the semantic/pragmatic level there is a metonymic association between recapitulating the content of a mental or speech event to that of constructing a hypothetical mental or speech event which can be imputed to a particular speaker.

Traugott and König (1991) suggest that inferencing is involved in certain cases of metonymic shift. They identify Horn's (1984) R-Principle, which is speaker-based, as the one relevant for grammaticalization. It enjoins speakers: "Make your contribution necessary. Say no more than you must." According to this principle speakers say as little as they can, and hearers are invited to infer more. Since the checkout woman is directly addressing the hearer to whom she imputes a hypothetical question, to use *say* would be to commit herself to saying too much since she is representing as speech something which was not actually said. Given the social asymmetry in the service encounter, she does not have the right to speak directly for the customer. To go on the record in this way would be to invite the inference that she has evidence for the proposition she reports as dialogue. By choosing *like* she leaves open the possibility that other hearers may augment to the domain of de re what she as the speaker situates in the textual domain of de dicto. Thus, we have a channel from the proposition *say that X > be like X*.

Like is less strongly informative as a channel cue than *say* (or *go*), which imply the act of vocalization. Thus, *like* is not, strictly speaking, referentially equivalent to or exchangable with *say*, as we suggested in our comments on examples (1) and (2). In this sense Tannen is right when she says (1986, 323) that *like* is next to no introducer at all (see above, 245–46). Discourses with *like* are not generally supported by a graphic verbal introducer with explicit lexical content (see, however, our examples 31, 32, and 41). Although report clauses introduced by *like* preserve some of the grammatical hallmarks of the indirect form in that the clause containing the quotation is introduced by a frame containing a complementizer, they do not always show the deictic shifts typical of the indirect mode. Pragmatically, however, the effects are those of the indirect mode in that the speaker stands in a relation of reduced responsibility and commitment to the truth of the report.

At the same time that this construction blurs the distinction between the direct and indirect mode, it also blurs the distinction between speech and thought. Since there is a subtle and often fuzzy boundary between reported speech and thought, *like* is a good choice since it creates only an example of something that could have been said or thought without implying the kind of commitment that *say* does.

The relation between mental verbs and verbs of saying has sometimes been used as a basis for theories about the relationship between language and thought. Vendler (1972), for instance, has pointed out a strong semantic correlation between mental verbs, such as *know*, and speech act verbs or verbs of saying. He argues that there are significant parallels between forms of thought and forms of speaking, so that you can say whatever you think and think almost whatever you say. Vendler claims that in English these two classes of verbs are practically isomorphic. Analyses of discourse in other languages have also documented the close relationship between reported speech and the description of mental states and events. Reported speech seems to be the primary means of representing mental states and events in discourse in Aguarana, a language of Peru (Larson 1978).

In taking these ideas further, Traugott (1986) has postulated that where both nonspeech-act and speech-act verb meanings coexist, the former will precede the latter in time. Thus, the direction of change will be from mental verb to speech-act verb. This is another manifestation of her general principles (i) and (ii), which predict that meanings will tend to shift from propositional to interpersonal, or, in other words, meanings become increasingly discourse-based or speaker-based. Since mental verbs like *think* and *know* are propositional in nature, and since speech-act verbs are interactive, the speech-act verbs can be expected to be later developments. The speech-act meanings are metalinguistic in that they refer to the described situation as a discourse situation. This suggests that 'having in mind' seems to be cognitively more fundamental than 'asserting that'. In (55) we have another case which offers evidence for the close affinity between thinking and speaking. The speaker seems to be on the point of introducing her thought as a quotation introduced by *like*, but then changes her mind and reports her ideas indirectly.

55. My mother said, "David where are you," and he just came right out. I was like, I thought I lost him. I really thought I lost him. [DL/SR]

Conclusions

The case of *like* raises a number of issues about the process and mechanism of grammaticalization. We will consider here briefly just two of these before we relate our historical discussion to the sociolinguistic findings mentioned earlier. One is the extent to which the semantics of particular lexical sources or the functions of grammatical categories determine the kind of grammaticalization that can be undergone. Traugott (1982), for instance, mentions the use of what were originally prepositions indicating position and directionality as aspect markers. She asks what it is about the spatial relation encoded in the meaning of *up* which allows it to become a perfective particle, as in *finish up*. Or similarly, what is it about the semantics of *on* which allows it to become a durative particle, as in *keep on*? The standard view on this has been that the new aspectual meanings are the result of a kind of fading or figurative extension of the concrete meanings of the original adverbs.[14]

What is it then about the meanings of verbs like *go* and markers such as *like*, which do not lexicalize explicitly the speech act of saying, that allows them to be used in quotation? Verbs of motion have a variety of metaphorical extensions. Their role in the grammaticalization of tense systems is well known (see Fleischman 1982).[15] Given that tense is basically a deictic category, it follows that deictic discourse sequencers such as *come* and *go* should be used in marking tense. If we take the speaker as a deictic center, it is easy to see how the future can be represented as an event which is coming toward the speaker or one which the speaker is going toward. Clark (1974) has offered a deixis-based explanation for idioms involving *come* and *go*, which express a change of state and evaluative viewpoints. Thus, it may be the case that the use of verbs of motion as quotation devices suggests that *come/go* and *like* occupy opposing places on a proximal-distal scale (see also Lange 1985). Verbs of motion point mainly forward and outward to the act of vocalization which is projected beyond the speaker, while *like* draws the listener to the internal state of the speaker in introducing constructed dialogue that dramatizes internalized feelings. In this respect, we might think of *like* as proximal and *go* as distal. This interpretation is reinforced by the frequent use of *like* for the speaker's discourse when the speaker is author, and *go* when the speaker animates someone else's discourse. We have already noted how the semantics of *like* is implicated in the discourse interpretations it has. In this respect the grammaticalization process, whereby *like* comes to introduce a mimetic performance, is in Haiman's terms (1989, 167, n. 1) motivated since in its traditional meaning *like* means "similar to."

This brings us to our second question, which concerns the extent to which the presuppositional implications of a lexical item permit the bleaching process which Meillet and others see as typical of grammaticalization. Hymes (1974, 149), for instance, says that "lexical elements and phrases, if they acquire grammatical function in a social or stylistic sense, may lose their earlier lexical force in their new paradigmatic relationship." We noted in our earlier discussion of *-ly* above, that after grammaticalization it lost not only the behavioral and coding properties of an independent lexeme, but also its semantics. Bleaching in this instance has been complete, though we noted the coexistence of the suffix *like*.

Traugott (1986) points out that there has been a tendency to use the term "bleaching" both for pragmaticization of meaning and for the syntacticization that leads to dummy markers. She notes that, although the first process may give rise to the second, they are not the same process but probably have been treated as one only because of the uncertain role of pragmatics in grammar. In its early stages, grammaticalization actually involves an increase in pragmatic meaning. What has happened to *like* does not involve bleaching of meaning, but rather an increase of pragmatic significance pertaining to the speaker's attitude. Both the semantic and grammatical status of *like* permit its extension to more and more contexts, eventually including the quotative function.

It may be that there is a greater propensity for grammaticalization in languages like English due to the multifunctionality of many items in its lexicon. Bauer (1983, 226), for example, notes that conversion has no demonstrated limitations in English since all form classes seem to be eligible and are able to produce words of almost any form class, particularly the open classes. Moreover, there is no reason to believe that the components of grammar identified by Halliday and Hasan (1976) are discrete. In fact, they are expressly not. Their model provides for an analysis of clauses on all three levels, so an element of clause structure can be assigned a function on each level. Because all items are multifunctional, this allows a certain amount of "leakage" between the components.

Now we can return to the implications of the sociolinguistic distribution of *like*. Why should *like* in its function of quotative complementizer be found most frequently in the informal conversational style of young people, especially women? In this connection, it is interesting that Nordberg (1984, 20) offers the following impression of young Swedish people's speech: "One thing you are struck by when listening to young people's conversations and discussions for a long time is what an incredible lot of opinions they express. It is far commoner for views, values, and feelings to be conveyed than reports, descriptions, and arguments, which, in my experience, take up considerably more time in adult speech." He characterizes adolescent style as emotional and implicit. There is also a high use of onomatopoeic elements. He interprets this as a reflection of the order in which speech functions are learned in childhood. The expressive or interpersonal function is primary. The frequent expression of value judgments and heavy reliance on paralinguistic and prosodic devices for achieving communicative purposes are stylistic features which are developed and play a dominant role in the early stages of language acquisition. They are of course also features of what Tannen and others have called "involved style" and are typically found in high concentration in what Wolfson (1982) calls "performed narrative," and Goffman (1981), a "replaying." Among these are direct speech, repetition, expressive noises and sound effects, and gestures (Wolfson 1982, 25). We argued above that the reason why direct speech is seen to be more vivid lies in the fact that the emotive, affective aspects of speech present considerable problems of incorporation for the indirect mode. Dialogue creates involvement because it makes it possible for listeners to come closer to imagining the recounted action or speech rather than hearing about it.

While direct speech is apparently universal, indirect speech is not. Why should this be so? Li (1986, 40) suggests that the reasons for the absence of indirect speech in the language of the Paez are cultural rather than linguistic. A Paez person is not allowed to assume the responsibility for the speech of another. Thus, in some cultures, one cannot freely adopt the perspective of others; the "natural" viewpoint is that of the original speaker. This shows the bias in the general assumption that the original speech act is somehow basic and indirect speech is therefore a modification because the speaker has to alter his perspective. Ebert (1986, 157) points out that from the pragmatic perspective, it is direct speech that is shifted because it requires the speaker to take another's point of view and to construct or infer what the other said or was thinking.

However, the primacy of direct speech can be seen too in children's language development. The Piagetian view of children emphasizes their egocentric perspective up until the age of 8 (see Piaget 1926). However, studies have shown that, even when young children play on their own, they construct appropriate dialogue for the different characters they pretend to speak for. In her study of children's reports of dialogues shown on video sequences, Hickmann (1982) found that there was a developmental progression in ability to transform dialogue into cohesive texts. The youngest children (4-year-olds) tended to focus on the dialogue participants and the events and states of the speech event, but not on the dialogue. When the younger children did focus on the dialogue and report it, they didn't use direct or indirect quotation frames to separate the act of reporting from reported speech. They depended on pitch and intonation to separate different speakers. The older children (ages 7–10) used direct quotation frames. In English the relative linguistic complexity of the indirect mode of reporting has to be taken into account. Performing a narrative through the use of direct quotation may be a simplifying device for speakers, particularly immature ones, because it allows them to avoid some of the more problematic aspects of syntactic and semantic incorporation, such as deictic shifting required in the indirect mode. Thus, while pragmatically it may be easier to maintain one's own perspective in reporting events, linguistically it may represent the marked option.[16] Discourses introduced by *like* preserve the pragmatic force of reduced responsibility conveyed by the indirect mode, but allow the speaker to sidestep the syntactic and semantic problems of incorporation.

Nordberg also notes the role of peer group solidarity in enforcing speech style. Since youth culture is more uniform than adult culture, young people can rely more easily on an implicit code which evokes shared experience. Young narrators seek the affective involvement with their audiences and rely on their support for interpretation. Another reason for the higher incidence of reported direct rather than indirect speech among young people, which Nordberg does not note, may also derive from aspects of peer group interactional conventions. Storytellings require the consent of others in the speech event because they interrupt the normal turntaking exchanges of conversation. A successful storyteller must gain and hold the floor. When we are with peers, where rights to speech are presumably equal, one could hypothesize that there is more pressure not only to recount an experience worth hearing about, but to recount it in such a way that it is worth listening to. Presenting a narrative by reenacting it as a series of speech exchanges also simulates the normal exchange pattern of conversation and may therefore be perceived as less of an interruption than a narrative presented entirely from one's own perspective. Thus the use of style features characteristic of performed narrative may reflect the nature of one's contractual obligations to others in the speech event.

The pattern of sex differentiation which we found is also not surprising in at least two respects. For one thing, it has been demonstrated that adolescents in western urban societies are generally socialized within and interact in single-sex peer groups. Thus, the peer group is an important source of many sex-specific ways of using language and behaving, some of which continue into adulthood (see, e.g., Cheshire 1982 and Romaine 1984, §6.3). Many have noted the greater emphasis in female groups on communicating affect and emotional involvement and the use of strategies which appeal to group concerns rather than provoke conflict and competition (see Maltz and Borker 1982). To the extent that *like* can be used to convey thought at the same time as it allows the speaker some leeway in commitment to what was said by another, it is consistent with many of the goals and values associated with the female communicative style.[17]

While young people's casual conversation may provide an important potential source of language change, it is possible that *like* represents a case of change in apparent rather than real time. Nevertheless, as in other changes believed to be in progress which have been observed, *like* shows familiar hallmarks. Thus, in the case of high rising intonation in Australian English, Guy et al. (1986, 230) comment that it "has the social distribution characteristic of a change in progress: higher rates of usage among working-class speakers, teenagers, and women."[18]

We believe the use of quotative *like* is spreading. We have observed it in the colloquial speech of educated people in their 30s, and even occasionally in print. It has just come to the notice of the media in a *New York Times* article by Bernstein (1988), who reports that *like* is now used by some young people "as a substitute for the straightforward verb 'to say.'" He gives examples from the conversation of two teen-age girls and cites some comments from a 14-year-old girl. Although Underhill's (1988) work is also mentioned, as we have seen, he does not deal with quotative *like*.

Most changes are in circulation for some time before they are noticed. The use of *like* as a conjunction, we have shown above, persisted for many centuries before attracting the condemnation of grammarians. It is widely in use and has now gained marginal acceptability. Likewise, the nonquotative discourse *like* has probably been used for over a century, though only now are scholars studying it seriously. Quotative *like* is just beginning to be noticed, though as far as we know, ours is the first and only detailed study of its historical origins.

Acknowledgements

We would like to thank Ronald Butters, Nancy Dorian, Bengt Nordberg, and Deborah Tannen for commenting on an earlier version of this paper. We have incorporated some of their suggestions here. We would also like to thank Jane Frank for examples (46), (49), and (64), quoted here. Examples from our corpus are followed by our initials [DL/SR]; those from others are followed by the appropriate information.

Notes

1. There is indeed some evidence that earlier *say*, when used as a speech act verb, was usually associated with a religious or legal binding force (see Dirven et al. 1982).

2. Milroy and Milroy (1977) have observed the use of frames such as *here's me, here's him* in Belfast English without verbs of saying, which alternate with *I says, he says*, and so on. See also Stein (1990). Nordberg (1984) also found unbracketed quotation in the speech of Swedish adolescents. Quotation is signalled paralinguistically by a change in timbre, voice quality, intonation, gestures, facial expression, etc. rather than by lexical bracketing. Tannen (1986, 318–19) says that, in the data she studied, nearly a quarter of the instances of direct speech in American English conversational narratives made no use of a lexicalized introducer. This was also true for Greek stories. Literary dialogue, however, relied on explicit framing to a much greater extent. In Tannen's view this difference between the two media reflects the greater versatility introduced by voice in spoken dialogue.

3. Others have made further distinctions among speaker roles. Fillmore (1981), for example, distinguishes between the speaker who represents as opposed to the speaker who quotes or reports. Todorov (1970) and others distinguish between the speaker as actor and initiator of the speech act and evaluator of the propositional content, i.e., as an interactant vis-à-vis the speech event itself, and as a participant in the event or state of affairs that is characterized in the proposition. Todorov uses the terms SUJET D'ÉNONCIATION ('subject to the act of utterance') and SUJET D'ÉNONCÉ ('subject of what is uttered'). Bakhtin (1973) speaks of the polyphonic nature of discourse.

4. See, for example, distinctions such as *histoire* vs. *discours* (Benveniste 1959), *besprochene* vs *erzählte Welt* (Weinrich 1964), *showing* vs. *telling* (Scholes and Kellog 1966), direct, indirect and free indirect style, stream of consciousness, etc. (Banfield 1982).

5. We have not been entirely comprehensive here. We have not included the use of *like* as a main verb, which is etymologically unrelated (<ME *lician*) to *like* in its function as preposition and conjunction (<OE *gelic*; cf. German *gleich*). The main verb *like* has also undergone some changes. Although the precise nature of these is debated (see Allen 1986), it seems clear that they did not have anything to do with the developments we discuss here. There is also a regionally restricted use of *like* as a quasi-modal verb, e.g., Southern American English: *He* LIKE *to fell down and broke his leg*. This development may be related to verbal constructions with *was/(had) like* + infinitive of the kind noted by Visser (1970, 223) and go back as far as the fourteenth century (cf. *Cursor Mundi*, 3452, *Hir liif was likest to be ded*). There are other common uses of *like*, particularly with experiencer or perception verbs, e.g., *It sounds like a bad time for John. The car looked like new.* Cf. also the colloquial *feel* + *like*, e.g., *I feel like [having] a pizza* and *He ran like crazy*. These seem related to the use of *like* as a preposition and conjunction. We have also not discussed related uses such as *likeness, likewise*, etc.

6. Quirk et al. (1972, 755n) observe that *like*, elsewhere a preposition, is sometimes used as a subordinator to replace *as* in manner clauses or *as if* in clauses of comparison, e.g., *It's just like I imagined.* and *He talked to me like his dog.* Even they, however, consider these usages (particularly the second one) somewhat substandard, especially in British English. Historically, *like* was used on its own as a conjunction and also together with *as* from the fourteenth century onwards. Like many other double complementizer constructions in Middle English (e.g., *while that, which that*, etc.), these were simplified, so that now there are certain restrictions on the number and type of forms allowed in COMP (see,

e.g., the analysis in Lightfoot 1979). In standard English only *as* was acceptable, but colloquial speech possibly always favored *like*. There are even instances of *like as if* (Cf. the example given in the OED 1971, 285 from Cleridge: "I held the letter in my hand *like as if* I was stupid").

7. Jespersen (1942, 406–8) notes some cases where formations with both are possible, e.g., *godly/godlike, gentlemanly/gentleman-like*, but not **ladily* (but rather *womanly)/ladylike*. The semantic differences are not always obvious (cf. the contrast between *homely/home-like*). The speaker of modern English does not connect *-ly* with *like*, as is obvious from the fact that even adverbs already ending in *-ly* can take *like* as an additional modifier. Jespersen (418) cites a literary example, "jumping on him suddenly *like*."

8. Goffman (1974, 537) has suggested that there are "rules of mimicry" which vary from culture to culture and within a speech community from one category of speaker to another. Interestingly, in Ayr it is only middle-class speakers who mimic lower-class speakers and not the reverse (Macaulay 1988).

9. The ideational or propositional component has to do with the resources a language has for talking about something. It is the main locus for truth conditional relations. The textual component contains the resources a language has for creating cohesive discourse. These include connectives like *but, therefore, because*, etc., items which can only be understood in terms of pragmatic discourse functions. The expressive or interpersonal component concerns the resources a language has for expressing personal attitudes to what is being talked about, to the text itself, and to others in the speech event or situation. These include items like the modals, which express the speaker's assessment of possibility of occurrence of events and situations.

10. Depending on one's choice of grammatical framework, it may not be necessary to postulate a process of recategorization to account of the use of *like* as a complementizer. It has been recognized at least since Jespersen that prepositions can take a full range of clauses, both finite and nonfinite. In English the formal identity of items such as *after, before, since*, etc., in their use as both prepositions and conjunctions, as in (i) and (ii), has been recognized within some generative treatments of syntactic categories (see, e.g., Emonds 1976, Radford 1988, and also Borseley 1986). Both uses of *after* would be regarded as systematically related. If we assume that both instances are prepositions, then in (i) *after* takes an NP complement, while in (ii) it takes a clausal complement. Thus, with regard to the types of complements they can take, prepositions behave very much like verbs.

    i.   We went to visit John after supper.
    ii. We went to visit John after we had eaten supper.

11. Another interesting development which shows some similarity to what has happened to *like* can be observed in some northern varieties of British English, where *but* has taken on the function of discourse marker and can occur sentence-finally, e.g., *I really don't want it but*. The usual use of *but* in standard English as a conjunction (e.g., *John bought a new car but isn't happy with it*) illustrates a movement from the propositional to textual. Like a number of other conjunctions in English, it was originally a spatial term or deictic (< OE *butan* 'on the outside'; cf. modern Dutch *buiten* "outside"). Now it is primarily a marker of a textual relation, though it can still be used as a preposition (e.g., *He ate all the cakes but one*). The northern British English development illustrates an additional shift into the interpersonal component.

12. Cf. these citations from the OED (1971, 283): Orm [1200, 3572]: "Hire sune wass

hym lic"; *Cursor Mundi* [1300, 18861] "Þe tanes es to þe toþer liche"; Robt Cicyle [1370; 58]: "he rode non odur lyke." The extension of postpositions to clause linking morphology has been noted by Genetti (1986).

13. If the suffix -*like* is regarded as the "starting" point for the grammaticalization of the discourse use of *like*, as suggested by Jespersen, and is also implicated in the grammaticalization of *like* as a marker of reported speech, we are dealing with a case where an item which is originally morphological has taken on syntactic and discourse functions. Thus, yesterday's morphology is today's syntax and discourse. (cf. Givón 1971, however, who suggests the opposite in his dictum: "Today's morphology is yesterday's syntax"). However, this would be a case of degrammaticalization, or regrammaticalization, where a bound form becomes free or relexicalized (cf. Kurylowicz's 1975 use of the term DEGRAMMATICALIZATION to refer to cases in which a derivational category grammaticalizes to an inflectional category, which then lexicalizes or degrammaticalizes to a derivational category).

14. Traugott (1982, 249–50) says that the semantic shift in the particles from directionality to boundedness or nonboundedness is a manifestation of a move from more to less concrete. In her view, however, the bleaching is unmotivated and is therefore a case of "de-iconization." Brinton (1988), however, argues for recognition of a coexistence of spatial and nonspatial meanings of varying intensities. In her view the change involves neither bleaching from spatial to aspect meaning nor a shift from concrete to abstract. Due to the isomorphism between physical movement and event movement, there has been a metonymic shift in focus from direction to goal orientation, i.e., from one kind of spatial meaning to another.

15. Fleischman (1982, 178) says that *come* futures are far less common than *go* futures, though systematic sampling suggests this asymmetry is perhaps illusory (see Bybee et al. 1991). The fact that Swedish is one of the languages which makes use of *come* in a future construction is probably linked with the choice of *come* rather than *go* as a verb of saying since languages rarely use both *come* and *go* in their tense systems (cf., however, French, where *come* is used in a past construction and *go* in the future; Traugott 1978, 377).

16. Spears (1982) has discussed the use of *come* and *go* in Black English as semi-auxiliaries which encode aspects of speaker attitudes.

17. Evidence to support this comes from the acquisition of Japanese, where Clancy (1985, 436–39), for example, reports that one of the earliest forms to emerge is sentence-final *tte* after reported speech and sounds. This is the complementizer used with verbs of saying and other nonfactive predicates. It was acquired before any other complement types or conjoined sentences were used. This means that, in a language like Japanese, children explicitly mark reported speech as early as 20 months. Too, Schieffelin (1985, 542) found the use of the quotative verb *say* preceded by a sentential object to report the speech of others was frequent in Kaluli-speaking children from the age of 26 months. Clancy (1985, 439) attributes the earlier acquisitions of quotation by Japanese children in comparison with English-speaking children to both cultural and linguistic factors. There is no grammatical distinction between direct and indirect speech within embedded quotation. The earliest occurrences of *tte* are morphological rather than syntactic. They are used as sentence-final particles first. Structures which could be embedded in verbs of saying can be used first as simple sentences ending in *tte*. Clancy also found that Japanese mothers frequently report speech and sounds when interacting with their children.

18. In some respects *like* can function as a hedging device (see also Underhill 1988, 240–41). This would be compatible with evidence suggesting that hedges are

more frequently used by women and by those of subordinate social status. Thus, there may be some truth in Jespersen's suggestion that *like* is used by inferiors when addressing superiors. See also Johnstone 1987 on the role of authority in alternation in the conversational historical present.

References

Allen, C.L. (1986) 'Reconsidering the History of *like*', *Journal of Linguistics* 22: pp. 375–410.
American Heritage Dictionary of the English Language, (1969) Ed. William Morris. Boston: Houghton Mifflin.
Anderson, S.R. and Kiparsky, P. (eds.), (1973) *Festschrift for Morris Halle*, New York: Holt.
Bakhtin, M. (1973) *Problems of Dostoevsky's Poetics*, Trans. R.W. Rotsel. A. Arbor: University of Michigan Press.
Bally, C. (1912) 'Le style indirect libre en français moderne', *Germanisch-Romanische Monatsschrift* 4: pp. 544–56, 597–606.
Bauer, L. (1983) *English Word Formation*, Cambridge: Cambridge University Press.
Benveniste, E. (1959) 'De la subjectivité dans le langage', *Journal de Psychologie* 51: pp. 257–65.
Bernstein, R. (1988) 'Is "Teenspeak", like, English?', *New York Times*, Sept., 15, p. 20.
Borseley, R.D. (1986) 'Prepositional Complementizers in Welsh', *Journal of Linguistics* 22: pp. 67–84.
Brotherton, P. (1976) 'Aspects of the Relationship between Speech Production, Hesitation and Social Class', Diss. University of Melbourne.
Bybee, J.L., Pagliuca, W. and Perkins, R. (1991) 'Back to the Future', Traugott and Heine (forthcoming).
Butters, R.R. (1980) 'Narrative *Go* "Say"', *American Speech* 55: pp. 304–07.
—— (1982) 'Editor's Note [on *be like* 'think']', *American Speech* 57: pp. 149.
—— (1989) *The Death of Black English: Divergence and Convergence in Black and White Vernaculars*, Bamberger Beitrage zur englischen Sprachwissenschaft, Frankfurt: Lang, p. 25.
Cheshire, J. (1982) *Variation in an English Dialect*, Cambridge: Cambridge University Press.
Clancy, P.M. (1985) 'The Acquisition of Japanese', Slobin (1985), pp. 373–524.
Clark, E.V. (1974) 'Normal States and Evaluative Viewpoints', *Language* 50: pp. 316–22.
Claudi, U. and Heine, B. (1986) 'On the Metaphorical Base of Grammar', *Studies in Language* 10: pp. 297–335.
Coulmas, F. (1986a) 'Reported Speech: Some General Issues', Coulmas (1986c), pp. 1–28.
—— (1986b) 'Direct and Indirect Speech in Japanese', Coulmas (1986c), pp. 161–78.
—— (ed.), (1986c) *Direct and Indirect Speech*, Berlin: De Gruyter.
Dirven, R., Goosens, L., Putseys, Y. and Vorlat, E. (1982) *The Scene of Linguistic Action and Its Perspectivization by* Speak, Talk, Say *and* Tell, Amsterdam: Benjamins.
Eckert, P. (1990) 'Cooperative Competition in Adolescent "Girl Talk",' *Discourse Processes* 13: pp. 91–122.
Emonds, J.E. (1976) *A Transformational Approach to English Syntax*, New York: Academic.
Feagin, C. (1980) 'Woman's Place in Nonstandard Southern Whitesh: Not So Simple', in R. Shuy and A. Shnukal (eds.), *Language Use and the Uses of Language*, Washington: Georgetown University Press, pp. 88–97.

Fillmore, C.J. (1981) 'Pragmatics and the Description of Discourse', in P. Cole (ed.), *Radical Pragmatics*, New York: Academic.

Fleischman, S. (1982) *The Future in Thought and Language: Diachronic Evidence from Romance*, Cambridge: Cambridge University Press.

Fonagy, I. (1986) 'Reported Speech in Hungarian.', Coulmas (1986c), pp. 255–310.

Genetti, C. (1986) 'The Development of Subordinators from Postpositions in Bodic Languages', *Proceedings of the Twelfth Annual Meeting of the Berkeley Linguistics Society.* (ed.), V. Mikiforidu, M. VanClay, M. Niepokuj and D. Fedr, Berkeley: Dept. of Linguistics, University of California, pp. 387–400.

Givón, T. (1971) 'Historical Syntax and Synchronic Morphology: An Archaeologist's Field Trip', *Papers from the Seventh Regional Meeting of the Chicago Linguistic Society*, Chicago: Chicago Linguistic Society, pp. 394–415.

—— (1980) 'The Binding Hierarchy and the Typology of Complements', *Studies in Language* 5: pp. 333–78.

Goffman, E. (1974) *Frame Analysis*, New York: Harper.

—— (1981) 'Footing', *Forms of Talk*, Philadelphia: University of Pennsylvania Press, pp. 124–59.

Guy, G., Horvath, B., Vonwiller, J., Daisley, E. and Rogers, I. (1986) 'An Intonational Change in Progress in Australian English', *Language in Society* 15: pp. 23–51.

Haberland, H. (1986) 'Reported Speech in Danish', Coulmas (1986c), pp. 219–54.

Haiman, J. (1989) 'Alienation in Grammar', *Studies in Language* 13: pp. 129–70.

Halliday, M.A.K. and Hasan, R. (1976) *Cohesion in English*, London: Longman.

Heine, B., Claudi, U. and Hünnemeyer, F. (1991) 'From cognition to Grammar', Traugott and Heine (1991).

Hickmann, M. (1982) 'The Development of Narrative Skills: Pragmatic and Metapragmatic Aspects of Discourse Cohesion', Diss. University of Chicago.

Horn, L.R. (1984) 'Toward a New Taxonomy for Pragmatic Inference: Q-based and R-Based Implicature', in D. Schiffrin (ed.), *Meaning, Form, and Use in Context*, Washington: Georgetown Universtiy Press, pp. 11–42.

Hymes, D. (1974) *Foundations in Sociolinguistics: An Ethnographic Approach*, Philadelphia: University of Pennyslvania Press.

Jakobson, R. (1971) 'Shifters, Verbal Categories, and the Russian Verb', in R. Jakobson (ed), *Selected Writings II*, The Hague: Mouton, pp. 130–47.

Jespersen, O. (1942) *A Modern English Grammar on Historical Principles. Part VI. Morphology*, Copenhagen: Ejnar Munksgaard, London: Allen and Unwin.

Johnstone, B. (1987) 'He says . . . So I Said: Verb Tense Alternation and Narrative Depictions of Authority in American English', *Linguistics* 25: pp. 33–52.

—— (1988) 'Gender and Power in Midwestern Personal Story Telling', Conference on Discourses of Power, Tempe, Arizona.

Kurylowicz, J. (1975) 'The Evolution of Grammatical Categories', *Esquisses linguistiques* II. Munich, pp. 38–54.

Kvavik, K.H. (1986) 'Characteristics of Direct and Reported Speech Prosody: Evidence from Spanish', Coulmas (1986c), pp. 333–60.

Lakoff, R. (1973) *Language and Woman's Place*, New York: Harper.

Lange, D. (1985) 'The Pragmatic Roles of *says*, *goes*, and *like* as Verbs of Saying', Unpublished ms. Dept of Linguistics, Georgetown University.

—— (1986) 'Attitudes of Teenagers toward Sex-Marked Language', Unpublished ms. Dept of Linguistics, Georgetown University.

—— (1988) 'Using *like* to Introduce Constructed Dialogue: How *like* Contributes to Discourse Coherence', Master's thesis, Georgetown University.

Larson, M.L. (1978) *The Functions of Reported Speech in Discourse*, Summer Institute of Linguistics Publications in Linguistics, 59, Dallas: SIL and University of Texas at Arlington.

Leech, G. and Short, M.N. (1981) *Style in Fiction*, London: Longman.

Lightfoot, D.W. (1979) *Principles of Diachronic Syntax*, Cambridge: Cambridge University Press.

Linden, E. (1986) *Silent Partners*, New York: Times books.

—— (1982) 'Deixis and Subjectivity: Loquor, Ergo Sum?' in R.J. Jarvella and W. Klein (eds.), *Speech, Place and Action: Studies in Deixis and Related Topics*, New York: Wiley, pp. 101–24.

Macaulay, R.K.S. (1985) 'The Narrative Skills of a Scottish Coal Miner', in M. Görlach (ed.), *Focus on Scotland*, Amsterdam: Benjamins, pp. 101–24.

—— (1991) 'Locating Dialect in Discourse: The Language of Honest Men and Bonnie Lassies.' New York: Oxford University Press.

McFadden, C. (1976) *The Serial. A Year in the Life of Marin County*, New York: Knopf. Rpt. London: Pan Books, 1978.

Maltz, D. and Borker, R. (1982) 'A Cultural Approach to Male-Female Miscommunication', in J. Gumperz (ed.), *Language and Social Identity*, Cambridge: Cambridge University Press, pp. 195–217.

Massamba, D.P.B. (1986) 'Reported Speech in Swahili', Coulmas (1986c), pp. 99–120.

Meillet, A. (1912) 'L'évolution des formes grammaticales', *Scientia* 12.

Miller, J. (n.d.) 'Syntax and Discourse in a Corpus of Spoken Scottish English', Working Paper SSRC Grant 5152/1. Dept of Linguistics, University of Edinburgh.

Milroy, L. and Milroy, J. (1977) 'Speech and context in an urban setting', *Belfast Working Papers in Language and Linguistics* 2.

Nordberg, B. (1984) 'Om ungdomars samstalsstil. Några preliminara iakttagelser',- *Nysvenska Studier* 64: 5–27.

Östman, J.O. (1982) 'The Symbiotic Relationship between Pragmatic Particles and Impromptu Speech', in N.E. Enkvist (ed.), *Impromptu Speech: A Symposium*, Abo: Abo Akademi, pp. 147–77.

OED. Oxford English Dictionary, 1971, Oxford: Oxford University Press.

Page, N. (1988) *Speech in the English Novel*, 2nd (ed.), London: MacMillan.

Piaget, J. (1926) *The Language and Thought of the Child*, New York: Harcourt.

Polanyi, L. (1982) 'Literary Complexity in Everyday Storytelling', in D. Tannen. (ed.), *Spoken and Written Language: Exploring Orality and Literacy*, Norwood, N.J.: Albex, pp. 155–70.

Quirk, R., Greenbaum, S., Leech, G. and Svartvik, J. (1972) *A Grammar of Contemporary English*, London: Longman.

Radford, A. (1988) *Transformational Grammar*, Cambridge: Cambridge University Press.

Rimmer, S.E. (1988) 'Sociolinguistic Variability in Oral Narrative', Diss. Aston University.

Romaine, S. (1984) *The Language of Children and Adolescents: The Acquisition of Communicative Competence*, Oxford: Blackwell.

—— (1985) 'Grammar and Style in Children's Narratives', *Linguistics* 23: pp. 83–104.

Schieffelin, B.B. (1985) 'The Acquisition of Kaluli', Slobin (1985), pp. 525–94.

Schiffrin, D. (1987) *Discourse Markers*, Cambridge: Cambridge University Press.

Scholes, R.E. and Kellogg, R. (1966) *The Nature of Narrative*, Oxford: Oxford University Press.

Slobin, D.I. (ed.), (1985) *The Crosslinguistic Study of Language Acquisition*, Hillsdale, N.J.: Erlbaum.

Spears, A.K. (1982) 'The Black English Semi-Auxiliary *come*', *Language* 58: pp. 850–72.

Stein, E. (1990) '*I'm sittin' there*: Another New Quotative?', *American Speech* 65: p. 303.

Tannen, D. (1986) 'Introducing Constructed Dialogue in Greek and American Conversational and Literary Narrative', Coulmas (1986c), pp. 311–32.
—— (1987) 'Repetition and Variation as Spontaneous Formulaicity in Conversation', *Language* 63: pp. 574–606.
—— (1990) 'Gender Differences in Conversational Coherence: Physical Alignment and Topical Cohesion', To appear in B. Dorval. (ed.), *Conversational Coherence and Its Development*, Norwood, NJ: Ablex.
Todorov, T. (ed.), (1970) *L'Énonciation*, Paris: Didier and Larousse.
Traugott, E.C. (1978) 'On the Expression of Spatio-Temporal Relations in Language', in J.H. Greenberg (ed.), *Universals of Human Language. Vol. 3, Word Structure*, Stanford: Stanford University Press pp. 369–400.
—— (1981) 'The Sociolinguistics of Minority Dialect in Literary Prose', *Proceedings of the Seventh Annual Meeting of the BerkeleyLinguistics Society*, Berkeley: Deptartment of Linguistics, University of California.
—— (1982) 'From Propositional to Textual and Expressive Meanings: Some Semantic-Pragmatic Aspects of Grammaticalization', in W.P. Lehmann and Y. Malkiel, (eds.), *Perspectives on Historial Linguistics*, Amsterdam: Benjamins, pp. 245–71.
—— (1986) 'From Polysemy to Internal Semantic Reconstruction', *Proceedings of the Berkeley Linguistics Society 12*, Berkeley: Dept. of Linguistics, University of California, pp. 539–50.
Traugott, E.C. and Pratt, M.L. (1980) *Linguistics for Students of Literature*, New York: Harcourt.
Traugott, E.C. and Heine, B. (eds.) (1991) *Approaches to Grammaticalization*, 2 vols., Amsterdam: Benjamins.
Traugott, E.C. and König, E. (1991) 'The Semantics-Pragmatics of Grammaticalization Revisited', Traugott and Heine (forthcoming).
Trudgill, P. (1972) 'Sex, Covert Prestige and Linguistic Change in Urban British English', *Language in Society* 1: pp. 179–96.
Underhill, R. (1988) '*Like* Is, Like, Focus', *American Speech* 63: pp. 234–46.
Vendler, Z. (1972) *Res Cogitans, an Essay in Rational Psychology*, Cornell: Cornell University Press.
Visser, F. Th. (1970) *An Historical Syntax of the English Language. Part One. Syntactical Units with One Verb*, 2nd (ed.), Leiden: Brill.
Vološinov, V.N. (1930) *Marksizm i filosofija jazyka*, Leningrad: Institute for Comparative History of Occidental and Oriental Languages and Literatures. *Marxism and the Philosophy of Language*, Trans. Ladislav Matejka and I.R. Titunik, New York: Seminar, 1973.
Weinrich, H. (1964) *Tempus: besprochene und erzählte Welt*, Stuttgart: Kohlhammer.

10

Children's voices: talk, knowledge and identity

Janet Maybin

Originally published in D. Graddol, J. Maybin and B. Stierer, eds, *Researching Language and Literacy in Social Context* (Multilingual Matters, 1994).

Introduction: the dialogic model

Much of the research on talk in school over the last twenty years has focused on teacher–pupil dialogue (e.g. Sinclair & Coulthard, 1975; Barnes, 1976; Edwards & Furlong, 1978; Edwards & Mercer, 1987), with a relatively small number of researchers looking at pupil–pupil talk in small groups set up by the teacher or researchers with particular learning tasks (e.g. Barnes & Todd, 1977; Phillips, 1987; Bennett & Cass, 1989). There has been considerable interest in what kinds of talk might be the most effective for helping pupils gain curriculum knowledge and understanding. Very little, however, is known about the structure of children's own undirected informal talk, or the processes of learning which it might be supporting. In this article[1] I want to look at some examples of informal talk between 10–12 year olds from various different contexts across the school day. I shall discuss the structure and function of this talk in relation to the children's negotiation and construction of knowledge and understanding.

There is plenty of theoretical justification for seeing peer group talk as an important site for learning. Vygotsky (1978, 1986) suggests that language mediates between the cognitive development of the individual on the one hand and that individual's cultural and historical environment on the other. Children's conceptual development occurs first through social interaction and dialogue before these dialogues are internalised as 'inner speech' to provide an individual resource for reflection and planning. Vygotsky goes so far as to argue that the internal processes of cognitive development can operate 'only when the child is interacting with people in his environment or with his peers' (1978: 90). If this is so, then children's conversations with each other, (as well as their talk with adults), should provide a rich site for looking at the ways in which they are constructing meanings and knowledge. From an educational point of view, it would also be useful to know more about the relationship between talk and learning in children's informal, naturally occurring conversations, since much of the research has focused on more tightly structured, pre-arranged learning contexts.

In order to research children's naturally occurring talk, I would suggest that we need to move away from the transmission model of communication which characterizes talk essentially as a medium for the conveying of information, with varying degrees of effectiveness, from a speaker to a listener. Although this model is still powerful within educational discourse, it cannot begin to address the complexities of informal talk. A more useful framework is what Wells (1992) calls the dialogic model, which he sees as drawing heavily on the constructivist ideas of Piaget and Vygotsky. In this model understandings are constructed between people, through dialogue, and are shaped by the social and cultural context of the interaction. Talk is not a transparent conduit through which knowledge is passed, but an integral part of how understanding is collaboratively accomplished.

The dialogic model is also associated with the work of Volosinov and Bakhtin[2] who suggest that there is a complex chaining relationship between utterances and responses both within and across conversations. Every utterance is always also a response, implicitly or explicitly, to some previous utterance either from within the immediate conversation or from some previous occasion, and every utterance also anticipates and takes into account its own possible responses. One cannot therefore judge the meaning of any particular utterance in isolation, but only in the context of its relationships with other related utterances. As well as the dialogic relationships between utterances, Bakhtin suggests that dialogues are set up within utterances by our taking on and reproducing other people's voices either directly through speaking their words as if they were our own, or through the use of reported speech. Like Vygotsky, Bakhtin and Volosinov see language as socially and culturally formed, and therefore they argue our use of it inevitably conveys particular value judgements and commitments. As Bakhtin puts it, we learn words not from dictionaries but from people's mouths, and these words are always overpopulated with the meanings of others. They invoke particular connotations, contexts, and power relationships, and there is a struggle within any one utterance between these previous meanings and the speaker's current conversational purposes. We have no alternative but to use the words of others, but we do have some choice over whose voices we appropriate, and how we reconstruct the voices of others within our own speech. Because of the value laden nature of language this selective assimilation of the words of others, Bakhtin suggests, is part of 'the ideological becoming of a human being' (1981: 341).

The research reported here constitutes an attempt to operationalise this dialogic model, and to use it as a basis for analysing children's talk. In relation to my own data, I shall try to unpick part of the collaborative process through which meanings are constructed in informal talk. I also want to examine how children take on and reproduce the voices of others as a central part of their meaning making. I hope to show that informal talk is an important site for the construction of knowledge and understanding and that children's language practices are closely tied up with their developing identities as people and their 'ideological becoming', as they move from childhood into adolescence.

Researching the talk

Some of the most powerful research into language in context which recognises the social constitution of its meaning comes from anthropologists working in the ethnography of communication tradition. It is they who coined the term 'language practices', to emphasise the embeddedness of language in everyday social life. Hymes argues that language should be studied 'as situated in the flux and pattern of communicative events' (1977: 5), and he shows how the different layers of context within any particular social situation contribute to the meaning of the language being used: for example, the meaning of a joke told at a party will derive from the words used, the content of the conversation in which the joke occurs, the kind of party it is, and from cultural understandings about what counts as funny, appropriate, and so on. Developing from Hymes' work, Heath's detailed accounts of literacy events and practices in specific communities illustrate how rather than acquiring abstract, disembedded skills and knowledge, children are inducted into particular social practices and culturally valued ways of taking meaning from texts, of being particular kinds of readers, and so on.

I found that Hymes and Heath's notion of language events and language practices and their practical unpicking of the contextual constitution of meaning provided me with a helpful guide to the collection and analysis of data. They show the close integration of oral and literate practices, and the complexities of language use which children have to learn in addition to its formal features. Their approach, grounded in the actions of real people in real events, complements Bakhtin's more theoretical and politically sensitive discussion of intertextual references, and Vygotsky's ideas about the social and cultural nature of dialogue and thought.

I carried out my fieldwork in two middle schools serving council estates in a new town in south-east England. Almost all of the 10–12 year old children were monolingual English speakers. Few had been born in the estate where they now lived and many had moved home four or five times, often as a result of the break-up or reconstitution of family units. In the first school I focused on the conversations of a ten year old girl, Julie, described by her teachers as a fairly 'typical' average-ability talkative child. I fixed a radio microphone on her (she carried the transmitter in the pocket of her skirt or shorts) and recorded all her conversations over three consecutive days from when she arrived in school at 8.45am until she left for home at 3.00pm. The microphone picked up everything Julie said (including, for instance, sotto voce comments to her neighbour while the teacher was addressing the class), and everything that was said to her, or within her hearing. I used a small personal cassette recorder to record other children in the class and this was also carried around by various children at break time. I made observation notes as unobtrusively as possible from the back of the classroom, and collected copies of texts read or written by the children being recorded. On the third day I informally interviewed Julie, a friend of hers called Kirsty and a number of other children about some of the topics cropping up on the tapes.

In the second school I carried out a similar but longer study over three weeks, focusing on two groups of friends: three girls and three boys (including Martie and Darren who figure in the extracts below). Each of these six wore the radio microphone in turn, and I again used a small personal recorder to collect the talk of other children in the class, kept observation notes, and collected copies of texts. I began to realise that I needed more than my observation notes to understand many of the references made in children's conversations, and after the three weeks' recording I interviewed all of the 35 children in the class in friendship pairs and talked with them about themes in the tapes and about their own personal interests and relationships. As well as providing useful background information about the different layers of context for my other recorded talk, these interviews unexpectedly generated a rich variety of anecdotes, accounts and explanations about quite intimate aspects of children's lives. Two extracts from my interview with Karlie and Nicole are discussed later in this article.

I believe my position within both schools as a friendly outsider who didn't fit the more familiar roles of teacher, work experience student or pupil helped keep my interactions with the children relaxed and informal, and also meant that they were more explicit with me in their interview accounts and explanations than they would have been with someone who was more familiar with their circumstances. In both schools the children appeared to trust my promise that no-one except myself would listen to the tapes of the interviews, or those of their talk during the day. Most of the time I was recording the children appeared to have forgotten or become bored with the fact that they were being taped.

The researching of people's private conversations does of course raise particular ethical issues, and perhaps more especially in the case of children because of the very asymmetrical relationship of power between the researcher and the researched. Fishman (1978) who studied private conversations between adult couples within their homes asked them to listen to the tapes she had collected and indicate any material which they did not want her to use (in fact, surprisingly little needed to be erased). Such procedures are not always followed with children who are often willing and vulnerable research subjects, particularly in the school context where they are in a sense held captive, and usually delighted to receive extra adult attention and a change from normal routines. In my own research it would have been impracticable to ask children to listen to the six hours of recordings which I was collecting each day, but I often, at their request, played parts of the tapes in which they figured back to them at breaktime and I tried to answer their questions about my research as fully and clearly as possible. Near the beginning of the study I played a couple of tapes of teacher–pupil dialogue to the teacher, and discussed with her how these dialogues might be supporting children's learning. I was careful not to play the tapes of talk between children or discuss their contents with anyone other than the children concerned. My contact with adults during the study was kept to a minimum. I obtained parental permission through the school for my main study and in both schools the headteachers had an interest in research and greatly supported and facilitated my work. At the end of the longer three week study I submitted a brief written report of general findings which I thought might be useful, to the head and the class teacher.

In both schools I managed to collect an extensive amount of naturally occurring talk between children from a wide variety of contexts across the school day. I shall now go on to discuss what I think are significant features in the structure and content of this talk, and to suggest some ways in which it serves to construct forms of knowledge for the children.

Collaboration and provisionality

As I listened to the tapes and transcribed them, one of the first things that struck me was the extent to which classroom activities were not just accompanied by talk but were being actually defined and accomplished through talk.

Readings, for instance, were not only something happening between individuals and texts, but were being collaboratively accomplished between children and adults through dialogue. In the first transcript example Julie, Kirsty and Sharon have returned from a scavenging expedition in the school grounds, and Julie is drawing a snail on the card where they are going to mount their findings. Kirsty and a parent helper, Mrs Reilly, have just brought a book on snails across from the class library. At one point in the extract below Julie also has a parallel conversation with a pupil who is reading a puzzle magazine and trying to make up as many words as possible out of the word 'peanut'.

In the transcriptions which follow, interrupted speech is shown by a slant (/), simultaneous speech by a bracket ([) and incomprehensible speech by a dotted line (. . .).

	Julie:	I'll just write 'This was drawn by bla bla bla'
	Kirsty:	It's got thousands of teeth (reads) 'Its long tongue is covered with thousands of tiny teeth'. He's got thousands of teeth.
5	Julie:	He has, he's got thousands of teeth, that little snail has.
	Sharon:	Look at its trail (teacher comes over)
	Julie:	Miss it's got hundreds and . . . it's got thousands and thousands of teeth/
10	Kirsty:	/on its long tongue
	Teacher:	It's got what?
	Kirsty:	Thousands of teeth. It says here.
	Mrs Reilly:	Those are tentacles. It's got four tentacles.
	Julie:	Yea, teeth, teeth.
15	Mrs Reilly:	(reads) 'to touch, feel and smell, and it breathes through [the hole in its side.'
	Julie:	[teeth
	Mrs Reilly:	So there must be a hole somewhere.
	Julie:	'eat' (a suggestion to the pupil with the puzzle
20		magazine)

	Mrs Reilly:	We saw its eyes, didn't we? At the end of its tentacles and it can only see light and dark.
	Julie:	(to puzzle magazine pupil) 'tune'
	Pupil:	It can only be three letters/
25	Julie:	/(reads) 'or more'. Three letters or more.
	Kirsty:	Miss its got a thousand- thousands of teeth on its tongue.
	Sharon:	Yes, cause we went into the library. Mrs Reilly and Kirsty went into the library to look it up.
30	Teacher:	What's that, the snail?
	Sharon:	Yea.
	Pupil:	Miss, where's the sellotape?
	Sharon:	And it breathes through its side.
	Kirsty:	It breathes [through . . . its side
35	Sharon:	[it's got this little hole/
	Kirsty:	/It breathes through a hole in its side.
	Mrs Reilly:	Mrs Smiley (their language teacher) would be interested in this.
	Teacher:	Where are its eyes then?
40	Kirsty:	These little things are for feeling.

There are a number of different people who are engaged in what might be called 'reading' in this extract. Although it is only Kirsty and Mrs Reilly who read directly from the text in the library book (lines 2 and 15), Julie and Sharon are also centrally involved in relating information in the book to the snail in front of them. Julie and Kirsty in lines 8–10 and Sharon and Kirsty in lines 34–36 collaborate and reproduce pieces of information from the text for the teacher. Although they are not decoding a text in front of them, they are also centrally involved in the reading event. This involvement is very social in nature, for instance the talk involves a lot of 'duetting' (Falk, 1980; Coates, 1994) where one girl starts an utterance and another completes it. Also, the pupils' extraction and announcement of surprising and news-worthy pieces of information to each other and the teacher is accomplish-ing social as well as intellectual ends. This is one particular way of engaging with the text and using it. Mrs Reilly illustrates an alternative approach and could be said to be performing a rather different kind of reading. Her approach was characteristic of the way the teachers in my recordings tended to encourage pupils to relate to science texts, and I believe that it reflects the way knowledge is constructed in teacher–pupil dialogues. She tries to get the girls to use the text as a frame for organizing how to look at the snail – to reconstruct their experience of it in the light of information from the book about its teeth, tentacles, eyes and breathing mechanism. She links direct observation with information in the text '"it breathes through the hole in its side" . . . so there must be a hole some-where'; 'We saw its eyes, didn't we . . . and it can only see light and dark'. Thus direct empirical experience of the snail is mediated through the authority of the text. In more formal classroom talk the teacher's approach to using the text will probably be the dominant one and it may not even be apparent that children are using rather different ways of engaging with it. In this less formal situation, however, where the power relationships between speakers are more symmetrical, the talk can provide evidence of a number of different kinds of reading and of a more active struggle between authorized and other approaches.

The parallel, unofficial literacy event connected with the puzzle magazine represents another kind of collaborative reading which occurred frequently in my data: the attempt to interpret instructions in order to carry out an activity. The example below also illustrates this kind of process. Julie, Kirsty and Sharon have finished with the book on snails and are now looking at their list for the scavenging hunt to decide how to display their findings. Julie starts by reading out the instruction which asked them to collect 'a small creature'.

Julie:	Ah look (reads) 'A small creature, be very careful' cause here it is. We've got to draw that, we've got to draw the snail. I've drawn . . . /
Kirsty	/(points to a dead insect on the table) That's our small creature.
Julie:	No that's what we're doing for our small creature (points to snail)
Sharon:	He's dead, in 'e, he's dead.
Mrs Reilly:	It's a greenfly
Kirsty:	It was, but . . . /
Sharon:	/That's not our creature
Julie:	The snail is our creature.
Kirsty:	Get hold of it and glue it on.
Julie:	No, you're not meant to glue the snail on, we're meant to draw a picture of it, you . . . /
Kirsty:	/(looks at Julie's picture) Is that meant to be a snail?
Julie:	Yea
Kirsty:	I can't see its tentacles.

The interpretation of the instruction 'a small creature' here highlights the close relationship between the social and cognitive aspects of talk. It depends not on some kind of category criteria (e.g., can an insect count as a 'creature'), but on the outcome of the tustle for power between Julie and Kirsty. For Mrs Reilly the insect on the table may represent a species which can be usefully labelled, but for the girls the task of matching items to the list they have been given, and the business of managing their own relationships, are closely intertwined. Interestingly, Kirsty refers back to the authority of the library book, by using the term 'tentacles', to lend added weight to her dismissal of Julie's drawing.

In the extract above Julie's interpretation of the written instruction (that they should use the snail and that she should draw it) seems to be the one that will be acted on and carried forwards as the negotiated outcome from that discussion. But the children's talk I collected is often rather more ambiguous in terms of meaning and outcome. The next extract illustrates how particular meanings can be challenged or changed within the space of one brief snatch of conversation. Julie's class were drawing a picture as part of followup work to their teacher's reading from 'The Silver Sword', and the exchange below occurred shortly after the teacher announced that pupils would be getting their school reports to take home at the end of the week.

Pupil 1:	Since I started at this school I've only been to see Mr. Clayson once/
Pupil 2:	/Neither have I.
Julie:	(gasps) I've been there about ten times . . . always going to Clayson every single day. Wak wak wak because she's been a good girl! I normally go there because I say I've been involved, when I'm not. I stick up for my other friends.
Pupil 3:	I know, you're trying to get your nose in and things
Julie:	I'm not, I'm sticking up for my friends and I say that I was doing it as well.

At the opening of this conversation it might be assumed that there is a shared understanding about the significance of being sent to the head-teacher: it is a fairly awesome punishment meted out for particularly naughty behaviour. Julie however undermines this meaning in a number of ways. She jokes that she goes to the head's office every day, caricatures what happens to her there (corporal punishment was not used in the school), and inverts the normal relationship between behaviour and punishment. In addition, she suggests that loyalty to one's friends should take precedence over honesty, as defined in school terms. Thus the initial meaning of being sent to the headteacher is radically subverted by Julie, who suggests that in her case punishment constitutes a martyrdom to friendship rather than a just response to bad behaviour. Julie's meaning is however itself contested by a third pupil, who claims that her actions should not be interpreted as loyalty, but as nosiness. The issue is never resolved and, as in many other conversations, a number of possible meanings are carried forwards, any of which may be drawn on in future dialogues.

Ambiguity of meaning is especially apparent in the next piece of transcript, where Julie and David are sitting together eating their sandwiches at lunchtime. I would suggest that the way Julie sets up and manages this ambiguity is an intrinsic part of her accomplishment of particular conversational purposes.

Julie:	Do you know where I live? Right if you go along Redlea the only blue door, that's where I live. The only blue door in Redlea.
David:	Only?
Julie:	Right, if you can't get through, go to my next door neighbour's, that side . . ., go through her place, jump over the fence and go down my path.
David:	Which number do you bang on?
Julie:	One three four. And if you can't get through, go to . . . go round to number one three two, go through the fence, over the wood . . . /
David:	/you got a bike?
Julie:	Puncture . . . got lost. I got skates. I can hold onto the back of your bike and go oooooh! (pause) Do you really go out with thingy – Ma-

David:	Who?
Julie:	Mellie
David:	No.
Julie:	What, did she chuck you? Why? (pause) Do you think Warren will mind if I move onto your table?
David:	No. It's my table, I was the first one on it, so I own it.
Julie:	You don't, the school does. What's the hottest part of the sun? What's the hottest part of the sun? (pause) Page 3!

The conversation starts off in a child's world of knocking on each other's doors after school to go out and play. Julie's question about whether David is going out with Mellie, however, retrospectively adds a different kind of meaning to her previous invitation. It seems she was not just suggesting a casual children's game, but was also tentatively exploring the possibility of a boyfriend/girlfriend relationship between herself and David. Her response to his stated ownership of the classroom table also provides mixed messages. On the one hand she quickly contradicts his assumption of dominance, 'you don't, the school does', but she follows this up immediately with a joke 'what's the hottest part of the Sun?' which relies for its humour on a pun between the sun and the *Sun* newspaper, with its regular page 3 photograph of a naked female model.

In one sense Julie is using language as a resource, drawing on both childhood and teenage discourses to negotiate her relationship with David, whose response will to some extent determine which meanings are carried forwards. But these discourses are also themselves shaping the choices of meanings available. The words 'go out with', 'chuck' and 'hot' all have specific cultural connotations, and invoke particular kinds of gender relations. Thus although language may be a resource, it is not a neutral one, but rather pushes Julie towards taking up particular positions and values. The ambiguity and provisionality of her approach allow Julie a way of trying out and testing these positions and values in relation to her own experience.

The next extract also illustrates this kind of exploration of teenage roles and concerns. In addition it shows the sensitivity of talk to context, and how different contexts can invoke very different forms of discourse. The transcript starts in the maths class, where Julie is working out how much each of a number of customers in a cafe will have to pay for their meals. She has just added up 'Tom Ato's' bill.

Julie:	Three pounds twelve I make Tom Ato. Back in a second. Miss, can I go to the toilet please?
Teacher:	Yes alright.
	(sound of Julie's heels as she goes down the corridor. When she enters the toilets the accoustics on the tape change abruptly, with the tiled walls making the voices echo. Carol and Nicole are already there)
Julie:	Oh, hi. Where did you get your hair permed?
Nicole:	(indistinct)
Julie:	You're not going out with Sasha, are you?
Nicole:	Yea.

Julie:	Are you?
Nicole:	Yea, I hope so (laughs)
Julie:	You've got darker skin than me, I've got a sun tan. (pause) (to Carol) I should think so too, it's disgusting, that skirt is! Aii . . . don't! (Nicole starts tapping her feet on the tiled floor) Do you do tap dancing? (both girls start tapping their feet and singing)
Julie and Nicole:	'I just called to say I love you / And I mean it, from the bottom of my heart.'
Julie:	Caught you that time, Carol- ooh! What's the matter, Carol, don't show your tits! (laughs) (to Nicole) I went like this to Carol, I says, I pulls down her top, I went phtt 'don't show your tits!' (Nicole laughs). (Julie leaves the toilets, walks down the corridor, reenters the classroom, and sits down.)
Julie:	Turn over – six plates of chips – oh I've nearly finished my book. I've got one page to do.

The conversation in the toilets seems to belong to a different world from that in the maths classroom. The vocabulary is different, the subject matter is different, and the role of the girls is different. They are no longer pupils straining to interpret the teacher's instructions and produce a neat, acceptable piece of work, but young adolescents concerned with trying out particular notions of femininity. Personal worth here is determined not by how quickly and accurately sums can be completed, but by how attractive you are to boys, and how much experience you have had in 'going out' with them. The authoritative voice is not the text book, but the pop song; the institutional authority of the school seems to fall away at the toilet door. Julie, however, makes the switch between these two different kinds of discourse without any apparent effort or hesitation.

The taking on of voices

In the extracts above there are a number of instances where children invoke voices carrying particular kinds of power within their conversations; textbooks, library books and popular songs are all quoted as sources of authority in different contexts. I also have examples of children quoting teachers or other adults, particularly where they are trying to win an argument or put a point more strongly. And frequently within their conversations they repeat each other's words, or their own words from a previous occasion. Sometimes, as in the first example about the snails book, it becomes difficult to ascribe exact ownership to the voice for a particular utterance. In this second part of the article I want to use Bakhtin and Volosinov's ideas about the invoking of voices within utterances to show in relation to my own data how these can explain some of the complexity of the way in which different layers of meaning are built up in children's conversations.

As I discussed earlier, Bakhtin and Volosinov see our use of other people's voices as part of the negotiation of our own ideological development, and as setting up complex dialogic relationships within and across utterances, which are an important part of meaning making.

We often reproduce other people's voices unattributed, as if they were our own and of course it is impossible to always trace when this is happening. In the example below, however, Karlie subsequently identifies the voice she has reproduced. This extract comes from my interview with Karlie and Nicole; I had just asked Nicole who else lived at her house and Karlie mentioned that Nicole's sister had recently had a baby.

	Janet:	So does your sister live quite near you?
	Nicole:	She lives with us
	Karlie:	Cause ⌈ she's only quite young
	Nicole:	⌊ she's young, she's sixteen
	Janet:	Ah right
6	Karlie:	She did the best thing about it though, didn't she, Nicole?
	Nicole:	She didn't tell a soul, no-one, that she was pregnant
	Karlie:	Until she was due, when she got into hospital, then she told them
	Nicole:	On Saturday night she had pains in her stomach and come the following Sunday my mum was at work and my sister come to the pub and my aunt Ella was in it and my sister went in there and said 'I've got pains in my stomach' so my auntie Ella went and got my mum, and took her to hospital, and my mum asked her if she was due on and she said 'No, I've just come off' and when they got her to hospital they said 'Take her to maternity'. My mum was crying!
	Janet:	Your mum didn't realise she was pregnant?
	Nicole:	No, and my mum slept with her when she was ill!
22	Karlie:	My dad said she did – Terri did the best thing about it – her sister's Terri
	Nicole:	Or if she did tell, as she's so young, she weren't allowed to have him.

Karlie initially provides what appears to be her own evaluation of Terri's decision to conceal her pregnancy (line 6), but in line 22 we learn that this evaluation was originally made by her father. In reproducing or appropriating his voice, Karlie is also taking on and communicating his judgment as if it were her own. This is a particularly obvious example of how taking on someone else's voice also involves taking on a value position, but Bakhtin and Volosinov would argue that, since language is ideologically saturated, our words *always* convey value judgements, and our reproduction of the words of others must always be a political act.

In addition to taking on voices wholesale, as it were, we can frame the words we reproduce in particular ways which create a distance between our own voice and the voice we are invoking. One of the most obvious ways in which the children in my study reproduced other peoples' voices was through reported speech in their anecdotes. Apart from its force as a way of creating a context away from the here and now, the dialogue of an anecdote sets up a second conversational layer within which a particular theme can be explored in more depth. As we shall see in the examples below, anecdotes also create their own resonances and additional themes.

New dialogic relationships are set up between the speaker's voice and the voices they invoke in the anecdote, and between the themes of the anecdote. and of the conversation in which it occurs (Volosinov, 1973; Bakhtin, 1986). Many of the children's anecdotes were told almost entirely through reconstructed dialogue, and I want to look at two of those now.

In the first example, Julie is talking to Kirsty while they mount their findings from the scavenging hunt. They have been discussing their anxiety about the amount of swearing on the tapes I was collecting. When Julie states firmly that 'children aren't meant to swear', Kirsty responds, 'If people swear at them, they can swear back'. A few minutes later, Julie returns to the subject.

Julie:	I swore at my mum the other day because she started, she hit me
Kirsty:	What did you do?
Julie:	I swore at my mum, I says, 'I'm packing my cases and I don't care what you say' and she goes 'Ooh?' and (I go) 'yea!'. I'm really cheeky to my mother

Julie's story here provides her with an opportunity to explore the question she is discussing with Kirsty in a bit more detail. Although partly agreeing with Kirsty's statement that if people swear at you then you can swear back, Julie is arguing extreme provocation in her case: her mother hit her and she felt like leaving home. In these exceptional circumstances, she seems to be suggesting, it is permissable to swear, although it is still being 'really cheeky'.

Julie's story also however has a particular resonance as one of a chain of anecdotes she tells her friends about her somewhat picaresque relationship with her mother. The theme of resisting or subverting adult authority is also a familiar one in her stories generally (like her visits to the headteacher in the example quoted earlier above). Julie's account of swearing at her mother will therefore be read by Kirsty in terms of themes around responses to adult authority, and relationships between mothers and daughters, as well as in relation to their current conversation. Julie's anecdote is thus operating simultaneously at the level of a reported dialogue between herself and her mother, and as part of the conversation with Kirsty. The theme of the reported dialogue, her relationship with her mother, and the theme of the conversation with Kirsty, when it is permissable to swear, are of course not totally unconnected. They both involve issues of power and authority, the cultural appropriateness of particular kinds of language behaviour, and the potential of oral language to contest or subvert particular power relationships.

In reporting her mother's speech, Julie is not expected by Kirsty to reproduce her mother's words exactly as she heard them. She in fact manufactures a voice for her mother, to fit in with the purpose of the story. In the next example, Darren also manufactures his own and a man's voice in an anecdote told while children are queueing in the playground, waiting to go in to lunch. There was always a lot of noise and milling about in the queue, and anecdotes told in this context need to be extremely arresting and lively in order to hold their audience. At this point, one child has just sworn at another.

> Martie: I said that to a real man and he went, he went 'dick head' [and
>   I went] 'of course I am!' (laughter) And he goes 'erm!' (growl-
>   ing and laughter)
> Darren: This man called me a fucking bastard, right, I go 'back to you',
>   he goes 'come here', I go 'come on, then' and he's got about
>   size 10 trainers and he chased me, right, and then when he got,
>   he catched me, right, like that, and he goes 'who's fucking
>   saying?' And I goes 'fuck off', I says 'fuck off' and he goes,
>   he goes, 'Do you want a fight?' I go 'not tonight, darling' and
>   he goes 'piss off!'

Again, this anecdote opens up the possibility for constructing meanings through the relationships between the different conversation layers, and through the links these make with the themes and voices of other contexts, and with the speakers' previous conversational history. In the boys' con-versations they often seem to be jostling for position, capping each other's comments with a more impressive contribution. Here, Darren's story is a response to Martie's rather abbreviated anecdote. It is more developed, the man is more frightening, and the turnaround at the end more dramatic and ingenious. As well as providing a turn in the immediate conversation, it also contributes to a recurring theme in the boys' talk concerning their toughness and canniness, which are important aspects of the way they present themselves to each other. And it echoes the concern of Julie's anecdote about how far adult authority can and should be contested.

Within the dialogue Darren, like Julie, uses reported dialogue to tell his story. But Darren doesn't just create voices for himself and the man. He also, inside the story at the point when things are getting really alarming, portrays himself as taking on a different voice ('not tonight, darling'). Darren adopts a slightly higher pitched voice at this point, portraying what could be either a woman or a homosexual man rejecting a partner's advances. The use of this voice, as in Julie's 'I'm packing my cases', invokes a particular scenario or scenarios with associated relationships. In Darren's case, calling up this particular speech genre changes the relationship between himself and the man in a way which defuses the situation through humour and signals a kind of submission which still enables him to main-tain face rather more successfully than Martie did in his story. This is Darren's internal intention, as it were, within the context of the anecdote. There is also his intention as a speaker who is following and hoping to decisively cap Martie's contribution, and the manufacture of voices within Darren's anecdote also contributes towards this conversational aim. There is thus a complex nesting of different conversational contexts: from the recurring conversational theme about canniness and resisting authority and of language itself as a means of doing so, to Darren's and Martie's con-versation, to the reported interchange between Martie and the man, to the scenario invoked by 'not tonight, darling'.

Volosinov (1973) explores at some length how novelists' voices enter and colour the voices of their characters, and how the perspective of a particular character can be conveyed through what is ostensibly a piece of authorial description. The interplay between an author's and a character's voice can sometimes be used to produce an ironic effect, where we hear both voices as it were simultaneously. This can also happen orally, in the use of reported speech. In the next example Geoffrey provides an ironic parody of his own voice in order to clarify a misunderstanding. Sarah also ironically assumes the concerned voice of a naive mother who thinks her daughter's bruises have come from fighting. The conversation occurs while the children are queueing in the school corridor, waiting for the coach to arrive which will take them swimming. Darren has just pretended to give Sherri a love bite.

Sherri:	(laughing) My mum thinks I've been in fights again!
Sarah:	What do your mum go? 'Who gave you a big bruise?' (laughter)
Terry:	I'll give her a double bruise, aha!
Darren:	I gave her one on the arm
	. . . .
Geoffrey:	Oi, you could never give someone a lovebite on the arm, could you, could you? You can't!
Sherri:	You can, if you've got a T-shirt on.
Geoffrey:	Yea I mean, look, it's really exciting look, let's get down to there, next time it'll be your finger! (noise of kissing).

Both Sarah and Geoffrey frame their use of irony – 'What do your mum go?' and 'Yes, I mean, look . . .', and they adopt a particular tone to convey the naivity of the person whose voice they are using. Sarah pitches the mother's voice high, as if she were addressing a young child, and Geoffrey puts on an excited, enthusiastic voice to show just how ridiculous such enthusiasm would be. He is trying to explain to Sherri that he was not asking whether it is physically possible to bite an arm, but whether it is culturally appropriate, and we are aware of Geoffrey's authorial voice mocking his own exaggerated parody. (Some features of these manufactured voices are inevitably lost in the written medium of this article).

Both Volosinov and Bakhtin, like Vygotsky, suggest that conversations are internalised to become inner dialogues. Thus individual thought processes also involve the taking on of voices which provide responses to voices heard in previous conversations, and which call up particular relationships and contexts. The last extract comes again from the interview with Karlie and Nicole. Karlie has explained that she sometimes goes to visit her Dad in prison, and I ask her what it is like doing that. Karlie answers me by representing her feelings at the prison as a kind of inner dialogue, which involves invoking her own voice as if she were talking first to herself, and then to her dad.

Karlie:	It's like – it's just loads and loads of bars. So you think 'What's my dad doing in here, he didn't do nothing' because he got accused by chopping someone's hand off so – and it weren't true,. . . . and you get in there, and you're seeing him, and you

think 'Come with us, come with us, you can't stay in here cause it's not true really, is it?' so you think 'You can come with us now, you can get out', but it's just not true.

When I was trying to punctuate this transcribed talk with speech marks it was difficult to make out where one voice ends and another starts or to identify particular audiences. Sometimes Karlie seems to be addressing herself, sometimes her father, sometimes myself and sometimes previous voices she has heard. It's difficlt to know, for example, to whom her final 'it's just not true' is addressed, and whether it refers to the crime of which her father is accused or to the possibility of taking him home with her, or to both. The fragmented nature of the dialogues invoked in Karlie's response to my question would suggest that her talk here is close to what Vygotsky calls 'inner speech', where dialogues we have had and those which we might have with other people feed into our internal thought processes. This utterance then has its own internal business: Karlie is struggling to come to terms with her father's imprisonment, and positioning herself in relation to the differing accounts of his guilt which she has heard people give. She is also, at the level of my interview conversation with her, constructing the voices in the representation of her inner dialogue in order to convey a particular presentation of herself to me and to Nicole.

Conclusion

I shall now try to summarize some main points about the structure and purposes of children's informal talk, in relation to their construction of meanings and understanding.

(1) Most of the talk is highly collaborative. Children complete each other's utterances, repeat something another child had just said, echo the voice of the teacher or of a text they have been reading, and frequently use reported speech in relating incidents or anecdotes. Meanings do not seem to be generated within one mind and then communicated to another through talk; rather, they are collaboratively and interactionally constructed between people.

(2) Talk, like writing, can create and hold a context away from the here and now, for example in anecdotes. The here and now is also to a large extent constructed and established through talk, whether it is negotiating and contesting ways of engaging with a text, the working through of a relationship between children in the course of carrying out a classroom activity, or discussing one's hair style in the school cloakroom.

(3) Social and cognitive aspects of talk are closely integrated, and utterances are multi-functional, that is, one utterance can (and usually does) serve a number of different cognitive and social purposes simultaneously. It is therefore not possible to separate out 'talk for conveying information' from 'talk for maintaining social relations', as is suggested in the Cox Report (DES, 1989) for example.

(4) The meanings and knowledge which children are jointly negotiating and constructing are provisional, and frequently contested. There is a fluidity about them which contrasts with the more clearly defined, fixed forms of knowledge circulating in the official curriculum through more formal teacher-pupil dialogue, worksheets and text-books.

(5) Associated with this provisionality, there is often an ambiguity in individual utterances; out of a range of possible meanings it is the respondent, not the speaker, who chooses a particular interpretation, which may then in its turn be reinterpreted or subverted. This ambiguity disperses the responsibility for the meaning and purposes of particular utterances between the participants in the conversation, rather than lodging it with the speaker. It can also provide a creative function for the speaker who may be 'over interpreted' and be taken to mean far more than she intended. She then has the opportunity to go along with, or refute, a meaning which is being imputed to her.

(6) Language is a resource for making meaning, but it is not a neutral one. Language choices bring with them particular values and positions, so that individuals are inducted into cultural practices. The provisionality and ambiguity of informal talk helps children to negotiate the complex relationship between individual purposes and cultural authority, and to develop their own personal identities.

(7) One of the ways in which children construct personhood, and build up the contextual layers in their talk, is through the reporting and taking on of other people's voices. The articulation of different conversational layers, the cross-cutting dialogues and the references out to other contexts and longer term themes all serve to create a particularly rich resource for negotiating and constructing meaning.

It would be theoretically inconsistent if I did not end by saying something about my own purposes in framing and reproducing children's voices within this article. Part of my motivation for the research comes from a dissatisfaction with the over-simplistic and misleading transmission model of communication which still influences so much of educational policy and the training of teachers. I have tried to show that an alternative, dialogic model is more appropriate for exploring the way children talk and learn. I am also unhappy about the widespread assumptions that some children's language use is deficient, or essentially different in quality from the language believed necessary for educational purposes. I hope that I have countered such assumptions by demonstrating something of the richness of the resource which all children have at their disposal, and the intensity and urgency of their endeavours to achieve understanding.

Notes

1. This article revises and brings together the analysis and discussion of data in Maybin, 1991 and 1993.
2. There is some controversy about whether works published under Volosinov's name were in fact written by Bakhtin. The 1973 translators of *Marxism and the*

Philosophy of Language however claim that the weight of evidence supports Volosinov's authorship.

References

Bakhtin, M. (1981) 'Discourse in the novel', in *The Dialogic Imagination*, Austin: University of Texas Press.
Bakhtin, M. (1986) *Speech Genres and Other Late Essays* (ed.), Caryl Emerson and Michael Holquist). Austin: University of Texas Press.
Barnes, D. (1976) *From Communication to Curriculum*, Harmondsworth: Penguin.
Barnes, D. and Todd, F. (1977) *Communication and Learning in Small Groups*, London: Routledge and Kegan Paul.
Bennett, N. and Cass, A. (1989) 'The effects of group composition on group inter-active processes and pupil understanding', *British Educational Research Journal* 15 (1), pp. 19–32.
Clark, K. and Holquist, M. (1984) *Mikhail Bakhtin*, Cambridge, MA: Harvard University Press.
Coates, J. (1994) 'No gap, lots of overlap: turn-taking patterns in the talk of women friends', In D. Graddol, J. Maybin and B. Stierer (eds.), *Researching Language and Literacy in Social Context*, Clevedon: Multilingual Matters.
DES (1989) (The Cox Report) *English for Ages 5 to 16*, London: HMSO.
Edwards, A.D. and Furlong, V.J. (1978) *The Language of Teaching*, London: Heinemann.
Edwards, D. and Mercer, N. (1987) *Common Knowledge: The Development of Under-standing in the Classroom*, London: Methuen.
Falk, J. (1980) 'The conversational duet', *Proceedings of the 6th Annual Meeting of the Berkley Linguistics Society*, Vol. 6, pp. 507–14.
Fishman, P. (1978) 'Interaction: The work women do', *Social Problems* 25 (4), pp. 397–406.
Heath, S.B. (1983) *Ways with Words*, Cambridge: Cambridge University Press.
Hymes, D. (1977) *Foundations in Sociolinguistics: An Ethnographic Approach*, London: Tavistock.
Maybin, J. (1991) 'Children's informal talk and the construction of meaning', *English in Education* 25 (2), pp. 34–49.
—— (1993) 'Dialogic relationships and the construction of knowledge in children's informal talk', in D. Graddol, L. Thompson and M. Byram (eds.), *Language and Culture*, Clevedon: British Association for Applied Linguistics/Multilingual Matters.
Phillips, T. (1987) 'Beyond lip-service: Discourse development after the age of nine', in M. Mayor and A. Pugh (eds.), *Language, Communication and Education*, London: Croom Helm/The Open University.
Sinclair, J. and Coulthard, R. (1975) *Towards an Analysis of Discourse: The English used by Teachers and Pupils*, London: Oxford University Press.
Volosinov, V.N. (1973) *Marxism and the Philosophy of Language*, New York: Seminar Press.
Vygotsky, L. (1978) *Mind in Society: The Development of Higher Psychological Processes (ed. M. Cole et al.)*, Cambridge: Harvard University Press.
—— (1986) *Thought and Language*, Cambridge: MA: MIT Press.
Wells, G. (1992) 'The centrality of talk in education', in K. Norman (ed.), *Thinking Voices: The Work of the National Oracy Project*, London: Hodder and Stoughton.

11

Two styles of narrative construction and their linguistic and educational implications

James Paul Gee

Originally published in *Discourse Processes*, 12 (1989).

Introduction

In this paper I will offer a linguistic analysis of two stories: a story told to a group of her peers by an 11-year-old black girl (who I will call "Leona") and a story to a sympathetic adult female by an 11-year-old white middle-class girl (who I will call "Sandy"). Sandy exemplifies in her use of language a style highly compatible with school-based values in regard to the use of language in speech and writing. Leona's style, on the other hand, though often misunderstood in the school context, is one found in many cultures across the world, and often associated with great verbal mastery. The goals of the analysis are: 1) to offer a view of psycholinguistically relevant structures that I take to be universally characteristic of spoken narratives, 2) to delineate other aspects of narrative construction that vary across social groups, and 3) to point to some of the educational implications of both of these aspects of narrative, in particular, with regard to literacy.

Lines and stanzas

Though we are often not consciously aware of it, speech is produced in little spurts, each of which usually contains a single piece of new information, has a unitary intonation contour, is often separated from other such spurts by a slight pause or hesitation, and is most often a single clause long though it can be somewhat shorter or longer (Chafe, 1979, 1980, 1984). These small spurts I will call, following Chafe's early work (1979, 1980), "idea units." Below, I give an example of some idea units from Leona's story to her peers:

> this lady was all cleanin'
> and stuff like that
> she said
> "you have an ear infection

> an
> an everything is going well
> but there's something in your ear
> you know"
> an I was like
> "yea
> I know"

Idea units, together with the speech errors and disfluencies characteristic of all spontaneous speech (which I have not tried to fully indicate here), appear to reflect the on-line planning and production of speech, the mind actively at work (Gee, 1986a). The simple clause appears, however, to be the basic linguistic unit underlying this process (Halliday, 1985). In fact, if we remove speech errors and disfluencies, which characterize all speech, and place pieces of clauses back together, we get an "ideal" structure that reflects quite clearly the overall shape and patterning of a text, the "ideal" or underlying structure the mind is "aiming" at. This ideal structure contains what I will call "lines," each one of which is a simple clause, a verb of saying and what is said, or a "heavy" pre- or postclausal modifier, for example, something like "and then you know just all of a sudden." Lines tend to begin with conjunctions like: "and" or "but." For example, below I put Leona's idea units above into lines:

> this lady was all cleanin an stuff like that
> she said: "you have an ear infection
> an everything is going well
> but there's something in your ear, you know"
> an I was like: "yeah, I know"

Both Leona (the working-class black girl) and Sandy (the middle-class white girl) group their lines into what I will call "stanzas." A stanza is a group of lines about a single topic; they capture a single "vignette." The function of a stanza is to mark perspective: At the beginning of each stanza a new point of view is taken either by means of a shift of focal participants or change in the time or framing of events (Scollon & Scollon, 1981). Comments and evaluative statements are often placed in separate stanzas. Stanzas are marked by a variety of linguistic devices, including often "topic chaining" (the first line contains a noun phrase which is referred back to in each subsequent line by a pronoun), phonological, rhythmic, syntactic, and/or semantic patterning of words and phrases across the lines of the stanza, and patterns of pausing and rate (we will see some of these features below). The lines above make up a stanza; they capture one speech exchange between the nurse and Leona. In the Appendix to this paper I give the line and stanza structure of Leona's story to her peers and Sandy's story. One can clearly see how each stanza represents a change of character, event, location, time, or narrative function, and I have labeled each stanza to reflect this. A detailed step-by-step defense of the demarcation of these texts into stanzas is given in Gee (1987). Such line and stanza structure has been found in a wide variety of cultures, and has heretofore been most

often associated with so-called "oral (non-literate) cultures" and their traditional stories and myths (Hymes, 1977, 1980, 1981, 1982; Scollon & Scollon, 1981; Tedlock, 1977, 1978, 1983). I would argue, however, that it is
"built into" the human narrative production system, though such line and
stanza structure can be more or less obscured, I believe, in middle-class
adult "literate" speech (Gee, 1986a; Law, 1986).

When we look at the stanza structure in the girls' stories, we find an
interesting sort of "isochrony." Both girls organize their stanzas around
something like four lines as a base or norm (after Stanza 6 all but one of
Leona's stanzas are either four lines long or made up of an introductory
line plus four tightly patterned lines; for Sandy, 19 of her 25 stanzas are four
lines long). I don't insist on "4" as any special number here (though it is
intriguing how often stanzas in English formal poetry are four lines long;
see Turco, 1968). Rather, what I am interested in is the fact that stanzas are
relatively short and pretty evenly balanced across the text as a whole. It is
for this reason, together with the fact that they are an important domain of
internal patterning (see discussion below), that I call them "stanzas," rather
than, say, "paragraphs" or "extended sentences" (Chafe, 1980).

Lines and stanzas and literacy

Line and stanza structure, though it has not been much studied outside
the domain of anthropological studies of "oral cultures," has important
implications for school-based literacy studies. While lines and stanzas are
a pervasive feature of children's speech, children from different social
groups pattern language within stanzas differently. Furthermore, there
is reason also to believe that in school poor writers "translate" their
line and stanza structure into writing differently than good writers. For
an example I will take one good writer and one poor writer from a study
of a group of good and poor high school writers (female, white working-
class) (Gordon, 1986). Fig. 11.1 gives two stanzas from the opening of
each girl's oral story and next to them the first four sentences from their
written version of the same stories. The figure is meant to exemplify
characteristics that hold across the texts as wholes. The poor writer tends
to map each one of her stanzas into a single sentence in her written text,
though she does not retain the order of her stanzas from her speech in her
written text (e.g., sentence 3 corresponds to stanza 4, sentence 4 to stanza
2). The good writer, however, maps each of her stanzas into two or more
sentences, and while these sentences may rearrange the order of information within a stanza, the order of the stanzas as wholes is retained across
the written text. The good writer also arranges information in her speech
differently than the poor writer. She tends to state background information in the first part of each stanza and then give the main focused
information at the end. And she uses lexical and syntactic devices to
clearly mark this background-foreground structuring (e.g., the "when"
clause spreading over the first three lines in Stanza 1 and the series of
progressive forms over the first three lines in Stanza 2 mark the background parts of these stanzas). She utilizes lexical and syntactic devices to

POOR WRITER

Speech

Stanza 1
This was last year
I woke up for school getting ready
I was getting dressed
and I got a pain in my neck

Stanza 2
so I told my sister
I asked her should I go to school
cause I never missed a day in school
and she said if your neck hurts
you should stay home

Writing

Sentence 1 (= Stanza 3, not shown)

Sentence 2 (= Stanza 1)
I woke up one morning and got a sharp pain in my neck.

Sentence 3 (= Stanza 4, not shown)

Sentence 4 (= Stanza 2)
My sister said I shouldn't go even though I wasn't absent.

GOOD WRITER

Speech

Stanza 1
OK when I was about five years old
and John-he's my brother
he was about eleven
we got up real early one Saturday
to make orange juice and watch cartoons

Stanza 2
and we were standing in between the kitchen and the dining room
and we were stirring up the orange juice
and just kidding around
and I looked over to the front door
and there was this man
standing there looking into our house

Writing

Sentences 1 and 2 (= Stanza 1)
It happened early one Saturday morning when John and I got up to
make some orange juice and watch the Saturday morning cartoons. I
was about five; he was around eleven

Sentences 3 and 4 (= Stanza 2)
As we stood between the kitchen and the dining room, the early
morning sun peeking out over the housetops, I glanced at the front
door ahead of me. A dark, shadowed mysterious figure stood spying
into our front door window!

**Fig.11.1 Mapping between the line and stanza structure of speech and the sentence
structure of writing for a poor and a good high school writer**

a yet further extent in her writing to carry out foregrounding and back-grounding, though she also rearranges material for effect (e.g., stressing the age differences between herself and her brother in the written version – they play a role later in the story). The poor writer tends to simply juxta-pose lines in her speech and sentences in her writing without marking out their informational relations. The two girls have a different attitude toward the written text. The poor writer sees each sentence as a topical unit analogous to her stanzas, while the good writer sees sentences as domains wherein lexical, syntactic, and cohesive devices structure information within and across sentences, the topical units of her stanzas translating into several sentences. In Givón's (1979) terms, the poor writer uses the "pragmatic" (topic-based) mode in her speech and writing, while the good writer uses a more "syntactic" mode in both, in an increasing degree as she moves from speech to writing.

Differences between Leona and Sandy: language within stanzas

Leona and Sandy differ significantly in how they organize information within and across their stanzas. Leona adopts a method that is in many respects similar to styles found in "oral cultures" (and it is this style that has made some believe that lines and stanzas occur only in such cultures, because it foregrounds line and stanza structure so clearly). On the other hand, Sandy adopts a method similar in some regards to that seen in the good writer discussed above. Leona's style is to create patterns out of the lines of her stanzas through the use of such devices as sound play, repeti-tion (of sounds, words, and phrases), syntactic and semantic parallelism, changes of rate, loudness, stress and pitch, and patterns of rhythm gener-ally. Below, I give five example stanzas from Leona's story to her peers, displaying some of the patterning created by these devices (to the extent that they can be shown in print):

STANZA 2

all right,	I got this thing	
	MY ear's all buggin me	an everything
	MY ear was all buggin me	
and	I was cryin	
	I was all:	oooh, oooh, oooh
	I was doin all that	

STANZA 6

"*All* right,	. . . there"	
	sitting there,	oooh, oooh, oooh
	sittin there, and *all*	
an she's	at *all*"	oooh, oooh, oooh
all: "		

STANZA 12

she didn't	PAY that CAB DRIVER
she jus'	WALKED OUT
she jus'	SLAMMed that DOOR
she said:	COME ON RONA

STANZA 16

she said	"you have an ear infection	
	an everything is going well	
	but there's something in your ear	you know"
I was like:	. . . yeah . . .	I know"

STANZA 17B

put that medicine in my ear
an I was grubbin out on that food
I was grubbin out on that food: mmm, mmm
an I was grubbin out on that food: an everythin

In addition to the obvious patterns created by repetition and parallelism, we can note that stanza 9 is said very rapidly, with increasing rate, pitch, and loudness as it progresses. It is made up of short lines with heavy stresses on its content words. Then stanzas 10 and 11 are said more slowly, with a great deal of enactment, each containing a pair of turns of speech between a nurse and the mother (in the order: mother-nurse-nurse-mother). Leona changes her voice for each speaker, and ends the two stanzas with the mother's, "I ain't got no money now" said quite loudly and with increased rate. Then stanza 12 is said much like 9, with increasing rate, pitch and loudness, short lines and heavy stresses. Leona uses throughout the story a variety of voices and emphatic and paralinguistic devices to enact the different speakers and their feelings and attitudes (her mother, various nurses, and herself in and out of distress). In fact, we can distinguish two related, but separable, aspects to Leona's style. First, it is *spatializing* in that it creates an intricate pattern of crisscrossing and interlocking relationships that render the lines of the stanza a simultaneously whole, rather than linear sequence. Similar devices are formalized in traditional poetry in many cultures, and paradigmatically exemplified in the Hebrew poetry of the Bible (e.g., the Psalms) or the poetry of Walt Whitman (Berlin, 1985; Jakobson, 1978, 1980; Jackobson & Pomorska, 1983). And it is *performative* or *enactive* in that it utilizes various dramatic and expressive devices to create a dramatic performance that the listener is enactively caught up in (cf. Wolfson, 1982 and her category of "performed narratives"). There is some reason to believe that these two features do not always co-occur in cultures, though both spatialization and performed narratives are common across the world.

Sandy's stanzas are also tightly patterned, but in a different way. She uses the information structure of the content of her stanzas (namely relations like topic-focus or background information-foreground information), as well as the analytic structure of the actions she describes, to build up patterns for her stanzas. For example, consider the following four stanzas:

STANZA 1
TOPIC: . . . we have THIS PARK near our house
COMMENT: . . . it really stinks
but   TOPIC: me and my friend Sarah were over there
COMMENT: we were playing on the swings

STANZA 4
ACTION: I threw a rock at him
RESULT OF ACTION: it missed him
INTENTION: I made sure it missed him
RESULT OF INTENTION: it just banged on the slide

STANZA 20
BACKGROUND (SETTING): next day we go over there
FOREGROUND (SETTING): he was up in the tree
—
BACKGROUND (SETTING): he has rocks and sand up there
FOREGROUND (ACTION): he started throwin sand at us

STANZA 21
BACKGROUND (SETTING: reason for action): Debbie got sand thrown
at her
FOREGROUND (SETTING: preparation for action): she goes up to tree
—
BACKGROUND (SETTING: preparation for action): she took the bucket
of sand
FOREGROUND (ACTION): and dumped it over his head

Once again, the patterns more or less speak for themselves. In stanza 1 we get a topic introduced (park), then a comment about it (stinks). The second two lines then constitute a further comment (but we play there anyway) on the first two as topic (the park that stinks), and these two are themselves broken down into topic (over there) and comment (we play). Sandy often uses an explicit signal (like "but" here or "because" in stanza 2, see Appendix) to mark how the second two lines of a stanza relate to the first two. Stanzas 20 and 21 also show how Sandy moves from background to foreground in the first two lines of a stanza, and then treats the second two lines as foreground vis-a-vis the first two as background, while ordering these latter two lines as foreground to background between themselves. Thus, often her stanzas have a structure something like: First Line is to Second Line as Third Line is to Fourth, and First Line–Second Line as a Pair are to Third Line–Fourth Line as a Pair as First Line is to Second or Third is to Fourth, that is, (1: 2):: (3: 4). Notice that this device ties the stanza tightly together semantically, while at the same time rendering sequence crucial, that is, line 2 carries 1 forward just as 3 carries 2 forward, and lines 3/4 carry 1/2 forward, either in terms of the analysis of action or the analysis of information structure.

I think it is the case that one would readily concede that Leona's style relates more closely to devices we associate with literary writing, rather than with expository prose, while Sandy's, despite being used in a narrative, bears some similarity to the sorts of linear and analytic devices we associate with exposition, rather than literary prose. This is one of the senses in which Sandy's style is more oriented towards school-based sorts of literacy, which tend to stress (outside of creative writing classes) expository sorts of writing, speaking, and thinking (Gee, 1986b; Heath, 1983; Romaine, 1984; Scribner & Cole, 1981). We will see additional implications of this sort below.

Differences between Leona and Sandy: organization of whole texts

The same sort of differences that we saw in how Leona and Sandy shape their language within stanzas show up in how they organize their texts as wholes. Just as Sandy's stanzas have something like the linear and analytic structure of a syllogism, so too does her text as a whole. We can schematize her text as a whole as below (see the Appendix, which displays the three major divisions of the story, labeling them Beginning, Middle, and End):

SANDY'S TEXT

BEGINNING (PART 1)
CHILDREN FIGHTING → MOTHER INTERVENES → (FAILED RESOLUTION) ⇓

MIDDLE (PART 2)
CHILDREN FIGHTING → MOTHER INTERVENES → (FAILED RESOLUTION) ⇓

END (PART 3)
CHILDREN FIGHTING →   0[ZERO]   → REAL RESOLUTION

Sandy creates a structure that could go on forever (children fighting → mother intervenes → failed resolution → children fighting, etc.). By Part 3 of a story we expect once again to get an intervention attempt on the part of the parent, but our expectation is frustrated. This is a perfect device for closure (Smith, 1968), and leads us to see the fact that the children settle the conflict by themselves, without parental intervention, as significant. The point to notice here is how sequential and "logical" Sandy's structure is. It is the fact that Part 2 follows Part 1 with an identical structure which sets up the expectations for Part 3, and these can then be frustrated, as a device for both closure and meaning. Further, the three parts have an almost syllogistic structure: The 0 in Part 3 (absence of parent) is to the parental intervention of Parts 1 and 2 as the Successful Resolution of Part 3 is to the Failed Ones of Part 1 and 2. We can almost "deduce" a successful resolution for Part 3 from the absence of parental intervention. In fact, in Part 3, the misbehaving boy runs home to his mother (to be socialized?), the exact inverse of the other mothers coming out to the children in Parts 1 and 2 (and failing to socialize the child).

Leona's story is shaped quite differently. Her story is not unified (like Sandy's) by a single setting, rather it features a fluid movement between places. Its unity is thematic. Her first scene starts with leaving the grandmother's house, then two bouts of pain bracket the vignette about getting ice cream. Finally, this opening, which lacks any single focus, ends by a staged arrival at the first hospital (stanza 5: "an then the hospital was there"). Leona announces the main part of her narrative by saying "and this is the funny part" (stanza 6). She then uses the cab stanzas (11 and 12) to make a very fluid transition from one hospital to another – effectively making the transition and adding a whole ministory about the cab. The cab transition is quite well handled: The mother fails to pay the cab driver, while moving from one institution that will not treat her because she cannot pay to another that mistreats her even though (perhaps because) there she does not have to pay. The cab stanzas move us from one hospital to another both physically and thematically. Stanzas 16 and 17 appear somewhat tacked on. I have argued elsewhere (Gee, 1987) that 16 is added to the main development of the story so that the tone does not end on "hot" but rather on "cool," and stanza 17 serves as a coda and end of the story at the same time that it achieves closure by returning us full circle to the home world.

Leona organizes her text in a "self-reflexive" way that makes it turn back on itself, so to speak. She organizes by what has been called "the principle of the echo" (Havelock, 1963; Ong, 1982), that is, later stanzas of her text bear thematic and structural similarity to earlier ones and thus "echo" them (much like a rhyme). This principle is just the analog at the whole text level of what she does within her stanzas, where repetition and parallelism cause various lines and parts of lines to "echo" others within the stanza. Thus, note how the recurrent earache in stanza four echoes the earache in stanza 2, and thus brackets the ice cream stanza in 3. Fig. 11.2 shows some of the thematic echoes in the main body of the text (labeled DEVELOPMENT in the Appendix).

Notice how the two middle stanzas 10 and 11 are both arguments between the nurse and the mother, first about treatment and then about the cab. On either side of these stanzas are stanzas that also match (9 and 12), both being instances of the mother's anger, first at the nurse, then at the cab. Furthermore, these stanzas (9 and 12) have nearly identical form; both are made up of very short lines and are said very rapidly (more rapidly than the surrounding text). On the outside of either of these are stanzas (8 and 13) that match also in representing the mistreatment which Leona and her mother received at each hospital, the first refusing to help, and the second spitting the slip (which means they do not have to pay) in the mother's face. The stanzas outside these (7 and 14) match in that they are both about having to wait at the respective hospitals (note "for about ten minutes, or what not" in 8, and "for a good fifteen minutes" in 14). Finally, stanza 6 begins the main line of the story, while 15 reprises it.

Leona's use of the principle of the echo spatializes her text as a whole (makes us simultaneously relate parts of it as a whole, rather than take it simply in a linear chronological fashion), just as it spatialized her stanzas. While Sandy does reiterate the logical structure of the parts of her story, she does not "rhyme" the language and themes of her stanzas. At both the level of individual stanzas and at the level of the texts as wholes, Sandy stresses what the language refers to (content) as an organizing principle, while Leona shapes the language itself to create pattern. The distinction between

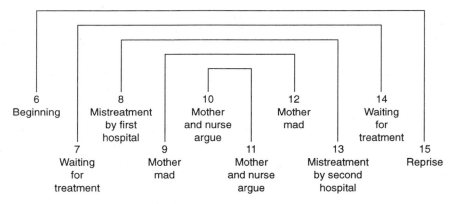

Fig. 11.2 Some thematic echoes in the main body of the text (labeled DEVELOPMENT in the Appendix)

Sandy's style and Leona's is analogous to the principle that differentiates prose (exposition) from poetry.

Quantitative comparisons: Leona to her peers and to a white adult

Leona's style and its import can also be seen clearly if we compare it in quantitative terms both to Sandy's and to a version of Leona's story which she told to a sympathetic, but nonintimate white adult male (not reprinted here, see Gee, 1987). We might expect that to the white male (being adult, white, and connected to a university-based research project) Leona would switch her narrative style, perhaps in the direction of Sandy's (since at the phonological and syntactic level the middle class tends to set the norms towards which nonstandard speakers shift in more formal speech, see Hudson, 1980; Labov, 1972a, 1972b). Table 11.1 below gives data on a variety of factors that are meant to capture the stylistic differences between Leona and Sandy.

First, what the labels in the table mean: "Informative lines" are lines which carry new information; they advance the story, however trivially. "Expressive lines" are lines that carry emotive, performative, or expressive content, but do not advance the narrative line of the story. "Other lines" are lines that are neither informative or expressive, being either extra-narrative comments or old information, that is, content expressed elsewhere in the story. "Line links" treats the way one line is linked to the line that immediately precedes it (or the stanza that precedes it if it is the first line of a stanza), thus measuring a certain type of cohesion. I distinguish four types of links: A temporally linked line is linked to the previous line by a relation of temporal contiguity; a logically linked line is linked to the previous line by a nontemporal information-relevant relation such as commenting, explanation, intention, result, exception, exemplification, "because," "instead," and so forth. An expressively linked line is linked to the previous line by an expressive or emotive relation (including exact and stylistically varied repetitions and acting out/performed lines). Unlinked lines are lines that bear none of the above linkage relations to the previous line. "Speech and Sound" categorizes lines that include speech or one or more sound effects. And, finally, "Performed Narrative Features" gives information about features of speech that have been taken to be characteristic of performed narratives (aside from speech and sound effects): demonstratives, the present tense for past action, and semantically empty expressions like "and all that stuff," "and like that," "and all" that encourage hearers to add in their own equivalent experience as to what "stuff like that" is like.

Table 11.1 shows clearly that Leona and Sandy differ in style, with Leona using in her story to her peers more expressive lines and less informative ones than Sandy, using more expressive links and less temporal and logical ones, and using more features indicative of performed narratives (speech and sound effects, and demonstratives, present tense for past action, and contextualizers). These differences do not mean that there is more substantive information in Sandy's story. Both stories are informative and have a strong sense of plot. The numerical differences simply reflect the fact that the girls use different linguistic devices to shape their stanzas. Sandy uses temporal/logical linkage almost exclusively, and these make her text seem very connected and sequential as we move through it linearly from beginning to end. Leona's smaller percentage of such links will make the text seem unconnected and nonsequential if we are not paying attention to, or do not know how to encode, her expressive and pattern-creating devices. Sandy's style bears the hallmarks of school-based essay-text literacy, and unfortunately children like Leona are often judged as if they were aiming

Table 11.1 Informational, expressive, and contextual design of Leona's story to her peers, a version of the same story to a white adult, and Sandy's story (to a white female adult)

	Leona to peers (%)	Leona to adult (%)	Sandy (%)
Informative lines	56	56	86
Expressive lines	24	7	2
Other	20	37	12
Line links			
Temporal	48	58	59
Logical	9	25	31
Expressive	30	9	1
Unlinked	13	9	9
Speech and sound	33	11	16
Performed narrative features:	11	6	6

Figures represent percentage of lines containing the relevant feature out of total lines of each story. See text for details.

for this style and missing it, rather than doing something quite different, and doing it well (Gee, 1986b).

When Leona tells her story to the white male, she appears to switch to Sandy's style, increasing her temporal and logical links and lowering all measures of performed narratives. However, the increase in temporal and logical links is actually caused by her dropping the expressive aspects of her narrative: As expressive lines are dropped, lines which were separated by this expressive material and which may be related temporally or logically have a greater chance to get next to each other. In fact, as Table 11.1 shows, Leona does not actually increase the number of her informative lines – she just greatly lowers the number of expressive ones and increases lines that are neither informative or expressive ("other"). This increase in "other" lines represents lines in the story to the adult which are not similar to anything Sandy does, nor to what Leona does to her peers. They are nonexpressive sorts of repetition and extranarrative comments, mainly "knowledge checks" she runs on the adult ("you know how . . ."). Thus, it is not so much that Leona switches to new devices, similar to those used by Sandy, as she speaks to the adult, but that she drops performance aspects of her style, as well as some of her spatialization devices (which is not directly reflected in Table 11.1). In fact, a content-based analysis of her two versions (to peers and adult) shows the same thing: While both versions are about equally long, the content of seven of the stanzas in the story to the peers is simply missing in the story to the adult (which sometimes uses two or more stanzas to say what she took one stanza to say to the peers). And all these missing stanzas involve the expression of anger, agonistic relations, or Leona's fear and dismay, that is, emotive and expressive information. Presumably, Leona has dropped the enactive/performative aspects of her style because she lacks "social permission" in the face of the white male to fully utilize her own style, a style that reflects her cultural identity and sense of self.

Since narrative style is associated with one's cultural identity and presentation of self (Goffman, 1981; for connections between speech style and sense of self in black culture, see Abrahams, 1976; Erickson, 1984; Kochman, 1972, 1981), a change in style can amount to a change in social identity (Scollon & Scollon, 1981). We know from Leona's history in school that the school has not given Leona full access to the uses of language and literacy that would ensure she could switch to Sandy's style. But the matter is deeper too: Such a style is connected with another culture's mode of expression, presentation of self, and way of making sense, encapsulating values that may, in fact, at points conflict with Leona's cultural values. The school does not understand or value Leona's mode of expression, doesn't see its connection to a culture and sense of self, and doesn't understand the full implications of asking Leona to switch that style. It does not give her access to the instruction that would ensure she could so switch, let alone do so in a way that does not threaten her own sense of self. It is not only prejudice that stands in the way. Our ignorance of how humans make sense, of how different ways of making sense interrelate in cross-cultural communication, and of how to teach people to use, understand, and appreciate alternative modes of making sense beyond the ones they acquired as children also stands in the way. I believe linguistics has a role to play in removing both these blocks.

References

Abrahams, R.D. (1976) *Talking black*, Rowley, MA: Newbury House.

Berlin, A. (1985) *The dynamics of biblical parallelism*, Bloomington, IN: Indiana University Press.

Cazden, C. (1988) *Classroom discourse: The language of teaching and learning*, Portsmouth, NH: Heinemann.

Cazden, C., Michaels, S. and Tabors, P. (1985) 'Spontaneous repairs in sharing time narratives: The intersection of metalinguistic awareness, speech event and narrative style', in S.W. Freedman (ed.), *The acquisition of written language: Revision and response*, Norwood, NJ: Ablex.

Chafe, W.L. (1979) 'The flow of thought and the flow of language', in T. Givón (ed.), *Syntax and semantics 12: Discourse and syntax*, New York: Academic.

Chafe, W.L. (1980) 'The deployment of consciousness in the production of a narrative', in W.L. Chafe (ed.), *The pear stories: Cognitive, cultural, and linguistic aspects of narrative production*, Norwood, NJ: Ablex.

Chafe, W. (1984) *Cognitive constraints on information flow*, (Berkeley Cognitive Science Report No. 26). Berkeley, CA: University of California.

Collins, J. (1985) 'Some problems and purposes of narrative analysis in educational research', *Journal of Education, 167*, pp. 57–70.

Erickson, F. (1984) 'Rhetoric, anecdote, and rhapsody: Coherence strategies in a conversation among Black American adolescents', in D. Tannen (ed.), *Coherence in spoken and written discourse*, Norwood, NJ: Ablex.

Gee, J.P. (1985) 'The narrativization of experience in the oral style', *Journal of Education, 167*, pp. 9–35.

Gee, J.P. (1986a) 'Units in the production of narrative discourse', *Discourse Processes, 9*, pp. 391–422.

Gee, J.P. (1986b) 'Orality and literacy: From *The Savage Mind* to *Ways with Words*', *TESOL Quarterly, 20*, pp. 719–746.

Gee, J.P. (1987) 'Commonalities and differences in narrative construction: A linguistic examination of a black and a white girl's stories', Unpublished manuscript, Department. of Linguistics, University of Southern California.

Givón, T. (1979) *On understanding grammar*, New York: Academic.

Goffman, E. (1981) *Forms of talk*, Philadelphia: University of Pennsylvania Press.

Gordon, S. (1986) *Oral discourse and literate prose: An analysis*, Unpublished doctoral thesis, Boston University.

Havelock, E.A. (1963) *Preface to Plato*, Cambridge, MA: Harvard University Press.

Halliday, M.A.K. (1985) *An introduction to functional grammar*, London: Edward Arnold.

Heath, S.B. (1983) *Ways with words: Language, life, and work in communities and classrooms*, Cambridge, England: Cambridge University Press.

Hudson, R.A. (1980) *Sociolinguistics*, Cambridge, England: Cambridge University Press.

Hymes, D. (1977) 'Discovering oral performance and measured verse in American Indian narrative', *New Literary History, 8*, pp. 431–457.

Hymes, D. (1980) 'Particle, pause and pattern in American Indian narrative verse', *American Indian Culture and Research Journal, 4*, pp. 7–51.

Hymes, D. (1981) *'In vain I tried to tell you': Essays in Native American ethnopoetics*, Philadelphia: PA: University of Pennsylvania Press.

Hymes, D. (1982) 'Narrative form as a "grammar" of experience: Native American and a glimpse of English', *Journal of Education, 164*, pp. 121–142.

Jakobson, R. (1978, 1980) *Selected writings:, III: Poetry of grammar and grammar of poetry; V: On verse, its masters and explorers*, Hawthorne, NY: Mouton.

Jakobson, R. and Pomorska, K. (1983) *Dialogues*, Cambridge, MA: MIT Press.

Kochman, T. (ed.), (1972) *Rappin' and stylin' out: Communication in urban black America*, Urbana, IL: University of Illinois Press.

Kochman, T. (1981) *Black and white styles in conflict*, Chicago, IL: University of Chicago Press.

Labov, W. (1972a) *Sociolinguistic patterns*, Philadelphia, PA: University of Pennsylvania Press.

Labov, W. (1972b) *Language in the inner city*, Philadelphia, PA: University of Pennsylvania Press.

Law, S-P. (1986) 'An analysis of a Chinese narrative', Unpublished manuscript, Deptartment. of Psychology, Boston University.

Michaels, S. (1981) ' "Sharing time: " Children's narrative styles and differential access to literacy', *Language in Society, 10*, pp. 423–442.

Michaels, S. (1985) 'Hearing the connections in children's oral and written discourse', *Journal of Education, 167*, pp. 36–56.

Michaels, S. and Cazden, C. (1986) 'Teacher/child collaboration as oral preparation for literacy', in B. Schieffelin (ed.), *Acquisition of literacy: Ethnographic perspectives*, Norwood, NJ: Ablex.

Michaels, S. and Cook-Gumperz, J. (1979) 'A study of sharing time with first-grade students: Discourse narratives in the classroom', in *Proceedings of the Fifth Annual Meetings of the Berkeley Linguistics Society*, Berkeley: University of California Press.

Michaels, S. and Collins, J. (1984) 'Oral discourse styles: Classroom interaction and the acquisition of literacy', in D. Tannen (ed.), *Coherence in spoken and written discourse*, Norwood, NJ: Ablex.

Michaels, S. and Foster, M. (1985) 'Peer–peer learning: Evidence from kid-run sharing time', in A. Jagger and M. Smith-Burke (ed.), *Kid watching: Observing the language learner*, Urbana, IL: National Council of Teachers of English, pp. 143–158.

Ong, W.S.J. (1982) *Orality and literacy: The technologizing of the word*, London: Methuen.

Romaine, S. (1984) *The language of children and adolescents: The acquisition of communicative competence*, Oxford, England: Basil Blackwell.

Scollon, R. and Scollon, S.B.K. (1981) *Narrative, literacy, and face in interethnic communication*, Norwood, NJ: Ablex.

Scribner, S. and Cole, M. (1981) *The psychology of literacy*, Cambridge, MA: Harvard University Press.

Smith, B.H. (1968) *Poetic closure: A study of how poems end*, Chicago: University of Chicago Press.

Tedlock, D. (1977) 'Toward an oral poetics', *New Literary History, 8*, pp. 507–519.

Tedlock, D. (1978) *Finding the center: Narrative poetry of the Zuni Indians*, Lincoln, NE: University of Nebraska Press.

Tedlock, D. (1983) *The spoken word and the work of interpretation*, Philadelphia, PA: University of Pennsylvania Press.

Turco, L. (1968) *The book of forms*, New York: E.P. Dutton.

Wolfson, N. (1982) *CHP: The conversational historical present in American English narratives*, Dordrecht, Holland: Foris.

Appendix: Leona's story to peers and Sandy's story

Leona's hospital story as told to peers

FRAME:

I'll tell you about my ear ache, o.k?
all right, this is what happened

BEGINNING

1. AT GRANDMOTHER'S
I was just up there
I was up my grandmother's house
especially for like like two weeks, or three
well not two weeks, two days or three, or more like that, a couple of ah shoot, I
should say days

2. EAR ACHE
all right, I got this thing
my ear's all buggin me an everything
my ear was all buggin me
and I was cryin
I was all: oooh oooh oooh, oooh oooh
I was doin all that
and my mother put alcohol on though

3. ICE-CREAM
and then what happened was
and then what happened
I was just let alone
an I bought myself an ice-cream
I thought that would make me feel better
I was all shuup, shuup, shuup, you know

4. EAR ACHE
And then, you know, just all of a sudden
I just got this terrible feelin
after I stopped eatin ice cream, and what not
like, oh shoot, oh go:: d
my ear was killin me
an I was sayin: "ma:: ma:: "

5. GOING TO FIRST HOSPITAL
an we got on the train to go home
an my mother said: "let's go to the hospital"
we had to walk down this LONG DARK street
about FIVE MILES, or somethin like that

???[aside – line cannot be heard]

we had to walk down this long street
an then the hospital was there

DEVELOPMENT

6. TALK TO RECEPTIONIST
and this is the funny part
"All right, you wait in there"
I'm sittin there, oooh oooh oooh
my mother's sittin there, talking to this lady and all
an, she's all, "excuse me, madam, can I help you at all", oooh oooh oooh

7. INTO THE EMERGENCY
an then we went in the emergency
because we didn't make an appointment or notin
my mother's in there, for about ten minutes, or what not
I'm still cryin
she's talkin to this lady

8. WE CAN'T HELP YOU
and they said: "well we can't help you here
cuz this is a here regular hospital"
we're blaa blaa blaa
and they kept goin on and on

9. MOTHER'S ANGER AT THE NURSE
my mother got real mad
start steamin at that lady
she was all cussin her out
yellin naa naa naa
                    [increasing rate over these lines]

10. MOTHER-NURSE ARGUE ABOUT TREATMENT
and then she goes: "what happened if my daughter was die'in", an all that
stuff
she was all: "well um excuse me miss
if you want to pay the bill
we can see you right away, my way"

11. MOTHER-NURSE ARGUE ABOUT CAB
an then she called my hospital doctor up on the phone
I was like ooooooh, still me cryin
and my mother was cussin that lady out
an then this lady goes: "why don't you take a cab/"
my mother say: "I ain't got no *money now*"

12. MOTHER'S ANGER AT THE CAB
an then they sent a cab down for her cuz she have no money
she didn't pay that cab driver
she jus' walked out
she jus' slammed that door
she said: "come on Rona"
                    [increasing rate over these lines]

13. GETTING THE "BILL"
an then they gave me this consumation, or something like that, for the bill
this lady wrote it up
an spit it in my mother's face
???pssst (kissing sound) "thank you", like that
boy I was upset

14. HAD TO WAIT
and then we had to wait for a good fifteen minutes
just to get help
now isn't that, come on, what if I was goin deaf, or something
you know what I mean

15. REPRISE
that's when I had that bad ear ache
I was like: "oh god, am I gonna die?"
I says: "no what if I die?", oooooh
I was just cryin there like that

16. LEONA AND THE NURSE CLEANING HER EAR
this lady was all cleanin, an like that
she said: "you have an ear inFECTION
an everything is going well
but there's something in your ear, you know"
an I was like: "yeah, I know"

END

STANZA 17A. GRUBBING OUT ON FOOD
an that's about all
we went home
I: grubbed out on SOME FOOD
wait you see

STANZA 17B.
put that medicine in my ear
an I was grubbin out on that food
I was grubbin out, shuuk shuuk, mmm mmm
an I was grubbin out on the food, an everything, mmm

FRAME:

all right
[Name of child], it's your turn

Sandy's park narrative as told to female adult

BEGINNING (PART 1)

1. PARK
well see, we have this park near our house
and it really stinks
but me and my friend Sarah were over there
and we were playin on the swings

2. "THE KID"
and this other kid
we call "tin head cans," or whatever
because he goes around through garbage and stuff and picks up cans
and brings em to the store to get the money

3. NAME CALLING
and so we're playin

and he starts callin us names
and so we call him names back
and then he starts talkin about our mothers

4. GIRL THROWS ROCK
so I take a rock and I threw it at him
it missed him
I made sure it missed him
it just banged on the slide

5. KID THROWS ROCKS
and then he started throwing rocks at us
and now he was throwin rocks
and he was spittin and everything else
he wouldn't dare have hit us with it though

6. MOTHER TRIES TO INTERVENE
and my mother was going down the street, okay?
and she saw him spittin at us
so my mother was trying to go over to his house
but she couldn't find 'im

7. JEREMY AND ERICA
and instead she went to Jeremy and Erica's house
they're brats
they do everything he does
except they get buckets and they dump 'em on people, and stuff like that

8. MOTHER ARRIVES AT KID'S PLACE
and so then him and my mother went over there
and she went up to where he was sittin
and I was telling my mother that he was up to the tree
and I told him that my mother was coming

9. MOTHER & KID TALK
and my mother came up
and she goes: "what's your name?"
and he goes: "I'm not gonna tell you,
you're not my mother"

10. TURNS OUT KID HAS PROBLEM
and my mother started calling him names and stuff like that
and then it turns out that he has this problem
like cause he's got some disease or somethin
and he doesn't quite know how to make friends, or anything like that

MIDDLE (PART 2)

11. KID HITS GIRLS
and one day we went over there, another day
he starts swingin chains around, okay?
and he whips Sarah with a chain
and whipped me with a padlock that was on the chain

12. GIRL THREATENS KID
and I didn't do anything,
but I grabbed him, okay?

and I go: "you hit me again
and you're gonna be in so much trouble you're not gonna believe it"

13. KIDS SWINGS SWING
so instead he starts swinging a swing
he wasn't on it
he just started swinging it
he swung it into me

14. GIRL KICKS KID
I go up to him
and I kicked him so hard he was like ahhhhhh
and he fell after I kicked him
I kicked him in both of his shins so it really hurt
and he'd get big bruises on his shins

15. MARK FROM PADLOCK
and the mark I had from the padlock was about a lump
   it was about like that
and the mark went—oohhhh
and it was all black and blue
and you could see the shape of the padlock

16. MOTHER INTERVENES
and then, let's see, Sarah's mother starts talkin to him
not to Jay – we finally found out his name was Jay
and started talkin to his mother
and the mother said: "I'll be glad to pay any hospital bills and anything like
that"

17. KID'S APOLOGY TO SARAH
and Sarah goes: "all I want him to do is apologize"
and he goes, like this: "I *did* apologize"
and Sarah, yeah, like, "oh you wanna be my friend,
after you whipped me with a chain?"

18. KID'S WHIPPING OF SARAH
he whipped her in the n—
he whipped once in her leg
and once in her arm
and once on her stomach

19. GIRL REPLIES TO KID'S APOLOGY
and then I go like this
after he yells at her like: "I'm sorry, I'm sorry"
and I go like this: "oh yeah that's a great way to make friends
whip people with chains and say 'hi I wanna be your friend'
that's dumb"

END (PART 3)

20. KID THROWS SAND
and so then the next day we went over there
he was up in the tree
and he has a bunch of rocks and a bucket of sand up there, kay?
and he started throwin sand at us

21. DEBBIE THROWS SAND AT KID
and Debbie Moraine got sand thrown at her
she goes up to the tree
she took the bucket of sand
and dumped it over his head

22. KID RUNS HOME CRYING
and he went home screamin and cryin
he's thirteen
and he went home screamin and cryin
and told his mother

STANZA 23: EVERYBODY RUNS
and everybody ran
cause they didn't want to get in trouble

24. KID CAUSES NO MORE TROUBLE
and then he doesn't cause any trouble anymore
cept when people start with him

[big pause]

25. KID HAS A PROBLEM
he's dumb
you threaten his life and he laughs
he's got some problem

12

Cultural differences in the organization of academic texts: English and German

Michael Clyne

Originally published in *Journal of Pragmatics*, 11 (1987).

Introduction

This paper reports on a project which aims at describing differences in discourse patterns which sometimes operate as a barrier to the exchange of scholarship between two related cultures. I shall first discuss the genesis of the project and the importance of education systems in transmitting culture-bound discourse norms. I shall then outline the aims, methods and corpus of the project, and the results that have been obtained, referring also to a testing program currently in progress. Finally I shall attempt some tentative explanations of the cultural differences. The project will eventually have five dimensions: linguistic (textual analysis), psycholinguistic (text processing), social psychological (attitudes to textual organization), sociocultural (the cultural background to possible differences in textual organization and attitudes), and applied (implications for foreign language teaching and translation).

Essay-writing norms

The project evolved out of a smaller study (Clyne (1980, 1981)) whose results I will briefly summarize here because of its relevance to the present research. It was found that the rules for writing essays, which form the basis for assessment in non-language subjects in Australian (and British) matriculation examinations but not in many European countries, are less rigid in Germany than in Britain or Australia. A study of four years of Matriculation examiners' reports in the state of Victoria (Australia) revealed a requirement of *linearity* in discourse structure and '*relevance*' (i.e. narrowly limiting the area covered, determined by the wording of the question, and exclusion of anything beyond this, even if the information is correct). A preliminary contrastive study was made of expectations of discourse patterns in English and German, based on (a) English and German essay-writing manuals, and (b) one set of upper secondary school assignments each (in three subjects) from different Australian and West German schools, together with marks and teachers' comments.

The following expectations of discourse could be deduced for English but *not* for German:

(1)   Essay form is essential for most upper secondary school assignments. (This does not apply to the U.S. where the big composition thrust is in the first year of tertiary education.)
(2)   The aim of an essay should be deduced strictly from the wording of the topic or question, which needs to be defined at the beginning. (In German-speaking countries, the wording of the topic or question is usually more general and does not need to be considered carefully by the student.)
(3)   *Relevance* is advocated as the primary virtue to be striven for in the construction of an essay. (In German, there appear to be few limitations on inclusion of material for the emphasis is almost entirely on the extent and correctness of content.)
(4)   The end of one paragraph should lead to the beginning of the next, which (especially in the U.S.) should generally be a topic sentence.
(5)   Repetition is deemed undesirable. (In German, where digressions are tolerated more, a logical development may entail more recapitulation.)

Expectations (3), (4) and (5) are all tantamount to requiring a linear development of texts.

This does not necessarily mean that these expectations do not play some part in German-speaking countries, but they are certainly not as important as, for instance, in Australia, where essay-writing techniques are drilled for years.

The norms for discourse apply not only for secondary schooling. It was noted, in connection with the preliminary study (Clyne (1981)), that English-speaking academics will sometimes impose norms similar to those of the examiners on their peers and comment harshly on their discourse patterns in reviews while German-speaking reviewers rarely mention such formal matters.

German academic register

Students entering German universities do not know or follow most of the Anglo-Saxon essay rules prescribed in English-speaking countries. They are, however, in the process of acquiring an academic register of the kind described in various papers in Bungarten (1981). Apart from *Fachsprache*, the technical terms of the discipline concerned, the German academic register is marked by the following:

(a)   Agentless passives, and impersonal and reflexive constructions (Polenz (1981), see also Siliakus (1984)), e.g.:
A's allgemeiner Begriff *empfiehlt sich.*
(b)   Hedged performatives using modals *kann, muß* and *darf* and passive infinitives,[1] e.g.:
Wir *können* allgemeine Übereinstimmung *voraussagen.*

Ein Kreis von Entscheidungen *ist zu kennzeichnen* als Aggression.
'Empty' discourse markers, such as *Es fragt sich, ob nicht* . . . are prevalent.

(c) A large number of nominalizations and compound nouns (see also Siliakus (1984)).

(d) Syntactic complexity (Siliakus (1984)); Although Beneš's (1981) sample of 100 sentences from each of ten disciplines bears this out only for Sociology and Linguistics (and not for Chemistry, Zoology, Medicine, Technology, History, Mathematics, and Logic).

This German academic register is used, among other things, to confirm the status of the writer (Hartung (1983)). It may be found also in high-quality newspapers such as the *Frankfurter Allgemeine* and accounts for the formal differences in language between high-quality and mass-circulation newspapers being greater in West Germany than in English-speaking countries.

Another feature of German academic discourse, 'digressiveness', which is not mentioned in the existing literature, is of functional importance in texts of the German tradition. In many books (especially dissertations) and some articles written by Germans, the *Exkurs* has become institutionalized. It provides more general or peripheral information that enables writers to work their way towards their conclusions. The *Exkurs* has neither a conceptual equivalent nor a translation equivalent in English, although I have occasionally seen 'excursus' or 'excursion' in English texts written by Germans. *Exhurse* necessarily have to be followed by some repetition of the main line of argument in order to maintain logical progression.

Grammatical structures and discourse patterns
Questions of linearization (linearity vs. digressiveness) which will be discussed in detail in this article, cannot be completely separated from grammatical considerations. German participial clauses and left-branching constructions force the German reader to interrupt his/her train of thought, e.g.:

Die von dem in der vergangenen Woche nach Südkorea zurückgekehrten Exilpolitiker Kim unterstützte. Oppositionspartei konnte trotz des die Regierungspartei begünstigende Wahlsystems überraschend viele Stimmen gewinnen.
'The opposition party supported by exile politician Kim who had returned to South Korea last week was able to win a surprisingly large number of votes in spite of the voting system favouring the government.' From TV news, cited in Greiner (1985: 45).

and:

. . . da diese Veröffentlichung, die erst jetzt, wo die Ergebnisse schon ohnehin bekannt sind, erschienen ist . . .
'. . . that this publication which has only appeared now when the results were known anyway . . . '

It could be claimed perhaps that the structure of German has contributed to linearity not having normative status as it does for English speakers. (See section 2.) However, the tendency towards digressiveness in texts by French, Italians and Russians (cf. Kaplan (1972a)), whose languages are structured differently to German, 'suggests that it might be cultural deter-minants rather than linguistic typologies that underlie degree of linearity in discourse. (See 'Sociocultural perspective' below.)

Significance of comparison

A comparison of the sources cited above would give support to a hypoth-esis that the formal marker of the scientifically credible text is the *discourse pattern* in English-speaking countries and the *level of abstraction* (character-ized by certain linguistic features) in German-speaking countries. In the present project we are focusing only on *discourse patterns*, in texts by English- and German-speaking scholars.

If English- and German-educated scholars do apply different formal criteria to judge the acceptability of academic writings, and cultural differ-ences make them susceptible to such judgments, international academic exchange and cooperation may suffer. If, as Bungarten (1981) has shown, academic register signals group solidarity, it can be counterproductive across cultures, with the same register causing some people to 'switch off'. Internationalization and academic emigration have, however, led to some alleviation of differences with adaptation towards Anglo-Saxon pat-terns (in natural sciences) or German-type 'in-group' registers (in some social sciences).

The present study

Outline
The present project, which started at the beginning of 1983, is concerned with three issues – differences in linearization between texts produced by English- and German-educated scholars, differences in their processing of texts, and variations in their perception of discourse patterns. So far the first part of the project is at an advanced stage, but testing on the other two parts has only recently begun. The corpus comprises articles and working papers by linguists and sociologists. For the German speakers we are analyzing scholarly texts written in either English or German, English functioning, to an increasing extent, as an international *lingua franca* of scholars (Baldauf and Jernudd (1983), Thogmartin (1980)).

The kinds of questions we are asking are: To what extent do texts by English- and German-educated scholars differ in their degree of linearity? Is there inter-cultural variation in discourse tempo through differences in the length of text segments, which are not in proportion to their role in the text? How does the text evolve?

By 'English-' and 'German-educated', I mean authors who not only are native speakers of the language but also received their schooling and most of their tertiary education in the language. Sociology and Linguistics were selected as the disciplines in accordance with my own interests, the position of the disciplines as a social science and a discipline near the intersection of humanities and social sciences respectively, and the different nature of the

English- and German-speaking contribution. American Linguistics has recently made a strong impact on German Linguistics whereas German Sociology has greatly influenced the discipline in the U.S. As may be expected, it is difficult to distinguish between 'cultural styles' and differences determined by individuals and schools. Similarly, we cannot take it for granted that discourse structures are the same for Americans, British and Australians or for East and West Germans, Austrians and Swiss.

Corpus
We have completed analyses of 52 texts, 17 in German, written by German speakers, 9 in English by German speakers, 26 in English by English speakers. The same number of texts (16 Linguistics, 10 Sociology) by German and English speakers were drawn from the two disciplines. Included in the corpus are texts by American, British and Australian scholars and by West and East German scholars.[2]

The texts were selected randomly but the choice was vetted to ensure a reasonable spread according to the following criteria: author's sex, type of discourse (e.g. working paper, published article), topic, length, purpose (e.g. to publicize a new theory, new direction in the discipline, data analysis, political/social application), and intended audience (people who know the field, general readers, specialist readers from the same discipline but a different field). Highly philosophical and epistemological texts from sociological schools were not included because of the specific features of these texts. In each case, a text by a German-educated scholar was found that matched one by an English-educated scholar (or vice versa) according to the above-mentioned criteria.

Methodology
Although the method I have devised focuses on broader organizational aspects of discourse, some 'lower level' phenomena, such as deixis and lexical cohesion, are analyzed separately where necessary. However, the stress is on coherence. For each text the following analyses are carried out, all of which concern linearization:

(1) *Hierarchy of text*: Which macropropositions[3] are dependent on which others? Is there more discourse subordination or discourse co-ordination?
(2) *Dynamics of text*: How is the text developed, in terms of a main argument and subsidiary arguments? How is the reader informed about this development and helped to understand the text?
(3) *Symmetry*: How long are the various sections of the text in comparison? How long are the text segments containing different macropropositions? Are there marked discrepancies in their length? Are data (and quotations) embedded in the text or more loosely attached?
(4) *Uniformity*: Are parallel text segments (say, sections with parallel content) structured in the same order or according to the same conventions?

All these analyses are intended also to contribute to the issue of linearity and digressiveness in texts by English and German speakers. For each digressive text, the function of the digressions is noted.

The normative requirement of the early placement of definitions in

English calls for a comparative examination with texts by German-educated scholars. Another matter we are investigating is the presence or absence, and positioning of topic sentences. Where a topic sentence does not occur, we are attempting to ascertain what corresponding cohesive structures are employed (e.g. bridge sentences between paragraphs).

Diagrams are drawn to represent the above aspects of the study. The hierarchy of the text (propositional dependency; discourse co-ordination vs. subordination) is shown by a tree, which also indicates the size of the branches (according to the number of lines they take up). Fig. 12.1 is a compressed tree diagram of a more co-ordinating text. It consists of two main parts (one on language acquisition and one on language teaching), each of which has two main subdivisions, each in turn with several main macropropositions on which depend a number of levels of macropropositions. Some related propositions are introduced in different parts of the text (e.g. under the acquisition and didactic headings), following unrelated propositions. Such related propositions are linked by a dotted line. Fig. 12.2 is a compressed tree diagram of a more subordinating text. Here the macropropositions all derive from the one starting point, and one follows the other directly and chronologically. A number of arguments are not followed up, so that there is one fairly linear development. The text depicted in Fig. 2 is reproduced in part in the appendix (text A), and a detailed tree is given in Fig. 12.5, to give a better idea of our working method.

As the tree is a static means of representation indicating dependency relationships and not evolution of the text, a graph is constructed to show the dynamics of the text. The graph is a strictly chronological and concrete representation. Each macroproposition is indicated by a node. The centre line along the Y-axis represents the macropropositions of the main argument. Other arguments are indicated by lines to the left and right. A line connects the nodes of the various arguments according to their appearance in the text. Fig. 12.3 is the graph of a more linear text, in which each text segment and macroproposition follow directly from the ones before them. (See also the appendix, text A). Fig. 12.4 is the graph of a digressive text, in which theoretical segments on discourse (to the right) are inserted into a treatise on discourse development in second language acquirers (to the left). The few attempts at integration are indicated by the nodes in the middle. For instance, some indices of lower level grammatical competence in a second language acquirer are followed by macropropositions concerning the definition of narrative, the roles of narrative, the way in which this temporal structure is expressed, and the devices used. (See box in Fig. 12.4.) Then the author reverts to the corpus and shows how the informant approaches the various problems of temporal reference.

The corpus includes both English and German texts by German-educated scholars so that the relative usefulness of interference, interlanguage and pidginization can be assessed as explanatory models for differences between the academic discourse produced by English- and German-educated scholars.

Both the research assistants who have worked on the textual analysis with me are German native speakers who have received their primary and

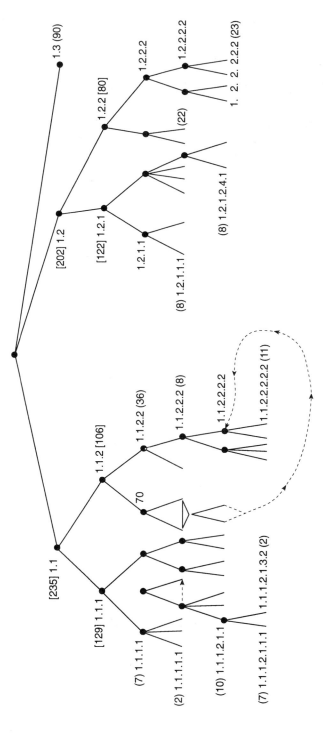

Fig. 12.1 Compressed tree of text with mainly discourse co-ordination, showing propositional dependencies. The figures in parentheses indicate the respective lengths of the propositions involved, in terms of lines: ( ) denotes the actual length of the proposition referred to; [ ] denotes the extent of the propositions involved, including those dependent.

secondary education in West Germany and most of their tertiary education in Australia. This corrects any bias due to my own background – Australian-born bilingual, educated in Australia with some exposure (through study, teaching and research overseas) to the West-German university system. In cases of uncertainty or disagreement on the categorization of texts, we have been able to draw on the assistance of colleagues and graduate students in the German Department with different degrees of bicultural experience. Such co-operation is essential due to the necessarily subjective and non-quantifiable element in the analysis of *broad* (top-level) discourse phenomena in long texts and particularly in determing cut-off points between categories (see next section).

Results

The following have emerged as tendencies in our texts:

Linearity
Irrespective of the norms of essay-writing (see above), there are texts by both English and German speakers that are more or less linear. But more texts by German speakers than by English speakers have shown major 'digressions' as shown in Table 12.1.

Table 12.1

Linearity	English-speaking authors (%)	German-speaking authors (%)
Linear	57	23
Slightly digressive	43	54
Very digressive	–	23

A text is deemed to be 'slightly digressive' if:

(a) some propositions are not dependent on the overarching proposition (macroproposition) of the section of the text in which they are situated,
(b) some propositions do not follow the macroproposition on which they depend, and/or
(c) some text segments are inserted inside another topic segment on a different topic.

If all or some of these patterns persist throughout a paper, it is regarded as 'very digressive'. As regards text segments, for example, in an article on remigration, a linear development:

(i)   occupational status of returnees
(ii) changes in occupational status
(iii) impact of several variables on occupational composition
(iv) occupational representation of returnee population in general

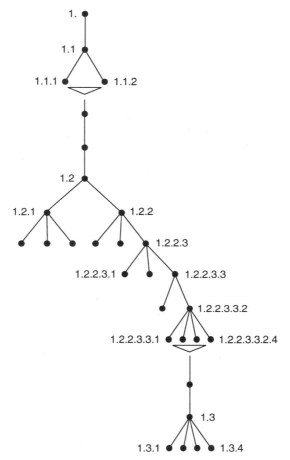

Fig. 12.2 Compressed tree of text with mainly discourse subordination, showing propositional dependencies. The actual (macro) propositions have been replaced by numbers. (For a detailed tree, see Fig. 12.5.)

is interrupted by a self-contained section on factors affecting occupational mobility, which could have preceded all the other sections.

In an article on the relation between language, society and thought, propositions relating to the societal dependence of linguistic signs are interrupted for ten lines by those relating to the macroproposition: 'Non-linguistic signs bear societal character'.

Symmetry
There is also a greater tendency to asymmetry in the German texts in both textual and propositional balance. A text is deemed to be characterized by 'textual asymmetry' if some sections of the paper are much longer than others and by 'propositional asymmetry' if there is an imbalance in the

(R.Shuy. 'The decade ahead for applied sociolinguistics')

On theory and application and how it influences modern sociolinguistic research

Theory and application
– a rigid linear theory-application model was of little use since sociolinguistics deals with real problems of society

– in a triangular model real human problems are related to both theory and application

– SL has flourished over the last decade because it has been sensitive to the triangular 'problem-theory-application' model

– there has also been an inclusion of previously excluded domains as linguistics expanded its focus

Applied SL in past decade
– applied SL in last decade has adhered to the emphases of the disciplines in which they operated:
  • interference phenomena
  • language attitudes, beliefs, values
  • issues of language planning

Applied SL in the next decade
– of interest will be:

  • analysis of discourse style
  • revelation of language functions
  • SL will also be used by other disciplines:
    – medicine
    – business and commerce
    – language and law

– the field of language and law seems to be most promising

  • the optimism is due to various conditions
– some scholars deserve praise for their pioneer work

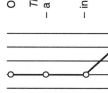

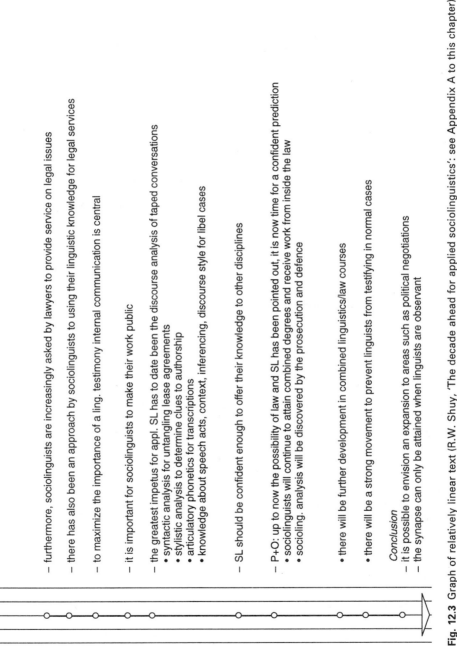

Fig. 12.3 Graph of relatively linear text (R.W. Shuy, 'The decade ahead for applied sociolinguistics'; see Appendix A to this chapter)

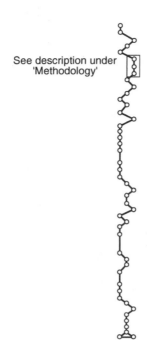

See description under
'Methodology'

Fig. 12.4 Graph of digressive text

length of related propositions branching from the same macroproposition. An example of textual asymmetry is a text dealing with four structural dimensions of German trade unions in 1914. In the description of the individual dimensions one, bureaucratization, occupies $2\frac{2}{3}$ times as much space as the other three. Propositional asymmetry occurs, for instance, in an article on the future of Sociolinguistics. Propositions dependent on 'applied Sociolinguistics will make itself relevant and useful in business and commerce' occupy 8 lines, while propositions dependent on 'one discipline with an interest in applied sociolinguistics will be medicine' take up 30 lines. (Both macropropositions, in turn, depend on 'there will be a focus on the uses of sociolinguistics by other disciplines'.) (See appendix.) It is often digressions that make German texts asymmetrical. (See Table 12.2.).

We must take into account that the texts by German speakers have a much higher lexical density (see Table 12.3) than those by English speakers.

Hierarchy
The texts written by Germans exhibit more subordination at the discourse level in the hierarchy of propositions than do those written by English speakers (see Table 12.4 and Figs. 12.1 and 12.2).

Functions of digression in German
German texts may be 'digressive', either because digression has a function in the text or because they are not well-planned texts, or for a combination of the two reasons. However, in virtually all cases, 'digressiveness' in German is functional.

The main functions of 'digression' in German are to provide theory, ideology, 'qualification' or additional information, or to enter into polemic with another author. This is done in the form of a longer or shorter *Exkurs*. When digressions with such functions are very long, as they often are, they contribute to textual asymmetry (see Table 12.5).
Some examples:

(a) Theoretical. In a working paper on the temporal organization of narratives in a group of second language learners, fairly brief analyses of the grammars of the informants are separated by a lengthy self-contained treatise on the theoretical issue (cf. Fig. 12.4).
(b) Historical. A historical interlude on the nature of Spanish Liberalism within an article on Basque Nationalism (see appendix, text B).
(c) Polemic. An article on white-collar trades unions turns, in the middle, into a retort against another scholar, covering areas beyond the ones under investigation in the article.
(d) Additional information. For part of a paper on the use of theoretical constructs in empirical research and their validity in acculturation studies in developing countries, the examples become an end in themselves.
(c) Ideological. A discussion of anti-democratic tendencies in Western Rationalism and of Science as Art in a paper describing and advocating action-oriented acquisition and teaching of a second language. It interrupts an exposition of action orientation:
   (i) action orientation is different to practice orientation,
   (ii) action orientation is different to theories of action, and precedes the proposition,
   (iii) action orientation clarifies the interdependence between researcher and learner.

Digression as well as textual asymmetry in German is often due to (obligatory) theoretical sections being not adequately integrated into an empirical paper, or vice versa.

Digression in English
On the other hand, about 65% of the 'digressive' or 'slightly digressive' English texts by English speakers result from faulty planning, sometimes from an unsuccessful attempt at conciseness. Some manifestations in our corpus:

(i) The text introduces new propositions in the conclusion.
(ii) The author appears to forget the main thesis in the latter part of the paper and forms her conclusion on the basis of only one aspect.
(iii) In a paper on flaws in research methods, the author abandons his main topic in a middle section which focuses on research without flaws.

(4) the distance between theoretical and applied sociolinguistics is not always a clearcut one

(4) the distinction between theory and application is often misperceived as being linear from theory to application

(2) what is not perceived as theoretical is often considered less academic

Theory and application

(15) the development of sociolinguistics took place in close contact with real problems of society, where the linear theory-application model had no place

(8) the old linear theory application model can be replaced by an iterative triangular model

(7) in the new model real human problems are inextricably related to both application and theory

(4) application without theory is sheer methodology

(2) theory without application is mere speculation

(2) theory or application absent from a real human problem is mere academic display

(3) sociolinguistics in the past decade has flourished because it has been sensitive towards the triangular problem-theory-application model

(9) it is difficult to separate cause and effect in the recent interdisciplinary surge in language function

(7) there has been a gradual inclusion of previously excluded domains as linguistics expanded its focus

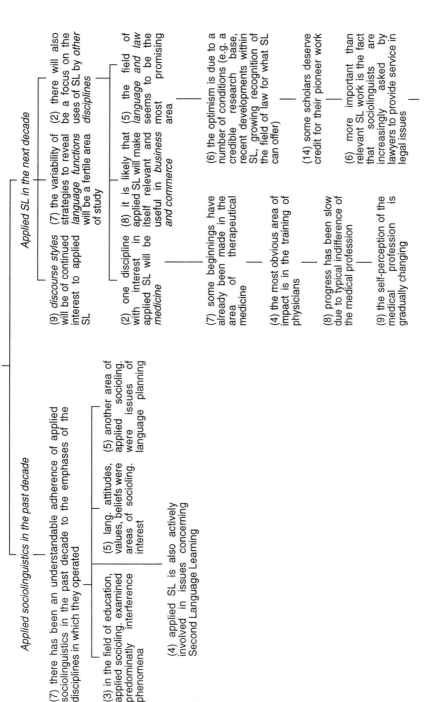

Applied sociolinguistics in the past decade

(7) there has been an understandable adherence of applied sociolinguistics in the past decade to the emphases of the disciplines in which they operated

(3) in the field of education, applied socioling. examined predominatly interference phenomena

(5) lang. attitudes, values, beliefs were areas of socioling. interest

(5) another area of applied socioling. were issues of language planning

(4) applied SL is also actively involved in issues concerning Second Language Learning

Applied SL in the next decade

(9) *discourse styles* will be of continued interest to applied SL

(7) the variability of strategies to reveal *language functions* will be a fertile area of study

(2) there will also be a focus on the uses of SL by *other disciplines*

(2) one discipline with interest in applied SL will be *medicine*

(8) it is likely that applied SL will make itself relevant and useful in *business and commerce*

(5) the field of *language and law* seems to be the most promising area

(7) some beginnings have already been made in the area of therapeutical medicine

(4) the most obvious area of impact is in the training of physicians

(8) progress has been slow due to typical indifference of the medical profession

(9) the self-perception of the medical profession is gradually changing

(6) the optimism is due to a number of conditions (e.g. a credible research base, recent developments within SL, growing recognition of the field of law for what SL can offer)

(14) some scholars deserve credit for their pioneer work

(6) more important than relevant SL work is the fact that sociolinguists are increasingly asked by lawyers to provide service in legal issues

Fig. 12.5 Detailed version of graph in Fig. 12.2

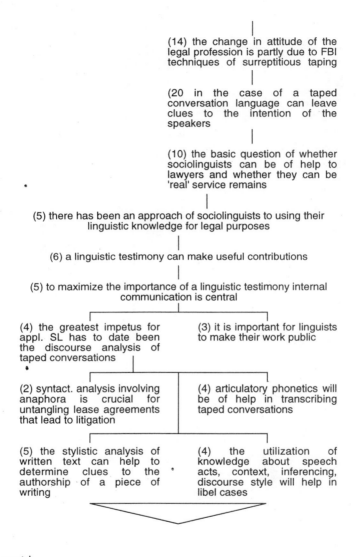

(14) the change in attitude of the legal profession is partly due to FBI techniques of surreptitious taping

(20 in the case of a taped conversation language can leave clues to the intention of the speakers

(10) the basic question of whether sociolinguists can be of help to lawyers and whether they can be 'real' service remains

(5) there has been an approach of sociolinguists to using their linguistic knowledge for legal purposes

(6) a linguistic testimony can make useful contributions

(5) to maximize the importance of a linguistic testimony internal communication is central

(4) the greatest impetus for appl. SL has to date been the discourse analysis of taped conversations

(3) it is important for linguists to make their work public

(2) syntact. analysis involving anaphora is crucial for untangling lease agreements that lead to litigation

(4) articulatory phonetics will be of help in transcribing taped conversations

(5) the stylistic analysis of written text can help to determine clues to the authorship of a piece of writing

(4) the utilization of knowledge about speech acts, context, inferencing, discourse style will help in libel cases

Fig. 12.5 contd

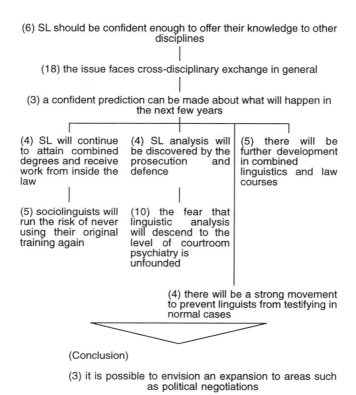

(6) SL should be confident enough to offer their knowledge to other disciplines

(18) the issue faces cross-disciplinary exchange in general

(3) a confident prediction can be made about what will happen in the next few years

(4) SL will continue to attain combined degrees and receive work from inside the law	(4) SL analysis will be discovered by the prosecution and defence	(5) there will be further development in combined linguistics and law courses
(5) sociolinguists will run the risk of never using their original training again	(10) the fear that linguistic analysis will descend to the level of courtroom psychiatry is unfounded	

(4) there will be a strong movement to prevent linguists from testifying in normal cases

(Conclusion)

(3) it is possible to envision an expansion to areas such as political negotiations

(4) the synapse can only be attained when linguists are observant, creative, and entrepreneurial

Fig. 12.5 contd

Table 12.2

Symmetry	English-speaking		German-speaking	
	Textual (%)	Propositional (%)	Textual (%)	Propositional (%)
Rather symmetrical	54	42	15	8
Slightly asymmetrical	23	42	27	31
Very asymmetrical	23	16	58	61

Table 12.3

Lexical density [a]	English-speaking authors	German-speaking authors
	447	247

[a] Average number of words per macroproposition.

Table 12.4

Hierarchy	English-speaking (%)	German-speaking (%)
Mainly subordination	19	38
Mainly co-ordination	31	27
Both	50	35

Table 12.5 Digressions in texts by Germans (major digressions only)

Theoretical	5	Historical	5
Polemic	7	Ideological	1
Additional information	6	New perspectives	2

Discontinuity
Texts by German speakers are more likely to be characterized by discontinuity, i.e. leaving an argument in mid-air and starting a new one (see Table 12.6). Such features become more conspicuous in the absence of advance organizers (see 'Advance organizers' below).

Ordering in English
A lack of uniformity in the ordering of constituent parts of parallel segments was recorded in only one text in English by a German speaker (evidently the result of faulty planning).

Table 12.6

Discontinuity	English-speaking authors (%)	German-speaking authors (%)
None	80	50
Slight	12	12
Marked	8	38

Table 12.7

Position of advance organizers	English-speaking authors (%)	German-speaking authors (%)
At or near beginning of text	59	42
Later in text	41	58

Advance organizers
English-educated scholars are more likely than German-educated colleagues to use advance organizers which explain the path and organization of
a paper, and to place them at the start of it. They sometimes mark digressions ('I will now digress . . . ', or 'Let us briefly digress to . . . '). So, even if
the paper of an English-educated author is not quite linear, people know
what to expect and it may be easier to understand. Where the advance
organizers are given by a German author, they are often in an obscure
location, almost as if to express embarrassment about this formal adherence
to the conventions of an international journal. Text B in the appendix has
advance organizers both at the start and in the course of the paper.

Definition
Where a main term is explained, which is more probable in a text by an
English speaker than in one by a German, this is far more likely to take
place at or near the start of the text if the author is English-educated.
However, in one English text by a German the word *status* is defined after
being used 44 times. In a German text by a German, the key term, *handlungsorientiert* (action oriented), is ultimately defined after occurring 20
times. The original definition is not adequate to the needs of the text so
that another definition is formulated without reference to the previous one.
(*Handlung*, which is basic to *Handlungsorientiert*, is defined after both sections.) The definition process in some German papers is seen as developing
in the course of the whole text (see Table 12.8).

Sentence types
The occurrence of topic and other sentences at the beginning of a paragraph
depends partly on the function of the text. However, English-educated
scholars (especially Americans) seem more likely to use topic sentences

Table 12.8

Definitions	English-speaking authors (%)	German-speaking authors (%)
Immediately	73	12
Later	4	19
Not at all	23	69

Table 12.9

Sentence types (beginning of paragraph)	English-speaking authors (%)	German-speaking authors (%)
Topic sentences	62	48
Enumerating sentences	38	23
Bridge sentences	–	29

than do the German-educated. The introductory sentence in a paragraph written by a German-educated scholar is far more likely to be a bridge sentence (referring back to the previous paragraph or another paragraph), e.g.:

> Wenn an dieser Polemik etwas dran ist, dann gibt es im Kreis der Betreiber offensichtlich Probleme mit der Legitimation.
> 'If there is anything in this polemic, there are obviously legitimation problems within the circle of participants.'

Texts presenting statistical data will employ enumerating sentences in paragraph-initial position (see Table 12.9).

Data integration
Examples, statistics and quotations are less likely to be embedded in the text by German-speaking scholars, who will sometimes present them in unintegrated fashion, e.g. at the end, in unexplained chunks or tables or in footnotes. In several German texts, macropropositions are expressed as statistics, e.g. '65 per cent of the respondents finished primary school, 10.3 per cent secondary school, and 20.2 per cent did not finish school at all. On an average, the respondents completed 6.7 years at school, although 18.7 per cent of the returnees visited school less than 6 years'. The data are deemed to be integrated if virtually all examples, statistics and quotations are embedded in the text and hardly at all integrated if, for instance, numerous statistics are expressed as propositions, or there are several tables the information of which is not taken up in the main body of the text (see Table 12.10).

All these phenomena contribute to the relative differences in linearity we have been discussing.

Actually, footnotes sometimes facilitate a compromise between a more

Table 12.10

Data Integration	English-speaking authors (%)	German-speaking authors (%)
Entirely	69	7
Partly	23	64
Hardly at all	8	29

Table 12.11

	English texts by German speakers (%)	German texts by German speakers (%)
Linearity		
Linear	11	36
Slightly digressive	56	47
Very digressive	33	17
Total symmetry		
Rather symmetrical	11	17
Slightly asymmetrical	33	24
Very asymmetrical	56	59

digressive and a more linear text in that they enable obligatory historical or theoretical 'digressions' which characterize some German academic discourse to be included in a co- or sub-text without their disrupting the linear flow of the main text. In this respect the Harvard system, which originated in the U.S. but is now widely used in linguistics and some social sciences in West Germany, by minimizing footnotes, has perhaps contributed to less linearity in texts by Germans.[4] On the other hand, in some texts, some macropropositions are divided between the main body of the discourse and a co-text in a footnote.

English texts by Germans
German-speaking scholars now writing in both languages whom I have interviewed are aware of the difficulties they are encountering with English discourse patterns. However, English texts by German scholars tend to contain the same cultural discourse patterns as German texts (see Table 12.11).

These patterns are more marked, in fact, in English texts by Germans perhaps because of the author's general problems in composing texts in a second language. Such texts do make concessions to English norms in 'lower level' routines such as advance organizers (see Table 12.12).

Table 12.12

Advance organizers	English texts by German speakers (%)	German texts by German speakers (%)
	89	47

Table 12.13

Beginnings	10
Endings	2
Beginnings and endings	5
Neither	16

GDR texts

Texts by GDR scholars intended for international consumption tend to follow similar patterns to comparable ones by West Germans. However, those East German texts written principally for local consumption – e.g. those published in the scientific journals of universities – frequently begin and/or end with a section relating their topic to Socialism. This does not apply where the topic is political and the Socialist element basic to the text (e.g. 'Herder, Humboldt and Marx'; 'Communist work education as the core of Communist education in the vocational colleges of the GDR'). Of the 44 papers in numbers 1/2 of the *Wissenschaftliche Zeitschrift der Humboldt-Universität, 1985*, 11 fell into this category. Of the remainder, 17 had political beginnings and/or endings and 16 did not (see Table 12.13).

The difference is often due to the topic, 'Leadership and control of preparation for self-education' lending itself more to – or necessitating more – a political linkage than does 'General pedagogical foundations of the development of process theory'. East German scholars themselves have a term for the Socialist closing routine – 'ideologisches Schwänzchen'. It would appear that 'ideologische Köpfchen' now predominate. East German texts mainly for local consumption tend to be very compressed (perhaps an outcome of a wish to save paper), with a high level of data integration. They are often characterized by discontinuity due to their high lexical density (186 words per macroproposition: 277 for West German texts) (see Table 12.14).

Disciplines

Are there patterns that are constant across the cultures but characteristic of the 'sub-culture' of one or other discipline? The only things that have emerged from our corpus are more discourse subordination in sociological texts, and a greater tendency to employ advance organizers and to introduce definitions and advance organizers earlier in sociological texts than in linguistic ones, as shown in Table 12.15.

Table 12.14

	Texts by East Germans (%)	Texts by West Germans (%)
Data integration		
Entirely integrated	76	–
Partly integrated	12	69
Not at all	12	31
Discontinuity		
Not at all	42	58
Slight	–	21
Marked	58	21

Table 12.15

	Sociological (%)	Linguistic (%)
Hierarchy		
More subordination	45	19
More co-ordination	25	31
Both	30	50
Advance organizers		
Yes	75	62
At or near beginning	64	53
Definitions		
Immediately	50	38
Later	10	13
Not at all	40	49

Sociocultural perspective

It is too early to assess which sociocultural and historical factors are involved in the oganizational differences between English and German academic discourse. Some diachronic studies may contribute an answer to this problem. Neustupný, while accepting the existence of 'national' types of communication systems, emphasizes 'developmental stages' (1978: 27–29, 148–49, 255). The 'modern' stage, based on a more differentiated role for individuals, may lead to their dependence on selling their verbal produce. A 'modern' communication can be expected to be more ordered in its discourse rules than the preceding ('early modern') and following ('contemporary') stages.

338   *Michael Clyne*

The place of essay-writing in the education systems of English- and German-speaking countries will no doubt play an important role in explaining the differences in discourse organization (see 'Essay-writing norms' above). The following will play an important role as well.

Intellectual styles
In his studies of 'Teutonic' (German-based) intellectual style – partly comparisons with 'Saxonic' (Anglo-American-based), 'Gallic' (French-based) and 'Nipponic' (Japanese-based) intellectual styles – Galtung (1979, 1981) concludes that 'Teutonic' arguments have to be derived from the theoretical principles with empirical reality existing only in relation to a system. 'Teutonic' and 'Gallic' styles are strong in paradigm analysis as well as theory, while 'Saxonic' and 'Nipponic' styles focus on description based on data analysis. 'Teutonic' intellectual style is more monologue-oriented, involving a test of strength, in contrast to 'Saxonic' style, which promotes dialogue and debate leading to *rapprochement* between viewpoints. Galtung stresses the importance, in the 'Teutonic' tradition, of membership of a school, which may be indicated through a particular use of language. Galtung's observations, though not based on empirical data, may serve to explain some of the linguistic issues we have discussed. Of particular significance here is his assertion (1981: 15):

> Die teutonische wie auch die gallische Form der Theoriekonstruktion erfordern ein sprachliches Vermögen, das nur wenige meistern (. . .) Die sachsonische - die US-Varianten mehr noch als die UK-Varianten – und die nipponischen Praktiken sind toleranter, demokratischer, weniger elitär.

> 'The Teutonic as well as the Gallic form of theory construction requires a language competence attained by few (. . .) The Saxonic – the U.S. variants even more than the U.K. ones – and the Nipponic practices are more tolerant and democratic, less elitist.

While these findings help account for some aspects of German academic register, theoretical 'digressions' and the greater proximity of English academic texts to non-academic ones, the above-mentioned 'Saxonic' tolerance does not seem to extend to texts organized according to the norms of other cultural traditions (Clyne (1980, 1981)).

German and 'Anglo-Saxon' attitudes to learning and content
The frequently expressed English-speaking examiners' remark (Clyne (1980)) that knowledge is no more important than the way in which it is presented, i.e. the adherence to particular discourse norms, could be regarded as sacrilege from a German point of view.

Knowledge is idealized in the German tradition. Consequently, texts by Germans are less designed to be easy to read. Their emphasis is on providing readers with knowledge, theory, and stimulus to thought. (This point was made by several of the people I interviewed, and it is raised in Greiner's (1985) popular article.) In both cultural traditions, there is a cooperation between author and reader, with the author engaged in what Candlin and Saedi (1983) term an elaborative process and the reader's perspective being a reductive process. In English-speaking countries, most of the onus falls on writers to make their texts readable, whereas it is the readers who have to make the extra effort in German-speaking countries so that they can understand the texts, especially if the author is an academic.

Just as it is the reader's responsibility to understand a German text (to gain *Verständnis*) rather than of the writer to make it understandable (*verständlich*), a piece of German academic writing concentrates on the subject (*Sache, Gegenstand*), the content. As Greiner (1985: 45) puts it: "Nicht er [der deutsche Professor] spricht, sondern die Wissenschaft aus ihm." 'Not he (the German Professor) speaks, but scholarship through him.' *Wissenschaft* (scholarship) is mystified; because of its exalted nature, it does not need to be readily comprehended.

Cultural parallels

It may be possible to find parallels in other aspects of the cultures to contrast a more linear one with a less linear one. Candidates for such contrasts would be the practice of queuing in Britain, which has not 'caught on' much in German-speaking countries; Anglo-American rules for the conduct of meetings, such as only one motion being before the chair at a time and the amendment (if adopted) becoming the motion; and the earlier German system of writing addresses on envelopes (Clyne (1981)).[5] Such differences have become less marked in recent years. In any case it is doubtful whether such parallels have a place in (socio)-linguistic research.

Closing remarks

The cultural norms for German academic interaction which have been described by Galtung entail what, from an 'Anglo-Saxon' point of view could be perceived as content digressions. These, in turn, will bring about a less linear text. Restrictions on such 'content digressions' in English-speaking countries will, from a German point of view, lead to a conclusion based on a more limited perspective.

In view of the importance of international communication between scholars, it is vital for scholars to understand the cultural basis of many discourse patterns.[6] Differences between English and German discourse are but one small example. I would recommend that this issue be raised in Languages for Special Purposes courses, for mastery of discourse conventions appears to be one of the prerequisites to power on the international academic scene. Also, native English speakers need to be confronted, within their graduate courses, with the problem of how to communicate with non-native speakers in an international context. Above all, it is imperative for the cultural basis of discourse structures to be recognized and for variant patterns to be appreciated and respected.

Notes

1. Incidentally, understatement appears to be more characteristic of books and papers than of spontaneous spoken discourse in German, whereas the reverse could be said for English.
2. This paper, written in 1987, refers to the situation in Germany before unification. – *Eds.*
3. By macroproposition I mean superordinated propositions which summarize the arguments of a number of (other) propositions in the text. They represent the intended meaning of that part of the text (see Van Dijk (1980: 192, 206)).
4. The Harvard system prescribes that bibliographical references be incorporated in parentheses in the text, e.g. Smith (1970: 15).
5. For instance: (Name) Herrn Wolfgang Schmidt
   (Postcode and place-name) 53 *Bonn*
   (Street, house number, apartment number) Struwelpeterstraße 15/14
6. The same goes for sub-cultural differences within a discipline. As Neustupný (1978: 36) puts it: "If any further progress and integration in linguistics is to come, we must first learn how to accept not merely variation in language, but to the same extent, how to accept variation in linguistics". The same goes for sociology and other social sciences.

References

Antos, G. (1982) *Grundlagen einer Theorie des Formulierens*, Tübingen: Niemeyer.

Baldauf, R.B. and Jernudd, B.H. (1983) 'Language of publications as a variable in scientific communication', *Australian Review of Applied Linguistics* 6: pp. 97–108.

Ballstaedt, S.-P., Mandl, H., Schnotz, W. and Tergan, S.-D. (1981) *Texte verstehen – Texte gestalten*, Munich: Urban and Schwarzenbach.

Benes, E. (1981) 'Die formale Struktur der wissenschaftlichen Fachsprache in syntaktischer Hinsicht', in T. Bungarten, (ed.), 1981, pp. 185–212.

Bungarten, T. (ed.), (1981) *Wissenschaftssprache*, Munich: Fink.

Chang, S.-J. (1983) 'Contrastive studies of English and Korean', *Annual Review of Applied Linguistics* 3: pp. 85–98.

Clyne, M.G. (1980) 'Writing, testing and culture', *The Secondary Teacher* 11: pp. 13–16.

Clyne, M.G. (1981) 'Culture and discourse structure', *Journal of Pragmatics* 5: pp. 61–66.

Clyne, M.G. (1983) 'Contrastive studies of English and German', *Annual Review of Applied Linguistics* 3: pp. 38–49.

Eggington, W.G. (1987) 'Written academic discourse in Korean. Implications for effective communication', to appear in U. Connor and R.B. Kaplan, (eds.), *Writing across languages*. Reading, MA.: Addison Wesley, pp. 172–189.

Galtung, J. (1979) *Paper on methodology*, (= Theory and Methods of Social Science Research 2.) Copenhagen: Ejlers.

Galtung, J. (1981) 'Struktur, Kultur und intellektueller Stil', (Lecture given at the Free University) Berlin.

Givón, T. (1983a) 'Topic and continuity in discourse: Introduction', in T. Givón, (ed.), (1983b) pp. 7–41.

Givón, T. (ed.), (1983b) *Topic and continuity in discourse. A quantitative cross-language study*, Amsterdam: John Benjamins.

Greiner, U. (1985) 'were ai wulld laik du go', *Die Zeit*, Nr. 20, 10 May 1985: pp. 45–46.

Grimes, J.E. (1975) *The thread of discourse*, The Hague: Mouton.

Groeben, N. (1982) *Leserpsychologie, Textverständlichkeit*, Münster: Aschendorff.

Halliday, M.A.K. and Hasan, R. (1976) *Cohesion in English*, London: Langman.

Hartung, W. (1983) 'Strukturebenen und ihre Einheiten in Diskussionstexten', *Linguistische Studien* A. 112, Berlin: Akademie der Wissenschaften, pp. 193–228.

Hinds, J. (1980) 'Japanese expository prose', *International Journal of Human Communication* 13: pp. 117–158.

Hinds, J. (1983a) 'Contrastive rhetoric: Japanese and English', *Text* 3: pp. 183–195.

Hinds, J. (1983b) 'Topic continuity in Japanese', in T. Givón, 1983b: pp. 47–93.

Hinds, J. (1983c) 'Contrastive studies of English and Japanese', *Annual Review of Applied Linguistics* 3: pp. 78–84.

Hinds, J. (1984) 'Retention of information using a Japanese style of presentation', *Studies in Language* 8: pp. 45–69.

Kachru, Y. (1983) 'Contrastive studies of English and Hindi', *Annual Review of Applied Linguistics* 3: pp. 50–77.

Kaplan, R.R. (1972a) 'Cultural thought patterns in inter-cultural education', in K. Croft, (ed.), *Readings on English as a second language*, Cambridge, MA: Winthrop, pp. 246–262.

Kaplan, R.B. (1972b) *The anatomy of rhetoric*, Philadelphia, PA: Center for Curriculum Development.

Kintsch, W. (1974) *The representation of meaning in memory*, Hillsdale, NJ: Erlbaum.

Kintsch, W. and Greene, E. (1978) 'The role of culture-specific schemata in the comprehension and recall of stories', *Discourse Processing* 1: pp. 1–13.

Kintsch, W. and van Dijk, T. (1978) 'Towards a model of text comprehension and production', *Psychological Review* 85: pp. 363–394.

Langer, I., Schulz von Thun, F. and Tausch, R. (1974) 'Verständlichkeit in Schule?' Verwaltung, *Politik und Wissenschaft*. Munich: Reinhardt.

Leap, W.C. (1983) 'Contrastive studies of English and American Indian languages', *Annual Review of Applied Linguistics* 3: pp. 24–37.

Levelt, W.J.M. (1981) 'The speaker's linearization problem', *Philosophical Transactions of the Royal Society of London*.

Longacre, R.E. (1972) *An anatomy of speech notions*, Lisse: Peter de Ridder.

Longacre, R.E. and Woods, F. (eds.), (1977) *Discourse grammar: Studies in indigenous languages of Columbia, Panama and Ecuador*, Dallas: S.I.L.

Meyer, B.J.F. (1975) *The organization of prose and its effects on memory*, Amsterdam: Elsevier.

Neustupný, J.V. (1975) 'Review of E. Haugen, "The Ecology of Language"', *Language* 51: pp. 236–242.

Neustupný, J.V. (1978) *Post-structural approaches to language*, Tokyo: Tokyo University Press.

Pandharipande, R. (1983) 'Contrastive studies of English and Marathi', *Annual Review of Applied Linguistics* 3: pp. 118–136.

Polenz, P. von (1981) 'Über die Jargonisierung von Wissenschaftssprache und wider die Deagentivierung', in T. Bungarten, (ed.), (1981) pp. 85–110.

Rumelhart, D.E. (1975) 'Notes on a schema for stories', in D.G. Bobrow and A. Collins, (eds.), *Representation and Understanding*, New York: Academic Press.

Schank, R.C. and Abelson, A.P. (1977) *Scripts, plans, goals and understanding*, Hillsdale, NJ: Erlbaum.

Siliakus, H. (1984) 'Some syntactic features of linguistic texts', Review of Applied Linguistics 65: pp. 57–77.

Sinclair, J. and Coulthard, J.M. (1975) *Towards an analysis of discourse*, London: Oxford University Press.
Smith, L. (ed.), (1987) *'Discourse across cultures'*, London: Prentice Hall.
Thogmartin, C. (1980) 'Which language for students in social sciences?', *Anthropological Newsletter* 21: p. 6.
Tsao, F.-F. (1983) 'Contrastive studies of English and Mandarin', *Annual Review of Applied Linguistics* 3: pp. 99–117.
Van Dijk, T. (1977) *Text and context*, London: Longman.
Van Dijk, T. (1980) *Textwissenschaft*, Munich: dtv.

Appendices

The text segments in Appendices A and B are reproduced to illustrate our working methods. For a detailed tree and graph of the text segment in Appendix A, see Figs. 12.2 and 12.5.

Appendix A: text by a speaker of English

Roger W. Shuy, 'The decade ahead for applied sociolinguistics', *International Journal of the Sociology of Language* 45 (1984), 101–5.

Unlike other academic disciplines or subdisciplines, sociolinguistics has not often placed the labels of 'theoretical' vs. 'applied' on itself. Because of this, it may not seem obvious that such a thing as applied socioinguistics is in any way distinct from theoretical sociolinguistics. Perhaps it is not and, if not, so much the better, for the distinction between theory and application is, at best, a blurry one which is frequently misperceived as linear, i.e. from theory to application. That is, many theoretical linguists view their work as primary, an end in itself. That which is not viewed as theoretical is of less significance academically, is much less highly valued, and is seen as 'derivative'.

Theory and application

The development of sociolinguistics, with origins throughout history, but with great leaps of visibility in the 1970s, occurred outside this linear 'theory to application' model. For one thing, the beginning point of sociolinguistic work was not the development and honing of theory in and for itself. Quite the contrary; sociolinguists began with a real problem of society. Many were concerned about educational issues that grew out of minority language or dialect use. Others were concerned about human problems of power, equality, and justice. Still others focused on communication problems of a more general nature, whether or not these problems concerned social or linguistic minorities. As it turned out, the linear 'theory → application' model had no real place in such concerns, partly because the theories had not yet been developed (e.g. a theory which would account for linguistic variability or a theory that would account for communicative competence, not just linguistic competence) and partly because the overriding concern of sociolinguistics was on solving the social or educational problem rather than on perfecting their theories. Replacing the old linear 'theory → application' model was one which might be best represented as an iterative, triangular one:

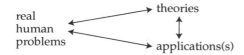

In this model, the sociolinguists can begin at any point on the triangle and move in any other direction (in fact, the beginning point is commonly at the human-problem entry point, but any other entry is possible). If entry is at the problem point, the problem determines the theories to be used. If entry is at the application point, the problem determines the theories to be used. If entry is at the theory point, the human problem still determines the application to be used.

But there is more. Note that the arrows are double-headed. By this I mean that feedback goes both ways. In cases where real human problems are involved, theory cannot be abstract or divorced from application. If the weakness of recent applied linguistics has been its separation from linguistic theory, so has the weakness of recent theoretical linguistics been its separation from real human problems. Adequate engagement in real human problems requires the selection and development of both theory and application. Application without theory is mere methodology (an error much of applied linguistics has fallen into). Theory without application is mere speculation (an error which much of theoretical linguistics has fallen into). Theory or application absent from a real human problem is mere academic display. Life is in the doing. Faith without works is dead. Works without causes or reasons for working are frivolous.

Sociolinguistics in the past decade has shown evidence of sensitivity to this triangular problem-theory-application model. For this reason it has flourished. Language variability is being accounted for in both linguistic and social theories. It is difficult to separate cause from effect in many of the recent developments in linguistics and other social sciences, but the recent surge of interest in language function can be seen in many fields. Did this come about as a result of the sociolinguists' concern for a satisfactory and full explanation of language variability? Did it emerge as a result of the theoretical linguists' discontent with autonomous syntax? Did it result from the efforts of philosophers to account for speech acts or pragmatics of natural language? Is it the result of the ethnographer's concern for communicative competence? The answer is probably 'yes' to all of these. As linguists expanded their focus from phonology, morphology, and syntax to a focus on meaning, it became more and more necessary to approach domains which were previously excluded from this form-dominated discipline. At the same time, linguists also began to expand their horizons from the sound and word-level analyses of the 1950s and early 1960s to sentence-level analyses in the 1960s and 1970s. More recently, this focus is even larger, leading to what is now called discourse analysis, the focus on spoken or written language units larger than the sentence.

Applied sociolinguistics in the past decade

It is only natural that the major contributions of applied sociolinguistics in the past decade were in keeping with the emphasis of the disciplines in which they existed. Linguists were studying language forms. Many sociolinguists also studied language forms.

In the field of education, applied sociolinguists attempted to point out the interference of a child's native dialect on his acquisition of oral standard English, reading skills, comprehension, test-taking, and written composition. Applied sociolinguists were also active in educational issues of second-language learning and teaching, particularly in bilingual education, again focusing primarily on language forms, predicting areas of interference, suggesting approaches to deal with such areas, and preparing materials to suit such situations.

Language attitudes, values, and beliefs were another area of focus by sociolinguists in the past decade. Studies of teachers' attitudes toward the language use of their students formed some helpful guidelines for instructional practice. Small efforts were also made to relate subjective reactions to language use to other human areas such as employability.

Larger issues of language planning, particularly in multilingual countries, formed still another area of applied sociolinguistics in the past decade. Sociolinguistic surveys, language attitude measures, and policy analyses and procedures were carried out with the intention of assisting third world nations, in particular, in the thorny problems of selecting official languages.

Applied sociolinguistics in the next decade

Discourse styles.   Such work will undoubtedly continue in the next decade, although the focus will also turn to matters larger than language forms. Variability of discourse styles will be one such newer focus. We now know pretty well which language forms will be difficult for an English speaker, for example, to learn as s/he acquires a new language such as Arabic. But we know very little about how such a person will need to restructure topic focus, elaboration, and perlocutionary effect to suit the Arabic culture. Issues of directness vs. indirectness, associated, as they are, not only with politeness but also with the accepted forms of rhetorical development, are vast areas for future applied sociolinguistic analysis across languages and cultures.

Language functions. Likewise, variability of strategies used to reveal language functions will be a fertile area of study in the coming decade. The recent interest in language functions, such as promising, denying, requesting, clarifying, asserting, etc., has revealed a multitude of various strategies used to accomplish these functions. Such strategies vary by age groups, ethnicity, culture, and other dimensions as yet unknown, offering an exciting prospect for increasing our knowledge about sociolinguistic aspects of language use.

Application to other fields.   Along with this growth in applied sociolinguistics toward discourse styles and language function variability will come a focus on the uses of sociolinguistics by other recognized disciplines, such as medicine.

Medicine.   Beginnings have already been made in the area of therapeutic discourse by Labov and Fanshel (1977) and in doctor-patient communicaiton by Ford (1976), Shuy (1976, 1977), Mischler (1982), and Fisher (1982). At least part of the reason why the application of applied sociolinguistics has not made greater advances in this area is because the field of medicine has not felt a particularly strong need for it.

The most obvious area of impact is in the training of physicians, yet relatively few medical schools have seen fit to adjust their curricula to include aspects of delivery of services. The focus continues to be on the technological aspect of medicine rather than on the interaction of doctor and patient. Nursing programs have made far greater advances in this area, but a great deal more is possible. With the possible exception of the training curriculum for social workers, techniques of interviewing are generally slighted. It appears either that a groundswell of public outrage against the verbal interaction in medical delivery has not yet emerged or that the medical profession has not yet cared enough to respond to it. Perhaps this is not surprising since the medical profession is so highly revered, in many countries at least.

The self-perception of the medical profession is showing evidence of change. The Henry J. Kaiser Family Foundation and the Association of American Medical Colleges have undertaken a three-year study of American medical education. One of the study's most hopeful conclusions is that doctors must be taught to interview and listen to their patients and that they should ' . . . develop sensitivity for the unique qualities of each human being and learn that physicians are accorded trust and confidence that goes beyond technical ability' (*Los Angeles Times*, January 14, 1983, p. V5). Such an attitude, if heeded, suggests a fertile area of work for applied sociolinguistics in the decade ahead.

Business. Building on the work of Merritt (1976), Geiss (1982), Garfinkel (1978), Coleman (i.p.), Tsuda (1983), Kumatoriya (1982), and others in the recent decade, it is likely that applied sociolinguistics will continue to find ways to make itself relevant and useful to the world of commerce. The microwork of Merritt (1976) in the service encounter opened the door to a structural analysis of this important speech event and gave emphasis to the fact that business is, indeed, conducted in language. Likewise, Garfinkel (1978), Geiss (1982), Coleman (i.p.), and Kumatoriya (1982) have been exploring the murky area of language in advertising, especially television advertising.

Law. It is the field of language and law, however, which appears to offer great promise for applied sociolinguistics in the next decade. As such, this area of application can serve as a model or case study for other fields in which the emerging tools, theory, and insights of sociolinguistics can be utilized. The field of law seems to be a growth potential area for future applied sociolinguistic work as a result of a number of conditions, including (1) a credible research base; (2) the recent development within sociolinguistics of research and theory which appear to be applicable to legal issues; (3) the growing recognition of the field of law for the service that sociolinguistics can offer; and (4) the willingness of some scholars to stick their necks out and leap into the middle of issues that had hitherto seemed separate, foreign, and dangerous.

Appendix B: text by a speaker of German

An example of a more 'digressive' (German) text. The four categories 'Path and Organization', 'Definition of Terms', 'Discontinuity' and 'Digressiveness' are indicated by footnotes. M. Heiberg, Insiders/outsiders: Basque nationalism, *Archives Européennes de Sociologie* 16 (1975), 169–71.

The material which I will try to analyse is largely historical and relates to the initial period of Basque nationalism at the turn of the last century. Moreover, the historical material will be presented only cursorily since the main emphasis on the paper is theoretical. It is believed that the Basque nationalism of today is incomprehensible if there is no theoretical understanding of the factors which led to its emergence in the 1890s. Furthermore, this paper does not purport to prove its conclusions. It is rather a tentative exploration of one theoretical line which may or may not eventually be useful. This paper is divided into three sections. The first section presents the historical material. The second will give an analysis of the specific character of Basque nationalism. By modifying the theory of Ernst Gellner and illustrating it with the Basque material, the third part will attempt to put nationalism into a general theoretical framework.[1]

I

As a preliminary to any study of the Basques, and especially to a study of Basque nationalism, the crucial position of the Basque *fueros*, or local privileges, must be discussed. These *fueros* were the foundation of Basque social, political and economic life from the twelfth and thirteenth century when they were first formulated until 1840 when they were finally revoked. As a symbol of Basque autonomy, the return of the *fueros* has always constituted a major demand of the Basque nationalists. On one level, the *fueros* were charters granted in the Middle Ages to particular Basque provinces and regions allowing local autonomy in return for political allegiance to the kings of Spain or the kings of France. The privileges granted by the *fueros* enabled the Basques to have their own courts, parliament, coinage, militia, customs boundaries and to be free from outside taxation. Moreover, the ordinances of the *fueros* covered nearly every aspect of Basque life from marriage and dowry to inheritance and political participation. Most importantly, the *fueros* guaranteed that the Basques were not to be integrated into either France or Castile.

But the full significance of the *fueros* extends even deeper than this. When the *fueros* are referred to in documents, the phrase *fueros, buenos usos y costumbres* ('fueros, good practices and customs') is almost always used. The *fueros* when first granted did not introduce unfamiliar innovations into the Basque provinces, but rather they molded and made formal the existing institutions of the time. As one author has put it, the *fueros* were 'first customs and later law', and as such were derived from the very fabric of the social structure itself. The *fueros* were formed to fit and protect the needs of a rural society whose social outlook in the main was one of peasant egalitarianism.[2] However, existing in enclosed pockets within this rural society from the thirteenth century onwards were urban, mercantile centers. Compressing drastically, the opposition between urban and rural gave rise to a fierce antagonism marked at times by bloody demonstrations. It was a duality of 'open land', *la tierra liena*, against closed, walled cities whose influence and power were gradually increasing. As a result two political apparatuses developed; one fitted to a prosperous rural people and the other adjusted to the needs of a mercantile class of traders. The conflict of interests which developed between the urban centers and rural areas became a crucial factor in the Carlist wars.

The Carlist wars

To attempt to understand the Carlism of the 19th century which was nominally a doctrine concerning the rightful heir to the Spanish throne, it is essential to understand the Liberalism that was so popular in certain political and social circles at the time; and what this Spanish Liberalism signified to the prosperous, rural Basques. Furthermore, the fanatical Carlism of Navarra which was centered around the religious reunification of Spain must be distinguished from the more pragmatic Carlism of Vizcaya and Guipuzcoa which revolved around the preservation of the *fueros*. Before we start, however, it might be useful to examine very briefly two topics; the rural conditions of the Basques, and the differences between the four Spanish Basque provinces.[3]

As Gerald Brenan has put it, rainfall is a critical factor in Spain, and in the Basque provinces rainfall is ample. An even distribution of resources combined with regular rainfall produced in the Basque provinces a large and prosperous yeoman class. Agrarian reformers attributed the prosperity of the Basque countryside to the *caserio*, the rural, self-sufficient farmstead, which is the most prominent feature of the Basque rural landscape. The *caserio*, the concrete symbol of the Basque family, was founded on the small landholding which consisted of about ten to fifteen hectares. The *caserio* was an autonomous and self-supporting unit. Social and economic links between *caserios* were weak. Augmenting this system of small farms were communal forest and grazing lands which played an indispensable role in maintaining the general affluence of the Basques. In the Basque region a person's first loyalty was always directed toward the farmstead rather than toward a village which in the Spanish sense hardly existed.

But this view of the typical Basque countryside based on the *caserio* was by and large confined to Guipuzcoa and Vizcaya. In Alava and parts of Navarra the land is dryer, villages tend to replace farmhouses as the focal points, the presence of a landed gentry as evidenced by castles and fortresses is a more marked feature, and the Spanish crops of vines and wheat become more prominent. Some differences between the four provinces can be traced to geographical factors. Vizcaya and Guipuzcoa have been isolated from the rest of Spain by the Cantabrian mountain range; and historically have been more oriented toward the sea and the rest of Europe. Navarra, on the other hand, is cut off from France by the Pyrenees on one side, is separated from Guipuzcoa and Vizcaya by the Cantabrian, and merges with Aragon to the south. Alava, landlocked like Navarra, blends gradually into Old Castile, and has the climate and appearance of the Castilian *meseta*. Of further note is the fact that both Navarra and Alava have remained, unlike the two other Basque provinces, almost completely rural and isolated from industrial centers until the last ten to fifteen years.[4]

Having said this much we can now turn our attention to the opposed ideologies of Liberalism and Carlism . . . (Continuation of note 3.)

Notes to Appendix B

1. Example of 'Path and Organization'. The author indicates and explicitly outlines the conceptual structuring of the text.
2. Example of 'Definition of Terms'. The term 'fueros', an understanding of which is, according to the author, crucial for the ensuing discussion, is worked into the main argument while at the same time defined.
3. Example of 'Discontinuity'. The argument (related to Carlism and Liberalism) is left unfinished for the time being and taken up again later in the text.
4. Example of 'Digressiveness'. The main argument (see preceding note) is abandoned. Instead the author inserts a segment on a topic ('rural conditions of the Basques' and 'differences between the four Basque provinces') which at this stage of the discussion is peripheral to the main argument. Also note that the author seems to be well aware of the less 'linear' nature of this segment, as it is pragmatically marked ('Before we start, however, it might be useful to examine . . . ').

13

Judging the facts: an analysis of one text in its institutional context

Michael Stubbs

Originally published in M. Stubbs, *Text and Corpus Analysis* (Blackwell, 1996).

There are no brute facts. (Firth, 1957, p. 29)

There is a great field for practical semantics in the contextualization of crucial words in judicial remarks and judgements. (Firth, 1935, p. 69)

In this paper I discuss various principles which underlie people's interpretation of language, especially language which is ambiguous and complex. My examples are from language in courtrooms, where such interpretation can have important consequences. The courtroom examples, and all the illustrative examples, are mainly authentic, attested 'real' language. Occasionally it has been convenient to modify (for example, to abbreviate) or invent an example. The following conventions are used to mark the source of examples:

[A]   actual, authentic, attested data
[M]   modified data
[I]   invented, intuitive, introspective data

Organization of the paper

I discuss several examples from the large literature on legal language, especially examples concerning the connotations which words can convey. Other examples are then taken from the transcript of a judge's summing-up (about 5,800 words) at the end of a criminal trial. I have selected for analysis four linguistic features which are widely discussed in general textual studies or in studies of courtroom language: modal verbs (used ambiguously in English to express possibility or permission), presuppositions (central to the representation of innocence or guilt), syntactic complexity (relevant to the comprehensibility of spoken language) and the connotations of individual lexical items. Comparative data on the individual lexical items are drawn from a corpus of 120 million words of written and spoken English. Concordances are used to show patterns of language use: the technique involves using a computer program to locate every occurrence of a target word in a corpus together with the words that occur on either side of it.

The main purpose of the analysis is to discuss whether lexical and grammatical features of a judge's style could influence a jury. That is, could linguistic factors affect a legal decision? I cannot prove that a jury did interpret a summing-up in a particular way: I cannot look inside their minds. But I can attempt to show that patterns of language are likely to be interpreted in a certain way, because that is how they are likely to be interpreted in everyday life. The linguist has to try and show how a reasonable person, doing his or her best to understand, is likely to interpret language.

I will show that, while the summing-up is very careful and explicit about some aspects of the jury's required decision, there are nevertheless instances where the language is unclear. A basic principle of the analysis presented here is that meanings are conveyed not only by individual words and their combination in sentences, but also by patterns of discourse and by breaks in those patterns.

The transcript of the judge's summing-up is from a case in which I was employed as an expert witness to prepare a report for a hearing in the Appeals Court. The defendant had been found guilty, and had appealed on the grounds that the summing-up had been biased against him.[1] The use of linguistic analysis in the courtroom provides striking examples of linguistics being applied to important social issues, often in circumstances where the outcome of the analysis could have considerable practical consequences, especially for a defendant (for example, Atkinson and Drew (1979), Berg-Seligson (1990), Harris (1984a, b), Levi (1992), O'Barr (1981, 1982), Walter (1988); see further Stubbs (1996: 122–4)). When linguistic analysis is applied in such circumstances, the standards of proof attainable in text analysis require a very careful statement.

In addition, courtroom language provides striking examples of the mediation of reality by language. It is a commonplace to lawyers that criminal cases are not tried on the 'facts', but on the spoken testimony of witnesses. The only access which the jury, judge and lawyers have to the facts is via the accounts which different witnesses give, and there are always at least two competing versions of these facts, from prosecution and defence.

Interactions in social institutions

Much discourse analysis studies face-to-face casual conversation between social equals, since this is arguably the most frequent and most basic kind of social interaction. However, many of the interactions which are crucial to people's lives take place within social institutions – such as schools and universities, doctors' surgeries and hospitals, police stations and courtrooms – where very different language conventions operate. And much of this talk, in meetings, examinations (of many kinds), consultations, interviews, negotiations and so on, has the purpose of reaching a decision.

In such settings, the Gricean cooperative principle (Grice, 1967/1975) may not always hold. There may be confrontation and conflict, as well as cooperation. This is the case in the courtroom, where Gricean maxims (be truthful be informative, be relevant, be clear) are supplemented by other conventions.

There is an increasing amount of such institutionalized discourse in modern highly industrialized societies. And it is within such institutions that strangers, from different social classes and language backgrounds, are in interaction with each other. There are therefore likely to be misunderstandings in precisely those encounters which lead to important decisions in people's lives.

The linguistic encoding of facts

In a court of law, the utmost social significance of language is evident. Language is action, and under certain circumstances, speech acts themselves may be criminal acts: consider slander, libel and defamation, threats, blackmail, bribery or perjury (Kniffka, 1981; Shuy, 1993). But speech acts in the courtroom itself are also social action. For example, a defendant's *admission* of guilt will have real consequences. And the *verdict* given by a jury and the judge's *sentencing* are speech acts in the strong sense of utterances which create a state of affairs in the world.

Furthermore, courtrooms are highly institutionalized and depend on special rules of language use: not only elaborate forms of address and ultra-politeness (such as *M'Lud, My Learned Friend*), but rules restricting leading questions (in examination-in-chief, though not in cross-examination) and restricting what may be said (for example, rules about hearsay evidence). Such rules may be at variance with everyday conversation. For example, it is common for casual conversation to consist of repeating and commenting on what other people have said: witnesses in a trial are not allowed to repeat such hearsay evidence, and many witnesses find this restriction difficult to understand and very difficult to obey.

A trial is aimed at resolving a dispute between two versions of reality, and language counts for everything. In the British adversarial or accusatorial system (sometimes also called the sporting theory of justice), truth is expected to emerge from opposing representations. The defence and prosecution prepare their cases separately and in secret, and resolving the conflicting accounts depends largely on the linguistic skills of those involved on the day in question. Very little is cut and dried beforehand, since no independent legal mind has looked at the case as a whole before the trial (Berlins and Dyer, 1989, p. 125). Witnesses and lawyers attempt to present, in the language they use, an unambiguous definition of past events. And what the jury (and others) have access to is not the facts themselves, but multiple definitions of the facts expressed in language: a case is always tried on facts as they are made to appear in testimony. For a jury, the crucial courtroom audience, it is therefore not possible to separate what happened from the words used to talk about it (O'Barr, 1982, p. 97, provides a good statement of these points).

Furthermore, the presentation of these versions is carried out at an abstract and formalized level. There are various links in the chain which the jury does not see, since the defendant will have instructed solicitors who have in turn instructed barristers. The lawyers themselves also have no access to the facts except via their interviews with their client and possibly other people involved. And, in the court itself, the plaintiff and defendant are not allowed to confront each other directly. Their versions are presented via barristers to the judge and jury, with many constraints on the permitted form of evidence. In American courts, members of the jury are forbidden to make independent visits to the scene of an incident: they may consider only facts as they are presented in court (O'Barr, 1982, p. 42), and this is generally also true of cases in Britain.

The underlying propositional structure of all the discourse in a jury trial, even if it lasts days, weeks or months, is very simple. There are just two conflicting propositions:

> The prosecution says: "You did it."
> The defence says: "No, I didn't."

This is a very clear case of the linguistic and social construction of reality. A jury always has to contend with conflicting versions of reality, at least two, from the prosecution and the defence, but possibly many more. The evidence is mainly what witnesses say in the witness box (and also what expert witnesses may have reported in writing). And at the end of a trial, the closing speeches from prosecuting and defending counsel and the judge's summing-up are further interpretations of these interpretations, conflicting summaries of original testimony and so on.

The basic discourse sequence of a jury trial (at least the parts which take place in the presence of the jury), which shows the sequence of conflicting versions of events, is as follows:

The jury are sworn in.

The Clerk of Court reads the indictment and says: 'To those charges the defendant has pleaded not guilty, and it is your task to say whether he (or she) is guilty or not guilty.'

Prosecuting counsel's opening speech.

Evidence.

Prosecuting counsel's examination of witness.

Defending counsel's cross-examination of witness.

Prosecuting counsel's re-examination of witness.

Repeated for witnesses 1 to n . . .

'That is the case for the prosecution.'

Defending counsel's opening speech.

Defending counsel's examination of witness.

Prosecuting counsel's cross-examination of witness.

Defending counsel's re-examination of witness.

Usually starting with the defendant, then repeated for witnesses 1 to *n* . . .

'That is the case for the defence.'

End of evidence.

Prosecuting counsel's closing speech.

Defending counsel's closing speech.

Judge's summing-up.

The jury retire to consider their verdict, then return, and the foreman/woman gives the verdict.

If guilty:

Prosecuting counsel's presentation of defendant's 'antecedents': personal details and previous convictions, if any.

Defending counsel's plea in mitigation.

Judge's sentence.

There can be variations on the pattern: for example, there may be more than one barrister on each side; defence counsel usually does not make an opening speech unless the case is complex; prosecuting and defending counsel do not always cross-examine and re-examine; the judge may ask questions, and so may the jury in written form.

Because the law relies on interpretations of language, the standards by which words are interpreted are inevitably different for the legal profession and the lay public, and it is inevitable that judge and jury will use language differently. People interpret discourse according to their own conventions, and it is therefore very likely that the jury are not always able to suspend their common-sense interpretations of language in ways the court may require of them. This is another potential source of misunderstandings.

Words and connotations

It is a general principle of language use that the same event can be referred to in an indefinitely large number of ways. If witnesses or counsel talk about events using certain terms, it is likely that the jury will also use these terms to think about them.

Danet (1980) analyses an American case where a doctor carried out a late abortion which led to his being convicted of manslaughter, and where vocabulary was an explicit concern in the trial itself. In such a case, one might say: *the fetus was aborted* or *the baby was murdered*. Although each phrase can be used to refer to the same external reality, very different moral points of view are encoded, and different assumptions about offence and guilt are implied. During the trial, the lawyers negotiated the different connotations of terms such as *products of conception, fetus, male human being, male child, baby boy* (and many others). When, as here, the meaning of an act is itself ambiguous (When does life begin? What do we mean by a person?), then it is impossible to separate what happened from the language used to talk about it. And such semantic choices, with their presuppositions, are crucial to the outcome of the trial: if no person existed, then no man-slaughter could have occurred.

There is always a category shift when one moves from ways of talking to ways of thinking. And it is impossible to discover what effect such lexical choices actually had on the jury. But one can analyse the points of view from which such lexical choices are made, the incommensurable frames of reference they assume and the presuppositions they make. For example, *baby boy* connotes helplessness, in a caring frame of reference which presupposes that there is a life to be ended. Words such as *fetus, abortion* and *termination* assume a medical frame of reference, rather than a criminal one. No terms are neutral. Choice of words expresses an ideological position.

In a much cited experiment, relevant to courtroom cases, Loftus and Palmer (1974) provide empirical evidence that lexical choices can influence perception and memory. They showed people a film of a traffic accident, and then asked questions such as *How fast were the cars going when they hit each other?* But they varied the question by using different verbs, and this influenced people's estimates of the speed. Higher estimates were given with verbs such as SMASH and COLLIDE than with BUMP and CONTACT. Furthermore, when they were asked *Did you see any broken glass?* (there was none in the film), people who had been asked about the cars *smashing* into each other were more likely to say "yes". That is, using the word SMASH triggered preconceptions both about speed and about likely consequences (broken glass). Individual words evoked a frame of reference in which various assumptions were made.

In this experimental case, subjects had direct access to the event itself, in the form of the film, yet language still influenced their perception and memory. In a real trial the jury have no such access: they have nothing but the words used in the courtroom, which makes it even more plausible that words will influence assumptions.

Such connotations can be seen in characteristic collocates (words which habitually co-occur). In a 120 million word corpus, I studied the collocates of the simple past tense forms in the semantic field of "hit". HIT itself has a wide range of uses, often metaphorical and/or in fixed phrases (*hit for six, hit rock bottom*). Collocates show this wide range:

> areas, badly, bottom, car, earthquake, flooding, hard, hardest, jackpot, recession, sales, six, target

BUMP has connotations of clumsiness. *Bumped* collocates with

> accidentally, car, head, lurched, stumbled

COLLIDE is used predominantly with large vehicles. *Collided* collocates with

> aircraft, car, jet, lorry, mid-air, plane, ship, tanker, train, trawler, vehicle

SMASH has connotations of crime and violence. *Smashed* collocates with

> bottles, broke, bullet, car(s), glass(es), looted, police, windscreen, window(s)

STRIKE has more metaphorical uses or is used with natural disasters. *Struck* collocates with

> blow, disaster, earthquake, lightning, tragedy

The data

I will now take examples from the summing-up by the judge at the end of a case of assault occasioning actual bodily harm. This is the technical name for an offence which can cover serious incidents, and can carry a prison sentence of up to five years (Clarkson, 1987, p. 119). In common-sense terms, the present case concerned a minor incident. One man was accused of hitting and slightly bruising another man, and the jury found the defendant guilty. Following O'Barr (1982), I will discuss whether apparently minor differences in presentational style may make major differences in the evaluation of accounts of events.

The data are the written transcript of the judge's spoken summing-up. During a trial, the judge takes detailed long-hand notes of testimony, and uses these notes to sum up at the end. Short-hand records and/or audio-recordings of everything that is said in court, including the summing-up, are made by official court reporters, and these can later be used to prepare transcripts. I have had no access to the testimony given in the case, and cannot therefore comment on the fairness of the summing-up in the sense of how accurately it summarizes what witnesses said. I can look only at internal features of the summing-up itself.

I also have no way of evaluating the accuracy of the transcript. Court reporters are supposed to transcribe verbatim what is said in court, but Walker (1990) studies how they transform in many ways what is said, by prescriptively tidying up features of normal spoken language. However, since it is the transcript itself which is considered in any appeal, that is what is relevant to my analysis here.

Analysis of the data

O'Barr (1982, pp. 16ff) provides good examples of legal language of various kinds. Some legal language is highly formal. Examples from the summing-up include

> a material inconsistency; learned defence Counsel

It is also often repetitive. Examples from the data include

> wholly separate and distinct; you and you alone; thinks or seems to think; well and good; the first and most important; honest and genuine mistakes; a statement or statements; unless and until; untruthful and deliberate lying, reliability and accuracy; how far you can or ought to or do rely

Some examples are tautologies: lying is, by definition, untruthful and deliberate. But such pairs or lists of near synonyms are a common general characteristic of legal English. Compare well known examples such as without let or hindrance; null and void; to have and to hold; each and every; breaking and entering; rest residue and remainder

These double or triple constructions derive partly from early legal English, where French/Latin and Anglo-Saxon terms were used alongside each other. Clerks were not sure if the terms meant the same, so they put in both for safety, on the belt and braces principle (O'Barr, 1982, p. 16).

However, on occasion, the judge uses doublets or triplets where the words do differ significantly in meaning:

intentionally or recklessly applied *unlawful* force
unlawful and *intentional or reckless* application of force

These are everyday words, but they have technical legal meanings which are discussed at length in books on law. For example, Clarkson (1987, pp. 58ff, 64ff) discusses: *intentional, malicious, negligent* and *reckless* (as in *reckless driving*). But the judge gives no warning to the jury that they have technical meanings: they may assume that this is part of his stylistic habit of being verbose. On the other hand, it would be dangerous if their meaning in the law departed too far from everyday meanings, since it is juries of ordinary men and women who have to interpret such phrases. Jury cases are designed for those who are not legally trained, and who are therefore dependent on everyday language and how it is understood.

Jurors also have to use common-sense reasoning to assess the credibility and plausibility of competing interpretations of events. (O'Barr (1982, pp. 42–6) discusses the centrality of such demeanour evidence, but the complete lack of guidelines to evaluate it.) In interpreting the summing-up, jury members will therefore be asking themselves, just as they do with everyday conversation: The judge said X, but what did he mean? What was he implying? Why did he phrase it in that way? What was he trying to tell us?

Counsel for the prosecution and defence give, in their closing speeches, accounts which are inevitably in opposition: interpretations which explicitly attempt to show the defendant in a bad or good light. But the judge's summing-up should be from an independent, impartial source. The judge's role is to decide legal issues, not to express views on the facts or on the witnesses, and certainly not on the result (Berlins and Dyer, 1989, pp. 102ff, Jones, 1983, pp. 121ff). In terms of content, a summing-up has essentially two parts: directions and explanations of the law, and a summary of the main points of evidence, concentrating on what is in dispute or seems contradictory. The judge is the judge of the law, and gives the jury directions on how they must interpret the law. If he or she gets this wrong, this could be the basis of an appeal. But the jury are the judges of the facts, and they must make inferences about who is to be believed about what happened. This basic distinction accounts both for things which a judge says and for the way in which they are said.

The judge in the present case made explicit to the jury several problematic aspects of language use in the courtroom. He drew the jury's attention to the inevitably selective nature of his summing-up. He recommended the jury to disregard his comments if they did not find them helpful. He directed the jury to disregard the content of what witnesses had previously said in statements to the police, even if this contradicts what they said in court. He distinguished between everyday interpretative principles (such as there's no smoke without fire) and the more rigorous interpretative principles required by the court. He directed the jury that, if they were not sure of the defendant's guilt, then they must find him not guilty. He commented on the technical, legal meaning of several terms. He repeated several times that it is for the prosecution to prove guilt, not for the defence to prove innocence. He pointed out that the defendant is inevitably under stress, and that this could affect his perceived credibility.

Some of these instructions, as the judge himself is pointing out, are at variance with how language is interpreted in everyday life. For example, it is probably a legal fiction that words can be 'struck from the record'. It is unlikely that a jury can simply forget some parts of what has been said to them. In fact, asking that they be ignored may, on the contrary, draw attention to them. So, the judge's remarks show that he is very sensitive to discrepancies between court procedures and everyday communication (O'Barr, 1982, pp. 6, 41, 94, 102).

Length and discourse markers
The summing-up covers 11 pages of official transcript: about 5,850 words. It probably took between 35 and 45 minutes to deliver. The jury could not possibly have retained all the details, and would therefore be susceptible to overall impressions created by the language used. Many research studies have been done on lectures (which are typically similar in length to this summing-up): Bligh (1972) reviews over 60 studies on how successfully listeners can retain material presented as lectures. One finding (Bligh, 1972; Beard, 1972) is that listeners' attention is typically high at the beginning of a lecture, and falls, with local peaks and troughs, until just before the end, when it rises somewhat. In addition, audiences experience micro-sleeps which result in temporary complete loss of attention.

The judge is doubtless aware of this, and marks the beginning of sections in his summing-up, to attract the attention of the jury to significantly new points, usually by saying: *Well, members of the jury . . . .* Such markers are, however, less frequent in the second half of the summing-up, when the jury's attention is likely to be flagging. The two cases which do occur in the second half both preface comments on alleged inconsistencies in the defence testimony. The judge marks clearly when he is coming to the end:

Well, members of the jury, there we are. At the end of the day, . . .

The jury are most likely to have retained points made at the beginning, after such markers of discourse organizations, and right at the end, when they realize the concluding points are being made.

Connotations of individual words
The case involved two men. It was not in dispute who was involved, but only whether or not one had struck the other. Words which convey connotations of emotion or violence are therefore particularly relevant to interpretations of conflicting testimony.

The words *aggravate, aggravated, annoyed, irritation, mad* and *temper* occurred several times (see Concordance 1). Such repetition is likely to make an idea salient for the jury. A similar case occurs with *reeled* (quoted from a prosecution witness): this occurs several times (see Concordance 1), with reference to the plaintiff falling backward after he had been allegedly assaulted by the defendant. The word carries an implication that the plaintiff was struck or pushed, and/or became giddy, etc., and is likely to be remembered by the jury, both because of the repetition and because it paints a small dramatic picture. The verb has connotations of staggering, unsteadiness, dizziness, jerky movements, and of violence and disaster.

Examples [all A] from a general corpus show that the word connotes confusion and/or violence due to some outside force:

sends the pulse racing and the senses reeling

reeling from shock

blood trickled into his mouth as he reeled backward

bashing X on the ear and sending him reeling backward

the man was reeling drunk

the markets reeled under the uncertainty

the shipping industry is still reeling from last March's Exxon Valdez disaster

I also checked the most frequent and typical collocates of REEL in a large (120 million word) corpus, using methods discussed in detail in Stubbs 1996: 172–6. These connotations are confirmed by characteristic collocates of the word forms *reeled* and *reeling*. (I omitted *reel* and *reels* to avoid irrelevant phrases such as *Scottish reel* and *reels of cotton*.) The collocates included

blow, blows, drunk, mind, senses, send, sent, shock

Modal verbs
Meanings are conveyed not only by individual words, but by patterns of words used by a speaker. Words take part of their meaning from the context in which they occur.

Concordance 2 provides a concordance of all examples of the words *may* and *might* (24 plus 7 instances). The majority occur in phrases such as:

you may think (that)	12 instances
you may feel (that)	2 instances
you may remember	2 instances
you may/might find	3 instances
you may/might ask/say to yourselves	4 instances

Because it is the jury who are the judges of the facts, and because therefore the judge cannot pass judgement on those facts, it is almost inevitable that a summing-up will contain phrases of the kind *you may think, . . . and it is entirely for you to decide . . .* [A], when discussing inconsistences in testimony. However, the modal verb *may* is ambiguous in English. It can denote permission (*you may go now: I've finished* [I]), or possibility (*he may go,*

All personal and place names have been changed in these data.
Mr P = plaintiff. Mr D = defendant.
Mr DWA = defence witness A, etc.

ar what was said. I saw Mr D lift his arm up and the other man reeled, his hat fell off and he fell against the wall." Mr D seems to have gesticulated. "I think his hand caught Mr P because he reeled. He did catch him. Mr P reeled against the wall." Now, his hand caught Mr P because he reeled. He did catch him. Mr P reeled against the wall." Now, members of the jury, it was put to tep and went backwards towards the shop, P was in the mews and reeled around saying, "I've been hit, I've been hit." I said, "Don't t. What else would I do with it? The man was clearly trying to aggravate me. He didn't aggravate me at all." And then Mr D with it? The man was clearly trying to aggravate me. He didn't aggravate me at all." And then Mr D said this, and you may it was perhaps a rather curious answer for somebody who wasn't aggravated at all. Taking off Mr P's hat, he said, "It was my way s was this just the last straw for Mr D? Had he been wound up, aggravated as he put it, by Mr P and did he lose his temper and he said, "It was my way of showing that I wasn't particularly annoyed." Now, you're going to have to ask yourselves was knock his hat off when striking Mr P's head in an explosion of irritation over this petty matter? "P was walking out and I was u are satisfied so that you are sure that this man allowed his irritation to boil over and he lost control of himself and struck to have their special little bin and it has been driving Mr D mad for a long time that everybody roundabout uses it as if it were wound up, aggravated as he put it, by Mr P and did he lose his temper and knock his hat off when striking Mr P's

Concordance 1 REEL, AGGREGATE, etc. in Judge's summing-up

evidence to remind you of what was said here. When I sum up may very well make comments upon the evidence. If you agree that resulted in bruising. That is what it comes dow to, you may think. That is the prosecution's case. And let me make this hat is no offence and the verdict is not guilty. However, Mr P may have suffered an injury, whether because he was shocked by it the defence, not for the defence to prove its case. An you may think that there are three different types of witnesses. The e doctor. He examined me." Well, there was some confusion, you may think, as to whether Mr P spoke just to Mrs PWA or to some that is a material inconsistency, pay attention to it, but you may think really it doesn't matter a great deal. She said, "I . I saw Mr P sway and fall against the wall of the close." You may think this is a rather more emphatic description of her evi in her statement. The reason I remind you of this is that you may feel that this helps you in deciding whether there might have n Mrs PWA and Mr P to trump up a case against Mr D because you may think to yourselves, if there was such a conspiracy, one thing Mr interviewing Mr DWA and Mr DWB, the defence witnesses, and you may think that there is some force in this criticism, that a thorough right eye. And, members of the jury, one of the questions you may care to ask yourselves is this: if Mr D did not cause any y ed when I give evidence on oath." That is the first point. You may also take it into account as part of the evidence as a whole b side him and said nothing because there was no point." And you may remember that is rather different from what his Counsel sug didn't aggravate me at all." And then Mr D said this, and you may think it was perhaps a rather curious answer for somebody nce to swearing and so forth. And then Mr D was asked what you may think a pertinent question: "Well, why didn't you tell that to th ver made by Mr D to any bad language by the defendant, and you may ask yourselves if this was the reason why Mr D returned the Land Rover and was carrying a computer to the shop which, you may remember, was totally different from what both Mr D and Mr bin, but they take no notice." Then he said this which is, you may think, a quite significant and important piece of evidence: Mr laughing and continued working." And, members of the jury, you may think that is slightly different from the general picture given b the end of the day, if you think that is what happened or what may have happened – because it is not for this defendant to prove ause it is not for this defendant to prove his innocence; what may have happened is that the defendant just removed Mr P's hat if you are satisfied so that you are sure as to that, then you may feel that the prosecution has proved its case and it will be number, either a lady or a man, who acts as your foreman. You may find it very helpful for you to appoint a foreman at the er, guilty or not guilty, on which you are all agreed, and you may think that in this case you will be able to do so. However, ct according to the evidence and that is the true verdict. You might find yourselves in the opposite frame of mind. You might . You might find yourselves in the opposite frame of mind. You might say to yourselves, "We are satisfied so that we are sure that circumstances, no problem – verdict, decision not guilty. You might find yourselves, however, somewhere in between. You You might find yourselves, however, somewhere in between. You might say to yourselves, "Well, maybe he's guilty and maybe he ou come to the conclusion that that is what did happen or what might have happened – because it is not for Mr D to prove that that n a review of all the evidence, that all this defendant did or might have done was simply thumb and forefinger to lift off Mr hat you may feel that this helps you in deciding whether there might have been a conspiracy between Mrs PWA and Mr P to *or he may not* [I]). Further, it is well known that there is significant social class variation in speaker's uses of modal verbs. *May* is largely restricted to middle class Anglo-English (e.g. Brown and Miller, 1980).

In the following cases, *may* is used as a true modal of possibility. Mr P is the plaintiff. Mr D is the defendant.

Mr P *may* have suffered an injury . . . because . . .

but *you may think* really it doesn't matter a great deal

that is what happened or what *may* have happened . . . what *may* have happened is . . .

In one case, the judge expresses a proposition in the *may*-clause, and then denies it:

you may think that x, . . . but the fact is that y

In one case, it is unclear whether the intended interpretation is *may* of permission ("this would be permissible evidence") or *may* of possibility ("it is possible that x"):

you may also take it into account

But in the majority of cases there seems to be no tentativeness intended at all. In these cases, *may* is used without its literal meanings of permission or possibility:

when I sum up I *may very well* make some comments upon the evidence

It is surely certain that he will.

what the Crown has to prove is x . . . that is what it comes down to, *you may think*

In context, this seems a definitive summary of the essential issue.

you may think that there are three different types of witnesses

The categorization which follows seems comprehensive.

there was some confusion, *you may think*, as to . . .

In context, it seems clear that there was.

In several cases, because of the evaluative adjectives and adverbs (italicized), the judge appears to be telling the jury what he himself thinks:

you may think this is a *rather more emphatic* description

you may think it was perhaps a *rather curious* answer

Mr D was asked what *you may think* a *pertinent* question

which is, *you may think*, a *quite significant and important* piece of evidence
and, members of the jury, *you may think* that is *slightly different*

(These adverb–adjective constructions seem to me to have middle class connotations, but I admit I have no corpus evidence of this.)

In contrast to *may*, all occurrences of *might* are genuine modals of possibility (see again Concordance 2). This is further evidence that *may* is used in a different way.

In summary, because of the structure of a summing-up, phrases such as *you may think* almost inevitably occur frequently. However,

- *may* occurs only in some social dialects of British English;
- it has two main meanings, permission and possibility;
- it is used in different senses in the summing-up;
- it sometimes signals possibility, but more often, it signals what the judge himself thinks.

The last case occurs because a pattern is established within the summing-up: the pattern has a micro-history in the text and becomes part of the judge's style. Uncertain instances are likely to be interpreted in line with the pattern. Thus, the implication of phrases such as *you may think that x* can become: "it would be reasonable or natural for you to think that x, (or even) I am instructing you to accept that x".

A key instance is therefore a comment towards the end of the summing-up:

> *you may feel* that the prosecution has proved its case

I comment further on this example below.

Presuppositions
In discussions of guilt and innocence, presuppositions about the defendant's actions and emotions are important to the messages conveyed. I use the term *presuppositions* in a linguistic, not psychological, sense. I cannot know what was in the judge's mind, but I can identify presuppositions in the words he used. It would then be natural for a jury to conclude that these presuppositions were actually held by the judge. If, for example, I say

> John's brother has been abroad for years [I]

then my sentence presupposes that "John has a brother". And it would be natural for you to conclude that I actually believe that he has a brother.

In simple cases, a test for presupposition is that it remains constant in negative or interrogative versions of the clause. Consider this example: the first version is attested (but see below) in the summing-up.

> this man allowed his irritation to boil over [A]
> this man did not allow his irritation to boil over [M]
> did this man allow his irritation to boil over? [M]

All three versions presuppose that "this man was irritated". The attested version further asserts that "he allowed his irritation to boil over".

Almost any sentence at all contains presuppositions, usually several. But the following are cases where presuppositions imply that the defendant is guilty of an offence, and that this is a natural thing to think or is taken for granted. I identify presuppositions in the italicized sections of the judge's remarks [all A], and make them explicit between double quote marks. Mr D is the defendant.

Some presuppositions are conveyed by tense forms of the verb, as in

it has been *driving Mr D mad for a long time* (presupposition: "Mr D has been mad/annoyed for a long time, and is still mad/annoyed")

or by individual verbs, as in

had he [Mr D] been . . . aggravated *as he put it?* (presuppositions: "Mr D has said he was aggravated")

what Mr D *admits* is that he did it twice (presupposition: "Mr D did something wrong and/or he did something which he or someone else had previously denied")

he [the defendant] *starts off* entitled to be believed (presupposition: "the situation then changes")

Contrast a formulation such as *He is entitled to be believed* [I], which would convey no such presupposition.

Sometimes the presuppositions are difficult to interpret, because they are embedded in hypothetical constructions. A fuller context for the first example above is

but on the other hand if you are satisfied so that you are sure that this man allowed his irritation to boil over . . . [A]

The presupposition is embedded under the projecting clause *you are sure that.*

any offence, *let alone one as unpleasant as this*

The presupposition ("an unpleasant offence has occurred") is embedded under the hypothetical *any.*

he is likely to be convicted of *this assault upon that old man*

whether it is likely that a person with such a character would have committed *this offence*

The presuppositions ("an assault on that old man occurred"; and "this offence occurred") are embedded under projecting clauses containing a hypothetical *likely.*

Such presuppositions are crucial in the present case, since what is at stake is the definition of certain events. If it is assumed that an act did occur, and was thereby an offence, then there is only one possible actor.

Syntactic complexity
O'Barr (1981, p. 395; 1982, p. 27) discusses American research on jury instructions which shows that they are 'poorly understood by most jurors'. In particular, he discusses one syntactic construction as 'the basis of the incomprehensibility of typical jury instructions'. Most sentences in English have the main verb early, followed by qualifying clauses. Sentences which consist of complex qualifying clauses, followed by the main verb, are more difficult to understand.

Consider this example from the summing-up:

> . . . a verdict of guilty . . . *and* that is the true verdict

This occurs at the end of a complex sequence of qualifying clauses, concerning hypothetical states of affairs:

> if you are in that state of mind, then, although obviously it is unpleasant to find any fellow human being guilty of any offence, let alone one as unpleasant as this, it will be your duty to return a *verdict of guilty* because you have sworn to return a true verdict according to the evidence *and that is the true verdict* [A, italicization added]

In outline, the sequence is:

> if you [the jury] are in that state of mind
> then, although *a*
> let alone *b*
> it will be your duty to *c* [main clause]
> because *d*
> and that is the true verdict [main clause]

In addition, the syntax is ambiguous. The final clause could be taken to mean: "the true verdict is guilty". The ambiguity results from the use of *and*, which stands in an unclear relation to the preceding conditional. (Contrast: "*If* you are in that state of mind, *then* that is the true verdict.")

Another case of syntactic ambiguity is this:

> however, Mr P may have suffered an injury . . . because he fell back and hurt himself

Again, the intended logical link with the preceding point is unclear. Is the judge directing the jury that if this is what happened, then this *would* count as assault, or *would not*? This point seems crucial to the jury's decision. In this connection, the phrase *occasioning actual bodily harm* is used three times. Again, the implication of causality is unclear. It is unclear (to me) whether *occasioning*, in this technical phrase, is intended to include both direct and indirect causation. (In fact, the jury requested clarification from the judge on precisely this point about causation. The judge clarified that direct causation was meant.)

Almost the very last thing the judge says, before he refers to arrangements for lunch, and likely to be remembered for that reason alone, is

> *you may feel* that the prosecution has proved its case and it will be your distasteful duty to return a verdict of guilty

Again this occurs after a complex sequence of *if*-clauses:

> Well, members of the jury, there we are. At the end of the day, if you think that is what happened or what may have happened – because it is not for this defendant to prove his innocence; what may have happened is that the defendant just removed Mr P's hat by lifting it off between his thumb and forefinger and dropping it to the ground – verdict not guilty. But, on the other hand, if you are satisfied so that you are sure that this man allowed his

irritation to boil over and he lost control of himself and struck out at P's head, hitting his – knocking his hat off and then striking his head, and that resulted in that bruising about which we have heard, if you are satisfied so that you are sure as to that, then *you may feel that the prosecution has proved its case and it will be your distasteful duty to return a verdict of guilty* [italicization added]

Here the sequence is

at the end of the day, if you think *x*

because *a* . . .

what may have happened is *b* . . .

but . . . if you are satisfied that *c* and *d*

and that resulted in *e*

if you are satisfied so that you are sure as to that

then *you may feel* that . . .

The clauses also follow *you may feel*, as discussed above. It is therefore easy to interpret this as a direction or suggestion to the jury to find the defendant guilty.

Conclusion

Linguists should always be prepared to state what degree of confidence they have in their analyses, and this responsibility is particularly important when the analysis could have important social consequences. I will therefore draw attention to some aspects of my analysis.

I think it likely that members of the jury interpreted utterances in the summing-up in line with the interpretative principles which I have set out. In particular, features of the language are likely to have led the jury to believe (correctly or not) that the judge thought that the defendant was guilty, and that this was a natural thing to think.

I am very aware that there are many features of the data which I have not analysed. Even for a text as short as 5,000 words or so, there are no methods of comprehensive text analysis: a listing of all presuppositions in all clauses would be very many times longer than the original text, and less comprehensible. However, it is possible to select for analysis features (such as modal verbs) which many different studies have shown to convey important social meanings.

There are always interpretative jumps when one moves from ways of talking to ways of thinking, and from normal strategies of interpretation to actual interpretations of a given text: it is impossible to discover how a jury actually understood a given summing-up. However, I can identify principles and strategies (also demonstrated in other studies) which reasonable people will use, when they are trying to be cooperative and to understand what is being said to them.

Such analysis certainly involves selection, but it makes use of empirical evidence in other comparable studies. In addition, comparative corpus data can provide direct empirical evidence about the connotations of words. In other work (Stubbs 1996), I discuss methods of making more systematic comparisons between what occurs and what might be expected to occur, and between individual instances and norms.

This paper has provided examples, from one social context, of how language mediates our understanding of past events. Such mediation is very widespread. For example, historians also try to understand past events which can no longer be directly observed. Like participants in a courtroom, they have no unmediated access to the past, but must rely on contemporary witnesses and on various forms of documentation. Their primary sources of evidence are predominantly written documents (plus other forms of statistical material and so on). And secondary sources take the form of contemporary commentaries or more recent interpretations by other historians. (For detailed case studies on language and history see Corfield, 1991.)

Students will be able to think of many other cases where the 'same' past event is represented differently in different texts, such as history books for children of different ages, or newspapers of different political persuasions. Analyses could provide interesting student projects on how facts are represented in texts.

Note

My report was considred in the Court of Appeal, where it failed as a ground for appeal. The Lord Chief Justice ruled that 'what the meaning is of the language used by a learned Judge in the course of his directions to the jury is a matter for this Court to determine and is not a matter for any linguistic expert'.

References

Atkinson, M. and Drew, P. (1979) *Order in Court*, London: Macmillan.
Beard, R. (1972) *Teaching and Learning in Higher Education*, 2nd edn. Harmondsworth: Penguin.
Berg-Seligson, S. (1990) *The Bilingual Courtroom*, Chicago and London: University of Chicago Press.
Berlins, M. and Dyer, C. (1989) *The Law Machine*, 3rd edn. Harmondsworth: Penguin.
Bligh, D.A. (1972) *What's the Use of Lectures?*, 3rd edn. Harmondsworth: Penguin.
Brown, E.K. and Miller J. (1980) *The Syntax of Scottish English*, Report to Social Science Research Council.
Clarkson, C.M.V. (1987) *Understanding Criminal Law*, London: Fontana.
Corfield, P.J. (ed.) (1991) *Language, History and Class*, Oxford: Blackwell.
Danet, B. (1980) '"Baby" or "fetus": language and the construction of reality in a manslaughter trial', *Semiotica* 32(1–2): pp. 187–219.
Firth, J.R. (1935) 'The technique of semantics', *Transactions of the Philological Society*: pp. 36–72.
—— (1957) 'A synopsis of linguistic theory', 1930–1955, *Studies in Linguistic Analysis*, special volume (Philological Society): pp. 1–32.
Grice, H.P. (1967/1975) 'Logic and conversation', MS, Harvard University,

reprinted in P. Cole and J.L. Morgan, (eds.), *Syntax and Semantics*, III. New York: Academic Press: pp. 41–58.

Harris, S. (1984a) 'Questions as a mode of control in magistrates courts', *International Journal of the Sociology of Language* 49: pp. 5–27.

—— (1984b) 'The form and function of threats in court', *Language and Communication* 4(4): pp. 247–71.

Jones, A. (1983) *Jury Services*, London: Robert Hale.

Kniffka, H. (1981) 'Der Linguist als Gutachter bei Gericht', in G. Peuser and S. Winter, (eds.), *Angewandte Sprachwissenschaft: Grundfragen, Bereiche, Methoden*, Bonn: Bouvier: pp. 584–634.

Levi, J.N. (1992) 'On the adequacy of Illinois jury instructions for capital sentencing', paper presented to 1992 meeting of the Law and Society Association, Philadelphia.

Loftus, E.F. and Palmer, J.C. (1974) 'Reconstruction of automobile destruction: an example of the interaction between language and memory', *Journal of Verbal Learning and Verbal Behavior* 13: pp. 585–9.

O'Barr, W.M. (1981) 'The language of the law', in C.A. Ferguson and S. Brice Heath, (eds.), *Language in the USA*, Cambridge: Cambridge University Press: pp. 386–406.

—— (1982) *Linguistic Evidence: Language, Power and Strategy in the Courtroom*, London: Academic Press.

Shuy, R.W. (1993) *Language Crimes*, Oxford: Blackwell.

Stubbs, M. (1996) *Text and Corpus Analysis*, Oxford: Blackwell.

Walker, A.G. (1990) 'Language at work in the law', in J.N. Levi and A.G. Walker, (eds.), *Language in the Judicial Process*, New York and London: Plenum: pp. 203–44.

Walter, B. (1988) *The Jury Summation as Speech Genre*, Amsterdam and Philadelphia: Benjamins.

14

Principles of critical discourse analysis

Teun A. van Dijk

Originally published in a longer version in *Discourse & Society*, 4 (1993).

Introduction

This paper discusses some principles, aims and criteria of a 'critical' discourse analysis (CDA). It tries to answer (critical) questions such as 'What *is* critical discourse analysis (anyway)?', 'How is it different from other types of discourse analysis?', 'What are its aims, special methods, and especially what is its theoretical foundation?' Also, it acknowledges the need to examine, in rather practical terms, how one goes about doing a 'critical' analysis of text and talk.

In general, the answers to such questions presuppose a study of the relations between discourse, power, dominance, social inequality and the position of the discourse analyst in such social relationships. Since this is a complex, multidisciplinary – and as yet underdeveloped – domain of study, which one may call 'sociopolitical discourse analysis', only the most relevant dimensions of this domain can be addressed here.

Although there are many directions in the study and critique of social inequality, the way we approach these questions and dimensions is by focusing on *the role of discourse in the (re)production and challenge of dominance.* Dominance is defined here as the exercise of social power by elites, institutions or groups, that results in social inequality, including political, cultural, class, ethnic, racial and gender inequality. This reproduction process may involve such different 'modes' of discourse–power relations as the more or less direct or overt support, enactment, representation, legitimation, denial, mitigation or concealment of dominance, among others. More specifically, critical discourse analysts want to know what structures, strategies or other properties of text, talk, verbal interaction or communicative events play a role in these modes of reproduction.

This paper is biased in another way: we pay more attention to 'top–down' relations of dominance than to 'bottom–up' relations of resistance, compliance and acceptance. This does not mean that we see power and dominance merely as unilaterally 'imposed' on others. On the contrary, in many situations, and sometimes paradoxically, power and even power abuse may seem 'jointly produced', e.g. when dominated groups are persuaded, by whatever means, that dominance is 'natural' or otherwise legitimate. Thus, although an analysis of strategies of resistance and challenge is crucial for our understanding of actual power and dominance relations in society, and although such an analysis needs to be included in a broader theory of power, counter-power and discourse, our critical approach prefers to focus on the elites and their discursive strategies for the maintenance of inequality.

From a discourse analytical and sociopolitical point of view it is tempting to study the relations between discourse structures and power structures more or less directly. This will often be effective and adequate. For instance, we may assume that directive speech acts such as commands or orders may be used to enact power, and hence also to exercise and to reproduce dominance. Similarly, we may examine the style, rhetoric or meaning of texts for strategies that aim at the concealment of social power relations, for instance by playing down, leaving implicit or understating the responsible agency of powerful social actors in the events represented in the text.

However, the relationships involved and the conditions on reproduction are more complicated than that. For instance, social inequality, at the societal level, is not simply or always reproduced by individual (speech) acts such as commands. This may be obvious from commands appropriately and legitimately executed in relationships of more or less 'accepted' everyday power relations, such as those between parents and children, between superiors and subordinates, or between police officers and citizens. Hence, special social conditions must be satisfied for such discourse properties to contribute to the reproduction of dominance. The same is true for all other properties of text and talk, and hence for all text-context relations. Apparently, what is involved in dominance are questionable *conditions* of legitimacy or acceptability, including what is usually called 'abuse' of power, and especially also possibly negative *effects* of the exercise of power, namely social inequality.

Another major complication we must address is the fact that typical macro-notions such as group or institutional power and dominance, as well as social inequality, do not directly relate to typical micro-notions such as text, talk or communicative interaction. This not only involves the well-known problem of macro–micro relations in sociology, but also, and perhaps even more interestingly, the relation between society, discourse and social cognition. Indeed, we argue that in order to relate discourse and society, and hence discourse and the reproduction of dominance and inequality, we need to examine in detail the role of social representations in the minds of social actors. More specifically, we hope to show that social cognition is the necessary theoretical (and empirical) 'interface', if not the 'missing link', between discourse and dominance. In our opinion, neglect of such social cognitions has been one of the major theoretical shortcomings of most work in critical linguistics and discourse analysis.

This paper does not discuss the historical backgrounds and developments of critical perspectives in the study of language, discourse and communication. Nor does it provide a full bibliography of such work. Depending on the discipline, orientation, school or paradigm involved, these lines of development are traced back, if not – as usual – to Aristotle, then at least to the philosophers of the Enlightenment or, of course, to Marx, and more recently to the members of the Frankfurt School (Adorno, Benjamin and others) and its direct or indirect heirs in and after the 1960s, among whom Jürgen Habermas plays a primary role (Geuss, 1981; Jay, 1973; Slater, 1977). Another line of influence and development, also more or less (neo-) marxist, is the one going back to Gramsci, and his followers in France and the UK, including most notably Stuart Hall and the other members of the Centre for Contemporary Cultural Studies (Corcoran, 1989; Hall, 1981). Likewise, first in France, later also in the UK and the USA, we can trace the influence of the work of Althusser (1971), Foucault (see, e.g., Foucault, 1980) and Pêcheux (1982), among others. Finally, we should emphasize the exemplary role of feminist scholarship in the critical approach to language and communication (for a bibliography, see Thorne et al., 1983).

Although often dealing with 'language', 'text' or 'discourse' in many (usually rather philosophical) ways, most of this work does not explicitly and systematically deal with discourse structures. We had to wait for the various contributions in critical linguistics and social semiotics, first and primarily in the UK and Australia, to get a more detailed view of the other side of the relationship, namely an analysis of the structures of text and image, even if such linguistic and semiotic approaches usually did not aim to provide sophisticated sociopolitical analyses (Chilton, 1985; Fairclough, 1989; Fowler et al., 1979; Hodge and Kress, 1988; Kress and Hodge, 1979). From a different perspective, the same critical approach characterizes much of the work in some directions of German and Austrian sociolinguistics, e.g. on language use of/with immigrant workers, language barriers, fascism and anti-semitism (Dittmar and Schlobinski, 1988; Ehlich, 1989; Wodak, 1985, 1989; Wodak et al., 1987, 1989, 1990; Wodak and Menz, 1990), some of which goes back to the critical sociolinguistic paradigm of Bernstein (1971–5).

It is our ultimate aim, then, though not realizable in this single paper, to eventually contribute to a theoretical, descriptive, empirical and critical framework in which discourse analyses and sociopolitical analyses are deeply integrated and both are as sophisticated as possible.

Principles and aims of critical discourse analysis

The questions raised above about the aims and the specific nature of CDA should be answered by a detailed technical discussion about the place of discourse analysis in contemporary scholarship and society. Such a discussion should specify, inter alia, the criteria that are characteristic of work in CDA. Instead, we shall simply, and perhaps naïvely, summarize such criteria by saying that in our opinion CDA should deal primarily with the discourse dimensions of power abuse and the injustice and inequality that result from it. Let us spell out some implications of such a lofty overall aim (see also Mey, 1985; O'Barr, 1984; Steiner, 1985).

First, the focus on dominance and inequality implies that, unlike other domains or approaches in discourse analysis, CDA does not primarily aim to contribute to a specific discipline, paradigm, school or discourse theory.

It is primarily interested and motivated by pressing social issues, which it hopes to better understand through discourse analysis. Theories, descriptions, methods and empirical work are chosen or elaborated as a function of their relevance for the realization of such a sociopolitical goal. Since serious social problems are naturally complex, this usually also means a multidisciplinary approach, in which distinctions between theory, description and 'application' become less relevant. This focus on fundamental understanding of social problems such as dominance and inequality does not mean ignoring theoretical issues. On the contrary, without complex and highly sophisticated theories no such understanding is possible. Central to this theoretical endeavour is the analysis of the complex relationships between dominance and discourse.

Unlike other discourse analysts, critical discourse analysts (should) take an explicit sociopolitical stance: they spell out their point of view, perspective, principles and aims, both within their discipline and within society at large. Although not in each stage of theory formation and analysis, their work is admittedly and ultimately political. Their hope, if occasionally illusory, is change through critical understanding. Their perspective, if possible, is that of those who suffer most from dominance and inequality. Their critical targets are the power elites that enact, sustain, legitimate, condone or ignore social inequality and injustice. That is, one of the criteria of their work is solidarity with those who need it most. Their problems are 'real' problems, that is the serious problems that threaten the lives or well-being of many, and not primarily the sometimes petty disciplinary problems of describing discourse structures, let alone the problems of the powerful (including the 'problems' the powerful have with those who are less powerful, or with those who resist it). Their critique of discourse implies a political critique of those responsible for its perversion in the reproduction of dominance and inequality. Such a critique should not be ad hoc, individual or incidental, but general, structural and focused on groups, while involving power relations between groups. In this sense, critical discourse scholars should also be social and political scientists, as well as social critics and activists. In other words, CDA is unabashedly normative: any critique by definition presupposes an applied ethics.

However, unlike politicians and activists, critical discourse analysts go beyond the immediate, serious or pressing issues of the day. Their structural understanding presupposes more general insights, and sometimes indirect and long-term analyses of fundamental causes, conditions and consequences of such issues. And unlike most social and political scientists, critical discourse scholars want to make a more specific contribution, namely to get more insight into the crucial role of discourse in the reproduction of dominance and inequality.

Critical discourse analysis is far from easy. In my opinion it is by far the toughest challenge in the discipline. As suggested above, it requires true multidisciplinarity, and an account of intricate relationships between text, talk, social cognition, power, society and culture. Its adequacy criteria are not merely observational, descriptive or even explanatory (Fairclough, 1985). Ultimately, its success is measured by its effectiveness and relevance, that is, by its contribution to change. In that respect, modesty is mandatory:

academic contributions may be marginal in processes of change, in which especially those who are directly involved, and their acts of resistance, are the really effective change agents. This has become particularly clear from large processes of change such as class struggles, decolonization, the Civil Rights Movement and the Women's Movement. Yet, although occasionally marginal, academics have also shown their presence and contributions in these movements. Critical discourse analysts continue this tradition: the 1990s are replete with persistent problems of oppression, injustice and inequality that demand their urgent attention.

Such aims, choices and criteria of CDA have implications for scholarly work. They monitor theory formation, analytical method and procedures of empirical research. They guide the choice of topics and relevancies. Thus, if immigrants, refugees and (other) minorities suffer from prejudice, discrimination and racism, and if women continue to be subjected to male dominance, violence or sexual harassment, it will be essential to examine and evaluate such events and their consequences essentially from their point of view. That is, such events will be called 'racist' or 'sexist' if knowledgeable Blacks or women say so, despite white or male denials. There cannot be an aloof, let alone a 'neutral', position of critical scholars. Critical scholars should not worry about the interests or perspectives of those in power, who are best placed to take care of their own interests anyway. Most male or white scholars have been shown to despise or discredit such partisanship, and thereby show how partisan they are in the first place, e.g. by ignoring, mitigating, excluding or denying inequality. They condemn mixing scholarship with 'politics', and thereby they do precisely that. Some, even more cynically and more directly, collude with dominance, e.g. by 'expert' advice, support and legitimation of the (western, middle-class, white, male, heterosexual, etc.) power elites. It is this collusion that is one of the major topics of critical discourse analysis.

Most of this has been said many times, in many modes and styles of formulation, both within and outside of science and scholarship. Yet, within the framework of this paper it does not hurt to repeat such statements, which may be trivialities for some, 'unscientific slogans' for others, and basic principles for us. What counts, henceforth, is only to draw the consequences for adequate critical research.

Power and dominance

One crucial presupposition of adequate critical discourse analysis is understanding the nature of social power and dominance. Once we have such an insight, we may begin to formulate ideas about how discourse contributes to their reproduction. To cut a long philosophical and social scientific analysis short, we assume that we here deal with properties of relations between social groups. That is, while focusing on *social* power, we ignore purely personal power, unless enacted as an individual realization of group power, that is, by individuals as group members. Social power is based on privileged *access* to socially valued resources, such as wealth, income, position, status, force, group membership, education or knowledge. Below we shall see that special access to various genres, forms or contexts of discourse and communication is also an important power resource (for further details on the concept of power, see, e.g. Clegg, 1989; Lukes, 1986).

Power involves *control*, namely by (members of) one group over (those of) other groups. Such control may pertain to *action* and *cognition*: that is, a powerful group may limit the freedom of action of others, but also influence their minds. Besides the elementary recourse to force to directly control action (as in police violence against demonstrators, or male violence against women), 'modern' and often more effective power is mostly cognitive, and enacted by persuasion, dissimulation or manipulation, among other strategic ways to *change the minds of others in one's own interests*. It is at this crucial point where *discourse* and critical discourse analysis come in: managing the mind of others is essentially a function of text and talk. Note, though, that such mind management is not always bluntly manipulative. On the contrary, dominance may be enacted and reproduced by subtle, routine, everyday forms of text and talk that appear 'natural' and quite 'acceptable'. Hence, CDA also needs to focus on the discursive strategies that legitimate control, or otherwise 'naturalize' the social order, and especially relations of inequality (Fairclough, 1985).

Despite such complexities and subtleties of power relations, critical discourse analysis is specifically interested in power *abuse*, that is, in breaches of laws, rules and principles of democracy, equality and justice by those who wield power. To distinguish such power from legitimate and acceptable forms of power, and lacking another adequate term, we use the term '*dominance*'. As is the case with power, dominance is seldom total. It may be restricted to specific domains, and it may be contested by various modes of *challenge*, that is, counter-power. It may be more or less consciously or explicitly exercised or experienced. Many more or less subtle forms of dominance seem to be so persistent that they seem natural until they begin to be challenged, as was/is the case for male dominance over women, White over Black, rich over poor. If the minds of the dominated can be influenced in such a way that they accept dominance, and act in the interest of the powerful out of their own free will, we use the term *hegemony* (Gramsci, 1971; Hall et al., 1977). One major function of dominant discourse is precisely to manufacture such consensus, acceptance and legitimacy of dominance (Herman and Chomsky, 1988).

The concept of hegemony, and its associated concepts of consensus, acceptance and the management of the mind, also suggests that a critical analysis of discourse and dominance is far from straightforward, and does not always imply a clear picture of villains and victims. Indeed, we have already suggested that many forms of dominance appear to be 'jointly produced' through intricate forms of social interaction, communication and discourse. We hope that critical discourse analysis will be able to contribute to our understanding of such intricacies.

Power and dominance are usually *organized* and *institutionalized*. The social dominance of groups is thus not merely enacted, individually, by its group members, as is the case in many forms of everyday racism or sexual harassment. It may also be supported or condoned by other group members, sanctioned by the courts, legitimated by laws, enforced by the police, and ideologically sustained and reproduced by the media or text-books. This social, political and cultural organization of dominance also implies a *hierarchy of power*: some members of dominant groups and orga-nizations have a special role in planning, decision-making and control over the relations and processes of the enactment of power. These (small) groups will here be called the *power elites* (Domhoff, 1978; Mills, 1956). For our discussion, it is especially interesting to note that such elites also have special access to discourse: they are literally the ones who have most to *say*. In our discourse analytical framework, therefore, we define elites pre-cisely in terms of their 'symbolic power' (Bourdieu, 1982), as measured by the extent of their discursive and communicative scope and resources.

Discourse and access

We have suggested that one of the social resources on which power and dominance are based is the privileged access to discourse and communica-tion. Access is an interesting but also a rather vague analytical notion (Van Dijk, 1989b, 1993b). In our case it may mean that language users or com-municators have more or less freedom in the use of special discourse genres or styles, or in the participation in specific communicative events and contexts. Thus, only parliamentarians have access to parliamentary debates and top managers to meetings in the boardroom. People may have more or less active or passive access to communicative events, as is usually the case for journalists, professors or bosses when writing for, or speaking to, a more or less passive audience. Similarly, participants may have more or less control over the variable properties of the (course of) discourse and its conditions and consequences, such as their planning, setting, the presence of other participants, modes of participation, overall organization, turn-taking, agenda, topics or style.

An analysis of the various modes of discourse access reveals a rather surprising parallelism between social power and discourse access: the more discourse genres, contexts, participants, audience, scope and text character-istics they (may) actively control or influence, the more powerful social groups, institutions or elites are. Indeed, for each group, position or institu-tion, we may spell out a 'discourse access profile'. Thus, top business managers have exclusive access to executive board meetings, in which the most powerful is usually associated with the 'chair', who also controls the agenda, speech acts (e.g. who may command whom), turn allocation (who is allowed to speak), decision-making, topics and other important and consequential dimensions of such institutional talk. At the same time, managers have access to business reports and documents, or can afford to have those written for them; they have preferential access to the news media, as well as to negotiations with top politicians and other top man-agers. Similar profiles may be sketched for presidents, prime ministers, political party leaders, newspaper editors, anchor(wo)men, judges, profes-sors, doctors or police officers.

Similarly, lack of power is also measured by its lack of active or con-trolled access to discourse: in everyday life, most 'ordinary' people only have active access to conversations with family members, friends or colleagues. They have more or less passive access to bureaucrats in public agencies or to professionals (e.g. doctors, teachers, police officers). In other situations they may be more or less controlled participants, onlookers, consumers or users, e.g. as media audiences, suspects in court, or as a topic in the news media (but often only when they are victims or perpetrators of crime and catastrophe). Modest forms of counter-power exist in some discourse and communication forms, as is the case for 'letters to the Editor', carrying or shouting slogans in demonstrations, or asking critical questions in the classroom.

In the same way as power and dominance may be institutionalized to enhance their effectivity, access may be organized to enhance its impact: given the crucial role of the media, powerful social actors and institutions have organized their media access by press officers, press releases, press conferences, PR departments, and so on (Gans, 1979; Tuchman, 1978). The same is more generally true for the control of public opinion, and hence for the manufacture of legitimation, consent and consensus needed in the reproduction of hegemony (Margolis and Mauser, 1989).

In sum, for the purpose of the theory sketched here, power and dominance of groups are measured by their control over (access to) discourse. The crucial implication of this correlation is not merely that discourse control is a form of social action control, but also and primarily that it implies the conditions of control over the minds of other people, that is, the management of social representations. More control over more properties of text and context, involving more people, is thus generally (though not always) associated with more influence, and hence with hegemony.

Social cognition

Whereas the management of discourse access represents one of the crucial social dimensions of dominance, that is, who is allowed to say/write/hear/read what to/from whom, where, when and how, we have stressed that 'modern' power has a major cognitive dimension. Except in the various forms of military, police, judicial or male force, the exercise of power usually presupposes mind management, involving the influence of knowledge, beliefs, understanding, plans, attitudes, ideologies, norms and values. Ultimately, the management of modes of access is geared towards this access to the public mind, which we conceptualize in terms of social cognition. Socially shared representations of societal arrangements, groups and relations, as well as mental operations such as interpretation, thinking and arguing, inferencing and learning, among others, together define what we understand by social cognition (Farr and Moscovici, 1984; Fiske and Taylor, 1991; Wyer and Srull, 1984).

Discourse, communication and (other) forms of action and interaction are monitored by social cognition (Van Dijk, 1989a). The same is true for our understanding of social events or of social institutions and power relations. Hence social cognitions mediate between micro- and macro-levels of society, between discourse and action, between the individual and the group. Although embodied in the minds of individuals, social cognitions are social because they are shared and presupposed by group members, monitor social action and interaction, and because they underlie the social and cultural organization of society as a whole (Resnick et al., 1991).

For our theoretical purposes, then, social cognitions allow us to link dominance and discourse. They explain the production as well as the understanding and influence of dominant text and talk. The complex cognitive theories involved in such processes cannot be explained in detail here. Indeed, many of their elements are as yet unknown. We know a little about how texts are produced and understood, how their information is searched, activated, stored or memorized (Van Dijk and Kintsch, 1983). We know that knowledge plays a prominent role in these processes, e.g. in terms of knowledge structures such as 'scripts' (Schank and Abelson, 1977). Control of knowledge crucially shapes our interpretation of the world, as well as our discourse and other actions. Hence the relevance of a critical analysis of those forms of text and talk, e.g. in the media and education, that essentially aim to construct such knowledge.

Unfortunately, we know very little about the structure and operations of the 'softer' (or 'hotter') forms of social cognition, such as opinions, attitudes, ideologies, norms and values. We shall merely assume that these 'evaluative' social representations also have a schematic form, featuring specific categories (as the schema men have about women, or whites have about blacks, may feature a category 'appearance': Van Dijk, 1987a). The 'contents' of such schematically organized attitudes are formed by general, socially shared opinions, that is, by evaluative beliefs. The general norms and values that in turn underlie such beliefs may be further organized in more complex, abstract and basic ideologies, such as those about immigrants, freedom of the press, abortion or nuclear arms. For our purposes, therefore, ideologies are the fundamental social cognitions that reflect the basic aims, interests and values of groups. They may (metaphorically and hence vaguely) be seen as the fundamental cognitive 'programmes' or 'operating systems' that organize and monitor the more specific social attitudes of groups and their members. What such ideologies look like exactly, and how they strategically control the development or change of attitudes, is as yet virtually unknown (see, however, e.g. Billig, 1982, 1991; Rosenberg, 1988; Windisch, 1985).

It is also increasingly accepted that concrete text production and interpretation are based on so-called models, that is, mental representations of experiences, events or situations, as well as the opinions we have about them (Johnson-Laird, 1983; Van Dijk, 1987b; Van Dijk and Kintsch, 1983). Thus, a newspaper report about (specific events in) the war in Bosnia is based on journalistic models of that war, and these models may in turn have been constructed during the interpretation of many source texts, e.g. of other media, key witnesses, or the press conferences of politicians. At the same time, such models are shaped by existing knowledge (about Yugoslavia, wars, ethnic conflict, etc.), and by more or less variable or shared general attitudes and ideologies.

Note that whereas knowledge, attitudes and ideologies are generalized representations that are socially shared, and hence characteristic of whole groups and cultures, specific models are – as such – unique, personal and contextualized: they define how one language user now produces or understands this specific text, even when large parts of such processes are not autobiographically but socially determined. In other words, models allow us to link the personal with the social, and hence individual actions and (other) discourses, as well as their interpretations, with the social order, and personal opinions and experiences with group attitudes and group relations, including those of power and dominance.

Here we touch upon the core of critical discourse analysis: that is, a detailed description, explanation and critique of the ways dominant discourses (indirectly) influence such socially shared knowledge, attitudes and ideologies, namely through their role in the manufacture of concrete models. More specifically, we need to know how specific discourse structures determine specific mental processes, or facilitate the formation of specific social representations. Thus, it may be the case that specific rhetorical figures, such as hyperboles or metaphors, preferentially affect the organization of models or the formation of opinions embodied in such models. Similarly, semantic moves may directly facilitate the formation or change of social attitudes, or they may do so indirectly, that is, through the generalization or decontextualization of personal models (including opinions) of specific events. In our account below of some major features of critical discourse analysis, therefore, we need to focus on these relations between discourse structures and the structures of social cognition. At the same time, this analysis of both discursive and cognitive structures must in turn be embedded in a broader social, political or cultural theory of the situations, contexts, institutions, groups and overall power relations that enable or result from such 'symbolic' structures.

Discourse structures

Within the broad social and cognitive framework sketched above, the theory and practice of critical discourse analysis focus on the structures of text and talk. If powerful speakers or groups enact or otherwise 'exhibit' their power in discourse, we need to know exactly *how* this is done. And if they thus are able to persuade or otherwise influence their audiences, we also want to know which discursive structures and strategies are involved in that process. Hence, the discursive reproduction of dominance, which we have taken as the main object of critical analysis, has two major dimensions, namely that of production and reception. That is, we distinguish between the enactment, expression or legitimation of dominance in the (production of the) various structures of text and talk, on the one hand, and the functions, consequences or results of such structures for the (social) minds of recipients, on the other. Discursive (re)production of power results *from* social cognitions of the powerful, whereas the situated discourse structures result *in* social cognitions. That is, in both cases we eventually have to deal with relations between discourse and cognition, and in both cases discourse structures form the crucial mediating role. They are truly the means of the 'symbolic' reproduction of dominance. [. . .]

Parliamentary discourse on ethnic affairs

To illustrate the general approach to critical discourse analysis sketched above, let us finally discuss some examples. These will be drawn from a study we did of the ways some western parliaments debate about ethnic affairs (Van Dijk, 1993a, ch. 3). This study is itself part of a project on 'elite discourse and racism' which seeks to show that the various elites (e.g. in politics, the media, academia, education and corporate business) play a prominent role in the reproduction of racism, and do so, sometimes subtly, through the respective discourse genres to which they have access. The project is part of our year-long research programme on discourse, communication and racism.

The study of parliamentary discourse focused on debates during the 1980s on immigration, ethnic relations, affirmative action and civil rights in the Netherlands, the UK, France, Germany and the USA. Such debates, unlike spontaneous conversations or arguments, usually consist of written depositions, with occasional spontaneous interruptions. Such statements are read and are intended for the parliamentary or congressional record, and are therefore heavily monitored. Except from extremist racist parties and arch-conservatives, therefore, explicitly and blatantly racist talk is exceptional for speakers of mainstream parties. On the contrary, the 'rhetoric of tolerance' in such debates is very prominent, and reflects underlying values of humanitarianism and civil rights, as is the case in the following examples from Germany and the USA. (All quotes are taken from the parliamentary records of the respective countries. Since some of the examples are translations, some details of a more subtle analysis of, for example, style must unfortunately be ignored.)

(1) I know no other country on this earth that gives more prominence to the rights of resident foreigners as does this bill in our country. (Germany, Herr Hirsch, 9 February 1990, p. 16279)

(2) This is a nation whose values and traditions now excite the world, as we all know. I think we all have a deep pride in American views, American ideals, American government, American principle, which excite hundreds of millions of people around the world who struggle for freedom. (US, Mr Foley, 2 August 1990, H6768)

Interestingly, all countries appear to make the same claim, namely to be the most tolerant one. For the discussion in this article it is especially important to emphasize that, besides the undeniable sincerity of many politicians and despite their humanitarian values, such nationalist rhetoric may also function as disclaimers that precede negative statements and decisions about minorities or immigrants. Indeed, in virtually all cases we examined, the decisions advocated by such speakers restrict the (immigration, litigation, residence, etc.) rights of immigrants or minorities. Similarly, all speakers, including the most racist ones, will emphatically deny that they or their country are racist. Even the leader of the National Front will say so:

(3) We are neither racist nor xenophobic. Our aim is only that, quite naturally, there be a hierarchy, because we are dealing with France, and France is the country of the French. (France, M. Le Pen, 7 July 1986, p. 3064)

There are many other versions of the classical disclaimer of the Apparent Denial: 'I have nothing against X, but . . . '. Also Le Pen uses 'only' to show that his denial is only apparent, and that the rest of his talk will blatantly express French superiority. Conservative speakers similarly deny racism, although they do so with a number of characteristic strategic moves:

(4) The French are not racist. But, facing this continuous increase of the foreign population in France, one has witnessed the development, in certain cities and neighbourhoods, of reactions that come close to xenophobia. (France, M. Pascua, 9 July 1986, p. 3053)

Instead of an Apparent Denial, we here find an Apparent Concession. That is, although racism as such is denied, it is conceded that there is a problem after all. This concession, however, is multiply hedged and embedded in euphemism and indirectness. First, racism is redefined as less serious sounding 'xenophobia'. Secondly, however, even this concession is hedged by the phrase 'reactions that come close to'. Thirdly, xenophobia is restricted by localization: 'in certain cities and neighbourhoods', which usually implies poor white inner city neighbourhoods. That is, as usual, the elites transfer racism 'down' to the lower class. Finally, xenophobia is explained and thereby half-excused by the initial clause 'facing this continuous increase of the foreign population in France', a presupposition which incidentally is false: compared to previous decades the percentage of immigrants has barely increased. This, then, is a characteristic example of political discourse on ethnic relations: denial, apparent concession, mitigation and justification of racism.

Obviously, negative decisions must be rationally defended, and we may therefore expect extensive statements about all the negative properties of immigration, residence, cultural conflicts, the reactions of the majority, and so on, especially by racist representatives, as is the case for those of the National Front in France. However, mainstream politicians also will commonly engage in more subtle moves of inferiorization, problematization and marginalization. Here is a more blatant example from the British House of Commons:

(5) . . . one in three children born in London today is of ethnic origin. . . . That is a frightening concept for the country to come to terms with. We have already seen the problems of massive Moslem immigration . . . unless we want to create major problems in the decades or the century ahead, we must not only stop immigration but must move to voluntary resettlement to reduce the immigrant population. (UK, Mr Janman, 20 June 1990, cols. 293–4)

Among the many other moves that characterize such parliamentary talk about 'them', we find those of *apparent sympathy* (we make these decisions for their own best interest), populism or *apparent democracy* (the people do not want more immigration) and *blaming the victim* (they are themselves to blame for, e.g., discrimination, unemployment, and so on) (see also Reeves, 1983). Overall, as in other forms of talk about minorities, also among the elites, we find a combination of positive self-presentation and many forms of negative other-presentation.

Within our present theoretical argument such examples may be analysed in different ways. Obviously, first of all, they are direct expressions of (political) power, by virtue of the special access representatives have to parliamentary debates (restricted only by the Speaker), and hence to the opinion formation of other parliamentarians, and indirectly to the media and the public. By expressing blatant prejudices, as does Mr Janman in example 5, such a powerful elite group member at the same time lends weight to the acceptability of racist opinions, and thereby directly enacts discursive discrimination against minorities and immigrants. Indeed, his contribution to the dominance of the white group most crucially consists of his influence on the Tory party in power, which is able to (and actually does) further restrict immigration. His talk is part of the discursively based decision process itself, and this decision may be racist in its own right when it specifically applies to non-European immigrants. In other words, political discourse directly enacts racism when being part of the decisions for actions or policies that cause or confirm ethnic or racial inequality. Since parliament in a democratic country is (theoretically) ultimately responsible for such decisions, we here witness the enactment of racism at the highest possible level. According to our thesis of the top–down direction of racism, this also means that all 'lower' groups and institutions (e.g. the police) may feel similarly entitled to develop or maintain similar prejudices and similarly engage in discrimination. A most dramatic example of such top–down influence may be observed in Germany, where a protracted discussion by politicians and the press about refugees conditioned the 'popular' racist attacks by skinheads against refugee reception centres in 1991 and 1992.

In other words, the reproduction of racism in parliamentary discourse is not limited to the enactment of inequality by political decision-makers, but also consists in influencing others, if only because of the credibility and respectability of MPs. MPs not only express their own opinions, or those of their party or social group, but also try to persuade others, such as the opposition, to adopt them. Also, such expressions may be seen as a legitimation or justification of decisions. Most importantly, though, their discourse contributes to the reproduction of racism through their coverage in the media, which spread them among the population at large. If adopted by the media, as is often the case, the negative models of immigrants or minorities underlying such statements will eventually be persuasively presented to the audience of the mass media. We have already seen that due to a lack of alternative, anti-racist elite discourses and media, and because of their own best interests and corresponding ideologies and attitudes, many members of the audience will tend to adopt such models. Such processes of persuasion involve not only persuasive argumentation and rhetoric, or congenial opinions, but also the authority with which the politicians and the media are able to present such models. The media have their own rich repertoire of means to further enhance and 'popularize' the sometimes abstract and technical language and opinions of the politicians, e.g. by spreading scare stories about 'massive' illegal immigration, welfare 'cheats', housing and employment shortages attributed to minorities, perceived cultural deviance (e.g. Islam) and especially 'black crime' (drugs, mugging, violence).

In sum, the enactment of (political) power as part of white group dominance in western countries is not limited to political decision-making and directly restricting the rights of minorities, but also, and perhaps more importantly, justifies and legitimates such acts through the manipulation of public opinion, usually through the mass media. This means that the politicians speak not only for their colleagues, but also for other elite groups, especially the media, and hence for the white population at large. In both cases the main aim is to form and change 'ethnic models' that may be used to make decisions or develop attitudes that may favour the unequal treatment of the Others, and thereby to reproduce white group dominance.

This is also the reason why politicians, as soon as they speak negatively about minorities or immigrants, will use the 'facts' that fit the stereotypical models that are derived from pre-existing popular attitudes they have helped to develop in the first place. Thus, they may invoke such proto-typical model-events as refugees living in expensive hotels, increasing unemployment, inner city 'riots', cultural (religious) conflicts (Rushdie, young Muslim women who are forced to wear the veil, or South Asian women forced into arranged marriages), immigrants bringing in drugs (if not AIDS), welfare scroungers, minorities who lightly accuse 'us' (employers, etc.) of discrimination, affirmative action programmes in employment and education that will 'favour' 'less qualified' minorities, and so on.

Reproducing racism in the British House of Commons
Finally, let us examine in somewhat more detail a longer example of such parliamentary discourse. This example was taken from a parliamentary debate held on 16 April 1985 in the British House of Commons and consists of several fragments from the leading speech by Mr Marcus Fox, Conservative representative of Shipley, about the so-called 'Honeyford affair'. Honeyford was the headmaster of a school in Bradford (UK), who was first suspended, then reinstated but finally dismissed (with a golden handshake) because of what the parents of his mostly Asian pupils, the Bradford City Council and their supporters saw as racist writings, e.g. in the right-wing *Salisbury Review* and the *Times Literary Supplement*, on multicultural education in general, and on his own students in particular. The affair soon became a national issue, in which Conservative politicians as well as the Conservative press fulminated against the 'race relations bullies' (also a phrase used by Mr Fox in his speech), who 'strike at the very root of our democracy . . . the freedom of speech'. Here is how Mr Fox begins this adjournment debate in the British Parliament:

> Mr. Marcus Fox (Shipley): This Adjournment debate is concerned with Mr. Ray Honeyford, the headmaster of Drummond Road Middle School, Bradford. This matter has become a national issue – not from Mr. Honeyford's choice. Its consequences go beyond the issue of race relations or, indeed, of education. They strike at the very root of our democracy and what we cherish in this House above all – the freedom of speech.
>
> One man writing an article in a small-circulation publication has brought down a holocaust on his head. To my mind, this was a breath of fresh air in the polluted area of race relations. . . .

Who are Mr. Honeyford's detractors? Who are the people who have persecuted him? They have one thing in common – they are all on the Left of British politics. The Marxists and the Trots are here in full force. We only have to look at their tactics, and all the signs are there. Without a thread of evidence, Mr. Honeyford has been villified as a racist. Innuendos and lies have been the order of the day. He has been criticised continuously through the media, yet most of the time he has been barred from defending himself and denied the right to answer those allegations by order of the education authority. The mob has taken to the streets to harass him out of his job. . . .

The race relations bullies may have got their way so far, but the silent majority of decent people have had enough. . . . The withdrawal of the right to free speech from this one man could have enormous consequences and the totalitarian forces ranged against him will have succeeded. (*Hansard*, 16 April 1985, cols 233–6)

To examine the enactment of power and dominance in this speech, and conversely the role of this speech in the reproduction of such dominance, we systematically discuss its major discourse dimensions. Recall that for all the dimensions, levels or properties of this speech that we analyse (and this analysis is far from exhaustive), the reproduction of dominance has two major aspects: the direct enactment or production of dominance, on the one hand, and the consequences of this speech in the process of the management of the public consensus on ethnic affairs, on the other. For instance, discrediting Asian parents is itself an act of verbal discrimination, indirectly restricting the civil rights of minorities. At the same time, such a discursive act may contribute to the formation of negative models about Asian parents and (other) anti-racists, which may be generalized to negative attitudes which in turn may influence discrimination by members of the white group at large.

Note that although our first task is to systematically examine the many textual and contextual properties of the exercise of dominance for this example, and to provide explicit evidence for such an account, analysis is not – and cannot be – 'neutral'. Indeed, the point of critical discourse analysis is to take a position. In this case, we take a position that tries to examine the speech of Mr Fox from the point of view of the opponents of Honeyford, thereby criticizing the dominant groups and institutions (e.g. Conservative politicians and journalists) who defended Honeyford and attacked multicultural education.

The analysis begins with various properties of the context, such as access patterns, setting and participants, and then examines the properties of the 'text' of the speech itself, such as its topics, local meanings, style and rhetoric. Of the many possible properties of the text and context of this speech we focus on those that most clearly exhibit the discursive properties of the exercise of dominance. For detailed theoretical explanations of these properties and their relevance for critical analysis, the reader is referred to our other work quoted in this paper (see, e.g., Van Dijk, 1984, 1987a, 1991, 1993a).

Access. As indicated above, Mr Fox's power as an MP is first of all defined by his active and more or less controlled access to the House of Commons and its debates.

Setting.   The power and authority of his speech is also signalled and maybe enhanced by elements of the setting, such as the location (the House of Commons) and its prestigious props, the presence of other MPs, and so on. Since television has recently entered the House of Commons, such symbols of parliamentary power are also relevant for the public 'overhearers' of parliamentary debates. Locally, Mr Fox's power and influence coincides with his having the floor, marked not only by his speaking, but also by his standing up while the other MPs are seated.

Genre.   Mr Fox also has special access to a genre only he and his colleagues are entitled to engage in, namely parliamentary debates. We have seen above that this is not merely 'talk', but constitutive of highest level political decision-making.

Communicative acts and social meanings.   Besides these broader social or political implications, this speech fragment from the House of Commons locally expresses or signals various social meanings and categories of social interaction. At the interaction level itself, therefore, politeness is signalled by the formal modes of address ('the Honourable Gentleman'), whereas political closeness may be marked by 'my friend . . . '. Since the politeness markers are mutual here, social power relations in the House seem to be equal. Note, though that Mr Fox is a member of a government party, which is able to control much of the parliamentary agenda, and which therefore is able to hold a parliamentary debate on Honeyford in the first place. That is, also among 'equals', political dominance may be at stake.

This is also the case at the semantic level, that is, relative to the social situation and events talked about by Mr Fox. By defending Mr Honeyford, Mr Fox attacks shared opponents, namely leftists or anti-racists. Because of his powerful position as an MP he adds considerable weight to the balance of this conflict between Honeyford and the parents of his students, as is also the case for the right-wing media supporting Honeyford. We see how the Conservative elites, who may otherwise be hardly interested in ordinary teachers, may take part in the struggle between racism and anti-racism, between 'British values' and the values of multiculturalism scorned by Mr Honeyford.

Indeed, rather surprisingly, Mr Honeyford was even personally received by former Prime Minister Margaret Thatcher at Number 10 Downing Street, which again signals the highest support for his case. Similarly, that a conflict of a headmaster becomes a topic of a parliamentary debate by itself already suggests the importance accorded to the conflict, and to the socio-political positions to be defended at all costs. Finally, by associating Honeyford's opponents (mostly Asian parents) with Marxists and 'Trots' not only means that the case of his opponents is discredited within the framework of a largely anti-communist consensus, but also, more politically, that the Labour opposition to which Mr Fox's speech is primarily addressed is thus attacked and discredited. Below we shall see how such attacks, marginalization, discrediting and other sociopolitical acts are enacted by properties of discourse. Here, it should be emphasized, however, that the ultimate functions of such a speech are not merely linguistic or communicative (expressing or conveying meaning), but political.

Participant positions and roles. Mr Fox obviously speaks in his role as MP, and as a member of the Conservative party, among several other social identities, such as being a politician, white and male. This position institutionally entitles him to put the Honeyford case on the parliamentary agenda if he and his party deem the issue to be of national interest. Hence, it is not only his role as Conservative MP that influences the structures and strategies of his speech, but also his identity as a member of the white dominant group, and especially his identity as a member of the white elites. Thus, his party-political position explains why he attacks Labour, and the Left in general, his being an MP influences his alleged concern for democracy and the freedom of speech, and his being white his collusion with racist practices and his aggressions against Indian parents and their supporters.

Speech acts. Most of Mr Fox's speech consists of assertions, and also, at the global level of macro-speech acts, he primarily accomplishes an assertion. However, we have observed that, indirectly, he also accuses Honeyford's 'detractors' of vilification, lying and intimidation. At the same time, he thereby accuses and attacks the Labour opposition, whom he sees as opponents of Honeyford. In parliament his accusations and allegations may be met with appropriate defence by his sociopolitical equals. Not so, however, beyond the boundaries of parliament, where his accusations may be heard (literally, over the radio) or read (when quoted in the press) by millions, who may thus be exposed to biased information about Honeyford's opponents (most of whom are not Marxists or Trotskyites at all). For our CDA perspective, this means that the function and the scope of speech participants may largely define the effectiveness and 'authority' of their speech acts. Indeed, other supporters of Honeyford may legitimate their position by referring to such accusations in parliament.

Macrosemantics: topics. The topic of the debate in the British House of Commons, as signalled by Mr Fox himself ('This Adjournment debate is concerned with . . . '), is clearly 'the Honeyford case'. Propositionally, however, the topic may be defined in various ways, e.g. as 'Honeyford wrote disparaging articles about his Asian students and about multicultural education more generally', 'Honeyford has been accused of racism' and 'Honeyford is being vilified by anti-racist detractors'. It is the latter topic that is being construed by Mr Fox. At the same time, however, topics have sociopolitical implications, and these implications are made explicit by Mr Fox: the debate is not only about Honeyford, or even about race relations and education, but about the 'very root of our democracy', namely about free speech. This example shows how events, including discourse about such events, are represented, at the macro-level, as a function of underlying norms and values, that is, within the framework of dominant ideologies. That is, Mr Fox and other supporters of Honeyford, including the Conservative media, interpret Honeyford's racist articles and his attack on multicultural education as a 'breath of fresh air', and hence as an example of justified criticism, whereas his opponents are categorized as restricting free speech, and hence as being intolerant and undemocratic. This reversal of the application of values is well known in anti-anti-racist rhetoric, where those who combat ethnic and racial intolerance are themselves accused of intolerance, namely of the 'freedom' to 'tell the truth' about ethnic relations (for further detail, see also Van Dijk, 1991).

Relevant for our discussion here is that Mr Fox as an MP has the power not only to define and redefine the topics of debate, but also to define the situation. That is, the point is no longer whether or not Honeyford has insulted his students and their parents, or whether or not a teacher of a largely multicultural school is competent when he attacks the principles of multiculturalism, but whether the critique levelled against him is legitimate in the first place. By generalizing the topic even beyond race relations and education to a debate about democracy and free speech, Mr Fox at the same time defines both his and Mr Honeyford's opponents – including Labour – as being against free speech and democracy, and hence as enemies of the British state and its fundamental values. By thus redefining the topic at issue, Mr Fox no longer merely defends Mr Honeyford, but also reverses the charges and attacks the Left. He thereby conceals the fundamentally undemocratic implications of racism, and manipulates his secondary audience, namely the public at large, into believing that Mr Honeyford is merely a champion of free speech, and that his opponents are attacking British values if not democracy in general. As we shall see below, most of his speech tries to persuasively support that topical 'point'.

Superstructures: text schemata. One major form of text schema is argumentation. In Mr Fox's speech, as in parliamentary debates in general, argumentation plays a prominent role. As we have seen above, his main political point coincides with his argumentative 'position', which consists of his opinion that an attack against Honeyford is an attack against democracy and the freedom of speech. How does he support such a position? His first argument is a negative description of the facts: one man who writes in a 'small-circulation' publication has brought a 'holocaust' on his head. In other words, whatever Honeyford has written, it was insignificant (while published in a 'small-circulation' publication), and the reaction was massively destructive (a 'holocaust'). Moreover, what he wrote was also a 'breath of fresh air in the polluted area of race relations' and hence not only not reprehensible, but laudable. For Mr Fox, it follows that a massive attack against laudable critique is a threat to the freedom of speech, and hence to democracy.

We see that we need several steps to 'make sense' of Mr Fox's argument, and that such a reconstruction needs to be based on the subjective arguments and attitudes of the arguer. After all, Mr Honeyford *was* able to speak his mind, so that the freedom of speech was not in danger. To equate criticism or even attacks against him with a threat to the freedom of speech and to democracy is, therefore, from another point of view, hardly a valid argument, but a hyperbole, a rhetorical figure we also find in the insensitive hyperbolic use of the term 'holocaust'. To fully understand this argument, however, we need more than a reconstruction of Mr Fox's attitudes. We need to know, for instance, that anti-racist critique in the UK is more generally discredited by right-wing politicians and media as a limitation of free speech, because it does not allow people to 'tell the truth' about ethnic relations in general, or about multicultural education in particular. Hence the reference to the 'polluted area of race relations'.

The second sequence of arguments focuses on Honeyford's 'detractors', by whom Honeyford has been allegedly 'vilified as a racist'. By categorizing such opponents as 'Marxists and Trots', and by claiming they have been engaged in lies and innuendo and even 'harassed him out of his job', Mr Fox details how, in his opinion, free speech is constrained, while at the same time discrediting Honeyford's opponents as communists, and as 'totalitarian forces', that is, in his view, as the enemies of freedom and democracy. A third component in this argumentative schema is the claim that Honeyford is helpless and is not allowed to defend himself. He even ranges the media among the opponents of Honeyford, although most of the vastly dominant Conservative press supported him.

In sum, the argument schema features the following steps (propositions or macropropositions), of which the implicit arguments are marked with square brackets:

Arguments

1. Honeyford wrote an original and deserved critique of multicultural education.
2. His opponents attacked and harassed him massively.
2.1 [Massive attack and harassment of critics is an attack against free speech]
2.2 His opponents are totalitarian communists.
2.1.1. [Totalitarian communists are against freedom and democracy]

Conclusion

3. By attacking Honeyford, his opponents limit the freedom of speech and attack democracy itself.

Interestingly, the argument, if valid, would also apply to Mr Fox's argument itself, because by thus attacking from his powerful position as an MP, and given the massive attacks against Honeyford's opponents in the right-wing press, we might conclude, probably with much more reason, that the freedom to criticize racist publications is delegitimated, if not constrained. That is, Honeyford's opponents hardly have access to the mass media as Honeyford and his supporters had. Indeed, their arguments, if heard at all, are usually ignored or negatively presented in much of the press. On the other hand, Honeyford got the unusual privilege to explain his opinions in several long articles he was invited to write for the *Daily Mail*.

The validity of Mr Fox's argument itself, however, hinges upon his definition of the situation, which is not only biased, but also unfounded: Honeyford's critics are not Marxists and Trotskyites (at least, not all or even most of them), they did not prevent him from writing what he wanted to write, and, apart from protests, demonstrations and picketing of his school, they did not harass him. Moreover, the majority of the press did not attack him, but supported him. What happened, however, was that he was suspended because he had publicly derogated his Asian students and their parents, and thus, for the education authority, he had failed as a headmaster.

From our CDA perspective, the point of this brief analysis of the argumentative schema of (part of) Mr Fox's speech is that a powerful and influential speaker, namely an MP, whose arguments may be quoted in the media, may misrepresent the facts, discredit anti-racists as being undemocratic and against free speech, while at the same time supporting and legitimating racist publications. Unless his audience knows the facts, and unless it knows the opponents of Mr Honeyford and their arguments, it may thus be manipulated into believing that Mr Fox's argument is valid, and thereby associate those who oppose racism with 'totalitarian' methods. This indeed is very common in the press, not only on the Right, and Mr Fox reinforces such a negative evaluation of the struggle against racism. Ultimately, therefore, Mr Fox legitimates racism and enacts the dominance of the white group, not only by marginalizing anti-racism, but also by discrediting multicultural policies in education. His political power as an MP is thus paired with his symbolic, discursive power consisting in controlling the minds of his (secondary) audience, namely the media, other elites and finally the public at large.

Local meaning and coherence.   Few levels of analysis are as revealing and relevant for a critical analysis as the semantic study of local 'meanings', including the propositional structures of clauses and sentences, relations between propositions, implications, presuppositions, vagueness, indirectness, levels of description, and so on. We have seen that, in general, dominance is semantically signalled by positive self-presentation and negative other-presentation or derogation. We may expect, therefore, that the various semantic modes of meaning also reflect such an overall strategy, e.g. by concealing negative properties of the own group (racism), and emphasizing or inventing those of the Others (the 'intolerance' of anti-racism).

(a) *Level of specificity and degree of completeness.* In a semantic analysis, discourses may be studied as describing events at several levels of specificity (in general abstract terms or in lower level details), and – at each such level – more or less completely. Irrelevant or dispreferred information is usually described at higher levels and less completely, and preferred information in over-complete, detailed ways. One of the most conspicuous forms of over-completeness in discourse is the irrelevant negative categorization of participants in order to delegitimate or marginalize their opinions or actions. This also happens in Mr Fox's speech, where (at least from the point of view of the Asian parents) he irrelevantly categorizes Honeyford's critics as Marxists or Trotskyites. For him and much of his anti-communist audience this implies an association of the political-ideological enemy (the communists) with his moral/social enemy (the anti-racists). At the same time, Mr Fox's argument, as we have seen, is also seriously incomplete, because (in this fragment) it says nothing about the nature of what Mr Honeyford has written. It does, however, detail the many alleged negative actions of his opponents. He does not summarize their actions by saying that Honeyford was 'criticized' or even 'attacked', but mentions lies, vilification, harassment, etc. In this case, thus, incompleteness is a semantic property of argumentation, but also a more general move of concealment and positive self-presentation: Honeyford's racist articles are not discussed in detail, but only positively described, at a higher level of specificity, as 'a breath of fresh air'.

(b) Perspective. Little analysis is necessary to identify the perspective and point of view displayed in Mr Fox's speech: he defends Honeyford openly, supports his view explicitly, and severely attacks and marginalizes Honeyford's opponents. However, Mr Fox also speaks as an MP – he refers to 'this House' – and as a defender of democracy. Using the politically crucial pronoun 'our' in 'our democracy', he also speaks from the perspective of a staunch defender of democracy. This identification is of course crucial for a right-wing MP and for someone who openly supports someone who has written racist articles. Finally, he claims to be the voice of the 'silent majority of decent people', a well-known populist ploy in Conservative rhetoric. This also means that the parents of the Asian children in Bradford do not belong to this majority of 'decent people'. On the contrary, they have been categorized as, or with, the enemy on the Left.

(c) Implicitness: implications, presuppositions, vagueness. Spelling out the full presuppositions and other implications of Mr Fox's speech would amount to specifying the complex set of beliefs about the Honeyford case (the Honeyford-model of Mr Fox, and those of his audience and critics), as well as the general opinions on which his evaluations and arguments are based, as we have seen above. Hence, we only mention a few examples. If the matter has become a national issue 'not from Mr Honeyford's choice' this strongly implies that others, namely his opponents, have made a national issue of it, whereas it also (weakly) implies that Mr Honeyford's publication in a widely read national newspaper (*Times Literary Supplement*) and later in the *Daily Mail* did nothing to contribute to the national issue. The use of 'small-circulation' as a modifier of 'publication' implies that, given the small audience of the publication (he probably refers to the extremist right-wing *Salisbury Review*), the publication is 'insignificant' and hence 'not worth all the fuss' and certainly not worth the ensuing 'holocaust'. The major presupposition of this speech, however, is embodied in Mr Fox's rhetorical question: 'Who are the people who have persecuted him?', presupposing that there actually *were* people who 'persecuted' him. Finally, important for the political power-play in parliament are the implications of his categorization of Honeyford's opponents as being 'all on the Left of British politics', which immediately addresses Mr Fox's opponents in the House of Commons: Labour. By vilifying Honeyford's opponents, and anti-racists generally, as communists, as undemocratic and as enemies of free speech, he implies that such is also the case for Labour.

(d) Local coherence. There is one interesting coherence feature in Mr Fox's speech, namely when he begins a new sentence with the definite noun phrase 'The mob'. Since no mob has been mentioned before in his text, we

must assume either that this phrase generically refers to an (unspecified) mob, or that the phrase corefers, as is clearly his intention, to the previously mentioned discourse referents (Honeyford's detractors, etc.). Such coreference is permissible only if the qualification of previously identified participants is presupposed. In other words, Mr Fox, in line with right-wing news reports about Honeyford's critics, implicitly qualifies Honeyford's opponents as a 'mob', and presupposes this qualification in a following sentence. This is one of Mr Fox's discursive means to derogate his opponents. In other words, coherence may presuppose ideologically based beliefs.

Style: variations of syntax, lexicon and sound

(a) *Lexical style.* Mr Fox's lexical style is characteristic not only of parliamentary speeches, featuring technical political terms such as 'Adjournment debate', or of 'educated' talk in general, as we see in 'intellectual' words such as 'innuendo', 'detractors', 'totalitarian forces' or 'vilified'. He also uses the well-known aggressive populist register of the tabloids when he characterizes his and Honeyford's opponents as 'Trots', 'mob', and especially as 'race relations bullies'. That is, Mr Fox's lexicalization multiply signals his power, his political and moral position, as well as his persuasive strategies in influencing his (secondary) audience, namely the British public.

(b) *Syntactic style.* The syntax of Mr Fox's speech shows a few examples of semantically controlled topicalization and other forms of highlighting information. Thus, in the fourth sentence, the object of the predicate 'to strike at', namely 'the freedom of speech', is placed at the end of the sentence, after its qualifying clause ('what we cherish in this House above all'), in order to emphasize it – a well-known strategy of syntactic and rhetorical 'suspense'. Conversely, 'without a thread of evidence' is fronted somewhat later in his speech so as to specify from the outset of the sentence that Honeyford's vilification was without grounds. Note also the agentless passives: By whom, indeed, was Honeyford continuously criticized in the media? Surely not by Marxists and Trotskyites, who have no access to mainstream publications in Britain.

(c) *Anaphora and deictics.* In our discussion of the perspective and point of view in Mr Fox's speech we have already suggested his multiple political and social 'positions' and with whom Mr Fox identifies. Position and identification also determine the use of pronouns and deictic expressions (like 'this' in 'this Adjournment debate' which signals Mr Fox's participation in the debate). Most significant in this fragment, however, is the use of 'our' in 'our democracy', a well-known political possessive pronoun in much Conservative rhetoric. Obviously, Mr Fox signals himself as participating in 'our democracy', which may refer to British democracy, or western democracy, or the kind of democracy as it is interpreted by Mr Fox. The rest of his argument, however, clearly shows that the Left, and especially Marxists, Trotskyites, and the supporters of Mr Honeyford, are excluded from this definition of democracy, because they allegedly violate the freedom of speech.

Rhetoric.   Within the ecological domain, Mr Fox finds both a contrastive comparison and two metaphors to identify Honeyford's original ideas ('breath of fresh air') and the 'polluted' atmosphere of race relations. Again, after associating Honeyford's opponents with Nazis, he now associates them with polluters, a new officially certified enemy. Interestingly, as we have seen earlier, we may interpret such qualifications also as reversals, since it is precisely the extreme Right that is politically more inclined to condone fascism and industrial pollution, and not the radical Left Mr Fox is speaking about. That is, in attacking the Left, right-wing speakers often make use of classical accusations of the Left itself, simply by 'inverting' them, and as if to deny their own lack of a democratic zeal, for instance in supporting someone who writes racist articles.

Also the rest of the speech makes full use of the usual tricks from the rhetorical bag: rhetorical questions ('Who are Mr Honeyford's detractors?', etc.), parallelisms (the repeated questions), alliterations ('full force'), and especially contrasts between US and THEM, as in 'race relations bullies' and 'the majority of decent people', in general, and between the lone hero ('One man . . . ') and his opponents (Marxists, Trots, totalitarian forces, mob, vilification, lies, etc.), in particular. These rhetorical features emphasize what has been expressed and formulated already at the semantic, syntactic and lexical (stylistic) levels of his speech, namely the positive presentation of Honeyford (US, Conservatives, etc.), on the one hand, and the negative presentation of the Others (the Left, anti-racists, Asian parents), on the other.

Final remark.   Hence, the dominance expressed, signalled and legitimated in this speech does not merely reside in the political realm of the House of Commons, for instance in Mr Fox's role of MP, and as representative of a government party that is entitled to hold a debate about the Honeyford affair in parliament. Similarly, by attacking the Left he not only attacks Labour, as may be expected from a Tory speaker. Rather, the dominance involved here extends beyond parliament, namely to the media and especially to the public at large when Mr Fox uses his political influence to publicly support a teacher of students whose parents think he writes racist things, and especially in order to discredit and marginalize both these parents and their supporters. Indeed, the rest of this speech, not analysed here, sketches in more detail what he sees as a wonderful teacher, while at the same time denying, as is common in much elite discourse, the racist nature of Honeyford's writings. That is, Mr Fox's power, authority and dominance is not merely that of being an influential MP. Rather, his authority, namely in establishing what racism is, is that of a member of the white elite. It is in this way, therefore, that such a speech indirectly supports the system of ethnic-racial dominance, that is, racism.

Conclusions

There are many ways to do 'critical' discourse analysis. Paradigms, philosophies, theories and methods may differ in these many approaches, and these may sometimes also be related to 'national' differences, e.g. between 'French', 'German', 'British' or 'American' directions of research. Unfortunately, this is also one of the reasons why there has been much mutual neglect and ignorance among these different approaches. International, theoretical and methodological integration would obviously benefit the realization of a common aim, namely to analyse, understand and combat inequality and injustice.

Against this background, this paper discusses some of the more general properties of what we see as a viable critical discourse analysis. In order to avoid paradigm controversies as well as superficial eclecticism, we therefore first of all argued for a multidisciplinary and issue-oriented approach: theories, methods or disciplines are more relevant if they are (also) able to contribute to the main aim of the critical approach, namely the understanding of social inequality and injustice. This means, among other things, that we presuppose a serious analysis of the very conditions and modalities of inequality, e.g. in terms of social power, dominance and their reproduction. In a critical study, such an analysis is not limited to a sociological or political-scientific account of dominance or patterns of access to social resources. Rather, positions and perspectives need to be chosen, for instance, against the power elites and in solidarity with dominated groups, as we have tried to illustrate in our analysis of the speech of Mr Fox in the British parliament. Such choices influence virtually all levels of theory and method.

Critical discourse analysis can only make a significant and specific contribution to critical social or political analyses if it is able to provide an account of the role of language, language use, discourse or communicative events in the (re)production of dominance and inequality. We have tried to show that there are two major dimensions along which discourse is involved in dominance, namely through the enactment of dominance in text and talk in specific contexts, and more indirectly through the influence of discourse on the minds of others. In the first case, dominant speakers may effectively limit the 'communicative rights' of others, e.g. by restricting (free access to) communicative events, speech acts, discourse genres, participants, topics or style. In the second case, dominant speakers control the access to public discourse and hence are able to indirectly manage the public mind. They may do so by making use of those structures and strategies that manipulate the mental models of the audience in such a way that 'preferred' social cognitions tend to be developed, that is, social cognitions (attitudes, ideologies, norms and values) that are ultimately in the interest of the dominant group.

Both cases show the relevance of a socio-cognitive interface between discourse and dominance: it is theoretically essential to understand that there is no other way to relate macro-level notions such as group dominance and inequality with micro-level notions as text, talk, meaning and understanding. Indeed, the crucial notion of reproduction, needed to explain how discourse plays a role in the reproduction of dominance, presupposes an account that relates discourse structures to social cognitions, and social cognitions to social structures.

We illustrated our argument with a brief analysis of the ways in which racism is being reproduced in western societies through parliamentary discourse. Although seldom blatantly racist, such more or less 'moderate' discourse may nevertheless enact white group power, e.g. through the authority of MPs, while at the same time manipulating the public mind in such a way that ethnocentric or racist policies can be legitimated. Such a critical analysis is primarily geared towards the demystification of the self-proclaimed ethnic and racial tolerance of the elites, and the challenging of their widespread denial of racism.

To conclude, a few words of caution and hesitation are in order. We have stressed that, facing the real issues and problems of today's world, discourse analysis, whether critical or not, may not make much difference, unless we are able to contribute to stimulating a critical perspective among our students or colleagues. To do that, we should persuade them not merely by our views or arguments, but also with our expertise. Although many studies in critical discourse analysis have shown that our results so far are encouraging, our expertise is still very limited.

Finally, this paper has sketched a rather simplified picture of power, dominance and their relations to discourse. Although we stressed that actual power relations are often subtle and indirect, and not simply top–down, the thrust of our argument has been to focus on the elites and their discourses. This choice is not motivated by the wish to picture these elites as the villains in a simplistic story of social inequality, but rather to focus on the unique access of these elites to public discourse, and hence on their role in the discursive management of the public mind. That is, they are the most obvious target of the critical approach in discourse analysis.

References

Althusser, L. (1971) *Lenin and Philosophy and Other Essays*, New York: Monthly Review Press.

Bernstein, B. (1971–5) *Class, Codes, Control* (3 vols), London: Routledge & Kegan Paul.

Billig, M. (1982) *Ideology and Social Psychology*, Oxford: Blackwell.

Billig, M. (1991) *Ideology and Opinions*, London: Sage.

Bourdieu, P. (1982) *Ce que parler veut dire* (What speaking means), Paris: Fayard.

Chilton, P. (ed.), (1985) *Language and the Nuclear Arms Debate: Nukespeak Today*, London: Pinter.

Clegg, S.R. (1989) *Frameworks of Power*, London: Sage.

Corcoran, F. (1989) 'Cultural Studies: From Old World to New World', in J.A. Anderson (ed.), *Communication Yearbook 12*, pp. 601–17. Newbury Park, CA: Sage.

Dittmar, N. and Schlobinksi, P. (eds.), (1988) *The Sociolinguistics of Urban Vernaculars: Case Studies and Their Evaluation*, Berlin: de Gruyter.

Domhoff, G.W. (1978) *The Powers That Be: Processes of Ruling Class Domination in America*, New York: Random House (Vintage Books).

Ehlich, K. (ed.), (1989) *Sprache im Faschismus*, Frankfurt: Suhrkamp.

Fairclough, N.L. (1985) 'Critical and Descriptive Goals in Discourse Analysis', *Journal of Pragmatics* 9: pp. 739–63.

Fairclough, N. (1989) *Language and Power*, London: Longman.

Farr, R.M. and Moscovici, S. (eds.), (1984) *Social Representations*, Cambridge: Cambridge University Press.

Fiske, S.T. and Taylor, S.E. (1991) *Social Cognition*, 2nd edn. New York: McGraw-Hill.

Foucault, M. (1980) *Power/Knowledge: Selected Writings and Other Interviews 1972–1977*, (ed.), C. Gordon. New York: Pantheon.

Fowler, R., Hodge, B., Kress, G. and Trew, T. (1979) *Language and Control*, London: Routledge & Kegan Paul.

Gans, H. (1979) *Deciding What's News*, New York: Pantheon Books.

Geuss, R. (1981) *The Idea of Critical Theory: Habermas and the Frankfurt School*, Cambridge: Cambridge University Press.

Gramsci, A. (1971) *Selections from the Prison Notebooks*, New York: International Publishers.

Hall, S. (1981) 'Cultural Studies: Two Paradigms', in T. Bennett, G. Martin, C. Mercer and J. Woollacott (eds.), *Culture, Ideology and Social Process*, pp. 19–37. London: Batsford Academic and Educational.

Hall, S., Lumley, B. and McLennan, G. (1977) 'Gramsci on Ideology', in Centre for Contemporary Cultural Studies (ed.) *Politics and Ideology: Gramsci*, London: Hutchinson, pp. 45–76.

Herman, E.S. and Chomsky, N. (1988) *Manufacturing Consent: The Political Economy of the Mass Media*, New York: Pantheon Books.

Hodge, R. and Kress, G. (1988) *Social Semiotics*, Cambridge: Polity.

Jay, M. (1973) *The Dialectical Imagination: A History of the Frankfurt School and the Institute of Social Research 1923–1950*, Boston: Little, Brown.

Johnson-Laird, P.N. (1983) *Mental Models*, Cambridge: Cambridge University Press.

Kress, G. and Hodge, B. (1979) *Language and Ideology*, London: Routledge & Kegan Paul.

Lukes, S. (ed.), (1986) *Power*, Oxford: Blackwell.

Margolis, M. and Mauser, G.A., (eds.), (1989) *Manipulating Public Opinion: Essays on Public Opinion as a Dependent Variable*, Brooks/Cole.

Mey, J. (1985) *Whose Language: A Study in Linguistic Pragmatics*, Amsterdam: Benjamins.

Mills, C.W. (1956) *The Power Elite*, London: Oxford University Press.

O'Barr, W.M. (1984) 'Asking the Right Questions about Language and Power', in C. Kramarae, M. Schulz and W.M. O'Barr (eds.), *Language and Power*, Beverly Hills, CA: Sage, pp. 260–80.

Pêcheux, M. (1982) *Language, Semantics and Ideology*, New York: St Martin's Press.

Reeves, F. (1983) *British Racial Discourse*, Cambridge: Cambridge University Press.

Resnick, L.B., Levine, J.M. and Teasley, S.D., (eds.), (1991) *Perspectives on Socially Shared Cognition*, Washington, D.C.: American Psychological Association.

Rosenberg, S.W. (1988) *Reason, Ideology, and Politics*, Princeton, NJ: Princeton University Press.

Schank, R.C. and Abelson, R.P. (1977) *Scripts, Plans, Goals, and Understanding: An Inquiry into Human Knowledge Structures*, Hillsdale, NJ: Erlbaum.

Slater, P. (1977) *Origin and Significance of the Frankfurt School: A Marxist Perspective*, London: Routledge & Kegan Paul.

Steiner, E. (1985) 'Towards a Critical Linguistics', in P. Chilton (ed.), *Language and the Nucleur Arms Debate: Nukespeak Today*, London: Pinter, pp. 213–30.

Thorne, B., Kramarae, C. and Henley, N., (eds.), (1983) *Language, Gender and Society*, Rowley, MA: Newbury House.

Tuchman, G. (1978) *Making News: A Study in the Construction of Reality*, New York: Free Press.

Van Dijk, T.A. (1984) *Prejudice in Discourse*, Amsterdam: Benjamins.

Van Dijk, T.A. (1987a) *Communicating Racism*, Newbury Park, CA: Sage.

Van Dijk, T.A. (1987b) 'Episodic Models in Discourse Processing', in R. Horowitz and S.J. Samuels (eds.), *Comprehending Oral and Written Language*, New York: Academic Press, pp. 161–96.

Van Dijk, T.A. (1989a) 'Social Cognition and Discourse', in H. Giles and R.P. Robinson (eds) *Handbook of Social Psychology and Language*, Chichester: Wiley, pp. 163–83.

Van Dijk, T.A. (1989b) 'Structures of Discourse and Structures of Power', in J.A. Anderson (ed.) *Communication Yearbook 12*, Newbury Park, CA: Sage, pp. 18–59.

Van Dijk, T.A. (1991) *Racism and the Press*, London: Routledge.

Van Dijk, T.A. (1993a) *Elite Discourse and Racism*, Newbury Park, CA: Sage.

Van Dijk, T.A. (1993b) 'Discourse, Power and Access', in C.R. Caldas (ed.), *Studies in Critical Discourse Analysis*, London: Routledge (in press).

Van Dijk, T.A. and Kintsch, W. (1983) *Strategies of Discourse Comprehension*, New York: Academic Press.

Windisch, U. (1985) *Le raisonnement et le parler quotidiens*, Lausanne: L'Age d'Homme.

Wodak, R. (1985) 'The Interaction between Judge and Defendant', in T.A. van Dijk (ed.), *Handbook of Discourse Analysis, Vol. 4: Discourse Analysis in Society*, London: Academic Press, pp. 181–91.

Wodak, R. (ed.), (1989) *Language, Power and Ideology*, Amsterdam: Benjamins.

Wodak, R., De Cillia, R., Blüml, K. and Andraschko, E. (1987) *Sprache und Macht*, Vienna: Deuticke.

Wodak, R. and Menz, F. (eds.), (1990) *Sprache in der Politik – Politik in der Sprache: Analysen zum öffentlichen Sprachgebrauch*, Klagenfurt: Drava.

Wodak, R., Menz, F. and Lalouschek, J. (1989) *Sprachbarrieren: Die Verständigungskrise der Gesellschaft*, Vienna: Atelier.

Wodak, R., Nowak, P., Pelikan, J., Gruber, H., De Cillia, R. and Mitten, R. (1990) '*Wir sind alle unschuldige Täter*': *Diskurshistorische Studien zum Nachkriegsantisemitismus*, Frankfurt am Main: Suhrkamp.

Wyer, R.S. and Srull, T.K. (eds.), (1984) *Handbook of Social Cognition* (3 vols), Hillsdale, NJ: Erlbaum.

Index